TEACHINGS OF PRESIDENTS OF THE CHURCH

JOSEPH SMITH

Published by
The Church of Jesus Christ of Latter-day Saints
Salt Lake City, Utah

Your comments and suggestions about this book would be appreciated. Please submit them to Curriculum Development, 50 East North Temple Street, Room 2420, Salt Lake City, UT 84150-3220 USA. E-mail: cur-development@ldschurch.org

Please list your name, address, ward, and stake. Be sure to give the title of the book. Then offer your comments and suggestions about the book's strengths and areas of potential improvement.

Printed in the United States of America

English approval: 8/00

Contents

"Joseph Smith, the Prophet and Seer of the Lord, has done more, save Jesus only, for the salvation of men in this world, than any other man that ever lived in it. . . . He lived great, and he died great in the eyes of God and his people" (D&C 135:3).

Introduction

The First Presidency and the Quorum of the Twelve Apostles have established the *Teachings of Presidents of the Church* series to help you deepen your understanding of the restored gospel and draw closer to the Lord through the teachings of latter-day Presidents of the Church. As the Church adds volumes to this series, you will build a collection of gospel reference books for your home. The volumes in this series are designed to be used both for personal study and for quorum and class instruction.

This book features the teachings of the Prophet Joseph Smith, who was called of God to open the dispensation of the fulness of times in these latter days. Between his vision of the Father and the Son in the spring of 1820 and his martyrdom in June 1844, he established The Church of Jesus Christ of Latter-day Saints and brought forth the fulness of the gospel, never again to be taken from the earth.

Personal Study

As you study the teachings of the Prophet Joseph Smith, seek the inspiration of the Spirit. Remember Nephi's promise: "He that diligently seeketh shall find; and the mysteries of God shall be unfolded unto them, by the power of the Holy Ghost" (1 Nephi 10:19). Begin your study with prayer, and continue to pray and ponder in your heart as you read.

At the end of each chapter, you will find questions and scripture references that will help you understand and apply Joseph Smith's teachings. Consider reviewing them before you read the chapter.

Also consider the following suggestions:

- Look for key words and phrases. If you find a word you do not understand, use a dictionary or another source to better understand its meaning. Write a note in the margin to help you remember what you have learned about the word.

- Think about the meaning of Joseph Smith's teachings. You may want to mark phrases and sentences that teach particular gospel principles or touch your mind and heart, or you may want to write your thoughts and feelings in the margins.
- Reflect on experiences you have had that relate to the Prophet's teachings.
- Ponder how Joseph Smith's teachings apply to you. Think about how the teachings relate to concerns or questions you have. Decide what you will do as a result of what you have learned.

Teaching from This Book

This book can be used to teach at home or at church. The following suggestions will help you.

Focus on Joseph Smith's Words and the Scriptures

The Lord has commanded that we teach "none other things than that which the prophets and apostles have written, and that which is taught [us] by the Comforter through the prayer of faith" (D&C 52:9). He also declared that "the elders, priests and teachers of this church shall teach the principles of my gospel, which are in the Bible and the Book of Mormon, in the which is the fulness of the gospel" (D&C 42:12).

Your assignment is to help others understand the Prophet Joseph Smith's teachings and the scriptures. Do not set this book aside or prepare lessons from other materials. Dedicate a significant portion of the lesson to reading Joseph Smith's teachings in this book and discussing their meaning and application.

Encourage participants to bring this book to church so that they will be better prepared to participate in class discussions.

Seek the Guidance of the Holy Ghost

As you pray for help and prepare diligently, the Holy Ghost will guide your efforts. He will help you emphasize the portions of each chapter that will encourage others to understand and apply the gospel.

When you teach, pray in your heart that the power of the Spirit will accompany your words and the class discussions. Nephi said, "When a man speaketh by the power of the Holy Ghost the power of the Holy Ghost carrieth it unto the hearts of the children of men" (2 Nephi 33:1; see also D&C 50:13–22).

Prepare to Teach

The chapters in this book have been organized to help you prepare to teach. The "From the Life of Joseph Smith" section in each chapter provides information about Joseph Smith's life and early Church history that can be used in introducing and teaching the lesson. The "Teachings of Joseph Smith" section is divided into several subsections, with headings that summarize the main points in the chapter. These headings can serve as an outline from which you can teach. The final section, "Suggestions for Study and Teaching," provides questions and scriptures that relate to the teachings.

You will be more effective in your teaching when you do the following:

1. *Study the chapter.* Read the chapter to become confident in your understanding of Joseph Smith's teachings. You will teach with greater sincerity and power when his words have influenced you personally (see D&C 11:21). As you read, keep in mind the needs of those you teach. You may want to mark doctrines and principles in the chapter that you feel will help them.

2. *Decide which portions to use.* Each chapter contains more than you will be able to teach in one lesson. Rather than try to cover the entire chapter, prayerfully select doctrines and principles that you feel will be most helpful for those you teach. For example, you could choose to focus on one or two subsections and a few questions that will help the participants discuss the principles in the sections you have chosen.

3. *Decide how to introduce the lesson.* To spark interest at the beginning of the lesson, you might share a personal experience or ask participants to read a story from the beginning of the chapter or look at a picture in the chapter. Then you could

ask, "What does this story (or picture) teach about the main topic of the chapter?" Other options for beginning a lesson include reading a scripture or a quotation from the chapter or singing a hymn. Another helpful idea is to let participants know what the main points of the lesson will be. You may also want to remind participants of the previous lesson from this book by asking them to recall events, people, principles, or doctrines that were discussed.

4. *Decide how to encourage discussion.* This is where you should spend most of the lesson time because participants learn doctrines and principles best when they participate in the discussion of them. Review the suggestions for conducting edifying discussions on pages xi–xii of this book. You might use questions from "Suggestions for Study and Teaching" at the end of the chapter. You might also prepare some of your own questions using the following suggestions:

   - Ask questions that help participants look for facts, events, doctrines, and principles. These types of questions help participants focus on specific truths you wish to emphasize and become familiar with specific information in the Prophet's teachings. For example, after identifying a specific quotation, you could ask, "What are some of the key words or phrases in this quotation?" or "What is the topic of this quotation?"
   - Ask questions that help participants think about the doctrines and principles that Joseph Smith taught. These types of questions encourage participants to examine and share their thoughts and feelings about Joseph Smith's teachings. For example, "Why do you think this teaching is important?" or "What thoughts or feelings do you have about this quotation?" or "What does this teaching mean to you?"
   - Ask questions that encourage participants to compare what they learn from the Prophet's teachings to their own thoughts, feelings, and experiences. For example, "What experiences have you had that relate to what the Prophet Joseph Smith said?"

- Ask questions that help participants apply what is being taught to their own lives. These questions help participants think about ways they can live according to Joseph Smith's teachings. For example, "What is Joseph Smith encouraging us to do? In what ways can we apply what he said?" Remind participants that they will learn not only from what is said, but also from revelation directly to them (see D&C 121:26).

5. *Decide how to conclude the lesson.* You may choose to quickly summarize the lesson or ask one or two participants to do so. As prompted by the Spirit, testify of the teachings you have discussed. You may also want to invite others to share their testimonies. Encourage those you teach to follow the promptings they have received from the Holy Ghost.

As you prepare to teach, you may want to look for ideas in *Teaching, No Greater Call* (36123), part B, chapters 14, 16, 28, and 29; or in the *Teaching Guidebook* (34595).

Conduct Edifying Discussions

The following suggestions will help you encourage and conduct edifying discussions:

- Seek the guidance of the Holy Ghost. He may prompt you to ask certain questions or to include certain people in the discussion.
- Help participants focus on Joseph Smith's teachings. Have them read his words to generate discussion and to answer questions. If the discussion begins to stray from the topic or becomes speculative or contentious, redirect the discussion by referring back to an event, doctrine, or principle in the chapter.
- As appropriate, share experiences that relate to the teachings in the chapter.
- Encourage participants to share their thoughts, ask questions, and teach one another (see D&C 88:122). For example, you could ask them to comment on what others have said, or you could direct one question to several participants.
- Do not be afraid of silence after you ask a question. Often those you teach need time to think or to look in their books before they share ideas, testimonies, and experiences.

- Listen sincerely, and seek to understand everyone's comments. Express gratitude for their participation.
- When participants share several ideas, consider listing the ideas on the chalkboard or asking someone else to do so.
- Look for different ways to include participants in the discussion. For example, you might have them discuss questions in small groups or with the person sitting next to them.
- Consider contacting one or two participants in advance. Ask them to come to class ready to answer one of the questions you have prepared.
- Use a hymn, especially a hymn of the Restoration, to reinforce the discussion of a gospel truth. Singing a hymn is also an effective way to introduce or conclude a lesson.
- Do not end a good discussion just because you want to cover all the material you have prepared. What matters most is that participants feel the influence of the Spirit and grow in their commitment to live the gospel.

Teachings for Our Day

This book deals with teachings of the Prophet Joseph Smith that have application to our day. For example, this book does not discuss such topics as the Prophet's teachings regarding the law of consecration as applied to stewardship of property. The Lord withdrew this law from the Church because the Saints were not prepared to live it (see D&C 119, section heading). This book also does not discuss plural marriage. The doctrines and principles relating to plural marriage were revealed to Joseph Smith as early as 1831. The Prophet taught the doctrine of plural marriage, and a number of such marriages were performed during his lifetime. Over the next several decades, under the direction of the Church Presidents who succeeded Joseph Smith, a significant number of Church members entered into plural marriages. In 1890, President Wilford Woodruff issued the Manifesto, which discontinued plural marriage in the Church (see Official Declaration 1). The Church of Jesus Christ of Latter-day Saints no longer practices plural marriage.

Information about Sources Quoted in This Book

The teachings of the Prophet Joseph Smith presented in this book have been taken from several categories of source materials: the Prophet's sermons, articles prepared for publication by the Prophet or under his direction, the Prophet's letters and journals, recorded recollections of those who heard the Prophet speak, and some of the Prophet's teachings and writings that were later canonized in the scriptures. Many of Joseph Smith's teachings have been quoted from the *History of the Church.* For further information about these sources, see the appendix.

A number of unpublished sources are quoted in this work. Spelling, punctuation, capitalization, and grammar have been standardized where necessary to improve readability. Paragraph divisions have also been inserted or altered to improve readability. Where the quotations come from published source materials, the sources have been quoted without alteration, unless otherwise noted. All material within square brackets has been added by the editors of this book, unless otherwise noted.

Historical Summary

The following chronology provides a brief historical framework for the teachings of the Prophet Joseph Smith presented in this book.

1805, December 23:	Born in Sharon, Windsor County, Vermont, the fifth child of eleven in the family of Joseph Smith Sr. and Lucy Mack Smith.
ca. 1813: *(age 7)*	Contracts typhoid fever; complications require surgery on his left leg. At this time, the Smith family was living in West Lebanon, New Hampshire, one of several places to which the family moved between 1808 and 1816 in search of opportunities for work.
1816: *(age 10)*	Moves with his family to the village of Palmyra, New York.
ca. 1818–19: *(age 12 or 13)*	Moves with his family from the village of Palmyra to a log home in Palmyra Township, New York.
1820, early spring: *(age 14)*	Prays in the woods near his home. Visited by God the Father and Jesus Christ. Asks which sect he should join. The Savior tells him that they are all wrong and he should join none of them.
1823, September 21–22: *(age 17)*	Visited by Moroni, who tells him of the Lord's work on the earth in the last days and of the Book of Mormon. Sees the gold plates, which are buried in a nearby hill, but is forbidden to take them at that time.

1825: *(age 19)*	Moves with his family from the log home to a newly built frame home on their farm in Manchester Township, New York.
1827, January 18: *(age 21)*	Marries Emma Hale of Harmony, Pennsylvania; they are married in South Bainbridge, New York.
1827, September 22:	Obtains the plates from Moroni, after having met with Moroni on September 22 each year since 1823.
1827, December: *(age 22)*	Moves to Harmony, Pennsylvania, to escape from a mob in Palmyra and Manchester that is trying to steal the plates. Shortly thereafter, begins translating the Book of Mormon.
1828, February:	Martin Harris shows a copy of some characters from the gold plates to noted scholars, including Charles Anthon and Samuel L. Mitchill in New York City.
1828, June–July:	116 manuscript pages of the translation of the Book of Mormon are lost while in the possession of Martin Harris.
1829, April 5: *(age 23)*	Oliver Cowdery arrives in Harmony to serve as scribe for the Book of Mormon; translation resumes on April 7.
1829, May 15:	With Oliver Cowdery, receives the Aaronic Priesthood from John the Baptist. Joseph and Oliver baptize one another in the Susquehanna River.
1829, May–June:	With Oliver Cowdery, receives the Melchizedek Priesthood from the ancient Apostles Peter, James, and John near the Susquehanna River between Harmony, Pennsylvania, and Colesville, New York.

1829, June:	Completes the translation of the Book of Mormon at the Peter Whitmer Sr. farm in Fayette Township, New York. The Three Witnesses see the plates and the angel Moroni in Fayette; the Eight Witnesses see and handle the plates in Palmyra Township.
1830, March 26: *(age 24)*	The first printed copies of the Book of Mormon become available to the public at Egbert B. Grandin's bookstore in Palmyra.
1830, April 6:	Formally organizes the Church at the home of Peter Whitmer Sr. in Fayette (see D&C 20:1). At first the official name of the Church is the Church of Christ. On May 3, 1834, the name is changed to The Church of the Latter Day Saints. On April 26, 1838, the name is changed by revelation to The Church of Jesus Christ of Latter-day Saints (see D&C 115:4).
1830, June:	At the Lord's command, begins an inspired revision of the Bible, now known as the Joseph Smith Translation of the Bible.
1830, June 9:	Holds the first conference of the Church in Fayette.
1830, September:	Moves from Harmony, Pennsylvania, to Fayette, New York. Between December 1827 and this time, Joseph and Emma lived in Harmony, but Joseph traveled periodically to Manchester, Fayette, and Palmyra to work on matters pertaining to the Book of Mormon translation, arrange for the publication of the Book of Mormon, organize the Church, preside over the Church's first conference, and attend to other Church duties.

1830, September:	Receives a revelation that missionaries are to "go unto the Lamanites" to preach the gospel (D&C 28:8; see also 30:5–6; 32:1–3). In October, four elders depart on a mission to teach in Indian territory west of the state of Missouri.
1830, December: *(age 25)*	Receives a revelation that the Saints are to gather to Ohio (see D&C 37).
1831, early February:	After traveling more than 250 miles from New York, arrives in Kirtland, Ohio.
1831, July 20:	In Independence, Jackson County, Missouri, receives a revelation identifying Independence as the "center place" of Zion (see D&C 57:1–3).
1831, August 2:	Presides as Sidney Rigdon dedicates Jackson County, Missouri, as the land of Zion.
1831, August 3:	Dedicates a temple site in Independence.
1832, January 25: *(age 26)*	Sustained as the President of the High Priesthood in Amherst, Ohio.
1832, March 8:	Organizes the First Presidency, with Sidney Rigdon and Jesse Gause as counselors, in Kirtland. On March 18, 1833, Frederick G. Williams replaces Jesse Gause.
1832, December 27–28: *(age 27)*	Receives a commandment to build a temple in Kirtland (see D&C 88:119–20).
1833, January:	Begins the School of the Prophets.

1833, July 2:	Completes his initial work on the inspired translation of the Bible, now known as the Joseph Smith Translation of the Bible. From this work came the book of Moses and Joseph Smith—Matthew, now contained in the Pearl of Great Price.
1833, July 20:	A mob destroys the press in Independence, Missouri, on which the Book of Commandments is being printed, as well as most of the printed pages. In September 1835 the revelations from the Book of Commandments, as well as other revelations, are published in Kirtland in the first edition of the Doctrine and Covenants.
1833, July 23:	Cornerstones are laid for the Kirtland Temple.
1833, December 18:	Joseph Smith Sr. is ordained Patriarch to the Church.
1834, May–July: *(age 28)*	Leads Zion's Camp from Kirtland, Ohio, to Clay County, Missouri, to bring relief to Saints expelled from their homes in Jackson County, Missouri. Returns to Kirtland after receiving a revelation that the Saints must "wait for a little season for the redemption of Zion" (D&C 105:9).
1835, February 14: *(age 29)*	Organizes the Quorum of the Twelve Apostles.
1835, February 28:	Organizes a Quorum of the Seventy.
1835, July:	Obtains Egyptian papyri containing writings of Abraham.
1836, March 27: *(age 30)*	Dedicates the Kirtland Temple (see D&C 109).

1836, April 3:	Jesus Christ appears to Joseph Smith and Oliver Cowdery in the Kirtland Temple and accepts the temple. Moses, Elias, and Elijah also appear and commit priesthood keys to Joseph and Oliver. (See D&C 110.)
1837, June: *(age 31)*	Sends elders from Kirtland and Upper Canada to serve as missionaries in England, the first mission outside of North America.
1838, January 12: *(age 32)*	Leaves Kirtland for Far West, Missouri, to escape mob violence.
1838, March 14:	Arrives in Far West and establishes Church headquarters there.
1838, April 27:	Initiates the writing of his history, published serially as the "History of Joseph Smith" in Church periodicals beginning in 1842; later republished as *History of the Church.*
1838, October 27:	Missouri governor Lilburn W. Boggs issues the infamous "Extermination Order." This order and severe persecution cause the Saints to leave Missouri for Illinois during the winter and spring of 1838–39.
1838, December 1:	Imprisoned with other Church leaders in Liberty, Missouri.
1839, March 20: *(age 33)*	From Liberty Jail, writes an epistle to the Saints, portions of which are later canonized in Doctrine and Covenants 121, 122, and 123.
1839, mid-April:	While being transferred on a change of venue from Gallatin to Columbia, Missouri, is allowed by his guards to escape.

1839, April 22:	Rejoins his family in Quincy, Illinois.
1839, May 10:	Moves with his family into a small log house in Commerce, Illinois. Later renames the city Nauvoo.
1839, November 29:	Visits Martin Van Buren, the president of the United States, in Washington, D.C., seeking redress for Missouri injustices. While there, he also petitions the United States Congress for help.
1840, August 15: *(age 34)*	Publicly announces the doctrine of baptism for the dead at a funeral in Nauvoo. Baptisms for the dead are first performed in the Mississippi River and local streams.
1840, September:	In an address by the First Presidency to the Church, announces that the time has come to begin building a temple in Nauvoo.
1841, February 4: *(age 35)*	Elected lieutenant general of the newly organized Nauvoo Legion, a unit of the Illinois state militia.
1841, April 6:	Cornerstones are laid for the Nauvoo Temple.
1841, November 21:	The first baptisms for the dead in the Nauvoo Temple are performed in a wooden font built and dedicated before the rest of the temple is completed.
1842, February–October: *(age 36)*	Serves as editor of the *Times and Seasons,* the Church periodical in Nauvoo.
1842, March 1:	Publishes the Wentworth Letter in the *Times and Seasons;* in March and May, also publishes the book of Abraham in the *Times and Seasons.*

1842, March 17:	Organizes the Female Relief Society of Nauvoo, with Emma Smith as president.
1842, May 4:	Administers the first endowment ordinances in an upper room of his Red Brick Store.
1842, May 19:	Elected mayor of Nauvoo.
1843, July 12: *(age 37)*	Records a revelation on the new and everlasting covenant, including the eternal nature of the marriage covenant (see D&C 132).
1844, January 29: *(age 38)*	Announces his candidacy for the presidency of the United States of America.
1844, March:	In a meeting with the Twelve Apostles and others, charges the Twelve to govern the Church in the event of his death, explaining that he has conferred upon them all the ordinances, authority, and keys necessary to do so.
1844, June 27:	Martyred with his brother Hyrum at the jail in Carthage, Illinois.
1844, June 29:	Buried with Hyrum in Nauvoo, Illinois.

At the time of the First Vision, Joseph Smith was living with his family in a log home in Palmyra, New York.

The Life and Ministry of Joseph Smith

"Joseph Smith, the Prophet and Seer of the Lord, has done more, save Jesus only, for the salvation of men in this world, than any other man that ever lived in it" (D&C 135:3). This astonishing declaration describes a man who was called of God at the age of 14 and lived only to the age of 38. Between Joseph Smith's birth in Vermont in December 1805 and his tragic death in Illinois in June 1844, marvelous things occurred. God the Father and His Son, Jesus Christ, appeared to him, teaching him more about the nature of God than had been known for centuries. Ancient prophets and apostles bestowed sacred priesthood power upon Joseph, making him a new, authorized witness of God in this last dispensation. An incomparable outpouring of knowledge and doctrine was revealed through the Prophet, including the Book of Mormon, the Doctrine and Covenants, and the Pearl of Great Price. Through him, the Lord's true Church was organized once again upon the earth.

Today, the work that commenced with Joseph Smith moves forward throughout the world. Of the Prophet Joseph Smith, President Wilford Woodruff testified: "He was a prophet of God, and he laid the foundation of the greatest work and dispensation that has ever been established on the earth."[1]

Ancestry and Childhood

Joseph Smith was a sixth-generation American, his ancestors having emigrated from England to America in the 1600s. The Prophet's ancestors typified the characteristics often associated with the early generations of Americans: they believed in God's directing care over them, they had a strong work ethic, and they diligently served their families and their country.

Joseph Smith's parents, Joseph Smith Sr. and Lucy Mack Smith, married in 1796 in Tunbridge, Vermont. They were a hardworking and God-fearing couple who started their married life under favorable financial circumstances. Unfortunately, Joseph Smith Sr. lost his first farming homestead and suffered a number of financial reverses in subsequent years. The Smith family was forced to move several times as their father tried to make a living by farming the wooded hills of New England, hiring out to work on other farms, operating a mercantile business, or teaching school.

Joseph Smith Jr. was born on December 23, 1805, in Sharon, Vermont, the fifth of eleven children. He was named after his father. The children in the Smith family were, in order of birth: an unnamed son (who died shortly after birth), Alvin, Hyrum, Sophronia, Joseph, Samuel, Ephraim (who lived less than two weeks), William, Katharine, Don Carlos, and Lucy.[2]

Evidence of the Prophet's extraordinary character emerged early in his life. The Smiths were living in West Lebanon, New Hampshire, when a deadly epidemic of typhoid fever attacked many in the community, including all the Smith children. While the other children recovered without complication, Joseph, who was about seven years old, developed a serious infection in his left leg. Dr. Nathan Smith of Dartmouth Medical School at nearby Hanover, New Hampshire, agreed to perform a new surgical procedure to try to save the boy's leg. As Dr. Smith and his colleagues prepared to operate, Joseph asked his mother to leave the room so she would not have to witness his suffering. Refusing liquor to dull the pain and relying only on his father's reassuring embrace, Joseph bravely endured as the surgeon bored into and chipped away part of his leg bone. The surgery was successful, although Joseph walked the next several years with crutches and showed signs of a slight limp the rest of his life.

In 1816, after facing repeated crop failures, Joseph Smith Sr. moved his family from Norwich, Vermont, to Palmyra, New York, hoping to find a more prosperous situation. "Being in indigent circumstances," recalled the Prophet in later years, "[we] were obliged to labor hard for the support of a large family . . . , and as it required the exertions of all that were able to render any assistance for the support of the family, therefore we were deprived of

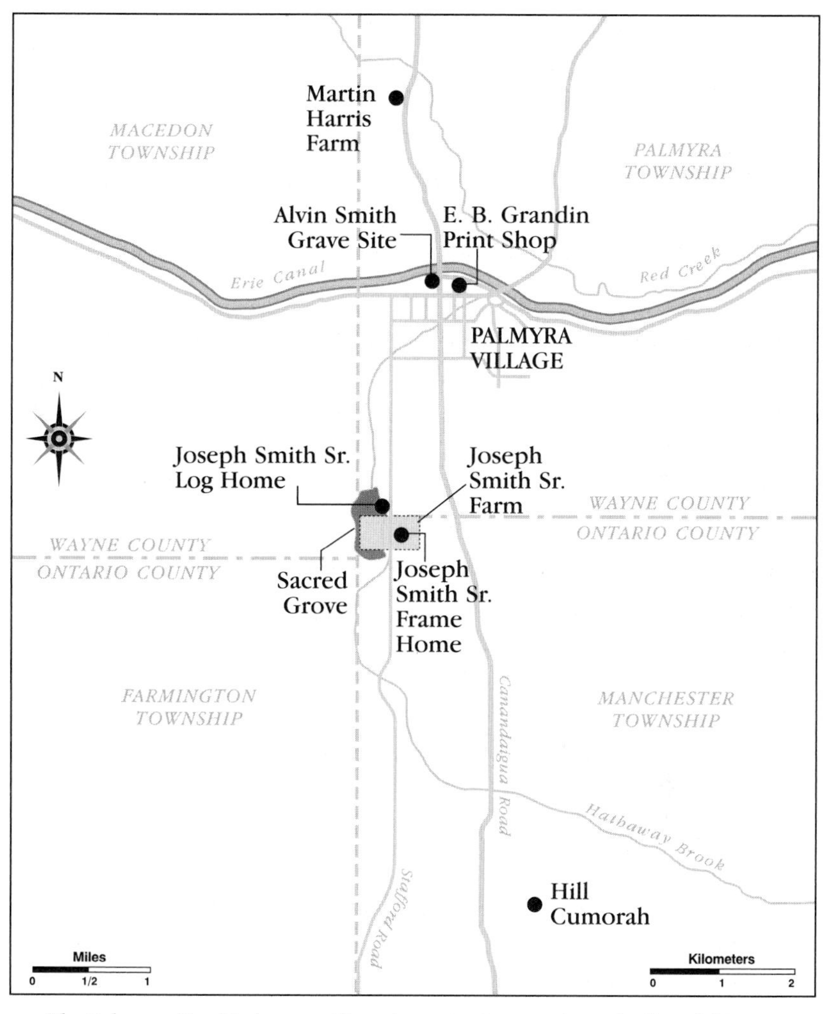

The Palmyra, New York, area. Many important events in early Church history occurred here, including the First Vision and the visits of Moroni to Joseph Smith.

the benefit of an education. Suffice it to say, I was merely instructed in reading, writing, and the ground rules of arithmetic."[3]

The First Vision

Joseph Smith wrote of his early training: "I was born . . . of goodly parents who spared no pains to instruct me in the Christian religion."[4] But, like many other Christians, Joseph's parents recognized that some of the gospel principles taught by

The Sacred Grove about 1907. In the spring of 1820, young Joseph Smith went to this grove of trees near his home to pray to the Lord for guidance.

Jesus and His Apostles were absent from contemporary churches. In the Palmyra area in 1820, several different Christian denominations were trying to win converts. Joseph's mother, two of his brothers, and his older sister joined the local Presbyterian church, but Joseph, along with his father and his brother Alvin, held back. Though only a boy, Joseph was deeply concerned about his own standing before God and about the confusion among the various religious groups.

During his study of the scriptures, 14-year-old Joseph became impressed by a passage from the book of James: "If any of you lack wisdom, let him ask of God, that giveth to all men liberally, and upbraideth not; and it shall be given him" (James 1:5). Inspired by this promise from the Lord, Joseph went into the woods near his home to pray on a spring day in 1820. Kneeling down, he offered up the desires of his heart to God. Immediately he was seized upon by the powers of darkness, which entirely overcame him and made him fear that he would be destroyed. Then, in response to his fervent prayer, the heavens were opened and he was delivered from his unseen enemy. In a pillar of light brighter than the sun, he saw two Personages standing above him in the air. One spoke, calling the boy by name, and said, "This is My Beloved Son. Hear Him!" (Joseph Smith—History 1:17).

In this glorious manifestation, God the Father and His Son, Jesus Christ, appeared in person to young Joseph. Joseph conversed with the Savior, who told him to join none of the churches of his day, for "they were all wrong" and "all their creeds were an abomination in his sight; . . . they teach for doctrines the commandments of men, having a form of godliness, but they deny the power thereof" (Joseph Smith—History 1:19). Joseph was also promised "that the fullness of the Gospel should at some future time be made known unto [him]."[5] After centuries of darkness, the word of God and the reality of God the Father and His Son, Jesus Christ, had been revealed to the world through this youthful and pure vessel.

The Visits of Moroni

Three years passed, during which Joseph Smith's declaration that he had seen God was treated with scorn and derision by others in his community. The young Prophet, now 17 years of age, wondered what awaited him. On the evening of September 21, 1823, he prayed earnestly for direction and for forgiveness of his youthful "sins and follies" (Joseph Smith—History 1:29). In answer to his prayer, light filled his attic bedroom, and a heavenly messenger named Moroni appeared. "[He] proclaimed himself to be an angel of God," Joseph recalled, "sent to bring the joyful tidings that the covenant which God made with ancient Israel was at hand to be fulfilled, that the preparatory work for the second coming of the Messiah was speedily to commence; that the time was at hand for the Gospel in all its fullness to be preached in power, unto all nations that a people might be prepared for the Millennial reign. I was informed that I was chosen to be an instrument in the hands of God to bring about some of His purposes in this glorious dispensation."[6]

Moroni also told Joseph that a compilation of ancient writings, engraved on gold plates by ancient prophets, was buried in a nearby hill. This sacred record described a people whom God had led from Jerusalem to the Western Hemisphere 600 years before Jesus's birth. Moroni was the last prophet among these people and had buried the record, which God had promised to bring forth in the latter days. Joseph Smith was to translate this sacred work into English.

For the next four years, Joseph was to meet Moroni at the hill each September 22 to receive further knowledge and instructions. He would need these years of preparation and personal refinement in order to translate the ancient record. He had to be equal to the task of bringing forth a work whose purpose was to convince "Jew and Gentile that Jesus is the Christ, the Eternal God, manifesting himself unto all nations" (title page of the Book of Mormon).

Establishing God's Kingdom on Earth

Translation of the Book of Mormon Begins

Emma Smith

While he waited to receive the gold plates, Joseph Smith helped provide for his family's temporal needs. In 1825 he went to Harmony, Pennsylvania, to work for Josiah Stowell. There he boarded with the family of Isaac and Elizabeth Hale and met their daughter Emma, a tall, dark-haired schoolteacher. On January 18, 1827, Joseph and Emma were married in South Bainbridge, New York.

Although their marriage would be tested by the deaths of children, financial difficulties, and Joseph's frequent absences from home in fulfillment of his duties, Joseph and Emma always loved one another deeply.

On September 22, 1827, four years after he first saw the plates, Joseph was at last entrusted with them. But once the plates were in his keeping, a local mob made repeated and strenuous efforts to steal them. To avoid this persecution, in December 1827 Joseph and Emma returned to Harmony, where Emma's parents lived. Once established there, Joseph began the translation of the plates.

In early 1828, Martin Harris, a prosperous farmer from Palmyra, received a testimony of the Lord's latter-day work and traveled to Harmony to help Joseph with the translation. By June of that year, Joseph's work on the translation had resulted in 116 pages of manuscript. Martin repeatedly asked the Prophet for permission to take the manuscript to his home in Palmyra to show to certain family members. The Prophet petitioned the Lord and was told no, but he asked the Lord two more times and finally Martin was allowed to take the manuscript. While the manuscript was in Palmyra, it was lost, never to be recovered. The Lord took the Urim and Thummim and the plates from the Prophet for a time, leaving him humbled and repentant. In a revelation from the Lord, Joseph learned that he must always fear God more than men (see D&C 3). Thereafter, though he was only 22 years old, his life was marked by complete dedication to following every command of the Lord.

On April 5, 1829, Oliver Cowdery, a schoolteacher a year younger than Joseph, arrived at Joseph's home in Harmony. In answer to prayer, he had received a testimony of the truthfulness of the Prophet's work. Two days later, the work of translation began again, with Joseph dictating and Oliver writing.

Restoration of the Priesthood of God

As Joseph and Oliver worked on the translation of the Book of Mormon, they read the account of the Savior's visit to the ancient Nephites. As a result, they decided to seek guidance from the Lord about baptism. On May 15, 1829, they went to the banks of the Susquehanna River, near Joseph's home in Harmony, to pray. To their amazement, a heavenly being visited them, announcing himself as John the Baptist. He conferred upon them the Aaronic Priesthood and instructed them to baptize and ordain each other. Later, as promised by John the Baptist, the ancient Apostles Peter, James, and John also appeared to Joseph and Oliver and bestowed upon them the Melchizedek Priesthood and ordained them Apostles.

Before these visitations, Joseph and Oliver had possessed knowledge and faith. But after the appearances of the heavenly messengers, they also had authority—the priesthood power and authority of God necessary to establish His Church and to perform the ordinances of salvation.

Publication of the Book of Mormon and Organization of the Church

During April and May of 1829, the Prophet's work of translation at his home in Harmony was increasingly interrupted by persecution. As a result, Joseph and Oliver moved temporarily to Fayette Township, New York, to finish the translation at the home of Peter Whitmer Sr. The translation was completed in June, less than three months after Oliver began serving as the Prophet's scribe. By August, Joseph had contracted with publisher Egbert B. Grandin of Palmyra to print the volume. Martin Harris mortgaged his farm to Mr. Grandin to ensure payment of the printing costs, and he later sold 151 acres of his farm to pay off the mortgage. The Book of Mormon was available for sale to the public in Grandin's bookstore on March 26, 1830.

On April 6, 1830, just eleven days after the Book of Mormon was advertised for sale, a group of about 60 people assembled in the log home of Peter Whitmer Sr. in Fayette, New York. There Joseph Smith formally organized the Church, later designated by revelation as The Church of Jesus Christ of Latter-day Saints (see D&C 115:4). It was a joyous occasion, with a great outpouring of the Spirit. The sacrament was administered, believers were baptized, the gift of the Holy Ghost was bestowed, and men were ordained to the priesthood. In a revelation received during the meeting, the Lord designated Joseph Smith as the leader of the

Replica of the Peter Whitmer Sr. home in Fayette, New York. This reconstructed home stands on the site where the Prophet formally organized the Church on April 6, 1830.

Church: "a seer, a translator, a prophet, an apostle of Jesus Christ, an elder of the church through the will of God the Father, and the grace of your Lord Jesus Christ" (D&C 21:1). The Church of Jesus Christ was once again established on the earth.

Kirtland, Ohio: Expansion of the Church

As Church members enthusiastically shared the truth they had found, the infant Church grew rapidly. Soon branches were established in the New York towns of Fayette, Manchester, and Colesville. In September 1830, shortly after Joseph and Emma Smith moved from Harmony, Pennsylvania, to Fayette, the Lord revealed to the Prophet that missionaries should "go unto the Lamanites" living on the western edge of Missouri (D&C 28:8). The journey of the missionaries took them through the Kirtland, Ohio, area, where they met a religious group searching for the truth and converted some 130 of them, including Sidney Rigdon, who later became a member of the First Presidency. The group of Saints in Kirtland grew to several hundred as members shared the gospel with those around them.

Important sites in early Church history and the life of the Prophet Joseph Smith.

As the Church grew in New York, opposition to the Church grew as well. In December 1830, the Prophet received a revelation instructing Church members to "go to the Ohio" (D&C 37:1), more than 250 miles away. In the next few months, the great majority of the New York Saints sold their property, often at great loss, and made the sacrifices necessary to gather to Kirtland, Ohio. Joseph and Emma Smith were among the first to start for Ohio, arriving in Kirtland about February 1, 1831.

Two Gathering Places for the Saints

In June of 1831, while the Church was growing strong in Kirtland, the Lord directed the Prophet and other Church leaders to travel to Missouri. There He would reveal to them "the land of [their] inheritance" (see D&C 52:3–5, 42–43). During June and July 1831, the Prophet and others traveled the nearly 900 miles from Kirtland to Jackson County, Missouri, which was on the western fringe of American settlement. Shortly after he arrived, the Prophet received a revelation from the Lord stating that "the land of Missouri . . . is the land which I have appointed and consecrated for the gathering of the saints. Wherefore, this is the land of promise, and the place for the city of Zion. . . . The place which is now called Independence is the center place; and a spot for the temple is lying westward" (D&C 57:1–3).

In fulfillment of prophecies made by ancient biblical prophets, 25-year-old Joseph Smith began to lay the foundation of the city of Zion in America. In August 1831, he presided over the dedication of the land as a gathering place and dedicated a temple site. A short time later, the Prophet returned to Ohio, where he encouraged some of the faithful to gather to Missouri. Hundreds of Saints endured the rigors of 19th-century travel on the American frontier and made their way to their new home in Missouri.

From 1831 to 1838, Church members lived in both Ohio and Missouri. The Prophet, members of the Quorum of the Twelve, and many Church members lived in Kirtland, while other members of the Church gathered to Missouri and were led by their priesthood leaders there, under the direction of the Prophet. Church leaders corresponded by letter and frequently traveled between Kirtland and Missouri.

Continuing Revelation

While he lived in the Kirtland area, the Prophet received many revelations from the Lord concerning the latter-day restoration of the gospel. In November 1831, Church leaders decided to publish many of the revelations in a compilation to be known as the Book of Commandments. The book was to be printed in Independence, Missouri. But in July 1833, mobs destroyed the press and many of the printed sheets. Except for a few copies of the book that were saved, the Book of Commandments never became available to the membership of the Church. In 1835 the revelations intended for the Book of Commandments, as well as many other revelations, were published in Kirtland as the Doctrine and Covenants.

While living in the Kirtland area, the Prophet also continued his work on the Joseph Smith Translation of the Bible, a work he had begun in 1830, as commanded by the Lord. Many plain and precious things had been lost from the Bible over the centuries, and the Prophet was guided by the Spirit to make corrections to the text of the King James Version of the Bible and to restore information that had been lost. This work led to the restoration of important gospel truths, including many revelations now included in the Doctrine and Covenants. Although the Prophet intended to publish his revision of the Bible, pressing matters, including persecution, kept him from publishing it in its entirety in his lifetime.

As part of his inspired revision of the Bible, Joseph Smith received the revelation that is now the book of Moses and an inspired translation of Matthew 24, which is now called Joseph Smith—Matthew. In 1835, the Prophet began translating the book of Abraham from ancient Egyptian papyri that the Church had purchased. All of these translations later became part of the Pearl of Great Price.

Among the revelations the Prophet received in Kirtland were those that established the general governance of the Church. Under the direction of the Lord, Joseph Smith organized the First Presidency in 1832.[7] He organized the Quorum of the Twelve Apostles and a Quorum of the Seventy in 1835. A stake was

The Kirtland Temple about 1900. This temple was built at great sacrifice by the Saints but had to be abandoned after persecution drove them from Kirtland.

organized in Kirtland in 1834. During this period, he also established Aaronic and Melchizedek Priesthood quorums to minister to the needs of local Church members.

The First Temple in This Dispensation

As one of the most important parts of the Restoration, the Lord revealed to Joseph Smith the need for holy temples. In December 1832, the Lord commanded the Saints to begin building a temple in Kirtland, Ohio. Although many Church members lacked adequate housing, employment, and food, they responded enthusiastically to the Lord's command, the Prophet working alongside them.

On March 27, 1836, Joseph Smith dedicated the temple amid a pentecostal outpouring of the Spirit. A week later, on April 3, 1836, some of the most significant events in religious history occurred. The Lord Jesus Christ appeared to Joseph Smith and Oliver Cowdery in the temple, declaring, "I have accepted this house, and my name shall be here; and I will manifest myself to my people in mercy in this house" (D&C 110:7). Three messengers from Old Testament dispensations—Moses, Elias, and Elijah—also appeared. They restored priesthood keys and authority long lost to the earth. The Prophet Joseph Smith now had the authority to gather Israel from the four parts of the earth and to seal families together for time and all eternity. (See D&C 110:11–16.) This restoration of priesthood keys followed the Lord's pattern of giving to the Prophet "line upon line, precept upon precept; here a little, and there a little" (D&C 128:21) until the fulness of Jesus Christ's gospel was restored to the earth.

Preaching the Everlasting Gospel

Throughout the Prophet's ministry, the Lord directed him to send missionaries to "preach the gospel to every creature" (D&C 68:8). The Prophet himself felt the burden of this charge and left his home and family many times to proclaim the gospel. In the early years of the Church, missionaries were called to preach in various parts of the United States and Canada.

Then, in the summer of 1837, the Prophet was inspired to send elders to England. The Prophet directed Heber C. Kimball, a member of the Quorum of the Twelve, to lead a small group of missionaries in this great undertaking. Leaving his family almost destitute, Elder Kimball departed with faith that the Lord would guide him. Within a year, approximately 2,000 people had joined the Church in England. Joseph Smith subsequently sent members of the Twelve to Great Britain to serve from 1839 to 1841, and this mission was also remarkably successful. By 1841, more than 6,000 people had embraced the gospel. Many of these emigrated to America, revitalizing and fortifying the Church during very difficult times.

Leaving Kirtland

The Saints in Kirtland had suffered persecution almost from the time they arrived there, but opposition intensified in 1837 and 1838. "In relation to the kingdom of God," the Prophet said, "the devil always sets up his kingdom at the very same time in opposition to God."[8] The Prophet felt the brunt of the hostility, both from enemies outside the Church and from apostates who had turned against him. He was unjustly accused of many crimes, harassed in court in dozens of unfounded criminal and civil cases, and forced to hide from those who sought his life. But he stood faithful and courageous in the midst of almost constant trouble and opposition.

Finally, the persecution in the Kirtland area became intolerable. In January 1838, the Prophet and his family were forced to leave Kirtland and take refuge in Far West, Missouri. By the end of the year, most of the Saints in Kirtland had followed him, leaving behind their homes and their beloved temple.

The Saints in Missouri

Expulsion from Jackson County and the March of Zion's Camp

While the Saints in Kirtland were striving to strengthen the Church in their area, many other Church members were doing the same in Jackson County, Missouri. Latter-day Saints began settling in the county in the summer of 1831. Two years later, they numbered some 1,200 Saints, or about one-third of the population there.

The arrival of so many Saints troubled the longtime settlers in the area. The Missourians feared loss of political control to the newcomers, who were mostly from the northern part of the United States and did not support the southern practice of slavery. The Missourians were also suspicious of unique Latter-day Saint doctrines—such as belief in the Book of Mormon, new revelation, and the gathering to Zion—and they resented Latter-day Saints for trading primarily among themselves. Mobs and the local militia soon began harassing the Saints and, in November 1833, drove them from Jackson County. Most of the Saints fled north across the Missouri River into Clay County, Missouri.

Joseph Smith was deeply concerned about the plight of the Missouri Saints. In August 1833 he wrote from Kirtland to Church leaders in Missouri: "Brethren, if I were with you I should take an active part in your sufferings, and although nature shrinks, yet my spirit would not let me forsake you unto death, God helping me. Oh, be of good cheer, for our redemption draweth near. O God, save my brethren in Zion."[9]

In February 1834, Joseph Smith received a revelation directing him to lead an expedition from Kirtland to Missouri to assist the suffering Saints and help restore them to their lands in Jackson County (see D&C 103). In response to the Lord's command, the Prophet organized a group called Zion's Camp for the march to Missouri. In May and June of 1834, the group, which eventually included more than 200 members, made its way westward across Ohio, Indiana, Illinois, and Missouri. They were beset by many difficulties, including an outbreak of cholera. On June 22, 1834, when the expedition neared Jackson County, the Prophet received a revelation disbanding the camp. However, the Lord promised that Zion would be redeemed in His own time. (See D&C 105:9–14.) After organizing a stake in Clay County with David Whitmer as president, the Prophet returned to Ohio.

Although Zion's Camp did not recover the properties of the Saints, it provided invaluable training for future leaders of the Church, for the participants learned principles of righteous leadership from the example and teachings of the Prophet. In a meeting of the members of Zion's Camp and other Church members held in Kirtland on February 14, 1835, the Prophet organized the Quorum of the Twelve Apostles. Two weeks later, he organized a Quorum of the Seventy. Nine of the members of the Quorum of the Twelve and all of the members of the Quorum of the Seventy had been part of Zion's Camp.

Settlement in Northern Missouri

Large numbers of Church members continued to live in Clay County, Missouri, until 1836, when the residents of that county said they could no longer provide a place of refuge. The Saints therefore began moving into northern Missouri, most of them settling in Caldwell County, a new county organized by the state legislature to accommodate the displaced Latter-day Saints. In 1838 they were joined by a large body of Saints who had been forced to abandon Kirtland. The Prophet and his family arrived that March in Far West, the thriving Latter-day Saint settlement in Caldwell County, and established Church headquarters there. In April the Lord directed Joseph Smith to build a temple in Far West (see D&C 115:7–16).

Unfortunately, peace was short-lived for the Saints in northern Missouri. In the fall of 1838, mobs and militia again harassed and attacked Latter-day Saints. When Church members retaliated and defended themselves, Joseph Smith and other Church leaders were arrested on charges of treason. In November they were imprisoned in Independence and then in Richmond, Missouri; and on December 1, they were taken to the jail in Liberty, Missouri. That winter, the Prophet and his companions languished under inhumane conditions. They were confined to the jail's dungeon—a dark, cold, and unsanitary cellar—and given food so bad that they could not eat until driven to it by hunger. The Prophet described his condition and that of the Saints as "a trial of our faith equal to that of Abraham."[10]

Liberty Jail, where the Prophet Joseph Smith was imprisoned during the winter of 1838–39.

While the Prophet was imprisoned, thousands of Latter-day Saints, including the Prophet's own family, were forced from their Missouri homes during the winter and spring of 1838–39. On March 7, 1839, Emma wrote to Joseph from Quincy, Illinois: "No one but God knows the reflections of my mind and the feelings of my heart when I left our house and home and almost all of everything that we possessed excepting our little children, and took my journey out of the state of Missouri, leaving you shut up in that lonesome prison."[11] Under the direction of Brigham Young and other Church leaders, the Saints were led eastward to Illinois.

The Nauvoo Years

Beloved Leader of His People

In April 1839, the Prophet and his companions were transferred on a change of venue from Liberty Jail to Gallatin, Missouri. While the prisoners were being transferred yet again, from Gallatin to Columbia, Missouri, the guards allowed them to escape their unjust confinement. They made their way to Quincy, Illinois, where the main body of the Church had assembled after fleeing from Missouri. Soon, under the Prophet's direction, most of the Saints began to settle 50 miles north at Commerce, Illinois, a village on a bend of the Mississippi River. Joseph renamed the city Nauvoo, and in the following years members and new converts flocked to Nauvoo from the United States, Canada, and Great Britain, making it one of the most populated areas in Illinois.

Joseph and Emma settled near the river in a small log home, which served as the Prophet's office in the early days of Nauvoo. He farmed for a living and later ran a general store. But because his Church and civic duties demanded much of his time, the Prophet often found it difficult to provide for the temporal needs of his family. In October 1841 his personal possessions were listed as "old Charley (a horse) given him in Kirtland, two pet deer, two old turkeys and four young ones, the old cow given him by a brother in Missouri, his old Major (a dog), . . . and a little household furniture."[12]

The Mansion House in Nauvoo. The Prophet Joseph Smith and his family moved into this home in August 1843.

In late August 1843 the Prophet and his family moved across the street to a newly constructed two-story home called the Mansion House. Joseph and Emma now had four living children. They had buried six beloved children over the years, and one more child would be born after Joseph's death. The eleven children in the family of Joseph and Emma Smith were: Alvin, born in 1828, who died shortly after birth; twins Thadeus and Louisa, born in 1831, who died shortly after birth; adopted twins Joseph and Julia, born to John and Julia Murdock in 1831 and taken in by Joseph and Emma after Sister Murdock died in childbirth (11-month-old Joseph died in 1832)[13]; Joseph III, born in 1832; Frederick, born in 1836; Alexander, born in 1838; Don Carlos, born in 1840, who died at the age of 14 months; a son born in 1842, who died the same day he was born; and David, born in 1844, almost five months after his father was martyred.

Throughout his ministry, the Prophet loved to be among the Saints. Of the city of Nauvoo and its inhabitants he said, "This is the loveliest place and the best people under the heavens."[14] In return, the Saints loved him and felt that he was their friend, often calling him "Brother Joseph." One convert observed, "There was a personal magnetism about him which drew all people who became acquainted with him to him."[15] "He does not pretend to be a man without failings and follies," one Nauvoo resident wrote. "He is a man that you could not help liking; . . . neither is he puffed up with his greatness as many suppose, but on the contrary is familiar with any decent man."[16] William Clayton, an English convert, wrote home from Nauvoo about the Prophet, saying, "Truly I wish I was such a man."[17]

The Prophet delivered many discourses in Nauvoo, and Church members loved to hear him, for he taught the revealed truths of the gospel with power. Angus M. Cannon recalled: "I never heard him speak when it did not electrify my whole being and make my whole soul glorify the Lord."[18] Brigham Young declared: "I never did let an opportunity pass of getting with the Prophet Joseph and of hearing him speak in public or in private, so that I might draw understanding from the fountain from which he spoke, that I might have it and bring it forth when it was needed. . . . Such moments were more precious to me than all the wealth of the world."[19]

Joseph Smith's leadership extended beyond his religious responsibilities. In Nauvoo, the Prophet was involved in civil, legal, business, educational, and military service. He wanted the city of Nauvoo to offer all the advantages and opportunities of cultural and civic progress to its citizens. In January 1844, in large measure because he was disappointed that state and federal officials failed to provide redress for the rights and property taken from the Saints in Missouri, Joseph Smith announced his candidacy for the presidency of the United States of America. Although most observers recognized that he had little chance of being elected, his candidacy drew public attention to the widespread violation of the constitutionally guaranteed rights of the Saints. All people, the Prophet once declared, "have equal rights to partake of the fruits of the great tree of our national liberty."[20]

Holiness to the Lord: Building a Temple to God in Nauvoo

When the Saints had been forced to leave Kirtland, they had left behind the temple they had worked so hard to build. But

The Nauvoo Temple in the mid-1840s. The temple was burned in 1848 after the Saints were forced to leave Nauvoo, and some of the walls were later destroyed by a tornado, leaving the remaining walls so weakened that they had to be razed.

they would once again have a holy temple in their midst, for the Lord commanded them to begin building a temple in Nauvoo. The work began in the fall of 1840, with the cornerstones being laid on April 6, 1841, in a ceremony presided over by the Prophet. The construction of the Nauvoo Temple was one of the most significant building projects in what was then western America. Building the temple required the Saints to make tremendous sacrifices, for with steady immigration into the developing city, Church members in general were poor.

The Prophet began teaching the doctrine of baptism for the dead as early as August 15, 1840. Since the temple was in the early stages of construction, the Saints initially performed baptisms for the dead in local rivers and streams. In January 1841, the Lord revealed that this practice could continue only until baptisms could be performed in the temple (see D&C 124:29–31). During the summer and fall of 1841, the Saints built a temporary wooden baptismal font in the newly excavated basement of the temple. Baptisms for the dead were first performed in this font on November 21, 1841.

In 1841 the first sealings of couples were performed, and in 1843 the Prophet dictated the revelation that describes the eternal nature of the marriage covenant (see D&C 132). The doctrines in this revelation had been known by the Prophet since 1831.[21] As commanded by God, he also taught the doctrine of plural marriage.

Because the temple would not be completed for some time, Joseph Smith chose to go forward with the temple endowment outside its sacred walls. On May 4, 1842, in the upper room of his Red Brick Store in Nauvoo, the Prophet administered the first endowments to a small group of brethren, including Brigham Young. The Prophet did not live to see the Nauvoo Temple completed. However, in 1845 and 1846, thousands of Saints received the temple endowment from Brigham Young and others who had received these blessings from the Prophet.

Joseph Smith's Ministry Draws to a Close

While the Saints initially enjoyed relative peace in Nauvoo, clouds of persecution increasingly billowed around the Prophet, and he sensed that his earthly mission was drawing to its close. At a memorable meeting in March 1844, the Prophet charged the Twelve to govern the Church after his death, explaining that they now had all the keys and authority necessary to do so. Wilford Woodruff, a member of the Quorum of the Twelve at that time, later declared: "I bear my testimony that in the early spring of 1844, in Nauvoo, the Prophet Joseph Smith called the Apostles together and he delivered unto them the ordinances of the church and kingdom of God. And all the keys and powers that

God had bestowed upon him, he sealed upon our heads, and he told us we must round up our shoulders and bear off this kingdom, or we would be damned. . . . His face was as clear as amber, and he was covered with a power that I had never seen in any man in the flesh before."[22] After the Prophet's death, responsibility for the Church and kingdom of God upon the earth would rest with the Quorum of the Twelve Apostles.

In June 1844 a charge of riot was brought against the Prophet. Though he was acquitted of this charge in Nauvoo, the governor

Carthage Jail, where the Prophet Joseph Smith and his brother Hyrum were martyred on June 27, 1844.

of Illinois, Thomas Ford, insisted that Joseph submit to trial for the same charge in Carthage, Illinois, the seat of Hancock County. When the Prophet and his brother Hyrum arrived in Carthage, they were freed on bail for the original charge but were then charged with treason against the state of Illinois and incarcerated in the local jail.

During the hot and sultry afternoon of June 27, 1844, a mob with blackened faces stormed the jail and murdered Joseph and Hyrum Smith. About three hours later, Willard Richards and John Taylor, who had been in the jail with the martyrs, sent a melancholy message to Nauvoo: "Carthage Jail, 8:05 o'clock, p.m., June 27th, 1844. Joseph and Hyrum are dead. . . . The job was done in an instant."[23] At the age of 38, the Prophet Joseph Smith had sealed his testimony with his blood. His work in mortality completed, the Church and kingdom of God set in place for the last time on earth, Joseph Smith fell to the bullets of assassins. Of the Prophet Joseph Smith, the Lord Himself testified: "I did call upon [Joseph Smith] by mine angels, my ministering servants, and by mine own voice out of the heavens, to bring forth my work; which foundation he did lay, and was faithful; and I took him to myself. Many have marveled because of his death; but it was needful that he should seal his testimony with his blood, that he might be honored and the wicked might be condemned" (D&C 136:37–39).

Joseph Smith, the great prophet, seer, and revelator of the latter days, was a valiant and obedient servant of the Most High. President Brigham Young attested: "I do not think that a man lives on the earth that knew him any better than I did; and I am bold to say that, Jesus Christ excepted, no better man ever lived or does live upon this earth. I am his witness."[24]

Notes

1. Wilford Woodruff, *Deseret News: Semi-Weekly,* Nov. 25, 1873, p. 1.
2. Because only nine of the eleven children of Joseph Smith Sr. and Lucy Mack Smith lived past infancy, family members generally referred to their family as consisting of nine children. Also, the name of Joseph's sister Katharine was spelled several ways during her lifetime, including Catherine.
3. Joseph Smith, History 1832, p. 1; Letter Book 1, 1829–35, Joseph Smith, Collection, Church Archives, The Church of Jesus Christ of Latter-day Saints, Salt Lake City, Utah.

4. Joseph Smith, History 1832, p. 1; Letter Book 1, 1829–35, Joseph Smith, Collection, Church Archives.
5. *History of the Church,* 4:536; from a letter from Joseph Smith written at the request of John Wentworth and George Barstow, Nauvoo, Illinois, published in *Times and Seasons,* Mar. 1, 1842, p. 707.
6. *History of the Church,* 4:536–37; from a letter from Joseph Smith written at the request of John Wentworth and George Barstow, Nauvoo, Illinois, published in *Times and Seasons,* Mar. 1, 1842, p. 707.
7. The original First Presidency was composed of Joseph Smith as President and Sidney Rigdon and Jesse Gause as counselors. Some months after Jesse Gause became a member of the First Presidency, he left the Church. On March 18, 1833, Frederick G. Williams was set apart as a counselor in the First Presidency.
8. *History of the Church,* 6:364; from a discourse given by Joseph Smith on May 12, 1844, in Nauvoo, Illinois; reported by Thomas Bullock.
9. Postscript written by Joseph Smith on a letter from Oliver Cowdery to Church leaders in Jackson County, Missouri, Aug. 10, 1833, Kirtland, Ohio, Church Archives.
10. *History of the Church,* 3:294; from a letter from Joseph Smith and others to Edward Partridge and the Church, Mar. 20, 1839, Liberty Jail, Liberty, Missouri.
11. Letter from Emma Smith to Joseph Smith, Mar. 7, 1839, Quincy, Illinois; in Letter Book 2, 1837–43, p. 37, Joseph Smith, Collection, Church Archives.
12. *History of the Church,* 4:437–38; punctuation modernized; from a letter from the Twelve Apostles to the "Brethren Scattered Abroad on the Continent of America," Oct. 12, 1841, Nauvoo, Illinois, published in *Times and Seasons,* Oct. 15, 1841, p. 569.
13. In May 1831, shortly after the deaths of their own newborn twins, Joseph and Emma Smith adopted the newborn twins of Church members John and Julia Murdock. The Murdock twins were named Joseph and Julia. Sister Murdock had died in childbirth, and Brother Murdock, who now had five motherless children, asked the Smiths to care for the twins.
14. *History of the Church,* 6:554; statement made by Joseph Smith on June 24, 1844, in Nauvoo, Illinois; reported by Dan Jones.
15. Mary Isabella Horne, "Testimony of Sister M. Isabella Horne," *Woman's Exponent,* June 1910, p. 6.
16. Letter from George W. Taggart to his brothers in New Hampshire, Sept. 10, 1843, Nauvoo, Illinois; in Albert Taggart, Correspondence, 1842–48 and 1860, Church Archives.
17. Letter from William Clayton to Church members in Manchester, England, Dec. 10, 1840, Nauvoo, Illinois, Church Archives.
18. Angus M. Cannon, in "Joseph, the Prophet," *Salt Lake Herald Church and Farm Supplement,* Jan. 12, 1895, p. 212.
19. Brigham Young, *Deseret News: Semi-Weekly,* Sept. 15, 1868, p. 2.
20. *History of the Church,* 3:304; from a letter from Joseph Smith and others to Edward Partridge and the Church, Mar. 20, 1839, Liberty Jail, Liberty, Missouri.
21. See Doctrine and Covenants 132, section heading.
22. Wilford Woodruff, statement made on Mar. 12, 1897, in Salt Lake City, Utah; in Journal History of The Church of Jesus Christ of Latter-day Saints, Mar. 12, 1897, p. 2.
23. *History of the Church,* 6:621–22; from a directive from Willard Richards and John Taylor, June 27, 1844, Carthage, Illinois.
24. Brigham Young, *Deseret News,* Aug. 27, 1862, p. 65.

"I saw a pillar of light exactly over my head, above the brightness of the sun, which descended gradually until it fell upon me."

CHAPTER 1

The First Vision: The Father and the Son Appear to Joseph Smith

"I saw two Personages, whose brightness and glory defy all description, standing above me in the air. One of them spake unto me, calling me by name and said, pointing to the other—This is My Beloved Son. Hear Him!"

From the Life of Joseph Smith

Following the death and resurrection of Jesus Christ, apostasy gradually became widespread. The Savior's Apostles were rejected and slain, His teachings were corrupted, and the priesthood of God was taken from the earth. The ancient prophet Amos had foretold a time of apostasy and spiritual darkness: "Behold, the days come, saith the Lord God, that I will send a famine in the land, not a famine of bread, nor a thirst for water, but of hearing the words of the Lord: and they shall wander from sea to sea, and from the north even to the east, they shall run to and fro to seek the word of the Lord, and shall not find it" (Amos 8:11–12).

One of those seeking the word of the Lord that had been lost from the earth was Joseph Smith, a young man living in the rural township of Palmyra, New York, in 1820. Joseph was a strong and active young man with fair skin, light brown hair, and blue eyes, the fifth of eleven children in the family of Joseph Smith Sr. and Lucy Mack Smith. He worked long hours helping his father and older brothers fell trees and plant crops on his family's thickly wooded, hundred-acre farm. By his mother's account, he was "a remarkably quiet, well-disposed child,"[1] who was "much more given to reflection and deep study" than any of his siblings.[2] Young Joseph worked to help support his family and so was able to obtain only enough formal education to know the basics of reading, writing, and arithmetic.

During this time, a spirit of religious fervor was sweeping through the region of western New York where the Smith family lived. The Smiths, like many others, attended the revivals of the Christian denominations in the area. While some of his family members joined with one of the churches, Joseph did not. He later wrote about this time:

"My mind became seriously impressed with regard to the all important concerns for the welfare of my immortal soul, which led me to searching the scriptures, believing, as I was taught, that they contained the word of God. Thus applying myself to them and my intimate acquaintance with those of different denominations led me to marvel exceedingly, for I discovered that they did not adorn their profession by a holy walk and godly conversation agreeable to what I found contained in that sacred depository. This was a grief to my soul. . . .

"I pondered many things in my heart concerning the situation of the world of mankind—the contentions and divisions, the wickedness and abominations, and the darkness which pervaded the minds of mankind. My mind became exceedingly distressed, for I became convicted of my sins, and by searching the scriptures I found that mankind did not come unto the Lord, but that they had apostatized from the true and living faith, and there was no society or denomination that built upon the gospel of Jesus Christ as recorded in the New Testament, and I felt to mourn for my own sins and for the sins of the world."[3]

Young Joseph Smith's search for truth led him into a grove of trees to ask God for the wisdom he needed. In answer to his prayer, Heavenly Father and Jesus Christ appeared to him, opening the way for the restoration of the gospel in the latter days. This marvelous event is recounted in Joseph Smith's simple yet eloquent words.

Teachings of Joseph Smith

Joseph Smith's search for truth teaches that scripture study and sincere prayer invite revelation.

Joseph Smith—History 1:5, 7–13: "There was in the place where we lived an unusual excitement on the subject of religion. It commenced with the Methodists, but soon became general among all the sects in that region of country. Indeed, the whole district of country seemed affected by it, and great multitudes united themselves to the different religious parties, which created no small stir and division amongst the people, some crying, 'Lo, here!' and others, 'Lo, there!' Some were contending for the Methodist faith, some for the Presbyterian, and some for the Baptist. . . .

"I was at this time in my fifteenth year. My father's family was proselyted to the Presbyterian faith, and four of them joined that church, namely, my mother, Lucy; my brothers Hyrum and Samuel Harrison; and my sister Sophronia.

"During this time of great excitement my mind was called up to serious reflection and great uneasiness; but though my feelings were deep and often poignant, still I kept myself aloof from all these parties, though I attended their several meetings as often as occasion would permit. In process of time my mind became somewhat partial to the Methodist sect, and I felt some desire to be united with them; but so great were the confusion and strife among the different denominations, that it was impossible for a person young as I was, and so unacquainted with men and things, to come to any certain conclusion who was right and who was wrong.

"My mind at times was greatly excited, the cry and tumult were so great and incessant. The Presbyterians were most decided against the Baptists and Methodists, and used all the powers of both reason and sophistry to prove their errors, or, at least, to make the people think they were in error. On the other hand, the Baptists and Methodists in their turn were equally zealous in endeavoring to establish their own tenets and disprove all others.

"Never did any passage of scripture come with more power to the heart of man than this did at this time to mine."

"In the midst of this war of words and tumult of opinions, I often said to myself: What is to be done? Who of all these parties are right; or, are they all wrong together? If any one of them be right, which is it, and how shall I know it?

"While I was laboring under the extreme difficulties caused by the contests of these parties of religionists, I was one day reading the Epistle of James, first chapter and fifth verse, which reads: *If any of you lack wisdom, let him ask of God, that giveth to all men liberally, and upbraideth not; and it shall be given him.*

"Never did any passage of scripture come with more power to the heart of man than this did at this time to mine. It seemed to enter with great force into every feeling of my heart. I reflected on it again and again, knowing that if any person needed wisdom from God, I did; for how to act I did not know, and unless I could get more wisdom than I then had, I would never know; for the teachers of religion of the different sects understood the same passages of scripture so differently as to destroy all confidence in settling the question by an appeal to the Bible.

"At length I came to the conclusion that I must either remain in darkness and confusion, or else I must do as James directs, that is, ask of God. I at length came to the determination to 'ask of God,' concluding that if he gave wisdom to them that lacked wisdom, and would give liberally, and not upbraid, I might venture."[4]

Joseph Smith was delivered from the power of the enemy of all righteousness.

Joseph Smith—History 1:14–16: "So, in accordance with this, my determination to ask of God, I retired to the woods to make the attempt. It was on the morning of a beautiful, clear day, early in the spring of eighteen hundred and twenty. It was the first time in my life that I had made such an attempt, for amidst all my anxieties I had never as yet made the attempt to pray vocally.

"After I had retired to the place where I had previously designed to go, having looked around me, and finding myself alone, I kneeled down and began to offer up the desires of my heart to God. I had scarcely done so, when immediately I was seized upon by some power which entirely overcame me, and had such an astonishing influence over me as to bind my tongue so that I could not speak. Thick darkness gathered around me, and it seemed to me for a time as if I were doomed to sudden destruction.

"But, exerting all my powers to call upon God to deliver me out of the power of this enemy which had seized upon me, and at the very moment when I was ready to sink into despair and abandon myself to destruction—not to an imaginary ruin, but to the power of some actual being from the unseen world, who had such marvelous power as I had never before felt in any being—just at this moment of great alarm, I saw a pillar of light exactly over my head, above the brightness of the sun, which descended gradually until it fell upon me."[5]

Heavenly Father and Jesus Christ appeared to Joseph in answer to his humble prayer.

Joseph Smith—History 1:17–20: "It no sooner appeared than I found myself delivered from the enemy which held me bound. When the light rested upon me I saw two Personages, whose brightness and glory defy all description, standing above me in the air. One of them spake unto me, calling me by name and said, pointing to the other—*This is My Beloved Son. Hear Him!*

"My object in going to inquire of the Lord was to know which of all the sects was right, that I might know which to join. No sooner, therefore, did I get possession of myself, so as to be able to speak, than I asked the Personages who stood above me in the light, which of all the sects was right (for at this time it had never entered into my heart that all were wrong)—and which I should join.

"I was answered that I must join none of them, for they were all wrong; and the Personage who addressed me said that all their creeds were an abomination in his sight; that those professors were all corrupt; that: 'they draw near to me with their lips, but their hearts are far from me, they teach for doctrines the commandments of men, having a form of godliness, but they deny the power thereof.'

"He again forbade me to join with any of them; and many other things did he say unto me, which I cannot write at this time. When I came to myself again, I found myself lying on my back, looking up into heaven. When the light had departed, I had no strength; but soon recovering in some degree, I went home. And as I leaned up to the fireplace, mother inquired what the matter was. I replied, 'Never mind, all is well—I am well enough off.' I then said to my mother, 'I have learned for myself that Presbyterianism is not true.' It seems as though the adversary was aware, at a very early period of my life, that I was destined to prove a disturber and an annoyer of his kingdom; else why should the powers of darkness combine against me? Why the opposition and persecution that arose against me, almost in my infancy?"[6]

When our testimonies are strong, persecution cannot cause us to deny what we know to be true.

Joseph Smith—History 1:21–26: "Some few days after I had this vision, I happened to be in company with one of the Methodist preachers, who was very active in the before mentioned religious excitement; and, conversing with him on the subject of religion, I took occasion to give him an account of the vision which I had had. I was greatly surprised at his behavior; he treated my communication not only lightly, but with great contempt, saying it was all of the devil, that there were no such things as visions or revelations in these days; that all such things had ceased with the apostles, and that there would never be any more of them.

"I soon found, however, that my telling the story had excited a great deal of prejudice against me among professors of religion, and was the cause of great persecution, which continued to increase; and though I was an obscure boy, only between fourteen and fifteen years of age, and my circumstances in life such as to make a boy of no consequence in the world, yet men of high standing would take notice sufficient to excite the public mind against me, and create a bitter persecution; and this was common among all the sects—all united to persecute me.

"It caused me serious reflection then, and often has since, how very strange it was that an obscure boy, of a little over fourteen years of age, and one, too, who was doomed to the necessity of obtaining a scanty maintenance by his daily labor, should be thought a character of sufficient importance to attract the attention of the great ones of the most popular sects of the day, and in a manner to create in them a spirit of the most bitter persecution and reviling. But strange or not, so it was, and it was often the cause of great sorrow to myself.

"However, it was nevertheless a fact that I had beheld a vision. I have thought since, that I felt much like Paul, when he made his defense before King Agrippa, and related the account of the vision he had when he saw a light, and heard a voice; but still there were but few who believed him; some said he was dishonest, others said he was mad; and he was ridiculed and reviled.

But all this did not destroy the reality of his vision. He had seen a vision, he knew he had, and all the persecution under heaven could not make it otherwise; and though they should persecute him unto death, yet he knew, and would know to his latest breath, that he had both seen a light and heard a voice speaking unto him, and all the world could not make him think or believe otherwise.

"So it was with me. I had actually seen a light, and in the midst of that light I saw two Personages, and they did in reality speak to me; and though I was hated and persecuted for saying that I had seen a vision, yet it was true; and while they were persecuting me, reviling me, and speaking all manner of evil against me falsely for so saying, I was led to say in my heart: Why persecute me for telling the truth? I have actually seen a vision; and who am I that I can withstand God, or why does the world think to make me deny what I have actually seen? For I had seen a vision; I knew it, and I knew that God knew it, and I could not deny it, neither dared I do it; at least I knew that by so doing I would offend God, and come under condemnation.

"I had now got my mind satisfied so far as the sectarian world was concerned—that it was not my duty to join with any of them, but to continue as I was until further directed. I had found the testimony of James to be true—that a man who lacked wisdom might ask of God, and obtain, and not be upbraided."[7]

Suggestions for Study and Teaching

Consider these ideas as you study the chapter or as you prepare to teach. For additional help, see pages vii–xii.

- Review pages 27–31. Think about how Joseph Smith provides an example for us as we seek answers to our questions. As you study his account of the First Vision, what do you learn about reading the scriptures? about pondering? about prayer?
- Review page 32. Think about the truths Joseph Smith learned about God the Father and Jesus Christ when he received the First Vision. Why must each of us have a testimony of the First Vision?

- When Joseph told others of the First Vision, many people became prejudiced against him and persecuted him (page 33). Why do you think people reacted in this way? Ponder Joseph's response to the persecution (pages 33–34). How can we follow his example when we face persecution or other trials?
- When you first learned of the First Vision, what effect did the account have on you? What effect has it had on you since then? In what ways have you been strengthened as you have studied the account again in this chapter?

Related Scriptures: Isaiah 29:13–14; Joel 2:28–29; Amos 3:7; Mormon 9:7–9

Notes

1. Lucy Mack Smith, "The History of Lucy Smith, Mother of the Prophet," 1845 manuscript, p. 72, Church Archives, The Church of Jesus Christ of Latter-day Saints, Salt Lake City, Utah. Lucy Mack Smith, the Prophet's mother, dictated her history, which includes much about the Prophet's life, to Martha Jane Knowlton Coray beginning in 1844 and continuing into 1845. Martha Coray referred to this early manuscript as "History rough manuscript." Later in 1845, Lucy Mack Smith, Martha Coray, and Martha's husband, Howard Coray, revised and expanded the earlier manuscript. The 1845 manuscript is titled "The History of Lucy Smith, Mother of the Prophet." This book quotes from the 1844–45 manuscript except in a few instances when the 1845 manuscript includes material that is not found in the 1844–45 manuscript.
2. Lucy Mack Smith, "The History of Lucy Smith, Mother of the Prophet," 1844–45 manuscript, book 4, p. 1, Church Archives.
3. Joseph Smith, History 1832, pp. 1–2; Letter Book 1, 1829–35, Joseph Smith, Collection, Church Archives.
4. Joseph Smith—History 1:5, 7–13. On several occasions the Prophet Joseph Smith wrote or dictated detailed accounts of the First Vision. Quotations in this chapter are from the First Vision account first published in 1842 in "History of Joseph Smith," *Times and Seasons,* Mar. 15, 1842, pp. 726–28; Apr. 1, 1842, pp. 748–49; and later included in the Pearl of Great Price and published in the *History of the Church,* vol. 1, pp. 1–8. This is the official scriptural account. The Prophet Joseph Smith prepared this account in 1838 and 1839 with the help of his scribes.
5. Joseph Smith—History 1:14–16.
6. Joseph Smith—History 1:17–20.
7. Joseph Smith—History 1:21–26.

In the First Vision, Joseph Smith learned for himself that the Father and the Son are individual beings and that man is fashioned in God's image—truths that are essential in understanding our actual relationship to our Father in Heaven.

CHAPTER 2

God the Eternal Father

"The purposes of our God are great, His love unfathomable, His wisdom infinite, and His power unlimited; therefore, the Saints have cause to rejoice and be glad."

From the Life of Joseph Smith

Among Joseph Smith's progenitors were many who sought to know the true God in their day. Joseph's own parents were deeply spiritual, and although they did not find the full truth about God in the churches around them, they honored the Bible as God's word and made prayer a part of daily life. The Prophet's brother William recalled: "My father's religious habits were strictly pious and moral. . . . I was called upon to listen to prayers both night and morning. . . . My parents, father and mother, poured out their souls to God, the donor of all blessings, to keep and guard their children and keep them from sin and from all evil works. Such was the strict piety of my parents."[1] William also said: "We always had family prayers since I can remember. I well remember father used to carry his spectacles in his vest pocket, . . . and when us boys saw him feel for his specs, we knew that was a signal to get ready for prayer, and if we did not notice it mother would say, 'William,' or whoever was the negligent one, 'get ready for prayer.' After the prayer we had a song we would sing; I remember part of it yet: 'Another day has passed and gone, We lay our garments by.' "[2]

This early spiritual training sank deep into young Joseph Smith's soul. When he became concerned about his eternal welfare and sought to know which church to join, he knew he could turn to God for answers:

"I learned in the scriptures that God was the same yesterday, today, and forever, that he was no respecter to persons, for he was God. For I looked upon the sun, the glorious luminary of the earth, and also the moon rolling in [its] majesty through the heavens and also the stars shining in their courses; and the earth also upon which I stood, and the beast of the field and the fowls of heaven and the fish of the waters; and also man walking forth upon the face of the earth in majesty and in the strength of beauty, [with] power and intelligence in governing the things which are so exceedingly great and marvelous, even in the likeness of him who created them.

"And when I considered upon these things my heart exclaimed, Well hath the wise man said it is a fool that saith in his heart there is no God [see Psalm 53:1]. My heart exclaimed, All these bear testimony and bespeak an omnipotent and omnipresent power, a Being who maketh laws and decreeth and bindeth all things in their bounds, who filleth eternity, who was and is and will be from all eternity to eternity. And when I considered all these things and that that Being seeketh such to worship him as worship him in spirit and in truth [see John 4:23], therefore I cried unto the Lord for mercy, for there was none else to whom I could go and obtain mercy."[3]

Joseph's faithful prayer for mercy and wisdom was answered with the First Vision. That vision gave the young Prophet far greater knowledge about God than any of the churches of his day possessed, knowledge that had been lost to the world for centuries. In the First Vision, Joseph learned for himself that the Father and the Son are individual beings, that Their power is greater than the power of evil, and that man is indeed fashioned in God's image—truths that are essential in understanding our actual relationship to our Father in Heaven.

Other revelations about the nature of God followed, including many that are now in our latter-day scriptures. As God's chosen instrument in restoring gospel truth to the world, the Prophet testified of God throughout his ministry. "I am going to inquire after God," he declared, "for I want you all to know Him, and to be familiar with Him. . . . You will then know that I am His servant; for I speak as one having authority."[4]

Teachings of Joseph Smith

God is the loving Father of all mankind and the source of all that is good.

"While one portion of the human race is judging and condemning the other without mercy, the Great Parent of the universe looks upon the whole of the human family with a fatherly care and paternal regard; He views them as His offspring, and without any of those contracted feelings that influence the children of men, causes 'His sun to rise on the evil and on the good, and sendeth rain on the just and on the unjust.' [Matthew 5:45.]"[5]

"We admit that God is the great source and fountain from whence proceeds all good; that He is perfect intelligence, and that His wisdom is alone sufficient to govern and regulate the mighty creations and worlds which shine and blaze with such magnificence and splendor over our heads, as though touched with His finger and moved by His Almighty word. . . . The heavens declare the glory of a God, and the firmament showeth His handiwork [see Psalm 19:1]; and a moment's reflection is sufficient to teach every man of common intelligence, that all these are not the mere productions of *chance,* nor could they be supported by any power less than an Almighty hand."[6]

"God sees the secret springs of human action, and knows the hearts of all living."[7]

"The purposes of our God are great, His love unfathomable, His wisdom infinite, and His power unlimited; therefore, the Saints have cause to rejoice and be glad, knowing that 'this God is our God forever and ever, and He will be our Guide until death.' [Psalm 48:14.]"[8]

When we comprehend the character of God, we comprehend ourselves and know how to approach Him.

"There are but a very few beings in the world who understand rightly the character of God. The great majority of mankind do not comprehend anything, either that which is past, or that which is to come, as it respects their relationship to God. They do not know, neither do they understand the nature of that relationship; and consequently they know but little above the brute beast, or more than to eat, drink and sleep. This is all man knows about God or His existence, unless it is given by the inspiration of the Almighty.

"If a man learns nothing more than to eat, drink and sleep, and does not comprehend any of the designs of God, the beast comprehends the same things. It eats, drinks, sleeps, and knows nothing more about God; yet it knows as much as we, unless we are able to comprehend by the inspiration of Almighty God. If men do not comprehend the character of God, they do not comprehend themselves. I want to go back to the beginning, and so lift your minds into more lofty spheres and a more exalted understanding than what the human mind generally aspires to.

". . . The scriptures inform us that 'This is life eternal that they might know thee, the only true God, and Jesus Christ whom thou hast sent.' [John 17:3.]

"If any man does not know God, and inquires what kind of a being He is,—if he will search diligently his own heart—if the declaration of Jesus and the apostles be true, he will realize that he has not eternal life; for there can be eternal life on no other principle.

"My first object is to find out the character of the only wise and true God, and what kind of a being He is. . . .

"God Himself was once as we are now, and is an exalted man, and sits enthroned in yonder heavens! That is the great secret. If the veil were rent today, and the great God who holds this world in its orbit, and who upholds all worlds and all things by His power, was to make Himself visible,—I say, if you were to see Him today, you would see Him like a man in form—like yourselves in all the person, image, and very form as a man; for Adam was created in the very fashion, image and likeness of God, and received instruction from, and walked, talked and conversed with Him, as one man talks and communes with another. . . .

". . . Having a knowledge of God, we begin to know how to approach Him, and how to ask so as to receive an answer. When we understand the character of God, and know how to come to

"Having a knowledge of God, we begin to know how to approach Him, and how to ask so as to receive an answer."

Him, He begins to unfold the heavens to us, and to tell us all about it. When we are ready to come to Him, He is ready to come to us."[9]

In the Godhead there are three separate and distinct personages.

Articles of Faith 1:1: "We believe in God, the Eternal Father, and in His Son, Jesus Christ, and in the Holy Ghost."[10]

Joseph Smith taught the following in April 1843, later recorded in Doctrine and Covenants 130:22: "The Father has a body of flesh and bones as tangible as man's; the Son also; but the Holy Ghost has not a body of flesh and bones, but is a personage of Spirit. Were it not so, the Holy Ghost could not dwell in us."[11]

"I have always declared God to be a distinct personage, Jesus Christ a separate and distinct personage from God the Father, and that the Holy Ghost was a distinct personage and a Spirit: and these three constitute three distinct personages and three Gods."[12]

"That which is without body or parts is nothing. There is no other God in heaven but that God who has flesh and bones."[13]

The Godhead is in perfect unity, and God the Father presides.

"There is much said about God and the Godhead. . . . The teachers of the day say that the Father is God, the Son is God, and the Holy Ghost is God, and they are all in one body and one God. Jesus prayed that those that the Father had given him out of the world might be made one in them, as they were one [see John 17:11–23]. . . .

"Peter and Stephen testify that they saw the Son of Man standing on the right hand of God. Any person that had seen the heavens opened knows that there are three personages in the heavens who hold the keys of power, and one presides over all."[14]

"Everlasting covenant was made between three personages before the organization of this earth and relates to their dispensation of things to men on the earth. These personages . . . are called God the first, the Creator; God the second, the Redeemer; and God the third, the Witness or Testator."[15]

"[It is] the province of the Father to preside as the Chief or President, Jesus as the Mediator, and the Holy Ghost as the Testator or Witness. The Son [has] a tabernacle and so [does] the Father, but the Holy Ghost is a personage of spirit without tabernacle."[16]

"The scripture says, 'I and my Father are one' [John 10:30], and again that the Father, Son and Holy Ghost are one, and these three agree in the same thing [see 1 John 5:7–8]. So did the Savior pray to the Father, 'I pray not for the world, but for those whom ye gave me out of the world, that we might be one,' or to say, be of one mind in the unity of the faith [see John 17:9, 11]. But everyone being a different or separate person, so are God and Jesus Christ and the Holy Ghost separate persons, but they all agree in one or the selfsame thing."[17]

Suggestions for Study and Teaching

Consider these ideas as you study the chapter or as you prepare to teach. For additional help, see pages vii–xii.

- Review pages 37–38, noting how young Joseph Smith saw evidence of an "omnipotent and omnipresent power" in the world around him. As you have observed the world around you, what have you seen that bears testimony of God?
- Review the first section of the chapter (page 39), looking for teachings that reveal the character of God. How can these teachings help us "rejoice and be glad"?
- Joseph Smith taught, "The Great Parent of the universe looks upon the whole of the human family with a fatherly care and paternal regard" (page 39). What are your thoughts and feelings as you ponder this statement?
- Read the paragraph that begins at the bottom of page 39 and also the next paragraph. Why is it impossible to comprehend ourselves if we do not comprehend the character of God?
- The Prophet Joseph Smith testified that God the Father, Jesus Christ, and the Holy Ghost are "three distinct personages." He also taught that They are one (page 42). In what ways are the members of the Godhead one? (For some examples, see page 42.)
- In what ways can parents nurture children's love for their Heavenly Father? (For some examples, see page 37.)

Related Scriptures: John 8:17–19; Hebrews 1:1–3; 12:9; Moses 1:3–6, 39

Notes

1. William Smith, Notes on Chambers' life of Joseph Smith, ca. 1875, Church Archives, The Church of Jesus Christ of Latter-day Saints, Salt Lake City, Utah.
2. William Smith, interview by E. C. Briggs and J. W. Peterson, Oct. or Nov. 1893, originally published in *Zion's Ensign* (periodical published by the Reorganized Church of Jesus Christ of Latter Day Saints, now called Community of Christ); reprinted in *Deseret Evening News,* Jan. 20, 1894, p. 2; punctuation modernized.
3. Joseph Smith, History 1832, pp. 2–3; Letter Book 1, 1829–35, Joseph Smith, Collection, Church Archives.

4. *History of the Church,* 6:305; from a discourse given by Joseph Smith on Apr. 7, 1844, in Nauvoo, Illinois; reported by Wilford Woodruff, Willard Richards, Thomas Bullock, and William Clayton.
5. *History of the Church,* 4:595; from "Baptism for the Dead," an editorial published in *Times and Seasons,* Apr. 15, 1842, p. 759; Joseph Smith was the editor of the periodical.
6. *History of the Church,* 2:12, 14; paragraph divisions altered; from "The Elders of the Church in Kirtland, to Their Brethren Abroad," Jan. 22, 1834, published in *Evening and Morning Star,* Feb. 1834, p. 136; Mar. 1834, p. 142.
7. *History of the Church,* 1:317; from a letter from Joseph Smith to William W. Phelps, Jan. 11, 1833, Kirtland, Ohio; this letter is incorrectly dated Jan. 14, 1833, in *History of the Church.*
8. *History of the Church,* 4:185; from a letter from Joseph Smith and his counselors in the First Presidency to the Saints, Sept. 1840, Nauvoo, Illinois, published in *Times and Seasons,* Oct. 1840, p. 178.
9. *History of the Church,* 6:303–5, 308; capitalization modernized; paragraph divisions altered; from a discourse given by Joseph Smith on Apr. 7, 1844, in Nauvoo, Illinois; reported by Wilford Woodruff, Willard Richards, Thomas Bullock, and William Clayton; see also the appendix in this book, page 562, item 3.
10. Articles of Faith 1:1.
11. Doctrine and Covenants 130:22; instructions given by Joseph Smith on Apr. 2, 1843, in Ramus, Illinois.
12. *History of the Church,* 6:474; from a discourse given by Joseph Smith on June 16, 1844, in Nauvoo, Illinois; reported by Thomas Bullock.
13. Quoted by William Clayton, reporting an undated discourse given by Joseph Smith in Nauvoo, Illinois; in L. John Nuttall, "Extracts from William Clayton's Private Book," p. 7, Journals of L. John Nuttall, 1857–1904, L. Tom Perry Special Collections, Brigham Young University, Provo, Utah; copy in Church Archives.
14. *History of the Church,* 5:426; from a discourse given by Joseph Smith on June 11, 1843, in Nauvoo, Illinois; reported by Wilford Woodruff and Willard Richards.
15. Quoted by William Clayton, reporting an undated discourse given by Joseph Smith in Nauvoo, Illinois; in L. John Nuttall, "Extracts from William Clayton's Private Book," pp. 10–11, Journals of L. John Nuttall, 1857–1904, L. Tom Perry Special Collections, Brigham Young University, Provo, Utah; copy in Church Archives.
16. Quoted by William P. McIntire, reporting a discourse given by Joseph Smith in early 1841 in Nauvoo, Illinois; William Patterson McIntire, Notebook 1840–45, Church Archives. William McIntire made brief reports of several discourses given by Joseph Smith in Nauvoo in early 1841. This book quotes from four of these reports, none of which is dated.
17. Quoted by George Laub, in compilation of excerpts from Joseph Smith's discourses, ca. 1845; George Laub, Reminiscences and Journal Jan. 1845–Apr. 1857, pp. 29–30, Church Archives.

CHAPTER 3

Jesus Christ, the Divine Redeemer of the World

"Salvation could not come to the world without the mediation of Jesus Christ."

From the Life of Joseph Smith

Years before Joseph Smith was born, his paternal grandfather felt inspired that something would happen in his family that "would revolutionize the world."[1] Joseph Smith's history records: "My grandfather, Asael Smith, long ago predicted that there would be a prophet raised up in his family, and my grandmother was fully satisfied that it was fulfilled in me. My grandfather Asael died in East Stockholm, St. Lawrence county, New York, after having received the Book of Mormon, and read it nearly through; and he declared that I was the very Prophet that he had long known would come in his family."[2]

As the Prophet of the Restoration, one of Joseph Smith's most important roles was to testify of Jesus Christ. He was blessed to enjoy a personal knowledge of the divinity of Jesus Christ and to understand His role as the Redeemer of the world. This knowledge began with the First Vision, in which young Joseph saw Heavenly Father and Jesus Christ and heard the Father declare, "This is My Beloved Son. Hear Him!" (Joseph Smith—History 1:17). In this sacred experience, Joseph was privileged to receive instruction from the Savior of the world.

Nearly twelve years later, on February 16, 1832, the Prophet was translating the Bible, with Sidney Rigdon as his scribe, in the home of John Johnson in Hiram, Ohio. After the Prophet translated John 5:29, which describes the resurrection of those who are good and those who are evil, a vision was opened to Joseph and Sidney, and they saw and conversed with the Savior:

The Savior appeared to Joseph Smith and Oliver Cowdery in the Kirtland Temple. "The veil was taken from our minds," Joseph said, "and the eyes of our understanding were opened. We saw the Lord standing upon the breastwork of the pulpit."

"By the power of the Spirit our eyes were opened and our understandings were enlightened, so as to see and understand the things of God—even those things which were from the beginning before the world was, which were ordained of the Father, through his Only Begotten Son, who was in the bosom of the Father, even from the beginning; of whom we bear record; and the record which we bear is the fulness of the gospel of Jesus Christ, who is the Son, whom we saw and with whom we conversed in the heavenly vision. . . .

"And we beheld the glory of the Son, on the right hand of the Father, and received of his fulness; and saw the holy angels, and them who are sanctified before his throne, worshiping God, and the Lamb, who worship him forever and ever.

"And now, after the many testimonies which have been given of him, this is the testimony, last of all, which we give of him: That he lives!

"For we saw him, even on the right hand of God; and we heard the voice bearing record that he is the Only Begotten of the Father—that by him, and through him, and of him, the worlds are and were created, and the inhabitants thereof are begotten sons and daughters unto God" (D&C 76:12–14, 20–24).

Joseph Smith saw the Savior again on April 3, 1836. The Prophet and Oliver Cowdery had retired to the west pulpit in the Kirtland Temple. They bowed themselves in solemn prayer, after which the Savior appeared before them. The Prophet declared:

"The veil was taken from our minds, and the eyes of our understanding were opened. We saw the Lord standing upon the breastwork of the pulpit, before us; and under his feet was a paved work of pure gold, in color like amber. His eyes were as a flame of fire; the hair of his head was white like the pure snow; his countenance shone above the brightness of the sun; and his voice was as the sound of the rushing of great waters, even the voice of Jehovah, saying: I am the first and the last; I am he who liveth, I am he who was slain; I am your advocate with the Father" (D&C 110:1–4).

From such experiences, the Prophet gained firsthand knowledge and became a special witness of the divinity of the Savior.

Teachings of Joseph Smith

In all dispensations, God's people have relied on the Atonement of Christ for the remission of their sins.

"Salvation could not come to the world without the mediation of Jesus Christ."[3]

"God . . . prepared a sacrifice in the gift of His own Son, who should be sent in due time to prepare a way, or open a door through which man might enter into the Lord's presence, whence he had been cast out for disobedience. From time to time these glad tidings were sounded in the ears of men in different ages of the world down to the time of Messiah's coming.

"By faith in this atonement or plan of redemption, Abel offered to God a sacrifice that was accepted, which was the firstlings of the flock. Cain offered of the fruit of the ground, and was not accepted, because he could not do it in faith; he could have no faith, or could not exercise faith contrary to the plan of heaven. It must be shedding the blood of the Only Begotten to atone for man, for this was the plan of redemption, and without the shedding of blood was no remission. And as the sacrifice was instituted for a type by which man was to discern the great Sacrifice which God had prepared, to offer a sacrifice contrary to that, no faith could be exercised, because redemption was not purchased in that way, nor the power of atonement instituted after that order; consequently Cain could have no faith; and whatsoever is not of faith, is sin. But Abel offered an acceptable sacrifice, by which he obtained witness that he was righteous, God Himself testifying of his gifts [see Hebrews 11:4].

"Certainly, the shedding of the blood of a beast could be beneficial to no man, except it was done in imitation, or as a type, or explanation of what was to be offered through the gift of God Himself—and this performance done with an eye looking forward in faith on the power of that great Sacrifice for a remission of sins. . . .

". . . We cannot believe that the ancients in all ages were so ignorant of the system of heaven as many suppose, since all that were ever saved, were saved through the power of this great plan of redemption, as much before the coming of Christ as since; if not, God has had different plans in operation (if we may so express it), to bring men back to dwell with Himself. And this we cannot believe, since there has been no change in the constitution of man since he fell; and the ordinance or institution of offering blood in sacrifice was only designed to be performed till Christ was offered up and shed His blood—as said before—that man might look forward in faith to that time. . . .

"That the offering of sacrifice was only to point the mind forward to Christ, we infer from these remarkable words of Jesus to the Jews: 'Your Father Abraham rejoiced to see my day: and he saw it, and was glad' [John 8:56]. So, then, because the ancients offered sacrifice it did not hinder their hearing the Gospel; but served, as we said before, to open their eyes, and enable them to look forward to the time of the coming of the Savior, and rejoice in His redemption. . . . We conclude that whenever the Lord revealed Himself to men in ancient days, and commanded them to offer sacrifice to Him, that it was done that they might look forward in faith to the time of His coming, and rely upon the power of that atonement for a remission of their sins. And this they have done, thousands who have gone before us, whose garments are spotless, and who are, like Job, waiting with an assurance like his, that they will see Him in the *latter day* upon the earth, even in their flesh [see Job 19:25–26].

"We may conclude, that though there were different dispensations, yet all things which God communicated to His people were calculated to draw their minds to the great object, and to teach them to rely upon God alone as the author of their salvation, as contained in His law."[4]

Because Jesus Christ rose from the dead, all mankind will be resurrected.

"The fundamental principles of our religion are the testimony of the Apostles and Prophets, concerning Jesus Christ, that He died, was buried, and rose again the third day, and ascended into heaven; and all other things which pertain to our religion are only appendages to it. But in connection with these, we believe

"The Lamb of God hath brought to pass the resurrection, so that all shall rise from the dead."

in the gift of the Holy Ghost, the power of faith, the enjoyment of the spiritual gifts according to the will of God, the restoration of the house of Israel, and the final triumph of truth."[5]

" 'As in Adam all die, even so in Christ shall all be made alive;' all shall be raised from the dead [1 Corinthians 15:22]. The

Lamb of God hath brought to pass the resurrection, so that all shall rise from the dead."[6]

"God has appointed a day in which He will judge the world, and this He has given an assurance of in that He raised up His Son Jesus Christ from the dead—the point on which the hope of all who believe the inspired record is founded for their future happiness and enjoyment; because, 'If Christ be not risen,' said Paul to the Corinthians, 'your faith is vain; ye are yet in your sins. Then they also which are fallen asleep in Christ have perished' [1 Corinthians 15:17–18]. . . .

"Christ Himself has assuredly risen from the dead; and if He has risen from the dead, He will, by His power, bring all men to stand before Him: for if He has risen from the dead the bands of the temporal death are broken that the grave has no victory. If then, the grave has no victory, those who keep the sayings of Jesus and obey His teachings have not only a promise of a resurrection from the dead, but an assurance of being admitted into His glorious kingdom; for, He Himself says, 'Where I am there also shall my servant be' [John 12:26]."[7]

"Those who have died in Jesus Christ may expect to enter into all that fruition of joy when they come forth, which they possessed or anticipated here. . . . I am glad I have the privilege of communicating to you some things which, if grasped closely, will be a help to you when earthquakes bellow, the clouds gather, the lightnings flash, and the storms are ready to burst upon you like peals of thunder. Lay hold of these things and let not your knees or joints tremble, nor your hearts faint; and then what can earthquakes, wars and tornadoes do? Nothing. All your losses will be made up to you in the resurrection, provided you continue faithful. By the vision of the Almighty I have seen it. . . .

"God has revealed His Son from the heavens and the doctrine of the resurrection also; and we have a knowledge that those we bury here God will bring up again, clothed upon and quickened by the Spirit of the great God; and what mattereth it whether we lay them down, or we lay down with them, when we can keep them no longer? Let these truths sink down in our hearts, that we may even here begin to enjoy that which shall be in full hereafter."[8]

Through the Atonement of Christ and obedience to the gospel, we can become joint heirs with Jesus Christ.

"I believe in the Divinity of Jesus Christ, and that He died for the sins of all men, who in Adam had fallen."[9]

Articles of Faith 1:3: "We believe that through the Atonement of Christ, all mankind may be saved, by obedience to the laws and ordinances of the Gospel."[10]

"After God had created the heavens and the earth, he came down and on the sixth day said, 'Let us make man in our own image.' In whose image? In the image of the Gods created they them, male and female, innocent, harmless, and spotless, bearing the same character and the same image as the Gods [see Genesis 1:26–27]. And when man fell he did not lose his image, but his character still retained the image of his Maker. Christ, who is the image of man, is also the express image of his Father's person [see Hebrews 1:3]. . . . Through the atonement of Christ and the resurrection, and obedience to the gospel, we shall again be conformed to the image of his Son, Jesus Christ [see Romans 8:29]; then we shall have attained to the image, glory, and character of God."[11]

"The Father of our spirits [provided] a sacrifice for His creatures, a plan of redemption, a power of atonement, a scheme of salvation, having as its great objects, the bringing of men back into the presence of the King of heaven, crowning them in the celestial glory, and making them heirs with the Son to that inheritance which is incorruptible, undefiled, and which fadeth not away."[12]

"The scripture says those who will obey the commandments shall be heirs of God and joint heirs with Jesus Christ. . . . 'The Spirit itself beareth witness with our spirit that we are the children of God, and if children, then heirs of God, and joint heirs with Jesus Christ, if so be that we suffer with him in the flesh that we may be also glorified together.' [See Romans 8:16–17.]"[13]

"How consoling to the mourners when they are called to part with a husband, wife, father, mother, child, or dear relative, to know that, although the earthly tabernacle is laid down and dissolved, they shall rise again to dwell in everlasting burnings in immortal glory, not to sorrow, suffer, or die any more, but they shall be heirs of God and joint heirs with Jesus Christ."[14]

Jesus Christ is perfect, pure, and holy, and He has called us to be like Him.

"Who, among all the Saints in these last days, can consider himself as good as our Lord? Who is as perfect? Who is as pure? Who is as holy as He was? Are they to be found? He never transgressed or broke a commandment or law of heaven—no deceit was in His mouth, neither was guile found in His heart. . . . Where is one like Christ? He cannot be found on earth."[15]

"The creature was made subject to vanity, not willingly, but Christ subjected the same in hope [see Romans 8:20]—all are subjected to vanity while they travel through the crooked paths and difficulties which surround them. Where is the man that is free from vanity? None ever were perfect but Jesus; and why was He perfect? Because He was the Son of God, and had the fullness of the Spirit, and greater power than any man."[16]

"When still a boy [Jesus Christ] had all the intelligence necessary to enable Him to rule and govern the kingdom of the Jews, and could reason with the wisest and most profound doctors of law and divinity, and make their theories and practice to appear like folly compared with the wisdom He possessed."[17]

"The commandments of our Lord, we hope are constantly revolving in your hearts, teaching you, not only His will in proclaiming His Gospel, but His meekness and perfect walk before all, even in those times of severe persecutions and abuse which were heaped upon Him by a wicked and adulterous generation. Remember, brethren, that He has called you unto holiness; and need we say, to be like Him in purity? How wise, how holy; how chaste, and how perfect, then, you ought to conduct yourselves in His sight; and remember, too, that His eyes are continually upon you."[18]

"When we reflect upon the holiness and perfections of our great Master, who has opened a way whereby we may come unto

"When we reflect upon the holiness and perfections of our great Master, . . . our hearts melt within us for his condescension."

him, even by the sacrifice of himself, our hearts melt within us for his condescension. And when we reflect also, that he has called us to be perfect in all things, that we may be prepared to meet him in peace when he comes in his glory with all the holy angels, we feel to exhort our brethren with boldness, to be humble and prayerful, to walk indeed as children of the light and of the day, that they may have grace to withstand every temptation, and to overcome every evil in the worthy name of our Lord Jesus Christ. For be assured, brethren, that the day is truly near when the Master of the house will rise up and shut the door, and none but such as have on a wedding garment will be permitted to enjoy a seat at the marriage supper! [See Matthew 22:1–14.]"[19]

Suggestions for Study and Teaching

Consider these ideas as you study the chapter or as you prepare to teach. For additional help, see pages vii–xii.

- Review the accounts of Joseph Smith's visions of the Savior (pages 45–47). What are your thoughts and feelings as you ponder these experiences?
- Anciently, animal sacrifices helped the Lord's people "open their eyes, and . . . look forward to the time of the coming of the Savior, and rejoice in His redemption" (page 49). What are some things that help you look to the Savior today?
- Read the paragraph that begins at the bottom of page 49. Note that in this statement, an appendage is something that is connected to something of greater importance, such as a branch that is connected to the trunk of a tree. Why do you think the testimonies of the apostles and prophets concerning the Savior's Atonement and Resurrection are the "fundamental principles of our religion"? How might you approach your service at home and in the Church if you remember that all other things are appendages to these principles?
- Review the Prophet Joseph's teachings about the resurrection (pages 49–51). What comfort do you receive from knowing that "all your losses will be made up to you in the resurrection, provided you continue faithful"? In what ways can a knowledge of the resurrection help us "begin to enjoy that which shall be in full hereafter"?
- As you review pages 52–53, ponder what the Savior has done so we can become joint heirs with Him. Consider ways you can show Him your gratitude for His atoning sacrifice.
- On pages 53–54, the Prophet Joseph Smith mentions many of the Savior's attributes. What other attributes do you think of when you ponder the life and mission of the Savior? Think about something you can do to become more like Him.

Related Scriptures: Isaiah 53:1–12; 2 Nephi 9:5–26; D&C 20:21–29

Notes

1. Reported by George A. Smith, *Deseret News,* Aug. 12, 1857, p. 183.
2. *History of the Church,* 2:443; from "History of the Church" (manuscript), book B-1, addenda, p. 5, Church Archives, The Church of Jesus Christ of Latter-day Saints, Salt Lake City, Utah.
3. *History of the Church,* 5:555; from a discourse given by Joseph Smith on Aug. 27, 1843, in Nauvoo, Illinois; reported by Willard Richards and William Clayton.
4. *History of the Church,* 2:15–17; punctuation modernized; paragraph divisions altered; from "The Elders of the Church in Kirtland, to Their Brethren Abroad," Jan. 22, 1834, published in *Evening and Morning Star,* Mar. 1834, p. 143.
5. *History of the Church,* 3:30; from an editorial published in *Elders' Journal,* July 1838, p. 44; Joseph Smith was the editor of the periodical.
6. *History of the Church,* 6:366; from a discourse given by Joseph Smith on May 12, 1844, in Nauvoo, Illinois; reported by Thomas Bullock.
7. *History of the Church,* 2:18–19; paragraph divisions altered; from "The Elders of the Church in Kirtland, to Their Brethren Abroad," Jan. 22, 1834, published in *Evening and Morning Star,* Mar. 1834, p. 144.
8. *History of the Church,* 5:361–62; paragraph divisions altered; from a discourse given by Joseph Smith on Apr. 16, 1843, in Nauvoo, Illinois; reported by Wilford Woodruff and Willard Richards.
9. *History of the Church,* 4:78; from a letter from Matthew L. Davis to Mary Davis, Feb. 6, 1840, Washington, D.C., reporting a discourse given by Joseph Smith on Feb. 5, 1840, in Washington, D.C.
10. Articles of Faith 1:3.
11. Quoted by James Burgess, in compilation of excerpts from Joseph Smith's discourses; James Burgess, Journals, 1841–48, vol. 2, Church Archives.
12. *History of the Church,* 2:5; from "The Elders of the Church in Kirtland, to Their Brethren Abroad," Jan. 22, 1834, published in *Evening and Morning Star,* Feb. 1834, p. 135.
13. Quoted by George Laub, in compilation of excerpts from Joseph Smith's discourses, ca. 1845; George Laub, Reminiscences and Journal Jan. 1845–Apr. 1857, p. 31, Church Archives.
14. *History of the Church,* 6:306; from a discourse given by Joseph Smith on Apr. 7, 1844, in Nauvoo, Illinois; reported by Wilford Woodruff, Willard Richards, Thomas Bullock, and William Clayton.
15. *History of the Church,* 2:23; from "The Elders of the Church in Kirtland, to Their Brethren Abroad," Jan. 22, 1834, published in *Evening and Morning Star,* Apr. 1834, p. 152.
16. *History of the Church,* 4:358; from a discourse given by Joseph Smith on May 16, 1841, in Nauvoo, Illinois; reported in *Times and Seasons,* June 1, 1841, pp. 429–30.
17. *History of the Church,* 6:608; from instructions given by Joseph Smith on June 27, 1844, in Carthage Jail, Carthage, Illinois; reported by Cyrus H. Wheelock.
18. *History of the Church,* 2:13; from "The Elders of the Church in Kirtland, to Their Brethren Abroad," Jan. 22, 1834, published in *Evening and Morning Star,* Mar. 1834, p. 142.
19. Letter from Joseph Smith and high priests to the brethren in Geneseo, New York, Nov. 23, 1833, Kirtland, Ohio, Church Archives.

CHAPTER 4

The Book of Mormon: Keystone of Our Religion

"I told the brethren that the Book of Mormon was the most correct of any book on earth, and the keystone of our religion."

From the Life of Joseph Smith

More than three years had passed since the morning in 1820 when Joseph Smith had prayed to know which church he should join. The young Prophet was now 17 years old, and he desired to know his standing before God and to receive forgiveness. On the night of September 21, 1823, Joseph retired to his attic bedroom in his family's log home in Palmyra, New York, but he stayed awake after the others in the room had gone to sleep, earnestly praying to know more about God's purposes for him. "I betook myself to prayer and supplication to Almighty God," he said, "for forgiveness of all my sins and follies, and also for a manifestation to me, that I might know of my state and standing before him; for I had full confidence in obtaining a divine manifestation, as I previously had one" (Joseph Smith—History 1:29).

In answer to his prayer, Joseph saw a light appear in his room that grew brighter and brighter until the room was "lighter than at noonday." A heavenly messenger appeared at his bedside, standing in the air, wearing a robe of "exquisite whiteness." (Joseph Smith—History 1:30–31.) This messenger was Moroni, the last Nephite prophet, who centuries earlier had buried the plates upon which the Book of Mormon was written and who now held the keys pertaining to this sacred record (see D&C 27:5). He had been sent to tell Joseph that God had forgiven his sins[1] and had a great work for him to do. As part of this work, Joseph was to go to a nearby hill, where a sacred record, written

Joseph Smith received the gold plates from Moroni on September 22, 1827. "I obtained them," the Prophet testified, "and the Urim and Thummim with them, by the means of which I translated the plates; and thus came the Book of Mormon."

on gold plates, was deposited. This record was written by prophets who had lived anciently upon the American continent. By the gift and power of God, Joseph was to translate the record and bring it forth to the world.

The next day, Joseph went to the hill where the Book of Mormon plates were buried. There he met Moroni and saw the plates, but was told that he would not receive them for four years. He was to begin an important period of preparation that would make him equal to the sacred task of translating the Book of Mormon. Joseph returned to the hill each September 22 for the next four years to receive further instructions from Moroni. (See Joseph Smith—History 1:33–54.) During these years, he also received "many visits from the angels of God unfolding the majesty and glory of the events that should transpire in the last days."[2]

This period of preparation also brought the blessing of marriage into the Prophet's life. In January 1827, he married Emma Hale, whom he had met while he was working in Harmony, Pennsylvania. Emma would be an important help to the Prophet throughout his ministry. On September 22, 1827, she went with him to the hill and waited nearby while Moroni delivered the plates into the Prophet's hands.

With the sacred record in his possession, Joseph soon discovered why Moroni had warned him to protect the plates (see Joseph Smith—History 1:59–60). A local mob began harassing the Prophet, making repeated efforts to steal the plates. On a wintry day in December 1827, hoping to find a place to work in peace, Joseph and Emma left the Smith family home to seek refuge with Emma's parents in Harmony. There the Prophet began the work of translation. The following February, Martin Harris, a friend of the Smiths from Palmyra, was inspired to go to Harmony to help the Prophet. With Martin as his scribe, Joseph moved forward with the translation of the sacred record.

The results of the Prophet's work would later be published as the Book of Mormon. This remarkable book, containing the fulness of the gospel, stands as a testimony of the truthfulness of The Church of Jesus Christ of Latter-day Saints and the prophetic mission of Joseph Smith.

Teachings of Joseph Smith

The Book of Mormon was translated by the gift and power of God.

In response to the question, "How and where did you obtain the Book of Mormon?" Joseph Smith responded: "Moroni, who deposited the plates in a hill in Manchester, Ontario county, New York, being dead and raised again therefrom, appeared unto me, and told me where they were, and gave me directions how to obtain them. I obtained them, and the Urim and Thummim with them, by the means of which I translated the plates; and thus came the Book of Mormon."[3]

"I was [told by Moroni] where were deposited some plates on which were engraven an abridgment of the records of the ancient Prophets that had existed on this continent. . . . These records were engraven on plates which had the appearance of gold; each plate was six inches wide and eight inches long, and not quite so thick as common tin. They were filled with engravings, in Egyptian characters, and bound together in a volume as the leaves of a book, with three rings running through the whole. The volume was something near six inches in thickness, a part of which was sealed. The characters on the unsealed part were small, and beautifully engraved. The whole book exhibited many marks of antiquity in its construction, and much skill in the art of engraving. With the records was found a curious instrument, which the ancients called 'Urim and Thummim,' which consisted of two transparent stones set in the rim of a bow fastened to a breast plate. Through the medium of the Urim and Thummim I translated the record by the gift and power of God."[4]

"By the power of God I translated the Book of Mormon from hieroglyphics, the knowledge of which was lost to the world, in which wonderful event I stood alone, an unlearned youth, to combat the worldly wisdom and multiplied ignorance of eighteen centuries, with a new revelation."[5]

"I wish to mention here that the title-page of the Book of Mormon is a literal translation, taken from the very last leaf, on the left hand side of the collection or book of plates, which

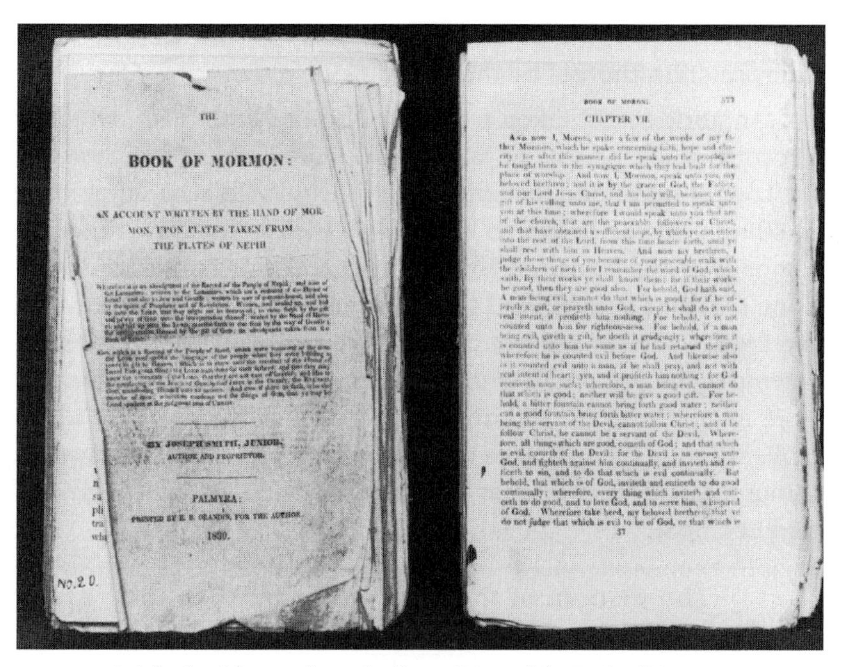
THE
BOOK OF MORMON:
AN ACCOUNT WRITTEN BY THE HAND OF MORMON, UPON PLATES TAKEN FROM THE PLATES OF NEPHI.

BY JOSEPH SMITH, JUNIOR,
AUTHOR AND PROPRIETOR.

PALMYRA:
PRINTED BY E. B. GRANDIN, FOR THE AUTHOR.
1830.

BOOK OF MORONI. 573
CHAPTER VII.

At left, the title page from the first edition of the Book of Mormon.

contained the record which has been translated, the language of the whole running the same as all Hebrew writing in general [that is, from right to left]; and that said title page is not by any means a modern composition, either of mine or of any other man who has lived or does live in this generation. . . . I give below that part of the title-page of the English version of the Book of Mormon, which is a genuine and literal translation of the title-page of the original Book of Mormon as recorded on the plates:

" 'THE BOOK OF MORMON.

" 'An account written by the hand of Mormon, upon Plates, taken from the Plates of Nephi.

" 'Wherefore, it is an abridgment of the record of the people of Nephi, and also of the Lamanites—Written to the Lamanites, who are a remnant of the house of Israel; and also to Jew and Gentile—Written by way of commandment, and also by the spirit of prophecy and of revelation—Written and sealed up, and hid up unto the Lord, that they might not be destroyed—To come forth by the gift and power of God unto the interpretation thereof—Sealed by the hand of Moroni, and hid up unto the

Lord, to come forth in due time by way of the Gentile—The interpretation thereof by the gift of God.

" 'An abridgment taken from the Book of Ether also, which is a record of the people of Jared, who were scattered at the time the Lord confounded the language of the people, when they were building a tower to get to heaven—Which is to show unto the remnant of the house of Israel what great things the Lord hath done for their fathers; and that they may know the covenants of the Lord, that they are not cast off forever—And also to the convincing of the Jew and Gentile that *Jesus* is the *Christ,* the *Eternal God,* manifesting himself unto all nations—And now, if there are faults they are the mistakes of men; wherefore, condemn not the things of God, that ye may be found spotless at the judgment-seat of Christ.' "[6]

The wisdom of the Lord is greater than the cunning of the devil.

By June 14, 1828, Joseph Smith's work on the translation of the Book of Mormon plates had resulted in 116 pages of manuscript. Then an incident occurred that taught the Prophet profound lessons about God's guiding hand in bringing forth this sacred record. The Prophet recorded: "Some time after Mr. Harris had begun to write for me, he began to importune me to give him liberty to carry the writings home and show them; and desired of me that I would inquire of the Lord, through the Urim and Thummim, if he might not do so. I did inquire, and the answer was that he must not. However, he was not satisfied with this answer, and desired that I should inquire again. I did so, and the answer was as before. Still he could not be contented, but insisted that I should inquire once more.

"After much solicitation I again inquired of the Lord, and permission was granted him to have the writings on certain conditions; which were, that he show them only to his brother, Preserved Harris; his own wife; his father and his mother; and a Mrs. Cobb, a sister to his wife. In accordance with this last answer, I required of him that he should bind himself in a covenant to me in a most solemn manner that he would not do otherwise than had been directed. He did so. He bound himself as I required of him, took the writings, and went his way. Notwithstanding, however, the great restrictions which he had been laid under, and the solemnity of the covenant which he had made with me, he did show them to others, and by stratagem they got them away from him, and they never have been recovered unto this day."[7]

In the preface to the first edition of the Book of Mormon, the Prophet declared that God's purposes could not be frustrated by the loss of the 116 pages: "As many false reports have been circulated respecting the [Book of Mormon], and also many unlawful measures taken by evil designing persons to destroy me, and also the work, I would inform you that I translated, by the gift and power of God, and caused to be written, one hundred and sixteen pages, the which I took from the Book of Lehi, which was an account abridged from the plates of Lehi, by the hand of Mormon; which said account, some person or persons have stolen and kept from me, notwithstanding my utmost exertions to recover it again—and being commanded of the Lord that I should not translate the same over again, for Satan had put it into their hearts to tempt the Lord their God, by altering the words, that they did read contrary from that which I translated and caused to be written; and if I should bring forth the same words again, or, in other words, if I should translate the same over again, they would publish that which they had stolen, and Satan would stir up the hearts of this generation, that they might not receive this work: but behold, the Lord said unto me, I will not suffer that Satan shall accomplish his evil design in this thing: therefore thou shalt translate from the plates of Nephi, until ye come to that which ye have translated, which ye have retained; and behold ye shall publish it as the record of Nephi; and thus I will confound those who have altered my words. I will not suffer that they shall destroy my work; yea, I will shew unto them that my wisdom is greater than the cunning of the Devil. [See D&C 10:38–43.]

"Wherefore, to be obedient unto the commandments of God, I have, through his grace and mercy, accomplished that which he hath commanded me respecting this thing."[8]

The Book of Mormon is the word of God.

"I told the brethren that the Book of Mormon was the most correct of any book on earth, and the keystone of our religion, and a man would get nearer to God by abiding by its precepts, than by any other book."[9]

Articles of Faith 1:8: "We believe the Bible to be the word of God as far as it is translated correctly; we also believe the Book of Mormon to be the word of God."[10]

"[The Book of Mormon] tells us that our Savior made His appearance upon this continent after His resurrection; that He planted the Gospel here in all its fulness, and richness, and power, and blessing; that they had Apostles, Prophets, Pastors, Teachers, and Evangelists, the same order, the same priesthood, the same ordinances, gifts, powers, and blessings, as were enjoyed on the eastern continent; that the people were cut off in consequence of their transgressions; that the last of their prophets who existed among them was commanded to write an abridgment of their prophecies, history, etc., and to hide it up in the earth, and that it should come forth and be united with the Bible for the accomplishment of the purposes of God in the last days."[11]

David Osborn was present when Joseph Smith preached in Far West, Missouri, in 1837. He recalled these words of the Prophet: "The Book of Mormon is true, just what it purports to be, and for this testimony I expect to give an account in the day of judgment."[12]

The scriptures cheer and comfort us and make us wise unto salvation.

"Connected with the building up of the Kingdom, is the printing and circulation of the Book of Mormon, Doctrine and Covenants, . . . and the new translation of the [Bible]. It is unnecessary to say anything respecting these works; those who have read them, and who have drunk of the stream of knowledge which they convey, know how to appreciate them; and although fools may have them in derision, yet they are calculated to make

The latter-day scriptures are published "so that the honest in heart may be cheered and comforted and go on their way rejoicing."

men wise unto salvation, and sweep away the cobwebs of superstition of ages, throw a light on the proceedings of Jehovah which have already been accomplished, and mark out the future in all its dreadful and glorious realities. Those who have tasted the benefit derived from a study of those works, will undoubtedly vie with each other in their zeal for sending them abroad throughout the world, that every son of Adam may enjoy the same privileges, and rejoice in the same truths."[13]

"[The latter-day scriptures are published] so that the honest in heart may be cheered and comforted and go on their way rejoicing, as their souls become exposed and their understanding enlightened by a knowledge of God's work through the fathers in former days, as well as what He is about to do in latter days to fulfill the words of the fathers."[14]

"We take the sacred writings into our hands, and admit that they were given by direct inspiration for the good of man. We believe that God condescended to speak from the heavens and declare His will concerning the human family, to give them just and holy laws, to regulate their conduct, and guide them in a direct way, that in due time He might take them to Himself, and make them joint heirs with His Son.

"But when this fact is admitted, that the immediate will of heaven is contained in the Scriptures, are we not bound as rational creatures to live in accordance to all its precepts? Will the mere admission that this is the will of heaven ever benefit us if we do not comply with all its teachings? Do we not offer violence to the Supreme Intelligence of heaven when we admit the truth of its teachings, and do not obey them? Do we not descend below our own knowledge, and the better wisdom which heaven has endowed us with, by such a course of conduct? For these reasons, if we have direct revelations given us from heaven, surely those revelations were never given to be trifled with, without the trifler's incurring displeasure and vengeance upon his own head, if there is any justice in heaven; and that there is must be admitted by every individual who admits the truth and force of God's teachings, His blessings and cursings, as contained in the sacred volume. . . .

". . . He that can mark the power of Omnipotence, inscribed upon the heavens, can also see God's own handwriting in the sacred volume: and he who reads it oftenest will like it best, and he who is acquainted with it, will know the hand wherever he can see it; and when once discovered, it will not only receive an acknowledgment, but an obedience to all its heavenly precepts."[15]

"O ye Twelve! and all Saints! profit by this important *Key*—that in all your trials, troubles, temptations, afflictions, bonds, imprisonments and death, see to it, that you do not betray heaven; that you do not betray Jesus Christ; that you do not betray the brethren; that you do not betray the revelations of God, whether in the Bible, Book of Mormon, or Doctrine and Covenants, or any other that ever was or ever will be given and revealed unto man in this world or that which is to come."[16]

Suggestions for Study and Teaching

Consider these ideas as you study the chapter or as you prepare to teach. For additional help, see pages vii–xii.

- Review the experiences Joseph Smith had between September 21, 1823, and September 22, 1827 (pages 57–59). How do you think these experiences prepared him to translate the gold plates? In what ways have you been prepared for callings from the Lord?
- Review the first full paragraph on page 62, noting the purposes of the Book of Mormon. In what ways have you seen these purposes fulfilled in your life and in the lives of others?
- As you ponder the Prophet's account of being commanded not to retranslate the 116 pages of manuscript that were lost (pages 62–63), what do you learn about God? How might an understanding of this account influence the decisions we make?
- Read the first paragraph on page 64. Note that in an arch made of stones, the keystone is placed at the top, holding all the other stones in place. In what ways is the Book of Mormon "the keystone of our religion"? How has the Book of Mormon helped you "get nearer to God"?
- Joseph Smith spoke of the blessings that come when we have "drunk of the stream of knowledge" in the scriptures and "tasted the benefit" of the word of God (pages 64–65). What do these expressions suggest to you about scripture study? What can we do to make our scripture study more meaningful?
- Read the paragraph beginning at the bottom of page 64. Why do you think that those who study the scriptures develop a zeal for sharing them with others? What can we do to share the Book of Mormon? What experiences have you had when you have shared the Book of Mormon or when someone has shared it with you?
- Read the last paragraph on page 65. What are some passages from the Book of Mormon that have "cheered and comforted" you? In what ways has the Book of Mormon enlightened your understanding?

Related Scriptures: Ezekiel 37:15–17; introduction to the Book of Mormon; 1 Nephi 13:31–42; 2 Nephi 27:6–26; D&C 20:6–15; Joseph Smith—History 1:29–54

Notes

1. See Joseph Smith, History 1832, p. 4; Letter Book 1, 1829–35, Joseph Smith, Collection, Church Archives, The Church of Jesus Christ of Latter-day Saints, Salt Lake City, Utah.
2. *History of the Church,* 4:537; from a letter from Joseph Smith written at the request of John Wentworth and George Barstow, Nauvoo, Illinois, published in *Times and Seasons,* Mar. 1, 1842, p. 707.
3. *History of the Church,* 3:28; from an editorial published in *Elders' Journal,* July 1838, pp. 42–43; Joseph Smith was the editor of the periodical.
4. *History of the Church,* 4:537; punctuation modernized; paragraph divisions altered; from a letter from Joseph Smith written at the request of John Wentworth and George Barstow, Nauvoo, Illinois, published in *Times and Seasons,* Mar. 1, 1842, p. 707.
5. *History of the Church,* 6:74; from a letter from Joseph Smith to James Arlington Bennet, Nov. 13, 1843, Nauvoo, Illinois; James Bennet's last name is incorrectly spelled "Bennett" in *History of the Church.*
6. *History of the Church,* 1:71–72; bracketed words in original; from "History of the Church" (manuscript), book A-1, pp. 34–35, Church Archives.
7. *History of the Church,* 1:21; punctuation modernized; paragraph divisions altered; from "History of the Church" (manuscript), book A-1, pp. 9–10, Church Archives.
8. Preface to the first (1830) edition of the Book of Mormon; paragraph divisions altered.
9. *History of the Church,* 4:461; from instructions given by Joseph Smith on Nov. 28, 1841, in Nauvoo, Illinois; reported by Wilford Woodruff.
10. Articles of Faith 1:8.
11. *History of the Church,* 4:538; punctuation modernized; from a letter from Joseph Smith written at the request of John Wentworth and George Barstow, Nauvoo, Illinois, published in *Times and Seasons,* Mar. 1, 1842, pp. 707–8.
12. Quoted by David Osborn, in "Recollections of the Prophet Joseph Smith," *Juvenile Instructor,* Mar. 15, 1892, p. 173.
13. *History of the Church,* 4:187; from a letter from Joseph Smith and his counselors in the First Presidency to the Saints, Sept. 1840, Nauvoo, Illinois, published in *Times and Seasons,* Oct. 1840, p. 179.
14. Letter from Joseph Smith to the *Times and Seasons,* about Mar. 1842, Nauvoo, Illinois; Miscellany, Joseph Smith, Collection, Church Archives; the letter was apparently not sent.
15. *History of the Church,* 2:11, 14; punctuation modernized; paragraph divisions altered; from "The Elders of the Church in Kirtland, to Their Brethren Abroad," Jan. 22, 1834, published in *Evening and Morning Star,* Feb. 1834, p. 136; Mar. 1834, p. 142.
16. *History of the Church,* 3:385; from a discourse given by Joseph Smith on July 2, 1839, in Montrose, Iowa; reported by Wilford Woodruff and Willard Richards. Elder Richards's record of this discourse was based on records of the discourse made by others. Elder Richards also used the records of others when recording the Prophet's discourse given on June 27, 1839, and the two discourses dated "about July 1839." These discourses will be referred to throughout this book.

C H A P T E R 5

Repentance

"Let us this very day begin anew, and now say, with all our hearts, we will forsake our sins and be righteous."

From the Life of Joseph Smith

On June 14, 1828, Martin Harris left Harmony, Pennsylvania, taking the first 116 manuscript pages translated from the gold plates to show to some of his family members in Palmyra, New York. The very next day, Joseph and Emma's first child was born, a son they named Alvin. The baby died that same day, and Emma's health declined until she was near death herself. The Prophet's mother later wrote: "For some time, [Emma] seemed to tremble upon the verge of the silent home of her infant. So uncertain seemed her fate for a season that in the space of two weeks her husband never slept one hour in undisturbed quiet. At the end of this time, his anxiety became so great about the manuscript that he determined, as his wife was now some better, that as soon as she had gained a little more strength he would make a trip to New York and see after the same."[1]

In July, at Emma's suggestion, the Prophet left Emma in her mother's care and traveled by stagecoach to his parents' home in Manchester Township, New York. The Prophet's trip covered about 125 miles and took two or three days to complete. Distraught about the loss of his firstborn son, worried about his wife, and gravely concerned about the manuscript, Joseph neither ate nor slept during the entire trip. A fellow traveler, the only other passenger on the stagecoach, observed the Prophet's weakened state and insisted on accompanying him for the 20-mile walk from the stagecoach station to the Smith home. For the last four miles of the walk, recalled the Prophet's mother, "the stranger was under the necessity of leading Joseph by his

Repentance is made possible through the atoning sacrifice of the Savior, Jesus Christ. "Search your hearts, and see if you are like God," the Prophet Joseph Smith declared. "I have searched mine, and feel to repent of all my sins."

arm, for nature was too much exhausted to support him any longer and he would fall asleep as he stood upon his feet."[2] Immediately upon reaching his parents' home, the Prophet sent for Martin Harris.

Martin arrived at the Smith home in the early afternoon, downcast and forlorn. He did not have the manuscript, he said, and did not know where it was. Hearing this, Joseph exclaimed, "Oh! My God, my God. . . . All is lost, is lost. What shall I do? I have sinned. It is I that tempted the wrath of God by asking him for that which I had no right to ask. . . . How shall I appear before the Lord? Of what rebuke am I not worthy from the angel of the Most High?"

As the day wore on, the Prophet paced back and forth in his parents' home in great distress, "weeping and grieving." The next day he left to return to Harmony, where, he said, "I commenced humbling myself in mighty prayer before the Lord . . . that if possible I might obtain mercy at his hands and be forgiven of all that I had done which was contrary to his will."[3]

The Lord severely chastised the Prophet for fearing man more than God, but assured him he could be forgiven. "Thou art Joseph," the Lord said, "and thou wast chosen to do the work of the Lord, but because of transgression, if thou art not aware thou wilt fall. But remember, God is merciful; therefore, repent of that which thou hast done which is contrary to the commandment which I gave you, and thou art still chosen, and art again called to the work" (D&C 3:9–10).

For a time, the Lord took the Urim and Thummim and the plates from Joseph. But these things were soon restored to him. "The angel was rejoiced when he gave me back the Urim and Thummim," the Prophet recalled, "and said that God was pleased with my faithfulness and humility, and loved me for my penitence and diligence in prayer, in the which I had performed my duty so well as to . . . be able to enter upon the work of translation again."[4] As Joseph moved forward in the great work before him, he was now fortified by the sweet feelings of receiving the Lord's forgiveness and a renewed determination to do His will.

Teachings of Joseph Smith

By repenting of our sins, we draw toward God and become more like Him.

Wilford Woodruff, while serving as a member of the Quorum of the Twelve, recorded: "Joseph the Seer arose in the power of God; reproved and rebuked wickedness before the people, in the name of the Lord God. He wished to say a few words to suit the condition of the general mass, and then said:

" 'I shall speak with authority of the Priesthood in the name of the Lord God. . . . Notwithstanding this congregation profess to be Saints, yet I stand in the midst of all [kinds of] characters and classes of men. If you wish to go where God is, you must be like God, or possess the principles which God possesses, for if we are not drawing towards God in principle, we are going from Him and drawing towards the devil. Yes, I am standing in the midst of all kinds of people.

" 'Search your hearts, and see if you are like God. I have searched mine, and feel to repent of all my sins.

" 'We have thieves among us, adulterers, liars, hypocrites. If God should speak from heaven, He would command you not to steal, not to commit adultery, not to covet, nor deceive, but be faithful over a few things. . . . Is not God good? Then you be good; if He is faithful, then you be faithful. Add to your faith virtue, to virtue knowledge, and seek for every good thing. The Church must be cleansed, and I proclaim against all iniquity.' "[5]

"You must be innocent, or you cannot come up before God: if we would come before God, we must keep ourselves pure, as He is pure. The devil has great power to deceive; he will so transform things as to make one gape at those who are doing the will of God. . . . Iniquity must be purged out from the midst of the Saints; then the veil will be rent, and the blessings of heaven will flow down—they will roll down like the Mississippi river."[6]

"Let not any man publish his own righteousness, for others can see that for him; sooner let him confess his sins, and then he will be forgiven, and he will bring forth more fruit."[7]

"All hearts must repent and be pure, and God will regard them and bless them in a manner that they could not be blessed in any other way."[8]

It is the will of God that we forsake our sins and put away evil from among us.

"Hear it, all ye ends of the earth—all ye priests, all ye sinners, and all men. Repent! Repent! Obey the gospel. Turn to God."[9]

"Let us this very day begin anew, and now say, with all our hearts, we will forsake our sins and be righteous."[10]

"The infidel will grasp at every straw for help until death stares him in the face, and then his infidelity takes its flight, for the realities of the eternal world are resting upon him in mighty power; and when every earthly support and prop fails him, he then sensibly feels the eternal truths of the immortality of the soul. We should take warning and not wait for the death-bed to repent; as we see the infant taken away by death, so may the youth and middle aged, as well as the infant be suddenly called into eternity. Let this, then, prove as a warning to all not to procrastinate repentance, or wait till a death-bed, for it is the will of God that man should repent and serve Him in health, and in the strength and power of his mind, in order to secure His blessing, and not wait until he is called to die."[11]

"The sacrament was administered to the Church [on March 1, 1835]. Previous to the administration, I spoke of the propriety of this institution in the Church, and urged the importance of doing it with acceptance before the Lord, and asked, How long do you suppose a man may partake of this ordinance unworthily, and the Lord not withdraw His Spirit from him? How long will he thus trifle with sacred things, and the Lord not give him over to the buffetings of Satan until the day of redemption! . . . Therefore our hearts ought to be humble, and we to repent of our sins, and put away evil from among us."[12]

"Repentance is a thing that cannot be trifled with every day. Daily transgression and daily repentance is not that which is pleasing in the sight of God."[13]

Just as the prodigal son was welcomed home by his father, our Heavenly Father is willing to "forgive sins, and restore to favor all those who are willing to humble themselves before Him."

The Prophet Joseph Smith wrote the following to his brother William Smith after William became angry with him and treated him with contempt: "[I have spoken to you] for the express purpose of endeavoring to warn, exhort, admonish, and rescue you from falling into difficulties and sorrows, which I foresaw you plunging into, by giving way to that wicked spirit, which you call your passions, which you should curb and break down, and put under your feet; which if you do not, you never can be saved, in my view, in the Kingdom of God. God requires the will of His creatures to be swallowed up in His will."[14]

Our Heavenly Father is willing to forgive those who repent and return to Him with full purpose of heart.

In 1835 Joseph Smith received a letter from Harvey Whitlock, who had apostatized from the Church and desired to return to full fellowship. The Prophet responded: "I have received your letter of the 28th of September, 1835, and I have read it twice, and it gave me sensations that are better imagined than described; let it suffice that I say that the very flood gates of my heart were broken up—I could not refrain from weeping. I thank God that it has entered into your heart to try to return to the Lord, and to this people, if it so be that He will have mercy upon you. I have inquired of the Lord concerning your case; these words came to me:

"Revelation to Harvey Whitlock.

" 'Verily, thus saith the Lord unto you—Let him who was my servant Harvey, return unto me, and unto the bosom of my Church, and forsake all the sins wherewith he has offended against me, and pursue from henceforth a virtuous and upright life, and remain under the direction of those whom I have appointed to be pillars and heads of my Church. And behold, saith the Lord your God, his sins shall be blotted out from under heaven, and shall be forgotten from among men, and shall not come up in mine ears, nor be recorded as a memorial against him, but I will lift him up, as out of deep mire, and he shall be exalted upon the high places, and shall be counted worthy to stand among princes, and shall yet be made a polished shaft in my quiver for bringing down the strongholds of wickedness among those who set themselves up on high, that they may take counsel against me, and against my anointed ones in the last days. Therefore, let him prepare himself speedily and come unto you, even to Kirtland. And inasmuch as he shall hearken unto all your counsel from henceforth, he shall be restored unto his former state, and shall be saved unto the uttermost, even as the Lord your God liveth. Amen.'

"Thus you see, my dear brother, the willingness of our heavenly Father to forgive sins, and restore to favor all those who are willing to humble themselves before Him, and confess their sins, and forsake them, and return to Him with full purpose of heart, acting no hypocrisy, to serve Him to the end [see 2 Nephi 31:13].

"Marvel not that the Lord has condescended to speak from the heavens, and give you instructions whereby you may learn your duty. He has heard your prayers and witnessed your humility, and holds forth the hand of paternal affection for your return; the angels rejoice over you, while the Saints are willing to receive you again into fellowship."[15]

"There is never a time when the spirit is too old to approach God. All are within the reach of pardoning mercy, who have not committed the unpardonable sin."[16]

Suggestions for Study and Teaching

Consider these ideas as you study the chapter or as you prepare to teach. For additional help, see pages vii–xii.

- As you read the account of the Prophet's reaction to the loss of the 116 pages (pages 69–71), what insights do you gain about Joseph Smith? What do you learn from his example about repentance?
- Review the section beginning on page 72. As you ponder the teachings in this chapter, take time to search your heart, as the Prophet counseled. Think about what you need to do—and what you need to stop doing—to become more like God.
- Ponder Joseph Smith's warnings against procrastinating our repentance (pages 73–74). What are some possible consequences of procrastinating repentance?
- Study the Prophet Joseph's counsel about turning to God and humbling ourselves before Him (pages 73–76). Why would repentance be incomplete without humility? What do you think it means to "return to [God] with full purpose of heart"? (page 76).
- Read the revelation Joseph Smith received for Harvey Whitlock, noting the Lord's promises if Brother Whitlock would sincerely repent (page 75). What are your thoughts or feelings as you ponder "the willingness of our heavenly Father to forgive sins, and restore [us] to favor"?

Related Scriptures: 2 Corinthians 7:9–10; Mosiah 4:10–12; Alma 34:31–38; D&C 1:31–33; 58:42–43

Notes

1. Lucy Mack Smith, "The History of Lucy Smith, Mother of the Prophet," 1844–45 manuscript, book 7, pp. 1–2, Church Archives, The Church of Jesus Christ of Latter-day Saints, Salt Lake City, Utah.
2. Lucy Mack Smith, "The History of Lucy Smith, Mother of the Prophet," 1844–45 manuscript, book 7, p. 5, Church Archives.
3. Quoted by Lucy Mack Smith, "The History of Lucy Smith, Mother of the Prophet," 1844–45 manuscript, book 7, pp. 6–9, Church Archives.
4. Quoted by Lucy Mack Smith, "The History of Lucy Smith, Mother of the Prophet," 1844–45 manuscript, book 7, p. 11, Church Archives.
5. *History of the Church,* 4:588; bracketed words in original; punctuation and capitalization modernized; paragraph divisions altered; from a discourse given by Joseph Smith on Apr. 10, 1842, in Nauvoo, Illinois; reported by Wilford Woodruff.
6. *History of the Church,* 4:605; paragraph divisions altered; from a discourse given by Joseph Smith on Apr. 28, 1842, in Nauvoo, Illinois; reported by Eliza R. Snow.
7. *History of the Church,* 4:479; from a discourse given by Joseph Smith on Dec. 19, 1841, in Nauvoo, Illinois; reported by Wilford Woodruff.
8. Discourse given by Joseph Smith on Apr. 28, 1842, in Nauvoo, Illinois; reported by Eliza R. Snow, in Relief Society, Minute Book Mar. 1842–Mar. 1844, p. 34, Church Archives.
9. *History of the Church,* 6:317; from a discourse given by Joseph Smith on Apr. 7, 1844, in Nauvoo, Illinois; reported by Wilford Woodruff, Willard Richards, Thomas Bullock, and William Clayton.
10. *History of the Church,* 6:363; from a discourse given by Joseph Smith on May 12, 1844, in Nauvoo, Illinois; reported by Thomas Bullock.
11. *History of the Church,* 4:553–54; punctuation modernized; from a discourse given by Joseph Smith on Mar. 20, 1842, in Nauvoo, Illinois; reported by Wilford Woodruff.
12. *History of the Church,* 2:204; from the minutes of a Church council meeting held on Mar. 1, 1835, in Kirtland, Ohio.
13. *History of the Church,* 3:379; from a discourse given by Joseph Smith on June 27, 1839, in Commerce, Illinois; reported by Willard Richards.
14. *History of the Church,* 2:342; from a letter from Joseph Smith to William Smith, Dec. 18, 1835, Kirtland, Ohio.
15. *History of the Church,* 2:314–15; punctuation modernized; from a letter from Joseph Smith to Harvey Whitlock, Nov. 16, 1835, Kirtland, Ohio.
16. *History of the Church,* 4:425; from the minutes of a Church conference held on Oct. 3, 1841, in Nauvoo, Illinois, published in *Times and Seasons,* Oct. 15, 1841, p. 577.

John the Baptist restored the Aaronic Priesthood to Joseph Smith and Oliver Cowdery on May 15, 1829, saying, "Upon you my fellow servants, in the name of Messiah, I confer the Priesthood of Aaron."

CHAPTER 6

The Mission of John the Baptist

"John [the Baptist] held the Aaronic Priesthood, and was a legal administrator, and the forerunner of Christ, and came to prepare the way before him."

From the Life of Joseph Smith

In Harmony, Pennsylvania, during the winter of 1828–29, Joseph Smith continued to work on the translation of the Book of Mormon, but the work progressed slowly. Not only did Joseph have to work on his farm to provide for his family, but he had no full-time scribe to assist him. In this time of need, he recalled, "I cried unto the Lord that he would provide for me to accomplish the work whereunto he had commanded me."[1] The Lord promised that He would provide the help Joseph Smith needed to continue the work of translation (see D&C 5:34). On April 5, 1829, a young schoolteacher named Oliver Cowdery accompanied the Prophet's brother Samuel to Harmony to meet Joseph. Oliver had heard about the plates while staying in the home of the Prophet's parents and, after praying about the matter, had received personal revelation that he was to write for the Prophet. On April 7, the two men began the work of translation, with Oliver as scribe.

As Joseph and Oliver were translating from the plates, they read the Savior's instructions to the Nephites regarding baptism for the remission of sins.[2] On May 15, they went to a wooded area near the Prophet's home to ask the Lord for more understanding about this important ordinance. "Our souls were drawn out in mighty prayer," Oliver Cowdery recalled, "to know how we might obtain the blessings of baptism and of the Holy Spirit, according to the order of God, and we diligently sought for the right of the fathers and the authority of the holy priesthood, and the power to administer in the same."[3]

Joseph Smith recorded what happened in answer to their prayer: "While we were thus employed, praying and calling upon the Lord, a messenger from heaven descended in a cloud of light, and having laid his hands upon us, he ordained us, saying: *Upon you my fellow servants, in the name of Messiah, I confer the Priesthood of Aaron, which holds the keys of the ministering of angels, and of the gospel of repentance, and of baptism by immersion for the remission of sins; and this shall never be taken again from the earth until the sons of Levi do offer again an offering unto the Lord in righteousness.*

"He said this Aaronic Priesthood had not the power of laying on hands for the gift of the Holy Ghost, but that this should be conferred on us hereafter. . . .

"The messenger who visited us on this occasion and conferred this Priesthood upon us, said that his name was John, the same that is called John the Baptist in the New Testament, and that he acted under the direction of Peter, James and John, who held the keys of the Priesthood of Melchizedek, which Priesthood, he said, would in due time be conferred on us" (Joseph Smith—History 1:68–70, 72).

The coming of John the Baptist was a significant event in the life of the Prophet Joseph Smith and in the progress of God's kingdom on earth. Although Joseph Smith had seen God the Father and Jesus Christ, had been visited by heavenly messengers, and had received the gold plates and the ability to translate them, he had not yet been given the authority and power of the priesthood. Now Aaronic Priesthood power had been restored to earth, and the power of the Melchizedek Priesthood would soon be restored. Joseph Smith had become a legal administrator in God's kingdom.

Teachings of Joseph Smith

John the Baptist fulfilled the important missions of preparing the way before the Savior and baptizing Him.

"I attended [a] meeting at the Temple [on January 29, 1843]. . . . I stated that there were two questions which had been asked me concerning my subject of the last Sabbath, which I had promised to answer in public, and would improve this opportunity.

"The question arose from the saying of Jesus—'Among those that are born of women there is not a greater prophet than John the Baptist; but he that is least in the kingdom of God is greater than he.' [Luke 7:28.] How is it that John was considered one of the greatest of prophets? His miracles could not have constituted his greatness. [See John 10:41.]

"First. He was entrusted with a divine mission of preparing the way before the face of the Lord. Whoever had such a trust committed to him before or since? No man.

"Secondly. He was entrusted with the important mission, and it was required at his hands, to baptize the Son of Man. Whoever had the honor of doing that? Whoever had so great a privilege and glory? Whoever led the Son of God into the waters of baptism, and had the privilege of beholding the Holy Ghost descend in the form of a dove, or rather in the *sign* of the dove, in witness of that administration? The sign of the dove was instituted before the creation of the world, a witness for the Holy Ghost, and the devil cannot come in the sign of a dove. The Holy Ghost is a personage, and is in the form of a personage. It does not confine itself to the *form* of the dove, but in *sign* of the dove. The Holy Ghost cannot be transformed into a dove; but the sign of a dove was given to John to signify the truth of the deed, as the dove is an emblem or token of truth and innocence.

"Thirdly. John, at that time, was the only legal administrator in the affairs of the kingdom there was then on the earth, and holding the keys of power. The Jews had to obey his instructions or be damned, by their own law; and Christ Himself fulfilled all righteousness in becoming obedient to the law which He had given to Moses on the mount, and thereby magnified it and made it honorable, instead of destroying it. The son of Zacharias wrested the keys, the kingdom, the power, the glory from the Jews, by the holy anointing and decree of heaven, and these three reasons constitute him the greatest prophet born of a woman.

"Second question:—How was the least in the kingdom of heaven greater than he? [See Luke 7:28.]

"In reply I asked—Whom did Jesus have reference to as being the least? Jesus was looked upon as having the least claim in God's kingdom, and [seemingly] was least entitled to their credulity as a prophet; as though He had said—'He that is considered the least among you is greater than John—that is I myself.' "[4]

There must be legal administrators in the kingdom of God.

"Some say the kingdom of God was not set up on the earth until the day of Pentecost, and that John [the Baptist] did not preach the baptism of repentance for the remission of sins; but I say, in the name of the Lord, that the kingdom of God was set up on the earth from the days of Adam to the present time. Whenever there has been a righteous man on earth unto whom God revealed His word and gave power and authority to administer in His name, and where there is a priest of God—a minister who has power and authority from God to administer in the ordinances of the gospel and officiate in the priesthood of God, there is the kingdom of God; and, in consequence of rejecting the Gospel of Jesus Christ and the Prophets whom God hath sent, the judgments of God have rested upon people, cities, and nations, in various ages of the world, which was the case with the cities of Sodom and Gomorrah, that were destroyed for rejecting the Prophets. . . .

"As touching the Gospel and baptism that John preached, I would say that John came preaching the Gospel for the remission of sins; he had his authority from God, and the oracles of God were with him, and the kingdom of God for a season seemed to rest with John alone. The Lord promised Zacharias that he should have a son who was a descendant of Aaron, the

Lord having promised that the priesthood should continue with Aaron and his seed throughout their generations. Let no man take this honor upon himself, except he be called of God, as was Aaron [see Hebrews 5:4]; and Aaron received his call by revelation. . . .

"But, says one, the kingdom of God could not be set up in the days of John, for John said the kingdom was at hand. But I would ask if it could be any nearer to them than to be in the hands of John. The people need not wait for the days of Pentecost to find the kingdom of God, for John had it with him, and he came forth from the wilderness crying out, 'Repent ye, for the kingdom of heaven is nigh at hand' [Matthew 3:2], as much as to say, 'Out here I have got the kingdom of God and I am coming after you; I have got the kingdom of God, and you can get it, and I am coming after you; and if you don't receive it, you will be damned;' and the scriptures represent that all Jerusalem went out unto John's baptism [see Matthew 3:5–6]. There was a legal administrator, and those that were baptized were subjects for a king; and also the laws and oracles of God were there; therefore the kingdom of God was there; for no man could have better authority to administer than John; and our Savior submitted to that authority Himself, by being baptized by John; therefore the kingdom of God was set up on the earth, even in the days of John. . . .

". . . Christ came according to the words of John [see Mark 1:7], and He was greater than John, because He held the keys of the Melchizedek Priesthood and kingdom of God, and had before revealed the priesthood of Moses, yet Christ was baptized by John to fulfill all righteousness [see Matthew 3:15]. . . .

". . . [Jesus] says, 'Except a man be born of water and of the Spirit, he cannot enter into the kingdom of God;' and, 'heaven and earth shall pass away, but my words shall not pass away.' [John 3:5; Matthew 24:35.] If a man is born of water and of the Spirit, he can get into the kingdom of God. It is evident the kingdom of God was on the earth, and John prepared subjects for the kingdom, by preaching the Gospel to them and baptizing them, and he prepared the way before the Savior, or came as a forerunner,

The Savior went to John the Baptist to be baptized because John "held the Aaronic Priesthood, and was a legal administrator."

and prepared subjects for the preaching of Christ; and Christ preached through Jerusalem on the same ground where John had preached. . . . John . . . preached the same Gospel and baptism that Jesus and the apostles preached after him. . . .

"Whenever men can find out the will of God and find an administrator legally authorized from God, there is the kingdom of God; but where these are not, the kingdom of God is not. All the ordinances, systems, and administrations on the earth are of no use to the children of men, unless they are ordained and authorized of God; for nothing will save a man but a legal administrator; for none others will be acknowledged either by God or angels."[5]

"John [the Baptist] held the Aaronic Priesthood, and was a legal administrator, and the forerunner of Christ, and came to prepare the way before him. . . . John was a priest after the order of Aaron before Christ. . . .

"The keys of the Aaronic Priesthood were committed unto him, and he was as the voice of one crying in the wilderness, saying, 'Prepare ye the way of the Lord and make his paths straight.' [Matthew 3:3.] . . .

"The Savior said unto John, I must be baptized by you. Why so? To answer my decrees [see Matthew 3:15]. . . . Jesus had no legal administrator [except] John.

"There is no salvation between the two lids of the Bible without a legal administrator."[6]

A person who has the spirit of Elias has a preparatory work assigned to him by the Lord.

"It is the spirit of Elias I wish first to speak of; and in order to come at the subject, I will bring some of the testimony from the Scripture and give my own.

"In the first place, suffice it to say, I went into the woods to inquire of the Lord, by prayer, His will concerning me, and I saw an angel [John the Baptist], and he laid his hands upon my head, and ordained me to a Priest after the order of Aaron, and to hold the keys of this Priesthood, which office was to preach repentance and baptism for the remission of sins, and also to baptize. But I was informed that this office did not extend to the laying on of hands for the giving of the Holy Ghost; that that office was a greater work, and was to be given afterward; but that my ordination was a preparatory work, or a going before, which was the spirit of Elias; for the spirit of Elias was a going before to prepare the way for the greater, which was the case with John the Baptist. He came crying through the wilderness, 'Prepare ye the way of the Lord, make his paths straight.' [Matthew 3:3.] And they were informed, if they could receive it, it was the spirit of Elias [see Matthew 11:14]; and John was very particular to tell the people, he was not that Light, but was sent to bear witness of that Light [see John 1:8].

"He told the people that his mission was to preach repentance and baptize with water; but it was He that should come after him that should baptize with fire and the Holy Ghost [see Matthew 3:11].

"If he had been an imposter, he might have gone to work beyond his bounds, and undertook to have performed ordinances which did not belong to that office and calling, under the spirit of Elias.

"The spirit of Elias is to prepare the way for a greater revelation of God, which [the spirit of Elias] is the Priesthood of Elias, or the Priesthood that Aaron was ordained unto. And when God sends a man into the world to prepare for a greater work, holding the keys of the power of Elias, it was called the doctrine of Elias, even from the early ages of the world.

"John's mission was limited to preaching and baptizing; but what he did was legal; and when Jesus Christ came to any of John's disciples, He baptized them with fire and the Holy Ghost. . . . John did not transcend his bounds, but faithfully performed that part belonging to his office; and every portion of the great building should be prepared right and assigned to its proper place; and it is necessary to know who holds the keys of power, and who does not, or we may be likely to be deceived.

"That person who holds the keys of Elias hath a preparatory work. . . . The spirit of Elias was revealed to me, and I know it is true; therefore I speak with boldness, for I know verily my doctrine is true."[7]

Suggestions for Study and Teaching

Consider these ideas as you study the chapter or as you prepare to teach. For additional help, see pages vii–xii.

- Read the accounts of John the Baptist conferring the Aaronic Priesthood on Joseph Smith and Oliver Cowdery (pages 79–80, 85). What effect did this event have on Joseph and Oliver? What effect has this event had on your life?
- Read the first full paragraph on page 80, noting that John the Baptist called Joseph and Oliver his "fellow servants." In what ways might this phrase help priesthood holders? In what ways might this phrase influence our interaction with young men who hold the Aaronic Priesthood?

- Review the section of the chapter that begins on page 81. What are your thoughts and feelings about John the Baptist and the mission he performed during his mortal life?
- The Prophet Joseph taught that John the Baptist was a "legal administrator" (pages 82–85). What do you think the term "legal administrator" means as it relates to the priesthood? Why is there "no salvation . . . without a legal administrator"? (page 85).
- As you read the final section in the chapter (pages 85–86), review also the definition for the term "Elias" given in the Bible Dictionary (see Bible Dictionary, page 663). What is the spirit of Elias? How did John the Baptist prepare the way for the coming of the Savior?
- Joseph Smith said that the conferral of the Aaronic Priesthood is "a preparatory work" because it prepares the way for something greater (page 85). What can Aaronic Priesthood holders do to prepare to receive the Melchizedek Priesthood? What can parents, grandparents, teachers, and leaders do to help them prepare?

Related Scriptures: Matthew 3:1–17; 1 Nephi 10:7–10; Joseph Smith Translation, Matthew 3:43–46

Notes

1. Joseph Smith, History 1832, p. 6; Letter Book 1, 1829–35, Joseph Smith, Collection, Church Archives, The Church of Jesus Christ of Latter-day Saints, Salt Lake City, Utah.
2. Oliver Cowdery, quoted in Joseph Smith—History 1:71, footnote; from a letter from Oliver Cowdery to William W. Phelps, Sept. 7, 1834, Norton, Ohio, published in *Messenger and Advocate,* Oct. 1834, p. 15.
3. Oliver Cowdery, statement recorded Sept. 1835 in "The Book of Patriarchal Blessings, 1834," pp. 8–9; Patriarchal Blessings, 1833–2005, Church Archives.
4. *History of the Church,* 5:260–61; bracketed word in final paragraph in original; capitalization modernized; from a discourse given by Joseph Smith on Jan. 29, 1843, in Nauvoo, Illinois; reported by Willard Richards and an unidentified *Boston Bee* correspondent. The *Boston Bee* letter was written on Mar. 24, 1843, in Nauvoo, Illinois, and published in *Times and Seasons,* May 15, 1843, p. 200. See also appendix, page 562, item 3.
5. *History of the Church,* 5:256–59; spelling and punctuation modernized; from a discourse given by Joseph Smith on Jan. 22, 1843, in Nauvoo, Illinois; reported by Wilford Woodruff.
6. Discourse given by Joseph Smith on July 23, 1843, in Nauvoo, Illinois; Joseph Smith, Collection, Addresses, July 23, 1843, Church Archives.
7. *History of the Church,* 6:249–51; paragraph divisions altered; from a discourse given by Joseph Smith on Mar. 10, 1844, in Nauvoo, Illinois; reported by Wilford Woodruff.

The Prophet's father, Joseph Smith Sr., was baptized on April 6, 1830. As his father came out of the water, the Prophet "covered his face in his father's bosom and wept aloud for joy."

CHAPTER 7

Baptism and the Gift of the Holy Ghost

"The baptism of water, without the baptism of fire and the Holy Ghost attending it, is of no use; they are necessarily and inseparably connected."

From the Life of Joseph Smith

In Joseph Smith's time, the Susquehanna River flowed in large, winding bends through forests of hardwood trees and pine, surrounded by rolling hills and fields of grain. The largest river in Pennsylvania, it was a central part of the landscape around Harmony, Pennsylvania. Because the river was close to his home and offered quiet, secluded spots, the Prophet sometimes withdrew there to think and to pray.

It was to the bank of this river that the Prophet and Oliver Cowdery went on May 15, 1829, to pray about the importance of baptism. In answer to their prayer, John the Baptist appeared to them, conferring the Aaronic Priesthood on them and commanding them to baptize each other. The blessing they had been seeking could now be performed in the proper way and with the power and authority of God. Going down into the river, they baptized one another, with Joseph baptizing Oliver first, as John had directed. Joseph then laid his hands on the head of Oliver and ordained him to the Aaronic Priesthood, and Oliver did the same for Joseph. The Prophet recalled:

"We experienced great and glorious blessings from our Heavenly Father. No sooner had I baptized Oliver Cowdery, than the Holy Ghost fell upon him, and he stood up and prophesied many things which should shortly come to pass. And again, so soon as I had been baptized by him, I also had the spirit of prophecy, when, standing up, I prophesied concerning the rise of this Church, and many other things connected with the Church, and this generation of the children of men. We were filled with the Holy Ghost, and rejoiced in the God of our salvation" (Joseph Smith—History 1:73).

The blessings of baptism were soon extended to other believers. Later in the month of May, the Prophet's younger brother Samuel came to visit Joseph and Oliver in Harmony. "We . . . labored to persuade him concerning the Gospel of Jesus Christ, which was now about to be revealed in its fulness," the Prophet stated. Samuel received a testimony of the work, and Oliver Cowdery baptized him, after which Samuel "returned to his father's house, greatly glorifying and praising God, being filled with the Holy Spirit."[1] In June, the Prophet baptized his older brother Hyrum, who had long been a steadfast believer in the Prophet's message. "From this time forth many became believers," Joseph recorded, "and some were baptized whilst we continued to instruct and persuade."[2]

The Prophet was especially grateful to see his father, Joseph Smith Sr., baptized. The Prophet had a deep love for his father, who had been the first to believe his message after he was first visited by Moroni. Joseph Smith Sr. was baptized on April 6, 1830, the day the Church was organized. The Prophet's mother, Lucy Mack Smith, recalled: "Joseph stood on the shore when his father came out of the water, and as he took him by the hand he cried out, '. . . I have lived to see my father baptized into the true church of Jesus Christ,' and he covered his face in his father's bosom and wept aloud for joy as did Joseph of old when he beheld his father coming up into the land of Egypt."[3]

On the day the Church was organized, many Saints who had previously been baptized received the gift of the Holy Ghost by the power of the Melchizedek Priesthood. The Prophet Joseph Smith taught emphatically the need for both baptism and the laying on of hands for the gift of the Holy Ghost. "The baptism of water, without the baptism of fire and the Holy Ghost attending it, is of no use," he declared. "They are necessarily and inseparably connected. An individual must be born of water and the spirit in order to get into the kingdom of God."[4]

Teachings of Joseph Smith

The ordinance of baptism is necessary for exaltation.

"God has set many signs on the earth, as well as in the heavens; for instance, the oak of the forest, the fruit of the tree, the herb of the field—all bear a sign that seed hath been planted there; for it is a decree of the Lord that every tree, plant, and herb bearing seed should bring forth of its kind, and cannot come forth after any other law or principle.

"Upon the same principle do I contend that baptism is a sign ordained of God, for the believer in Christ to take upon himself in order to enter into the kingdom of God, 'for except ye are born of water and of the Spirit ye cannot enter into the kingdom of God,' said the Savior [see John 3:5]. It is a sign and a commandment which God has set for man to enter into His kingdom. Those who seek to enter in any other way will seek in vain; for God will not receive them, neither will the angels acknowledge their works as accepted, for they have not obeyed the ordinances, nor attended to the signs which God ordained for the salvation of man, to prepare him for, and give him a title to, a celestial glory; and God has decreed that all who will not obey His voice shall not escape the damnation of hell. What is the damnation of hell? To go with that society who have not obeyed His commands.

"Baptism is a sign to God, to angels, and to heaven that we do the will of God, and there is no other way beneath the heavens whereby God hath ordained for man to come to Him to be saved, and enter into the kingdom of God, except faith in Jesus Christ, repentance, and baptism for the remission of sins, and any other course is in vain; then you have the promise of the gift of the Holy Ghost."[5]

"Upon looking over the sacred pages of the Bible, searching into the prophets and sayings of the apostles, we find no subject so nearly connected with salvation, as that of baptism. . . . Let us understand that the word *baptise* is derived from the Greek verb *baptiso,* and means to immerse. . . .

". . . It may not be amiss to introduce the commissions and commands of Jesus himself on the subject.—He said to the twelve, or rather eleven at the time: 'Go ye therefore, and teach all nations, baptising them in the name of the Father, and of the Son, and of the Holy Ghost: teaching them to observe all things whatsoever I have commanded you': Thus it is recorded by Matthew [Matthew 28:19–20]. In Mark we have these important words: 'Go ye into all the world, and preach the gospel to every creature. He that believeth and is baptised shall be saved, and he that believeth not shall be damned' [Mark 16:15–16]. . . .

". . . 'Nicodemus, a ruler of the Jews, . . . came to Jesus by night, and said unto him, Rabbi, we know that thou art a teacher come from God: for no man can do these miracles that thou doest, except God be with him. Jesus answered and said unto him, Verily, verily, I say unto thee, except a man be born again he cannot see the kingdom of God. Nicodemus saith unto him, How can a man be born when he is old? can he enter the second time into his mother's womb, and be born?—Jesus answered, Verily, verily, I say unto thee, Except a man be born of water, and of the Spirit, he cannot enter into the kingdom of God' [John 3:1–5].

"This strong and positive answer of Jesus, as to water baptism, settles the question: If God is the same yesterday, to day, and forever; it is no wonder he is so positive in the great declaration: 'He that believes and is baptised shall be saved, and he that believes not shall be damned!' [Mark 16:16.] There was no other name given under heaven, nor no other ordinance admitted, whereby men could be saved: No wonder the Apostle said, being 'buried with him in baptism,' ye shall rise from the dead! [Colossians 2:12.] No wonder Paul had to arise and be baptised and wash away his sins [see Acts 9:17–18]."[6]

In all dispensations, Saints have been baptized in the name of Jesus Christ.

"The ancients who were actually the fathers of the church in the different ages, when the church flourished on the earth, . . . were initiated into the kingdom by baptism, for it is self evident in the scripture—God changes not. The Apostle says the gospel

Alma baptizing in the waters of Mormon. Joseph Smith taught, "Before the Saviour came in the flesh, 'the saints' were baptised in the name of Jesus Christ to come, because there never was any other name whereby men could be saved."

is the power of God unto salvation unto them that believe; and also informs us that life and immortality were brought to light through the gospel [see Romans 1:16; 2 Timothy 1:10]. . . .

"Now taking it for granted that the scriptures say what they mean, and mean what they say, we have sufficient grounds to go on and prove from the Bible that the gospel has always been the same; the ordinances to fulfil its requirements, the same; and the officers to officiate, the same; and the signs and fruits resulting from the promises, the same: therefore, as Noah was a preacher of righteousness he must have been baptised and ordained to the priesthood by the laying on of the hands, etc. For no man taketh this honor upon himself except he be called of God as was Aaron [see Hebrews 5:4]. . . .

". . . It will be seen and acknowledged that if there was sin among men, repentance was as necessary at one time or age of the world as another—and that other foundation can no man lay than that is laid, which is Jesus Christ. If, then, Abel was a righteous man he had to become so by keeping the commandments;

if Enoch was righteous enough to come into the presence of God, and walk with him, he must have become so by keeping his commandments, and so of every righteous person, whether it was Noah, a preacher of righteousness; Abraham, the father of the faithful; Jacob, the prevailer with God; Moses, the man who wrote of Christ, and brought forth the law by commandment, as a school master to bring men to Christ; or whether it was Jesus Christ himself, who had no need of repentance, having done no sin; according to his solemn declaration to John:—now let me be baptised: for no man can enter the kingdom without obeying this ordinance: for thus it becometh us to fulfil all righteousness [see Joseph Smith Translation, Matthew 3:43]. Surely, then, if it became John and Jesus Christ, the Saviour, to fulfil all righteousness to be baptised—so surely, then, it will become every other person that seeks the kingdom of heaven to go and do likewise; for he is the door, and if any person climbs up any other way, the same is a thief and a robber! [See John 10:1–2.]

"In the former ages of the world, before the Saviour came in the flesh, 'the saints' were baptised in the name of Jesus Christ to come, because there never was any other name whereby men could be saved; and after he came in the flesh and was crucified, then the saints were baptised in the name of Jesus Christ, crucified, risen from the dead and ascended into heaven, that they might be buried in baptism like him, and be raised in glory like him, that as there was but one Lord, one faith, one baptism, and one God and father of us all [see Ephesians 4:5–6], even so there was but one door to the mansions of bliss."[7]

Children who die before the age of accountability do not need to be baptized; they are redeemed by the Atonement of Jesus Christ.

"Baptism is for remission of sins. Children have no sins. Jesus blessed them and said, 'Do what you have seen me do.' Children are all made alive in Christ, and those of riper years through faith and repentance."[8]

"The doctrine of baptizing children, or sprinkling them, or they must welter in hell, is a doctrine not true, not supported in

Holy Writ, and is not consistent with the character of God. All children are redeemed by the blood of Jesus Christ, and the moment that children leave this world, they are taken to the bosom of Abraham."[9]

The Prophet Joseph Smith described the following as part of a vision he received on January 21, 1836, later recorded in Doctrine and Covenants 137:1, 10: "The heavens were opened upon us, and I beheld the celestial kingdom of God, and the glory thereof. . . . I also beheld that all children who die before they arrive at the years of accountability are saved in the celestial kingdom of heaven."[10]

After baptism by water, we receive the Holy Ghost by the laying on of hands.

"The gospel requires baptism by immersion for the remission of sins, which is the meaning of the word in the original language—namely, to bury or immerse. . . . I further believe in the gift of the Holy Ghost by the laying on of hands, [as evidenced] by Peter's preaching on the day of Pentecost, Acts 2:38. You might as well baptize a bag of sand as a man, if not done in view of the remission of sins and getting of the Holy Ghost. Baptism by water is but half a baptism, and is good for nothing without the other half—that is, the baptism of the Holy Ghost. The Savior says, 'Except a man be born of water and of the Spirit, he cannot enter into the kingdom of God.' [John 3:5.]"[11]

Daniel Tyler recalled an address the Prophet gave in Springfield, Pennsylvania, in 1833: "During his short stay he preached at my father's residence, a humble log cabin. He read the 3rd chapter of John. . . . Explaining the 5th verse, he said, 'To be born of water and of the Spirit' meant to be immersed in water for the remission of sins and receive the gift of the Holy Ghost thereafter. This was given by the laying on of the hands of one having authority given him of God."[12]

"Being born again, comes by the Spirit of God through ordinances."[13]

"Baptism is a holy ordinance preparatory to the reception of the Holy Ghost; it is the channel and key by which the Holy

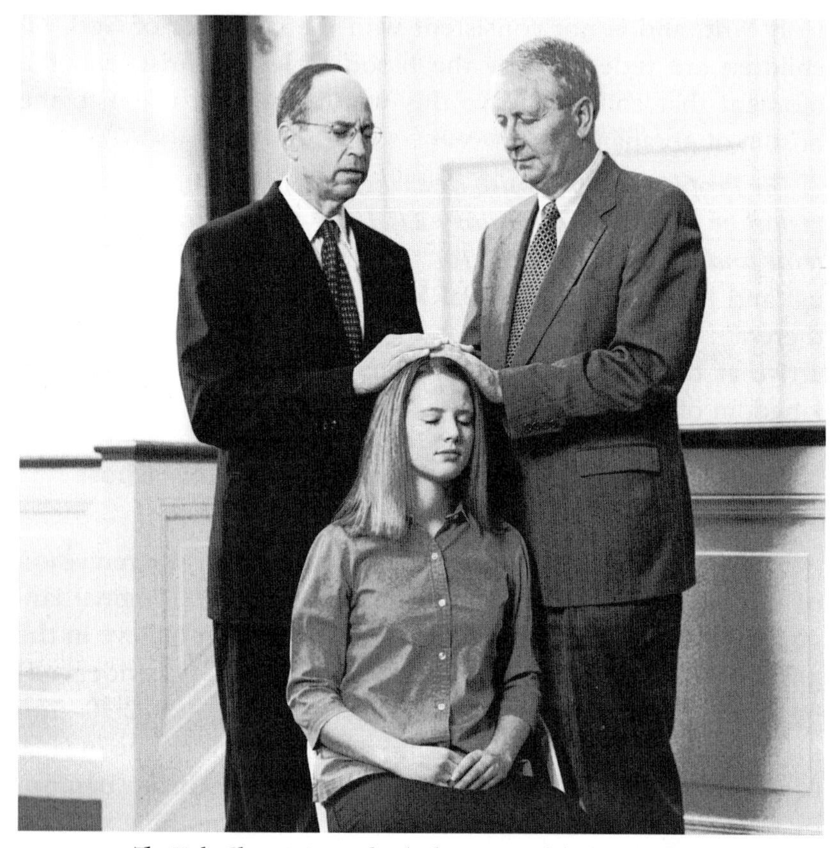

The Holy Ghost is "given by the laying on of the hands of one having authority given him of God."

Ghost will be administered. The Gift of the Holy Ghost by the laying on of hands, cannot be received through the medium of any other principle than the principle of righteousness."[14]

"What if we should attempt to get the gift of the Holy Ghost through any other means except the signs or way which God hath appointed—would we obtain it? Certainly not; all other means would fail. The Lord says do so and so, and I will bless you.

"There are certain key words and signs belonging to the Priesthood which must be observed in order to obtain the blessing. The sign [taught by] Peter was to repent and be baptized for the remission of sins, with the promise of the gift of the Holy Ghost; and in no other way is the gift of the Holy Ghost obtained [see Acts 2:38].

"There is a difference between the Holy Ghost and the gift of the Holy Ghost. Cornelius received the Holy Ghost before he was baptized, which was the convincing power of God unto him of the truth of the Gospel, but he could not receive the gift of the Holy Ghost until after he was baptized. Had he not taken this sign or ordinance upon him, the Holy Ghost which convinced him of the truth of God, would have left him. [See Acts 10:1–48.] Until he obeyed these ordinances and received the gift of the Holy Ghost, by the laying on of hands, according to the order of God, he could not have healed the sick or commanded an evil spirit to come out of a man, and it obey him; for the spirits might say unto him, as they did to the sons of Sceva: 'Paul we know and Jesus we know, but who are ye?' [See Acts 19:13–15.]"[15]

In December 1839, while they were in Washington, D.C., to seek redress for the wrongs done to the Missouri Saints, Joseph Smith and Elias Higbee wrote the following to Hyrum Smith: "In our interview with the President [of the United States], he interrogated us wherein we differed in our religion from the other religions of the day. Brother Joseph said we differed in mode of baptism, and the gift of the Holy Ghost by the laying on of hands. We considered that all other considerations were contained in the gift of the Holy Ghost."[16]

The gift of the Holy Ghost brings peace, joy, divine guidance, and other gifts into our lives.

"We believe in the gift of the Holy Ghost being enjoyed now, as much as it was in the Apostles' days; we believe that it [the gift of the Holy Ghost] is necessary to make and to organize the Priesthood, that no man can be called to fill any office in the ministry without it; we also believe in prophecy, in tongues, in visions, and in revelations, in gifts, and in healings; and that these things cannot be enjoyed without the gift of the Holy Ghost. We believe that the holy men of old spake as they were moved by the Holy Ghost, and that holy men in these days speak by the same principle; we believe in its being a comforter and a witness bearer, that it brings things past to our remembrance, leads us into all truth, and shows us of things to come; we believe that 'no man can know that Jesus is the Christ, but by the

Holy Ghost.' [See 1 Corinthians 12:3.] We believe in it [this gift of the Holy Ghost] in all its fullness, and power, and greatness, and glory."[17]

In February 1847, nearly three years after the Prophet Joseph Smith was martyred, he appeared to President Brigham Young and gave him this message: "Tell the people to be humble and faithful and sure to keep the Spirit of the Lord and it will lead them right. Be careful and not turn away the small still voice; it will teach [you what] to do and where to go; it will yield the fruits of the kingdom. Tell the brethren to keep their hearts open to conviction so that when the Holy Ghost comes to them, their hearts will be ready to receive it. They can tell the Spirit of the Lord from all other spirits. It will whisper peace and joy to their souls, and it will take malice, hatred, envying, strife, and all evil from their hearts; and their whole desire will be to do good, bring forth righteousness, and build up the kingdom of God. Tell the brethren if they will follow the Spirit of the Lord they will go right."[18]

Suggestions for Study and Teaching

Consider these ideas as you study the chapter or as you prepare to teach. For additional help, see pages vii–xii.

- Review pages 89–90, in which the Prophet Joseph Smith expressed the feelings he had when he and Oliver Cowdery were baptized and when his father was baptized. What memories do you have of your baptism or the baptisms of family members and friends? Consider recording these memories in your journal or life history.
- The statements on pages 91–94 are taken from messages Joseph Smith gave to people who had already been baptized. Why do you think baptized members of the Church need to be reminded of these truths? What new insights have you gained as you have studied these teachings?
- What might you say to a friend who believes that baptism is not necessary? What might you say to a friend who believes

that infants need to be baptized? (For some examples, see pages 94–95.)

- Read the second complete paragraph on page 95. Why is baptism "good for nothing" without the gift of the Holy Ghost? Joseph Smith said, "There is a difference between the Holy Ghost and the gift of the Holy Ghost" (page 97). From your experience, what are some of the blessings that can come into our lives when we have the gift of the Holy Ghost?
- Review the second paragraph on page 97. Why is the mode of baptism a significant difference between the restored Church and other churches? Why is the gift of the Holy Ghost a significant difference? In what ways are "all other considerations . . . contained in the gift of the Holy Ghost"?
- Study the last paragraph in the chapter (page 98). Think about how you can live to be worthy to receive and recognize the promptings of the Holy Ghost.

Related Scriptures: John 15:26; Romans 6:3–6; 2 Nephi 31:13; 3 Nephi 11:18–41; Moroni 8:1–23

Notes

1. *History of the Church,* 1:44; from "History of the Church" (manuscript), book A-1, p. 19, Church Archives, The Church of Jesus Christ of Latter-day Saints, Salt Lake City, Utah.
2. *History of the Church,* 1:51; from "History of the Church" (manuscript), book A-1, p. 23, Church Archives.
3. Lucy Mack Smith, "The History of Lucy Smith, Mother of the Prophet," 1844–45 manuscript, book 9, p. 12, Church Archives.
4. *History of the Church,* 6:316; from a discourse given by Joseph Smith on Apr. 7, 1844, in Nauvoo, Illinois; reported by Wilford Woodruff, Willard Richards, Thomas Bullock, and William Clayton.
5. *History of the Church,* 4:554–55; paragraph divisions altered; from a discourse given by Joseph Smith on Mar. 20, 1842, in Nauvoo, Illinois; reported by Wilford Woodruff; see also appendix, page 562, item 3.
6. "Baptism," an editorial published in *Times and Seasons,* Sept. 1, 1842, pp. 903–5; punctuation modernized; paragraph divisions altered; italics deleted; Joseph Smith was the editor of the periodical.
7. "Baptism," an editorial published in *Times and Seasons,* Sept. 1, 1842, pp. 904–5; punctuation modernized; italics deleted; Joseph Smith was the editor of the periodical.
8. *History of the Church,* 5:499; from a discourse given by Joseph Smith on July 9, 1843, in Nauvoo, Illinois; reported by Willard Richards; see also appendix, page 562, item 3.
9. *History of the Church,* 4:554; from a discourse given by Joseph Smith on Mar. 20, 1842, in Nauvoo, Illinois; reported by Wilford Woodruff; see also appendix, page 562, item 3.
10. Doctrine and Covenants 137:1, 10; vision given to Joseph Smith on Jan. 21, 1836, in the temple in Kirtland, Ohio.

11. *History of the Church,* 5:499; punctuation modernized; paragraph divisions altered; from a discourse given by Joseph Smith on July 9, 1843, in Nauvoo, Illinois; reported by Willard Richards; see also appendix, page 562, item 3.
12. Daniel Tyler, "Recollections of the Prophet Joseph Smith," *Juvenile Instructor,* Feb. 1, 1892, pp. 93–94; spelling and punctuation modernized; paragraph divisions altered.
13. *History of the Church,* 3:392; from a discourse given by Joseph Smith about July 1839 in Commerce, Illinois; reported by Willard Richards.
14. *History of the Church,* 3:379; paragraph divisions altered; from a discourse given by Joseph Smith on June 27, 1839, in Commerce, Illinois; reported by Willard Richards.
15. *History of the Church,* 4:555; from a discourse given by Joseph Smith on Mar. 20, 1842, in Nauvoo, Illinois; reported by Wilford Woodruff.
16. *History of the Church,* 4:42; from a letter from Joseph Smith and Elias Higbee to Hyrum Smith and other Church leaders, Dec. 5, 1839, Washington, D.C.; the president of the United States at the time was Martin Van Buren.
17. *History of the Church,* 5:27; first and third sets of bracketed words in original; from "Gift of the Holy Ghost," an editorial published in *Times and Seasons,* June 15, 1842, p. 823; Joseph Smith was the editor of the periodical.
18. Quoted by Brigham Young, in Brigham Young, Office Files, Brigham Young, Vision, Feb. 17, 1847, Church Archives.

CHAPTER 8

The Everlasting Priesthood

"The Melchizedek Priesthood . . . is the channel through which all knowledge, doctrine, the plan of salvation, and every important matter is revealed from heaven."

From the Life of Joseph Smith

After they received the Aaronic Priesthood and the ordinance of baptism, Joseph Smith and Oliver Cowdery experienced blessings they had never known before. The Prophet recorded: "Our minds being now enlightened, we began to have the scriptures laid open to our understandings, and the true meaning and intention of their more mysterious passages revealed unto us in a manner which we never could attain to previously, nor ever before had thought of" (Joseph Smith—History 1:74). With this additional insight, they pressed forward in their work of translating the Book of Mormon. But the Prophet had not yet received an important blessing—one that was necessary before he could organize the Church, establish priesthood offices and quorums, and confer the gift of the Holy Ghost. He had to receive the Melchizedek Priesthood.

As promised by John the Baptist, this blessing was given to Joseph and Oliver shortly after they received the Aaronic Priesthood. The ancient Apostles Peter, James, and John appeared to them in a secluded location near the Susquehanna River and conferred the Melchizedek Priesthood upon them. Joseph later declared that he heard "the voice of Peter, James, and John in the wilderness between Harmony, Susquehanna county, and Colesville, Broome county, on the Susquehanna river, declaring themselves as possessing the keys of the kingdom, and of the dispensation of the fulness of times!" (D&C 128:20).

The ancient Apostles Peter, James, and John conferred the Melchizedek Priesthood on Joseph Smith and Oliver Cowdery. "The keys [of the priesthood]," the Prophet declared, "have to be brought from heaven whenever the Gospel is sent."

In the years that followed, Joseph Smith was visited by many other priesthood holders from ancient times. These messengers from God came to restore the priesthood keys necessary to make the full blessings of the gospel available to God's children. They also came to tutor the prophet who would stand at the head of the dispensation of the fulness of times.

President John Taylor, the third President of the Church, explained: "Moses, Elijah, Elias and many of the leading characters mentioned in the Scriptures, who had operated in the various dispensations, came and conferred upon Joseph the various keys, powers, rights, privileges and [permissions] which they enjoyed in their times. . . . Whatever of knowledge, of intelligence, of Priesthood, of powers, of revelations were conferred upon those men in the different ages, were again restored to the earth by the ministration and through the medium of those who held the holy Priesthood of God in the different dispensations in which they lived."[1]

President Taylor also declared: "If you were to ask Joseph what sort of a looking man Adam was, he would tell you at once; he would tell you his size and appearance and all about him. You might have asked him what sort of men Peter, James and John were, and he could have told you. Why? Because he had seen them."[2]

In September 1842, the Prophet wrote a letter to the Church expressing his joy as he contemplated the knowledge and priesthood keys now restored to the earth: "And again, what do we hear? Glad tidings from Cumorah! Moroni, an angel from heaven, declaring the fulfilment of the prophets—the book to be revealed. . . . And the voice of Michael, the archangel; the voice of Gabriel, and of Raphael, and of divers angels, from Michael or Adam down to the present time, all declaring their dispensation, their rights, their keys, their honors, their majesty and glory, and the power of their priesthood; giving line upon line, precept upon precept; here a little, and there a little; giving us consolation by holding forth that which is to come, confirming our hope!" (D&C 128:20–21).

Teachings of Joseph Smith

The priesthood is everlasting and has been held by prophets in every dispensation.

"There has been a chain of authority and power from Adam down to the present time."[3]

"The Priesthood was first given to Adam; he obtained the First Presidency, and held the keys of it from generation to generation. He obtained it in the Creation, before the world was formed, as in Gen. 1:26, 27, 28. He had dominion given him over every living creature. He is Michael the Archangel, spoken of in the Scriptures. Then to Noah, who is Gabriel; he stands next in authority to Adam in the Priesthood; he was called of God to this office, and was the father of all living in his day, and to him was given the dominion. These men held keys first on earth, and then in heaven.

"The Priesthood is an everlasting principle, and existed with God from eternity, and will to eternity, without beginning of days or end of years [see Joseph Smith Translation, Hebrews 7:3]. The keys have to be brought from heaven whenever the Gospel is sent. When they are revealed from heaven, it is by Adam's authority.

"Daniel in his seventh chapter speaks of the Ancient of Days; he means the oldest man, our Father Adam, Michael; he will call his children together and hold a council with them to prepare them for the coming of the Son of Man [see Daniel 7:9–14]. He (Adam) is the father of the human family, and presides over the spirits of all men, and all that have had the keys must stand before him in this grand council. . . . The Son of Man stands before him, and there is given him glory and dominion. Adam delivers up his stewardship to Christ, that which was delivered to him as holding the keys of the universe, but retains his standing as head of the human family.

". . . The Father called all spirits before Him at the creation of man, and organized them. He (Adam) is the head, and was told to multiply. The keys were first given to him, and by him to others. He will have to give an account of his stewardship, and they to him.

"The Priesthood is everlasting. The Savior, Moses, and Elias [Elijah], gave the keys to Peter, James, and John, on the mount, when they were transfigured before him. The Priesthood is everlasting—without beginning of days or end of years; without father, mother, etc. If there is no change of ordinances, there is no change of Priesthood. Wherever the ordinances of the Gospel are administered, there is the Priesthood.

"How have we come at the Priesthood in the last days? It came down, down, in regular succession. Peter, James, and John had it given to them and they gave it to others. Christ is the Great High Priest; Adam next. Paul speaks of the Church coming to an innumerable company of angels—to God the Judge of all—the spirits of just men made perfect; to Jesus the Mediator of the new covenant [see Hebrews 12:22–24]."[4]

Prophets who held priesthood keys in ancient times have joined in bringing about the work of the last dispensation.

"I saw Adam in the valley of Adam-ondi-Ahman. He called together his children and blessed them with a patriarchal blessing. The Lord appeared in their midst, and he (Adam) blessed them all, and foretold what should befall them to the latest generation.

"This is why Adam blessed his posterity; he wanted to bring them into the presence of God. They looked for a city, etc., ['whose builder and maker is God'—Heb. 11:10]. Moses sought to bring the children of Israel into the presence of God, through the power of the Priesthood, but he could not. In the first ages of the world they tried to establish the same thing; and there were Eliases raised up who tried to restore these very glories, but did not obtain them; but they prophesied of a day when this glory would be revealed. Paul spoke of the dispensation of the fullness of times, when God would gather together all things in one, etc. [see Ephesians 1:10]; and those men to whom these keys have been given, will have to be there; and they without us cannot be made perfect.

"I saw Adam in the valley of Adam-ondi-Ahman. He called together his children and blessed them with a patriarchal blessing. The Lord appeared in their midst."

"These men are in heaven, but their children are on the earth. Their bowels yearn over us. God sends down men for this reason. 'And the Son of Man shall send forth His angels, and they shall gather out of His kingdom all things that give offense and them that do iniquity.' [Matthew 13:41.] All these authoritative characters will come down and join hand in hand in bringing about this work.

"The Kingdom of Heaven is like a grain of mustard seed. The mustard seed is small, but brings forth a large tree, and the fowls lodge in the branches. [See Mark 4:30–32.] The fowls are the angels. Thus angels come down, combine together to gather their children, and gather them. We cannot be made perfect without them, nor they without us; when these things are done, the Son of Man will descend, the Ancient of Days sit; we may come to an innumerable company of angels, have communion with and receive instructions from them."[5]

The priesthood ordinances have been established from the beginning and must be kept in the way God has appointed.

"Adam . . . was the first man, who is spoken of in Daniel as being the 'Ancient of Days' [Daniel 7:9], or in other words, the first and oldest of all, the great, grand progenitor of whom it is said in another place he is Michael, because he was the first and father of all, not only by progeny, but the first to hold the spiritual blessings, to whom was made known the plan of ordinances for the salvation of his posterity unto the end, and to whom Christ was first revealed, and through whom Christ has been revealed from heaven, and will continue to be revealed from henceforth. Adam holds the keys of the dispensation of the fullness of times; i.e., the dispensation of all the times have been and will be revealed through him from the beginning to Christ, and from Christ to the end of all the dispensations that are to be revealed. . . .

". . . [God] set the ordinances to be the same forever and ever, and set Adam to watch over them, to reveal them from heaven to man, or to send angels to reveal them. 'Are they not all ministering spirits, sent forth to minister for them who shall be heirs of salvation?' [Hebrews 1:14.]

"These angels are under the direction of Michael or Adam, who acts under the direction of the Lord. From the above quotation we learn that Paul perfectly understood the purposes of God in relation to His connection with man, and that glorious and perfect order which He established in Himself, whereby He sent forth power, revelations, and glory.

"God will not acknowledge that which He has not called, ordained, and chosen. In the beginning God called Adam by His own voice. 'And the Lord called unto Adam and said unto him, Where art thou? And he said, I heard thy voice in the garden, and I was afraid because I was naked, and hid myself.' [Genesis 3:9–10.] Adam received commandments and instructions from God: this was the order from the beginning.

"That he received revelations, commandments and ordinances at the beginning is beyond the power of controversy; else how did they begin to offer sacrifices to God in an acceptable manner? And if they offered sacrifices they must be authorized by ordination. We read in Genesis [4:4] that Abel brought of the firstlings of the flock and the fat thereof, and the Lord had respect to Abel and to his offering. . . .

"This, then, is the nature of the Priesthood; every man holding the Presidency of his dispensation, and one man holding the Presidency of them all, even Adam; and Adam receiving his Presidency and authority from the Lord, but cannot receive a fullness until Christ shall present the Kingdom to the Father, which shall be at the end of the last dispensation.

"The power, glory and blessings of the Priesthood could not continue with those who received ordination only as their righteousness continued; for Cain also being authorized to offer sacrifice, but not offering it in righteousness, was cursed. It signifies, then, that the ordinances must be kept in the very way God has appointed; otherwise their Priesthood will prove a cursing instead of a blessing."[6]

The Melchizedek Priesthood is the channel through which God reveals Himself and His purposes.

"There are two Priesthoods spoken of in the Scriptures, viz., the Melchizedek and the Aaronic or Levitical. Although there are two Priesthoods, yet the Melchizedek Priesthood comprehends the Aaronic or Levitical Priesthood, and is the grand head, and holds the highest authority which pertains to the Priesthood, and the keys of the Kingdom of God in all ages of the world to the latest posterity on the earth, and is the channel through which all knowledge, doctrine, the plan of salvation, and every important matter is revealed from heaven.

"Its institution was prior to 'the foundation of this earth, or the morning stars sang together, or the Sons of God shouted for joy' [see Job 38:4–7], and is the highest and holiest Priesthood, and is after the order of the Son of God, and all other Priesthoods are only parts, ramifications, powers and blessings belonging to the same, and are held, controlled, and directed by it. It is the channel through which the Almighty commenced revealing His glory at the beginning of the creation of this earth, and through which He has continued to reveal Himself to the children of men to the present time, and through which He will make known His purposes to the end of time."[7]

"The power of the Melchizedek Priesthood is to have the power of 'endless lives;' for the everlasting covenant cannot be broken. . . . What was the power of Melchizedek? 'Twas not the Priesthood of Aaron which administers in outward ordinances, and the offering of sacrifices. Those holding the fullness of the Melchizedek Priesthood are kings and priests of the Most High God, holding the keys of power and blessings. In fact, that priesthood is a perfect law of theocracy, and stands as God to give laws to the people, administering endless lives to the sons and daughters of Adam. . . .

" 'Without father, without mother, without descent, having neither beginning of days nor end of life, but made like unto the Son of God, abideth a priest continually.' [Hebrews 7:3.] The Melchizedek Priesthood holds the right from the eternal God, and not by descent from father and mother; and that priesthood is as eternal as God Himself, having neither beginning of days nor end of life. . . .

". . . The Levitical [Aaronic] Priesthood, consisting of priests to administer in outward ordinance, [is] made without an oath; but the Priesthood of Melchizedek is by an oath and covenant."[8]

"The Melchizedek High Priesthood [is] no other than the Priesthood of the Son of God; . . . there are certain ordinances which belong to the Priesthood, from which flow certain results. . . . One great privilege of the Priesthood is to obtain revelations of the mind and will of God. It is also the privilege of the Melchizedek Priesthood to reprove, rebuke, and admonish, as well as to receive revelation."[9]

"All priesthood is Melchizedek; but there are different portions or degrees of it. . . . All the prophets had the Melchizedek Priesthood."[10]

"I advise all to go on to perfection, and search deeper and deeper into the mysteries of Godliness. A man can do nothing for himself unless God direct him in the right way; and the priesthood is for that purpose."[11]

A man must be authorized of God and ordained to the priesthood to administer in the ordinances of salvation.

Articles of Faith 1:5: "We believe that a man must be called of God, by prophecy, and by the laying on of hands by those who are in authority, to preach the Gospel and administer in the ordinances thereof."[12]

"We believe that no man can administer salvation through the gospel, to the souls of men, in the name of Jesus Christ, except he is authorized from God, by revelation, or by being ordained by some one whom God hath sent by revelation, as it is written by Paul, Romans 10:14, 'And how shall they believe in him of whom they have not heard? and how shall they hear without a preacher? and how shall they preach, except they be sent?' And I will ask, how can they be sent without a revelation, or some other visible display of the manifestation of God? And again, Hebrews 5:4, 'And no man taketh this honor unto himself, but he that is called of God, as was Aaron.'—And I would ask, how was Aaron called, but by revelation?"[13]

"The angel told good old Cornelius that he must send for Peter to learn how to be saved [see Acts 10:21–22]: Peter could baptise, and angels could not, so long as there were legal officers in the flesh holding the keys of the kingdom, or the authority of the priesthood. There is one evidence still further on this point, and that is that Jesus himself when he appeared to Paul on his way to Damascus, did not inform him how he could be saved. He had set in the church firstly Apostles, and secondly prophets, for the work of the ministry, perfecting of the saints, etc. [see Ephesians 4:11–12]; and as the grand rule of heaven was that nothing should ever be done on earth without revealing the secret to his servants the prophets, agreeable to Amos 3:7, so Paul could not learn so much from the Lord relative to his duty in the common salvation of man, as he could from one of Christ's ambassadors called with the same heavenly calling of the Lord, and endowed with the same power from on high—so that what they loosed on earth, should be loosed in heaven; and what they bound on earth should be bound in heaven [see Matthew 16:19]."[14]

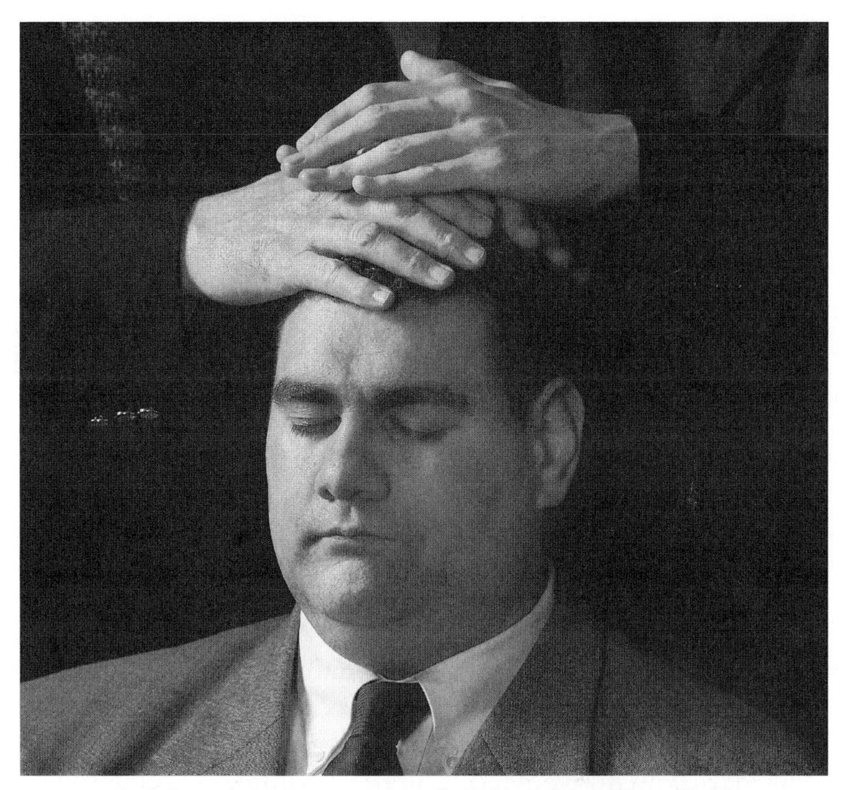

"We believe that a man must be called of God, by prophecy, and by the laying on of hands by those who are in authority, to preach the Gospel and administer in the ordinances thereof."

It is a great privilege to magnify any office of the priesthood.

"[The] Priesthood . . . may be illustrated by the figure of the human body, which has different members, which have different offices to perform; all are necessary in their place, and the body is not complete without all the members. . . . If a Priest understands his duty, his calling, and ministry, and preaches by the Holy Ghost, his enjoyment is as great as if he were one of the Presidency; and his services are necessary in the body, as are also those of Teachers and Deacons."[15]

Eliza R. Snow reported: "[Joseph Smith gave] instructions respecting the different offices, and the necessity of every individual acting in the sphere allotted him or her, and filling the several offices to which they are appointed. He spoke of the disposition of many men to consider the lower offices in the Church dishonorable, and to look with jealous eyes upon the standing of others who are called to preside over them; that it was the folly and nonsense of the human heart for a person to be aspiring to other stations than those to which they are appointed of God for them to occupy; that it was better for individuals to magnify their respective callings. . . . Everyone should aspire only to magnify his own office and calling."[16]

Suggestions for Study and Teaching

Consider these ideas as you study the chapter or as you prepare to teach. For additional help, see pages vii–xii.

- Review the account of Peter, James, and John conferring the Melchizedek Priesthood on Joseph Smith and Oliver Cowdery (page 101). What blessings have you and your family received because the Melchizedek Priesthood has been restored?
- Throughout this chapter, Joseph Smith testifies of a chain of priesthood authority through a succession of prophets. Why do you think this doctrine was important for him to teach in his day? Why do we need to understand this doctrine today? How does the chain of authority that Joseph Smith describes relate to a man's priesthood line of authority?
- As you read this chapter, note the Prophet Joseph Smith's use of the words *everlasting, eternal,* and *eternity.* What do these terms tell you about the nature and importance of the priesthood?
- Joseph Smith taught that God "set the ordinances to be the same forever and ever" and that "the ordinances must be kept in the very way God has appointed" (pages 107–8). How do these teachings increase your understanding of the ordinances of the gospel?
- Review the Prophet Joseph Smith's teachings about the Melchizedek Priesthood (pages 108–9). Think about how the Melchizedek Priesthood is necessary in all aspects of the gospel. What are your thoughts and feelings as you contemplate the Melchizedek Priesthood in this way?

- Review the final two paragraphs in the chapter (pages 111–12). How have you seen that each member of the Church plays an important part in the Lord's work? What can result if we "look with jealous eyes" at those who are called to serve as leaders in the Church? Think about what you can do to magnify your own calling.

Related Scriptures: Alma 13:1–12; D&C 27:5–14; 84:33–44, 109–10; 107:6–20; 121:34–46

Notes

1. John Taylor, *Deseret News: Semi-Weekly,* Apr. 18, 1882, p. 1; paragraph divisions altered.
2. John Taylor, *Deseret News: Semi-Weekly,* Mar. 20, 1877, p. 1.
3. *History of the Church,* 4:425; from the minutes of a Church conference held on Oct. 3, 1841, in Nauvoo, Illinois, published in *Times and Seasons,* Oct. 15, 1841, p. 577.
4. *History of the Church,* 3:385–88; punctuation modernized; from a discourse given by Joseph Smith about July 1839 in Commerce, Illinois; reported by Willard Richards.
5. *History of the Church,* 3:388–89; first set of bracketed words in second paragraph in original; punctuation modernized; from a discourse given by Joseph Smith about July 1839 in Commerce, Illinois; reported by Willard Richards.
6. *History of the Church,* 4:207–9; punctuation modernized; from a discourse prepared by Joseph Smith and read at a Church conference held on Oct. 5, 1840, in Nauvoo, Illinois.
7. *History of the Church,* 4:207; spelling and punctuation modernized; from a discourse prepared by Joseph Smith and read at a Church conference held on Oct. 5, 1840, in Nauvoo, Illinois.
8. *History of the Church,* 5:554–55; capitalization modernized; paragraph divisions altered; from a discourse given by Joseph Smith on Aug. 27, 1843, in Nauvoo, Illinois; reported by Willard Richards and William Clayton; see also appendix, page 562, item 3.
9. *History of the Church,* 2:477; punctuation modernized; from a discourse given by Joseph Smith on Apr. 6, 1837, in Kirtland, Ohio; reported by *Messenger and Advocate,* Apr. 1837, p. 487.
10. Quoted by William Clayton, reporting a discourse given by Joseph Smith on Jan. 5, 1841, in Nauvoo, Illinois; in L. John Nuttall, "Extracts from William Clayton's Private Book," p. 5, Journals of L. John Nuttall, 1857–1904, L. Tom Perry Special Collections, Brigham Young University, Provo, Utah; copy in Church Archives, The Church of Jesus Christ of Latter-day Saints, Salt Lake City, Utah.
11. *History of the Church,* 6:363; from a discourse given by Joseph Smith on May 12, 1844, in Nauvoo, Illinois; reported by Thomas Bullock.
12. Articles of Faith 1:5.
13. Letter from Joseph Smith to Isaac Galland, Mar. 22, 1839, Liberty Jail, Liberty, Missouri, published in *Times and Seasons,* Feb. 1840, p. 54; punctuation and capitalization modernized.
14. "Baptism," an editorial published in *Times and Seasons,* Sept. 1, 1842, p. 905; grammar modernized; Joseph Smith was the editor of the periodical.
15. *History of the Church,* 2:478; paragraph divisions altered; from a discourse given by Joseph Smith on Apr. 6, 1837, in Kirtland, Ohio; reported by *Messenger and Advocate,* Apr. 1837, p. 487.
16. *History of the Church,* 4:603, 606; paragraph divisions altered; from a discourse given by Joseph Smith on Apr. 28, 1842, in Nauvoo, Illinois; reported by Eliza R. Snow; see also appendix, page 562, item 3.

taste yea and i behold that the fruit thereof was white
to exceed all the whiteness that i had ever seen and as
i partook of the fruit thereof it filled my soul with ex-
ding great joy wherefore i began to be desirous that my family
should partake of it also for i knew that it was desirous
Above all other fruit and as i cast my eyes round about
it that perhaps i might discover my family also
and i beheld a river of water and it ran along and it was
near the tree of which i was partaking the fruit and
looked to behold from whence it came and i saw the
head thereof a little way off and at the head thereof i
beheld your Mother sariah and Sam and nephi and they
stood as if they knew not whither they should go and
it came to pass that i beckoned unto them and i also
did say unto them with a loud voice that they should
come unto me and partake of the fruite which was
desirable above all other fruit and it came to pass th
at they did come unto me and partake of the fruit
Also and it came to pass that i was desirous that Laman
And lemuel should come and partake of the fruit also
Wherefore i cast mine eyes toward the head of the river
that perhaps i might see them and it came to pass
that i saw them but they would not come unto
Me and partake of the fruit and i beheld a rod of
iron and it extended along the bank of the river
And led to the tree by which i stood and i also beh
eld a Strait and narrow path which came along
by the rod of iron even to the tree by which i stood
and it also led by the head of the fountain unto a
large and spacious field as if it had been a world
and i saw numberless concourses of people many of
whome are pressing forward that they might obtain
the path which led unto the tree by which i stood
and it came to pass that they did come forth and com
menced in the path which led to the tree and it came

A portion of a page from the original manuscript of the Book of Mormon. The words shown are part of Lehi's account of his vision of the tree of life, as found in 1 Nephi 8:11–23.

CHAPTER 9

Gifts of the Spirit

"If you will obey the Gospel with honest hearts, I promise you in the name of the Lord, that the gifts as promised by our Saviour will follow you."

From the Life of Joseph Smith

The title page of the Book of Mormon explains how this remarkable book of scripture would be made available to the world. In ancient times, the gold plates were "written and sealed up, and hid up unto the Lord, that they might not be destroyed." In the latter days, they were "to come forth by the gift and power of God" and be interpreted "by the gift of God." In fulfillment of these prophecies, God chose Joseph Smith to translate the sacred records. Clearly, Joseph's ability to translate the ancient characters did not come through education: he had only a grammar school knowledge of reading, writing, and arithmetic. His ability to translate records written centuries before in a language of which he had no knowledge came as a gift from God Himself.

Emma Smith, an early scribe in her husband's work, testified of this divine gift: "No man could have dictated the writing of the manuscripts unless he was inspired; for, when [I was] acting as his scribe, [Joseph] would dictate to me hour after hour; and when returning after meals, or after interruptions, he would at once begin where he had left off, without either seeing the manuscript or having any portion of it read to him."[1]

The Lord gave the Prophet vital temporal help that allowed him to go forward with the work of translation. Joseph Knight Sr., a friend of the Prophet, gave Joseph money and food on several occasions. At a particularly desperate time, Brother Knight traveled to the Prophet's home to give Joseph and Oliver "a barrel of mackerel and some lined paper for writing," along with "nine or ten bushels of grain and five or six bushels of taters [potatoes]."

Brother Knight recalled, "Joseph and Oliver . . . returned home and found me there with provisions, and they were glad, for they were out."[2]

During April and May 1829, persecution increasingly interrupted the Prophet's work of translating at his home in Harmony, Pennsylvania. Oliver Cowdery wrote to a friend, David Whitmer, telling him about the sacred work and asking him to allow the work to continue in the Whitmer home in Fayette, New York. In late May or early June 1829, the Prophet and Oliver traveled with David Whitmer in his one-horse wagon to the farm home of David's father, Peter Whitmer Sr. During the month of June, in an upstairs room of the Whitmer home, the translation was completed by the gift and power of God.

Oliver Cowdery described the marvelous experience of serving as the Prophet's scribe: "These were days never to be forgotten—to sit under the sound of a voice dictated by the inspiration of heaven, awakened the utmost gratitude of this bosom! Day after day I continued, uninterrupted, to write from his mouth, as he translated with the Urim and Thummim . . . the history or record called 'The Book of Mormon.' "[3]

During this time, Joseph Smith learned that the divine gift was with him only when he was worthy to be guided by the Spirit. David Whitmer recounted: "One morning when [Joseph Smith] was getting ready to continue the translation, something went wrong about the house and he was put out about it. Something that Emma, his wife, had done. Oliver and I went up stairs, and Joseph came up soon after to continue the translation, but he could not do anything. He could not translate a single syllable. He went down stairs, out into the orchard and made supplication to the Lord; was gone about an hour—came back to the house, asked Emma's forgiveness and then came up stairs where we were and the translation went on all right. He could do nothing save he was humble and faithful."[4]

Humbly and faithfully using the gift God gave him, the young Prophet accomplished the seemingly impossible task of translating almost the entire Book of Mormon between early April and the end of June 1829.

Teachings of Joseph Smith

We are each given gifts of the Spirit; each person's gifts are necessary in the Church.

Articles of Faith 1:7: "We believe in the gift of tongues, prophecy, revelation, visions, healing, interpretation of tongues, and so forth."[5]

"We . . . believe in prophecy, in tongues, in visions, and in revelations, in gifts, and in healings; and that these things cannot be enjoyed without the gift of the Holy Ghost."[6]

Amasa Potter recalled: "I remember the Prophet arising to preach to a large congregation in the grove west of the Temple in Nauvoo. He stated that he would preach on spiritual gifts. . . . Joseph stated that every Latter-day Saint had a gift, and by living a righteous life, and asking for it, the Holy Spirit would reveal it to him or her."[7]

"Paul says, 'To one is given the gift of tongues, to another the gift of prophecy, and to another the gift of healing;' and again: 'Do all prophesy? do all speak with tongues? do all interpret?' evidently showing that all did not possess these several gifts; but that one received one gift, and another received another gift—all did not prophesy, all did not speak in tongues, all did not work miracles; but all did receive the gift of the Holy Ghost; sometimes they spake in tongues and prophesied in the Apostles' days, and sometimes they did not. . . .

"The Church is a compact body composed of different members, and is strictly analogous to the human system, and Paul, after speaking of the different gifts, says, 'Now ye are the body of Christ and members in particular; and God hath set some in the Church, first Apostles, secondarily Prophets, thirdly Teachers, after that miracles, then gifts of healing, helps, governments, diversities of tongues. Are all Teachers? Are all workers of miracles? Do all speak with tongues? Do all interpret?' It is evident that they do not; yet are they all members of one body. All members of the natural body are not the eye, the ear, the head or the hand—yet the eye cannot say to the ear I have no need of thee, nor the head to the foot, I have no need of thee; they are all so many component parts in the perfect machine—the one body; and if one member suffer, the whole of the members suffer with it: and if one member rejoice, all the rest are honored with it. [See 1 Corinthians 12:9–10, 18–21, 26–30.]

"These, then, are all gifts; they come from God; they are of God; they are all the gifts of the Holy Ghost."[8]

We receive gifts of the Spirit through obedience and faith.

"Because faith is wanting, the fruits are. No man since the world was had faith without having something along with it. The ancients quenched the violence of fire, escaped the edge of the sword, women received their dead, etc. By faith the worlds were made. [See Hebrews 11:3, 34–35.] A man who has none of the gifts has no faith; and he deceives himself, if he supposes he has. Faith has been wanting, not only among the heathen, but in professed Christendom also, so that tongues, healings, prophecy, and prophets and apostles, and all the gifts and blessings have been wanting."[9]

"This winter [1832–33] was spent in translating the Scriptures; in the School of the Prophets; and sitting in conferences. I had many glorious seasons of refreshing. The gifts which follow them that believe and obey the Gospel, as tokens that the Lord is ever the same in His dealings with the humble lovers and followers of truth, began to be poured out among us, as in ancient days."[10]

Edward Stevenson was present when Joseph Smith preached in Pontiac, Michigan, in 1834. He recalled these words of the Prophet: "If you will obey the Gospel with honest hearts, I promise you in the name of the Lord, that the gifts as promised by our Saviour will follow you, and by this you may prove me to be a true servant of God."[11]

Gifts of the Spirit are usually received quietly and privately, without outward manifestations.

"Various and conflicting are the opinions of men in regard to the gift of the Holy Ghost. Some people have been in the habit of calling every supernatural manifestation the effects of the Spirit of God, whilst there are others that think there is no manifestation connected with it at all; and that it is nothing but a mere impulse of the mind, or an inward feeling, impression, or secret testimony or evidence, which men possess, and that there is no such a thing as an outward manifestation.

"It is not to be wondered at that men should be ignorant, in a great measure, of the principles of salvation, and more especially of the nature, office, power, influence, gifts, and blessings of the gift of the Holy Ghost; when we consider that the human family have been enveloped in gross darkness and ignorance for many centuries past, without revelation, or any just criterion [by which] to arrive at a knowledge of the things of God, which can only be known by the Spirit of God. Hence it not infrequently occurs, that when the Elders of this Church preach to the inhabitants of the world, that if they obey the Gospel they shall receive the gift of the Holy Ghost, that the people expect to see some wonderful manifestation, some great display of power, or some extraordinary miracle performed. . . .

"The human family are very apt to run to extremes, especially in religious matters, and hence people in general either want some miraculous display, or they will not believe in the gift of the Holy Ghost at all. If an Elder lays his hands upon a person, it is thought by many that the person must immediately rise and speak in tongues and prophesy; this idea is gathered from the circumstance of Paul laying his hands upon certain individuals who had been previously (as they stated) baptized unto John's baptism; which when he had done, they 'spake in tongues and prophesied.' [See Acts 19:1–6.] . . .

"We believe that the Holy Ghost is imparted by the laying on of hands of those in authority, and that the gift of tongues, and also the gift of prophecy are gifts of the Spirit, and are obtained through that medium; but then to say that men always prophesied and spoke in tongues when they had the imposition of hands, would be to state that which is untrue, contrary to the practice of the Apostles, and at variance with holy writ. . . .

". . . All the gifts of the Spirit are not visible to the natural vision, or understanding of man; indeed very few of them are. . . . Few of them could be known by the generality of men. Peter and John were Apostles, yet the Jewish court scourged them as impostors. Paul was both an Apostle and Prophet, yet they stoned him and put him into prison. The people knew nothing about it, although he had in his possession the gift of the Holy Ghost. Our Savior was 'anointed with the oil of gladness above his fellows' [Hebrews 1:9], yet so far from the people knowing Him, they said He was Beelzebub, and crucified Him as an impostor. Who could point out a Pastor, a Teacher, or an Evangelist by their appearance, yet had they the gift of the Holy Ghost?

"But to come to the other members of the Church, and examine the gifts as spoken of by Paul, we shall find that the world can in general know nothing about them, and that there are but one or two that could be immediately known, if they were all poured out immediately upon the imposition of hands. In [1 Corinthians 12:4–11], Paul says, 'There are diversities of gifts yet the same spirit, and there are differences of administrations but the same Lord; and there are diversities of operations, but it is the same God which worketh all in all. But the manifestation of the Spirit is given unto every man to profit withal. For to one is given, by the Spirit, the word of wisdom; to another, the word of knowledge by the same Spirit; to another faith, by the same Spirit; to another the gifts of healing, by the same Spirit; to another the working of miracles; to another prophecy; to another the discerning of spirits; to another divers kinds of tongues; to another the interpretation of tongues. But all these worketh that one and the self same spirit, dividing to each man severally as he will.'

"There are several gifts mentioned here, yet which of them all could be known by an observer at the imposition of hands? The word of wisdom, and the word of knowledge, are as much gifts as any other, yet if a person possessed both of these gifts, or received them by the imposition of hands, who would know it? Another might receive the gift of faith, and they would be as ignorant of it. Or suppose a man had the gift of healing or power to work miracles, that would not then be known; it would require time and circumstances to call these gifts into operation. Suppose a man had the discerning of spirits, who would be the wiser for it? Or if he had the interpretation of tongues, unless someone spoke in an unknown tongue, he of course would have to be silent; there are only two gifts that could be made visible—the gift of tongues and the gift of prophecy. These are things that are the most talked about, and yet if a person spoke in an unknown tongue, according to Paul's testimony, he would be a barbarian to those present [see 1 Corinthians 14:11]. They would say that it was gibberish; and if he prophesied they would call it nonsense. The gift of tongues is the smallest gift perhaps of the whole, and yet it is one that is the most sought after.

"So that according to the testimony of Scripture and the manifestations of the Spirit in ancient days, very little could be known about it by the surrounding multitude, except on some extraordinary occasion, as on the day of Pentecost. The greatest, the best, and the most useful gifts would be known nothing about by an observer. . . .

"The manifestations of the gift of the Holy Ghost, the ministering of angels, or the development of the power, majesty or glory of God were very seldom manifested publicly, and that generally to the people of God, as to the Israelites; but most generally when angels have come, or God has revealed Himself, it has been to individuals in private, in their chamber; in the wilderness or fields, and that generally without noise or tumult. The angel delivered Peter out of prison in the dead of night; came to Paul unobserved by the rest of the crew; appeared to Mary and Elizabeth without the knowledge of others; spoke to John the Baptist whilst the people around were ignorant of it.

"When Elisha saw the chariots of Israel and the horsemen thereof, it was unknown to others. When the Lord appeared to Abraham it was at his tent door; when the angels went to Lot, no person knew them but himself, which was the case probably with Abraham and his wife; when the Lord appeared to Moses, it was in the burning bush, in the tabernacle, or in the mountain top; when Elijah was taken in a chariot of fire, it was unobserved by the world; and when he was in a cleft of a rock, there was

"The power, majesty or glory of God [are] very seldom manifested publicly. . . . When the Lord appeared to Abraham it was at his tent door [see Genesis 18:1]."

loud thunder, but the Lord was not in the thunder; there was an earthquake, but the Lord was not in the earthquake; and then there was a still small voice, which was the voice of the Lord, saying, 'What doest thou here, Elijah?' [See 1 Kings 19:11–13.]

"The Lord cannot always be known by the thunder of His voice, by the display of His glory or by the manifestation of His power; and those that are the most anxious to see these things, are the least prepared to meet them, and were the Lord to manifest His power as He did to the children of Israel, such characters would be the first to say, 'Let not the Lord speak any more, lest we His people die.' [See Exodus 20:19.]"[12]

Suggestions for Study and Teaching

Consider these ideas as you study the chapter or as you prepare to teach. For additional help, see pages vii–xii.

- The Lord gave the Prophet Joseph Smith a gift to be able to translate the gold plates (pages 115–16). When has the Lord given you gifts to help you participate in His work?
- What can we learn from the story told by David Whitmer on page 116? What experiences in your own life have taught you that you must be worthy in order to use your spiritual gifts?
- Review the section that begins on page 117. In what ways does the Church benefit from having members with different gifts of the Spirit? How have you benefited from the spiritual gifts of others? When have you seen people with different gifts work together to help one another?
- Study the section on page 118. Think about some spiritual gifts that would strengthen you personally or help you serve the Lord and others. Determine what you will do to "seek . . . earnestly the best gifts" (D&C 46:8).
- Review the section that begins at the bottom of page 118. Think about or discuss the specific counsel you find about how spiritual gifts are manifested. Why is it important to remember that spiritual gifts are "very seldom manifested publicly"? (page 121). Why do you think that many spiritual gifts come quietly and privately? Why is it important to remember that many gifts require "time and circumstances to call [them] into operation"? (page 121).
- After reading this chapter, what would you say are some of the purposes of spiritual gifts?

Related Scriptures: 1 Corinthians 12:1–31; 3 Nephi 29:6; Moroni 10:6–23; D&C 46:8–33

Notes

1. Emma Smith, interview by Joseph Smith III, Feb. 1879, *Saints' Herald* (periodical published by the Reorganized Church of Jesus Christ of Latter Day Saints, now called Community of Christ), Oct. 1, 1879, p. 290.
2. Joseph Knight, Reminiscences, p. 6, Church Archives, The Church of Jesus Christ of Latter-day Saints, Salt Lake City, Utah.
3. Oliver Cowdery, quoted in Joseph Smith—History 1:71, footnote; from a letter from Oliver Cowdery to William W. Phelps, Sept. 7, 1834, Norton, Ohio, published in *Messenger and Advocate,* Oct. 1834, p. 14.
4. David Whitmer, interview by William H. Kelley and George A. Blakeslee, Sept. 15, 1881, *Saints' Herald,* Mar. 1, 1882, p. 68.
5. Articles of Faith 1:7.
6. *History of the Church,* 5:27; from "Gift of the Holy Ghost," an editorial published in *Times and Seasons,* June 15, 1842, p. 823; Joseph Smith was the editor of the periodical.
7. Amasa Potter, "A Reminiscence of the Prophet Joseph Smith," *Juvenile Instructor,* Feb. 15, 1894, p. 132.
8. *History of the Church,* 5:28–29; from "Gift of the Holy Ghost," an editorial published in *Times and Seasons,* June 15, 1842, pp. 823–24; Joseph Smith was the editor of the periodical.
9. *History of the Church,* 5:218; from instructions given by Joseph Smith on Jan. 2, 1843, in Springfield, Illinois; reported by Willard Richards.
10. *History of the Church,* 1:322; bracketed dates in original; from "History of the Church" (manuscript), book A-1, p. 270, Church Archives.
11. Quoted by Edward Stevenson, *Reminiscences of Joseph, the Prophet, and the Coming Forth of the Book of Mormon* (1893), p. 4.
12. *History of the Church,* 5:26–31; bracketed words in second paragraph in original; punctuation and grammar modernized; paragraph divisions altered; from "Gift of the Holy Ghost," an editorial published in *Times and Seasons,* June 15, 1842, pp. 823–25; Joseph Smith was the editor of the periodical.

CHAPTER 10

Prayer and Personal Revelation

"It is the privilege of the children of God to come to God and get revelation."

From the Life of Joseph Smith

By June 1829, many important events in the unfolding restoration of the gospel had already occurred. The heavens had been opened at the time of the First Vision and God had again spoken to men on earth. The Prophet Joseph Smith had received the Book of Mormon plates and was translating their sacred message. The holy priesthood had been restored, and the ordinance of baptism had been made available to God's children. Each of these events had occurred in answer to prayer as the Prophet sought guidance from the Lord.

As the work of translation drew to a close, the Prophet once again sought direction from the Lord. Because Moroni had instructed Joseph not to show the plates to anyone unless he was commanded to do so, Joseph had felt very much alone and heavily burdened with his responsibility as he translated the plates. However, he had discovered from the record itself that the Lord would provide three special witnesses who would testify to the world that the Book of Mormon was true (see 2 Nephi 11:3; Ether 5:2–4).

"Almost immediately after we had made this discovery," Joseph Smith recalled, "it occurred to Oliver Cowdery, David Whitmer and . . . Martin Harris (who had come to inquire after our progress in the work) that they would have me inquire of the Lord to know if they might not obtain of him the privilege to be these three special witnesses."[1] The Prophet prayed for direction and received a revelation declaring that the three men would be permitted to see the plates, as well as the sword of Laban, the Urim and Thummim, and the Liahona (see D&C 17).

In June 1829, Oliver Cowdery, David Whitmer, and Joseph Smith were privileged to see Moroni and the gold plates. A short time later on the same day, Martin Harris also saw the angel and the plates.

A few days later, the Prophet and the three men went into the woods near the Whitmer home in Fayette, New York, and began to pray for this great privilege to be granted to them. Martin withdrew, feeling unworthy. The Prophet recorded what then occurred: "We . . . had not been many minutes engaged in prayer, when presently we beheld a light above us in the air, of exceeding brightness; and behold, an angel [Moroni] stood before us. In his hands he held the plates which we had been praying for these to have a view of. He turned over the leaves one by one, so that we could see them, and discern the engravings thereon distinctly."[2] The men also heard the voice of God testifying of the truthfulness of the translation and commanding them to bear record of what they had seen and heard. Joseph then went to find Martin, who was praying elsewhere in the woods. They prayed together and saw the same vision and heard the same voice.

Joseph Smith's mother, who was visiting the Prophet in Fayette at this time, recalled her son's joy and relief after this manifestation: "When Joseph came in [to the Whitmer home], he threw himself down beside me. 'Father! Mother!' said he, 'you do not know how happy I am. The Lord has caused the plates to be shown to three more besides me, who have also seen an angel and will have to testify to the truth of what I have said, for they know for themselves that I do not go about to deceive the people. And I do feel as though I was relieved of a dreadful burden which was almost too much for me to endure. But they will now have to bear a part, and it does rejoice my soul that I am not any longer to be entirely alone in the world.' "[3]

Throughout his life, Joseph Smith would turn to God in prayer to seek the help and guidance he needed. A Church member recalled hearing him pray in Kirtland, Ohio, at a time of great personal difficulty: "Never until then had I heard a man address his Maker as though He was present listening as a kind father would listen to the sorrows of a dutiful child. . . . There was no ostentation, no raising of the voice as by enthusiasm, but a plain conversational tone, as a man would address a present friend. It appeared to me as though, in case the veil were taken away, I could see the Lord standing facing His humblest of all servants I had ever seen."[4]

Teachings of Joseph Smith

God will hear our prayers and speak to us today, just as He spoke to the ancient Saints.

"Seeing that the Lord has never given the world to understand by anything heretofore revealed that he had ceased forever to speak to his creatures when sought unto in a proper manner, why should it be thought a thing incredible that he should be pleased to speak again in these last days for their salvation?

"Perhaps you may be surprised at this assertion, that I should say for the salvation of his creatures in these last days, since we have already in our possession a vast volume of his word which he has previously given. But you will admit that the word spoken to Noah was not sufficient for Abraham, or it was not required of Abraham to leave the land of his nativity and seek an inheritance in a strange country upon the word spoken to Noah, but for himself he obtained promises at the hand of the Lord and walked in that perfection that he was called the friend of God. Isaac, the promised seed, was not required to rest his hope upon the promises made to his father, Abraham, but was privileged with the assurance of his approbation in the sight of heaven by the direct voice of the Lord to him.

"If one man can live upon the revelations given to another, might not I with propriety ask, why the necessity, then, of the Lord speaking to Isaac as he did, as is recorded in the 26th chapter of Genesis? For the Lord there repeats, or rather promises again, to perform the oath which he had previously sworn unto Abraham. And why this repetition to Isaac? Why was not the first promise as sure for Isaac as it was for Abraham? Was not Isaac Abraham's son? And could he not place implicit confidence in the word of his father as being a man of God? Perhaps you may say that he was a very peculiar man and different from men in these last days; consequently, the Lord favored him with blessings peculiar and different, as he was different from men in this age. I admit that he was a peculiar man and was not only peculiarly blessed, but greatly blessed. But all the peculiarity that I can discover in the man, or all the difference between him and men in this age, is that he was more holy and more perfect before God and came to him with a purer heart and more faith than men in this day.

"The same might be said on the subject of Jacob's history. Why was it that the Lord spake to him concerning the same promise after he had made it once to Abraham and renewed it to Isaac? Why could not Jacob rest contented upon the word spoken to his fathers?

"When the time of the promise drew nigh for the deliverance of the children of Israel from the land of Egypt, why was it necessary that the Lord should begin to speak to them? The promise or word to Abraham was that his seed should serve in bondage and be afflicted four hundred years, and after that they should come out with great substance. Why did they not rely upon this promise and, when they had remained in Egypt in bondage four hundred years, come out without waiting for further revelation, but act entirely upon the promise given to Abraham that they should come out? . . .

". . . I may believe that Enoch walked with God. I may believe that Abraham communed with God and conversed with angels. I may believe that Isaac obtained a renewal of the covenant made to Abraham by the direct voice of the Lord. I may believe that Jacob conversed with holy angels and heard the word of his Maker, that he wrestled with the angel until he prevailed and obtained a blessing. I may believe that Elijah was taken to heaven in a chariot of fire with fiery horses. I may believe that the saints saw the Lord and conversed with him face to face after his resurrection. I may believe that the Hebrew church came to Mount Zion and unto the city of the living God, the heavenly Jerusalem, and to an innumerable company of angels. I may believe that they looked into eternity and saw the Judge of all, and Jesus, the Mediator of the new covenant.

"But will all this purchase an assurance for me, or waft me to the regions of eternal day with my garments spotless, pure, and white? Or, must I not rather obtain for myself, by my own faith and diligence in keeping the commandments of the Lord, an assurance of salvation for myself? And have I not an equal privilege with the ancient saints? And will not the Lord hear my prayers and listen to my cries as soon as he ever did to theirs if I come to him in the manner they did?"[5]

We can make everything we undertake a subject of prayer.

Sarah Granger Kimball reported: "In the School of the Prophets . . . , when Joseph Smith was giving instruction to the brethren, he told them to make everything they undertook a subject of prayer."[6]

"Seek to know God in your closets, call upon him in the fields. Follow the directions of the Book of Mormon, and pray over, and for your families, your cattle, your flocks, your herds, your corn, and all things that you possess [see Alma 34:18–27]; ask the blessing of God upon all your labors, and everything that you engage in."[7]

"Slack not your duties in your families, but call upon God for his blessings upon you, and your families, upon your flocks and

"Slack not your duties in your families, but call upon God for his blessings upon you, and your families."

herds, and all that pertains to you—that you may have peace and prosperity—and while you are doing this, 'pray for the peace of Zion, for they shall prosper that love her.' [See Psalm 122:6.]"[8]

A prayer the Prophet recorded in August 1842 shows his desire for wisdom from God: "O Thou, who seest and knowest the hearts of all men . . . , look down upon Thy servant Joseph at this time; and let faith on the name of Thy Son Jesus Christ, to a greater degree than Thy servant ever yet has enjoyed, be conferred upon him, even the faith of Elijah; and let the lamp of eternal life be lit up in his heart, never to be taken away; and let the words of eternal life be poured upon the soul of Thy servant, that he may know Thy will, Thy statutes, and Thy commandments, and Thy judgments, to do them. As the dews upon Mount Hermon, may the distillations of Thy divine grace, glory, and honor, in the plenitude of Thy mercy, and power, and goodness, be poured down upon the head of Thy servant."[9]

When we pray in faith and simplicity, we receive the blessings God sees fit to bestow upon us.

"Supplicate at the throne of grace, that the Spirit of the Lord may always rest upon you. Remember that without asking we can receive nothing; therefore, ask in faith, and ye shall receive such blessings as God sees fit to bestow upon you. Pray not with covetous hearts that ye may consume it upon your lusts, but pray earnestly for the best gifts [see D&C 46:8–9]."[10]

"Virtue is one of the most prominent principles that enables us to have confidence in approaching our Father who is in heaven in order to ask wisdom at his hand. Therefore, if thou wilt cherish this principle in thine heart, thou mayest ask with all confidence before him and it shall be poured out upon thine head [see D&C 121:45–46]."[11]

"Let the prayers of the Saints to heaven appear, that they may enter into the ears of the Lord of Sabaoth, for the effectual prayers of the righteous avail much [see James 5:16]."[12]

Henry W. Bigler recalled: "Speaking about praying to our Father in heaven, I once heard Joseph Smith remark, 'Be plain and simple and ask for what you want, just like you would go to a neighbor and say, I want to borrow your horse to go to [the] mill.' "[13]

We can receive personal revelation through the Holy Ghost.

"It is the privilege of the children of God to come to God and get revelation. . . . God is not a respecter of persons; we all have the same privilege."[14]

"We believe that we have a right to revelations, visions, and dreams from God, our heavenly Father; and light and intelligence, through the gift of the Holy Ghost, in the name of Jesus Christ, on all subjects pertaining to our spiritual welfare; if it so be that we keep his commandments, so as to render ourselves worthy in his sight."[15]

"A person may profit by noticing the first intimation of the spirit of revelation; for instance, when you feel pure intelligence flowing into you, it may give you sudden strokes of ideas, so that by noticing it, you may find it fulfilled the same day or soon; (i.e.) those things that were presented unto your minds by the Spirit of God, will come to pass; and thus by learning the Spirit of God and understanding it, you may grow into the principle of revelation, until you become perfect in Christ Jesus."[16]

"I have an old edition of the New Testament in the Latin, Hebrew, German and Greek languages. . . . I thank God that I have got this old book; but I thank him more for the gift of the Holy Ghost. I have got the oldest book in the world; but I have got the oldest book in my heart, even the gift of the Holy Ghost. . . . The Holy Ghost . . . is within me, and comprehends more than all the world; and I will associate myself with him."[17]

"No man can receive the Holy Ghost without receiving revelations. The Holy Ghost is a revelator."[18]

John Taylor, while serving as President of the Quorum of the Twelve, reported: "I well remember a remark that Joseph Smith made to me upwards of forty years ago. Said he, 'Elder Taylor, you have been baptized, you have had hands laid upon your head for the reception of the Holy Ghost, and you have been ordained to the holy priesthood. Now, if you will continue to follow the leadings of that spirit, it will always lead you right. Sometimes it might be contrary to your judgment; never mind that, follow its dictates; and if you be true to its whisperings it will in time become in you a principle of revelation so that you will know all things.' "[19]

Suggestions for Study and Teaching

Consider these ideas as you study the chapter or as you prepare to teach. For additional help, see pages vii–xii.

- Note the importance of prayer in the experience of Joseph Smith and the Three Witnesses of the Book of Mormon (pages 125–27). How has prayer influenced your own experiences with the Book of Mormon? What other aspects of your life are influenced by prayer?
- What are your thoughts as you read the paragraph at the bottom of page 127? As you ponder this statement, consider what you might do to improve the way you "address [your] Maker."
- Why can't we rely solely on revelations from the past? (For some examples, see pages 128–30.) Why do we need continuing, personal revelation?
- Review the section that begins on page 130. Identify the Prophet's teachings concerning *when* we should pray and *what* we should pray about. How might these teachings help you in your personal prayers? How might they help families with family prayer?
- Study the Prophet's teachings on pages 131–32 about *how* we should pray. What is the value of using "plain and simple" language when we pray? How does living righteously give us confidence in approaching our Heavenly Father in prayer? What has helped you gain a testimony that God hears and answers prayers?
- Read the third full paragraph on page 132. When have you profited from noticing "the first intimation" of the Spirit prompting you? How can we learn to immediately recognize the whisperings of the Spirit when they come?

Related Scriptures: 1 Kings 19:11–12; James 1:5–6; Helaman 5:30; 3 Nephi 18:18–21; D&C 6:22–23; 8:2–3; 88:63–65

Notes

1. *History of the Church,* 1:52–53; from "History of the Church" (manuscript), book A-1, p. 23, Church Archives, The Church of Jesus Christ of Latter-day Saints, Salt Lake City, Utah.
2. *History of the Church,* 1:54; from "History of the Church" (manuscript), book A-1, pp. 24–25, Church Archives.
3. Lucy Mack Smith, "The History of Lucy Smith, Mother of the Prophet," 1844–45 manuscript, book 8, p. 11, Church Archives.
4. Daniel Tyler, in "Recollections of the Prophet Joseph Smith," *Juvenile Instructor,* Feb. 15, 1892, p. 127.
5. Letter from Joseph Smith to his uncle Silas Smith, Sept. 26, 1833, Kirtland, Ohio; in Lucy Mack Smith, "The History of Lucy Smith, Mother of the Prophet," 1845 manuscript, pp. 229–32, Church Archives.
6. Sarah Granger Kimball, in "R. S. Report," *Woman's Exponent,* Aug. 15, 1892, p. 30.
7. *History of the Church,* 5:31; from "Gift of the Holy Ghost," an editorial published in *Times and Seasons,* June 15, 1842, p. 825; Joseph Smith was the editor of the periodical.
8. "To the Saints of God," an editorial published in *Times and Seasons,* Oct. 15, 1842, p. 952; punctuation modernized; Joseph Smith was the editor of the periodical.
9. *History of the Church,* 5:127–28; paragraph divisions altered; from a Joseph Smith journal entry, Aug. 23, 1842, near Nauvoo, Illinois; this entry is incorrectly dated Aug. 22, 1842, in *History of the Church.*
10. Letter from Joseph Smith and John Whitmer to the Saints in Colesville, New York, Aug. 20, 1830, Harmony, Pennsylvania; in Newel Knight, Autobiography and Journal, ca. 1846–47, p. 129, Church Archives.
11. Statement written by Joseph Smith in Feb. 1840 in Philadelphia, Pennsylvania; original in private possession.
12. *History of the Church,* 6:303; from a discourse given by Joseph Smith on Apr. 7, 1844, in Nauvoo, Illinois; reported by Wilford Woodruff, Willard Richards, Thomas Bullock, and William Clayton.
13. Henry W. Bigler, in "Recollections of the Prophet Joseph Smith," *Juvenile Instructor,* Mar. 1, 1892, pp. 151–52.
14. Discourse given by Joseph Smith about July 1839 in Commerce, Illinois; reported by Willard Richards, in Willard Richards, Pocket Companion, pp. 75, 78–79, Church Archives.
15. Letter from Joseph Smith to Isaac Galland, Mar. 22, 1839, Liberty Jail, Liberty, Missouri, published in *Times and Seasons,* Feb. 1840, p. 54.
16. *History of the Church,* 3:381; from a discourse given by Joseph Smith on June 27, 1839, in Commerce, Illinois; reported by Willard Richards.
17. *History of the Church,* 6:307–8; paragraph divisions altered; from a discourse given by Joseph Smith on Apr. 7, 1844, in Nauvoo, Illinois; reported by Wilford Woodruff, Willard Richards, Thomas Bullock, and William Clayton.
18. *History of the Church,* 6:58; from a discourse given by Joseph Smith on Oct. 15, 1843, in Nauvoo, Illinois; reported by Willard Richards.
19. John Taylor, *Deseret News: Semi-Weekly,* Jan. 15, 1878, p. 1.

CHAPTER 11

The Organization and Destiny of the True and Living Church

"You know no more concerning the destinies of this Church and kingdom than a babe upon its mother's lap. You don't comprehend it. . . . This Church will fill North and South America—it will fill the world."

From the Life of Joseph Smith

In June 1829, the Prophet Joseph Smith completed the translation of the Book of Mormon. "Our translation drawing to a close," the Prophet stated, "we went to Palmyra, Wayne county, New York, secured the copyright, and agreed with Mr. Egbert B. Grandin to print five thousand copies for the sum of three thousand dollars."[1] Egbert B. Grandin was a young man, a year younger than Joseph Smith, who owned a printing shop in Palmyra. He had just purchased a new press with technology that made the printing process considerably faster. It was remarkable that the Prophet was able to find a printer in the rural town of Palmyra capable of printing so many copies of a lengthy volume like the Book of Mormon. Because printing the Book of Mormon was such a large and expensive project, Martin Harris mortgaged his farm to Mr. Grandin to ensure payment of the printing costs.

In the late summer of 1829, Joseph Smith, Martin Harris, and several others gathered at the printing shop to inspect the proof of the title page of the Book of Mormon, the first page of the book to be printed. When the Prophet declared that he was pleased with the appearance of the page, the printing went forward as quickly as possible. The work took about seven months to complete, and copies of the Book of Mormon were made available to the public on March 26, 1830.

In the late summer of 1829, Joseph Smith, Martin Harris, and several others gathered with the printer of the Book of Mormon, Egbert B. Grandin, to inspect the proof of the Book of Mormon's title page, the first page to be printed.

With the work of translating and publishing the Book of Mormon now completed, Joseph Smith moved forward to organize the Church. In the revelation now found in section 20 of the Doctrine and Covenants, the Lord revealed to the Prophet "the precise day upon which, according to His will and commandment, we should proceed to organize His Church once more here upon the earth."[2] The day specified was April 6, 1830.

"We . . . made known to our brethren," the Prophet said, "that we had received a commandment to organize the Church; and accordingly we met together for that purpose, at the house of Mr. Peter Whitmer, Sen., (being six in number,) on Tuesday, the sixth day of April, A.D., one thousand eight hundred and thirty."[3] Approximately 60 people crowded into the Whitmer home in Fayette, New York, completely filling two rooms in the home. Six of the men present were identified as the incorporators of the new Church in order to fulfill the law of New York—the Prophet Joseph Smith, Oliver Cowdery, Hyrum Smith, Peter Whitmer Jr., Samuel Smith, and David Whitmer.[4]

Although the Church was very small in the beginning, Joseph Smith had a prophetic sense of its grand destiny. Wilford Woodruff recalled that during a priesthood meeting at Kirtland, Ohio, in April 1834, the Prophet tried to awaken the brethren to a realization of the future state of God's kingdom on earth:

"The Prophet called on all who held the Priesthood to gather into the little log school house they had there. It was a small house, perhaps 14 feet square. But it held the whole of the Priesthood of the Church of Jesus Christ of Latter-day Saints who were then in the town of Kirtland. . . . When we got together the Prophet called upon the Elders of Israel with him to bear testimony of this work. . . . When they got through the Prophet said, 'Brethren, I have been very much edified and instructed in your testimonies here tonight, but I want to say to you before the Lord, that you know no more concerning the destinies of this Church and kingdom than a babe upon its mother's lap. You don't comprehend it.' I was rather surprised. He said, 'It is only a little handful of Priesthood you see here tonight, but this Church will fill North and South America—it will fill the world.' "[5]

Teachings of Joseph Smith

The true Church of Jesus Christ was organized by Joseph Smith in the dispensation of the fulness of times.

Joseph Smith reported the events of the meeting held on April 6, 1830, to organize the Church: "Having opened the meeting by solemn prayer to our Heavenly Father, we proceeded, according to previous commandment, to call on our brethren to know whether they accepted us as their teachers in the things of the Kingdom of God, and whether they were satisfied that we should proceed and be organized as a Church according to said commandment which we had received. To these several propositions they consented by a unanimous vote.

"I then laid my hands upon Oliver Cowdery, and ordained him an Elder of the 'Church of Jesus Christ of Latter-day Saints;' after which, he ordained me also to the office of an Elder of said Church. We then took bread, blessed it, and brake it with them; also wine, blessed it, and drank it with them. We then laid our hands on each individual member of the Church present, that they might receive the gift of the Holy Ghost, and be confirmed members of the Church of Christ. The Holy Ghost was poured out upon us to a very great degree—some prophesied, whilst we all praised the Lord, and rejoiced exceedingly. . . .

"We now proceeded to call out and ordain some others of the brethren to different offices of the Priesthood, according as the Spirit manifested unto us: and after a happy time spent in witnessing and feeling for ourselves the powers and blessings of the Holy Ghost, through the grace of God bestowed upon us, we dismissed with the pleasing knowledge that we were now individually members of, and acknowledged of God, 'The Church of Jesus Christ,' organized in accordance with commandments and revelations given by Him to ourselves in these last days, as well as according to the order of the Church as recorded in the New Testament."[6]

At the first general conference of the Church, held in Fayette, New York, on June 9, 1830, the sacrament was administered, several people were confirmed members of the Church, others

were ordained to offices in the priesthood, and the Holy Ghost was poured out upon the Saints. The Prophet Joseph Smith recorded: "Such scenes as these were calculated to inspire our hearts with joy unspeakable, and fill us with awe and reverence for that Almighty Being, by whose grace we had been called to be instrumental in bringing about, for the children of men, the enjoyment of such glorious blessings as were now at this time poured out upon us. To find ourselves engaged in the very same order of things as observed by the holy Apostles of old; to realize the importance and solemnity of such proceedings; and to witness and feel with our own natural senses, the like glorious manifestations of the powers of the Priesthood, the gifts and blessings of the Holy Ghost, and the goodness and condescension of a merciful God unto such as obey the everlasting Gospel of our Lord Jesus Christ, combined to create within us sensations of rapturous gratitude, and inspire us with fresh zeal and energy in the cause of truth."[7]

Christ's Church is organized according to the order of God.

"Christ was the head of the Church, the chief cornerstone, the spiritual rock upon which the Church was built, and the gates of hell shall not prevail against it [see Matthew 16:18; Ephesians 2:20]. He built up the Kingdom, chose Apostles and ordained them to the Melchizedek Priesthood, giving them power to administer in the ordinances of the gospel."[8]

" 'Christ . . . gave some Apostles, and some Prophets, and some Evangelists, and some Pastors and Teachers' [Ephesians 4:11]. And how were Apostles, Prophets, Pastors, Teachers and Evangelists chosen? By prophecy (revelation) and by laying on of hands:—by a divine communication, and a divinely appointed ordinance—through the medium of the Priesthood, organized according to the order of God, by divine appointment."[9]

"[The Book of Mormon] tells us that our Savior made His appearance upon this [the American] continent after His resurrection; that He planted the Gospel here in all its fulness, and richness, and power, and blessing; that they had Apostles, Prophets, Pastors, Teachers, and Evangelists; the same order, the same

priesthood, the same ordinances, gifts, powers, and blessings, as were enjoyed on the eastern continent."[10]

"An evangelist is a Patriarch. . . . Wherever the Church of Christ is established in the earth, there should be a Patriarch for the benefit of the posterity of the Saints, as it was with Jacob in giving his patriarchal blessing unto his sons."[11]

Articles of Faith 1:6: "We believe in the same organization that existed in the Primitive Church, namely, apostles, prophets, pastors, teachers, evangelists, and so forth."[12]

The Church of Jesus Christ of Latter-day Saints was formally organized by the Prophet Joseph Smith on April 6, 1830, at the home of Peter Whitmer Sr. in Fayette, New York. The latter-day Church is organized in the same way as the Church in the Savior's time, with "apostles, prophets, pastors, teachers, evangelists, and so forth."

The Church is led by the First Presidency, the Quorum of the Twelve Apostles, and the Quorums of the Seventy.

"I firmly believe in the prophets and apostles, Jesus Christ being the chief cornerstone, and speak as one having authority among them, and not as the scribes."[13]

"The Presidents or [First] Presidency are over the Church; and revelations of the mind and will of God to the Church, are to come through the Presidency. This is the order of heaven, and the power and privilege of [the Melchizedek] Priesthood."[14]

"What importance is there attached to the calling of these Twelve Apostles, different from the other callings or officers of the Church? . . . They are the Twelve Apostles, who are called to the office of the Traveling High Council, who are to preside over the churches of the Saints. . . . They are to hold the keys of this ministry, to unlock the door of the Kingdom of heaven unto all nations, and to preach the Gospel to every creature. This is the power, authority, and virtue of their apostleship."[15]

Orson Pratt, who served in the Quorum of the Twelve Apostles, reported: "The Lord . . . directed that the Quorum of the Twelve Apostles should be organized, whose business it would be to preach the Gospel to the nations, to the Gentiles first and then to the Jews. The Priesthood were called together after the building of the Kirtland Temple, and, in speaking of the Twelve Apostles, the Prophet Joseph said they had received the Apostleship with all the powers pertaining to the same, just as the ancient Apostles."[16]

Wilford Woodruff, the fourth President of the Church, reported: "Joseph called twelve Apostles. Who were they? The Lord said to him: 'The twelve are they who shall desire to take upon them my name with full purpose of heart; and if they desire to take upon them my name with full purpose of heart, they are called to go into all the world to preach my gospel unto every creature.' [D&C 18:27–28.] . . . When the Prophet Joseph organized the Quorum of the Twelve Apostles, he taught [the] principle of union to them. He gave them to understand that they must be of one heart and one mind, and they must take upon themselves fully the name of Christ; that if God commanded them to do anything they must go and do it."[17]

"The Seventies are to constitute traveling quorums, to go into all the earth, whithersoever the Twelve Apostles shall call them."[18]

"The Seventies are not called to serve tables [see Acts 6:1–2], . . . but are to preach the Gospel and build [the churches] up, and set others, who do not belong to these quorums, to preside over [the churches], who are High Priests. The Twelve also are . . . to bear the keys of the Kingdom to all nations, and unlock the door of the Gospel to them, and call upon the Seventies to follow after them, and assist them."[19]

Although the forces of evil may seek to destroy the Church, "no unhallowed hand can stop the work from progressing."

"Since the organization of the Church of Christ, . . . on the 6th of April, 1830, we have had the satisfaction of witnessing the spread of the truth into various parts of our land, notwithstanding its enemies have exerted their unceasing diligence to stop its course and prevent its progress; though evil and designing men have combined to destroy the innocent, . . . yet the glorious Gospel in its fullness is spreading and daily gaining converts; and our prayer to God is, that it may continue, and numbers be added of such as shall be eternally saved."[20]

"The Standard of Truth has been erected; no unhallowed hand can stop the work from progressing; persecutions may rage, mobs may combine, armies may assemble, calumny may defame, but the truth of God will go forth boldly, nobly, and independent, till it has penetrated every continent, visited every clime, swept every country, and sounded in every ear, till the purposes of God shall be accomplished, and the Great Jehovah shall say the work is done."[21]

"And again, another parable put [the Savior] forth unto them, having an allusion to the Kingdom that should be set up just previous to or at the time of the harvest, which reads as follows—'The Kingdom of Heaven is like a grain of mustard seed, which a man took and sowed in his field: which indeed is the least of all seeds: but, when it is grown, it is the greatest among herbs, and becometh a tree, so that the birds of the air come and lodge in the branches thereof.' [Matthew 13:31–32.] Now we can discover plainly that this figure is given to represent the Church as it shall come forth in the last days. Behold, the Kingdom of Heaven is likened unto it. Now, what is like unto it?

"Let us take the Book of Mormon, which a man took and hid in his field, securing it by his faith, to spring up in the last days, or in due time; let us behold it coming forth out of the ground, which is indeed accounted the least of all seeds, but behold it branching forth, yea, even towering with lofty branches and God-like majesty, until it, like the mustard seed, becomes the greatest of all herbs. And it is truth, and it has sprouted and come forth out of the earth, and righteousness begins to look down from heaven [see Psalm 85:11; Moses 7:62], and God is sending down His powers, gifts, and angels to lodge in the branches thereof.

"The Kingdom of Heaven is like unto a mustard seed. Behold, then, is not this the Kingdom of Heaven that is raising its head in the last days in the majesty of its God, even the Church of the Latter-day Saints, like an impenetrable, immovable rock in the midst of the mighty deep, exposed to the storms and tempests of Satan, that has, thus far, remained steadfast, and is still braving the mountain waves of opposition, which are driven by the tempestuous winds of sinking crafts, which have [dashed] and are still dashing with tremendous foam across its triumphant brow; urged onward with redoubled fury by the enemy of righteousness?"[22]

As part of his prayer at the dedication of the Kirtland Temple, later recorded in Doctrine and Covenants 109:72–76, the Prophet Joseph Smith said: "Remember all thy church, O Lord, with all their families, and all their immediate connections, with all their sick and afflicted ones, with all the poor and meek of the earth; that the kingdom, which thou hast set up without hands, may become a great mountain and fill the whole earth; that thy church may come forth out of the wilderness of darkness, and shine forth fair as the moon, clear as the sun, and terrible as an army with banners; and be adorned as a bride for that day when thou shalt unveil the heavens, and cause the mountains to flow down at thy presence, and the valleys to be exalted, the rough places made smooth; that thy glory may fill the earth; that when the trump shall sound for the dead, we shall be caught up in the cloud to meet thee, that we may ever be with the Lord; that our garments may be pure, that we may be clothed upon with robes of righteousness, with palms in our hands, and crowns of glory upon our heads, and reap eternal joy for all our sufferings."[23]

We each have the responsibility to strengthen the Church and do our part in building up the kingdom of God.

"The cause of God is one common cause, in which the Saints are alike all interested; we are all members of the one common body, and all partake of the same spirit, and are baptized into one baptism and possess alike the same glorious hope. The advancement of the cause of God and the building up of Zion is as much one man's business as another's. The only difference is, that one is called to fulfill one duty, and another another duty; 'but if one member suffers, all the members suffer with it, and if one member is honored all the rest rejoice with it, and the eye cannot say to the ear, I have no need of thee, nor the head to the foot, I have no need of thee;' party feelings, separate interests, exclusive designs should be lost sight of in the one common cause, in the interest of the whole [see 1 Corinthians 12:21, 26]."[24]

"Brethren and sisters, be faithful, be diligent, contend earnestly for the faith once delivered to the Saints [see Jude 1:3]; let every man, woman and child realize the importance of the work, and act as if success depended on his individual exertion alone; let all feel an interest in it, and then consider they live in a day, the contemplation of which animated the bosoms of kings, Prophets, and righteous men thousands of years ago—the prospect of which inspired their sweetest notes, and most exalted lays, and caused them to break out in such rapturous strains as are recorded in the Scriptures; and by and by we will have to exclaim, in the language of inspiration—

" 'The Lord has brought again Zion,
The Lord hath redeemed His people Israel.' [D&C 84:99.]"[25]

"The advancement of the cause of God and the building up of Zion is as much one man's business as another's. The only difference is, that one is called to fulfill one duty, and another another duty."

As recalled by Wilford Woodruff, Joseph Smith made the following declaration to members of the Twelve who were leaving for a mission to Great Britain in 1839: "No matter what may come upon you, round up your shoulders and bear it, and always sustain and defend the interests of the Church and Kingdom of God."[26]

Suggestions for Study and Teaching

Consider these ideas as you study the chapter or as you prepare to teach. For additional help, see pages vii–xii.

- Imagine what it was like to attend the priesthood meeting described on page 137. How do you think you would have felt if you had heard Joseph Smith prophesy that the Church would someday fill the world? Looking back now on that prophecy, what are your thoughts or feelings?
- Review pages 138–39, noting the actions taken at the organization of the Church and the first general conference. Joseph

Smith said, "Such scenes as these were calculated to inspire our hearts with joy unspeakable, and fill us with awe and reverence for [God]" (page 139). When have you had the feelings Joseph Smith described?

- Review Joseph Smith's teachings about the Church in Jesus's day and in Book of Mormon times (pages 139–40). How does the Church follow the same pattern today?
- Why do you think we need leaders who preside over the worldwide Church? (For some examples, see pages 141–42.) How have you been blessed through the service of the First Presidency, the Quorum of the Twelve Apostles, the Quorums of the Seventy, and the Presiding Bishopric?
- What are your thoughts or feelings as you read Joseph Smith's prophecies about the Church's destiny? (See pages 142–44.) In what ways can we participate in this work? (For some examples, see pages 144–45.)
- Joseph Smith taught, "Let every man, woman and child realize the importance of the work, and act as if success depended on his individual exertion alone" (page 144). Think about particular ways in which you can apply this counsel in your life.
- If someone asked you why you are a member of The Church of Jesus Christ of Latter-day Saints, what would you say?

Related Scriptures: Daniel 2:31–45; Mosiah 18:17–29; D&C 20:1–4; 65:1–6; 115:4–5

Notes

1. *History of the Church,* 1:71; from "History of the Church" (manuscript), book A-1, p. 34, Church Archives, The Church of Jesus Christ of Latter-day Saints, Salt Lake City, Utah.
2. *History of the Church,* 1:64; from "History of the Church" (manuscript), book A-1, p. 29, Church Archives.
3. *History of the Church,* 1:75–77; from "History of the Church" (manuscript), book A-1, p. 37, Church Archives.
4. New York law required from three to nine persons to organize or transact the business of a church. The Prophet chose to use six persons.
5. Wilford Woodruff, in Conference Report, Apr. 1898, p. 57; punctuation and capitalization modernized.
6. *History of the Church,* 1:77–79; paragraph divisions altered; from "History of the Church" (manuscript), book A-1, pp. 37–38, Church Archives.
7. *History of the Church,* 1:85–86; from "History of the Church" (manuscript), book A-1, p. 42, Church Archives.
8. Discourse given by Joseph Smith on July 23, 1843, in Nauvoo, Illinois; Joseph Smith, Collection, Addresses, July 23, 1843, Church Archives.

9. *History of the Church,* 4:574; from "Try the Spirits," an editorial published in *Times and Seasons,* Apr. 1, 1842, pp. 744–45; Joseph Smith was the editor of the periodical.
10. *History of the Church,* 4:538; from a letter from Joseph Smith written at the request of John Wentworth and George Barstow, Nauvoo, Illinois, published in *Times and Seasons,* Mar. 1, 1842, pp. 707–8.
11. *History of the Church,* 3:381; from a discourse given by Joseph Smith on June 27, 1839, in Commerce, Illinois; reported by Willard Richards.
12. Articles of Faith 1:6.
13. Letter from Joseph Smith to Isaac Galland, Mar. 22, 1839, Liberty Jail, Liberty, Missouri, published in *Times and Seasons,* Feb. 1840, p. 53; punctuation and capitalization modernized.
14. *History of the Church,* 2:477; from a discourse given by Joseph Smith on Apr. 6, 1837, in Kirtland, Ohio; reported by *Messenger and Advocate,* Apr. 1837, p. 487.
15. *History of the Church,* 2:200; paragraph divisions altered; from the minutes of a Church council meeting held on Feb. 27, 1835, in Kirtland, Ohio; reported by Oliver Cowdery.
16. Orson Pratt, *Millennial Star,* Nov. 10, 1869, p. 732.
17. Wilford Woodruff, *Deseret Weekly,* Aug. 30, 1890, p. 306; capitalization modernized.
18. *History of the Church,* 2:202; from "History of the Church" (manuscript), book B-1, p. 577, Church Archives.
19. *History of the Church,* 2:431–32; from instructions given by Joseph Smith on Mar. 30, 1836, in Kirtland, Ohio.
20. *History of the Church,* 2:22; from "The Elders of the Church in Kirtland, to Their Brethren Abroad," Jan. 22, 1834, published in *Evening and Morning Star,* Apr. 1834, p. 152.
21. *History of the Church,* 4:540; from a letter from Joseph Smith written at the request of John Wentworth and George Barstow, Nauvoo, Illinois, published in *Times and Seasons,* Mar. 1, 1842, p. 709.
22. *History of the Church,* 2:268; final bracketed word in original; punctuation, capitalization, and grammar modernized; from a letter from Joseph Smith to the elders of the Church, Dec. 1835, Kirtland, Ohio, published in *Messenger and Advocate,* Dec. 1835, p. 227.
23. Doctrine and Covenants 109:72–76; prayer offered by Joseph Smith on Mar. 27, 1836, at the dedication of the temple in Kirtland, Ohio.
24. *History of the Church,* 4:609; from "The Temple," an editorial published in *Times and Seasons,* May 2, 1842, p. 776; Joseph Smith was the editor of the periodical.
25. *History of the Church,* 4:214; from a report from Joseph Smith and his counselors in the First Presidency, Oct. 4, 1840, Nauvoo, Illinois, published in *Times and Seasons,* Oct. 1840, p. 188.
26. Quoted by Wilford Woodruff, *Deseret News: Semi-Weekly,* Mar. 20, 1883, p. 1.

Whether he was preaching to those around him or sending missionaries into the world, the Prophet Joseph Smith loved missionary work.

CHAPTER 12

Proclaim Glad Tidings to All the World

"Souls are as precious in the sight of God as they ever were; and the Elders [are] . . . to persuade and invite all men everywhere to repent, that they may become the heirs of salvation."

From the Life of Joseph Smith

After the Church was organized on April 6, 1830, Joseph Smith continued to proclaim the glad tidings of the gospel. During the month of April, he traveled to Colesville, New York, to visit his friend Joseph Knight Sr., who with his family had become interested in the gospel. The Prophet held meetings in the neighborhood, and "many began to pray fervently to Almighty God, that He would give them wisdom to understand the truth."[1] About two months later, on a second visit to Colesville, the Prophet found that a number of people who had heard the gospel now desired to be baptized. For these new converts, accepting the gospel took faith and courage, as the Prophet recorded:

"We appointed a meeting for the Sabbath, and on the afternoon of Saturday we erected a dam across a stream of water, which was convenient, for the purpose of there attending to the ordinance of baptism; but during the night a mob collected and tore down our dam, which hindered us from attending to the baptism on the Sabbath. . . . Early on Monday morning we were on the alert, and before our enemies were aware of our proceedings, we had repaired the dam, and the following thirteen persons [were] baptized, by Oliver Cowdery, viz.: Emma Smith; Hezekiah Peck and wife; Joseph Knight, Sen., and wife; William Stringham and wife; Joseph Knight, Jun.; Aaron Culver and wife; Levi [Hall]; Polly Knight; and Julia Stringham."[2]

That fall, the Lord revealed to Joseph Smith that Oliver Cowdery, Peter Whitmer Jr., Parley P. Pratt, and Ziba Peterson were to "go unto the Lamanites and preach my gospel unto them" (D&C 28:8; 30:5–6; 32:1–3). These missionaries traveled some 1,500 miles, preaching briefly among various Indian tribes, including the Seneca in New York, the Wyandot in Ohio, and the Delaware and Shawnee in Indian territory. However, the missionaries' greatest success came when they stopped in the area of Kirtland, Ohio. There they baptized about 130 converts, principally from among the Reformed Baptist congregation of Sidney Rigdon, thus opening what would become a gathering place for hundreds of Church members the following year. The missionaries also found some converts among the settlers in Jackson County, Missouri, where the city of Zion would later be established.

Whether he was preaching to those around him or sending missionaries into the world, the Prophet Joseph Smith loved missionary work. Elder Parley P. Pratt recorded the following experience that occurred in 1839: "While visiting with Brother Joseph in Philadelphia, [Pennsylvania,] a very large church was opened for him to preach in, and about three thousand people assembled to hear him. Brother Rigdon spoke first, and dwelt on the Gospel, illustrating his doctrine by the Bible. When he was through, Brother Joseph arose like a lion about to roar; and being full of the Holy Ghost, spoke in great power, bearing testimony of the visions he had seen, the ministering of angels which he had enjoyed; and how he had found the plates of the Book of Mormon, and translated them by the gift and power of God. He commenced by saying: 'If nobody else had the courage to testify of so glorious a message from Heaven, and of the finding of so glorious a record, he felt to do it in justice to the people, and leave the event with God.'

"The entire congregation were astounded; electrified, as it were, and overwhelmed with the sense of the truth and power by which he spoke, and the wonders which he related. A lasting impression was made; many souls were gathered into the fold. And I bear witness, that he, by his faithful and powerful testimony, cleared his garments of their blood. Multitudes were baptized in Philadelphia and in the regions around."[3]

Teachings of Joseph Smith

Because the world is in spiritual darkness, we should be diligent in preaching the gospel.

In 1834, Joseph Smith and other elders of the Church in Kirtland sent the following letter to the brethren in other areas: "Though our communications to you may be frequent, yet we believe they will be received on your part with brotherly feelings; and that from us your unworthy brethren, you will suffer a word of exhortation to have place in your hearts, as you see the great extent of the power and dominion of the prince of darkness, and realize how vast the numbers are who are crowding the road to death without ever giving heed to the cheering sound of the Gospel of our Lord Jesus Christ.

"Consider for a moment, brethren, the fulfillment of the words of the prophet; for we behold that darkness covers the earth and gross darkness the minds of the inhabitants thereof [see Isaiah 60:2], that crimes of every description are increasing among men; vices of great enormity are practiced; the rising generation growing up in the fullness of pride and arrogance; the aged losing every sense of conviction, and seemingly banishing every thought of a day of retribution; intemperance, immorality, extravagance, pride, blindness of heart, idolatry, the loss of natural affection, the love of this world, and indifference toward the things of eternity increasing among those who profess a belief in the religion of heaven, and infidelity spreading itself in consequence of the same; men giving themselves up to commit acts of the foulest kind and deeds of the blackest dye, blaspheming, defrauding, blasting the reputation of neighbors, stealing, robbing, murdering, advocating error and opposing the truth, forsaking the covenant of heaven, and denying the faith of Jesus—and in the midst of all this, the day of the Lord fast approaching when none except those who have on the wedding garment will be permitted to eat and drink in the presence of the Bridegroom, the Prince of Peace!

"Impressed with the truth of these facts, what can be the feelings of those who have been partakers of the heavenly gift and have tasted the good word of God and the powers of the world to come? [See Hebrews 6:4–5.] Who but those who can see the awful precipice upon which the world of mankind stands in this generation, can labor in the vineyard of the Lord without feeling a sense of the world's deplorable situation? Who but those who have duly considered the condescension of the Father of our spirits in providing a sacrifice for His creatures—a plan of redemption, a power of atonement, a scheme of salvation, having as its great objects, the bringing of men back into the presence of the King of heaven, crowning them in the celestial glory, and making them heirs with the Son to that inheritance which is incorruptible, undefiled, and which fadeth not away [see 1 Peter 1:4]—who but such can realize the importance of a perfect walk before all men, and a diligence in calling upon all men to partake of these blessings? How indescribably glorious are these things to mankind! Of a truth they may be considered tidings of great joy to all people; and tidings, too, that ought to fill the earth and cheer the hearts of every one when sounded in his ears."[4]

"The servants of God will not have gone over the nations of the Gentiles, with a warning voice, until the destroying angel will commence to waste the inhabitants of the earth, and as the prophet hath said, 'It shall be a vexation to hear the report.' [See Isaiah 28:19.] I speak thus because I feel for my fellow men; I do it in the name of the Lord, being moved upon by the Holy Spirit. Oh, that I could snatch them from the vortex of misery, into which I behold them plunging themselves, by their sins; that I might be enabled by the warning voice, to be an instrument of bringing them to unfeigned repentance, that they might have faith to stand in the evil day!"[5]

"May God enable us to perform our vows and covenants with each other, in all fidelity and righteousness before Him, that our influence may be felt among the nations of the earth, in mighty power, even to rend the kingdoms of darkness asunder, and triumph over priestcraft and spiritual wickedness in high places, and break in pieces all kingdoms that are opposed to the kingdom of Christ, and spread the light and truth of the everlasting Gospel from the rivers to the ends of the earth."[6]

The Prophet Joseph Smith admonished the Saints to call upon all people to partake of the blessings of the gospel. "How indescribably glorious are these things to mankind!"

Wilford Woodruff, the fourth President of the Church, recalled the following words of the Prophet Joseph Smith: "The world is full of darkness. Sin and wickedness is overwhelming the world as the waters cover the great deep. The devil rules over the world in a great measure. The world will war against you; the devil will, earth will, and hell will. But . . . you must preach the Gospel, do your duty, and the Lord will stand by you. Earth and hell shall not prevail against you."[7]

Our duty is to invite all mankind to repent, be baptized, receive the Holy Ghost, and become heirs of salvation.

"This we believe to be our duty—to teach to all mankind the doctrine of repentance, which we shall endeavor to show from the following quotations:

" 'Then opened He their understandings, that they might understand the scriptures, and said unto them, Thus it is written, and thus it behoved Christ to suffer, and to rise from the dead the third day: and that repentance and remission of sins should be preached in His name among all nations, beginning at Jerusalem' [Luke 24:45–47].

"By this we learn that it behoved Christ to suffer, and to be crucified, and rise again on the third day, for the express purpose that repentance and remission of sins should be preached to all nations.

" 'Then Peter said unto them, Repent, and be baptized every one of you in the name of Jesus Christ for the remission of sins, and ye shall receive the gift of the Holy Ghost. For the promise is unto you, and to your children, and to all that are afar off, even as many as the Lord our God shall call' [Acts 2:38–39].

"By this we learn that the promise of the Holy Ghost is made unto as many as those to whom the doctrine of repentance was to be preached, which was unto all nations. . . . Therefore we believe in preaching the doctrine of repentance in all the world, both to old and young, rich and poor, bond and free."[8]

"Souls are as precious in the sight of God as they ever were; and the Elders were never called to drive any down to hell, but to persuade and invite all men everywhere to repent, that they may become the heirs of salvation. It is the acceptable year of the Lord: liberate the captives that they may sing hosanna [see Isaiah 61:1–2]."[9]

"It should be the duty of the Elder to stand up boldly for the cause of Christ, and warn [the] people with one accord to repent and be baptized for the remission of sins, and for the Holy Ghost."[10]

"I will proceed to tell you what the Lord requires of all people, high and low, rich and poor, male and female, ministers and people, professors of religion and non-professors, in order that they may enjoy the Holy Spirit of God to a fulness and escape the judgments of God, which are almost ready to burst upon the nations of the earth. Repent of all your sins, and be baptized in water for the remission of them, in the name of the Father, and of the Son, and of the Holy Ghost, and receive the ordinance of the laying on of the hands of him who is ordained and sealed unto this power, that ye may receive the Holy Spirit of God; and this is according to the Holy Scriptures, and the Book of Mormon; and the only way that man can enter into the celestial kingdom. These are the requirements of the new covenant, or first principles of the Gospel of Christ."[11]

"It is required of all men, to have faith in the Lord Jesus Christ; to repent of all their sins and to be baptized (by one in authority) in the name of Jesus Christ for the remission of sins, and to have hands laid on them for the gift of the Holy Ghost, to constitute them a member in the Church of Jesus Christ of Latter-day Saints."[12]

Servants of the Lord go throughout the world to find those who are willing to accept the gospel of Jesus Christ.

"Send somebody to Central America and to all Spanish America; and don't let a single corner of the earth go without a mission."[13]

"We don't ask any people to throw away any good they have got; we only ask them to come and get more. What if all the world should embrace this Gospel? They would then see eye to eye, and the blessings of God would be poured out upon the people, which is the desire of my whole soul."[14]

"Thousands who have heard the Gospel have become obedient thereto, and are rejoicing in its gifts and blessings. Prejudice, with its attendant train of evil, is giving way before the force of truth, whose benign rays are penetrating the nations afar off. . . . The time was, when we were looked upon as deceivers, and that 'Mormonism' would soon pass away, come to naught, and be forgotten. But the time has gone by when it is looked upon as a transient matter, or a bubble on the wave, and it is now taking a deep hold in the hearts and affections of all those who are noble-minded enough to lay aside the prejudice of education, and investigate the subject with candor and honesty."[15]

"Some of the Twelve and others have already started for Europe [in September 1839], and the remainder of that mission we expect will go now in a few days. . . . The work of the Lord rolls on in a very pleasing manner, both in this and in the old country. In England many hundreds have of late been added to our numbers; but so, even so, it must be, for 'Ephraim he hath mixed himself among the people' [Hosea 7:8]. And the Savior He hath said, 'My sheep hear my voice' [John 10:27]; and also, 'He that heareth you, heareth me' [Luke 10:16]; and, 'Behold I will bring them again from the north country, and gather them from the coasts of the earth' [Jeremiah 31:8]. And as John heard the voice saying, 'Come out of her, my people' [Revelation 18:4], even so must all be fulfilled; that the people of the Lord may live when 'Babylon the great is fallen, is fallen' [Revelation 18:2]."[16]

In a letter written from Liberty Jail in March 1839, the Prophet Joseph Smith stated the following, later recorded in Doctrine and Covenants 123:12: "There are many yet on the earth among all sects, parties, and denominations, who are blinded by the subtle craftiness of men, whereby they lie in wait to deceive, and who are only kept from the truth because they know not where to find it."[17]

Suggestions for Study and Teaching

Consider these ideas as you study the chapter or as you prepare to teach. For additional help, see pages vii–xii.

- Review the second and third paragraphs on page 150. Why does it sometimes take courage to share our testimonies of the Restoration and the Book of Mormon? How can we develop such courage?
- Joseph Smith described the spiritual darkness of the world; then he testified of the "tidings of great joy" in the restored gospel (pages 151–53). How might these two thoughts inspire us to open our mouths and share the gospel?
- Read the first paragraph on page 153. When has the Lord stood by you in your missionary efforts?
- Ponder the scripture passages Joseph Smith quoted to remind us of our duty to teach the gospel to all mankind (pages 153–54). Think about or discuss what you and your family can do to share the gospel with others.
- Read the fourth paragraph on page 154, in which the Prophet speaks of missionary work as an effort to liberate the captives. In what ways might some people be considered captives? (For some examples, see pages 151–53.) In what ways can the first principles and ordinances of the gospel liberate them?
- Review the Prophet's invitation in the third paragraph on page 155. How might this invitation encourage people to learn

about the restored gospel? Review the fourth paragraph on page 155 and the last paragraph of the chapter. What can we do to help people "lay aside [their] prejudice" about the Church? How might our actions help people know where to find the truth?

- What blessings have come into your life as a result of your efforts to proclaim the gospel?

Related Scriptures: Mark 16:15–20; 2 Nephi 2:8; Alma 26:1–9, 26–37; D&C 42:6–9, 11–14; 88:77–83

Notes

1. *History of the Church,* 1:81; from "History of the Church" (manuscript), book A-1, pp. 39–40, Church Archives, The Church of Jesus Christ of Latter-day Saints, Salt Lake City, Utah.
2. *History of the Church,* 1:86–88; punctuation modernized; paragraph divisions altered; from "History of the Church" (manuscript), book A-1, pp. 42–43, Church Archives.
3. Parley P. Pratt, *Autobiography of Parley P. Pratt,* ed. Parley P. Pratt Jr. (1938), pp. 298–99; capitalization modernized.
4. *History of the Church,* 2:5–6; punctuation modernized; from "The Elders of the Church in Kirtland, to Their Brethren Abroad," Jan. 22, 1834, published in *Evening and Morning Star,* Feb. 1834, p. 135.
5. *History of the Church,* 2:263; from a letter from Joseph Smith to the elders of the Church, Nov. 1835, Kirtland, Ohio, published in *Messenger and Advocate,* Nov. 1835, p. 211.
6. *History of the Church,* 2:375; from the minutes of a council meeting of the First Presidency and the Twelve held on Jan. 16, 1836, in Kirtland, Ohio; reported by Warren Parrish.
7. Quoted by Wilford Woodruff, *Deseret News,* July 30, 1884, p. 434.
8. *History of the Church,* 2:255–56; paragraph divisions altered; from a letter from Joseph Smith to the elders of the Church, Sept. 1835, Kirtland, Ohio, published in *Messenger and Advocate,* Sept. 1835, pp. 180–81.
9. *History of the Church,* 2:229, footnote; from "To the Saints Scattered Abroad," *Messenger and Advocate,* June 1835, p. 138.
10. *History of the Church,* 2:263; from a letter from Joseph Smith to the elders of the Church, Nov. 1835, Kirtland, Ohio, published in *Messenger and Advocate,* Nov. 1835, p. 211.
11. *History of the Church,* 1:314–15; from a letter from Joseph Smith to N. C. Saxton, Jan. 4, 1833, Kirtland, Ohio; Mr. Saxton's name is incorrectly given as "N. E. Seaton" in *History of the Church.*
12. Editor's reply to a letter from Richard Savary, *Times and Seasons,* Mar. 15, 1842, p. 732; capitalization modernized; Joseph Smith was the editor of the periodical.
13. *History of the Church,* 5:368; from instructions given by Joseph Smith on Apr. 19, 1843, in Nauvoo, Illinois; reported by Willard Richards.
14. *History of the Church,* 5:259; from a discourse given by Joseph Smith on Jan. 22, 1843, in Nauvoo, Illinois; reported by Wilford Woodruff.
15. *History of the Church,* 4:336–37; spelling modernized; paragraph divisions altered; from a report from Joseph Smith and his counselors in the First Presidency, Apr. 7, 1841, Nauvoo, Illinois, published in *Times and Seasons,* Apr. 15, 1841, p. 384.
16. *History of the Church,* 4:8–9; punctuation modernized; from a letter from Joseph Smith to Isaac Galland, Sept. 11, 1839, Commerce, Illinois.
17. Doctrine and Covenants 123:12; a letter from Joseph Smith and others to Edward Partridge and the Church, Mar. 20, 1839, Liberty Jail, Liberty, Missouri.

In February 1831, Joseph Smith arrived in Kirtland, Ohio, walked into Newel K. Whitney's store, and said, "I am Joseph, the Prophet. . . . You've prayed me here; now what do you want of me?"

CHAPTER 13

Obedience: "When the Lord Commands, Do It"

"Live in strict obedience to the commandments of God, and walk humbly before Him."

From the Life of Joseph Smith

From December 1827 through August 1830, Joseph and Emma Smith lived in Harmony, Pennsylvania, the Prophet traveling periodically to New York to attend to Church business. In September 1830, Joseph and Emma moved to Fayette, New York, to join the Saints living in western New York. The following December, the Prophet received a revelation that would require the Church members in New York to make great sacrifices. They were to leave their homes, farms, and businesses and gather to Kirtland, Ohio (see D&C 37). There they would join with converts living in that vicinity to build up the Church and, as promised by the Lord, "be endowed with power from on high" (D&C 38:32). Joseph and Emma Smith were among the first to obey the Lord's command, leaving New York at the end of January 1831. They traveled over 250 miles to Kirtland by sleigh, in the middle of an especially severe winter, Emma being pregnant with twins.

Kirtland resident Newel K. Whitney was one of the first to welcome the Prophet, as described by his grandson Orson F. Whitney: "About the first of February, 1831, a sleigh containing four persons, drove through the streets of Kirtland and drew up at the door of Gilbert and Whitney's mercantile establishment. . . . One of the men, a young and stalwart personage, alighted, and springing up the steps, walked into the store and to where the junior partner was standing.

" 'Newel K. Whitney! Thou art the man!' he exclaimed, extending his hand cordially, as if to an old and familiar acquaintance.

" 'You have the advantage of me,' replied the [storekeeper], as he mechanically took the proffered hand—a half-amused, half-mystified look overspreading his countenance—'I could not call you by name, as you have me.'

" 'I am Joseph, the Prophet,' said the stranger, smiling. 'You've prayed me here; now what do you want of me?'

"Mr. Whitney, astonished, but no less delighted, as soon as his surprise would permit, conducted the party . . . across the street to his house on the corner, and introduced them to his wife [Elizabeth Ann]. She shared fully his surprise and ecstasy. Joseph said of this episode: 'We were kindly received and welcomed into the house of Brother N. K. Whitney. I and my wife lived in the family of Brother Whitney several weeks, and received every kindness and attention that could be expected.' [See *History of the Church,* 1:145–46.]"[1]

Orson F. Whitney declared: "By what power did this remarkable man, Joseph Smith, recognize one whom he had never before seen in the flesh? Why did not Newel K. Whitney recognize him? It was because Joseph Smith was a seer, a choice seer; he had actually seen Newel K. Whitney upon his knees, hundreds of miles away, praying for his coming to Kirtland. Marvelous—but true!"[2]

By May almost 200 more Saints from New York had made their way to Kirtland—some by sleigh or wagon, but most by barge on the Erie Canal and then by steamboat or schooner across Lake Erie. In this move to Kirtland, as in the many other challenging circumstances of his life, Joseph Smith led the Saints in following God's commandments, no matter how difficult the task.

Four years later, in the midst of the many pressures of leading the growing Church in Kirtland, the Prophet expressed the conviction that characterized his life: "No month ever found me more busily engaged than November; but as my life consisted of activity and unyielding exertions, I made this my rule: *When the Lord commands, do it.*"[3]

Teachings of Joseph Smith

When we seek to know God's will and do everything He commands us to do, the blessings of heaven will rest upon us.

"To get salvation we must not only do some things, but everything which God has commanded. Men may preach and practice everything except those things which God commands us to do, and will be damned at last. We may tithe mint and rue, and all manner of herbs, and still not obey the commandments of God [see Luke 11:42]. The object with me is to obey and teach others to obey God in just what He tells us to do. It mattereth not whether the principle is popular or unpopular, I will always maintain a true principle, even if I stand alone in it."[4]

"As a Church and a people it behooves us to be wise, and to seek to know the will of God, and then be willing to do it; for 'blessed is he that heareth the word of the Lord, and keepeth it,' say the Scriptures. 'Watch and pray always,' says our Savior, 'that ye may be accounted worthy to escape the things that are to come on the earth, and to stand before the Son of Man.' [See Luke 11:28; 21:36.] If Enoch, Abraham, Moses, and the children of Israel, and all God's people were saved by keeping the commandments of God, we, if saved at all, shall be saved upon the same principle. As God governed Abraham, Isaac and Jacob as families, and the children of Israel as a nation; so we, as a Church, must be under His guidance if we are prospered, preserved and sustained. Our only confidence can be in God; our only wisdom obtained from Him; and He alone must be our protector and safeguard, spiritually and temporally, or we fall.

"We have been chastened by the hand of God heretofore for not obeying His commands, although we never violated any human law, or transgressed any human precept; yet we have treated lightly His commands, and departed from His ordinances, and the Lord has chastened us sore, and we have felt His arm and kissed the rod; let us be wise in time to come and ever remember that 'to obey is better than sacrifice, and to hearken than the fat of rams.' [1 Samuel 15:22.]"[5]

"When the Lord commands, do it," Joseph Smith declared. The law of tithing, like all commandments given by the Lord, brings great blessings to those who obey it.

"When instructed, we must obey that voice, observe the laws of the kingdom of God, that the blessing of heaven may rest down upon us. All must act in concert, or nothing can be done, and should move according to the ancient Priesthood; hence the Saints should be a select people, separate from all the evils of the world—choice, virtuous, and holy. The Lord [is] going to make of the Church of Jesus Christ a kingdom of Priests, a holy people, a chosen generation [see Exodus 19:6; 1 Peter 2:9], as in Enoch's day, having all the gifts as illustrated to the Church in Paul's epistles and teachings to the churches in his day."[6]

"Any man may believe that Jesus Christ is the Son of God, and be happy in that belief, and yet not obey his commandments, and at last be cut down for disobedience to the Lord's righteous requirements."[7]

"Be virtuous and pure; be men of integrity and truth; keep the commandments of God; and then you will be able more perfectly to understand the difference between right and wrong—between the things of God and the things of men; and your path will be like that of the just, which shineth brighter and brighter unto the perfect day [see Proverbs 4:18]."[8]

Wilford Woodruff, while serving as a member of the Quorum of the Twelve, reported: "President Joseph . . . read the parable of the vine and its branches [see John 15:1–8], and explained it, and said, 'If we keep the commandments of God, we should bring forth fruit and be the friends of God, and know what our Lord did.' "[9]

God gives laws that will prepare us for celestial rest if we obey them.

"God will not command any thing, but what is peculiarly adapted in itself, to ameliorate [improve] the condition of every man under whatever circumstances it may find him, it matters not what kingdom or country he may be in."[10]

"The law of heaven is presented to man, and as such guarantees to all who obey it a reward far beyond any earthly consideration; though it does not promise that the believer in every age should be exempt from the afflictions and troubles arising from different sources in consequence of the acts of wicked men on earth. Still in the midst of all this there is a promise predicated upon the fact that it is the law of heaven, which transcends the law of man, as far as eternal life the temporal; and as the blessings which God is able to give, are greater than those which can be given by man. Then, certainly, if the law of man is binding upon man when acknowledged, how much more must the law of heaven be! And as much as the law of heaven is more perfect than the law of man, so much greater must be the reward if obeyed. . . . The law of God promises that life which is eternal, even an inheritance at God's own right hand, secure from all the powers of the wicked one. . . .

". . . God has in reserve a time, or period appointed in His own bosom, when He will bring all His subjects, who have obeyed His voice and kept His commandments, into His celestial rest. This rest is of such perfection and glory, that man has need of a preparation before he can, according to the laws of that kingdom, enter it and enjoy its blessings. This being the fact, God has given certain laws to the human family, which, if observed, are sufficient to prepare them to inherit this rest. This, then, we conclude, was the purpose of God in giving His laws to us. . . . All the commandments contained in the law of the Lord, have the sure promise annexed of a reward to all who obey, predicated upon the fact that they are really the promises of a Being who cannot lie, One who is abundantly able to fulfill every tittle of His word."[11]

Joseph Smith taught the following in April 1843, later recorded in Doctrine and Covenants 130:20–21: "There is a law, irrevocably decreed in heaven before the foundations of this world, upon which all blessings are predicated—and when we obtain any blessing from God, it is by obedience to that law upon which it is predicated."[12]

"All blessings that were ordained for man by the Council of Heaven were on conditions of obedience to the law thereof."[13]

Those who are faithful to the end will receive a crown of righteousness.

"Live in strict obedience to the commandments of God, and walk humbly before Him, and He will exalt thee in His own due time."[14]

"How careful men ought to be what they do in the last days, lest they are cut short of their expectations, and they that think they stand should fall, because they keep not the Lord's commandments; whilst you, who do the will of the Lord and keep His commandments, have need to rejoice with unspeakable joy, for such shall be exalted very high, and shall be lifted up in triumph above all the kingdoms of this world."[15]

"In the 22nd chapter of [Matthew's] account of the Messiah, we find the kingdom of heaven likened unto a king who made a marriage for his son [see Matthew 22:2–14]. That this son was the Messiah will not be disputed, since it was the kingdom of heaven that was represented in the parable; and that the Saints, or those who are found faithful to the Lord, are the individuals who will be found worthy to inherit a seat at the marriage supper, is evident from the sayings of John in the Revelation where he represents the sound which he heard in heaven to be like 'a great multitude,' or like 'the voice of mighty thunderings, saying, the Lord God Omnipotent reigneth. Let us be glad and rejoice, and give honor to Him; for the marriage of the Lamb is come, and His wife hath made herself ready. And to her was granted that she should be arrayed in fine linen, clean and white: For the fine linen is the righteousness of Saints' [Revelation 19:6–8].

"That those who keep the commandments of the Lord and walk in His statutes to the end, are the only individuals permitted to sit at this glorious feast, is evident from the following items in Paul's last letter to Timothy, which was written just previous to his death,—he says: 'I have fought a good fight, I have finished my course, I have kept the faith: henceforth there is laid up for me a crown of righteousness which the Lord, the righteous Judge, shall give me at that day: and not to me only, but unto all them also that love His appearing.' [2 Timothy 4:7–8.] No one who believes the account, will doubt for a moment this assertion of Paul which was made, as he knew, just before he was to take his leave of this world. Though he once, according to his own word, persecuted the Church of God and wasted it, yet after embracing the faith, his labors were unceasing to spread the glorious news: and like a faithful soldier, when called to give his life in the cause which he had espoused, he laid it down, as he says, with an assurance of an eternal crown.

"Follow the labors of this Apostle from the time of his conversion to the time of his death, and you will have a fair sample of industry and patience in promulgating the Gospel of Christ. Derided, whipped, and stoned, the moment he escaped the hands of his persecutors he as zealously as ever proclaimed the doctrine of the Savior. And all may know that he did not embrace the faith for honor in this life, nor for the gain of earthly goods. What, then, could have induced him to undergo all this toil? It was, as he said, that he might obtain the crown of righteousness from the hand of God. No one, we presume, will doubt the faithfulness of Paul to the end. None will say that he did not keep the faith, that he did not fight the good fight, that he did not preach and persuade to the last. And what was he to receive? A crown of righteousness. . . .

"Reflect for a moment, brethren, and enquire, whether you would consider yourselves worthy [of] a seat at the marriage feast with Paul and others like him, if you had been unfaithful? Had you not fought the good fight, and kept the faith, could you expect to receive? Have you a promise of receiving a crown of righteousness from the hand of the Lord, with the Church of the First Born? Here then, we understand, that Paul rested his hope in Christ, because he had kept the faith, and loved his appearing and from His hand he had a promise of receiving a crown of righteousness. . . .

". . . The ancients, though persecuted and afflicted by men, obtained from God promises of such weight and glory, that our hearts are often filled with gratitude that we are even permitted to look upon them while we contemplate that there is no respect of persons in His sight, and that in every nation, he that feareth God and worketh righteousness, is acceptable with Him [see Acts 10:34–35]. . . .

"We can draw the conclusion that there is to be a day when all will be judged of their works, and rewarded according to the same; that those who have kept the faith will be crowned with a crown of righteousness; be clothed in white raiment; be admitted to the marriage feast; be free from every affliction, and reign with Christ on the earth, where, according to the ancient promise, they will partake of the fruit of the vine new in the glorious kingdom with Him; at least we find that such promises were made to the ancient Saints. And though we cannot claim these promises which were made to the ancients, for they are not our property, merely because they were made to the ancient Saints, yet if we are the children of the Most High, and are called with the same calling with which they were called, and embrace the same covenant that they embraced, and are faithful to the testimony of our Lord as they were, we can approach the Father in the name of Christ as they approached Him, and for ourselves obtain the same promises.

"These promises, when obtained, if ever by us, will not be because Peter, John, and the other Apostles . . . walked in the fear of God and had power and faith to prevail and obtain them; but it will be because we, ourselves, have faith and approach God in

Paul testifying before King Agrippa.
"No one," Joseph Smith said, "will doubt the faithfulness of Paul to the end. . . .
And what was he to receive? A crown of righteousness."

the name of His Son Jesus Christ, even as they did; and when these promises are obtained, they will be promises directly to us, or they will do us no good. They will be communicated for our benefit, being our own property (through the gift of God), earned by our own diligence in keeping His commandments, and walking uprightly before Him."[16]

"We would remind you, brethren, of the fatigues, trials, privations, and persecutions, which the ancient saints endured for the sole purpose of persuading men of the excellency and propriety of the faith of Christ, were it in our opinion necessary, or if it would serve in any respect to stimulate you to labor in the vineyard of the Lord with any more diligence. But we have reason to believe (if you make the holy Scriptures a sufficient part of your studies), that their perseverance is known to you all; as also that they were willing to sacrifice the present honors and pleasures of this world, that they might obtain an assurance of a crown of life from the hand of our Lord; and their excellent example in labor, which manifests their zeal to us in the cause which they embraced, you are daily striving to pattern. And not only these examples of the Saints, but the commandments of our Lord, we hope are constantly revolving in your hearts, teaching you, not only His will in proclaiming His Gospel, but His meekness and perfect walk before all, even in those times of severe persecutions and abuse which were heaped upon Him by a wicked and adulterous generation.

"Remember, brethren, that He has called you unto holiness; and need we say, to be like Him in purity? How wise, how holy; how chaste, and how perfect, then, you ought to conduct yourselves in His sight; and remember, too, that His eyes are continually upon you. Viewing these facts in a proper light, you cannot be insensible, that without a strict observance of all His divine requirements, you may, at last, be found wanting; and if so, you will admit, that your lot will be cast among the unprofitable servants. We beseech you, therefore, brethren, to improve upon all things committed to your charge, that you lose not your reward."[17]

Suggestions for Study and Teaching

Consider these ideas as you study the chapter or as you prepare to teach. For additional help, see pages vii–xii.

- Read the final paragraph on page 160, focusing on the rule Joseph Smith adopted for his life. Think about specific commands you have recently received, through words of the living prophet or promptings of the Holy Ghost. How have you been blessed when you have obeyed these commands without hesitation?
- Review the first paragraph on page 161. Why do we sometimes have to "stand alone" to "maintain a true principle"? In what ways are we *not* alone at such times? (For some examples, see pages 161–63.) How can we help children and youth stay true to gospel principles even when it is unpopular to do so?

- Study the section that begins on page 163. For what reasons does God give us commandments? Why should we obey His commandments?
- Review Joseph Smith's teachings about Matthew 22:2–14 and 2 Timothy 4:7–8 (pages 164–68). Ponder how you would feel to be admitted to the marriage feast. What kind of people must we be to be worthy to be admitted? What do you think it means to fight a good fight and keep the faith? Think of someone you know who has fought a good fight and kept the faith. What can you learn from this person?
- The Prophet Joseph encouraged us to remember that the Lord has "called [us] unto holiness" (page 168). What does it mean to you to be called to holiness? How might our remembrance of this "calling" make a difference in our lives? in the lives of our family members and friends?

Related Scriptures: Exodus 20:1–17; John 7:17; 1 Nephi 3:7; D&C 58:26–29; Abraham 3:25

Notes

1. Orson F. Whitney, "Newel K. Whitney," *Contributor,* Jan. 1885, p. 125; punctuation and grammar modernized.
2. Orson F. Whitney, in Conference Report, Apr. 1912, p. 50.
3. *History of the Church,* 2:170; from "History of the Church" (manuscript), book B-1, p. 558, Church Archives, The Church of Jesus Christ of Latter-day Saints, Salt Lake City, Utah.
4. *History of the Church,* 6:223; from a discourse given by Joseph Smith on Feb. 21, 1844, in Nauvoo, Illinois; reported by Wilford Woodruff and Willard Richards.
5. *History of the Church,* 5:65; from "The Government of God," an editorial published in *Times and Seasons,* July 15, 1842, p. 857; Joseph Smith was the editor of the periodical.
6. *History of the Church,* 4:570; from a discourse given by Joseph Smith on Mar. 30, 1842, in Nauvoo, Illinois; reported by Eliza R. Snow; see also appendix, page 562, item 3.
7. *History of the Church,* 5:426; from a discourse given by Joseph Smith on June 11, 1843, in Nauvoo, Illinois; reported by Wilford Woodruff and Willard Richards; see also appendix, page 562, item 3.
8. *History of the Church,* 5:31; from "Gift of the Holy Ghost," an editorial published in *Times and Seasons,* June 15, 1842, p. 825; Joseph Smith was the editor of the periodical.
9. *History of the Church,* 4:478; capitalization modernized; from a discourse given by Joseph Smith on Dec. 19, 1841, in Nauvoo, Illinois; reported by Wilford Woodruff.
10. Letter from Joseph Smith to Isaac Galland, Mar. 22, 1839, Liberty Jail, Liberty, Missouri, published in *Times and Seasons,* Feb. 1840, p. 54.
11. *History of the Church,* 2:7–8, 12; from "The Elders of the Church in Kirtland, to Their Brethren Abroad," Jan. 22, 1834, published in *Evening and Morning Star,* Feb. 1834, pp. 135–36.

12. Doctrine and Covenants 130:20–21; instructions given by Joseph Smith on Apr. 2, 1843, in Ramus, Illinois.
13. Discourse given by Joseph Smith on July 16, 1843, in Nauvoo, Illinois; reported by Franklin D. Richards, in Franklin Dewey Richards, Scriptural Items, ca. 1841–44, Church Archives.
14. *History of the Church,* 1:408; from a letter from Joseph Smith to Vienna Jacques, Sept. 4, 1833, Kirtland, Ohio; Sister Jacques's last name is also sometimes spelled "Jaques," as in *History of the Church.*
15. *History of the Church,* 1:299; from a letter from Joseph Smith to William W. Phelps, Nov. 27, 1832, Kirtland, Ohio.
16. *History of the Church,* 2:19–22; punctuation modernized; paragraph divisions altered; from "The Elders of the Church in Kirtland, to Their Brethren Abroad," Jan. 22, 1834, published in *Evening and Morning Star,* Mar. 1834, p. 144.
17. *History of the Church,* 2:13; paragraph divisions altered; from "The Elders of the Church in Kirtland, to Their Brethren Abroad," Jan. 22, 1834, published in *Evening and Morning Star,* Mar. 1834, p. 142.

C H A P T E R 1 4

Words of Hope and Consolation at the Time of Death

"What have we to console us in relation to the dead? We have reason to have the greatest hope and consolation for our dead of any people on the earth."

From the Life of Joseph Smith

Bereavement at the death of loved ones repeatedly touched the life of the Prophet Joseph Smith. On June 15, 1828, in Harmony, Pennsylvania, Joseph and Emma's first son, Alvin, died a short time after birth. When Joseph and Emma moved from New York to Kirtland, Ohio, in February 1831, Emma was again pregnant, this time with twins. Shortly after Joseph and Emma's arrival in Kirtland, they moved to a cabin on the farm of Church member Isaac Morley. There, on April 30, little Thadeus and Louisa were born, but they did not long survive, dying within a few hours of their birth.

At the same time, in the nearby town of Warrensville, Ohio, Brother John Murdock lost his wife, Julia, who had just given birth to healthy twins. With a family that now included five children, Brother Murdock felt unable to care for the new arrivals, and he asked Joseph and Emma to adopt them as their own. This Joseph and Emma did, gratefully taking the two infants, named Joseph and Julia, into their family. Tragically, little Joseph died eleven months later in March 1832, a consequence of being exposed to the cold night air while suffering with measles when the Prophet was tarred and feathered by a mob. With this death, the grieving parents had laid to rest four of their first five children, leaving Julia as their only living child.

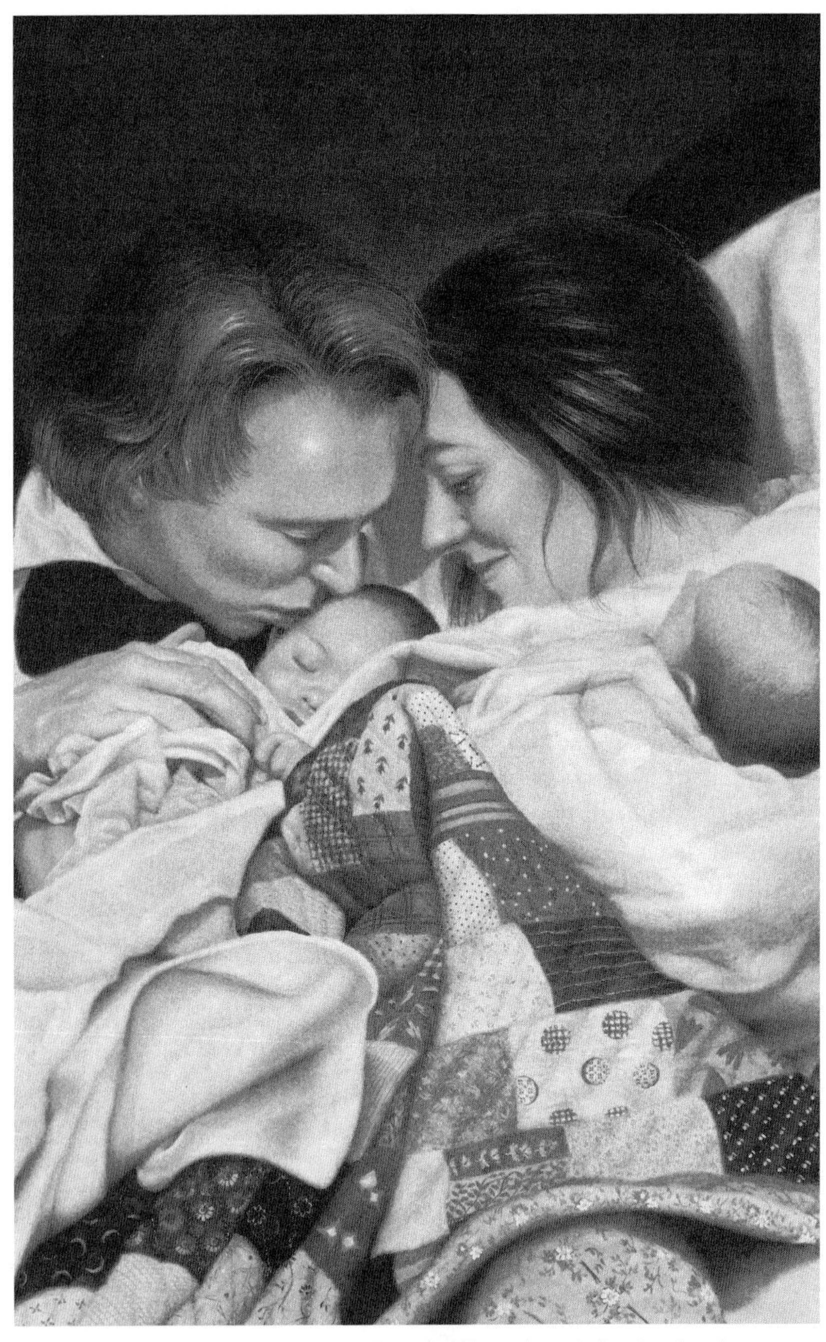

Joseph and Emma Smith with the twins they adopted shortly after their own infant twins died. Joseph and Emma gratefully took Joseph and Julia into their family, but little Joseph died in March 1832.

Of the eleven children of Joseph and Emma—nine born to them and two adopted—only five would live to adulthood: Julia, born in 1831; Joseph III, born in 1832; Frederick, born in 1836; Alexander, born in 1838; and David, born in November 1844, five months after his father's death. Joseph and Emma's 14-month-old son Don Carlos died in 1841, and a son born in 1842 died the same day he was born.

During his lifetime, Joseph Smith also lost three brothers to untimely deaths. Ephraim died soon after birth in 1810. Joseph's older brother Alvin died in 1823 at the age of 25, and his younger brother Don Carlos died in 1841, also at 25 years of age.

The Prophet suffered another great loss when his father, upon whom he relied for counsel and strength, died in Nauvoo, Illinois, in 1840. When Father Smith realized that his death was imminent, he called his family to his bedside. He spoke to his wife, saying, "When I look upon my children and realize that although they were raised up to do the Lord's work, yet they must pass through scenes of trouble and affliction as long as they live upon the earth, my heart is pained and I dread to leave you so surrounded by enemies."[1]

Then he spoke to each of his sons and daughters in turn, giving them his last blessing. As recorded by the Prophet's mother, he spoke these reassuring words to the Prophet Joseph:

" 'Joseph, my son, thou art called to a high and holy calling. Thou art even called to do the work of the Lord. Hold out faithful and you shall be blessed, and your children after you. You shall even live to finish your work.'

"At this Joseph cried out, weeping, 'Oh, my Father, will I?' 'Yes,' said his father, 'you shall live to lay out the plan of all the work which God has given you to do. This is my dying blessing on your head in the name of Jesus.' "[2]

Drawing upon these difficult experiences from his own life and his inspired understanding of the Savior's Atonement, the Prophet Joseph Smith was able to give much-needed comfort to many mourning Saints.

Teachings of Joseph Smith

When beloved family members or friends die, we have great comfort in knowing we will meet them again in the world to come.

The Prophet spoke at a Church conference in Nauvoo on April 7, 1844. He spoke about his friend King Follett, who had recently died: "Beloved Saints: I will call [for] the attention of this congregation while I address you on the subject of the dead. The decease of our beloved brother, Elder King Follett, who was crushed in a well by the falling of a tub of rock, has more immediately led me to this subject. I have been requested to speak by his friends and relatives, but inasmuch as there are a great many in this congregation who live in this city as well as elsewhere, who have lost friends, I feel disposed to speak on the subject in general, and offer you my ideas, so far as I have ability, and so far as I shall be inspired by the Holy Spirit to dwell on this subject. I want your prayers and faith that I may have the instruction of Almighty God and the gift of the Holy Ghost, so that I may set forth things that are true and which can be easily comprehended by you, and that the testimony may carry conviction to your hearts and minds of the truth of what I shall say. . . .

". . . I know that my testimony is true; hence, when I talk to these mourners, what have they lost? Their relatives and friends are only separated from their bodies for a short season: their spirits which existed with God have left the tabernacle of clay only for a little moment, as it were; and they now exist in a place where they converse together the same as we do on the earth. . . .

". . . What have we to console us in relation to the dead? We have reason to have the greatest hope and consolation for our dead of any people on the earth; for we have seen them walk worthily in our midst, and seen them sink asleep in the arms of Jesus. . . .

"You mourners have occasion to rejoice, speaking of the death of Elder King Follett; for your husband and father is gone to wait until the resurrection of the dead—until the perfection of the remainder; for at the resurrection your friend will rise in perfect felicity and go to celestial glory. . . .

"I am authorized to say, by the authority of the Holy Ghost, that you have no occasion to fear; for he is gone to the home of the just. Don't mourn, don't weep. I know it by the testimony of the Holy Ghost that is within me; and you may wait for your friends to come forth to meet you in the morn of the celestial world. . . .

"I have a father, brothers, children, and friends who have gone to a world of spirits. They are only absent for a moment. They are in the spirit, and we shall soon meet again. The time will soon arrive when the trumpet shall sound. When we depart, we shall hail our mothers, fathers, friends, and all whom we love, who have fallen asleep in Jesus. There will be no fear of mobs, persecutions, or malicious lawsuits and arrests; but it will be an eternity of felicity."[3]

Elder Lorenzo D. Barnes died while serving as a missionary in England. The Prophet spoke of his passing at a meeting held in the unfinished Nauvoo Temple: "I will tell you what I want. If tomorrow I shall be called to lie in yonder tomb, in the morning of the resurrection let me strike hands with my father, and cry, 'My father,' and he will say, 'My son, my son,' as soon as the rock rends and before we come out of our graves.

"And may we contemplate these things so? Yes, if we learn how to live and how to die. When we lie down we contemplate how we may rise in the morning; and it is pleasing for friends to lie down together, locked in the arms of love, to sleep and wake in each other's embrace and renew their conversation.

"Would you think it strange if I relate what I have seen in vision in relation to this interesting theme? Those who have died in Jesus Christ may expect to enter into all that fruition of joy when they come forth, which they possessed or anticipated here.

"So plain was the vision, that I actually saw men, before they had ascended from the tomb, as though they were getting up slowly. They took each other by the hand and said to each other, 'My father, my son, my mother, my daughter, my brother, my sister.' And when the voice calls for the dead to arise, suppose I am laid by the side of my father, what would be the first joy of my heart? To meet my father, my mother, my brother, my sister; and when they are by my side, I embrace them and they me. . . .

"More painful to me are the thoughts of annihilation than death. If I have no expectation of seeing my father, mother, brothers, sisters and friends again, my heart would burst in a moment, and I should go down to my grave. The expectation of seeing my friends in the morning of the resurrection cheers my soul and makes me bear up against the evils of life. It is like their taking a long journey, and on their return we meet them with increased joy. . . .

"To Marcellus Bates [a Church member whose wife had died] let me administer comfort. You shall soon have the company of your companion in a world of glory, and the friends of Brother Barnes and all the Saints who are mourning. This has been a warning voice to us all to be sober and diligent and lay aside mirth, vanity and folly, and to be prepared to die tomorrow."[4]

Parents who lose children in death will receive them in the resurrection just as they laid them down.

At the funeral of two-year-old Marian Lyon, the Prophet said: "We have again the warning voice sounded in our midst, which shows the uncertainty of human life; and in my leisure moments I have meditated upon the subject, and asked the question, why it is that infants, innocent children, are taken away from us, especially those that seem to be the most intelligent and interesting. The strongest reasons that present themselves to my mind are these: This world is a very wicked world; and it . . . grows more wicked and corrupt. . . . The Lord takes many away, even in infancy, that they may escape the envy of man, and the sorrows and evils of this present world; they were too pure, too lovely, to live on earth; therefore, if rightly considered, instead of mourning we have reason to rejoice as they are delivered from evil, and we shall soon have them again. . . .

". . . The only difference between the old and young dying is, one lives longer in heaven and eternal light and glory than the

Joseph Smith taught that young children "must rise just as they died" and that parents will greet their children with "the same loveliness in the celestial glory."

other, and is freed a little sooner from this miserable, wicked world. Notwithstanding all this glory, we for a moment lose sight of it, and mourn the loss, but we do not mourn as those without hope."[5]

"A question may be asked—'Will mothers have their children in eternity?' Yes! Yes! Mothers, you shall have your children; for they shall have eternal life, for their debt is paid."[6]

"Children . . . must rise just as they died; we can there hail our lovely infants with the same glory—the same loveliness in the celestial glory."[7]

President Joseph F. Smith, the sixth President of the Church, reported: "Joseph Smith taught the doctrine that the infant child that was laid away in death would come up in the resurrection as a child; and, pointing to the mother of a lifeless child, he said to her: 'You will have the joy, the pleasure and satisfaction of nurturing this child, after its resurrection, until it reaches the full stature of its spirit.' . . .

"In 1854, I met with my aunt [Agnes Smith], the wife of my uncle, Don Carlos Smith, who was the mother of that little girl

[Sophronia] that Joseph Smith, the Prophet, was speaking about, when he told the mother that she should have the joy, the pleasure, and the satisfaction of rearing that child, after the resurrection, until it reached the full stature of its spirit; and that it would be a far greater joy than she could possibly have in mortality, because she would be free from the sorrow and fear and disabilities of mortal life, and she would know more than she could know in this life. I met that widow, the mother of that child, and she told me this circumstance and bore testimony to me that this was what the Prophet Joseph Smith said when he was speaking at the funeral of her little daughter."[8]

Mary Isabella Horne and Leonora Cannon Taylor each lost a young child in death. Sister Horne recalled that the Prophet Joseph Smith gave the two sisters these words of comfort: "He told us that we should receive those children in the morning of the resurrection just as we laid them down, in purity and innocence, and we should nourish and care for them as their mothers. He said that children would be raised in the resurrection just as they were laid down, and that they would obtain all the intelligence necessary to occupy thrones, principalities and powers."[9]

While we mourn when loved ones die, we can trust that "the God of all the earth will do right."

At the funeral of 24-year-old Ephraim Marks, the Prophet declared: "It is a very solemn and awful time. I never felt more solemn; it calls to mind the death of my oldest brother, Alvin, who died in New York, and my youngest brother, Don Carlos Smith, who died in Nauvoo. It has been hard for me to live on earth and see these young men upon whom we have leaned for support and comfort taken from us in the midst of their youth. Yes, it has been hard to be reconciled to these things. I have sometimes thought that I should have felt more reconciled to have been called away myself if it had been the will of God; yet I know we ought to be still and know it is of God, and be reconciled to His will; all is right. It will be but a short time before we shall all in like manner be called: it may be the case with me as well as you."[10]

On June 6, 1832, Joseph Smith wrote to Emma Smith: "I was grieved to hear that Hyrum had lost his little child. I think we can in some degree sympathize with him, but we all must be reconciled to our lots and say the will of the Lord be done."[11]

On January 20, 1840, Joseph Smith wrote to Emma Smith: "I received a letter from Hyrum, which cheered my heart to learn that my family was all alive. Yet my heart mourns for those who have been taken from us, but not without hope, for I shall see them again and be with them. Therefore, we can be more reconciled to the dealings of God."[12]

"With respect to the deaths in Zion, we feel to mourn with those that mourn, but remember that the God of all the earth will do right."[13]

"There have been many deaths, which leaves a melancholy reflection, but we cannot help it. When God speaks from the heavens to call us hence, we must submit to His mandates."[14]

At the funeral of James Adams, the Prophet said: "I saw him first at Springfield, [Illinois,] when on my way from Missouri to Washington. He sought me out when a stranger, took me to his home, encouraged and cheered me, and gave me money. He has been a most intimate friend. . . . He has had revelations concerning his departure, and has gone to a more important work. When men are prepared, they are better off to go hence. Brother Adams has gone to open up a more effectual door for the dead. The spirits of the just are exalted to a greater and more glorious work; hence they are blessed in their departure to the world of spirits."[15]

Suggestions for Study and Teaching

Consider these ideas as you study the chapter or as you prepare to teach. For additional help, see pages vii–xii.

- What are your thoughts or feelings as you read the accounts on pages 171–73? How might these experiences have influenced the way the Prophet Joseph taught about death and resurrection?

- This chapter contains messages Joseph Smith shared with people who mourned the deaths of loved ones (pages 174–79). In these messages, the Prophet offered "hope and consolation" by teaching doctrines of the gospel and showing his hearers how those doctrines applied in their lives. As you think of loved ones who have died or who may soon die, what gospel truths bring you comfort? Why are these truths significant to you?
- Read the counsel Joseph Smith gave when speaking of Elder Barnes's death, including his counsel about "how to live and how to die" (pages 175–76). What does this counsel mean to you? Think about how your life might change as you remember his counsel.
- Review the Prophet's words to parents whose little children had died (pages 176–78). How can these doctrines provide hope to grieving parents?
- Study Joseph Smith's counsel about reconciling ourselves to God's will when loved ones die (pages 178–79). How does our decision to accept God's will influence our emotions? our words and our actions? In what ways might our decision help others?

Related Scriptures: John 20:1–29; Mosiah 16:7–8; Alma 40:11–12; Moroni 8:11–20; D&C 42:45–46

Notes

1. Joseph Smith Sr., quoted in Lucy Mack Smith, "The History of Lucy Smith, Mother of the Prophet," 1844–45 manuscript, book 18, p. 5, Church Archives, The Church of Jesus Christ of Latter-day Saints, Salt Lake City, Utah.
2. Joseph Smith Sr., blessing given to Joseph Smith shortly before Joseph Smith Sr.'s death on Sept. 14, 1840, in Nauvoo, Illinois; quoted in Lucy Mack Smith, "The History of Lucy Smith, Mother of the Prophet," 1845 manuscript, p. 298, Church Archives.
3. *History of the Church,* 6:302–3, 310–11, 315–16; bracketed word in original; paragraph divisions altered; from a discourse given by Joseph Smith on Apr. 7, 1844, in Nauvoo, Illinois; reported by Wilford Woodruff, Willard Richards, Thomas Bullock, and William Clayton; see also appendix, page 562, item 3.
4. *History of the Church,* 5:361–63; paragraph divisions altered; from a discourse given by Joseph Smith on Apr. 16, 1843, in Nauvoo, Illinois; reported by Wilford Woodruff and Willard Richards.
5. *History of the Church,* 4:553–54; from a discourse given by Joseph Smith on Mar. 20, 1842, in Nauvoo, Illinois; reported by Wilford Woodruff.

6. *History of the Church,* 6:316; from a discourse given by Joseph Smith on Apr. 7, 1844, in Nauvoo, Illinois; reported by Wilford Woodruff, Willard Richards, Thomas Bullock, and William Clayton; see also appendix, page 562, item 3.
7. *History of the Church,* 6:366; from a discourse given by Joseph Smith on May 12, 1844, in Nauvoo, Illinois; reported by Thomas Bullock.
8. Joseph F. Smith, "Status of Children in the Resurrection," *Improvement Era,* May 1918, p. 571.
9. Mary Isabella Horne, quoted in *History of the Church,* 4:556, footnote; from her statement given on Nov. 19, 1896, in Salt Lake City, Utah.
10. *History of the Church,* 4:587; from a discourse given by Joseph Smith on Apr. 9, 1842, in Nauvoo, Illinois; reported by Wilford Woodruff.
11. Letter from Joseph Smith to Emma Smith, June 6, 1832, Greenville, Indiana; Chicago Historical Society, Chicago, Illinois.
12. Letter from Joseph Smith to Emma Smith, Jan. 20, 1840, Chester County, Pennsylvania; Chicago Historical Society, Chicago, Illinois.
13. *History of the Church,* 1:341; from a letter from Joseph Smith to the brethren in Missouri, Apr. 21, 1833, Kirtland, Ohio.
14. *History of the Church,* 4:432; from a letter from Joseph Smith to Smith Tuttle, Oct. 9, 1841, Nauvoo, Illinois.
15. *History of the Church,* 6:51–52; from a discourse given by Joseph Smith on Oct. 9, 1843, in Nauvoo, Illinois; reported by Willard Richards and *Times and Seasons,* Sept. 15, 1843, p. 331; this issue of the *Times and Seasons* was published late.

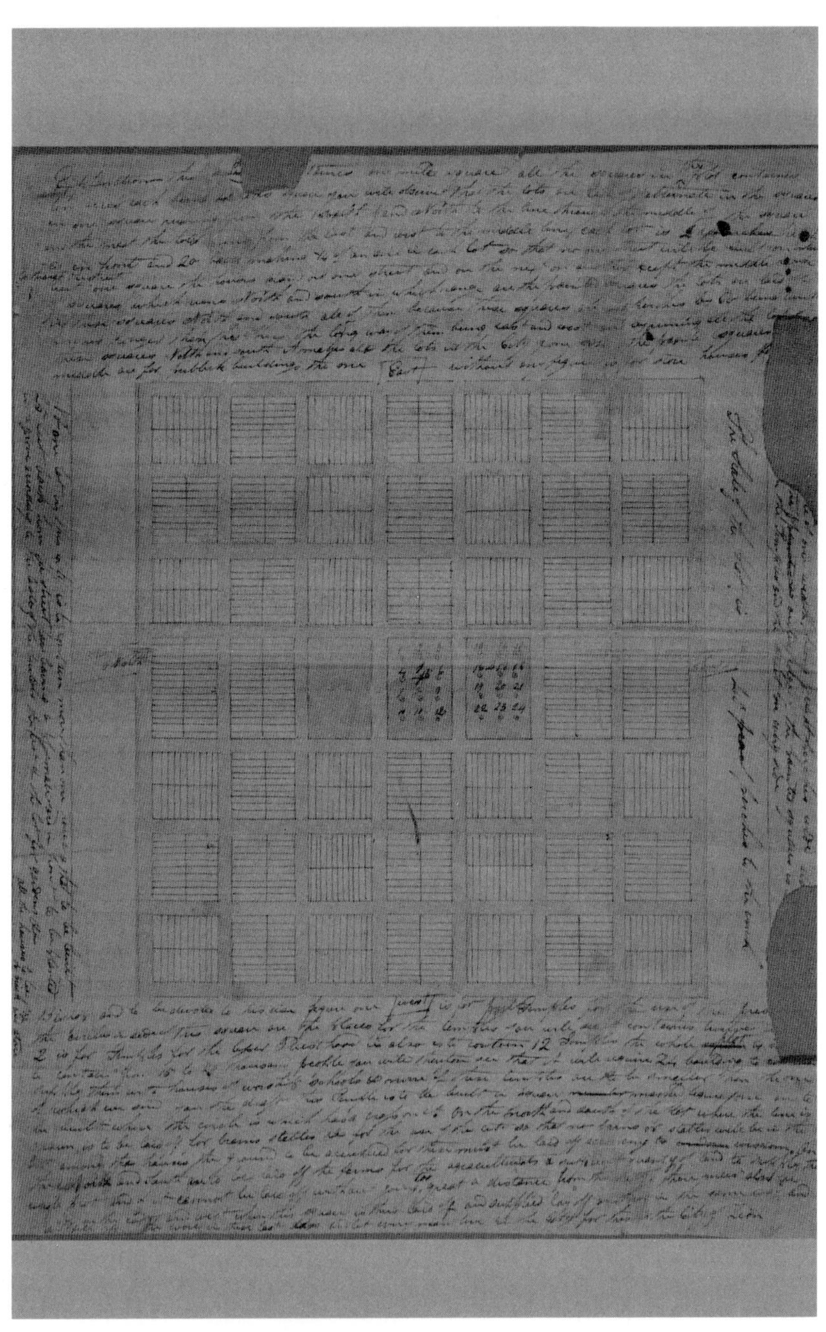

In 1833, Joseph Smith and Frederick G. Williams prepared this map for the city of Zion, to be built in Jackson County, Missouri. Public areas in the center are surrounded by 10-acre city blocks with half-acre home lots. The city was never built, but many of the plan's basic ideas were later used in Latter-day Saint settlements.

CHAPTER 15

Establishing the Cause of Zion

"The building up of Zion is a cause that has interested the people of God in every age; it is a theme upon which prophets, priests and kings have dwelt with peculiar delight."

From the Life of Joseph Smith

In early June 1831, just weeks after the gathering from New York to Ohio was complete, the Saints assembled in Kirtland for a conference of the Church. On June 7, the day after the conference ended, Joseph Smith received a revelation that turned Church members' thoughts toward Zion: "The next conference . . . shall be held in Missouri, upon the land which I will consecrate unto my people" (D&C 52:2).

The Saints were intensely interested in establishing Zion—a holy city, a peaceful refuge for the righteous fleeing the wickedness of the world. To prepare the Saints, the Lord had repeatedly counseled them to "seek to bring forth and establish the cause of Zion" (D&C 6:6; 11:6; 12:6; see also 14:6). Now Church leaders would be leaving immediately to determine the location of Zion. Joseph Smith, Sidney Rigdon, and others started the 900-mile journey to Jackson County, Missouri, on June 19, traveling by water, by coach, and for many miles on foot. The journey was difficult and strenuous, but the Prophet felt the Lord's protecting care: "Notwithstanding the corruptions and abominations of the times, and the evil spirit manifested towards us on account of our belief in the Book of Mormon, at many places and among various persons, yet the Lord continued His watchful care and loving kindness to us day by day; and we made it a rule wherever there was an opportunity, to read a chapter in the Bible, and pray; and these seasons of worship gave us great consolation."[1]

In mid-July, the Prophet arrived in western Missouri, a beautiful area of rolling, fertile prairie, thick with flowers. There, in reply to his pleading to know Zion's specific location, the Lord revealed that "the place which is now called Independence is the center place; and a spot for the temple is lying westward, upon a lot which is not far from the courthouse" (D&C 57:3) and that tracts of land should be purchased. On August 2, Joseph Smith and others met to begin the building of Zion. The Prophet recorded: "I assisted the Colesville branch of the Church to lay the first log, for a house, as a foundation of Zion in Kaw township, twelve miles west of Independence. The log was carried and placed by twelve men, in honor of the twelve tribes of Israel. At the same time, through prayer, the land of Zion was consecrated and dedicated by Elder Sidney Rigdon for the gathering of the Saints. It was a season of joy to those present, and afforded a glimpse of the future, which time will yet unfold to the satisfaction of the faithful."[2] The following day, the Prophet dedicated the temple site.

The Saints from Colesville, New York, were among the first Church members to settle in Missouri. They had made the arduous journey from New York to Kirtland, Ohio, but had lived in Ohio only a short time before being commanded to travel to Missouri. Polly Knight, a member of the Colesville branch, traveled to the land of Zion, only to die there a week later. Although she had been in failing health, she was determined to hold on. Her son wrote: "She quietly fell asleep in death, rejoicing in the new and everlasting covenant of the gospel and praising God that she had lived to see the land of Zion. . . . Brother Joseph Smith attended the funeral of my mother and addressed us in a very able and consoling manner."[3] Although the Prophet soon returned to Kirtland and continued to lead the Church from there until 1838, many Saints continued to move to Missouri.

The Saints worked diligently to build up Zion, but by late 1833, they had been driven out of their homes in Jackson County by severe persecution, leaving behind their dreams of establishing Zion and building a temple there. Through the Prophet Joseph Smith, the Lord revealed that the conditions for the redemption of Zion in that land were not yet fulfilled and that the establishment of Zion must "wait for a little season" (D&C 105:9).

Teachings of Joseph Smith

The Lord designated Jackson County, Missouri, as the land of Zion—a place where the Saints of Joseph Smith's day would gather and where the holy city of Zion would eventually be built.

"I received, by a heavenly vision, a commandment in June [1831], to take my journey to the western boundaries of the State of Missouri, and there designate the very spot which was to be the central place for the commencement of the gathering together of those who embrace the fullness of the everlasting Gospel. Accordingly I undertook the journey, with certain ones of my brethren, and after a long and tedious journey, suffering many privations and hardships, arrived in Jackson County, Missouri, and after viewing the country, seeking diligently at the hand of God, He manifested Himself unto us, and designated, to me and others, the very spot upon which He designed to commence the work of the gathering, and the upbuilding of an 'holy city,' which should be called Zion—Zion, because it is a place of righteousness, and all who build thereon are to worship the true and living God, and all believe in one doctrine, even the doctrine of our Lord and Savior Jesus Christ. 'Thy watchmen shall lift up the voice; with the voice together shall they sing: for they shall see eye to eye, when the Lord shall bring again Zion' [Isaiah 52:8]."[4]

In the early 1830s, the Saints attempted to lay the foundation of Zion in Jackson County, Missouri, as commanded by the Lord, but were unable to do so because they were not spiritually prepared. The Prophet Joseph Smith said the following about the time when Zion would be established: "I cannot learn from any communication by the Spirit to me, that Zion has forfeited her claim to a celestial crown, notwithstanding the Lord has caused her to be thus afflicted, except it may be some individuals, who have walked in disobedience, and forsaken the new covenant; all such will be made manifest by their works in due time. I have always expected that Zion would suffer some affliction, from what I could learn from the commandments which have been given. But I would remind you of a certain clause in one which says, that after *much* tribulation cometh the blessing [see D&C

58:4]. By this, and also others, and also one received of late, I know that Zion, in the due time of the Lord, will be redeemed; but how many will be the days of her purification, tribulation, and affliction, the Lord has kept hid from my eyes; and when I inquire concerning this subject, the voice of the Lord is: Be still, and know that I am God! All those who suffer for my name shall reign with me, and he that layeth down his life for my sake shall find it again. . . . May God grant that notwithstanding [our] great afflictions and sufferings, there may not anything separate us from [the] love of Christ [see Romans 8:35–39]."[5]

We build up the cause of Zion by becoming a people who are pure in heart and by working diligently with one heart and mind.

"The building up of Zion is a cause that has interested the people of God in every age; it is a theme upon which prophets, priests and kings have dwelt with peculiar delight; they have looked forward with joyful anticipation to the day in which we live; and fired with heavenly and joyful anticipations they have sung and written and prophesied of this our day; but they died without the sight; we are the favored people that God has made choice of to bring about the Latter-day glory; it is left for us to see, participate in and help to roll forward the Latter-day glory."[6]

"Anyplace where the Saints gather is Zion, which every righteous man will build up for a place of safety for his children."[7]

"There will be here and there a Stake [of Zion] for the gathering of the Saints. . . . There your children shall be blessed, and you in the midst of friends where you may be blessed. The Gospel net gathers of every kind.

". . . We ought to have the building up of Zion as our greatest object. . . . The time is soon coming, when no man will have any peace but in Zion and her stakes."[8]

"In regard to the building up of Zion, it has to be done by the counsel of Jehovah, by the revelations of heaven."[9]

"If Zion will not purify herself, so as to be approved of in all things, in His sight, He will seek another people; for His work will go on until Israel is gathered, and they who will not hear His

"Anyplace where the Saints gather is Zion, which every righteous man will build up for a place of safety for his children."

voice, must expect to feel His wrath. Let me say unto you, seek to purify yourselves, and also all the inhabitants of Zion, lest the Lord's anger be kindled to fierceness. Repent, repent, is the voice of God to Zion; and strange as it may appear, yet it is true, mankind will persist in self-justification until all their iniquity is exposed, and their character past being redeemed, and that which is treasured up in their hearts be exposed to the gaze of mankind. I say to you (and what I say to you I say to all,) hear the warning voice of God, lest Zion fall, and the Lord swear in His wrath the inhabitants of Zion shall not enter into His rest."[10]

"So long as unrighteous acts are suffered in the Church, it cannot be sanctified, neither can Zion be redeemed."[11]

"Let every one labor to prepare himself for the vineyard, sparing a little time to comfort the mourners; to bind up the brokenhearted; to reclaim the backslider; to bring back the wanderer; to re-invite into the kingdom such as have been cut off, by encouraging them to lay to while the day lasts, and work righteousness, and, with one heart and one mind, prepare to help redeem Zion, that goodly land of promise, where the willing and the obedient shall be blessed. . . .

"[We] pray our heavenly Father that you may be very prayerful, very humble, and very charitable; working diligently, spiritually and temporally, for the redemption of Zion, that the pure in heart may return with songs of everlasting joy to build up her waste places, and meet the Lord when He comes in His glory [see D&C 101:18]."[12]

Zion, the New Jerusalem, will be built upon the American continent.

Articles of Faith 1:10: "We believe in the literal gathering of Israel and in the restoration of the Ten Tribes; that Zion (the New Jerusalem) will be built upon the American continent."[13]

"The city of Zion spoken of by David, in the one hundred and second Psalm, will be built upon the land of America, 'And the ransomed of the Lord shall return, and come to Zion with songs and everlasting joy upon their heads' [Isaiah 35:10]; and then they will be delivered from the overflowing scourge that shall pass through the land. But Judah shall obtain deliverance at Jerusalem. [See Joel 2:32; Isaiah 26:20–21; Jeremiah 31:12; Psalm 1:5; Ezekiel 34:11–13.] These are testimonies that the Good Shepherd will put forth His own sheep, and lead them out from all nations where they have been scattered in a cloudy and dark day, to Zion, and to Jerusalem."[14]

"I shall begin by quoting from the prophecy of Enoch, speaking of the last days: 'Righteousness will I send down out of heaven, and truth will I send forth out of the earth, to bear testimony of mine Only Begotten, His resurrection from the dead [this resurrection I understand to be the corporeal body]; yea, and also the resurrection of all men; righteousness and truth will I cause to sweep the earth as with a flood, to gather out mine own elect from the four quarters of the earth, unto a place which I shall prepare, a holy city, that my people may gird up their loins, and be looking forth for the time of my coming, for there shall be my tabernacle, and it shall be called Zion, a New Jerusalem' [Moses 7:62].

"Now I understand by this quotation, that . . . righteousness and truth are to sweep the earth as with a flood. And now, I ask, how righteousness and truth are going to sweep the earth as with a flood? I will answer. Men and angels are to be co-workers in bringing to pass this great work, and Zion is to be prepared, even a new Jerusalem, for the elect that are to be gathered from the four quarters of the earth, and to be established an holy city, for the tabernacle of the Lord shall be with them. . . .

". . . 'Behold this people will I establish in this land, unto the fulfilling of the covenant which I made with your father Jacob, and it shall be a New Jerusalem.' [3 Nephi 20:22.] Now we learn from the Book of Mormon the very identical continent and spot of land upon which the New Jerusalem is to stand, and it must be caught up according to the vision of John upon the isle of Patmos.

"Now many will feel disposed to say, that this New Jerusalem spoken of, is the Jerusalem that was built by the Jews on the eastern continent. But you will see, from Revelation 21:2, there was a New Jerusalem coming down from God out of heaven, adorned as a bride for her husband; that after this, the Revelator was caught away in the Spirit, to a great and high mountain, and saw the great and holy city descending out of heaven from God. Now there are two cities spoken of here. As everything cannot be had in so narrow a compass as a letter, I shall say with brevity, that there is a New Jerusalem to be established on this continent, and also Jerusalem shall be rebuilt on the eastern continent [see Ether 13:1–12]. 'Behold, Ether saw the days of Christ, and he spake also concerning the house of Israel, and the Jerusalem from whence Lehi should come; after it should be destroyed, it should be built up again, a holy city unto the Lord, wherefore it could not be a New Jerusalem, for it had been in a time of old.' [Ether 13:4–5.]"[15]

"The Prophets have said concerning Zion in the last days: how the glory of Lebanon is to come upon her; the fir tree, the pine tree, and the box tree together, to beautify the place of His sanctuary, that He may make the place of His feet glorious [see Isaiah 60:13]. Where for brass, He will bring gold; and for iron, He will bring silver; and for wood, brass; and for stones, iron [see Isaiah 60:17]; and where the feast of fat things will be given to the just [see Isaiah 25:6]; yea, when the splendor of the Lord is brought to our consideration for the good of His people, the calculations of men and the vain glory of the world vanish, and we exclaim, 'Out of Zion the perfection of beauty, God hath shined.' [Psalm 50:2.]"[16]

Suggestions for Study and Teaching

Consider these ideas as you study the chapter or as you prepare to teach. For additional help, see pages vii–xii.

- In this chapter, notice how the Prophet Joseph Smith uses the word *Zion* to refer to specific places and to the Lord's people. How do these uses of the word help you understand what it means to build up Zion? (As you think about or discuss this question, consider reading Doctrine and Covenants 97:21.)
- In the paragraph beginning at the bottom of page 185, Joseph Smith tells of his desire to know when the city of Zion would be established in Jackson County, Missouri. What can we learn from the Lord's response to Joseph Smith's prayers?
- Read the second full paragraph on page 186, and then identify some places where the Saints gather. How can we build up Zion in these places?
- Review the third and fourth full paragraphs on page 186, and consider how stakes in the Church provide safety and peace. In what ways have you been blessed as you have gathered with other members of your stake?
- In what ways does the Prophet's counsel about building Zion apply in our homes?
- The Prophet Joseph taught that as part of the effort to build up Zion, we must purify ourselves individually. What are some ways we can follow this counsel? (For some examples, see pages 186–88.) Why do you think that individuals must be pure before Zion will be redeemed?
- Review Joseph Smith's prophecies about the two holy cities (pages 188–90). What part do we play in the fulfillment of these prophecies?

Related Scriptures: Revelation 21:1–27; D&C 45:65–71; 97:18–25; 103:1–7; Moses 7:16–21, 62–69

Notes

1. *History of the Church,* 1:188–89; from "History of the Church" (manuscript), book A-1, pp. 126–27, Church Archives, The Church of Jesus Christ of Latter-day Saints, Salt Lake City, Utah.
2. *History of the Church,* 1:196; from "History of the Church" (manuscript), book A-1, p. 137, Church Archives.
3. Newel Knight, Autobiography and Journal, ca. 1846, pp. 32, 34, Church Archives.
4. *History of the Church,* 2:254; from a letter from Joseph Smith to the elders of the Church, Sept. 1835, Kirtland, Ohio, published in *Messenger and Advocate,* Sept. 1835, pp. 179–80.
5. *History of the Church,* 1:453–54; paragraph divisions altered; from a letter from Joseph Smith to Edward Partridge and others, Dec. 10, 1833, Kirtland, Ohio.
6. *History of the Church,* 4:609–10; from "The Temple," an editorial published in *Times and Seasons,* May 2, 1842, p. 776; Joseph Smith was the editor of the periodical.
7. Quoted by Martha Jane Knowlton Coray, reporting a discourse given by Joseph Smith in Nauvoo, Illinois; Martha Jane Knowlton Coray, Notebook, Church Archives; this discourse is dated July 19, 1840, in Sister Coray's notebook, but the discourse was probably given at a later date.
8. *History of the Church,* 3:390–91; bracketed words in original; paragraph divisions altered; from a discourse given by Joseph Smith about July 1839 in Commerce, Illinois; reported by Willard Richards.
9. *History of the Church,* 5:65; from "The Government of God," an editorial published in *Times and Seasons,* July 15, 1842, p. 858; Joseph Smith was the editor of the periodical.
10. *History of the Church,* 1:316; spelling modernized; from a letter from Joseph Smith to William W. Phelps, Jan. 11, 1833, Kirtland, Ohio; this letter is incorrectly dated Jan. 14, 1833, in *History of the Church.*
11. *History of the Church,* 2:146; from a letter from Joseph Smith to Lyman Wight and others, Aug. 16, 1834, Kirtland, Ohio.
12. *History of the Church,* 2:229–30, footnote; punctuation modernized; paragraph divisions altered; from "To the Saints Scattered Abroad," *Messenger and Advocate,* June 1835, p. 138.
13. Articles of Faith 1:10.
14. *History of the Church,* 1:315; from a letter from Joseph Smith to N. C. Saxton, Jan. 4, 1833, Kirtland, Ohio; Mr. Saxton's name is incorrectly given as "N. E. Seaton" in *History of the Church.*
15. *History of the Church,* 2:260–62; punctuation modernized; first set of bracketed words in first paragraph in original; from a letter from Joseph Smith to the elders of the Church, Nov. 1835, Kirtland, Ohio, published in *Messenger and Advocate,* Nov. 1835, pp. 209–10.
16. *History of the Church,* 1:198; punctuation modernized; from "History of the Church" (manuscript), book A-1, p. 139, Church Archives.

When the Prophet Joseph Smith received revelations, he was often in the presence of other Church leaders, with someone recording his words as he received them from the Lord.

CHAPTER 16

Revelation and the Living Prophet

"The grand rule of heaven [is] that nothing should ever be done on earth without revealing the secret to his servants the prophets."

From the Life of Joseph Smith

In Kirtland, Ohio, the Prophet Joseph Smith received a flood of revelations, making this period of great importance in establishing the doctrine and government of the Church. When the Prophet received these revelations, he was often in the presence of other Church leaders, with someone recording his words as he received them from the Lord. The revelations frequently came to him in answer to prayer. Parley P. Pratt, who later became a member of the Twelve, was present when the Prophet received the revelation that is now Doctrine and Covenants 50. Elder Pratt recalled:

"After we had joined in prayer in his translating room, he dictated in our presence the following revelation. Each sentence was uttered slowly and very distinctly, and with a pause between each, sufficiently long for it to be recorded, by an ordinary writer, in long hand. . . . There was never any hesitation, reviewing, or reading back, in order to keep the run of the subject."[1]

Although some revelations had been copied by hand for personal use, Church members generally did not have them. Joseph Smith knew that the revelations of God were of such importance that they must be carefully preserved and made available to the world. In November 1831, at a special conference held in Hiram, Ohio, the Prophet and other Church leaders decided to publish a selection of the revelations the Prophet had received up to that time. After this decision was made, the Prophet received a divine communication that the Lord called "my preface unto the book of my commandments" (D&C 1:6). This revelation, which is now Doctrine and Covenants section 1, signified the Lord's approval for publication of the revelations and explained His purposes in giving them. "Search these commandments," the Lord declared, "for they are true and faithful, and the prophecies and promises which are in them shall all be fulfilled" (D&C 1:37). After hearing the revelation read back to him on the second day of the conference, the Prophet "arose and expressed his feelings and gratitude" for this manifestation of the Lord's approval.[2]

Following this conference, the Prophet recalled, "my time was occupied closely in reviewing the commandments and sitting in conference, for nearly two weeks; for from the first to the twelfth of November we held four special conferences. In the last . . . the conference voted that they prize the revelations to be worth . . . the riches of the whole earth." The conference also declared that the revelations are "the foundation of the Church in these last days, and a benefit to the world, showing that the keys of the mysteries of the kingdom of our Savior are again entrusted to man; and the riches of eternity [are] within the compass of those who are willing to live by every word that proceedeth out of the mouth of God."[3]

Handwritten copies of the revelations were taken to William W. Phelps in Missouri, to be published as the Book of Commandments. Brother Phelps, who had been commanded by the Lord to go to Missouri and become a printer for the Church (see D&C 57:11), soon began setting the type for the book. However, on July 20, 1833, a mob destroyed the press and most of the printed sheets. Some of the loose sheets were rescued by Church members and individually bound, but the book was never officially published. In 1835, the revelations intended for the Book of Commandments plus many additional revelations were published in Kirtland as the Doctrine and Covenants. With additional revelations that have been added since 1835, this book stands as a witness that God speaks today through His living prophet, the President of the Church, for the blessing and guidance of His Church.

Teachings of Joseph Smith

God has always guided His people and His Church through revelation.

Articles of Faith 1:9: "We believe all that God has revealed, all that He does now reveal, and we believe that He will yet reveal many great and important things pertaining to the Kingdom of God."[4]

"We never can comprehend the things of God and of heaven, but by revelation. We may spiritualize and express opinions to all eternity; but that is no authority."[5]

"The doctrine of revelation far transcends the doctrine of no revelation; for one truth revealed from heaven is worth all the sectarian notions in existence."[6]

"Salvation cannot come without revelation; it is in vain for anyone to minister without it. . . . No man can be a minister of Jesus Christ except he has the testimony of Jesus; and this is the spirit of prophecy [see Revelation 19:10]. Whenever salvation has been administered, it has been by testimony. Men of the present time testify of heaven and hell, and have never seen either; and I will say that no man knows these things without this."[7]

"Jesus in His teachings says, 'Upon this rock I will build my Church, and the gates of hell shall not prevail against it.' [Matthew 16:18.] What rock? Revelation."[8]

"The Church of Jesus Christ of Latter-day Saints was founded upon direct revelation, as the true Church of God has ever been, according to the Scriptures (Amos 3:7, and Acts 1:2); and through the will and blessings of God, I have been an instrument in His hands, thus far, to move forward the cause of Zion."[9]

The Prophet spoke at a Church conference in April 1834: "President Joseph Smith, Jun., read the second chapter of Joel's prophecy, prayed, and addressed the conference as follows: . . . 'We are differently situated from any other people that ever existed upon this earth; consequently those former revelations cannot be suited to our conditions; they were given to other people, who were before us; but in the last days, God was to call a remnant, in which was to be deliverance, as well as in Jerusalem and Zion [see Joel 2:32]. Now if God should give no more revelations, where will we find Zion and this remnant? . . .'

"The President then gave a relation of obtaining and translating the Book of Mormon, the revelation of the Priesthood of Aaron, the organization of the Church in 1830, the revelation of the High Priesthood, and the gift of the Holy Ghost poured out upon the Church, and said: 'Take away the Book of Mormon and the revelations, and where is our religion? We have none.' "[10]

The President of the Church is appointed to receive revelation from God for the Church; individuals may receive revelation for their own responsibilities.

"Jesus . . . set in the church firstly Apostles, and secondly prophets, for the work of the ministry, perfecting of the saints, etc.; . . . the grand rule of heaven [is] that nothing should ever be done on earth without revealing the secret to his servants the prophets, agreeable to Amos 3:7."[11]

In September 1830 Joseph and Emma Smith moved from Harmony, Pennsylvania, to Fayette, New York. When they arrived, they found that some Saints were being deceived by claims of false revelations: "To our great grief, . . . we soon found that Satan had been lying in wait to deceive, and seeking whom he might devour. Brother Hiram Page had in his possession a certain stone, by which he had obtained certain 'revelations' concerning the upbuilding of Zion, the order of the Church, etc., all of which were entirely at variance with the order of God's house, as laid down in the New Testament, as well as in our late revelations. As a conference meeting had been appointed for the 26th day of September, I thought it wisdom not to do much more than to converse with the brethren on the subject, until the conference should meet. Finding, however, that many, especially the Whitmer family and Oliver Cowdery, were believing much in the things set forth by this stone, we thought best to inquire of the Lord concerning so important a matter; and before [the] conference convened, we received the following:

"Revelation to Oliver Cowdery, given at Fayette, New York, September, 1830.

" '. . . Behold, verily, verily, I say unto thee, no one shall be appointed to receive commandments and revelations in this Church excepting my servant Joseph Smith, Jun., for he receiveth them even as Moses. And thou shalt be obedient unto the things which I shall give unto him. . . .

" 'And thou shalt not command him who is at thy head, and at the head of the church; for I have given him the keys of the mysteries, and the revelations which are sealed, until I shall appoint unto them another in his stead. . . .

" 'And again, thou shalt take thy brother, Hiram Page, between him and thee alone, and tell him that those things which he hath written from that stone are not of me, and that Satan deceiveth him; for, behold, these things have not been appointed unto him, neither shall anything be appointed unto any of this church contrary to the church covenants.

" 'For all things must be done in order, and by common consent in the church, by the prayer of faith.' [D&C 28:2–3, 6–7, 11–13.] . . .

"At length our conference assembled. The subject of the stone previously mentioned was discussed, and after considerable investigation, Brother Page, as well as the whole Church who were present, renounced the said stone, and all things connected therewith, much to our mutual satisfaction and happiness."[12]

"The Presidents or [First] Presidency are over the Church; and revelations of the mind and will of God to the Church, are to come through the Presidency. This is the order of heaven, and the power and privilege of [the Melchizedek] Priesthood. It is also the privilege of any officer in this Church to obtain revelations, so far as relates to his particular calling and duty in the Church."[13]

"We do not consider ourselves bound to receive any revelation from any one man or woman without his being legally constituted and ordained to that authority, and giving sufficient proof of it.

". . . It is contrary to the economy of God for any member of the Church, or any one, to receive instructions for those in authority, higher than themselves; therefore you will see the impropriety of giving heed to them; but if any person have a vision or a visitation from a heavenly messenger, it must be for his own benefit and instruction; for the fundamental principles, government, and doctrine of the Church are vested in the keys of the kingdom."[14]

The President of the Church conveys the word of God to us for our day and generation.

Heber C. Kimball

Heber C. Kimball, while serving as a counselor to President Brigham Young, reported: "Brother Joseph Smith many a time said to Brother Brigham and myself, and to others, that he was a representative of God to us, to teach and direct us and reprove the wrong doers."[15]

Wilford Woodruff, the fourth President of the Church, reported: "I will refer to a certain meeting I attended in the town of Kirtland in my early days. At that meeting some remarks were made . . . with regard to the living oracles and with regard to the written word of God. . . . A leading man in the Church got up and talked upon the subject, and said: 'You have got the word of God before you here in the Bible, Book of Mormon, and Doctrine and Covenants; you have the written word of God, and you who give revelations should give revelations according to those books, as what is written in those books is the word of God. We should confine ourselves to them.'

"When he concluded, Brother Joseph turned to Brother Brigham Young and said, 'Brother Brigham, I want you to take the stand and tell us your views with regard to the [living] oracles and the written word of God.' Brother Brigham took the stand, and he took the Bible, and laid it down; he took the Book of Mormon, and laid it down; and he took the Book of Doctrine and Covenants, and laid it down before him, and he said: 'There is the written word of God to us, concerning the work of God from the beginning of the world, almost, to our day. And now,' said he, 'when compared with the living oracles those books are nothing to me; those books do not convey the word of God direct to us now, as do the words of a Prophet or a man bearing the Holy Priesthood in our day and generation. I would rather have the living oracles than all the writing in the books.' That was the course he pursued. When he was through, Brother Joseph said to the congregation: 'Brother Brigham has told you the word of the Lord, and he has told you the truth.' "[16]

Brigham Young, the second President of the Church, recalled: "Many years ago the Prophet Joseph observed that if the people would have received the revelations he had in his possession and wisely acted upon them, as the Lord would dictate, they might in their power to do and understand have been many years ahead of what they then were."[17]

We sustain the President of the Church and other Church leaders by praying for them and heeding their counsel.

Joseph Smith recorded that the following occurred at the dedication of the Kirtland Temple on March 27, 1836: "I then made a short address, and called upon the several quorums, and all the congregation of Saints, to acknowledge the [First] Presidency as Prophets and Seers, and uphold them by their prayers. They all covenanted to do so, by rising.

"I then called upon the quorums and congregation of Saints to acknowledge the Twelve Apostles, who were present, as Prophets, Seers, Revelators, and special witnesses to all the nations of the earth, holding the keys of the kingdom, to unlock it, or cause it to be done, among them, and uphold them by their prayers, which they assented to by rising.

"I next called upon the quorums and congregation of Saints to acknowledge the presidents of Seventies . . . and to uphold them by their prayers, which they did by rising. . . .

"The vote was unanimous in every instance, and I prophesied to all, that inasmuch as they would uphold these men in their several stations, . . . the Lord would bless them; yea, in the name of Christ, the blessings of heaven should be theirs."[18]

"Like those who held up the hands of Moses [see Exodus 17:8–13], so let us hold up the hands of those who are appointed to direct the affairs of the Kingdom, so that they may be strengthened, and be enabled to prosecute their great designs, and be instrumental in effecting the great work of the last days."[19]

"Now for persons to do things, merely because they are advised to do them, and yet murmur all the time they are doing them, is of no use at all; they might as well not do them. There are those who profess to be Saints who are too apt to murmur, and find fault, when any advice is given, which comes in opposition to their feelings, even when they, themselves, ask for counsel; much more so when counsel is given unasked for, which does not agree with their notion of things; but brethren, we hope for better things from the most of you; we trust that you desire counsel, from time to time, and that you will cheerfully conform to it, whenever you receive it from a proper source."[20]

Eliza R. Snow recorded: "[Joseph Smith] said, if God has appointed him, and chosen him as an instrument to lead the Church, why not let him lead it through? Why stand in the way when he is appointed to do a thing? Who knows the mind of God? Does He not reveal things differently from what we expect? [The Prophet] remarked that he was continually rising, although he had everything bearing him down, standing in his way, and opposing; notwithstanding all this opposition, he always comes out right in the end. . . .

"He reproved those that were disposed to find fault with the management of the concerns of the Church, saying God had called him to lead the Church, and he would lead it right; those that undertake to interfere will be ashamed when their own folly is made manifest."[21]

Those who reject the living prophet will not progress and will bring upon themselves the judgments of God.

"Notwithstanding, literally speaking, that all knowledge comes from God, yet when it has been revealed, all men have not believed it as revelation at the time. . . .

"Noah was a perfect man, and his knowledge or revelation of what was to take place upon the earth . . . was not believed by the inhabitants of the earth."

"Noah was a perfect man, and his knowledge or revelation of what was to take place upon the earth gave him power to prepare and save himself and family from the destruction of the flood. This knowledge, or revelation, . . . was not believed by the inhabitants of the earth. They knew Adam was the first man, made in the image of God; that he was a good man; that Enoch walked with God three hundred and sixty-five years, and was translated to heaven without tasting death. But they could not endure the new revelation: the old we believe because our fathers did, but away with new revelations. And the flood swept them away. . . .

"The same principle . . . was signally manifest among the Jews when the Savior came in the flesh. [They] boasted of the old revelations, garnished the sepulchres of the dead, gave tithes of mint and anise, made long prayers for a pretense, and crossed sea and land to make proselytes, but yet when the new revelation came fresh from the mouth of the great I Am himself, they could not endure it—it was too much. It showed the corruptions of that generation, as others before, and they cried, away with him; crucify him! . . .

"Once more, the same course and language were used when the Book of Mormon came to this generation. The old revelation, the old patriarchs, pilgrims and apostles, were blessed. We believe in them, but the new ones we cannot abide."[22]

"The world always mistook false prophets for true ones, and those that were sent of God, they considered to be false prophets, and hence they killed, stoned, punished and imprisoned the true prophets, and these had to hide themselves 'in deserts and dens, and caves of the earth' [see Hebrews 11:38], and though the most honorable men of the earth, they banished them from their society as vagabonds, whilst they cherished, honored and supported knaves, vagabonds, hypocrites, impostors, and the basest of men."[23]

"I have not the least idea, if Christ should come to the earth and preach such rough things as He preached to the Jews, but that this generation would reject Him for being so rough. . . . Many men will say, 'I will never forsake you, but will stand by you at all times.' But the moment you teach them some of the mysteries of the kingdom of God that are retained in the heavens and are to be revealed to the children of men when they are prepared for them, they will be the first to stone you and put you to death. It was this same principle that crucified the Lord Jesus Christ, and will cause the people to kill the prophets in this generation.

"Many things are [inexplicable] to the children of men in the last days: for instance, that God should raise the dead; [they forget] that things have been hid from before the foundation of the world, which are to be revealed to babes in the last days.

"There are a great many wise men and women too in our midst who are too wise to be taught; therefore they must die in their ignorance, and in the resurrection they will find their mistake. Many seal up the door of heaven by saying, So far God may reveal and I will believe. . . .

"It always has been when a man was sent of God with the priesthood and he began to preach the fullness of the gospel, that he was thrust out by his friends, who are ready to butcher him if he teach things which they imagine to be wrong; and Jesus was crucified upon this principle."[24]

"Woe, woe be to that man or set of men who lift up their hands against God and His witness in these last days: for they shall deceive almost the very chosen ones!

". . . When a man goes about prophesying, and commands men to obey his teachings, he must either be a true or false prophet. False prophets always arise to oppose the true prophets and they will prophesy so very near the truth that they will deceive almost the very chosen ones."[25]

"In consequence of rejecting the Gospel of Jesus Christ and the Prophets whom God hath sent, the judgments of God have rested upon people, cities, and nations, in various ages of the world, which was the case with the cities of Sodom and Gomorrah, that were destroyed for rejecting the Prophets."[26]

William P. McIntire reported: "[Joseph Smith] prophesied that all those that made light of the revelations that were given, and of him and his words, would ere long cry and lament, . . . saying, Oh! that we had hearkened to the words of God and the revelations given."[27]

Suggestions for Study and Teaching

Consider these ideas as you study the chapter or as you prepare to teach. For additional help, see pages vii–xii.

- Review the account on pages 193–94, noting how the early Church members felt about the revelations received through Joseph Smith. What are your feelings about the Doctrine and Covenants?
- Read the fourth paragraph on page 195. Why do you think that "salvation cannot come without revelation"?
- Review pages 196–97. Why do you think people sometimes allow themselves to be deceived, as in the story about Hiram Page? What can we do to avoid being deceived by false prophets or false teachings?

- Review the last two full paragraphs on page 197 and the paragraph that continues onto page 198. How do we benefit from having only one man who can receive revelations for the entire Church? What experiences can you share in which the Lord has guided you in your specific responsibilities?
- On pages 198–99, read how Joseph Smith and Brigham Young responded when a man said we should confine ourselves to the revelations written in the scriptures. What would be missing from your life if you confined yourself to the standard works, without hearing the words of the living prophet? What can we do to follow the spirit of Brigham Young's counsel?
- What can we do to uphold the President of the Church and other Church leaders? (For some examples, see pages 199–200.) What counsel did the President of the Church give in the past general conference? In what ways have you been blessed as you have followed the prophet and other Church leaders?
- What are some ways in which people reject God's prophets? (For some examples, see pages 200–203.) What are some possible consequences of choosing not to follow the counsel of those the Lord has chosen to lead His Church?

Related Scriptures: Proverbs 29:18; Jacob 4:8; 3 Nephi 28:34; Mormon 9:7–9; D&C 21:1–6

Notes

1. Parley P. Pratt, *Autobiography of Parley P. Pratt,* ed. Parley P. Pratt Jr. (1938), p. 62; punctuation modernized; paragraph divisions altered.
2. "The Conference Minutes and Record Book of Christ's Church of Latter Day Saints 1838–39; 1844," entry for Nov. 2, 1831, p. 16, reported by John Whitmer, Church Archives, The Church of Jesus Christ of Latter-day Saints, Salt Lake City, Utah. This record book contains records from 1830 to 1844.
3. *History of the Church,* 1:235; from "History of the Church" (manuscript), book A-1, pp. 172–73, Church Archives.
4. Articles of Faith 1:9.
5. *History of the Church,* 5:344; from a discourse given by Joseph Smith on Apr. 8, 1843, in Nauvoo, Illinois; reported by Willard Richards and William Clayton.
6. *History of the Church,* 6:252; from a discourse given by Joseph Smith on Mar. 10, 1844, in Nauvoo, Illinois; reported by Wilford Woodruff.
7. *History of the Church,* 3:389–90; from a discourse given by Joseph Smith about July 1839 in Commerce, Illinois; reported by Willard Richards.
8. *History of the Church,* 5:258; from a discourse given by Joseph Smith on Jan. 22, 1843, in Nauvoo, Illinois; reported by Wilford Woodruff.

9. *History of the Church,* 6:9; from Joseph Smith, "Latter Day Saints," in I. Daniel Rupp, comp., *He Pasa Ekklesia [The Whole Church]: An Original History of the Religious Denominations at Present Existing in the United States* (1844), p. 404.
10. *History of the Church,* 2:52; punctuation modernized; paragraph divisions altered; from the minutes of a Church conference held on Apr. 21, 1834, in Norton, Ohio; reported by Oliver Cowdery.
11. "Baptism," an editorial published in *Times and Seasons,* Sept. 1, 1842, p. 905; grammar modernized; Joseph Smith was the editor of the periodical.
12. *History of the Church,* 1:109–11, 115; paragraph divisions altered; from "History of the Church" (manuscript), book A-1, pp. 53–55, 58, Church Archives; the date of Joseph and Emma's arrival in Fayette is incorrectly given as August 1830 in *History of the Church.*
13. *History of the Church,* 2:477; from a discourse given by Joseph Smith on Apr. 6, 1837, in Kirtland, Ohio; reported by *Messenger and Advocate,* Apr. 1837, p. 487.
14. *History of the Church,* 1:338; from a letter from Joseph Smith and Frederick G. Williams to John S. Carter, Apr. 13, 1833, Kirtland, Ohio.
15. Heber C. Kimball, *Deseret News,* Nov. 5, 1856, p. 274.
16. Wilford Woodruff, in Conference Report, Oct. 1897, pp. 22–23; punctuation modernized; paragraph divisions altered.
17. Brigham Young, *Deseret News,* Dec. 9, 1857, p. 316.
18. *History of the Church,* 2:417–18; from a Joseph Smith journal entry, Mar. 27, 1836, Kirtland, Ohio; see also *Messenger and Advocate,* Mar. 1836, p. 277.
19. *History of the Church,* 4:186; from a letter from Joseph Smith and his counselors in the First Presidency to the Saints, Sept. 1840, Nauvoo, Illinois, published in *Times and Seasons,* Oct. 1840, p. 178.
20. *History of the Church,* 4:45, footnote; from a letter from the First Presidency and high council to the Saints living west of Kirtland, Ohio, Dec. 8, 1839, Commerce, Illinois, published in *Times and Seasons,* Dec. 1839, p. 29.
21. *History of the Church,* 4:603–4; from a discourse given by Joseph Smith on Apr. 28, 1842, in Nauvoo, Illinois; reported by Eliza R. Snow; see also appendix, page 562, item 3.
22. "Knowledge Is Power," an editorial published in *Times and Seasons,* Aug. 15, 1842, pp. 889–90; spelling, punctuation, and grammar modernized; italics deleted; Joseph Smith was the editor of the periodical.
23. *History of the Church,* 4:574; punctuation modernized; from "Try the Spirits," an editorial published in *Times and Seasons,* Apr. 1, 1842, p. 744; Joseph Smith was the editor of the periodical.
24. *History of the Church,* 5:423–25; punctuation modernized; paragraph divisions altered; from a discourse given by Joseph Smith on June 11, 1843, in Nauvoo, Illinois; reported by Wilford Woodruff and Willard Richards; see also appendix, page 562, item 3.
25. *History of the Church,* 6:364; from a discourse given by Joseph Smith on May 12, 1844, in Nauvoo, Illinois; reported by Thomas Bullock.
26. *History of the Church,* 5:256–57; from a discourse given by Joseph Smith on Jan. 22, 1843, in Nauvoo, Illinois; reported by Wilford Woodruff.
27. William P. McIntire, reporting a discourse given by Joseph Smith in early 1841 in Nauvoo, Illinois; William Patterson McIntire, Notebook 1840–45, Church Archives.

"And the Lord God spake unto Moses, saying: . . . For behold, this is my work and my glory—to bring to pass the immortality and eternal life of man."

CHAPTER 17

The Great Plan of Salvation

"The great plan of salvation is a theme which ought to occupy our strict attention, and be regarded as one of heaven's best gifts to mankind."

From the Life of Joseph Smith

In September 1831, the Prophet Joseph Smith and his family moved 30 miles southeast of Kirtland to Hiram, Ohio, where they lived for about a year in the home of John and Alice (also known as Elsa) Johnson. In this home, the Prophet did much of his work on the Joseph Smith Translation of the Bible.

This important work, which the Prophet called a "branch of my calling,"[1] contributes significantly to our understanding of the plan of salvation. The Prophet began this work in June 1830 when the Lord commanded him to begin making an inspired revision of the King James Version of the Bible. The Prophet had long known that the Bible was not always clear on some important matters. He had noted that Moroni quoted some biblical passages to him "with a little variation from the way [they read] in our Bibles" (Joseph Smith—History 1:36). While translating 1 Nephi 13:23–29, he learned that many "parts which are plain and most precious" had been taken out of the Bible, including "many covenants of the Lord" (1 Nephi 13:26).

The Prophet later said: "I believe the Bible as it read when it came from the pen of the original writers. Ignorant translators, careless transcribers, or designing and corrupt priests have committed many errors. . . . Look at [Hebrews 6:1] for contradictions—'Therefore leaving the principles of the doctrine of Christ, let us go on unto perfection.' If a man leaves the principles of the doctrine of Christ, how can he be saved in the principles? This is a contradiction. I don't believe it. I will render it as it should be—'Therefore *not* leaving the principles of the doctrine of Christ, let us go on unto perfection.' "[2]

As guided by the Spirit, Joseph spent about three years going through the Bible, making thousands of corrections to the text and restoring information that had been lost. This restored information sheds marvelous light on many doctrines that are not clearly presented in the Bible as it exists today. These inspired revisions to the text of the Bible are known as the Joseph Smith Translation of the Bible. Hundreds of passages from the Joseph Smith Translation are now included in the Latter-day Saint edition of the King James Version of the Bible.

The Prophet's translation of the Bible was an important part of his own spiritual education and the unfolding restoration of gospel truth. As he revised the Old and New Testaments, he often received revelations clarifying or expanding upon biblical passages. In this way, the Prophet received many doctrines from the Lord, including those now found in Doctrine and Covenants 74, 76, 77, 86, and 91, and in portions of many other sections of the Doctrine and Covenants.

When the Prophet first began his translation of the Bible in June 1830, the Lord revealed to him a lengthy passage from the writings of Moses. This passage became chapter 1 of the book of Moses in the Pearl of Great Price. It records a vision in which Moses saw and conversed with God—a vision so remarkable that Joseph Smith called it "a precious morsel" and "a supply of strength."[3] In this vision, God taught Moses the fundamental purpose of the great plan of salvation:

"And the Lord God spake unto Moses, saying: . . . For behold, this is my work and my glory—to bring to pass the immortality and eternal life of man" (Moses 1:37, 39).

The doctrines, ordinances, and promises that constitute the plan of salvation were revealed to the earth in these latter days through the Prophet Joseph Smith. As one who clearly understood the importance of this plan, the Prophet declared: "The great plan of salvation is a theme which ought to occupy our strict attention, and be regarded as one of heaven's best gifts to mankind."[4]

Teachings of Joseph Smith

In the premortal world, Jesus Christ was chosen to be the Savior, and we chose to accept the plan of salvation.

"At the first organization in heaven we were all present and saw the Savior chosen and appointed and the plan of salvation made, and we sanctioned it."[5]

"The Lord [is] a priest forever, after the order of Melchizedek, and the anointed Son of God, from before the foundation of the world [see Psalm 110:4]."[6]

"The salvation of Jesus Christ was wrought out for all men, in order to triumph over the devil. . . . All will suffer until they obey Christ himself.

"The contention in heaven was—Jesus said there would be certain souls that would not be saved; and the devil said he would save them all, and laid his plans before the grand council, who gave their vote in favor of Jesus Christ. So the devil rose up in rebellion against God, and was cast down, with all who put up their heads for him."[7]

We are eternal beings; we can advance toward exaltation as we obey the laws of God.

The Prophet Joseph Smith received the following revelation from the Lord in May 1833, later recorded in Doctrine and Covenants 93:29: "Man was also in the beginning with God. Intelligence, or the light of truth, was not created or made, neither indeed can be." In April 1844, the Prophet taught: "I have another subject to dwell upon, which is calculated to exalt man. . . . It is associated with the subject of the resurrection of the dead,—namely, the soul—the mind of man—the immortal spirit. Where did it come from? All learned men and doctors of divinity say that God created it in the beginning; but it is not so: the very idea lessens man in my estimation. I do not believe the doctrine; I know better. Hear it, all ye ends of the world; for God has told me so; and if you don't believe me, it will not make the truth without effect. . . .

"I am dwelling on the immortality of the spirit of man. Is it logical to say that the intelligence of spirits is immortal, and yet that it has a beginning? The intelligence of spirits had no beginning, neither will it have an end. That is good logic. That which has a beginning may have an end. There never was a time when there were not spirits. . . .

". . . I take my ring from my finger and liken it unto the mind of man—the immortal part, because it had no beginning. Suppose you cut it in two; then it has a beginning and an end; but join it again, and it continues one eternal round. So with the spirit of man. As the Lord liveth, if it had a beginning, it will have an end. All the fools and learned and wise men from the beginning of creation, who say that the spirit of man had a beginning, prove that it must have an end; and if that doctrine is true, then the doctrine of annihilation would be true. But if I am right, I might with boldness proclaim from the house-tops that God never had the power to create the spirit of man at all. God himself could not create himself.

"Intelligence is eternal and exists upon a self-existent principle. It is a spirit from age to age and there is no creation about it. All the minds and spirits that God ever sent into the world are susceptible of enlargement.

"The first principles of man are self-existent with God. God himself, finding he was in the midst of spirits and glory, because he was more intelligent, saw proper to institute laws whereby the rest could have a privilege to advance like himself. The relationship we have with God places us in a situation to advance in knowledge. He has power to institute laws to instruct the weaker intelligences, that they may be exalted with himself, so that they might have one glory upon another, and all that knowledge, power, glory, and intelligence, which is requisite in order to save them in the world of spirits."[8]

"We consider that God has created man with a mind capable of instruction, and a faculty which may be enlarged in proportion to the heed and diligence given to the light communicated from heaven to the intellect; and that the nearer man approaches perfection, the clearer are his views, and the greater his enjoyments, till he has overcome the evils of his life and lost every desire for sin; and like the ancients, arrives at that point of faith where he is wrapped in the power and glory of his Maker, and is caught up to dwell with Him. But we consider that this is a station to which no man ever arrived in a moment."[9]

We came to earth to obtain a body, to gain knowledge, and to overcome through faith.

"All men know that they must die. And it is important that we should understand the reasons and causes of our exposure to the vicissitudes of life and of death, and the designs and purposes of God in our coming into the world, our sufferings here, and our departure hence. What is the object of our coming into existence, then dying and falling away, to be here no more? It is but reasonable to suppose that God would reveal something in reference to the matter, and it is a subject we ought to study more than any other. We ought to study it day and night, for the world is ignorant in reference to their true condition and relation [to God]."[10]

"The design of God before the foundation of the world was that we should take tabernacles [bodies], that through faithfulness we should overcome and thereby obtain a resurrection from the dead, in this wise obtaining glory, honor, power, and dominion."[11]

"We came to this earth that we might have a body and present it pure before God in the celestial kingdom. The great principle of happiness consists in having a body. The devil has no body, and herein is his punishment. He is pleased when he can obtain the tabernacle of man, and when cast out by the Savior he asked to go into the herd of swine, showing that he would prefer a swine's body to having none. All beings who have bodies have power over those who have not."[12]

"Salvation is for a man to be saved from all his enemies; for until a man can triumph over death, he is not saved. . . .

"The spirits in the eternal world are like the spirits in this world. When those have come into this world and received tabernacles, then died and again have risen and received glorified

"The design of God before the foundation of the world was that we should take tabernacles [bodies], that through faithfulness we should overcome."

bodies, they will have an ascendency over the spirits who have received no bodies, or kept not their first estate, like the devil. The punishment of the devil was that he should not have a habitation like men."[13]

"The principle of knowledge is the principle of salvation. This principle can be comprehended by the faithful and diligent; and every one that does not obtain knowledge sufficient to be saved will be condemned. The principle of salvation is given us through the knowledge of Jesus Christ.

"Salvation is nothing more nor less than to triumph over all our enemies and put them under our feet. And when we have power to put all enemies under our feet in this world, and a knowledge to triumph over all evil spirits in the world to come, then we are saved, as in the case of Jesus, who was to reign until He had put all enemies under His feet, and the last enemy was death [see 1 Corinthians 15:25–26].

"Perhaps there are principles here that few men have thought of. No person can have this salvation except through a tabernacle.

"Now, in this world, mankind are naturally selfish, ambitious and striving to excel one above another; yet some are willing to build up others as well as themselves. So in the other world there are a variety of spirits. Some seek to excel. And this was the case with Lucifer when he fell. He sought for things which were unlawful. Hence he was sent down, and it is said he drew many away with him; and the greatness of his punishment is that he shall not have a tabernacle. This is his punishment."[14]

God has given us moral agency and the power to choose good over evil.

"If men would acquire salvation, they have got to be subject, before they leave this world, to certain rules and principles, which were fixed by an unalterable decree before the world was. . . . The organization of the spiritual and heavenly worlds, and of spiritual and heavenly beings, was agreeable to the most perfect order and harmony: their limits and bounds were fixed irrevocably, and voluntarily subscribed to in their heavenly estate by themselves, and were by our first parents subscribed to upon the earth. Hence the importance of embracing and subscribing to principles of eternal truth by all men upon the earth that expect eternal life."[15]

"All persons are entitled to their agency, for God has so ordained it. He has constituted mankind moral agents, and given them power to choose good or evil; to seek after that which is good, by pursuing the pathway of holiness in this life, which brings peace of mind, and joy in the Holy Ghost here, and a fulness of joy and happiness at His right hand hereafter; or to pursue an evil course, going on in sin and rebellion against God, thereby bringing condemnation to their souls in this world, and an eternal loss in the world to come."[16]

"Satan cannot seduce us by his enticements unless we in our hearts consent and yield. Our organization is such that we can resist the devil; if we were not organized so, we would not be free agents."[17]

"The devil has no power over us only as we permit him; the moment we revolt at anything which comes from God, the devil takes power."[18]

On May 16, 1841, the Prophet addressed the Saints: "President Joseph Smith . . . observed that Satan was generally blamed for the evils which we did, but if he was the cause of all our wickedness, men could not be condemned. The devil could not compel mankind to do evil; all was voluntary. Those who resisted the Spirit of God, would be liable to be led into temptation, and then the association of heaven would be withdrawn from those who refused to be made partakers of such great glory. God would not exert any compulsory means, and the devil could not; and such ideas as were entertained [on these subjects] by many were absurd."[19]

Eliza R. Snow recorded: "[Joseph Smith] said he did not care how fast we run in the path of virtue. Resist evil, and there is no danger; God, men, and angels will not condemn those that resist everything that is evil, and devils cannot; as well might the devil seek to dethrone Jehovah, as overthrow an innocent soul that resists everything which is evil."[20]

Suggestions for Study and Teaching

Consider these ideas as you study the chapter or as you prepare to teach. For additional help, see pages vii–xii.

- What are some specific truths about the plan of salvation and the purpose of life that we know because of revelations to the Prophet Joseph Smith? How have these truths helped you?
- Joseph Smith taught that the plan of salvation is "a subject we ought to study more than any other" (page 211) and "a theme which ought to occupy our strict attention" (page 208). In what ways can we study the plan of salvation? As we go about our daily activities, what can we do to give the plan of salvation our strict attention? What are some ways we can teach the plan of salvation to others?
- Review Joseph Smith's teachings about the Council in Heaven and about our eternal nature (pages 209–11). How might

knowing of these doctrines be a blessing to you in your life on earth?

- The Prophet Joseph testified, "All the minds and spirits that God ever sent into the world are susceptible of enlargement" (page 210). What do you think this means? How might this truth influence the way you face challenges? the way you feel about your own worth and capabilities? the way you treat other people?
- Read the paragraph that begins at the bottom of page 210. Ponder the blessings we receive as we give "heed and diligence . . . to the light communicated from heaven."
- Review Joseph Smith's teachings about the significance of having a physical body (pages 211–13). How might this knowledge affect the way we care for our bodies?
- Read the last paragraph on page 213 and the first paragraph on page 214. Think about what these teachings mean to you as you exercise your agency. What are some specific things we can do to resist Satan's influence?

Related Scriptures: 2 Nephi 2:25; 9:6–12; Alma 34:31–33; D&C 76:25–32; 101:78; Abraham 3:22–25

Notes

1. *History of the Church,* 1:238; from "History of the Church" (manuscript), book A-1, p. 175, Church Archives, The Church of Jesus Christ of Latter-day Saints, Salt Lake City, Utah.
2. *History of the Church,* 6:57–58; paragraph divisions altered; from a discourse given by Joseph Smith on Oct. 15, 1843, in Nauvoo, Illinois; reported by Willard Richards; see also appendix, page 562, item 3.
3. *History of the Church,* 1:98; from "History of the Church" (manuscript), book A-1, miscellaneous papers, Church Archives.
4. *History of the Church,* 2:23; from "The Elders of the Church in Kirtland, to Their Brethren Abroad," Jan. 22, 1834, published in *Evening and Morning Star,* Apr. 1834, p. 152.
5. Quoted by William Clayton, reporting an undated discourse given by Joseph Smith in Nauvoo, Illinois; in L. John Nuttall, "Extracts from William Clayton's Private Book," p. 7, Journals of L. John Nuttall, 1857–1904, L. Tom Perry Special Collections, Brigham Young University, Provo, Utah; copy in Church Archives.
6. "Baptism," an editorial published in *Times and Seasons,* Sept. 1, 1842, p. 905; spelling and capitalization modernized; Joseph Smith was the editor of the periodical.
7. *History of the Church,* 6:314; from a discourse given by Joseph Smith on Apr. 7, 1844, in Nauvoo, Illinois; reported by Wilford Woodruff, Willard Richards, Thomas Bullock, and William Clayton.

8. *History of the Church,* 6:310–12; capitalization modernized; from a discourse given by Joseph Smith on Apr. 7, 1844, in Nauvoo, Illinois; reported by Wilford Woodruff, Willard Richards, Thomas Bullock, and William Clayton; see also appendix, page 562, item 3.
9. *History of the Church,* 2:8; from "The Elders of the Church in Kirtland, to Their Brethren Abroad," Jan. 22, 1834, published in *Evening and Morning Star,* Feb. 1834, p. 135.
10. *History of the Church,* 6:50; from a discourse given by Joseph Smith on Oct. 9, 1843, in Nauvoo, Illinois; reported by Willard Richards and *Times and Seasons,* Sept. 15, 1843, p. 331; this issue of the *Times and Seasons* was published late.
11. Quoted by Martha Jane Knowlton Coray, reporting a discourse given by Joseph Smith on May 21, 1843, in Nauvoo, Illinois; Martha Jane Knowlton Coray, Notebook, Church Archives.
12. Quoted by William Clayton, reporting an undated discourse given by Joseph Smith in Nauvoo, Illinois; in L. John Nuttall, "Extracts from William Clayton's Private Book," pp. 7–8, Journals of L. John Nuttall, 1857–1904, L. Tom Perry Special Collections, Brigham Young University, Provo, Utah; copy in Church Archives.
13. *History of the Church,* 5:403; from a discourse given by Joseph Smith on May 21, 1843, in Nauvoo, Illinois; reported by Willard Richards; see also appendix, page 562, item 3.
14. *History of the Church,* 5:387–88; from a discourse given by Joseph Smith on May 14, 1843, in Yelrome, Illinois; reported by Wilford Woodruff; see also appendix, page 562, item 3.
15. *History of the Church,* 6:50–51; paragraph divisions altered; from a discourse given by Joseph Smith on Oct. 9, 1843, in Nauvoo, Illinois; reported by Willard Richards and *Times and Seasons,* Sept. 15, 1843, p. 331; this issue of the *Times and Seasons* was published late; see also appendix, page 562, item 3.
16. *History of the Church,* 4:45, footnote; from a letter from the First Presidency and high council to the Saints living west of Kirtland, Ohio, Dec. 8, 1839, Commerce, Illinois, published in *Times and Seasons,* Dec. 1839, p. 29.
17. Quoted by William P. McIntire, reporting a discourse given by Joseph Smith in early 1841 in Nauvoo, Illinois; William Patterson McIntire, Notebook 1840–45, Church Archives.
18. Quoted by William Clayton, reporting an undated discourse given by Joseph Smith in Nauvoo, Illinois; in L. John Nuttall, "Extracts from William Clayton's Private Book," p. 8, Journals of L. John Nuttall, 1857–1904, L. Tom Perry Special Collections, Brigham Young University, Provo, Utah; copy in Church Archives.
19. *History of the Church,* 4:358; bracketed words in original; paragraph divisions altered; from a discourse given by Joseph Smith on May 16, 1841, in Nauvoo, Illinois; reported by *Times and Seasons,* June 1, 1841, p. 429.
20. *History of the Church,* 4:605; punctuation modernized; from a discourse given by Joseph Smith on Apr. 28, 1842, in Nauvoo, Illinois; reported by Eliza R. Snow.

CHAPTER 18

Beyond the Veil: Life in the Eternities

"[The righteous who have died] shall rise again to dwell in everlasting burnings in immortal glory, not to sorrow, suffer, or die any more, but they shall be heirs of God and joint heirs with Jesus Christ."

From the Life of Joseph Smith

Joseph Smith's work on the translation of the Bible led to a most remarkable vision of life in the eternities. On February 16, 1832, the Prophet was at work in the home of John Johnson in Hiram, Ohio, with Sidney Rigdon serving as his scribe. He was translating the Gospel of John. "From sundry revelations which had been received," the Prophet later said, "it was apparent that many important points touching the salvation of man had been taken from the Bible, or lost before it was compiled. It appeared self-evident from what truths were left, that if God rewarded every one according to the deeds done in the body, the term 'Heaven,' as intended for the Saints' eternal home, must include more kingdoms than one."[1]

The Prophet translated John 5:29, which describes how all "shall come forth" in the resurrection—"they that have done good, unto the resurrection of life; and they that have done evil, unto the resurrection of damnation." As he and Sidney pondered this scripture, a marvelous vision was opened to them. As the Prophet recorded: "By the power of the Spirit our eyes were opened and our understandings enlightened, so as to see and understand the things of God—even those things which were from the beginning before the world was, which were ordained of the Father, through his Only Begotten Son, who was in the bosom of the Father, even from the beginning" (D&C 76:12–13).

The restored John Johnson home in Hiram, Ohio.
In the Johnson home in February 1832, the Prophet Joseph Smith saw a vision of the three degrees of glory that God has prepared for His children.

In this glorious vision, the Prophet and Sidney Rigdon saw the Son of God at the right hand of the Father and "received of his fulness" (D&C 76:20). They saw the three kingdoms of glory that God has prepared for His children and learned who will inherit these kingdoms. They also saw Satan thrust out of the presence of God and the sufferings of those who allow themselves to be overcome by Satan.

This vision later became section 76 of the Doctrine and Covenants. The Prophet explained: "Nothing could be more pleasing to the Saints upon the order of the kingdom of the Lord, than the light which burst upon the world through the foregoing vision. Every law, every commandment, every promise, every truth, and every point touching the destiny of man, from Genesis to Revelation, where the purity of the scriptures remains unsullied by the folly of men, . . . witnesses the fact that that document is a transcript from the records of the eternal world. The sublimity of the ideas; the purity of the language; the scope for action; the continued duration for completion, in order that the heirs of salvation may confess the Lord and bow the knee; the rewards for faithfulness, and the punishments for sins, are so much beyond the narrow-mindedness of men, that every honest man is constrained to exclaim: *'It came from God.'* "[2]

Teachings of Joseph Smith

God has prepared three degrees of glory for His children.

"My text is on the resurrection of the dead, which you will find in the 14th chapter of John—'In my Father's house are many mansions.' [John 14:2.] It should be—'In my Father's kingdom are many kingdoms,' in order that ye may be heirs of God and joint-heirs with me. . . . There are mansions for those who obey a celestial law, and there are other mansions for those who come short of the law, every man in his own order."[3]

" 'But,' says one, 'I believe in one universal heaven and hell, where all go, and are all alike, and equally miserable or equally happy.'

"What! where all are huddled together—the honorable, virtuous, and murderers, and whoremongers, when it is written that they shall be judged according to the deeds done in the body? But St. Paul informs us of three glories and three heavens. He knew a man that was caught up to the third heaven [see 1 Corinthians 15:40–41; 2 Corinthians 12:2–4]. . . . Jesus said unto His disciples, 'In my Father's house are many mansions; if it were not so, I would have told you. I go to prepare a place for you, and I will come and receive you to myself, that where I am ye may be also.' [See John 14:2–3.]"[4]

"Go and read the vision in [Doctrine and Covenants 76]. There is clearly illustrated glory upon glory—one glory of the sun, another glory of the moon, and a glory of the stars; and as one star differeth from another star in glory, even so do they of the telestial world differ in glory, and every man who reigns in celestial glory is a God to his dominions. . . .

"Paul says, 'There is one glory of the sun, and another glory of the moon, and another glory of the stars; for one star differeth from another star in glory. So is also the resurrection of the dead.' [1 Corinthians 15:41–42.]"[5]

Those who receive the testimony of Jesus, receive the ordinances of the gospel, and overcome by faith will inherit the celestial kingdom.

The Prophet Joseph Smith saw the following in vision, later recorded in Doctrine and Covenants 76:50–59, 62, 68–70: "And again we bear record—for we saw and heard, and this is the testimony of the gospel of Christ concerning them who shall come forth in the resurrection of the just—they are they who received the testimony of Jesus, and believed on his name and were baptized after the manner of his burial, being buried in the water in his name, and this according to the commandment which he has given—that by keeping the commandments they might be washed and cleansed from all their sins, and receive the Holy Spirit by the laying on of the hands of him who is ordained and sealed unto this power; and who overcome by faith, and are sealed by the Holy Spirit of promise, which the Father sheds forth upon all those who are just and true.

"They are they who are the church of the Firstborn. They are they into whose hands the Father has given all things—they are they who are priests and kings, who have received of his fulness, and of his glory; and are priests of the Most High, after the order of Melchizedek, which was after the order of Enoch, which was after the order of the Only Begotten Son.

"Wherefore, as it is written, they are gods, even the sons of God—wherefore, all things are theirs, whether life or death, or things present, or things to come, all are theirs and they are Christ's, and Christ is God's. . . .

"These shall dwell in the presence of God and his Christ forever and ever. . . . These are they whose names are written in heaven, where God and Christ are the judge of all. These are they who are just men made perfect through Jesus the mediator of the new covenant, who wrought out this perfect atonement through the shedding of his own blood. These are they whose bodies are celestial, whose glory is that of the sun, even the glory of God, the highest of all, whose glory the sun of the firmament is written of as being typical."[6]

The Prophet Joseph Smith taught the following in May 1843, later recorded in Doctrine and Covenants 131:1–4: "In the celestial glory there are three heavens or degrees; and in order to obtain the highest, a man must enter into this order of the priesthood [meaning the new and everlasting covenant of marriage]; and if he does not, he cannot obtain it. He may enter into the other, but that is the end of his kingdom; he cannot have an increase."[7]

"Here, then, is eternal life—to know the only wise and true God; and you have got to learn how to be gods yourselves, and to be kings and priests to God, . . . by going from one small degree to another, and from a small capacity to a great one; from grace to grace, from exaltation to exaltation, until you attain to the resurrection of the dead, and are able to dwell in everlasting burnings, and to sit in glory, as do those who sit enthroned in everlasting power. . . .

". . . [The righteous who have died] shall rise again to dwell in everlasting burnings in immortal glory, not to sorrow, suffer, or

Those who inherit the celestial kingdom are "they whose bodies are celestial, whose glory is that of the sun, even the glory of God, the highest of all."

die any more, but they shall be heirs of God and joint heirs with Jesus Christ. What is it? To inherit the same power, the same glory and the same exaltation, until you arrive at the station of a god, and ascend the throne of eternal power, the same as those who have gone before."[8]

"They who obtain a glorious resurrection from the dead, are exalted far above principalities, powers, thrones, dominions and angels, and are expressly declared to be heirs of God and joint heirs with Jesus Christ, all having eternal power [see Romans 8:17]."[9]

The "honorable men of the earth," those who are not valiant in the testimony of Jesus, will inherit the terrestrial kingdom.

The Prophet Joseph Smith saw the following in vision, later recorded in Doctrine and Covenants 76:71–79: "And again, we saw the terrestrial world, and behold and lo, these are they who are of the terrestrial, whose glory differs from that of the church of the Firstborn who have received the fulness of the Father, even as that of the moon differs from the sun in the firmament.

"Behold, these are they who died without law; and also they who are the spirits of men kept in prison, whom the Son visited, and preached the gospel unto them, that they might be judged according to men in the flesh; who received not the testimony of Jesus in the flesh, but afterwards received it.

"These are they who are honorable men of the earth, who were blinded by the craftiness of men. These are they who receive of his glory, but not of his fulness. These are they who receive of the presence of the Son, but not of the fulness of the Father.

"Wherefore, they are bodies terrestrial, and not bodies celestial, and differ in glory as the moon differs from the sun. These are they who are not valiant in the testimony of Jesus; wherefore, they obtain not the crown over the kingdom of our God."[10]

Those who are wicked and do not receive the gospel or the testimony of Jesus will inherit the telestial kingdom.

The Prophet Joseph Smith saw the following in vision, later recorded in Doctrine and Covenants 76:81–85, 100–106, 110–12: "And again, we saw the glory of the telestial, which glory is that of the lesser, even as the glory of the stars differs from that of the glory of the moon in the firmament.

"These are they who received not the gospel of Christ, neither the testimony of Jesus. These are they who deny not the Holy Spirit. These are they who are thrust down to hell. These are they who shall not be redeemed from the devil until the last resurrection, until the Lord, even Christ the Lamb, shall have finished his work. . . .

"These are they who say they are some of one and some of another—some of Christ and some of John, and some of Moses, and some of Elias, and some of Esaias, and some of Isaiah, and some of Enoch; but received not the gospel, neither the testimony of Jesus, neither the prophets, neither the everlasting covenant.

"Last of all, these all are they who will not be gathered with the saints, to be caught up unto the church of the Firstborn, and received into the cloud.

"These are they who are liars, and sorcerers, and adulterers, and whoremongers, and whosoever loves and makes a lie. These are they who suffer the wrath of God on earth. These are they who suffer the vengeance of eternal fire. These are they who are cast down to hell and suffer the wrath of Almighty God, until the fulness of times, when Christ shall have subdued all enemies under his feet, and shall have perfected his work. . . .

"And [we] heard the voice of the Lord saying: These all shall bow the knee, and every tongue shall confess to him who sits upon the throne forever and ever; for they shall be judged according to their works, and every man shall receive according to his own works, his own dominion, in the mansions which are prepared; and they shall be servants of the Most High; but where God and Christ dwell they cannot come, worlds without end."[11]

The torment of the wicked is to know they have come short of the glory they might have enjoyed.

"God has decreed that all who will not obey His voice shall not escape the damnation of hell. What is the damnation of hell? To go with that society who have not obeyed His commands. . . . I know that all men will be damned if they do not come in the way which He hath opened, and this is the way marked out by the word of the Lord."[12]

"The great misery of departed spirits in the world of spirits, where they go after death, is to know that they come short of the glory that others enjoy and that they might have enjoyed themselves, and they are their own accusers."[13]

"There is no pain so awful as that of suspense. This is the punishment of the wicked; their doubt, anxiety and suspense cause weeping, wailing and gnashing of teeth."[14]

"A man is his own tormentor and his own condemner. Hence the saying, They shall go into the lake that burns with fire and brimstone [see Revelation 21:8]. The torment of disappointment in the mind of man is as exquisite as a lake burning with fire and brimstone. I say, so is the torment of man. . . .

". . . Some shall rise to the everlasting burnings of God, for God dwells in everlasting burnings, and some shall rise to the damnation of their own filthiness, which is as exquisite a torment as the lake of fire and brimstone."[15]

Suggestions for Study and Teaching

Consider these ideas as you study the chapter or as you prepare to teach. For additional help, see pages vii–xii.

- Joseph Smith and Sidney Rigdon were meditating about a verse of scripture when they received the revelation that is recorded in Doctrine and Covenants 76 (pages 217–19; see also D&C 76:15–19). What personal experiences have helped you understand that meditating can lead to increased understanding? As you study or discuss this chapter, as well as other chapters, take time to meditate about the truths you read.
- Read John 14:2–3 and 1 Corinthians 15:40–41. How do the teachings in this chapter help you understand these verses?
- In the description of those who will inherit celestial, terrestrial, and telestial glory, the phrase "the testimony of Jesus" is used five times (pages 220–24). What are the characteristics of a person who is "valiant in the testimony of Jesus"? What promises are given to those who are valiant in the testimony of Jesus?
- Read the last paragraph on page 220, giving special attention to the phrase "overcome by faith." What are some things we might need to overcome? How does faith in Jesus Christ help us overcome our problems in this life?
- Read the last full paragraph on page 221. In our eternal progression, why do you think we need to improve "from one small degree to another"? What experiences have you had that illustrate our need to learn and grow in this way?
- Review the second paragraph on page 223, which describes some of the people who will inherit the terrestrial kingdom. How can we avoid being "blinded by the craftiness of men"? What can we do to help others avoid being blinded?
- On page 224, look for words and phrases Joseph Smith used to describe the state of the wicked in the next life. What do these words and phrases communicate to you? How can a man be "his own tormentor and his own condemner"?

Related Scriptures: Alma 41:2–8; D&C 14:7; 76:20–49; 88:15–39

Notes

1. *History of the Church,* 1:245; punctuation modernized; from "History of the Church" (manuscript), book A-1, p. 183, Church Archives, The Church of Jesus Christ of Latter-day Saints, Salt Lake City, Utah.
2. *History of the Church,* 1:252–53; from "History of the Church" (manuscript), book A-1, p. 192, Church Archives.
3. *History of the Church,* 6:365; paragraph divisions altered; from a discourse given by Joseph Smith on May 12, 1844, in Nauvoo, Illinois; reported by Thomas Bullock.
4. *History of the Church,* 5:425–26; punctuation modernized; from a discourse given by Joseph Smith on June 11, 1843, in Nauvoo, Illinois; reported by Wilford Woodruff and Willard Richards; see also appendix, page 562, item 3.
5. *History of the Church,* 6:477–78; from a discourse given by Joseph Smith on June 16, 1844, in Nauvoo, Illinois; reported by Thomas Bullock; see also appendix, page 562, item 3.
6. Doctrine and Covenants 76:50–59, 62, 68–70; vision given to Joseph Smith and Sidney Rigdon on Feb. 16, 1832, in Hiram, Ohio.
7. Doctrine and Covenants 131:1–4; bracketed words in original; instructions given by Joseph Smith on May 16 and 17, 1843, in Ramus, Illinois.
8. *History of the Church,* 6:306; from a discourse given by Joseph Smith on Apr. 7, 1844, in Nauvoo, Illinois; reported by Wilford Woodruff, Willard Richards, Thomas Bullock, and William Clayton.
9. *History of the Church,* 6:478; from a discourse given by Joseph Smith on June 16, 1844, in Nauvoo, Illinois; reported by Thomas Bullock; see also appendix, page 562, item 3.
10. Doctrine and Covenants 76:71–79; vision given to Joseph Smith and Sidney Rigdon on Feb. 16, 1832, in Hiram, Ohio.
11. Doctrine and Covenants 76:81–85, 100–106, 110–12; vision given to Joseph Smith and Sidney Rigdon on Feb. 16, 1832, in Hiram, Ohio.
12. *History of the Church,* 4:554–55; paragraph divisions altered; from a discourse given by Joseph Smith on Mar. 20, 1842, in Nauvoo, Illinois; reported by Wilford Woodruff; see also appendix, page 562, item 3.
13. *History of the Church,* 5:425; from a discourse given by Joseph Smith on June 11, 1843, in Nauvoo, Illinois; reported by Wilford Woodruff and Willard Richards; see also appendix, page 562, item 3.
14. *History of the Church,* 5:340; from a discourse given by Joseph Smith on Apr. 8, 1843, in Nauvoo, Illinois; reported by Willard Richards and William Clayton.
15. *History of the Church,* 6:314, 317; punctuation modernized; from a discourse given by Joseph Smith on Apr. 7, 1844, in Nauvoo, Illinois; reported by Wilford Woodruff, Willard Richards, Thomas Bullock, and William Clayton.

C H A P T E R 1 9

Stand Fast through the Storms of Life

"Stand fast, ye Saints of God, hold on a little while longer, and the storm of life will be past, and you will be rewarded by that God whose servants you are."

From the Life of Joseph Smith

On the night of March 24, 1832, Joseph Smith had stayed up late caring for his 11-month-old son, Joseph, who was sick with the measles. The Smith family was then living in the John Johnson home in Hiram, Ohio. The Prophet had finally gone to sleep on a trundle bed when a mob of a dozen or more men who had been drinking whiskey broke into the home. The Prophet later described the events of that terrible night:

"The mob burst open the door and surrounded the bed in an instant, and . . . the first I knew I was going out of the door in the hands of an infuriated mob. I made a desperate struggle, as I was forced out, to extricate myself, but only cleared one leg, with which I made a pass at one man, and he fell on the door steps. I was immediately overpowered again; and they swore . . . they would kill me if I did not be still, which quieted me. . . .

"They then seized me by the throat and held on till I lost my breath. After I came to, as they passed along with me, about thirty rods from the house, I saw Elder Rigdon stretched out on the ground, whither they had dragged him by his heels. I supposed he was dead. I began to plead with them, saying, 'You will have mercy and spare my life, I hope.' To which they replied, '. . . Call on yer God for help, we'll show ye no mercy.' "

After some discussion, the mob "concluded not to kill me," the Prophet related, "but to beat and scratch me well, tear off my shirt and drawers, and leave me naked. . . . They ran back and

On the night of March 24, 1832, in Hiram, Ohio, Joseph Smith was dragged out of his home by an infuriated mob and covered with tar and feathers.

fetched the bucket of tar, when one exclaimed, with an oath, 'Let us tar up his mouth;' and they tried to force the tar-paddle into my mouth; I twisted my head around, so that they could not; and they cried out, '. . . Hold up yer head and let us giv ye some tar.' They then tried to force a vial into my mouth, and broke it in my teeth. All my clothes were torn off me except my shirt collar; and one man fell on me and scratched my body with his nails like a mad cat. . . .

"They then left me, and I attempted to rise, but fell again; I pulled the tar away from my lips, so that I could breathe more freely, and after a while I began to recover, and raised myself up, whereupon I saw two lights. I made my way towards one of them, and found it was Father Johnson's. When I came to the door . . . the tar made me look as if I were covered with blood, and when my wife saw me she thought I was all crushed to pieces, and fainted. . . .

"My friends spent the night in scraping and removing the tar, and washing and cleansing my body; so that by morning I was ready to be clothed again."

Even after this ordeal, the Prophet stood fast in carrying out his responsibilities to the Lord. The next day was the Sabbath. "The people assembled for meeting at the usual hour of worship," the Prophet recorded, "and among them came also the mobbers. . . . With my flesh all scarified and defaced, I preached to the congregation as usual, and in the afternoon of the same day baptized three individuals."[1] Joseph and Emma's son, Joseph, died five days after the mob attack as a result of being exposed to the cold night air while suffering from the measles.

Wilford Woodruff, the fourth President of the Church, said: "The Lord told Joseph that He would prove him, whether he would abide in His covenant or not, even unto death. He did prove him; and although [Joseph] had the whole world to contend against and the treachery of false friends to withstand, although his whole life was a scene of trouble and anxiety and care, yet, in all his afflictions, his imprisonments, the mobbings and ill treatment he passed through, he was ever true to his God."[2]

Teachings of Joseph Smith

Those who follow Jesus Christ will be tried and must prove themselves faithful to God.

"There is no safety, only in the arm of Jehovah. None else can deliver, and he will not deliver unless we do prove ourselves faithful to him in the severest trouble. For he that will have his robes washed in the blood of the Lamb must come up through great tribulation [see Revelation 7:13–14], even the greatest of all affliction."[3]

"The destinies of all people are in the hands of a just God, and He will do no injustice to any one; and this one thing is sure, that they who will live godly in Christ Jesus, shall suffer persecution [see 2 Timothy 3:12]; and before their robes are made white in the blood of the Lamb, it is to be expected, according to John the Revelator, they will pass through great tribulation [see Revelation 7:13–14]."[4]

"Men have to suffer that they may come upon Mount Zion and be exalted above the heavens."[5]

While suffering greatly during his imprisonment in Liberty Jail during the winter of 1838–39, Joseph Smith wrote to members of the Church: "Beloved brethren, we say unto you, that inasmuch as God hath said that He would have a tried people, that He would purge them as gold [see Malachi 3:3], now we think that this time He has chosen His own crucible, wherein we have been tried; and we think if we get through with any degree of safety, and shall have kept the faith, that it will be a sign to this generation, altogether sufficient to leave them without excuse; and we think also, it will be a trial of our faith equal to that of Abraham, and that the ancients will not have whereof to boast over us in the day of judgment, as being called to pass through heavier afflictions; that we may hold an even weight in the balance with them."[6]

"Trials will only give us the knowledge necessary to understand the minds of the ancients. For my part, I think I never could have felt as I now do, if I had not suffered the wrongs that

I have suffered. All things shall work together for good to them that love God [see Romans 8:28]."[7]

John Taylor

John Taylor, the third President of the Church, said: "I heard the Prophet Joseph say, in speaking to the Twelve on one occasion: 'You will have all kinds of trials to pass through. And it is quite as necessary for you to be tried as it was for Abraham and other men of God, and (said he) God will feel after you, and He will take hold of you and wrench your very heart strings, and if you cannot stand it you will not be fit for an inheritance in the Celestial Kingdom of God.' . . . Joseph Smith never had many months of peace after he received the truth, and finally he was murdered in Carthage jail."[8]

God will support and bless those who trust Him in their times of trial.

"The power of the Gospel will enable us to stand and bear with patience the great affliction that is falling upon us on all sides. . . . The harder the persecution the greater the gifts of God upon his church. Yea, all things shall work together for good to them who are willing to lay down their lives for Christ's sake."[9]

"My only hope and confidence is in that God who gave me being, in whom there is all power, who now is present before me, and my heart is naked before his eyes continually. He is my comforter, and he forsaketh me not."[10]

"I know in whom I trust; I stand upon the rock; the floods cannot, no, they shall not, overthrow me."[11]

After the Prophet was delivered from his imprisonment in Liberty Jail, he said the following about his experience: "Thank God, we have been delivered. And although some of our beloved brethren have had to seal their testimony with their blood, and have died martyrs to the cause of truth—

"Short though bitter was their pain,
Everlasting is their joy.

"Let us not sorrow as 'those without hope' [see 1 Thessalonians 4:13]; the time is fast approaching when we shall see them again and rejoice together, without being afraid of wicked men. Yes, those who have slept in Christ, shall He bring with Him, when He shall come to be glorified in His Saints, and admired by all those who believe, but to take vengeance upon His enemies and all those who obey not the Gospel.

"At that time the hearts of the widows and fatherless shall be comforted, and every tear shall be wiped from their faces. The trials they have had to pass through shall work together for their good, and prepare them for the society of those who have come up out of great tribulation, and have washed their robes and made them white in the blood of the Lamb. [See Romans 8:28; Revelation 7:13–14, 17.]"[12]

The Prophet wrote the following in a letter to the Saints on September 1, 1842, later recorded in Doctrine and Covenants 127:2: "And as for the perils which I am called to pass through, they seem but a small thing to me, as the envy and wrath of man have been my common lot all the days of my life. . . . Deep water is what I am wont to swim in. It all has become a second nature to me; and I feel, like Paul, to glory in tribulation; for to this day has the God of my fathers delivered me out of them all, and will deliver me from henceforth; for behold, and lo, I shall triumph over all my enemies, for the Lord God hath spoken it."[13]

The faithful do not murmur in affliction, but are thankful for God's goodness.

On December 5, 1833, the Prophet wrote to Church leaders presiding over the Saints who were being persecuted in Missouri: "Remember not to murmur at the dealings of God with His creatures. You are not as yet brought into as trying circumstances as were the ancient Prophets and Apostles. Call to mind a Daniel, the three Hebrew children [Shadrach, Meshach, and Abednego], Jeremiah, Paul, Stephen, and many others, too numerous to mention, who were stoned, sawn asunder, tempted, slain with the sword, and [who] wandered about in sheep skins and goat skins, being destitute, afflicted, tormented, of whom the world was not worthy. They wandered in deserts and in mountains, and hid in dens and caves of the earth; yet they all obtained a good report through faith [see Hebrews 11:37–39]; and amidst all their afflictions they rejoiced that they were counted worthy to receive persecutions for Christ's sake.

"We know not what we shall be called to pass through before Zion is delivered and established; therefore, we have great need to live near to God, and always to be in strict obedience to all His commandments, that we may have a conscience void of offense toward God and man. . . .

". . . Our trust is in God, and we are determined, His grace assisting us, to maintain the cause and hold out faithful unto the end, that we may be crowned with crowns of celestial glory, and enter into the rest that is prepared for the children of God."[14]

Five days later, the Prophet wrote to Church leaders and Saints in Missouri: "Let us be thankful that it is as well with us as it is, and we are yet alive and peradventure, God hath laid up in store great good for us in this generation, and may grant that we may yet glorify His name. I feel thankful that there have no more denied the faith; I pray God in the name of Jesus that you all may be kept in the faith unto the end."[15]

The Prophet's journal for January 1, 1836, records: "This being the beginning of a new year, my heart is filled with gratitude to God that He has preserved my life, and the lives of my family, while another year has passed away. We have been sustained and upheld in the midst of a wicked and perverse generation, although exposed to all the afflictions, temptations, and misery that are incident to human life; for this I feel to humble myself in dust and ashes, as it were, before the Lord."[16]

About his recovery from an illness in June 1837, the Prophet said: "This is one of the many instances in which I have suddenly been brought from a state of health, to the borders of the grave, and as suddenly restored, for which my heart swells with gratitude to my heavenly Father, and I feel renewedly to dedicate myself and all my powers to His service."[17]

"Our trust is in God, and we are determined, His grace assisting us, to maintain the cause and hold out faithful unto the end."

Confidence in God's power, wisdom, and love will help us avoid discouragement in times of trial.

"All difficulties which might and would cross our way must be surmounted. Though the soul be tried, the heart faint, and the hands hang down, we must not retrace our steps; there must be decision of character."[18]

"Having confidence in the power, wisdom, and love of God, the Saints have been enabled to go forward through the most adverse circumstances, and frequently, when to all human appearances, nothing but death presented itself, and destruction [seemed] inevitable, has the power of God been manifest, His glory revealed, and deliverance effected; and the Saints, like the children of Israel, who came out of the land of Egypt, and through the Red Sea, have sung an anthem of praise to his holy name."[19]

"I know that the cloud will burst, and Satan's kingdom be laid in ruins, with all his black designs; and that the Saints will come forth like gold seven times tried in the fire, being made perfect through sufferings and temptations, and that the blessings of heaven and earth will be multiplied upon their heads; which may God grant for Christ's sake."[20]

"Stand fast, ye Saints of God, hold on a little while longer, and the storm of life will be past, and you will be rewarded by that God whose servants you are, and who will duly appreciate all your toils and afflictions for Christ's sake and the Gospel's. Your names will be handed down to posterity as Saints of God."[21]

George A. Smith, who served as a counselor to President Brigham Young, received the following counsel from the Prophet Joseph Smith at a time of great difficulty: "He told me I should never get discouraged, whatever difficulties might surround me. If I was sunk in the lowest pit of Nova Scotia and all the Rocky Mountains piled on top of me, I ought not to be discouraged but hang on, exercise faith, and keep up good courage and I should come out on the top of the heap at last."[22]

Just a few days before the Prophet was martyred, at a time when he and the Saints knew that his life was in danger, Joseph took the hand of Abraham C. Hodge and said: "Now, Brother Hodge, let what will, come; don't deny the faith, and all will be well."[23]

Suggestions for Study and Teaching

Consider these ideas as you study the chapter or as you prepare to teach. For additional help, see pages vii–xii.

- Review the account on pages 227–29. Why do you think the Prophet Joseph Smith was able to endure the trials he experienced? What are your thoughts or feelings as you picture him with his "flesh all scarified and defaced," teaching a congregation?
- Read the third paragraph on page 230. How do you think suffering helps us prepare for exaltation? (For some examples, see pages 230–31.) What have you learned from your trials?
- Three times in this chapter, Joseph Smith assures us that "the trials [we] have had to pass through shall work together for [our] good" (page 232; see also page 231). How have you seen the truth of this statement?

- Read the third and fourth full paragraphs on page 231. What experiences can you share in which the Lord has comforted you in times of trial? What does it mean to you to "stand upon the rock"?
- Joseph Smith counseled the Saints not to murmur, or complain, about God's dealings with us (pages 232–33). In what ways can murmuring affect us? What are some ways we should respond to trials? (For some examples, see pages 232–35.)
- What does it mean to have "decision of character" when facing difficulties? (page 234).
- Read the Prophet's counsel to George A. Smith (page 235). How might this counsel help you when you face trials?

Related Scriptures: Psalm 55:22; John 16:33; Alma 36:3; Helaman 5:12; D&C 58:2–4; 90:24; 122:5–9

Notes

1. *History of the Church,* 1:261–64; italics deleted; from "History of the Church" (manuscript), book A-1, pp. 205–8, Church Archives, The Church of Jesus Christ of Latter-day Saints, Salt Lake City, Utah.
2. Wilford Woodruff, *Deseret News: Semi-Weekly,* Oct. 18, 1881, p. 1; punctuation and capitalization modernized.
3. Letter from Joseph Smith to William W. Phelps and others, Aug. 18, 1833, Kirtland, Ohio; Joseph Smith, Collection, Church Archives.
4. *History of the Church,* 1:449; from a letter from Joseph Smith to Edward Partridge and others, Dec. 5, 1833, Kirtland, Ohio.
5. *History of the Church,* 5:556; from a discourse given by Joseph Smith on Aug. 27, 1843, in Nauvoo, Illinois; reported by Willard Richards and William Clayton.
6. *History of the Church,* 3:294; from a letter from Joseph Smith and others to Edward Partridge and the Church, Mar. 20, 1839, Liberty Jail, Liberty, Missouri.
7. *History of the Church,* 3:286; from a letter from Joseph Smith to Presendia Huntington Buell, Mar. 15, 1839, Liberty Jail, Liberty, Missouri; Sister Buell's last name is incorrectly spelled "Bull" in *History of the Church.*
8. John Taylor, *Deseret News: Semi-Weekly,* Aug. 21, 1883, p. 1.
9. Letter from Joseph Smith to William W. Phelps and others, Aug. 18, 1833, Kirtland, Ohio; Joseph Smith, Collection, Church Archives.
10. Letter from Joseph Smith to William W. Phelps, July 31, 1832, Hiram, Ohio; Joseph Smith, Collection, Church Archives.
11. *History of the Church,* 2:343; from a letter from Joseph Smith to William Smith, Dec. 18, 1835, Kirtland, Ohio.
12. *History of the Church,* 3:330–31; punctuation modernized; from "Extract, from the Private Journal of Joseph Smith Jr.," *Times and Seasons,* Nov. 1839, p. 8.
13. Doctrine and Covenants 127:2; a letter from Joseph Smith to the Saints, Sept. 1, 1842, Nauvoo, Illinois.
14. *History of the Church,* 1:450; from a letter from Joseph Smith to Edward Partridge and others, Dec. 5, 1833, Kirtland, Ohio.

15. *History of the Church,* 1:455; paragraph divisions altered; from a letter from Joseph Smith to Edward Partridge and others, Dec. 10, 1833, Kirtland, Ohio.
16. *History of the Church,* 2:352; from a Joseph Smith journal entry, Jan. 1, 1836, Kirtland, Ohio.
17. *History of the Church,* 2:493; from "History of the Church" (manuscript), book B-1, pp. 762–63, Church Archives.
18. *History of the Church,* 4:570; from a discourse given by Joseph Smith on Mar. 30, 1842, in Nauvoo, Illinois; reported by Eliza R. Snow.
19. *History of the Church,* 4:185; from a letter from Joseph Smith and his counselors in the First Presidency to the Saints, Sept. 1840, Nauvoo, Illinois, published in *Times and Seasons,* Oct. 1840, p. 178.
20. *History of the Church,* 2:353; from a Joseph Smith journal entry, Jan. 1, 1836, Kirtland, Ohio.
21. *History of the Church,* 4:337; from a report from Joseph Smith and his counselors in the First Presidency, Apr. 7, 1841, Nauvoo, Illinois, published in *Times and Seasons,* Apr. 15, 1841, p. 385.
22. George A. Smith, "History of George Albert Smith by Himself," p. 49, George Albert Smith, Papers, 1834–75, Church Archives.
23. *History of the Church,* 6:546; punctuation modernized; from "History of the Church" (manuscript), book F-1, p. 147, Church Archives.

The Prophet's many responsibilities, as well as the persecutions he faced, often took him away from his family. While he and his brother Hyrum were imprisoned in Liberty Jail, the Prophet's wife, Emma, and their son Joseph came to visit him.

CHAPTER 20

A Heart Full of Love and Faith: The Prophet's Letters to His Family

"Remember that I am a true and faithful friend to you and the children forever. My heart is entwined around yours forever and ever. Oh, may God bless you all."

From the Life of Joseph Smith

In his prophetic calling, Joseph Smith was required to travel extensively to meet the needs of a rapidly expanding organization. After he identified Independence, Missouri, as the place for the building of Zion in the summer of 1831, the Church grew quickly there, as it continued to do in Kirtland, Ohio. From 1831 to 1838, the Church had two centers of population, one in Missouri and the other in Kirtland, where the Prophet lived. During this period, the Prophet made the arduous 900-mile journey to Missouri five times to oversee the development of the Church there.

In 1833 and again in 1837, Joseph Smith visited Upper Canada, teaching the gospel and strengthening branches. In 1834 and 1835, he traveled to Michigan to visit Church members. Over a period of years, he preached the gospel and conducted Church business in Springfield, Illinois; Boston and Salem, Massachusetts; Monmouth County, New Jersey; New York City and Albany, New York; Cincinnati, Ohio; Philadelphia, Pennsylvania; Washington, D.C.; and various other locations.

The Prophet's travels took him frequently away from his home and family, as did the persecutions he repeatedly faced. He was unjustly arrested and imprisoned numerous times, and he was the victim of dozens of unfounded lawsuits. For example, on July 27, 1837, the Prophet and several other Church leaders left

Kirtland to visit the Saints in Canada. When they reached Painesville, Ohio, they were "detained all day by malicious and vexatious lawsuits." Since they were not far from Kirtland, they started for home in order to rest and then begin their journey again the next day. "About sunset I got into my carriage to return home to Kirtland," the Prophet wrote. "At this moment the sheriff sprang into the carriage, seized my lines, and served another writ on me."[1]

The Prophet's many absences from home were a severe trial to him and to his family. His letters to Emma reveal the loneliness he experienced and the longing he felt for her and for their children. He wrote continually of his great love for his family and his faith in God. He also gave heartening assurances to his family, expressing optimism for the future in spite of the adversities they faced.

On April 1, 1832, the Prophet left home for his second journey to Missouri, only a week after he had been tarred and feathered by a mob and just two days after his adopted son had died. Surely his heart would have been heavy with sadness and concern for his wife, Emma, and for his only living child, Julia. While he was returning home the following month, anxious to rejoin his family, he was detained for several weeks in Greenville, Indiana. Bishop Newel K. Whitney, one of the Prophet's traveling companions, had severely injured his leg in a stagecoach accident and needed to convalesce before he could travel. During this time, the Prophet was poisoned in some manner, causing him to vomit so violently that he dislocated his jaw. He made his way to Bishop Whitney, who, though still bedridden, gave Joseph a priesthood blessing. The Prophet was immediately healed.

Shortly after this experience, the Prophet penned these lines to his wife: "Brother Martin [Harris] has arrived here and brought the pleasing news that our families were well when he left there, which greatly cheered our hearts and revived our spirits. We thank our Heavenly Father for his goodness unto us and all of you. . . . My situation is a very unpleasant one, although I will endeavor to be contented, the Lord assisting me. . . . I should like to see little Julia and once more take her on my knee and converse with you. . . . I subscribe myself your husband. The Lord bless you, peace be with you, so farewell until I return."[2]

Teachings of Joseph Smith

Family members pray for, comfort, and strengthen one another.

To Emma Smith on October 13, 1832, from New York City, New York: "This day I have been walking through the most splendid part of the city of New York. The buildings are truly great and wonderful, to the astonishing of every beholder. . . . After beholding all that I had any desire to behold, I returned to my room to meditate and calm my mind; and behold, the thoughts of home, of Emma and Julia, rush upon my mind like a flood and I could wish for a moment to be with them. My breast is filled with all the feelings and tenderness of a parent and a husband, and could I be with you I would tell you many things. . . .

"I feel as if I wanted to say something to you to comfort you in your peculiar trial and present affliction [Emma was pregnant at the time]. I hope God will give you strength that you may not faint. I pray God to soften the hearts of those around you to be kind to you and take the burden off your shoulders as much as possible and not afflict you. I feel for you, for I know your state and that others do not, but you must comfort yourself knowing that God is your friend in heaven and that you have one true and living friend on earth, your husband."[3]

To Emma Smith on November 12, 1838, from Richmond, Missouri, where he was being held prisoner: "I received your letter, which I read over and over again; it was a sweet morsel to me. O God, grant that I may have the privilege of seeing once more my lovely family in the enjoyment of the sweets of liberty and social life. To press them to my bosom and kiss their lovely cheeks would fill my heart with unspeakable gratitude. Tell the children that I am alive and trust I shall come and see them before long. Comfort their hearts all you can, and try to be comforted yourself all you can. . . .

"P.S. Write as often as you can, and if possible come and see me, and bring the children if possible. Act according to your own feelings and best judgment, and endeavor to be comforted, if possible, and I trust that all will turn out for the best."[4]

To Emma Smith on April 4, 1839, from the jail in Liberty, Missouri: "My dear Emma, I think of you and the children continually. . . . I want to see little Frederick, Joseph, Julia, and Alexander, Johanna [an orphan who was living with the Smiths], and old Major [the family dog]. And as to yourself, if you want to know how much I want to see you, examine your feelings, how much you want to see me, and judge for yourself. I would gladly walk from here to you barefoot and bareheaded and half-naked to see you and think it great pleasure, and never count it toil. . . . I bear with fortitude all my oppression; so do those that are with me. Not one of us has flinched yet."[5]

To Emma Smith on January 20, 1840, from Chester County, Pennsylvania: "I feel very anxious to see you all once more in this world. The time seems long that I am deprived of your society, but the Lord being my helper, I will not be much longer. . . . I am filled with constant anxiety and shall be until I get home. I pray God to spare you all until I get home. My dear Emma, my heart is entwined around you and those little ones. I want you to remember me. Tell all the children that I love them and will come home as soon as I can. Yours in the bonds of love, your husband."[6]

The responsibility to teach our children is always with us.

To Emma Smith on November 12, 1838, from Richmond, Missouri, where he was being held prisoner: "Tell little Joseph he must be a good boy; Father loves him with a perfect love. He is the eldest and must not hurt those that are smaller than him, but comfort them. Tell little Frederick Father loves him with all his heart; he is a lovely boy. Julia is a lovely little girl. I love her also. She is a promising child. Tell her Father wants her to remember him and be a good girl. Tell all the rest that I think of them and pray for them all. . . . Little Alexander is on my mind continually. O my affectionate Emma, I want you to remember that I am a true and faithful friend to you and the children forever. My heart is entwined around yours forever and ever. Oh, may God bless you all, amen. I am your husband and am in bands and tribulation."[7]

To Emma Smith on April 4, 1839, from the jail in Liberty, Missouri: "I want you should not let those little fellows forget me.

Tell them Father loves them with a perfect love, and he is doing all he can to get away from the mob to come to them. Do teach [the children] all you can, that they may have good minds. Be tender and kind to them; don't be fractious to them, but listen to their wants. Tell them Father says they must be good children and mind their mother. My dear Emma, there is great responsibility resting upon you in preserving yourself in honor and sobriety before them and teaching them right things, to form their young and tender minds that they begin in right paths and not get contaminated when young by seeing ungodly examples."[8]

To Emma Smith on November 9, 1839, from Springfield, Illinois: "I shall be filled with constant anxiety about you and the children until I hear from you and, in a particular manner, little Frederick. It was so painful to leave him sick. I hope you will watch over those tender offspring in a manner that is becoming a mother and a saint and try to cultivate their minds and [teach] them to read and be sober. Do not let them be exposed to the weather to take cold, and try to get all the rest you can. It will be a long and lonesome time during my absence from you. . . . Be patient until I come, and do the best you can. I cannot write what I want but believe me, my feelings are of the best kind towards you all."[9]

God is our friend, and we can trust Him in our times of adversity.

To Emma Smith on June 6, 1832, from Greenville, Indiana: "I have visited a grove which is just back of the town almost every day, where I can be secluded from the eyes of any mortal and there give vent to all the feelings of my heart in meditation and prayer. I have called to mind all the past moments of my life and am left to mourn and shed tears of sorrow for my folly in suffering the adversary of my soul to have so much power over me as he has had in times past. But God is merciful and has forgiven my sins, and I rejoice that he sendeth forth the Comforter unto as many as believe and humble themselves before him. . . .

"I will try to be contented with my lot, knowing that God is my friend. In him I shall find comfort. I have given my life into his

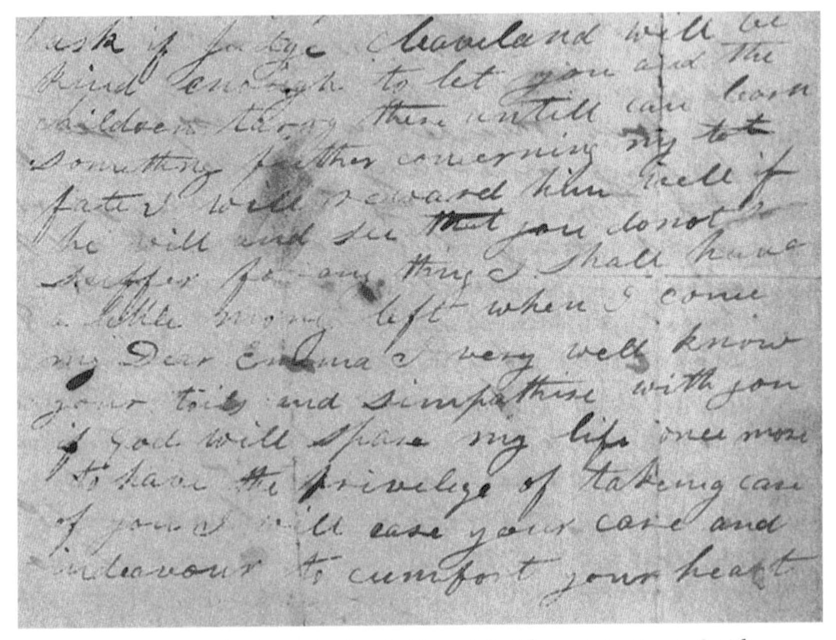
bask if Judge Cleaveland will be
kind enough to let you and the
children tarry there untill we can learn
something farther concerning my fat
fate I will reward him well if
he will and see that you donot
suffer for any thing I shall have
a little money left when I come
my Dear Emma I very well know
your toils and simpathise with you
if God will spare my life once more
to have the privelege of takeing care
of you I will ease your care and
indeavour to cumfort your heart

A portion of the letter the Prophet Joseph Smith wrote to Emma Smith from Liberty Jail on March 21, 1839.

hands. I am prepared to go at his call. I desire to be with Christ. I count not my life dear to me [except] to do his will."[10]

To Emma Smith on June 4, 1834, from the banks of the Mississippi River in western Illinois; the Prophet Joseph was traveling with Zion's Camp: "Every now and then our thoughts linger with inexpressible anxiety for our wives and our children—our kindred according to the flesh who are entwined around our hearts—and also our brethren and friends. . . . Tell Father Smith and all the family and brother Oliver [Cowdery] to be comforted and look forward to the day when the trials and tribulations of this life will be at an end, and we [will] all enjoy the fruits of our labor if we hold out faithful to the end, which I pray may be the happy lot of us all."[11]

To Emma Smith on November 4, 1838, from Independence, Missouri, where he was being held prisoner: "My dear and beloved companion of my bosom in tribulation and affliction, I would inform you that I am well and that we are all of us in good spirits as regards our own fate. . . . I have great anxiety about you and my lovely children. My heart mourns and bleeds for the brethren and sisters and for the slain of the people of God. . . . What God may do for us I do not know, but I hope for the best always in all circumstances. Although I go unto death, I will trust in God. What outrages may be committed by the mob I know not, but expect there will be but little or no restraint. Oh, may God have mercy on us. . . . God has spared some of us thus far; perhaps he will extend mercy in some degree toward us yet. . . .

"I cannot learn much for certainty in the situation that I am in, and can only pray for deliverance until it is meted out and take everything as it comes with patience and fortitude. I hope you will be faithful and true to every trust. I can't write much in my situation. Conduct all matters as your circumstances and necessities require. May God give you wisdom and prudence and sobriety, which I have every reason to believe you will [have].

"Those little children are subjects of my meditation continually. Tell them that Father is yet alive. God grant that he may see them again. O Emma, . . . do not forsake me nor the truth, but remember me; if I do not meet you again in this life, may God grant that we may meet in heaven. I cannot express my feelings; my heart is full. Farewell, O my kind and affectionate Emma. I am yours forever, your husband and true friend."[12]

To Emma Smith on March 21, 1839, from the jail in Liberty, Missouri: "My dear Emma, I very well know your toils and sympathize with you. If God will spare my life once more to have the privilege of taking care of you, I will ease your care and endeavor to comfort your heart. I want you to take the best care of the family you can. I believe you will do all you can. I was sorry to learn that Frederick was sick, but I trust he is well again and that you are all well. I want you to try to gain time and write to me a long letter and tell me all you can and even if old Major is alive yet and what those little prattlers say that cling around your neck. . . . Tell them I am in prison that their lives might be saved. . . .

"God ruleth all things after the counsel of his own will. My trust is in him. The salvation of my soul is of the most importance to me forasmuch as I know for a certainty of eternal things. If the heavens linger, it is nothing to me. I must steer my [ship] safe, which I intend to do. I want you to do the same. Yours forever."[13]

To Emma Smith on August 16, 1842, near Nauvoo, Illinois; the Prophet Joseph was hiding from his enemies: "I take the liberty to tender you my sincere thanks for the two interesting and consoling visits that you have made me during my almost exiled situation. Tongue cannot express the gratitude of my heart, for the warm and true-hearted friendship you have manifested in these things towards me. The time has passed away, since you left me, very agreeably thus far; my mind being perfectly reconciled to my fate, let it be what it may. . . .

"Tell the children it is well with their father as yet; and that he remains in fervent prayer to Almighty God for the safety of himself, and for you, and for them. Tell Mother Smith that it shall be well with her son, whether in life or in death; for thus saith the Lord God. Tell her that I remember her all the while, as well as Lucy [Joseph's sister], and all the rest. They all must be of good cheer. . . . Yours in haste, your affectionate husband until death, through all eternity; for evermore."[14]

Suggestions for Study and Teaching

Consider these ideas as you study the chapter or as you prepare to teach. For additional help, see pages vii–xii.

- Briefly review this chapter, noting Joseph Smith's feelings toward Emma and their children. What does his example teach about how we should speak and act in our families? What can we learn from Joseph and Emma Smith's efforts to write to one another and to see one another? What are some things you have done to show family members that you love them?
- The Prophet Joseph told Emma that he was "a true and faithful friend to [her] and the children forever," and he thanked her for her "warm and true-hearted friendship" (pages 242, 246). What can husbands and wives do to nurture their friendship?
- In his letters, Joseph Smith showed trust in Emma, expressing confidence that she would make good decisions and do all she could to take care of the family (page 245). How might such expressions of trust influence the relationship between a husband and a wife?

- Read the Prophet Joseph's message to his children in the second paragraph on page 246. How might it have helped his children to receive this news? During times of trial, what can parents do to show their children that they have faith in God?
- Review Joseph Smith's expressions of trust in God found on pages 243–46. Identify several of these expressions that are particularly touching to you. How can you apply these truths in your life?

Related Scriptures: Genesis 2:24; 1 Corinthians 11:11; Ephesians 5:25; Mosiah 4:14–15; D&C 25:5, 9, 14; 68:25–28

Notes

1. *History of the Church,* 2:502; spelling modernized; from "History of the Church" (manuscript), book B-1, p. 767, and addenda, p. 6, Church Archives, The Church of Jesus Christ of Latter-day Saints, Salt Lake City, Utah.
2. Letter from Joseph Smith to Emma Smith, June 6, 1832, Greenville, Indiana; Chicago Historical Society, Chicago, Illinois.
3. Letter from Joseph Smith to Emma Smith, Oct. 13, 1832, New York City, New York; Community of Christ Archives, Independence, Missouri.
4. Letter from Joseph Smith to Emma Smith, Nov. 12, 1838, Richmond, Missouri; Community of Christ Archives, Independence, Missouri.
5. Letter from Joseph Smith to Emma Smith, Apr. 4, 1839, Liberty Jail, Liberty, Missouri; Beinecke Library, Yale University, New Haven, Connecticut; copy in Church Archives. Johanna's full name was Johanna Carter; she was the orphaned daughter of John S. and Elizabeth Kenyon Carter.
6. Letter from Joseph Smith to Emma Smith, Jan. 20, 1840, Chester County, Pennsylvania; Chicago Historical Society, Chicago, Illinois.
7. Letter from Joseph Smith to Emma Smith, Nov. 12, 1838, Richmond, Missouri; Community of Christ Archives, Independence, Missouri.
8. Letter from Joseph Smith to Emma Smith, Apr. 4, 1839, Liberty Jail, Liberty, Missouri; Beinecke Library, Yale University, New Haven, Connecticut; copy in Church Archives.
9. Letter from Joseph Smith to Emma Smith, Nov. 9, 1839, Springfield, Illinois; Community of Christ Archives, Independence, Missouri; copy in Church Archives.
10. Letter from Joseph Smith to Emma Smith, June 6, 1832, Greenville, Indiana; Chicago Historical Society, Chicago, Illinois.
11. Letter from Joseph Smith to Emma Smith, June 4, 1834, from the banks of the Mississippi River in western Illinois; Letter Book 2, 1837–43, p. 58, Joseph Smith, Collection, Church Archives.
12. Letter from Joseph Smith to Emma Smith, Nov. 4, 1838, Independence, Missouri; Community of Christ Archives, Independence, Missouri; copy in Church Archives.
13. Letter from Joseph Smith to Emma Smith, Mar. 21, 1839, Liberty Jail, Liberty, Missouri; Joseph Smith, Collection, Church Archives.
14. *History of the Church,* 5:103, 105; paragraph divisions altered; from a letter from Joseph Smith to Emma Smith, Aug. 16, 1842, near Nauvoo, Illinois.

An upstairs room in the restored Newel K. Whitney store.
Joseph and Emma Smith lived in this store for more than a year, and the Prophet received many revelations here, including revelations about the coming of the Lord.

CHAPTER 21

The Second Coming and the Millennium

"We shall . . . do well to discern the signs of the times as we pass along, that the day of the Lord may not 'overtake us as a thief in the night.' "

From the Life of Joseph Smith

In September 1832, Joseph and Emma Smith and their sixteen-month-old daughter, Julia, moved from the Johnson farm in Hiram, Ohio, back to Kirtland. There they moved into the general store owned by Newel K. Whitney, where they would live for more than a year. The Smith family lived on the second floor of the store and part of the first floor that was not used for business. Joseph and Emma's son, Joseph Smith III, was born while the family lived in this store. The Prophet also received many revelations there.

One such revelation came on Christmas Day in 1832. The Prophet spent part of this day at home, deep in contemplation about the serious problems facing the nations of the world at that time. "Appearances of troubles among the nations became more visible this season than they had previously been since the Church began her journey out of the wilderness," the Prophet said.[1] Events in the United States were leading toward civil war, and outbreaks of deadly diseases were widespread throughout the world. While "praying earnestly on the subject,"[2] the Prophet received the revelation now found in section 87 of the Doctrine and Covenants. The Lord revealed to Joseph that before the Second Coming, war would be poured out upon all the nations and natural calamities would chasten the people:

"With the sword and by bloodshed the inhabitants of the earth shall mourn; and with famine, and plague, and earthquake, and the thunder of heaven, and the fierce and vivid lightning also, shall the inhabitants of the earth be made to feel the wrath, and indignation, and chastening hand of an Almighty God, until the consumption decreed hath made a full end of all nations. . . . Wherefore, stand ye in holy places, and be not moved, until the day of the Lord come; for behold, it cometh quickly, saith the Lord" (D&C 87:6, 8).

Two days later, on December 27, the Prophet received another revelation that contained much information about the Second Coming. On that day, a conference of high priests had gathered in the Prophet's "translating room," the room in the Whitney store where Joseph did much of his work on the Joseph Smith Translation of the Bible. The minutes of the conference record: "Brother Joseph arose and said, to receive revelation and the blessings of heaven it was necessary to have our minds on God and exercise faith and become of one heart and of one mind. Therefore he recommended all present to pray separately and vocally to the Lord for [Him] to reveal His will unto us concerning the upbuilding of Zion and for the benefit of the Saints."

Each high priest "bowed down before the Lord" and then spoke of his feelings and determination to keep the commandments of God.[3] Shortly thereafter, the Prophet began to receive the revelation from God that would later become section 88 of the Doctrine and Covenants. This revelation contains some of the scriptures' most detailed prophecies about the coming of the Lord and the establishment of a thousand-year period of peace (see D&C 88:86–116).

Through the Prophet Joseph Smith, the Lord revealed many prophecies concerning the Second Coming, the Millennium, and the turbulent time that will precede these events. This great outpouring of revelation is a testimony that Joseph Smith was truly a seer raised up by God. As the Book of Mormon testifies, "A seer can know of things which are past, and also of things which are to come, and by [him] shall all things be revealed, or, rather, shall secret things be made manifest, and hidden things shall come to light, and things which are not known shall be made known" (Mosiah 8:17).

Teachings of Joseph Smith

The signs of the Savior's coming are being fulfilled; the faithful will recognize these signs and have peace in perilous times.

"We shall . . . do well to discern the signs of the times as we pass along, that the day of the Lord may not 'overtake us as a thief in the night.' [See D&C 106:4–5.]"[4]

"I will prophesy that the signs of the coming of the Son of Man are already commenced. One pestilence will desolate after another. We shall soon have war and bloodshed. The moon will be turned into blood. I testify of these things, and that the coming of the Son of Man is nigh, even at your doors. If our souls and our bodies are not looking forth for the coming of the Son of Man; and after we are dead, if we are not looking forth, we shall be among those who are calling for the rocks to fall upon them [see Revelation 6:15–17]."[5]

"Dearly and beloved brethren, we see that perilous times have come, as was testified of [see 2 Timothy 3:1]. We may look, then, with most perfect assurance, for the fulfillment of all those things that have been written, and with more confidence than ever before, lift up our eyes to the luminary of day, and say in our hearts, Soon thou wilt veil thy blushing face. He that said, 'Let there be light,' and there was light [see Genesis 1:3], hath spoken this word. And again, Thou moon, thou dimmer light, thou luminary of night, shalt turn to blood.

"We see that everything is being fulfilled; and that the time shall soon come when the Son of Man shall descend in the clouds of heaven."[6]

"The earth will soon be reaped—that is, the wicked must soon be destroyed from off the face of the earth, for the Lord hath spoken it, and who can stay the hand of the Lord, or who is there that can measure arms with the Almighty, for at his commands the heavens and the earth must pass away. The day is fast hastening on when the restoration of all things shall be fulfilled, which all the holy prophets have prophesied of, even unto the gathering in of the house of Israel. Then shall come to pass that the lion shall lie down with the lamb, etc.

"But, brethren, be not discouraged when we tell you of perilous times, for they must shortly come, for the sword, famine, and pestilence are approaching. There shall be great destructions upon the face of this land, for ye need not suppose that one jot or tittle of the prophecies of all the holy prophets shall fail, and there are many that remain to be fulfilled yet. The Lord hath said that a short work will he make of it, and the righteous shall be saved if it be as by fire [see Romans 9:28; 1 Nephi 22:17]."[7]

"The scripture is ready to be fulfilled when great wars, famines, pestilence, great distress, judgments, etc., are ready to be poured out on the inhabitants of the earth."[8]

"We see that perilous times have truly come, and the things which we have so long expected have at last begun to usher in; but when you see the fig tree begin to put forth its leaves, you may know that the summer is nigh at hand [see Matthew 24:32–33]. There will be a short work on the earth. It has now commenced. I suppose there will soon be perplexity all over the earth. Do not let our hearts faint when these things come upon us, for they must come, or the word cannot be fulfilled."[9]

"I have asked of the Lord concerning His coming; and while asking the Lord, He gave a sign and said, 'In the days of Noah I set a bow in the heavens as a sign and token that in any year that the bow should be seen the Lord would not come; but there should be seed time and harvest during that year: but whenever you see the bow withdrawn, it shall be a token that there shall be famine, pestilence, and great distress among the nations, and that the coming of the Messiah is not far distant.' "[10]

"Judah must return, Jerusalem must be rebuilt, and the temple, and water come out from under the temple, and the waters of the Dead Sea be healed [see Ezekiel 47:1–9]. It will take some time to rebuild the walls of the city and the temple, etc.; and all this must be done before the Son of Man will make His appearance. There will be wars and rumors of wars, signs in the heavens above and on the earth beneath, the sun turned into darkness and the moon to blood, earthquakes in divers places, the seas heaving beyond their bounds; then will appear one grand sign of the Son of Man in heaven. But what will the world do? They will say it is a planet, a comet, etc. But the Son of Man will come as the sign of the coming of the Son of Man, which will be as the light of the morning cometh out of the east [see Joseph Smith—Matthew 1:26]."[11]

"[I] explained concerning the coming of the Son of Man; also that it is a false idea that the Saints will escape all the judgments, whilst the wicked suffer; for all flesh is subject to suffer, and 'the righteous shall hardly escape' [see D&C 63:34]; still many of the Saints will escape, for the just shall live by faith [see Habakkuk 2:4]; yet many of the righteous shall fall a prey to disease, to pestilence, etc., by reason of the weakness of the flesh, and yet be saved in the Kingdom of God. So that it is an unhallowed principle to say that such and such have transgressed because they have been preyed upon by disease or death, for all flesh is subject to death; and the Savior has said, 'Judge not, lest ye be judged.' [See Matthew 7:1.]"[12]

The Lord will not come until all things are fulfilled in preparation for His coming.

"The coming of the Son of Man never will be—never can be till the judgments spoken of for this hour are poured out: which judgments are commenced. Paul says, 'Ye are the children of the light, and not of the darkness, that that day should overtake you as a thief in the night.' [See 1 Thessalonians 5:4–5.] It is not the design of the Almighty to come upon the earth and crush it and grind it to powder, but he will reveal it to His servants the prophets [see Amos 3:7]."[13]

"Jesus Christ never did reveal to any man the precise time that He would come [see Matthew 24:36; D&C 49:7]. Go and read the Scriptures, and you cannot find anything that specifies the exact hour He would come; and all that say so are false teachers."[14]

Regarding a man who claimed to have seen the sign of the Son of Man, the Prophet Joseph Smith said: "He has not seen the sign of the Son of Man, as foretold by Jesus; neither has any man, nor will any man, until after the sun shall have been darkened and the moon bathed in blood; for the Lord hath not shown me any such sign; and as the prophet saith, so it must be—'Surely the Lord God will do nothing, but He revealeth His secret unto His servants the prophets.' (See Amos 3:7.) Therefore hear this, O earth: The Lord will not come to reign over the righteous, in this world, in 1843, nor until everything for the Bridegroom is ready."[15]

Those who are wise and faithful will be prepared when the Lord comes again.

"When I contemplate the rapidity with which the great and glorious day of the coming of the Son of Man advances, when He shall come to receive His Saints unto Himself, where they shall dwell in His presence, and be crowned with glory and immortality; when I consider that soon the heavens are to be shaken, and the earth tremble and reel to and fro; and that the heavens are to be unfolded as a scroll when it is rolled up; and that every mountain and island are to flee away, I cry out in my heart, What manner of persons ought we to be in all holy conversation and godliness! [See 2 Peter 3:11.]"[16]

"The earth is groaning under corruption, oppression, tyranny and bloodshed; and God is coming out of His hiding place, as He said He would do, to vex the nations of the earth. Daniel, in his vision, saw convulsion upon convulsion; he 'beheld till the thrones were cast down, and the Ancient of Days did sit;' and one was brought before him like unto the Son of Man; and all nations, kindred, tongues, and people, did serve and obey Him [see Daniel 7:9–14]. It is for us to be righteous, that we may be wise and understand; for none of the wicked shall understand; but the wise shall understand, and they that turn many to righteousness shall shine as the stars for ever and ever [see Daniel 12:3]."[17]

"Let the rich and the learned, the wise and the noble, the poor and the needy, the bond and the free, both black and white, take heed to their ways, and cleave to the knowledge of God, and execute justice and judgment upon the earth in righteousness, and prepare to meet the judge of the quick and the dead, for the hour of His coming is nigh."[18]

"Let us be wise in all things, and keep all the commandments of God, that our salvation may be sure. Having our armor ready and prepared against the time appointed and having on the whole armor of righteousness, we may be able to stand in that trying day [see Ephesians 6:13]."[19]

In December 1830, the Prophet Joseph Smith said the following in a letter to members of the Church in Colesville, New York: "May you all be faithful and wait for the time of our Lord, for his appearing is nigh at hand.

" 'But [of] the time and the season, brethren, ye have no need that I write unto you, for ye yourselves perfectly know that the day of the Lord so cometh as a thief in the night: for when they shall say peace and safety, then sudden destruction cometh upon them, as travail upon a woman, but they shall not escape.

" 'But ye, brethren, are not in darkness. . . . Therefore let us not sleep as do others, but let us watch and be sober, for they that sleep, sleep in the night, and they that be drunken are drunken in the night.

" 'But let us who be of the day, be sober, putting on the breastplate of faith and love, and for a helmet, the hope of salvation. For God hath not appointed us unto wrath, but to obtain salvation through our Lord Jesus Christ.' [1 Thessalonians 5:1–4, 6–9.]

"Wherefore, comfort one another, even as ye also do, for perilous times are at hand. . . . Peace is taken from the earth in part, and it will soon be in whole; yea, destructions are at our doors, and they soon will be in the houses of the wicked, and they that know not God.

"Yea, lift up your heads and rejoice, for your redemption draweth nigh. We are the most favored people that ever have been from the foundation of the world, if we remain faithful in keeping the commandments of our God. Yea, even Enoch, the seventh from Adam, beheld our day and rejoiced [see Moses 7:65–67], and the prophets from that day forth have prophesied of the Second Coming of our Lord and Savior, Jesus Christ, and rejoiced at the day of rest of the Saints; yea, and the Apostle of our Savior also did rejoice in his appearance in a cloud with the host of heaven, to dwell with man on the earth a thousand years [see Revelation 1:7]. Therefore we have reason to rejoice.

"Behold the prophecies of the Book of Mormon are fulfilling as fast as time can bring it about. The Spirit of the living God is upon me; therefore, who will say that I shall not prophesy. The time is soon at hand that we shall have to flee whithersoever the Lord will, for safety. Fear not those who are making you an offender for a word [see Isaiah 29:20–21], but be faithful in witnessing unto a crooked and a perverse generation that the day of the coming of our Lord and Savior is at hand. Yea, prepare ye the way of the Lord, make straight his path [see Matthew 3:3].

"Who will shrink because of offenses, for offenses must come, but woe to them by whom they come, for the rock must fall on them and grind them to powder [see Matthew 18:7; 21:43–44]. For the fulness of the Gentiles is come in, and woe will be unto them if they do not repent and be baptized in the name of our Lord and Savior, Jesus Christ, for the remission of their sins, and come in at the strait gate and be numbered with the house of Israel. For God will not always be mocked, and not pour out his wrath upon those that blaspheme his holy name, for the sword, famines, and destruction will soon overtake them in their wild career, for God will avenge, and pour out his vials of wrath, and save his elect [see Revelation 16:1].

"And all those who will obey his commandments are his elect, and he will soon gather them from the four winds of heaven, from one quarter of the earth to the other [see Matthew 24:31], to a place whithersoever he will; therefore, in your patience possess ye your souls [see Luke 21:19]."[20]

The Millennium will be a time of peace when the Savior will reign over the earth.

Articles of Faith 1:10: "We believe . . . that Christ will reign personally upon the earth; and, that the earth will be renewed and receive its paradisiacal glory."[21]

"The designs of God . . . have been . . . to establish peace and good will among men; to promote the principles of eternal truth; to bring about a state of things that shall unite man to his fellow

"The day is fast hastening on when the restoration of all things shall be fulfilled. . . . Then shall come to pass that the lion shall lie down with the lamb."

man; cause the world to 'beat their swords into plowshares, and their spears into pruning hooks' [Isaiah 2:4], make the nations of the earth dwell in peace, and to bring about the millennial glory, when 'the earth shall yield its increase, resume its [paradisiacal] glory, and become as the garden of the Lord.' . . .

"It has been the design of Jehovah, from the commencement of the world, and is His purpose now, to regulate the affairs of the world in His own time, to stand as a head of the universe, and take the reins of government in His own hand. When that is done, judgment will be administered in righteousness; anarchy and confusion will be destroyed, and 'nations will learn war no more.' [See Isaiah 2:4.] . . .

". . . Moses received the word of the Lord from God Himself; he was the mouth of God to Aaron, and Aaron taught the people, in both civil and ecclesiastical affairs; they were both one, there was no distinction; so will it be when the purposes of God shall be accomplished: when 'the Lord shall be King over the whole earth,' and 'Jerusalem His throne.' 'The law shall go forth from Zion, and the word of the Lord from Jerusalem.' [See Zechariah 14:9; Jeremiah 3:17; Micah 4:2.]

". . . 'He whose right it is, will possess the kingdom, and reign until He has put all things under His feet' [see Ezekiel 21:27; 1 Corinthians 15:27]; iniquity will hide its hoary head, Satan will be bound, and the works of darkness destroyed; righteousness will be put to the line, and judgment to the plummet, and 'he that fears the Lord will alone be exalted in that day.' [See Isaiah 2:11; 28:17.]"[22]

"That Jesus will be a resident on the earth a thousand [years] with the Saints is not the case, but will reign over the Saints and come down and instruct, as he did the five hundred brethren [see 1 Corinthians 15:6], and those of the first resurrection will also reign with him over the Saints."[23]

After the Millennium, the earth will be changed into a sanctified, celestial state.

"While at dinner, I remarked to my family and friends present, that when the earth was sanctified and became like a sea of glass, it would be one great urim and thummim, and the Saints could look in it and see as they are seen."[24]

"This earth will be rolled back into the presence of God and crowned with celestial glory."[25]

"After the little season [of Satan's last rebellion] is expired and the earth undergoes its last change and is glorified, then will all the meek inherit the earth, wherein dwelleth the righteous."[26]

The Prophet taught the following on April 2, 1843, later recorded in Doctrine and Covenants 130:9: "This earth, in its sanctified and immortal state, will be made like unto crystal and will be a Urim and Thummim to the inhabitants who dwell thereon, whereby all things pertaining to an inferior kingdom, or all kingdoms of a lower order, will be manifest to those who dwell on it; and this earth will be Christ's."[27]

Suggestions for Study and Teaching

Consider these ideas as you study the chapter or as you prepare to teach. For additional help, see pages vii–xii.

- Read the first two full paragraphs on page 250, and note the high priests' preparation to receive the revelation that is now section 88 of the Doctrine and Covenants. Think about how this account applies to you in your efforts to understand the prophecies of the Second Coming.
- Read the Prophet Joseph Smith's prophecies of the perilous times before the coming of the Lord (pages 251–53). How can we remain at peace even during such trials? Why do you think we need to know and understand the signs of the Second Coming? What signs of the Second Coming have been or are being fulfilled?
- Read the second full paragraph on page 253 and the third paragraph on page 255. What does the phrase "as a thief in the night" suggest about the Lord's coming? Why do you think the day of the Lord will not overtake the children of the light as a thief in the night?
- How can we prepare for the Second Coming of the Savior? (For some examples, see pages 254–56.) Think about how you will feel to see the Savior if you are prepared for His coming. As we prepare for the Second Coming, how can we avoid feelings of fear or alarm?
- Review Joseph Smith's prophecies about the Millennium (pages 256–58). What are your thoughts and feelings as you contemplate this period of time?

Related Scriptures: Micah 4:1–7; D&C 29:9–25; 45:36–71; 88:95–98, 110–15; Joseph Smith—Matthew 1:21–55

Notes

1. *History of the Church,* 1:301; from "History of the Church" (manuscript), book A-1, p. 244, Church Archives, The Church of Jesus Christ of Latter-day Saints, Salt Lake City, Utah.
2. Doctrine and Covenants 130:13; instructions given by Joseph Smith on Apr. 2, 1843, in Ramus, Illinois.
3. Kirtland High Council, Minutes Dec. 1832–Nov. 1837, entry for Dec. 27, 1832, pp. 3–4, reported by Frederick G. Williams, Church Archives.
4. *History of the Church,* 3:331; from "Extract, from the Private Journal of Joseph Smith Jr.," *Times and Seasons,* Nov. 1839, p. 9.
5. *History of the Church,* 3:390; from a discourse given by Joseph Smith about July 1839 in Commerce, Illinois; reported by Willard Richards.
6. *History of the Church,* 3:291; punctuation modernized; from a letter from Joseph Smith and others to Edward Partridge and the Church, Mar. 20, 1839, Liberty Jail, Liberty, Missouri.

7. Letter from Joseph Smith and John Whitmer to the Saints in Colesville, New York, Aug. 20, 1830, Harmony, Pennsylvania; in Newel Knight, Autobiography and Journal, ca. 1846–47, pp. 133–36, Church Archives.
8. *History of the Church,* 6:364; from a discourse given by Joseph Smith on May 12, 1844, in Nauvoo, Illinois; reported by Thomas Bullock.
9. *History of the Church,* 3:286; from a letter from Joseph Smith to Presendia Huntington Buell, Mar. 15, 1839, Liberty Jail, Liberty, Missouri; Sister Buell's last name is incorrectly spelled "Bull" in *History of the Church.*
10. *History of the Church,* 6:254; from a discourse given by Joseph Smith on Mar. 10, 1844, in Nauvoo, Illinois; reported by Wilford Woodruff; see also appendix, page 562, item 3.
11. *History of the Church,* 5:337; from a discourse given by Joseph Smith on Apr. 6, 1843, in Nauvoo, Illinois; reported by Willard Richards.
12. *History of the Church,* 4:11; punctuation modernized; from instructions given by Joseph Smith on Sept. 29, 1839, in Commerce, Illinois; reported by James Mulholland.
13. *History of the Church,* 5:336–37; from a discourse given by Joseph Smith on Apr. 6, 1843, in Nauvoo, Illinois; reported by Willard Richards.
14. *History of the Church,* 6:254; from a discourse given by Joseph Smith on Mar. 10, 1844, in Nauvoo, Illinois; reported by Wilford Woodruff.
15. *History of the Church,* 5:291; from a letter from Joseph Smith to the editor of the *Times and Seasons,* Feb. 28, 1843, Nauvoo, Illinois, published in *Times and Seasons,* Mar. 1, 1843, p. 113.
16. *History of the Church,* 1:442; from a letter from Joseph Smith to Moses Nickerson, Nov. 19, 1833, Kirtland, Ohio.
17. *History of the Church,* 5:65; from "The Government of God," an editorial published in *Times and Seasons,* July 15, 1842, p. 857; Joseph Smith was the editor of the periodical.
18. *History of the Church,* 6:93; from Joseph Smith's appeal to the state of Vermont, Nov. 29, 1843, Nauvoo, Illinois, published as *General Joseph Smith's Appeal to the Green Mountain Boys* (1843), p. 7.
19. Letter from Joseph Smith and others to Hezekiah Peck, Aug. 31, 1835, Kirtland, Ohio; in "The Book of John Whitmer," p. 80, Community of Christ Archives, Independence, Missouri; copy of "The Book of John Whitmer" in Church Archives.
20. Letter from Joseph Smith and John Whitmer to the Saints in Colesville, New York, Dec. 2, 1830, Fayette, New York; in Newel Knight, Autobiography and Journal, ca. 1846–47, pp. 198–206, Church Archives.
21. Articles of Faith 1:10.
22. *History of the Church,* 5:61, 63–65; punctuation modernized; from "The Government of God," an editorial published in *Times and Seasons,* July 15, 1842, pp. 855–57; Joseph Smith was the editor of the periodical.
23. Quoted by William P. McIntire, reporting a discourse given by Joseph Smith in early 1841 in Nauvoo, Illinois; William Patterson McIntire, Notebook 1840–45, Church Archives.
24. *History of the Church,* 5:279; from a Joseph Smith journal entry, Feb. 18, 1843, Nauvoo, Illinois.
25. Quoted by William Clayton, reporting an undated discourse given by Joseph Smith in Nauvoo, Illinois; in L. John Nuttall, "Extracts from William Clayton's Private Book," p. 8, Journals of L. John Nuttall, 1857–1904, L. Tom Perry Special Collections, Brigham Young University, Provo, Utah; copy in Church Archives.
26. Quoted by William P. McIntire, reporting a discourse given by Joseph Smith in early 1841 in Nauvoo, Illinois; William Patterson McIntire, Notebook 1840–45, Church Archives.
27. Doctrine and Covenants 130:9; instructions given by Joseph Smith on Apr. 2, 1843, in Ramus, Illinois.

CHAPTER 22

Gaining Knowledge of Eternal Truths

"A man is saved no faster than he gets knowledge."

From the Life of Joseph Smith

The Prophet Joseph Smith "loved learning," wrote George Q. Cannon. "He loved knowledge for its righteous power. Through the tribulations which had surrounded him from the day when first he made known to a skeptical world his communion with the heavens, he had been ever advancing in the acquisition of intelligence. The Lord had commanded him to study, and he was obeying. . . . His mind, quickened by the Holy Spirit, grasped with readiness all true principles, and one by one he mastered these branches and became in them a teacher."[1]

In 1833, the Prophet and a group of Kirtland Saints had a unique opportunity to study the gospel. In January of that year, in accordance with the Lord's command (see D&C 88:127–41), the Prophet organized the School of the Prophets to train priesthood holders for their work in the ministry and to prepare them to preach the gospel. The school was held in a second-floor room in the Newel K. Whitney store, where the Prophet lived. About 25 brethren attended, some traveling hundreds of miles for the privilege of studying the gospel in a room no larger than 11 by 14 feet. Many of these men would later become Apostles, Seventies, and other Church leaders. Though the Prophet and the other brethren occasionally studied language, they focused primarily on learning the doctrines of the gospel, diligently pursuing their studies from early morning until late afternoon. This school lasted for four months, and similar schools were later held in Kirtland and also in Missouri, which hundreds of people attended.

At a meeting of the School of the Prophets on February 27, 1833, the Prophet received the revelation known as the Word of Wisdom in the presence of several brethren. He then walked into the main room and read the revelation to the assembled brethren.

At the meeting of the school held on February 27, 1833, the Prophet received an important revelation. In the early days of the Church, the use of alcohol, tobacco, coffee, and tea was common in society and among Church members. As the Prophet saw the brethren using tobacco at the school, he became concerned. Brigham Young recalled: "When they assembled together in this room after breakfast, the first they did was to light their pipes, and, while smoking, talk about the great things of the kingdom. . . . Often when the Prophet entered the room to give the school instructions he would find himself in a cloud of tobacco smoke. This, and the complaints of his wife at having to clean so filthy a floor [from chewing tobacco], made the Prophet think upon the matter, and he inquired of the Lord relating to the conduct of the elders in using tobacco, and the revelation known as the Word of Wisdom was the result of his inquiry."[2]

Millions of people have followed the counsel in this revelation and have received temporal and spiritual blessings, including the "wisdom and great treasures of knowledge" promised to those who walk in obedience to God's commandments (D&C 89:19).

Treasures of spiritual knowledge were poured out upon the brethren attending the School of the Prophets, and they made great advances in their understanding of the gospel. At the meeting of the school held on March 18, 1833, Sidney Rigdon and Frederick G. Williams were set apart as the Prophet's counselors in the First Presidency. Afterward, the Prophet "exhorted the brethren to faithfulness and diligence in keeping the commandments of God, and gave much instruction for the benefit of the Saints, with a promise that the pure in heart should see a heavenly vision; and after remaining a short time in secret prayer, the promise was verified; for many present had the eyes of their understanding opened by the Spirit of God, so as to behold many things. . . . Many of the brethren saw a heavenly vision of the Savior, and concourses of angels, and many other things."[3]

The Prophet explained, "Great joy and satisfaction continually beamed in the countenances of the School of the Prophets, and the Saints, on account of the things revealed, and our progress in the knowledge of God."[4]

Teachings of Joseph Smith

The gospel of Jesus Christ embraces all truth; the faithful accept the truths God has revealed and put aside false traditions.

"Mormonism is truth; and every man who embraces it feels himself at liberty to embrace every truth: consequently the shackles of superstition, bigotry, ignorance, and priestcraft, fall at once from his neck; and his eyes are opened to see the truth, and truth greatly prevails over priestcraft. . . .

". . . Mormonism is truth, in other words the doctrine of the Latter-day Saints, is truth. . . . The first and fundamental principle of our holy religion is, that we believe that we have a right to embrace all, and every item of truth, without limitation or without being circumscribed or prohibited by the creeds or superstitious notions of men, or by the dominations of one another, when that truth is clearly demonstrated to our minds, and we have the highest degree of evidence of the same."[5]

In January 1843, Joseph Smith had a conversation with some people who were not members of the Church: "I stated that the most prominent difference in sentiment between the Latter-day Saints and sectarians was, that the latter were all circumscribed by some peculiar creed, which deprived its members the privilege of believing anything not contained therein, whereas the Latter-day Saints . . . are ready to believe all true principles that exist, as they are made manifest from time to time."[6]

"I cannot believe in any of the creeds of the different denominations, because they all have some things in them I cannot subscribe to, though all of them have some truth. I want to come up into the presence of God, and learn all things; but the creeds set up stakes [limits], and say, 'Hitherto shalt thou come, and no further' [Job 38:11]; which I cannot subscribe to."[7]

"I say to all those who are disposed to set up stakes for the Almighty, You will come short of the glory of God. To become a joint heir of the heirship of the Son, one must put away all his false traditions."[8]

"The great thing for us to know is to comprehend what God did institute before the foundation of the world. Who knows it? It is the constitutional disposition of mankind to set up stakes and set bounds to the works and ways of the Almighty. . . . That which hath been hid from before the foundation of the world is revealed to babes and sucklings in the last days [see D&C 128:18]."[9]

"When men open their lips against [the truth] they do not injure me, but injure themselves. . . . When things that are of the greatest importance are passed over by weak-minded men without even a thought, I want to see truth in all its bearings and hug it to my bosom. I believe all that God ever revealed, and I never hear of a man being damned for believing too much; but they are damned for unbelief."[10]

"When God offers a blessing or knowledge to a man, and he refuses to receive it, he will be damned. The Israelites prayed that God would speak to Moses and not to them; in consequence of which he cursed them with a carnal law."[11]

"I have always had the satisfaction of seeing the truth triumph over error, and darkness give way before light."[12]

Gaining knowledge of eternal truths is essential to obtaining salvation.

"Knowledge is necessary to life and godliness. Woe unto you priests and divines who preach that knowledge is not necessary unto life and salvation. Take away Apostles, etc., take away knowledge, and you will find yourselves worthy of the damnation of hell. Knowledge is revelation. Hear, all ye brethren, this grand key: knowledge is the power of God unto salvation."[13]

"Knowledge does away with darkness, suspense and doubt; for these cannot exist where knowledge is. . . . In knowledge there is power. God has more power than all other beings, because He has greater knowledge; and hence He knows how to subject all other beings to Him. He has power over all."[14]

"As far as we degenerate from God, we descend to the devil and lose knowledge, and without knowledge we cannot be saved, and while our hearts are filled with evil, and we are studying evil, there is no room in our hearts for good, or studying good. Is not God good? Then you be good; if He is faithful, then you be faithful. Add to your faith virtue, to virtue knowledge, and seek for every good thing [see 2 Peter 1:5].

". . . A man is saved no faster than he gets knowledge, for if he does not get knowledge, he will be brought into captivity by some evil power in the other world, as evil spirits will have more knowledge, and consequently more power than many men who are on the earth. Hence it needs revelation to assist us, and give us knowledge of the things of God."[15]

Joseph Smith taught the following in April 1843, later recorded in Doctrine and Covenants 130:18–19: "Whatever principle of intelligence we attain unto in this life, it will rise with us in the resurrection. And if a person gains more knowledge and intelligence in this life through his diligence and obedience than another, he will have so much the advantage in the world to come."[16]

Joseph Smith taught the following in May 1843, later recorded in Doctrine and Covenants 131:6: "It is impossible for a man to be saved in ignorance."[17]

We obtain knowledge of eternal truths through diligent study and prayer.

George A. Smith, while serving in the First Presidency, reported: "Joseph Smith taught that every man and woman should seek the Lord for wisdom, that they might get knowledge from Him who is the fountain of knowledge; and the promises of the gospel, as revealed, were such as to authorize us to believe, that by taking this course we should gain the object of our pursuit."[18]

The Prophet Joseph Smith wrote the following to a man who had recently joined the Church: "You remember the testimony which I bore in the name of the Lord Jesus, concerning the great work which He has brought forth in the last days. You know my manner of communication, how that in weakness and simplicity, I declared to you what the Lord had brought forth by the ministering of His holy angels to me for this generation. I pray that the Lord may enable you to treasure these things in your mind, for I

"I know that His Spirit will bear testimony to all who seek diligently after knowledge from Him."

know that His Spirit will bear testimony to all who seek diligently after knowledge from Him."[19]

The Prophet Joseph Smith wrote the following to a man who wanted to learn more about the Church: "Study the Bible, and as many of our books as you can get; pray to the Father in the name of Jesus Christ, have faith in the promises made to the fathers, and your mind will be guided to the truth."[20]

"The things of God are of deep import; and time, and experience, and careful and ponderous and solemn thoughts can only find them out. Thy mind, O man! if thou wilt lead a soul unto salvation, must stretch as high as the utmost heavens, and search into and contemplate the darkest abyss, and the broad expanse of eternity—thou must commune with God. How much more dignified and noble are the thoughts of God, than the vain imaginations of the human heart! . . .

". . . Let honesty, and sobriety, and candor, and solemnity, and virtue, and pureness, and meekness, and simplicity crown our heads in every place; and in fine, become as little children, without malice, guile or hypocrisy. And now, brethren, after your tribulations, if you do these things, and exercise fervent prayer and faith in the sight of God always, He shall give unto you knowledge by His Holy Spirit, yea by the unspeakable gift of the Holy Ghost [see D&C 121:26]."[21]

We gain knowledge of eternal truths a little at a time; we can learn all things as fast as we are able to bear them.

"It is not wisdom that we should have all knowledge at once presented before us; but that we should have a little at a time; then we can comprehend it."[22]

"When you climb up a ladder, you must begin at the bottom, and ascend step by step, until you arrive at the top; and so it is with the principles of the gospel—you must begin with the first, and go on until you learn all the principles of exaltation. But it will be a great while after you have passed through the veil before you will have learned them. It is not all to be comprehended in this world; it will be a great work to learn our salvation and exaltation even beyond the grave."[23]

Joseph Smith and his counselors in the First Presidency gave the following instructions to the Saints who were gathering to Nauvoo: "To those who . . . can assist in this great work, we say, let them come to this place; by so doing they will not only assist in the rolling on of the Kingdom, but be in a situation where they can have the advantages of instruction from the Presidency and other authorities of the Church, and rise higher and higher in the scale of intelligence until they can 'comprehend with all Saints what is the breadth and length, and depth and height; and to know the love of Christ which passeth knowledge.' [Ephesians 3:18–19.]"[24]

"God hath not revealed anything to Joseph, but what He will make known unto the Twelve, and even the least Saint may know all things as fast as he is able to bear them, for the day must come when no man need say to his neighbor, Know ye the Lord; for all shall know Him . . . from the least to the greatest [see Jeremiah 31:34]."[25]

Suggestions for Study and Teaching

Consider these ideas as you study the chapter or as you prepare to teach. For additional help, see pages vii–xii.

- Read the first paragraph on page 265. Think about habits or ideas that can "set bounds to the works and ways of the Almighty" in our lives. What do you think we need to do in order to embrace all the truth the Lord will give us?
- Review the last full paragraph on page 265. When has knowledge pushed darkness and doubt out of your life? Why do you think gaining knowledge of the truth is essential to receiving salvation? (For some examples, see pages 265–66.)
- From the teachings of the Prophet Joseph, we can see that Satan wants us to lose knowledge (pages 265–66) and that the Lord wants to give us knowledge (pages 266–68). What can we learn from this contrast?
- What can we do to increase our knowledge of the truth? (For some examples, see pages 261–63, 266–68.) Review the paragraph that begins at the bottom of page 267. Select a few of the characteristics listed in this paragraph. How does each of these characteristics prepare us to receive knowledge?
- Read the second full paragraph on page 268. What can we learn from comparing our learning of gospel principles to climbing a ladder? What have you done to continually increase in your knowledge of the gospel?
- What are your thoughts or feelings as you ponder the last paragraph in this chapter?

Related Scriptures: Proverbs 1:7; 1 Timothy 2:3–4; 2 Nephi 28:29–31; Alma 5:45–47; D&C 88:118

Notes

1. George Q. Cannon, *The Life of Joseph Smith, the Prophet* (1888), p. 189.
2. Brigham Young, *Deseret News: Semi-Weekly,* Feb. 25, 1868, p. 2; capitalization modernized.
3. *History of the Church,* 1:334–35; from the minutes of a meeting of the School of the Prophets held on Mar. 18, 1833, in Kirtland, Ohio; reported by Frederick G. Williams.

4. *History of the Church,* 1:334; from "History of the Church" (manuscript), book A-1, p. 281, Church Archives, The Church of Jesus Christ of Latter-day Saints, Salt Lake City, Utah.
5. Letter from Joseph Smith to Isaac Galland, Mar. 22, 1839, Liberty Jail, Liberty, Missouri, published in *Times and Seasons,* Feb. 1840, pp. 53–54; spelling and grammar modernized.
6. *History of the Church,* 5:215; from "History of the Church" (manuscript), book D-1, p. 1433, Church Archives.
7. *History of the Church,* 6:57; punctuation modernized; from a discourse given by Joseph Smith on Oct. 15, 1843, in Nauvoo, Illinois; reported by Willard Richards.
8. *History of the Church,* 5:554; paragraph divisions altered; from a discourse given by Joseph Smith on Aug. 27, 1843, in Nauvoo, Illinois; reported by Willard Richards and William Clayton.
9. *History of the Church,* 5:529–30; paragraph divisions altered; from a discourse given by Joseph Smith on Aug. 13, 1843, in Nauvoo, Illinois; reported by Willard Richards.
10. *History of the Church,* 6:477; from a discourse given by Joseph Smith on June 16, 1844, in Nauvoo, Illinois; reported by Thomas Bullock; see also appendix, page 562, item 3.
11. *History of the Church,* 5:555; from a discourse given by Joseph Smith on Aug. 27, 1843, in Nauvoo, Illinois; reported by Willard Richards and William Clayton.
12. Letter from Joseph Smith to Oliver Cowdery, Sept. 24, 1834, Kirtland, Ohio, published in *Evening and Morning Star,* Sept. 1834, p. 192.
13. Quoted by Martha Jane Knowlton Coray, reporting a discourse given by Joseph Smith on May 21, 1843, in Nauvoo, Illinois; Martha Jane Knowlton Coray, Notebook, Church Archives.
14. *History of the Church,* 5:340; capitalization modernized; paragraph divisions altered; from a discourse given by Joseph Smith on Apr. 8, 1843, in Nauvoo, Illinois; reported by Willard Richards and William Clayton.
15. *History of the Church,* 4:588; from a discourse given by Joseph Smith on Apr. 10, 1842, in Nauvoo, Illinois; reported by Wilford Woodruff.
16. Doctrine and Covenants 130:18–19; instructions given by Joseph Smith on Apr. 2, 1843, in Ramus, Illinois.
17. Doctrine and Covenants 131:6; instructions given by Joseph Smith on May 16 and 17, 1843, in Ramus, Illinois.
18. George A. Smith, *Deseret News: Semi-Weekly,* Nov. 29, 1870, p. 2.
19. *History of the Church,* 1:442; from a letter from Joseph Smith to Moses Nickerson, Nov. 19, 1833, Kirtland, Ohio.
20. *History of the Church,* 6:459; from a letter from Joseph Smith to Washington Tucker, June 12, 1844, Nauvoo, Illinois.
21. *History of the Church,* 3:295–96; paragraph divisions altered; from a letter from Joseph Smith and others to Edward Partridge and the Church, Mar. 20, 1839, Liberty Jail, Liberty, Missouri; parts of this letter were later included in the Doctrine and Covenants as sections 121, 122, and 123.
22. *History of the Church,* 5:387; from a discourse given by Joseph Smith on May 14, 1843, in Yelrome, Illinois; reported by Wilford Woodruff.
23. *History of the Church,* 6:306–7; from a discourse given by Joseph Smith on Apr. 7, 1844, in Nauvoo, Illinois; reported by Wilford Woodruff, Willard Richards, Thomas Bullock, and William Clayton; see also appendix, page 562, item 3.
24. *History of the Church,* 4:186; from a letter from Joseph Smith and his counselors in the First Presidency to the Saints, Sept. 1840, Nauvoo, Illinois, published in *Times and Seasons,* Oct. 1840, p. 179.
25. *History of the Church,* 3:380; from a discourse given by Joseph Smith on June 27, 1839, in Commerce, Illinois; reported by Willard Richards.

"How Good and How Pleasant It Is . . . to Dwell Together in Unity"

"A long pull, a strong pull, and a pull all together."

From the Life of Joseph Smith

On December 27, 1832, the Prophet Joseph Smith received a commandment from the Lord that the Saints were to begin building a temple in Kirtland (see D&C 88:119). On June 1, 1833, the Lord gave further instructions to the Prophet: "Now here is wisdom, and the mind of the Lord—let the house be built, not after the manner of the world . . . ; let it be built after the manner which I shall show unto three of you" (D&C 95:13–14).

A few days later, the Lord fulfilled His promise, giving Joseph Smith and his counselors in the First Presidency a remarkable vision in which they saw detailed plans for the temple. Frederick G. Williams, the Second Counselor in the First Presidency, later recalled: "Joseph [Smith] received the word of the Lord for him to take his two counselors, [Frederick G.] Williams and [Sidney] Rigdon, and come before the Lord, and He would show them the plan or model of the house to be built. We went upon our knees, called on the Lord, and the building appeared within viewing distance, I being the first to discover it. Then all of us viewed it together. After we had taken a good look at the exterior, the building seemed to come right over us."[1]

When Joseph Smith explained to a council of high priests the glorious plan that had been revealed to the First Presidency, the brethren were delighted and went out at once to choose a site—a spot in a wheat field the Smith brothers had planted the previous fall. Immediately Hyrum Smith ran to get a scythe to begin clearing the land for construction, exclaiming, "We are preparing

After Joseph Smith explained the plan of the Kirtland Temple, as revealed by the Lord, Hyrum Smith ran to get a scythe, exclaiming, "We are preparing to build a house for the Lord, and I am determined to be the first at the work."

to build a house for the Lord, and I am determined to be the first at the work."[2]

This sense of enthusiasm became a unifying emotion as the Saints worked and sacrificed to build the first temple in this dispensation. Under Emma Smith's direction, women made stockings, pantaloons, and jackets for the temple workmen. The women also made the curtains and carpets for the temple, with the work on the temple interior being directed by Brigham Young. Brother John Tanner sold his 2,200-acre farm in New York, arriving in Kirtland just in time to lend the Prophet the $2,000 to redeem the mortgage on the temple block, which was about to be foreclosed. To protect the temple from threatening mobs, men guarded the temple at night, sleeping in the same clothes they had worn as construction workers by day.

The Prophet declared: "Great preparations were making to commence a house of the Lord; and notwithstanding the Church was poor, yet our unity, harmony and charity abounded to strengthen us to do the commandments of God."[3]

Heber C. Kimball, who became a member of the Quorum of the Twelve a year before the temple was dedicated, described the great effort: "The whole church united in this undertaking, and every man lent a helping hand. Those who had no teams went to work in the stone quarry and prepared the stones for drawing to the house."[4] Elder Kimball also recalled: "Joseph said, 'Come, brethren, let us go into the stone-quarry and work for the Lord.' And the Prophet went himself in his tow frock and tow breeches [linen work clothes] and worked at quarrying stone like the rest of us. Then every Saturday we brought out every team to draw stone to the Temple, and so we continued until that house was finished; and our wives were all the time knitting, spinning and sewing, and . . . doing all kinds of work."[5]

The efforts of the Kirtland Saints were typical of the unity, sacrifice, and devotion that would make it possible for the Lord's purposes to be fulfilled in the years to come. This was one of many times when the Saints would pull together, heeding the admonition of the Prophet Joseph Smith: "A long pull, a strong pull, and a pull all together."[6]

Teachings of Joseph Smith

When we work together in unity, we can better accomplish the purposes of God.

"[We] feel rejoiced to meet the Saints at another General Conference [October 1840]. . . . The Saints are as zealous, untiring, and energetic as ever, in the great work of the last days; and [this] gives us joy and consolation, and greatly encourages us, while contending with the difficulties which necessarily lie in our way.

"Let the brethren ever manifest such a spirit, and hold up our hands, and we must, we will go forward; the work of the Lord shall roll forth, the Temple of the Lord be reared, the Elders of Israel be encouraged, Zion be built up, and become the praise, the joy, and the glory of the whole earth; and the song of praise, glory, honor, and majesty to Him that sitteth upon the throne, and to the Lamb for ever and ever, shall reverberate from hill to hill, from mountain to mountain, from island to island, and from continent to continent, and the kingdoms of this world become the kingdom of our God and His Christ [see Revelation 11:15].

"We are glad indeed to know that there is such a spirit of union existing throughout the churches, at home and abroad, on this continent, as well as on the islands of the sea; for by this principle, and by a concentration of action, shall we be able to carry into effect the purposes of our God."[7]

"[The Nauvoo Temple] is progressing with great rapidity; strenuous exertions are being made on every hand to facilitate its erection, and materials of all kinds are in a great state of forwardness, and by next fall we expect to see the building enclosed. . . . There have been frequently, during the winter, as many as one hundred hands quarrying rock, while at the same time multitudes of others have been engaged in hauling, and in other kinds of labor. . . .

"While the busy multitudes have thus been engaged in their several vocations performing their daily labor, and working one-tenth of their time, others have not been less forward in bringing in their tithings and consecrations for the same great object. Never since the foundation of this Church was laid, have we seen manifested a greater willingness to comply with the [requirements] of Jehovah, a more ardent desire to do the will of God, more strenuous exertions used, or greater sacrifices made than there have been since the Lord said, 'Let the Temple be built by the tithing of my people.' [See D&C 97:10–11.] It seemed as though the spirit of enterprise, philanthropy and obedience rested simultaneously upon old and young; and brethren and sisters, boys and girls, and even strangers, who were not in the Church, united with an unprecedented liberality in the accomplishment of this great work; nor could the widow, in many instances, be prevented, out of her scanty pittance, from throwing in her two mites.

"We feel at this time to tender to all, old and young, both in the Church and out of it, our unfeigned thanks for their unprecedented liberality, kindness, diligence, and obedience, which they have so opportunely manifested on the present occasion. Not that we are personally or individually benefitted in a pecuniary point of view, but when the brethren, as in this instance, show a unity of purpose and design, and all put their shoulder to the wheel, our care, labor, toil and anxiety are materially diminished, our yoke is made easy and our burden is light [see Matthew 11:30]."[8]

"Now, let me say once for all, like the Psalmist of old, 'How good and how pleasant it is for brethren to dwell together in unity.' 'As the precious ointment upon the head that ran down upon Aaron's beard, that went down to the skirts of his garments, as the dew of Hermon that descended upon the mountains of Zion,' is such unity; 'for there the Lord commanded the blessing, even life for evermore!' Unity is power. [See Psalm 133:1–3.]"[9]

We grow in unity as we strive to be obedient to God's laws and overcome our selfish feelings and prejudices.

In December 1840 the Prophet wrote to members of the Quorum of the Twelve and other priesthood leaders who were serving missions in Great Britain: "It is . . . very satisfactory to my mind, that there has been such a good understanding between you, and that the Saints have so cheerfully hearkened to counsel, and [striven] with each other in this labor of love, and in the promotion of truth and righteousness. This is as it should be in the Church of Jesus Christ; unity is strength. 'How pleasing it is for brethren to dwell together in unity!' [Psalm 133:1.] Let the Saints of the Most High ever cultivate this principle, and the most glorious blessings must result, not only to them individually, but to the whole Church—the order of the kingdom will be maintained, its officers respected, and its requirements readily and cheerfully obeyed. . . .

"Let the Saints remember that great things depend on their individual exertion, and that they are called to be co-workers with us and the Holy Spirit in accomplishing the great work of the last days; and in consideration of the extent, the blessings and glories of the same, let every selfish feeling be not only buried, but annihilated; and let love to God and man predominate, and reign triumphant in every mind, that their hearts may become like unto Enoch's of old, and comprehend all things, present, past and future, and come behind in no gift, waiting for the coming of the Lord Jesus Christ [see 1 Corinthians 1:7].

"The work in which we are unitedly engaged is one of no ordinary kind. The enemies we have to contend against are subtle and well skilled in maneuvering; it behooves us to be on the alert to concentrate our energies, and that the best feelings should exist in our midst; and then, by the help of the Almighty, we shall go on from victory to victory, and from conquest to conquest; our evil passions will be subdued, our prejudices depart; we shall find no room in our bosoms for hatred; vice will hide its deformed head, and we shall stand approved in the sight of heaven, and be acknowledged the sons of God.

"Let us realize that we are not to live to ourselves, but to God; by so doing the greatest blessings will rest upon us both in time and in eternity."[10]

"We would say to the Saints that come here [to Nauvoo], we have laid the foundation for the gathering of God's people to this place, and [we] expect that when the Saints do come, they will be under the counsel that God has appointed. . . . We are trying here to gird up our loins, and purge from our midst the workers of iniquity; and we hope that when our brethren arrive

"Unity is strength. 'How pleasing it is for brethren to dwell together in unity!' Let the Saints of the Most High ever cultivate this principle."

from abroad, they will assist us to roll forth this good work, and to accomplish this great design, that 'Zion may be built up in righteousness; and all nations flock to her standard;' that as God's people, under His direction, and obedient to His law, we may grow up in righteousness and truth; that when His purposes shall be accomplished, we may receive an inheritance among those that are sanctified."[11]

"We, all of us, have our friends, our connections, our families and associations; and we find that the ties of friendship . . . and brotherhood have indissolubly united us together with a thousand endearing associations; we have embraced the one common faith, even that 'which was once delivered to the saints.' [Jude 1:3.] We have been privileged with hearing the everlasting gospel, which has been delivered unto us by the spirit of prophecy, by the opening of the heavens, by the gift of the Holy

Ghost, by the ministering of angels, and by the power of God. . . . A kindred sympathy runs through the whole body, even the body of Christ, which, according to Paul's statement, is his church; and no one part of the body can be injured without the other parts feeling the pain, for says Paul, if one member suffer, all the members suffer with it; and if one member rejoice all the rest are honored with it [see 1 Corinthians 12:12–27]."[12]

The greatest temporal and spiritual blessings always flow from a unity of effort.

In January 1841 the Prophet Joseph Smith and his counselors in the First Presidency gave direction to Saints who were coming to Nauvoo from different parts of the world: "By a concentration of action, and a unity of effort, we can only accomplish the great work of the last days . . . , while our interests, both temporal and spiritual, will be greatly enhanced, and the blessings of heaven must flow unto us in an uninterrupted stream; of this, we think there can be no question.

"The greatest temporal and spiritual blessings which always flow from faithfulness and concerted effort, never attended individual exertion or enterprise. The history of all past ages abundantly attests this fact. . . .

"We would wish the Saints to understand that, when they come here, they must not expect perfection, or that all will be harmony, peace, and love; if they indulge these ideas, they will undoubtedly be deceived, for here there are persons, not only from different states, but from different nations, who, although they feel a great attachment to the cause of truth, have their prejudices of education, and, consequently, it requires some time before these things can be overcome. Again, there are many that creep in unawares, and endeavor to sow discord, strife, and animosity in our midst, and by so doing, bring evil upon the Saints. . . . Therefore, let those who come up to this place be determined to keep the commandments of God, and not be discouraged by those things we have enumerated, and then they will be prospered—the intelligence of heaven will be communicated to them, and they will, eventually, see eye to eye, and rejoice in the full fruition of that glory which is reserved for the righteous.

"In order to erect the Temple of the Lord, great exertions will be required on the part of the Saints, so that they may build a house which shall be accepted by the Almighty, and in which His power and glory shall be manifested. Therefore let those who can freely make a sacrifice of their time, their talents, and their property, for the prosperity of the kingdom, and for the love they have to the cause of truth, . . . unite with us in the great work of the last days, and share in the tribulation, that they may ultimately share in the glory and triumph."[13]

Suggestions for Study and Teaching

Consider these ideas as you study the chapter or as you prepare to teach. For additional help, see pages vii–xii.

- Think about the Prophet Joseph Smith's statement, "A long pull, a strong pull, and a pull all together" (page 273). What happens when an effort is not long enough or strong enough? What happens when people pull in different directions? How might we apply the Prophet's statement in our homes? in our Church callings?
- Read the first full paragraph on page 275. Why do our burdens become lighter when we work together? (For some examples, see pages 271–75.) What principles have helped you to work in greater unity with others?
- Review the first full paragraph on page 276. What are some dangers of selfishness? What can we do to annihilate selfish feelings within ourselves? How do you feel when you "let love to God and man predominate" in your heart?
- Review the paragraph that begins at the bottom of page 277. In what ways have you benefited from "ties of friendship" and "endearing associations" in your ward or branch? How do wards and branches benefit when "a kindred sympathy runs through the whole body"?

- Study the paragraph that begins at the bottom of page 278. Why do you think it is unwise to expect perfection in members of our wards and branches? When have you seen an imperfect group of people use their diverse talents and abilities for a common cause? What have been the results of this unified effort?

Related Scriptures: Matthew 18:19–20; John 17:6–26; Mosiah 18:21; 3 Nephi 11:29–30; D&C 38:24–27; Moses 7:18

Notes

1. Frederick G. Williams, quoted by Truman O. Angell, in Truman Osborn Angell, Autobiography 1884, pp. 14–15, Church Archives, The Church of Jesus Christ of Latter-day Saints, Salt Lake City, Utah.
2. Hyrum Smith, quoted in Lucy Mack Smith, "The History of Lucy Smith, Mother of the Prophet," 1844–45 manuscript, book 14, pp. 1–2, Church Archives.
3. *History of the Church,* 1:349; from "History of the Church" (manuscript), book A-1, pp. 296–97, Church Archives.
4. Heber C. Kimball, "Extracts from H. C. Kimball's Journal," *Times and Seasons,* Apr. 15, 1845, pp. 867–68.
5. Heber C. Kimball, *Deseret News,* May 27, 1863, p. 377; punctuation and capitalization modernized.
6. Quoted by Brigham Young, *Deseret News: Semi-Weekly,* Apr. 20, 1867, p. 2; punctuation modernized.
7. *History of the Church,* 4:212–13; punctuation modernized; paragraph divisions altered; from a report from Joseph Smith and his counselors in the First Presidency, Oct. 4, 1840, Nauvoo, Illinois, published in *Times and Seasons,* Oct. 1840, p. 187.
8. *History of the Church,* 4:608–9; punctuation and grammar modernized; from "The Temple," an editorial published in *Times and Seasons,* May 2, 1842, pp. 775–76; Joseph Smith was the editor of the periodical.
9. *History of the Church,* 6:70; from a letter from Joseph Smith to the Saints, Nov. 1, 1843, Nauvoo, Illinois, published in *Times and Seasons,* Nov. 1, 1843, pp. 376–77; this letter is incorrectly dated Nov. 8, 1843, in *History of the Church.*
10. *History of the Church,* 4:227, 230–31; spelling modernized; from a letter from Joseph Smith to the Twelve, Dec. 15, 1840, Nauvoo, Illinois, published in *Times and Seasons,* Jan. 1, 1841, pp. 258, 260–61; this letter is incorrectly dated Oct. 19, 1840, in *History of the Church.*
11. *History of the Church,* 5:65–66; from "The Government of God," an editorial published in *Times and Seasons,* July 15, 1842, p. 858; Joseph Smith was the editor of the periodical.
12. "To the Saints of God," an editorial published in *Times and Seasons,* Oct. 15, 1842, p. 951; spelling, punctuation, and capitalization modernized; Joseph Smith was the editor of the periodical.
13. *History of the Church,* 4:272–73; from a letter from Joseph Smith and his counselors in the First Presidency to the Saints, Jan. 15, 1841, Nauvoo, Illinois, published in *Times and Seasons,* Jan. 15, 1841, pp. 276–77.

CHAPTER 24

Leading in the Lord's Way

"I teach them correct principles, and they govern themselves."

From the Life of Joseph Smith

While the Saints in Kirtland began working and sacrificing to build a temple in their midst, the Saints in Jackson County, Missouri, were facing severe persecution. As increasing numbers of Church members moved to Missouri, tensions grew with long-time settlers. The Missourians feared losing political control, they were suspicious of the Church's unfamiliar religious beliefs, and they disliked the Saints' tendency to trade among themselves. Mobs became increasingly violent in their persecution of the Saints and, in November 1833, forced them out of their homes. Leaving most of their livestock and household belongings behind, the Saints fled north, primarily to Clay County, Missouri, where they found refuge for a time.

The Prophet Joseph Smith, who was living in Kirtland, was deeply concerned about the sufferings of the Saints in Missouri, and he longed to help them. In February 1834, the Lord revealed to him that he should organize a group of Saints to march to Jackson County. This group, called Zion's Camp, was to help recover the lands and property illegally taken from Church members. (See D&C 103:21–40.) The camp was officially organized on May 6, 1834, and eventually included over 200 people. The marchers, who were armed and organized as a military body, arrived near Jackson County in the middle of June, after traveling more than 900 miles.

The members of the camp walked long distances each day, often in oppressive heat with only inadequate food and bad water to sustain them. The close association with one another over many

Leaders in the Lord's kingdom "should be endowed with wisdom, knowledge, and understanding, in order to teach and lead the people of God."

weeks of travel, accompanied by weariness and hunger, led some of the men to quarrel with one another and criticize the Prophet.

Despite all the problems of this dangerous and difficult trip, Joseph Smith taught the members of the camp important principles of leadership as he led them day by day. Wilford Woodruff, a member of Zion's Camp who later became the fourth President of the Church, declared: "We gained an experience that we never could have gained in any other way. We had the privilege of beholding the face of the Prophet, and we had the privilege of traveling a thousand miles with him, and seeing the workings of the Spirit of God with him, and the revelations of Jesus Christ unto him and the fulfillment of those revelations."[1]

After the group arrived in Missouri, they began negotiations with state officials, but these attempts at peaceful resolution failed. When armed conflict seemed inevitable, the Prophet prayed for guidance and, on June 22, 1834, received a revelation disbanding the camp and declaring that Zion could not be redeemed at that time (see D&C 105). Concerning the members of the camp the Lord said, "I have heard their prayers, and will accept their offering; and it is expedient in me that they should be brought thus far for a trial of their faith" (D&C 105:19).

Zion's Camp did not accomplish its political objectives, but it had long-lasting spiritual results. In February 1835, when the Prophet organized the Quorum of the Twelve Apostles and the Quorum of the Seventy, nine of the Twelve Apostles and all of the Seventy had served in Zion's Camp. As recalled by Joseph Young, one of the original members of the Seventy, the Prophet explained to a group of these brethren: "God did not want you to fight. He could not organize His kingdom with twelve men to open the Gospel door to the nations of the earth, and with seventy men under their direction to follow in their tracks, unless He took them from a body of men who had offered their lives, and who had made as great a sacrifice as did Abraham."[2]

It was in Zion's Camp that Brigham Young, Heber C. Kimball, Wilford Woodruff, and others gained practical training that enabled them to lead the Saints from Missouri to Illinois in 1839 and later to the Salt Lake Valley. From their experience with the Prophet, these brethren had learned to lead in the Lord's way.

Teachings of Joseph Smith

Leaders teach correct principles and help those they lead learn to govern themselves.

John Taylor, the third President of the Church, reported: "Some years ago, in Nauvoo, a gentleman in my hearing, a member of the Legislature, asked Joseph Smith how it was that he was enabled to govern so many people, and to preserve such perfect order; remarking at the same time that it was impossible for them to do it anywhere else. Mr. Smith remarked that it was very easy to do that. 'How?' responded the gentleman; 'to us it is very difficult.' Mr. Smith replied, 'I teach them correct principles, and they govern themselves.' "[3]

Brigham Young, the second President of the Church, reported: "The question was asked a great many times of Joseph Smith, by gentlemen who came to see him and his people, 'How is it that you can control your people so easily? It appears that they do nothing but what you say; how is it that you can govern them so easily?' Said he, 'I do not govern them at all. The Lord has revealed certain principles from the heavens by which we are to live in these latter days. The time is drawing near when the Lord is going to gather out His people from the wicked, and He is going to cut short His work in righteousness, and the principles which He has revealed I have taught to the people and they are trying to live according to them, and they control themselves.' "[4]

In response to an accusation that he was seeking power, Joseph Smith said: "In relation to the power over the minds of mankind which I hold, I would say, It is in consequence of the power of truth in the doctrines which I have been an instrument in the hands of God of presenting unto them, and not because of any compulsion on my part. . . . I ask, Did I ever exercise any compulsion over any man? Did I not give him the liberty of disbelieving any doctrine I have preached, if he saw fit? Why do not my enemies strike a blow at the doctrine? They cannot do it: it is truth, and I defy all men to upset it."[5]

"A brother who works in the *St. Louis Gazette* office . . . wanted to know by what principle I got so much power. . . . I told him

I obtained power on the principles of truth and virtue, which would last when I was dead and gone."[6]

Leaders receive the wisdom they need from the Spirit and acknowledge the Lord's blessings to them.

"A man of God should be endowed with wisdom, knowledge, and understanding, in order to teach and lead the people of God."[7]

Joseph Smith wrote to members of the Quorum of the Twelve and other priesthood leaders who were serving missions in Great Britain: "I can say, that as far as I have been made acquainted with your movements, I am perfectly satisfied that they have been in wisdom; and I have no doubt, but that the Spirit of the Lord has directed you; and this proves to my mind that you have been humble, and your desires have been for the salvation of your fellow man, and not for your own aggrandizement, and selfish interests. As long as the Saints manifest such a disposition, their counsels will be approved of, and their exertions crowned with success.

"There are many things of much importance, on which you ask counsel, but which I think you will be perfectly able to decide upon, as you are more conversant with the peculiar circumstances than I am; and I feel great confidence in your united wisdom. . . .

"Beloved brethren, you must be aware in some measure of my feelings, when I contemplate the great work which is now rolling on, and the relationship which I sustain to it, while it is extending to distant lands, and thousands are embracing it. I realize in some measure my responsibility, and the need I have of support from above, and wisdom from on high, that I may be able to teach this people, which have now become a great people, the principles of righteousness, and lead them agreeable to the will of Heaven; so that they may be perfected, and prepared to meet the Lord Jesus Christ when He shall appear in great glory. Can I rely on your prayers to our heavenly Father on my behalf, and on all the prayers of all my brethren and sisters in England, (whom having not seen, yet I love), that I may be enabled to escape every stratagem of Satan, surmount every difficulty, and bring this people to the enjoyment of those blessings which are reserved for the righteous? I ask this at your hands in the name of the Lord Jesus Christ."[8]

In 1833 the Prophet and other Church leaders wrote to members in Thompson, Ohio, telling them that Brother Salmon Gee had been appointed to preside over them: "Our beloved Brother Salmon . . . has been ordained by us . . . to lead you and to teach the things which are according to godliness, in whom we have great confidence, as we presume also you have. We therefore say to you—yea, not us only, but the Lord also—receive you him as such, knowing that the Lord has appointed him to this office for your good, holding him up by your prayers, praying for him continually that he may be endowed with wisdom and understanding in the knowledge of the Lord, that through him you may be kept from evil spirits, and all strifes and dissensions, and grow in grace and in the knowledge of our Lord and Savior, Jesus Christ.

". . . Finally, brethren, pray for us, that we may be enabled to do the work whereunto we are called, that you may enjoy the mysteries of God, even a fulness."[9]

The Prophet gave the following counsel to a group of priesthood leaders to guide them in their discussions: "Each should speak in his turn and in his place, and in his time and season, that there may be perfect order in all things; and . . . every man . . . should be sure that he can throw light upon the subject rather than spread darkness, . . . which may be done by men applying themselves closely to study the mind and will of the Lord, whose Spirit always makes manifest and demonstrates the truth to the understanding of all who are in possession of the Spirit."[10]

"When the Twelve or any other witnesses stand before the congregations of the earth, and they preach in the power and demonstration of the Spirit of God, and the people are astonished and confounded at the doctrine, and say, 'That man has preached a powerful discourse, a great sermon,' then let that man or those men take care that they do not ascribe the glory unto themselves, but be careful that they are humble, and ascribe the praise and glory to God and the Lamb; for it is by the power of the Holy Priesthood and the Holy Ghost that they have power thus to speak. What art thou, O man, but dust? And from whom receivest thou thy power and blessings, but from God?"[11]

Leaders in the Lord's kingdom love those they serve.

"As I grow older, my heart grows tenderer for you. I am at all times willing to give up everything that is wrong, for I wish this people to have a virtuous leader. I have set your minds at liberty by letting you know the things of Christ Jesus. . . . I have nothing in my heart but good feelings."[12]

"Sectarian priests cry out concerning me, and ask, 'Why is it this babbler gains so many followers, and retains them?' I answer, It is because I possess the principle of love. All I can offer the world is a good heart and a good hand."[13]

A few days before he went to Carthage Jail, the Prophet expressed his love for the Saints: "God has tried you. You are a good people; therefore I love you with all my heart. Greater love hath no man than that he should lay down his life for his friends [see John 15:13]. You have stood by me in the hour of trouble, and I am willing to sacrifice my life for your preservation."[14]

Leaders in the Lord's kingdom teach through their service and example.

As the members of Zion's Camp marched from Kirtland, Ohio, to Missouri, they learned many leadership principles from their association with Joseph Smith. George A. Smith, a member of Zion's Camp, recalled: "The Prophet Joseph took a full share of the fatigues of the entire journey. In addition to the care of providing for the Camp and presiding over it, he walked most of the time and had a full proportion of blistered, bloody, and sore feet, which was the natural result of walking from 25 to 40 miles a day in a hot season of the year. But during the entire trip he never uttered a murmur or complaint, while most of the men in the Camp complained to him of sore toes, blistered feet, long drives, scanty supply of provisions, poor quality of bread, bad corn dodger [corn bread], frowsy [spoiled] butter, strong honey, maggoty bacon and cheese, etc. Even a dog could not bark at some men without their murmuring at Joseph. If they had to camp

"The Prophet was the first man at the rope in his bare feet," recalled a member of Zion's Camp. "This was characteristic of him in all times of difficulty."

with bad water, it would nearly cause rebellion. Yet we were the Camp of Zion, and many of us were prayerless, thoughtless, careless, heedless, foolish, or devilish, and yet we did not know it. Joseph had to bear with us and tutor us like children. There were many, however, in the Camp who never murmured and who were always ready and willing to do as our leader desired."[15]

The following are excerpts from the Prophet's history for May 1834: "Every night before retiring to rest, at the sound of the trumpet, we bowed before the Lord in the several tents, and presented our thank-offerings with prayer and supplication; and at the sound of the morning trumpet, about four o'clock, every man was again on his knees before the Lord, imploring His blessing for the day."[16]

May 27, 1834: "Notwithstanding our enemies were continually breathing threats of violence, we did not fear, neither did we hesitate to prosecute our journey, for God was with us, and His angels went before us, and the faith of our little band was unwavering. We know that angels were our companions, for we saw them."[17]

May 29, 1834: "I discovered that a part of my company had been served with sour bread, while I had received good, sweet bread from the same cook. I reproved Brother Zebedee Coltrin for this partiality, for I wanted my brethren to fare as well as I did."[18]

John M. Chidester, a member of Zion's Camp, recalled: "Zion's Camp, in passing through the State of Indiana, had to cross very bad swamps; consequently we had to attach ropes to the wagons to help them through, and the Prophet was the first man at the rope in his bare feet. This was characteristic of him in all times of difficulty.

"We continued our journey until we reached the [Wakenda] River, having traveled twenty-five miles without resting or eating. We were compelled to ferry this stream; and we found on the opposite side of it a most desirable place to camp, which was a source of satisfaction to the now weary and hungry men. On reaching this place the Prophet announced to the Camp that he felt impressed to travel on; and taking the lead, he invited the brethren to follow him.

"This caused a split in the camp. Lyman Wight and others at first refused to follow the Prophet, but finally came up. The sequel showed that the Prophet was inspired to move on a distance of some seven miles. It was reported to us afterwards that about eight miles below where we crossed the river a body of men was organized to come upon us that night."[19]

During the march of Zion's Camp, some of the participants murmured and complained. The Prophet chastised those involved and warned that disaster would strike if they did not repent. Although some heeded his counsel, others did not. Soon cholera broke out, and some members of the camp died. Orson Hyde, who later served in the Quorum of the Twelve, recalled: "Did the Prophet cease his anxiety for the welfare of the camp? Did he become alienated in his feelings from his friends in their hour of chastisement and tribulation? Did he turn to be their enemy because he had spoken hard things against them? No! His heart was melted with sympathy—his bosom glowed with love, compassion and kindness; and with a zeal and fidelity that became a devoted friend in the hour of peril, he personally ministered to the sick and dying; and aided in burying the dead. Every act of his during that severe trial gave additional assurances to the camp that with all their faults, he loved them still."[20]

Suggestions for Study and Teaching

Consider these ideas as you study the chapter or as you prepare to teach. For additional help, see pages vii–xii.

- Read the first paragraph on page 284. What strengths do you see in the Prophet Joseph Smith's approach to leadership? How do you think most people respond to such leadership?
- Review the Prophet's teachings about the need for leaders to receive wisdom from the Spirit (pages 285–87). What can help leaders receive the wisdom they need?
- Review the second full paragraph on page 285. Why are humility and selflessness essential characteristics for leaders? What other characteristics do you think leaders should have?
- Joseph Smith spoke openly of his love and tender feelings for the Saints (page 287). How do you know when a leader truly loves you? When have you been blessed through the love of a leader?
- Study the reports of Zion's Camp on pages 281–83 and 287–90. What qualities of leadership did the Prophet demonstrate?
- Think about your leadership responsibilities in your family, the Church, your profession, your school, the community, or elsewhere. Consider what you can do to follow Joseph Smith's example.

Related Scriptures: Exodus 18:13–26; Proverbs 29:2; Matthew 20:25–28; Alma 1:26; D&C 107:99–100

Notes

1. Wilford Woodruff, *Deseret News: Semi-Weekly,* Dec. 21, 1869, p. 1; spelling and capitalization modernized.
2. Quoted by Joseph Young Sr., in *History of the Church,* 2:182, footnote; from Joseph Young Sr., *History of the Organization of the Seventies* (1878), p. 14.
3. John Taylor, "The Organization of the Church," *Millennial Star,* Nov. 15, 1851, p. 339.
4. Brigham Young, *Deseret News: Semi-Weekly,* June 7, 1870, p. 3.
5. *History of the Church,* 6:273; from a discourse given by Joseph Smith on Mar. 24, 1844, in Nauvoo, Illinois; reported by Wilford Woodruff.
6. *History of the Church,* 6:343; from a Joseph Smith journal entry, Apr. 25, 1844, Nauvoo, Illinois.
7. *History of the Church,* 5:426; from a discourse given by Joseph Smith on June 11, 1843, in Nauvoo, Illinois; reported by Wilford Woodruff and Willard Richards.
8. *History of the Church,* 4:228–30; spelling and grammar modernized; from a letter from Joseph Smith to the Twelve, Dec. 15, 1840, Nauvoo, Illinois, published in *Times and Seasons,* Jan. 1, 1841, pp. 259–60; this letter is incorrectly dated Oct. 19, 1840, in *History of the Church.*
9. Letter from Joseph Smith and others to Church members in Thompson, Ohio, Feb. 6, 1833, Kirtland, Ohio; Letter Book 1, 1829–35, pp. 25–26, Joseph Smith, Collection, Church Archives, The Church of Jesus Christ of Latter-day Saints, Salt Lake City, Utah.
10. *History of the Church,* 2:370; from a Joseph Smith journal entry, Jan. 15, 1836, Kirtland, Ohio.
11. *History of the Church,* 3:384; from a discourse given by Joseph Smith on July 2, 1839, in Montrose, Iowa; reported by Wilford Woodruff and Willard Richards.
12. *History of the Church,* 6:412; from a discourse given by Joseph Smith on May 26, 1844, in Nauvoo, Illinois; reported by Thomas Bullock.
13. *History of the Church,* 5:498; from a discourse given by Joseph Smith on July 9, 1843, in Nauvoo, Illinois; reported by Willard Richards; see also appendix, page 562, item 3.
14. *History of the Church,* 6:500; from a discourse given by Joseph Smith on June 18, 1844, in Nauvoo, Illinois. The compilers of *History of the Church* combined verbal reports by several eyewitnesses into a single account of the discourse.
15. George A. Smith, "History of George Albert Smith by Himself," p. 30, George Albert Smith, Papers, 1834–75, Church Archives.
16. *History of the Church,* 2:64–65; from Heber C. Kimball, "Elder Kimball's Journal," *Times and Seasons,* Jan. 15, 1845, p. 771.
17. *History of the Church,* 2:73; from Heber C. Kimball, "Elder Kimball's Journal," *Times and Seasons,* Jan. 15, 1845, p. 772.
18. *History of the Church,* 2:75; from George A. Smith, "History of George Albert Smith by Himself," p. 17, George Albert Smith, Papers, 1834–75, Church Archives.
19. John M. Chidester, in "Recollections of the Prophet Joseph Smith," *Juvenile Instructor,* Mar. 1, 1892, p. 151; punctuation modernized.
20. Orson Hyde, *Deseret News,* July 30, 1853, p. 66.

The Prophet Joseph Smith teaching a group of brethren, including Brigham Young (left). Brigham Young said that the Prophet could "take the scriptures and make them so plain and simple that everybody could understand."

Truths from the Savior's Parables in Matthew 13

"The chariot wheels of the Kingdom are still rolling on, impelled by the mighty arm of Jehovah; and in spite of all opposition, will still roll on, until His words are all fulfilled."

From the Life of Joseph Smith

As construction on the Kirtland Temple neared completion, Joseph Smith and the Saints began to prepare themselves for the great blessings they would receive there. To help prepare the brethren for the temple dedication, a session of the School of the Elders began in November 1835. This school had been established in 1834, a continuation of the School of the Prophets held earlier.

Among other subjects, Joseph Smith and the other brethren studied Hebrew, the language in which most of the Old Testament was originally written. The Prophet's journal for this period shows that he studied Hebrew nearly every day, often for many hours a day. His journal entries include words such as "Spent the day in reading Hebrew" or "Attended school and read Hebrew."[1] On January 19, 1836, he recorded: "Spent the day at school. The Lord blessed us in our studies. This day we commenced reading in our Hebrew Bibles with much success. It seems as if the Lord opens our minds in a marvelous manner, to understand His word in the original language."[2] A month later, he wrote: "Attended the school and read and translated with my class as usual. My soul delights in reading the word of the Lord in the original."[3]

Joseph Smith's experience in the School of the Elders is just one evidence of his love for the scriptures. He studied the scriptures diligently, finding in them solace, knowledge, and inspiration throughout his life. Significantly, it was a passage from the Bible that led him to seek wisdom from God and receive the First Vision when he was just 14 years old (see James 1:5).

The Prophet's writings and sermons are filled with scriptural quotations and interpretations, for he had studied the scriptures so extensively that they became an integral part of his thinking. In his teachings, he quoted scriptures directly, he alluded to them, he paraphrased them, and he used them as the foundation for his sermons. "I know the scriptures and understand them," he declared in April 1844.[4]

His extraordinary knowledge of the scriptures allowed him to teach and interpret them with great power and clarity, and many who heard him speak remembered this ability. President Brigham Young recalled that the Prophet could "take the scriptures and make them so plain and simple that everybody could understand."[5]

Wandle Mace recalled: "I have listened to the Prophet Joseph Smith in public and in private, in sunshine and in shower, as many others have done as he taught them from the stand. And in my own, and in his house, I have been familiar with him . . . and do know that no man could explain the scriptures, throw them wide open to view so plainly that none could misunderstand their meaning, except he had been taught of God.

"I have sometimes felt ashamed of myself because, having studied the scriptures so much, even from a child, I had not seen that which was so plain when he touched them. He, as it were, turned the key, and the door of knowledge sprang wide open, disclosing precious principles, both new and old."[6]

The Prophet's knowledge of the scriptures is evident in the following letter, in which he gave a prophetic interpretation of the Savior's parables in Matthew 13. He taught that these parables describe the establishment of the Church in the Savior's time and its marvelous growth and destiny in the latter days.

Teachings of Joseph Smith

The Savior taught in parables so that those who believed in His teachings could gain greater light, while those who rejected His teachings would lose the light they had.

" 'And the disciples came and said unto [the Savior], Why speakest thou unto them in parables? [I would here remark, that the "them" made use of in this interrogation . . . refers to the multitude.] He answered and said unto them, [that is unto the disciples,] because it is given unto *you* to know the mysteries of the Kingdom of Heaven, but to *them,* [that is, unbelievers,] it is not given; for whosoever hath, to him shall be given, and he shall have more abundance; but whosoever hath not, from him shall be taken away even that he hath.' [Matthew 13:10–12.]

"We understand from this saying, that those who had been previously looking for a Messiah to come according to the testimony of the Prophets, and were then at that time looking for a Messiah, but had not sufficient light on account of their unbelief to discern Him to be their Savior, and He being the true Messiah, consequently they must be disappointed, and lose even all the knowledge, or have taken away from them all the light, understanding, and faith which they had upon this subject. Therefore he that will not receive the greater light, must have taken away from him all the light which he hath; and if the light which is in you becomes darkness, behold, how great is that darkness! 'Therefore,' says the Savior, 'speak I unto them in parables, because they seeing see not, and hearing they hear not, neither do they understand; and in them is fulfilled the prophecy of Esaias [Isaiah] which saith, By hearing ye shall hear, and shall not understand; and seeing ye shall see, and not perceive.' [Matthew 13:13–14.]

"Now we discover that the very reason assigned by this prophet [Isaiah], why they would not receive the Messiah, was, because they did not or would not understand; and seeing, they did not perceive; 'for this people's heart is waxed gross, and their ears are dull of hearing, their eyes have closed, lest at any time they should see with their eyes, and hear with their ears, and understand with their heart, and should be converted, and I should heal them.' [Matthew 13:15.] But what saith He to His disciples? 'Blessed are your eyes for they see, and your ears for they hear, for verily I say unto you, that many prophets and righteous men have desired to see those things which ye see, and have not seen them; and to hear those things which ye hear, and have not heard them.' [Matthew 13:16–17.]

"We again make remark here—for we find that the very principle upon which the disciples were accounted blessed, was because they were permitted to see with their eyes and hear with their ears—that the condemnation which rested upon the multitude that received not His saying, was because they were not willing to see with their eyes, and hear with their ears; not because they could not, and were not privileged to see and hear, but because their hearts were full of iniquity and abominations; 'as your fathers did, so do ye.' [Acts 7:51.] The prophet, foreseeing that they would thus harden their hearts, plainly declared it; and herein is the condemnation of the world; that light hath come into the world, and men choose darkness rather than light, because their deeds are evil. This is so plainly taught by the Savior, that a wayfaring man need not mistake it.

". . . Men are in the habit, when the truth is exhibited by the servants of God, of saying, All is mystery; they have spoken in parables, and, therefore, are not to be understood. It is true they have eyes to see, and see not, but none are so blind as those who will not see; and, although the Savior spoke this to such characters, yet unto His disciples he expounded it plainly; and we have reason to be truly humble before the God of our fathers, that He hath left these things on record for us, so plain, that notwithstanding the exertions and combined influence of the priests of Baal, they have not power to blind our eyes, and darken our understanding, if we will but open our eyes, and read with candor, for a moment."[7]

The parable of the sower shows the effects of preaching the gospel; it also shows that the Savior established His kingdom in the meridian of time.

"At the time the Savior spoke these beautiful sayings and parables contained in [Matthew 13], we find Him seated in a ship on account of the multitude that pressed upon Him to hear His words; and He commenced teaching them, saying:

" 'Behold, a sower went forth to sow, and when he sowed, some seeds fell by the way side, and the fowls came and devoured them up: some fell upon stony places, where they had not much earth; and forthwith they sprang up because they had no deepness of earth: and when the sun was up they were scorched: and because they had no root they withered away. And some fell among thorns; and the thorns sprung up and choked them: but other fell in good ground, and brought forth fruit, some an hundred fold, some sixty fold, some thirty fold. Who hath ears to hear, let him hear.' [Matthew 13:3–9.] . . .

"But listen to the explanation of the parable of the Sower: 'When any one heareth the word of the Kingdom, and understandeth it not, then cometh the wicked one, and catcheth away that which was sown in his heart.' Now mark the expression—that which was sown in his heart. 'This is he which receiveth seed by the way side.' [Matthew 13:19.] Men who have no principle of righteousness in themselves, and whose hearts are full of iniquity, and have no desire for the principles of truth, do not understand the word of truth when they hear it. The devil taketh away the word of truth out of their hearts, because there is no desire for righteousness in them.

" 'But he that receiveth seed in stony places, the same is he that heareth the word, and anon, with joy receiveth it; yet hath he not root in himself, but dureth for a while: for when tribulation or persecution ariseth because of the word, by and by, he is offended. He also that receiveth seed among the thorns, is he that heareth the word; and the care of this world, and the deceitfulness of riches choke the word, and he becometh unfruitful. But he that received seed into the good ground is he that heareth the word, and understandeth it, which also beareth fruit, and bringeth forth, some an hundred fold, some sixty, some thirty.' [Matthew 13:20–23.]

"Thus the Savior Himself explained unto His disciples the parable which He put forth, and left no mystery or darkness upon the minds of those who firmly believe on His words.

"Behold, a sower went forth to sow, and when he sowed, some seeds fell by the way side. . . . But other fell in good ground, and brought forth fruit."

"We draw the conclusion, then, that the very reason why the multitude, or the world, as they were designated by the Savior, did not receive an explanation upon His parables, was because of unbelief. To you, He says, (speaking to His disciples,) it is given to know the mysteries of the Kingdom of God [see Matthew 13:11]. And why? Because of the faith and confidence they had in Him. This parable was spoken to demonstrate the effects that are produced by the preaching of the word; and we believe that it has an allusion directly to the commencement, or the setting up, of the Kingdom in that age; therefore we shall continue to trace His sayings concerning this Kingdom from that time forth, even unto the end of the world."[8]

The parable of the wheat and tares teaches that the righteous and wicked will grow together until the end of the world, when the righteous will be gathered and the wicked burned.

" 'Another parable put He forth unto them, saying, [which parable has an allusion to the setting up of the Kingdom, in that age of the world also,] the Kingdom of Heaven is likened unto a man which sowed good seed in his field, but while men slept, his enemy came and sowed tares among the wheat, and went his way. But when the blade was sprung up, and brought forth fruit, then appeared the tares also; so the servants of the householder came and said unto him, Sir, didst not thou sow good seed in thy field? From whence, then, hath it tares? He said unto them, An enemy hath done this. The servants said unto him, Wilt thou then that we go and gather them up? But he said, Nay; lest while ye gather up the tares, ye root up also the wheat with them. Let both grow together until the harvest: and in the time of harvest I will say to the reapers, Gather ye together first the tares, and bind them in bundles to burn them, but gather the wheat into my barn.' [Matthew 13:24–30.]

"Now we learn by this parable, not only the setting up of the Kingdom in the days of the Savior, which is represented by the good seed, which produced fruit, but also the corruptions of the Church, which are represented by the tares, which were sown by the enemy, which His disciples would fain have plucked up, or cleansed the Church of, if their views had been favored by the Savior. But He, knowing all things, says, Not so. As much as to say, your views are not correct, the Church is in its infancy, and if you take this rash step, you will destroy the wheat, or the Church, with the tares; therefore it is better to let them grow together until the harvest, or the end of the world, which means the destruction of the wicked, which is not yet fulfilled. . . .

" '. . . His disciples came unto Him, saying, Declare unto us the parable of the tares of the field. He answered and said unto them,

He that soweth the good seed is the Son of Man; the field is the world; the good seed are the children of the Kingdom; but the tares are the children of the wicked one.' [Matthew 13:36–38.]

"Now let our readers mark the expression—'the field is the world, . . . the tares are the children of the wicked one, the enemy that sowed them is the devil, the harvest is the end of the world, [let them carefully mark this expression—*the end of the world,*] and the reapers are the angels.' [Matthew 13:38–39.]

"Now men cannot have any possible grounds to say that this is figurative, or that it does not mean what it says, for He is now explaining what He has previously spoken in parables; and according to this language, the end of the world is the destruction of the wicked; the harvest and the end of the world have an allusion directly to the human family in the last days, instead of the earth, as many have imagined, and that which shall precede the coming of the Son of Man, and the restitution of all things spoken of by the mouth of all the holy prophets since the world began; and the angels are to have something to do in this great work, for they are the reapers.

" 'As, therefore, the tares are gathered and burned in the fire, so shall it be in the end of the world' [Matthew 13:40]; that is, as the servants of God go forth warning the nations, both priests and people, and as they harden their hearts and reject the light of truth, these first being delivered over to the buffetings of Satan, and the law and the testimony being closed up, . . . they are left in darkness, and delivered over unto the day of burning; thus being bound up by their creeds, and their bands being made strong by their priests, [they] are prepared for the fulfillment of the saying of the Savior—'The Son of Man shall send forth His angels, and gather out of His Kingdom all things that offend, and them which do iniquity, and shall cast them into a furnace of fire; there shall be wailing and gnashing of teeth.' [Matthew 13:41–42.]

"We understand that the work of gathering together of the wheat into barns, or garners, is to take place while the tares are being bound over and preparing for the day of burning; that after the day of burnings, 'the righteous shall shine forth like the sun, in the Kingdom of their Father. Who hath ears to hear, let him hear' [Matthew 13:43]."[9]

The parable of the mustard seed teaches that the Church and kingdom of God, established in these last days, will spread throughout the earth.

"And again, another parable put He forth unto them, having an allusion to the Kingdom that should be set up just previous to or at the time of the harvest, which reads as follows—'The Kingdom of Heaven is like a grain of mustard seed, which a man took and sowed in his field: which indeed is the least of all seeds: but, when it is grown, it is the greatest among herbs, and becometh a tree, so that the birds of the air come and lodge in the branches thereof.' [Matthew 13:31–32.] Now we can discover plainly that this figure is given to represent the Church as it shall come forth in the last days. Behold, the Kingdom of Heaven is likened unto it. Now, what is like unto it?

"Let us take the Book of Mormon, which a man took and hid in his field, securing it by his faith, to spring up in the last days, or in due time; let us behold it coming forth out of the ground, which is indeed accounted the least of all seeds, but behold it branching forth, yea, even towering with lofty branches and God-like majesty, until it, like the mustard seed, becomes the greatest of all herbs. And it is truth, and it has sprouted and come forth out of the earth, and righteousness begins to look down from heaven [see Psalm 85:11; Moses 7:62], and God is sending down His powers, gifts, and angels to lodge in the branches thereof.

"The Kingdom of Heaven is like unto a mustard seed. Behold, then, is not this the Kingdom of Heaven that is raising its head in the last days in the majesty of its God, even the Church of the Latter-day Saints, like an impenetrable, immovable rock in the midst of the mighty deep, exposed to the storms and tempests of Satan, that has, thus far, remained steadfast, and is still braving the mountain waves of opposition, which are driven by the tempestuous winds of sinking crafts, which have [dashed] and are still dashing with tremendous foam across its triumphant brow; urged onward with redoubled fury by the enemy of righteousness? . . .

The Church is "like an impenetrable, immovable rock in the midst of the mighty deep, exposed to the storms and tempests of Satan, that has, thus far, remained steadfast."

"The . . . clouds of darkness have long been beating like mountain waves upon the immovable rock of the Church of the Latter-day Saints; and notwithstanding all this, the mustard seed is still towering its lofty branches, higher and higher, and extending itself wider and wider; and the chariot wheels of the Kingdom are still rolling on, impelled by the mighty arm of Jehovah; and in spite of all opposition, will still roll on, until His words are all fulfilled."[10]

The testimonies of the Three Witnesses and the latter-day scriptures are like the leaven that was hidden in meal; the parable of the net teaches about the worldwide gathering.

" 'And another parable spake He unto them. The Kingdom of Heaven is like unto leaven which a woman took and hid in three measures of meal till the whole was leavened.' [Matthew 13:33.]

It may be understood that the Church of the Latter-day Saints has taken its rise from a little leaven that was put into three witnesses. Behold, how much this is like the parable! It is fast leavening the lump, and will soon leaven the whole. . . .

" 'Again, the Kingdom of Heaven is like unto a net that was cast into the sea, and gathered of every kind, which when it was full they drew to shore, and sat down, and gathered the good into vessels, but cast the bad away.' [Matthew 13:47–48.] For the work of this pattern, behold the seed of Joseph, spreading forth the Gospel net upon the face of the earth, gathering of every kind, that the good may be saved in vessels prepared for that purpose, and the angels will take care of the bad. 'So shall it be at the end of the world—the angels shall come forth and sever the wicked from among the just, and cast them into the furnace of fire, and there shall be wailing and gnashing of teeth. Jesus saith unto them, Have you understood all these things? They say unto Him, Yea, Lord.' [Matthew 13:49–51.] And we say, yea, Lord; and well might they say, yea, Lord; for these things are so plain and so glorious, that every Saint in the last days must respond with a hearty Amen to them.

" 'Then said He unto them, therefore every scribe which is instructed in the Kingdom of Heaven, is like unto a man that is an householder, which bringeth forth out of his treasure things that are new and old.' [Matthew 13:52.]

"For the works of this example, see the Book of Mormon coming forth out of the treasure of the heart. Also the covenants given to the Latter-day Saints [the Doctrine and Covenants], also the translation of the Bible—thus bringing forth out of the heart things new and old, thus answering to three measures of meal undergoing the purifying touch by a revelation of Jesus Christ, and the ministering of angels, who have already commenced this work in the last days, which will answer to the leaven which leavened the whole lump. Amen."[11]

Suggestions for Study and Teaching

Consider these ideas as you study the chapter or as you prepare to teach. For additional help, see pages vii–xii.

- Review pages 293–94. What can we learn from the example of Joseph Smith to help us in our own scripture study?
- Review Joseph Smith's explanation of why the Savior sometimes taught with parables (pages 295–96). As we learn the truths of the gospel, what do you think it means to see with our eyes and hear with our ears? Why do you think light will be taken away from us if we are unwilling to receive greater light? Think about what you need to do to receive more gospel light.
- Study the parable of the sower (pages 296–99). In this parable, the Savior shows that the same gospel message produces different effects depending on how people receive it. Why is the word of God unable to grow in people "whose hearts are full of iniquity"? Why do tribulation and persecution lead some to set aside the word of God? In what ways might "the care of this world" and "the deceitfulness of riches" choke the word within us?
- How can we ensure that our "ground" is good when the word is planted in us? What can parents do to help children prepare their hearts to receive the word?
- In the parable of the wheat and the tares (pages 299–301), the wheat represents the righteous, or "the children of the Kingdom." The tares represent "the children of the wicked one." How can we remain faithful even though the "tares" are allowed to grow among the "wheat"? How does Doctrine and Covenants 86:1–7 help you understand the parable?
- In what ways is the Church today like the developing tree in the parable of the mustard seed? (For some examples, see pages 301–2.)
- Review pages 302–3. Note that leaven is a substance that causes bread dough to rise. In what ways are the latter-day scriptures like leaven for the Church? How are they like leaven

for you personally? How are the latter-day scriptures like treasures "that are new and old"?

- In the parable of the gospel net (page 303), why do you think it is significant that the net gathers fish of every kind? How is this parable being fulfilled today?

Related Scriptures: Luke 8:4–18; Alma 12:9–11; D&C 86:1–11; 101:63–68

Notes

1. *History of the Church,* 2:326, 387; from Joseph Smith journal entries, Dec. 7, 1835, and Jan. 29, 1836, Kirtland, Ohio.
2. *History of the Church,* 2:376; from a Joseph Smith journal entry, Jan. 19, 1836, Kirtland, Ohio.
3. *History of the Church,* 2:396; from a Joseph Smith journal entry, Feb. 17, 1836, Kirtland, Ohio.
4. *History of the Church,* 6:314; from a discourse given by Joseph Smith on Apr. 7, 1844, in Nauvoo, Illinois; reported by Wilford Woodruff, Willard Richards, Thomas Bullock, and William Clayton.
5. Brigham Young, *Deseret News,* Dec. 30, 1857, p. 340; spelling modernized.
6. Wandle Mace, Autobiography, ca. 1890, p. 45, Church Archives, The Church of Jesus Christ of Latter-day Saints, Salt Lake City, Utah.
7. *History of the Church,* 2:265–66; second, third, and fourth sets of bracketed words in first paragraph in original; punctuation and grammar modernized; from a letter from Joseph Smith to the elders of the Church, Dec. 1835, Kirtland, Ohio, published in *Messenger and Advocate,* Dec. 1835, pp. 225–26.
8. *History of the Church,* 2:264–67; punctuation and grammar modernized; paragraph divisions altered; from a letter from Joseph Smith to the elders of the Church, Dec. 1835, Kirtland, Ohio, published in *Messenger and Advocate,* Dec. 1835, pp. 225–26.
9. *History of the Church,* 2:267, 271; first set of bracketed words in first paragraph in original, and first set of bracketed words in fourth paragraph in original; punctuation and capitalization modernized; paragraph divisions altered; from a letter from Joseph Smith to the elders of the Church, Dec. 1835, Kirtland, Ohio, published in *Messenger and Advocate,* Dec. 1835, pp. 226–29.
10. *History of the Church,* 2:268, 270; bracketed word in third paragraph in original; punctuation, capitalization, and grammar modernized; from a letter from Joseph Smith to the elders of the Church, Dec. 1835, Kirtland, Ohio, published in *Messenger and Advocate,* Dec. 1835, pp. 227–28. See page xvi for information about changes in the official name of the Church.
11. *History of the Church,* 2:270, 272; punctuation and capitalization modernized; paragraph divisions altered; from a letter from Joseph Smith to the elders of the Church, Dec. 1835, Kirtland, Ohio, published in *Messenger and Advocate,* Dec. 1835, pp. 228–29.

"Another great and glorious vision burst upon us; for Elijah the prophet, who was taken to heaven without tasting death, stood before us."

CHAPTER 26

Elijah and the Restoration of the Sealing Keys

"How shall God come to the rescue of this generation? He will send Elijah the prophet."

From the Life of Joseph Smith

In the spring of 1836, after three years of work and sacrifice, the Kirtland Saints finally saw their beautiful temple complete, the first temple in this dispensation. On Sunday, March 27, more than 900 people gathered in the temple chapel and vestibule for the dedicatory service. Many others met in an overflow session in a nearby schoolroom, while still others listened outside the open windows of the temple. The Prophet himself helped to seat the faithful.

The congregation heard an address by Sidney Rigdon, a counselor in the First Presidency, and then joined together to sing "Now Let Us Rejoice" and "Adam-ondi-Ahman," written by William W. Phelps. Joseph Smith then rose to offer the dedicatory prayer, which he had received by revelation. In the prayer, he described many of the remarkable blessings that are bestowed upon those who come in worthiness to God's temples (see D&C 109). The choir sang "The Spirit of God," and the congregation then stood and gave the Hosanna Shout "with such power as seemed almost sufficient to raise the roof from the building."[1]

"Let thy house be filled," the Prophet said in the dedicatory prayer, "as with a rushing mighty wind, with thy glory" (D&C 109:37). This was literally fulfilled, for many Saints testified that heavenly beings were present during the dedication service. Eliza R. Snow recalled: "The ceremonies of that dedication may be rehearsed, but no mortal language can describe the heavenly manifestations of that memorable day. Angels appeared to some, while a sense of divine presence was realized by all present, and each heart was filled with 'joy inexpressible and full of glory' [see 1 Peter 1:8]."[2]

That evening, as the Prophet gathered with about 400 priesthood bearers in the temple, "a noise was heard like the sound of a rushing mighty wind, which filled the Temple, and all the congregation simultaneously arose, being moved upon by an invisible power." According to the Prophet, "many began to speak in tongues and prophesy; others saw glorious visions; and I beheld the Temple was filled with angels, which fact I declared to the congregation."[3]

In a meeting held in the temple a week later, on Sunday, April 3, manifestations of extraordinary significance occurred. After the Prophet assisted other Church leaders in administering the sacrament, he and Oliver Cowdery retired to the pulpit behind lowered curtains and knelt in solemn prayer. As they rose from prayer, the Savior Himself appeared to them and proclaimed His approval of the temple: "Behold, I have accepted this house, and my name shall be here; and I will manifest myself to my people in mercy in this house" (D&C 110:7).

After this vision closed, Joseph and Oliver saw three separate visions in which ancient prophets appeared to them to restore priesthood keys necessary for the latter-day work of the Lord. The prophet Moses appeared and committed to them "the keys of the gathering of Israel from the four parts of the earth." Elias came and committed to them "the dispensation of the gospel of Abraham." (See D&C 110:11–12.)

Then, in another glorious vision, Joseph and Oliver saw the prophet Elijah (see D&C 110:13–16). The coming of Elijah was so important that the ancient prophet Malachi had prophesied of it centuries earlier, and the Savior had repeated the prophecy to the Nephites (see Malachi 4:5–6; 3 Nephi 25:5–6; 26:1–2). Elijah came to commit to Joseph and Oliver the keys of sealing—the power to bind and validate in the heavens all ordinances performed on the earth. The restoration of the sealing power was necessary to prepare the world for the Savior's Second Coming, for without it, "the whole earth would be utterly wasted at his coming" (Joseph Smith—History 1:39).

Teachings of Joseph Smith

The ancient prophet Malachi foretold the coming of Elijah.

The Prophet Joseph Smith said the following about Moroni's visit to him on the evening of September 21, 1823, as recorded in Joseph Smith—History 1:36–39: "[Moroni] first quoted part of the third chapter of Malachi; and he quoted also the fourth or last chapter of the same prophecy, though with a little variation from the way it reads in our Bibles. Instead of quoting the first verse as it reads in our books, he quoted it thus:

"For behold, the day cometh that shall burn as an oven, and all the proud, yea, and all that do wickedly shall burn as stubble; for they that come shall burn them, saith the Lord of Hosts, that it shall leave them neither root nor branch.

"And again, he quoted the fifth verse thus: *Behold, I will reveal unto you the Priesthood, by the hand of Elijah the prophet, before the coming of the great and dreadful day of the Lord.*

"He also quoted the next verse differently: *And he shall plant in the hearts of the children the promises made to the fathers, and the hearts of the children shall turn to their fathers. If it were not so, the whole earth would be utterly wasted at his coming.*"[4]

Elijah appeared to Joseph Smith and Oliver Cowdery in the Kirtland Temple.

Joseph Smith described the appearance of the ancient prophet Elijah to him and Oliver Cowdery on April 3, 1836, in the Kirtland Temple, later recorded in Doctrine and Covenants 110:13–16: "Another great and glorious vision burst upon us; for Elijah the prophet, who was taken to heaven without tasting death, stood before us, and said:

"Behold, the time has fully come, which was spoken of by the mouth of Malachi—testifying that he [Elijah] should be sent, before the great and dreadful day of the Lord come—to turn the hearts of the fathers to the children, and the children to the fathers, lest the whole earth be smitten with a curse—therefore, the keys of this dispensation are committed into your hands; and by this ye may know that the great and dreadful day of the Lord is near, even at the doors."[5]

Elijah restored the sealing keys—the power and authority to bind in heaven all ordinances performed on earth.

" 'And I will send Elijah the Prophet before the great and terrible day of the Lord,' etc., etc. [see Malachi 4:5]. Why send Elijah? Because he holds the keys of the authority to administer in all the ordinances of the Priesthood; and [unless] the authority is given, the ordinances could not be administered in righteousness."[6]

The Prophet Joseph Smith said the following in a letter to the Saints, later recorded in Doctrine and Covenants 128:8–11: "The nature of this ordinance [baptism for the dead] consists in the power of the priesthood, by the revelation of Jesus Christ, wherein it is granted that whatsoever you bind on earth shall be bound in heaven, and whatsoever you loose on earth shall be loosed in heaven. . . .

"It may seem to some to be a very bold doctrine that we talk of—a power which records or binds on earth and binds in heaven. Nevertheless, in all ages of the world, whenever the Lord has given a dispensation of the priesthood to any man by actual revelation, or any set of men, this power has always been given. Hence, whatsoever those men did in authority, in the name of the Lord, and did it truly and faithfully, and kept a proper and faithful record of the same, it became a law on earth and in heaven, and could not be annulled, according to the decrees of the great Jehovah. This is a faithful saying. Who can hear it?

"And again, for the precedent, Matthew 16:18, 19: *And I say also unto thee, That thou art Peter, and upon this rock I will build my church; and the gates of hell shall not prevail against it. And I will give unto thee the keys of the kingdom of heaven: and whatsoever thou shalt bind on earth shall be bound in heaven; and whatsoever thou shalt loose on earth shall be loosed in heaven.*

"Now the great and grand secret of the whole matter, and the *summum bonum* of the whole subject that is lying before us, consists in obtaining the powers of the Holy Priesthood. For him to whom these keys are given there is no difficulty in obtaining a knowledge of facts in relation to the salvation of the children of men, both as well for the dead as for the living."[7]

Through the sealing power, families can be sealed for time and all eternity, and sacred ordinances can be performed for the dead.

"The spirit, power, and calling of Elijah is, that ye have power to hold the key of the revelation, ordinances, oracles, powers and endowments of the fullness of the Melchizedek Priesthood and of the kingdom of God on the earth; and to receive, obtain, and perform all the ordinances belonging to the kingdom of God, even unto the turning of the hearts of the fathers unto the children, and the hearts of the children unto the fathers, even those who are in heaven.

"Malachi says, 'I will send you Elijah the prophet before the coming of the great and dreadful day of the Lord: and he shall turn the heart of the fathers to the children, and the heart of the children to their fathers, lest I come and smite the earth with a curse.' [Malachi 4:5–6.]

"Now, what I am after is the knowledge of God, and I take my own course to obtain it. What are we to understand by this in the last days?

"In the days of Noah, God destroyed the world by a flood, and He has promised to destroy it by fire in the last days: but before it should take place, Elijah should first come and turn the hearts of the fathers to the children, etc.

"Now comes the point. What is this office and work of Elijah? It is one of the greatest and most important subjects that God has revealed. He should send Elijah to seal the children to the fathers, and the fathers to the children.

"Now was this merely confined to the living, to settle difficulties with families on earth? By no means. It was a far greater work. Elijah! what would you do if you were here? Would you confine your work to the living alone? No: I would refer you to the Scriptures, where the subject is manifest: that is, without us, they could not be made perfect, nor we without them; the

"We should be wise. The first thing you do, go and seal on earth your sons and daughters unto yourself, and yourself unto your fathers in eternal glory."

fathers without the children, nor the children without the fathers [see Hebrews 11:40].

"I wish you to understand this subject, for it is important; and if you will receive it, this is the spirit of Elijah, that we redeem our dead, and connect ourselves with our fathers which are in heaven, and seal up our dead to come forth in the first resurrection; and here we want the power of Elijah to seal those who dwell on earth to those who dwell in heaven. This is the power of Elijah and the keys of the kingdom of Jehovah. . . .

"Again: The doctrine or sealing power of Elijah is as follows:— If you have power to seal on earth and in heaven, then we should be wise. The first thing you do, go and seal on earth your sons and daughters unto yourself, and yourself unto your fathers in eternal glory."[8]

The coming of Elijah was a necessary preparation for the Second Coming of the Savior.

"The hearts of the children of men will have to be turned to the fathers, and the fathers to the children, living or dead, to prepare them for the coming of the Son of Man. If Elijah did not come, the whole earth would be smitten."[9]

"Elias is a forerunner to prepare the way, and the spirit and power of Elijah is to come after, holding the keys of power, building the Temple to the capstone, placing the seals of the Melchizedek Priesthood upon the house of Israel, and making all things ready; then Messiah comes to His Temple, which is last of all. . . . Elijah was to come and prepare the way and build up the kingdom before the coming of the great day of the Lord."[10]

"The world is reserved unto burning in the last days. He shall send Elijah the prophet, and he shall reveal the covenants of the fathers in relation to the children, and the covenants of the children in relation to the fathers."[11]

"How shall God come to the rescue of this generation? He will send Elijah the prophet. . . . Elijah shall reveal the covenants to seal the hearts of the fathers to the children, and the children to the fathers."[12]

Suggestions for Study and Teaching

Consider these ideas as you study the chapter or as you prepare to teach. For additional help, see pages vii–xii.

- When the Savior appeared in the Kirtland Temple, He told Joseph Smith and Oliver Cowdery, "I will manifest myself to my people in mercy in this house" (page 308). How was the restoration of the sealing keys a manifestation of the Lord's mercy? In what other ways does He manifest Himself in the temple?
- Study the third and fourth paragraphs on page 309. What do these two paragraphs teach about Elijah's mission that we do not learn from Malachi 4:5–6? What is significant about these differences?

- Study the explanation of the sealing power found on pages 310–11. What is the sealing power? Why is this power significant to you and your family?
- Read Joseph Smith's explanation of the work of Elijah (pages 311–12). What is the Spirit of Elijah? Why was it so important that Elijah come and fulfill his work in these latter days?
- What experiences have you had in which you have turned your heart to family members who have died? What can parents do to help their children turn their hearts to their ancestors?
- Read the paragraph that begins on the bottom of page 309 and the first paragraph on page 313. Why do you think the earth would have been "smitten with a curse" without the sealing power?

Related Scriptures: Helaman 10:4–10; D&C 132:45–46; 138:47–48; Bible Dictionary, "Elijah," p. 664

Notes

1. Eliza R. Snow, quoted in Edward W. Tullidge, *The Women of Mormondom* (1877), p. 94.
2. Eliza R. Snow, quoted in *The Women of Mormondom,* p. 95.
3. *History of the Church,* 2:428; from "History of the Church" (manuscript), book B-1, addenda, pp. 3–4, Church Archives, The Church of Jesus Christ of Latter-day Saints, Salt Lake City, Utah.
4. Joseph Smith—History 1:36–39.
5. Doctrine and Covenants 110:13–16; bracketed word in original; vision given to Joseph Smith and Oliver Cowdery on Apr. 3, 1836, in the temple in Kirtland, Ohio.
6. *History of the Church,* 4:211; from a discourse prepared by Joseph Smith and read at a Church conference held on Oct. 5, 1840, in Nauvoo, Illinois.
7. Doctrine and Covenants 128:8–11; a letter from Joseph Smith to the Saints, Sept. 6, 1842, Nauvoo, Illinois.
8. *History of the Church,* 6:251–53; spelling modernized; from a discourse given by Joseph Smith on Mar. 10, 1844, in Nauvoo, Illinois; reported by Wilford Woodruff.
9. *History of the Church,* 3:390; from a discourse given by Joseph Smith about July 1839 in Commerce, Illinois; reported by Willard Richards.
10. *History of the Church,* 6:254; spelling modernized; paragraph divisions altered; from a discourse given by Joseph Smith on Mar. 10, 1844, in Nauvoo, Illinois; reported by Wilford Woodruff.
11. *History of the Church,* 5:530; from a discourse given by Joseph Smith on Aug. 13, 1843, in Nauvoo, Illinois; reported by Willard Richards.
12. *History of the Church,* 5:555; paragraph divisions altered; from a discourse given by Joseph Smith on Aug. 27, 1843, in Nauvoo, Illinois; reported by Willard Richards and William Clayton.

CHAPTER 27

Beware the Bitter Fruits of Apostasy

"In all your trials, tribulations and sickness, in all your sufferings, even unto death, be careful you don't betray God, . . . be careful you don't apostatize."

From the Life of Joseph Smith

In the weeks before and after the completion of the Kirtland Temple in the spring of 1836, the Saints experienced a time of harmony and a rich outpouring of the gifts of the Spirit. But the Prophet Joseph Smith warned the Saints that if they did not continue to live righteously, their joy and unity would not last. Daniel Tyler said of this time: "All felt that they had a foretaste of heaven. In fact, there were several weeks in which we were not tempted of the devil; and we wondered whether the millennium had commenced. At [a meeting of priesthood brethren], the Prophet Joseph addressed us. Among other things he said: 'Brethren, for some time Satan has not had power to tempt you. Some have thought that there would be no more temptation. But the opposite will come; and unless you draw near to the Lord you will be overcome and apostatize.' "[1]

As that year wore on, a spirit of apostasy grew among some of the Saints in Kirtland. Some members became proud, greedy, and disobedient to the commandments. Some blamed Church leaders for economic problems caused by the failure of a Kirtland financial institution established by Church members. This failure occurred in 1837, the same year that a banking panic swept across the United States, compounding the Saints' economic problems. As many as two or three hundred members fell away from the Church in Kirtland, sometimes joining with those who opposed the Church to torment and even physically threaten the

Joseph Smith taught the importance of sustaining our Church leaders: "That man who rises up to condemn others, finding fault with the Church, saying that they are out of the way, while he himself is righteous, . . . that man is in the high road to apostasy."

Saints. Some apostates openly claimed that the Prophet was fallen and tried to have other men put in his place. Sister Eliza R. Snow recalled: "Many who had been humble and faithful to the performance of every duty—ready to go and come at every call of the Priesthood—were getting haughty in their spirits, and lifted up in the pride of their hearts. As the Saints drank in the love and spirit of the world, the Spirit of the Lord withdrew from their hearts."[2]

Of the Church's situation in May 1837, the Prophet lamented: "It seemed as though all the powers of earth and hell were combining their influence in an especial manner to overthrow the Church at once. . . . The enemy abroad, and apostates in our midst, united in their schemes, . . . and many became disaffected toward me as though I were the sole cause of those very evils I was most strenuously striving against."[3]

Despite these challenges, the large majority of the leaders and members of the Church remained faithful. Brigham Young, a member of the Quorum of the Twelve Apostles during this uncertain period, remembered a meeting at which some Church members were discussing how to depose the Prophet Joseph: "I rose up, and in a plain and forcible manner told them that Joseph was a Prophet and I knew it, and that they might rail and slander him as much as they pleased, [but] they could not destroy the appointment of the Prophet of God; they could only destroy their own authority, cut the thread that bound them to the Prophet and to God, and sink themselves to hell. Many were highly enraged at my decided opposition to their measures. . . .

"This meeting was broken up without the apostates being able to unite on any decided measures of opposition. This was a crisis when earth and hell seemed leagued to overthrow the Prophet and Church of God. The knees of many of the strongest men in the Church faltered. During this siege of darkness I stood close by Joseph, and with all the wisdom and power God bestowed upon me, put forth my utmost energies to sustain the servant of God and unite the quorums of the Church."[4]

Teachings of Joseph Smith

Losing confidence in Church leaders, criticizing them, and neglecting any duty required by God lead to apostasy.

"I will give you one of the *Keys* of the mysteries of the Kingdom. It is an eternal principle, that has existed with God from all eternity: That man who rises up to condemn others, finding fault with the Church, saying that they are out of the way, while he himself is righteous, then know assuredly, that that man is in the high road to apostasy; and if he does not repent, will apostatize, as God lives."[5]

Heber C. Kimball, while serving as a counselor to President Brigham Young, reported: "I will give you a key which Brother Joseph Smith used to give in Nauvoo. He said that the very step of apostasy commenced with losing confidence in the leaders of this church and kingdom, and that whenever you discerned that spirit you might know that it would lead the possessor of it on the road to apostasy."[6]

Wilford Woodruff, while serving in the Quorum of the Twelve, said: "Brother Joseph used to counsel us in this wise: 'The moment you permit yourselves to lay aside any duty that God calls you to perform, to gratify your own desires; the moment you permit yourselves to become careless, you lay a foundation for apostasy. Be careful; understand you are called to a work, and when God requires you to do that work do it.' Another thing he said: 'In all your trials, tribulations and sickness, in all your sufferings, even unto death, be careful you don't betray God, be careful you don't betray the priesthood, be careful you don't apostatize.' "[7]

Wilford Woodruff also said: "I remember Brother Joseph Smith visited myself, Brother [John] Taylor, Brother Brigham Young and several other missionaries, when we were about to take our mission to England. We were sick and afflicted, many of us. At the same time we felt to go. The Prophet blessed us, as also our wives and families. . . . He taught us some very important principles, some of which I here name. Brother Taylor, myself, George A. Smith, John E. Page and others had been called to fill the place of those [apostles] who had fallen away. Brother Joseph laid before us the cause of those men turning away from the commandments of God. He hoped we would learn wisdom by what we saw with the eye and heard with the ear, and that we would be able to discern the spirits of other men without being compelled to learn by sad experience.

"He then remarked that any man, any elder in this Church and kingdom, who pursued a course whereby he would ignore or, in other words, refuse to obey any known law or commandment or duty—whenever a man did this, neglected any duty God required at his hand in attending meetings, filling missions, or obeying counsel, he laid a foundation to lead him to apostasy and this was the reason those men had fallen. They had misused the priesthood sealed upon their heads. They had neglected to magnify their calling as apostles, as elders. They had used that priesthood to attempt to build themselves up and to perform some other work besides the building up of the kingdom of God."[8]

In 1840, a small, organized body of Church members continued to live in Kirtland, Ohio, although most of the Saints had gathered to Nauvoo, Illinois. In response to news that a Church member in Kirtland was trying to destroy the Saints' confidence in the First Presidency and other authorities of the Church, the Prophet wrote to a Church leader in Kirtland: "In order to conduct the affairs of the Kingdom in righteousness, it is all important that the most perfect harmony, kind feeling, good understanding, and confidence should exist in the hearts of all the brethren; and that true charity, love one towards another, should characterize all their proceedings. If there are any uncharitable feelings, any lack of confidence, then pride, arrogance and envy will soon be manifested; confusion must inevitably prevail, and the authorities of the Church set at naught. . . .

"If the Saints in Kirtland deem me unworthy of their prayers when they assemble together, and neglect to bear me up at the throne of heavenly grace, it is a strong and convincing proof to me that they have not the Spirit of God. If the revelations we have received are true, who is to lead the people? If the keys of the Kingdom have been committed to my hands, who shall open out the mysteries thereof?

"As long as my brethren stand by me and encourage me, I can combat the prejudices of the world, and can bear the contumely [harsh treatment] and abuse with joy; but when my brethren stand aloof, when they begin to faint, and endeavor to retard my progress and enterprise, then I feel to mourn, but am no less determined to prosecute my task, being confident that although my earthly friends may fail, and even turn against me, yet my heavenly Father will bear me off triumphant.

"However, I hope that even in Kirtland there are some who do not make a man an offender for a word [see Isaiah 29:21], but are disposed to stand forth in defense of righteousness and truth, and attend to every duty enjoined upon them; and who will have wisdom to direct them against any movement or influence calculated to bring confusion and discord into the camp of Israel, and to discern between the spirit of truth and the spirit of error.

"It would be gratifying to my mind to see the Saints in Kirtland flourish, but think the time is not yet come; and I assure you it never will until a different order of things be established and a different spirit manifested. When confidence is restored, when pride shall fall, and every aspiring mind be clothed with humility as with a garment, and selfishness give place to benevolence and charity, and a united determination to live by every word which proceedeth out of the mouth of the Lord is observable, then, and not till then, can peace, order and love prevail.

"It is in consequence of aspiring men that Kirtland has been forsaken. How frequently has your humble servant been envied in his office by such characters, who endeavored to raise themselves to power at his expense, and seeing it impossible to do so, resorted to foul slander and abuse, and other means to effect his overthrow. Such characters have ever been the first to cry out against the Presidency, and publish their faults and foibles to the four winds of heaven."[9]

Those who apostatize lose the Spirit of God, break their covenants, and often persecute members of the Church.

"Strange as it may appear at first thought, yet it is no less strange than true, that notwithstanding all the professed determination to live godly, apostates after turning from the faith of Christ, unless they have speedily repented, have sooner or later fallen into the snares of the wicked one, and have been left destitute of the Spirit of God, to manifest their wickedness in the eyes of multitudes. From apostates the faithful have received the severest persecutions. Judas was rebuked and immediately betrayed his Lord into the hands of His enemies, because Satan entered into him.

"There is a superior intelligence bestowed upon such as obey the Gospel with full purpose of heart, which, if sinned against, the apostate is left naked and destitute of the Spirit of God, and he is, in truth, nigh unto cursing, and his end is to be burned. When once that light which was in them is taken from them they become as much darkened as they were previously enlightened, and then, no marvel, if all their power should be enlisted against the truth, and they, Judas-like, seek the destruction of those who were their greatest benefactors.

"What nearer friend on earth, or in heaven, had Judas than the Savior? And his first object was to destroy Him. Who, among all the Saints in these last days, can consider himself as good as our Lord? Who is as perfect? Who is as pure? Who is as holy as He was? Are they to be found? He never transgressed or broke a commandment or law of heaven—no deceit was in His mouth, neither was guile found in His heart. And yet one that ate with Him, who had often drunk of the same cup, was the first to lift up his heel against Him. Where is one like Christ? He cannot be found on earth. Then why should His followers complain, if from those whom they once called brethren, and considered as standing in the nearest relation in the everlasting covenant, they should receive persecution?

"From what source emanated the principle which has ever been manifested by apostates from the true Church to persecute with double diligence, and seek with double perseverance, to destroy those whom they once professed to love, with whom they once communed, and with whom they once covenanted to strive with every power in righteousness to obtain the rest of God? Perhaps our brethren will say the same that caused Satan

"What nearer friend on earth, or in heaven, had Judas than the Savior? And his first object was to destroy Him."

to seek to overthrow the kingdom of God, because he himself was evil, and God's kingdom is holy."[10]

"There have always been, in every age of the church, those who have been opposed to the principles of virtue, who have loved the gain of this present world, followed the principles of unrighteousness, and have been the enemies of truth. . . . Those who have associated with us and made the greatest professions of friendship, have frequently been our greatest enemies and our most determined foes; if they became unpopular, if their interest or dignity was touched, or if they were detected in their iniquity, they were always the first to raise the hand of persecution, to calumniate [make false charges about] and vilify their brethren, and to seek the downfall and destruction of their friends."[11]

"Renegade 'Mormon' dissenters are running through the world and spreading various foul and libelous reports against us, thinking thereby to gain the friendship of the world, because they know that we are not of the world, and that the world hates us; therefore they [the world] make a tool of these fellows [the dissenters]; and by them try to do all the injury they can, and after that they hate them worse than they do us, because they find them to be base traitors and sycophants [flatterers]."[12]

Wilford Woodruff reported: "I attended [a] meeting at the [Kirtland] Temple [on February 19, 1837]. President Joseph Smith had been absent on business for the Church, but not half as long as Moses was in the mount away from Israel [see Exodus 32:1–8]; yet many of the people in Kirtland, if they did not make a calf to worship as did the Israelites, turned their hearts away from the Lord and from his servant Joseph, and had engaged in speculation and given way to false spirits, until they were darkened in their minds; and many were opposed to Joseph Smith, and some wished to appoint David Whitmer to lead the Church in his stead. In the midst of this cloud of dark spirits, Joseph returned to Kirtland, and this morning arose in the stand. He appeared much depressed; but soon the Spirit of God rested upon him, and he addressed the assembly in great plainness for about three hours, and put his enemies to silence.

"When he arose he said, 'I am still the President, Prophet, Seer, Revelator and Leader of the Church of Jesus Christ. God, and not man, has appointed and placed me in this position, and no man or set of men have power to remove me or appoint another in my stead, and those who undertake this, if they do not speedily repent, will burn their fingers and go to hell.' He reproved the people sharply for their sins, darkness and unbelief; the power of God rested upon him, and bore testimony that his sayings were true."[13]

Wilford Woodruff reported: "President Smith spoke in the afternoon [on April 9, 1837], and said in the name of the Lord that the judgments of God would rest upon those men who had professed to be his friends, and friends of humanity, and in building up Kirtland, a stake of Zion, but had turned traitors to him, and the interests of the kingdom of God, and had given power into the hands of our enemies against us; they had oppressed the poor Saints, and had brought distress upon them, and had become covenant breakers, for which they will feel the wrath of God."[14]

Daniel Tyler recalled: "Soon after the Prophet's arrival in Commerce (afterwards Nauvoo) from Missouri prison, Brother Isaac Behunin and myself made him a visit at his residence. His persecutions were the topic of conversation. He repeated many false, inconsistent and contradictory statements made by apostates, frightened members of the Church and outsiders. He also told how most of the officials who would fain have taken his life, when he was arrested, turned in his favor on forming his acquaintance. He laid the burden of the blame on false brethren. . . .

"When the Prophet had ended telling how he had been treated, Brother Behunin remarked: 'If I should leave this Church I would not do as those men have done: I would go to some remote place where Mormonism had never been heard of, settle down, and no one would ever learn that I knew anything about it.'

"The great Seer immediately replied: 'Brother Behunin, you don't know what you would do. No doubt these men once thought as you do. Before you joined this Church you stood on neutral ground. When the gospel was preached, good and evil were set before you. You could choose either or neither. There were two opposite masters inviting you to serve them. When you joined this Church you enlisted to serve God. When you did that you left the neutral ground, and you never can get back on to it. Should you forsake the Master you enlisted to serve, it will be by the instigation of the evil one, and you will follow his dictation and be his servant.' "[15]

If we follow the prophets and apostles and the revelations of the Church, we will not be led astray.

Orson Hyde, a member of the Quorum of the Twelve, reported: "Joseph the Prophet . . . said, 'Brethren, remember that the majority of this people will never go astray; and as long as you keep with the majority you are sure to enter the celestial kingdom.' "[16]

William G. Nelson reported: "I have heard the Prophet speak in public on many occasions. In one meeting I heard him say: 'I will give you a key that will never rust,—if you will stay with the majority of the Twelve Apostles, and the records of the Church, you will never be led astray.' The history of the Church has proven this to be true."[17]

Ezra T. Clark remembered: "I heard the Prophet Joseph say that he would give the Saints a key whereby they would never be led away or deceived, and that was: The Lord would never suffer a majority of this people to be led away or deceived by imposters, nor would He allow the records of this Church to fall into the hands of the enemy."[18]

Suggestions for Study and Teaching

Consider these ideas as you study the chapter or as you prepare to teach. For additional help, see pages vii–xii.

- Review the account on pages 315–17. Why do you think people can change from righteousness to apostasy in such a short time? What are some influences that cause people to apostatize today? What can we do to guard against such influences?
- What are some dangers of losing confidence in our Church leaders and criticizing them? (For some examples, see pages 318–20.) What can we do to maintain a feeling of respect and appreciation for our leaders? How can parents encourage their children to respect Church leaders?
- The Prophet taught, "The moment you permit yourselves to lay aside any duty that God calls you to perform, to gratify your own desires . . . , you lay a foundation for apostasy" (page 318). What does this statement mean to you?
- Read the story told by Daniel Tyler (page 324). Why do you think that those who have apostatized from the Church often fight so strongly against it? (For some examples, see pages 320–24.) How do you think we should respond to the words and actions of such people?
- Read the last three paragraphs of the chapter (pages 324–25). Why is it important for us to understand and use this "key" given by Joseph Smith?

Related Scriptures: 1 Nephi 8:10–33; Helaman 3:33–35; D&C 82:3, 21; 121:11–22

Notes

1. Daniel Tyler, "Incidents of Experience," in *Scraps of Biography* (1883), pp. 32–33.
2. Eliza R. Snow, *Biography and Family Record of Lorenzo Snow* (1884), p. 20; punctuation modernized.
3. *History of the Church,* 2:487–88; from "History of the Church" (manuscript), book B-1, p. 761, Church Archives, The Church of Jesus Christ of Latter-day Saints, Salt Lake City, Utah.
4. Brigham Young, in Historian's Office, Manuscript History of Brigham Young, 1844–46, vol. 1, p. 16, Church Archives.
5. *History of the Church,* 3:385; from a discourse given by Joseph Smith on July 2, 1839, in Montrose, Iowa; reported by Wilford Woodruff and Willard Richards.
6. Heber C. Kimball, *Deseret News,* Apr. 2, 1856, p. 26; spelling and capitalization modernized.
7. Wilford Woodruff, *Deseret News,* Dec. 22, 1880, p. 738.
8. Wilford Woodruff, *Deseret News: Semi-Weekly,* Sept. 7, 1880, p. 1; punctuation modernized; paragraph divisions altered.
9. *History of the Church,* 4:165–66; from a letter from Joseph Smith to Oliver Granger, July 1840, Nauvoo, Illinois.
10. *History of the Church,* 2:23; spelling, punctuation, and grammar modernized; paragraph divisions altered; from "The Elders of the Church in Kirtland, to Their Brethren Abroad," Jan. 22, 1834, published in *Evening and Morning Star,* Apr. 1834, p. 152.
11. "John C. Bennett," an editorial published in *Times and Seasons,* Aug. 1, 1842, p. 868; punctuation and grammar modernized; Joseph Smith was the editor of the periodical.
12. *History of the Church,* 3:230; first and second sets of bracketed words in original; from a letter from Joseph Smith to Church members in Caldwell County, Missouri, Dec. 16, 1838, Liberty Jail, Liberty, Missouri.
13. Wilford Woodruff, reporting a discourse given by Joseph Smith on Feb. 19, 1837, in Kirtland, Ohio; "History of Wilford Woodruff," *Deseret News,* July 14, 1858, p. 85; capitalization and grammar modernized; paragraph divisions altered.
14. Wilford Woodruff, reporting a discourse given by Joseph Smith on Apr. 9, 1837, in Kirtland, Ohio; "History of Wilford Woodruff," *Deseret News,* July 14, 1858, p. 86.
15. Daniel Tyler, in "Recollections of the Prophet Joseph Smith," *Juvenile Instructor,* Aug. 15, 1892, pp. 491–92; punctuation and grammar modernized.
16. Orson Hyde, *Deseret News: Semi-Weekly,* June 21, 1870, p. 3.
17. William G. Nelson, in "Joseph Smith, the Prophet," *Young Woman's Journal,* Dec. 1906, p. 543; paragraph divisions altered.
18. Ezra T. Clark, "The Testimony of Ezra T. Clark," July 24, 1901, Farmington, Utah; in Heber Don Carlos Clark, Papers, ca. 1901–74, typescript, Church Archives.

CHAPTER 28

Missionary Service: A Holy Calling, a Glorious Work

"After all that has been said, the greatest and most important duty is to preach the Gospel."

From the Life of Joseph Smith

During the last few years the Saints lived in Kirtland, many members and even some leaders of the Church apostatized. The Church seemed to be passing through a time of crisis. "In this state of things," the Prophet wrote, "God revealed to me that something new must be done for the salvation of His Church."[1] This "something new" was a revelation to send missionaries to England to preach the gospel.

Heber C. Kimball, a member of the Quorum of the Twelve, recalled: "About the first day of June 1837, the Prophet Joseph came to me, while I was seated in . . . the Temple, in Kirtland, and whispering to me, said, 'Brother Heber, the Spirit of the Lord has whispered to me, "Let my servant Heber go to England and proclaim my gospel and open the door of salvation to that nation."'"[2] Elder Kimball was overwhelmed by the thought of such an undertaking: "I felt myself one of the very weakest of God's servants. I asked Joseph what I should say when I got there; he told me to go to the Lord and He would guide me, and speak through me by the same spirit that [directed] him."[3]

The Prophet also extended calls to Orson Hyde, Willard Richards, and Joseph Fielding in Kirtland, and to Isaac Russell, John Snyder, and John Goodson in Toronto, Canada. These brethren were to join Elder Kimball on his mission to England. Gathering in New York City, they sailed on the ship *Garrick* for Great Britain on July 1, 1837. This first mission outside of North America brought some 2,000 converts into the Church during

Heber C. Kimball and Joseph Fielding in England being greeted by those who had joined the Church as a result of their missionary labors. "Glory to God, Joseph," Elder Kimball wrote to the Prophet, "the Lord is with us among the nations!"

the missionaries' first year in England. Elder Kimball wrote joyfully to the Prophet: "Glory to God, Joseph, the Lord is with us among the nations!"[4]

A second apostolic mission to Britain, involving most members of the Twelve under the leadership of Brigham Young, was directed by the Prophet from Nauvoo. Leaving in the fall of 1839, the Twelve arrived in England in 1840. There they began a labor that by 1841 would bring over 6,000 converts into the Church, fulfilling the Lord's promise that He would do "something new" for the salvation of His Church.

From Nauvoo, Joseph Smith continued to send missionaries throughout the world. Elder Orson Hyde landed in England in 1841 and later continued his assigned mission to Jerusalem. He carried a letter of recommendation from Joseph Smith recognizing "the bearer of these presents, a faithful and worthy minister of Jesus Christ, to be our agent and representative in foreign lands, to . . . converse with the priests, rulers and Elders of the Jews."[5] On October 24, 1841, Elder Hyde knelt on Jerusalem's Mount of Olives and petitioned Heavenly Father to dedicate and consecrate the land "for the gathering together of Judah's scattered remnants, according to the predictions of the holy prophets."[6] Elder Hyde then made his way to Germany, where he laid an initial foundation for the growth of the Church there.

On May 11, 1843, the Prophet called Elders Addison Pratt, Noah Rogers, Benjamin F. Grouard, and Knowlton F. Hanks to perform missions to the islands of the South Pacific. This was the first mission of the Church anywhere in that vast region. Elder Hanks died at sea, but Elder Pratt traveled to the Austral Islands, where he taught the gospel on the island of Tubuai. Elders Rogers and Grouard continued to Tahiti, where hundreds of people were baptized as a result of their labors.

Under the direction of Joseph Smith, the Saints were moving forward to fulfill the Lord's command: "Go ye into all the world; and unto whatsoever place ye cannot go ye shall send, that the testimony may go from you into all the world unto every creature" (D&C 84:62).

Teachings of Joseph Smith

Missionary service is a holy work; faith, virtue, diligence, and love enable us to do this work.

"After all that has been said, the greatest and most important duty is to preach the Gospel."[7]

In December 1840 Joseph Smith wrote to members of the Quorum of the Twelve and other priesthood leaders who were serving missions in Great Britain: "Be assured, beloved brethren, that I am no disinterested observer of the things which are transpiring on the face of the whole earth; and amidst the general movements which are in progress, none is of more importance than the glorious work in which you are now engaged; consequently I feel some anxiety on your account, that you may by your virtue, faith, diligence and charity commend yourselves to one another, to the Church of Christ, and to your Father who is in heaven; by whose grace you have been called to so holy a calling; and be enabled to perform the great and responsible duties which rest upon you. And I can assure you, that from the information I have received, I feel satisfied that you have not been remiss in your duty; but that your diligence and faithfulness have been such as must secure you the smiles of that God whose servants you are, and also the good will of the Saints throughout the world.

"The spread of the Gospel throughout England is certainly pleasing; the contemplation of which cannot but afford feelings of no ordinary kind in the bosom of those who have borne the heat and burden of the day, and who were its firm supporters and strenuous advocates in infancy, while surrounded with circumstances the most unpropitious, and its destruction threatened on all hands—like the gallant bark [boat] that has braved the storm unhurt, spreads her canvas to the breeze, and nobly cuts her way through the yielding wave, more conscious than ever of the strength of her timbers, and the experience and capability of her captain, pilot, and crew. . . .

"Love is one of the chief characteristics of Deity, and ought to be manifested by those who aspire to be the sons of God. A man filled with the love of God, is not content with blessing his family alone, but ranges through the whole world, anxious to bless the whole human race. This has been your feeling, and caused you to forego the pleasures of home, that you might be a blessing to others, who are candidates for immortality, but strangers to truth; and for so doing, I pray that heaven's choicest blessings may rest upon you."[8]

We teach the simple truths of the gospel with humility and meekness and avoid contending with others about their beliefs.

"Oh, ye elders of Israel, hearken to my voice; and when you are sent into the world to preach, tell those things you are sent to tell; preach and cry aloud, 'Repent ye, for the kingdom of heaven is at hand; repent and believe the Gospel.' Declare the first principles, and let mysteries alone, lest ye be overthrown. . . . Preach those things the Lord has told you to preach about—repentance and baptism for the remission of sins."[9]

"I spoke and explained concerning the uselessness of preaching to the world about great judgments, but rather to preach the simple Gospel."[10]

"The Elders [should] go forth . . . in all meekness, in sobriety, and preach Jesus Christ and Him crucified; not to contend with others on account of their faith, or systems of religion, but pursue a steady course. This I delivered by way of commandment; and all who observe it not, will pull down persecution upon their heads, while those who do, shall always be filled with the Holy Ghost; this I pronounced as a prophecy."[11]

"If there are any doors open for the Elders to preach the first principles of the gospel, let them not keep silence. Rail not against the sects; neither talk against their tenets. But preach Christ and him crucified, love to God, and love to man; . . . thereby, if possible, we may allay the prejudice of the people. Be meek and lowly of heart, and the Lord God of our fathers shall be with you forevermore."[12]

"Notice this *Key,* and be wise for Christ's sake, and your own soul's sake. Ye are not sent out to be taught, but to teach. Let

"Preach Christ and him crucified, love to God, and love to man. . . . Be meek and lowly of heart, and the Lord God of our fathers shall be with you forevermore."

every word be seasoned with grace. Be vigilant; be sober. It is a day of warning, and not of many words. Act honestly before God and man. . . . Be honest, open, and frank in all your [dealings] with mankind. [See D&C 43:15; 63:58.]"[13]

Before George A. Smith departed for a mission in 1835, he visited with the Prophet Joseph Smith, who was his cousin. George A. Smith recorded: "I called to see Cousin Joseph. He gave me a Book of Mormon, shook hands with me, and said, 'Preach short sermons, make short prayers, and deliver your sermons with a prayerful heart.' "[14]

We teach the gospel as directed by the Spirit.

"All are to preach the Gospel, by the power and influence of the Holy Ghost; and no man can preach the Gospel without the Holy Ghost."[15]

"As Paul said he had to become all things to all men, that he might thereby save some [see 1 Corinthians 9:22], so must the elders of the last days do; and, being sent out to preach the Gospel and warn the world of the judgments to come, we are sure, when they teach as directed by the Spirit, according to the revelations of Jesus Christ, that they will preach the truth and prosper without complaint. Thus we have no new commandment to give, but admonish elders and members to live by every word that proceedeth forth from the mouth of God [see Matthew 4:4], lest they come short of the glory that is reserved for the faithful."[16]

The Prophet spoke at a conference held in October 1839: "President [Joseph Smith] proceeded to give instruction to the Elders respecting preaching the Gospel, and pressed upon them the necessity of getting the Spirit, so that they might preach with the Holy Ghost sent down from heaven; to be careful in speaking on those subjects which are not clearly pointed out in the word of God, which lead to speculation and strife."[17]

On May 14, 1840, Joseph Smith wrote from Nauvoo to Elders Orson Hyde and John E. Page, who were on their way to a mission in the Holy Land: "Do not be discouraged on account of the greatness of the work; only be humble and faithful, and then you can say, 'What art thou, O great mountain! before Zerubbabel shalt thou be brought down.' [See Zechariah 4:7.] He who scattered Israel has promised to gather them; therefore inasmuch as you are to be instrumental in this great work, He will endow you with power, wisdom, might, and intelligence, and every qualification necessary; while your minds will expand wider and wider, until you can circumscribe the earth and the heavens, reach forth into eternity, and contemplate the mighty acts of Jehovah in all their variety and glory."[18]

We seek opportunities to teach the gospel and bear testimony of its truthfulness.

In the fall of 1832 Joseph Smith traveled with Bishop Newel K. Whitney from Kirtland, Ohio, to the eastern United States. On October 13, the Prophet wrote to Emma Smith from New York City: "When I reflect upon this great city like Nineveh not discerning their right hand from their left, yea, more than two hundred thousand souls, my bowels are filled with compassion towards them, and I am determined to lift up my voice in this city and leave the event with God, who holdeth all things in his hands and will not suffer a hair of our heads unnoticed to fall to the ground. . . .

"I have had some conversation with a few, which gave satisfaction, and one very beautiful young gentleman from Jersey, whose countenance was very solemn. He came and sat by my side and began to converse with me about the cholera, and I learned he had been seized with it and came very near dying with it. He said the Lord had spared him for some wise purpose. I took advantage of this and opened a long discourse with him. He received my teaching apparently with much pleasure and became very strongly attached to me. We talked till late at night and concluded to omit conversation till the next day. But having some business to do, he was detained until the boat was ready to go out and must leave. He came to me and bid me farewell, and we parted with much reluctance."[19]

Newel K. Whitney's wife, Elizabeth Ann, recalled her husband's 1832 journey to the eastern United States with Joseph Smith: "My husband traveled with Joseph the Prophet, through many of the Eastern cities, bearing their testimony and collecting means towards building a Temple in Kirtland, and also to purchase lands in Missouri. . . . He said to my husband, 'If they reject us they shall have our testimony, for we will write it and leave it upon their doorsteps and windowsills.' "[20]

In 1834 Joseph Smith preached in a schoolhouse in Pontiac, Michigan. Edward Stevenson was present and recalled the experience: "It was on those school grounds where two Mormon Elders introduced the restored Gospel in the year 1833; and in 1834 Joseph Smith the Prophet preached with such power as had not there ever before been witnessed in this nineteenth century. . . . I can very well remember many of the words of the boy Prophet as they were uttered in simplicity, but with a power which was irresistible to all present. . . .

"With uplifted hand he said: 'I am a witness that there is a God, for I saw Him in open day, while praying in a silent grove, in the spring of 1820.' He further testified that God, the Eternal Father, pointing to a separate personage, in the likeness of Himself, said: 'This is my Beloved Son, hear ye Him.' Oh, how these words thrilled

Each member of the Church has a responsibility to share the gospel. "All are to preach the Gospel," the Prophet Joseph Smith declared, "by the power and influence of the Holy Ghost."

my entire system, and filled me with joy unspeakable to behold one who, like Paul the apostle of olden time, could with boldness testify that he had been in the presence of Jesus Christ! . . .

". . . A succession of meetings were held, in which the Prophet was joined, and very interestingly, too, by the three witnesses to the Book of Mormon. During his visit to this branch the Prophet testified that he was instructed to organize a Church after the pattern of the Church which Jesus organized, with Twelve Apostles, Seventies, Elders, gifts and blessings, with signs following, as found recorded in the sixteenth chapter of Mark. . . . 'As a servant of God,' said Joseph, 'I promise you, inasmuch as you will repent and be baptized for the remission of your sins, you shall receive the Holy Ghost.' "[21]

While being taken from Far West, Missouri, in November 1838, to his imprisonment in Richmond, Missouri, the Prophet again taught the gospel: "We were visited by some ladies and gentlemen. One of the women came up, and very candidly inquired of the troops which of the prisoners was the Lord whom the 'Mormons' worshiped? One of the guard pointed to me with a significant smile, and said, 'This is he.' The woman then turning to me inquired whether I professed to be the Lord and Savior? I replied, that I professed to be nothing but a man, and a minister of salvation, sent by Jesus Christ to preach the Gospel.

"This answer so surprised the woman that she began to inquire into our doctrine, and I preached a discourse, both to her and her companions, and to the wondering soldiers, who listened with almost breathless attention while I set forth the doctrine of faith in Jesus Christ, and repentance, and baptism for remission of sins, with the promise of the Holy Ghost, as recorded in the second chapter of the Acts of the Apostles [see Acts 2:38–39].

"The woman was satisfied, and praised God in the hearing of the soldiers, and went away, praying that God would protect and deliver us."[22]

Dan Jones recalled that on the evening before the Prophet was martyred in Carthage Jail, the following occurred: "Joseph bore a powerful testimony to the guards of the divine authenticity of the Book of Mormon, the restoration of the Gospel, the administration of angels, and that the kingdom of God was again established upon the earth, for the sake of which he was then incarcerated in that prison, and not because he had violated any law of God or man."[23]

Suggestions for Study and Teaching

Consider these ideas as you study the chapter or as you prepare to teach. For additional help, see pages vii–xii.

- Review pages 327–29, noting the missionary efforts that were organized under the direction of the Prophet Joseph Smith. Have you been influenced in some way through the work of those early missionaries? If so, how?
- Read the paragraph that begins at the bottom of page 330, and consider why love influences us in the way the Prophet describes. What are some other characteristics we need in order to be effective missionaries? (For some examples, see pages 330–31.)

- Review the Prophet Joseph Smith's words about what missionaries should teach and how they should teach (pages 331–33). Why should we preach "the first principles" of the gospel? What can be the consequences of contending with others on the subject of religion? What do you think it means to "let every word be seasoned with grace" when preaching the gospel?
- Review the second full paragraph on page 332. In what ways has the Holy Ghost guided your efforts to share the gospel? Why can't we preach the gospel without the Holy Ghost?
- Review Joseph Smith's experiences recounted on pages 333–36. What can we learn about sharing the gospel from these experiences?
- In what ways can we actively seek opportunities to share the gospel with others? In what ways can we prepare ourselves for such opportunities? How can we involve our families in missionary work?

Related Scriptures: Matthew 28:19–20; 2 Nephi 2:8; Alma 26:26–37; D&C 4:1–7; 31:3–5

Notes

1. *History of the Church,* 2:489; from "History of the Church" (manuscript), book B-1, p. 761, Church Archives, The Church of Jesus Christ of Latter-day Saints, Salt Lake City, Utah.
2. Heber C. Kimball, "Synopsis of the History of Heber Chase Kimball," *Deseret News,* Apr. 14, 1858, p. 33; punctuation and capitalization modernized.
3. Heber C. Kimball, *Deseret News,* May 21, 1862, p. 370; capitalization modernized.
4. Quoted by Orson F. Whitney, in Conference Report, Oct. 1920, p. 33.
5. Letter of recommendation issued by Joseph Smith and others to Orson Hyde, Apr. 6, 1840, Nauvoo, Illinois, published in *Times and Seasons,* Apr. 1840, p. 86.
6. Orson Hyde, *A Voice from Jerusalem, or a Sketch of the Travels and Ministry of Elder Orson Hyde* (1842), p. 29.
7. *History of the Church,* 2:478; from a discourse given by Joseph Smith on Apr. 6, 1837, in Kirtland, Ohio; reported by *Messenger and Advocate,* Apr. 1837, p. 487.
8. *History of the Church,* 4:226–27; punctuation and grammar modernized; from a letter from Joseph Smith to the Twelve, Dec. 15, 1840, Nauvoo, Illinois, published in *Times and Seasons,* Jan. 1, 1841, p. 258; this letter is incorrectly dated Oct. 19, 1840, in *History of the Church.*
9. *History of the Church,* 5:344; spelling modernized; from a discourse given by Joseph Smith on Apr. 8, 1843, in Nauvoo, Illinois; reported by Willard Richards and William Clayton.
10. *History of the Church,* 4:11; from instructions given by Joseph Smith on Sept. 29, 1839, in Commerce, Illinois; reported by James Mulholland.
11. *History of the Church,* 2:431; from instructions given by Joseph Smith on Mar. 30, 1836, in Kirtland, Ohio.

12. Letter from Joseph Smith and others to Hezekiah Peck, Aug. 31, 1835, Kirtland, Ohio; in "The Book of John Whitmer," p. 80, Community of Christ Archives, Independence, Missouri; copy of "The Book of John Whitmer" in Church Archives.
13. *History of the Church,* 3:384; from a discourse given by Joseph Smith on July 2, 1839, in Montrose, Iowa; reported by Wilford Woodruff and Willard Richards.
14. George A. Smith, "History of George Albert Smith by Himself," p. 36, George Albert Smith, Papers, 1834–75, Church Archives.
15. *History of the Church,* 2:477; from a discourse given by Joseph Smith on Apr. 6, 1837, in Kirtland, Ohio; reported by *Messenger and Advocate,* Apr. 1837, p. 487.
16. *History of the Church,* 5:404; from a letter from Joseph Smith to the editor of the *Times and Seasons,* May 22, 1843, Nauvoo, Illinois, published in *Times and Seasons,* May 15, 1843, p. 199; this issue of the *Times and Seasons* was published late.
17. *History of the Church,* 4:13; from a discourse given by Joseph Smith on Oct. 6, 1839, in Commerce, Illinois; reported by *Times and Seasons,* Dec. 1839, p. 31.
18. *History of the Church,* 4:128–29; from a letter from Joseph Smith to Orson Hyde and John E. Page, May 14, 1840, Nauvoo, Illinois. Although Elder Hyde completed his mission to the Holy Land, Elder Page remained in the United States.
19. Letter from Joseph Smith to Emma Smith, Oct. 13, 1832, New York City, New York; Community of Christ Archives, Independence, Missouri.
20. Elizabeth Ann Whitney, "A Leaf from an Autobiography," *Woman's Exponent,* Oct. 1, 1878, p. 71; spelling, punctuation, and capitalization modernized.
21. Edward Stevenson, "The Home of My Boyhood," *Juvenile Instructor,* July 15, 1894, pp. 443–45; punctuation and grammar modernized; paragraph divisions altered.
22. *History of the Church,* 3:200–201; an account of a discourse given by Joseph Smith on Nov. 4, 1838, near the Missouri River, while being taken as a prisoner from Far West to Independence, Missouri; reported by Parley P. Pratt.
23. *History of the Church,* 6:600; an account of instructions given by Joseph Smith on June 26, 1844, in Carthage Jail, Carthage, Illinois; reported by Dan Jones.

CHAPTER 29

Living with Others in Peace and Harmony

"We want to live in peace with all men."

From the Life of Joseph Smith

One of the desires of the early Latter-day Saints was simply to be allowed to live their religion in peace. But wherever they moved, peace eluded them. In 1833, just two years after the dedication of a place of gathering in Missouri, mobs forced the Saints to leave Jackson County, Missouri (see page 281). Church members found temporary refuge in Clay County, Missouri, and then, in 1836, began moving into northern Missouri. Most of them settled in Caldwell County, a new county organized by the state legislature to accommodate the Saints. Far West, which served as the county seat, soon became a thriving Latter-day Saint settlement.

The Prophet Joseph Smith had continued to live in Kirtland, Ohio, but in January 1838, he was forced to leave, fearing for his life. With his family, he traveled the 900 miles to Far West, where he joined the Saints living there. Later in 1838, most of the Kirtland Saints sold or abandoned their homes and followed the Prophet to Missouri. To accommodate the Church members pouring into the area, the Prophet designated areas near Far West where the Saints could settle. In July 1838, cornerstones were dedicated for a temple in Far West, giving the Saints hope that they could establish a permanent settlement where they could enjoy prosperity and peace. Unfortunately, tensions similar to those they experienced in Jackson County soon divided them from local settlers, and in the fall of 1838, mobs and militia once again began to harass and attack Latter-day Saints.

One day the Prophet was visiting his parents' home in Far West, when a group of armed militiamen came in and announced

In Far West, Missouri, when a group of armed militiamen came to arrest Joseph Smith, he “looked upon them with a very pleasant smile and, stepping up to them, gave each of them his hand.”

that they had come to kill him for a supposed crime. Lucy Mack Smith, the Prophet's mother, described his gift for peacemaking:

"[Joseph] looked upon them with a very pleasant smile and, stepping up to them, gave each of them his hand in a manner which convinced them that he was neither a guilty criminal nor yet a cowering hypocrite. They stopped and stared as though a spectre had crossed their path.

"Joseph sat down and entered into conversation with them and explained to them the views and feelings of the people called Mormons and what their course had been, as also the treatment which they had met with from their enemies since the first outset of the Church. He told them that malice and detraction had pursued them ever since they entered Missouri, but they were a people who had never broken the laws to his knowledge. But if they had, they stood ready to be tried by the law. . . .

"After this, he rose and said, 'Mother, I believe I will go home. Emma will be expecting me.' Two of the men sprang to their feet, saying, 'You shall not go alone, for it is not safe. We will go with you and guard you.' Joseph thanked them, and they went with him.

"The remainder of the officers stood by the door while these were absent, and I overheard the following conversation between them:

"First Officer: 'Did you not feel strangely when Smith took you by the hand? I never felt so in my life.'

"Second Officer: 'I felt as though I could not move. I would not harm one hair of that man's head for the whole world.'

"Third Officer: 'This is the last time you will ever catch me coming to kill Joe Smith or the Mormons either.' . . .

"Those men who went with my son promised to go disband the militia under them and go home, and said that if he had any use for them, they would come back and follow him anywhere."[1]

Speaking the truth in a kind, forthright way, Joseph Smith overcame prejudice and hostility and made peace with many of those who had been his enemies.

Teachings of Joseph Smith

By striving to be peacemakers, we can live in greater harmony and love with others.

"Jesus said: 'Blessed are the peacemakers: for they shall be called the children of God.' [Matthew 5:9.] Wherefore if the nation, a single State, community, or family ought to be grateful for anything, it is peace.

"Peace, lovely child of heaven!—peace like light from the same great parent, gratifies, animates, and happifies the just and the unjust, and is the very essence of happiness below, and bliss above.

"He that does not strive with all his powers of body and mind, with all his influence at home and abroad—and cause others to do so too—to seek peace and maintain it for his own benefit and convenience, and for the honor of his State, nation, and country, has no claim on the clemency [mercy] of man; nor should he be entitled to the friendship of woman or the protection of government.

"He is the canker-worm to gnaw his own vitals; and the vulture to prey upon his own body; and he is, as to his own prospects and prosperity in life, a [destroyer] of his own pleasure.

"A community of such beings are not far from hell on earth, and should be let alone as unfit for the smiles of the free or praise of the brave.

"But the peacemaker, O give ear to him! for the words of his mouth and his doctrine drop like the rain, and distil as the dew. They are like the gentle mist upon the herbs, and as the moderate shower upon the grass.

"Animation, virtue, love, contentment, philanthropy, benevolence, compassion, humanity and friendship push life into bliss: and men, a little below the angels, exercising their powers, privileges, and knowledge according to the order, rules, and regulations of revelation, by Jesus Christ, dwell together in unity; and the sweet odor that is wafted by the breath of joy and satisfaction from their righteous communion is like the rich perfume from the consecrated oil that was poured upon the head of Aaron, or

In the Sermon on the Mount, the Savior taught, "Blessed are the peacemakers: for they shall be called the children of God."

like the luscious fragrance that rises from the field of Arabian spices. Yea, more, the voice of the peacemaker—

"It is like the music of the spheres—
It charms our souls and calms our fears;
It turns the world to Paradise,
And men to pearls of greater price."[2]

"Brethren beloved, continue in brotherly love; walk in meekness, watching unto prayer, that you be not overcome. Follow after peace, as said our beloved brother Paul, that you may be the children of our Heavenly Father [see Romans 14:19]."[3]

"Humanity towards all, reason and refinement to enforce virtue, and good for evil are . . . eminently designed to cure more disorders of society than an appeal to arms, or even argument untempered with friendship. . . . Our motto, then, is Peace with all! If we have joy in the love of God, let us try to give a reason of that joy, which all the world cannot gainsay or resist."[4]

"We want to live in peace with all men."[5]

We can cultivate peace by honoring one another and refusing to find fault.

"We [hope that] our brethren will be careful of one another's feelings, and walk in love, honoring one another more than themselves, as is required by the Lord."[6]

"The man who willeth to do well, we should extol his virtues, and speak not of his faults behind his back."[7]

"Now, in this world, mankind are naturally selfish, ambitious and striving to excel one above another; yet some are willing to build up others as well as themselves."[8]

"Let the Twelve and all Saints be willing to confess all their sins, and not keep back a part; and let [them] be humble, and not be exalted, and beware of pride, and not seek to excel one above another, but act for each other's good, and pray for one another, and honor our brother or make honorable mention of his name, and not backbite and devour our brother."[9]

"If you will put away from your midst all evil speaking, backbiting, and ungenerous thoughts and feelings: humble yourselves, and cultivate every principle of virtue and love, then will the blessings of Jehovah rest upon you, and you will yet see good and glorious days; peace will be within your gates, and prosperity in your borders."[10]

We can cultivate harmony in our communities by respecting the freedom of all people to believe according to their own conscience.

Articles of Faith 1:11: "We claim the privilege of worshiping Almighty God according to the dictates of our own conscience, and allow all men the same privilege, let them worship how, where, or what they may."[11]

"We deem it a just principle, and it is one the force of which we believe ought to be duly considered by every individual, that all men are created equal, and that all have the privilege of thinking for themselves upon all matters relative to conscience. Consequently, then, we are not disposed, had we the power, to deprive any one of exercising that free independence of mind which heaven has so graciously bestowed upon the human family as one of its choicest gifts."[12]

"I have the most liberal sentiments, and feelings of charity towards all sects, parties, and denominations; and the rights and liberties of conscience, I hold most sacred and dear, and despise no man for differing with me in matters of opinion."[13]

"The Saints can testify whether I am willing to lay down my life for my brethren. If it has been demonstrated that I have been willing to die for a 'Mormon,' I am bold to declare before Heaven that I am just as ready to die in defending the rights of a Presbyterian, a Baptist, or a good man of any other denomination; for the same principle which would trample upon the rights of the Latter-day Saints would trample upon the rights of the Roman Catholics, or of any other denomination who may be unpopular and too weak to defend themselves.

"It is a love of liberty which inspires my soul—civil and religious liberty to the whole of the human race. Love of liberty was diffused into my soul by my grandfathers while they dandled me on their knees. . . .

"If I esteem mankind to be in error, shall I bear them down? No. I will lift them up, and in their own way too, if I cannot persuade them my way is better; and I will not seek to compel any man to believe as I do, only by the force of reasoning, for truth will cut its own way."[14]

"We ought always to be aware of those prejudices which sometimes so strangely present themselves, and are so congenial to human nature, against our friends, neighbors, and brethren of the world, who choose to differ from us in opinion and in matters of faith. Our religion is between us and our God. Their religion is between them and their God."[15]

"When we see virtuous qualities in men, we should always acknowledge them, let their understanding be what it may in relation to creeds and doctrine; for all men are, or ought to be free, possessing unalienable rights, and the high and noble qualifications of the laws of nature and of self-preservation, to think and act and say as they please, while they maintain a due respect to the rights and privileges of all other creatures, infringing upon none. This doctrine I do most heartily subscribe to and practice."[16]

"All persons are entitled to their agency, for God has so ordained it. He has constituted mankind moral agents, and given them power to choose good or evil; to seek after that which is good, by pursuing the pathway of holiness in this life, which brings peace of mind, and joy in the Holy Ghost here, and a fulness of joy and happiness at His right hand hereafter; or to pursue an evil course, going on in sin and rebellion against God, thereby bringing condemnation to their souls in this world, and an eternal loss in the world to come. Since the God of heaven has left these things optional with every individual, we do not wish to deprive them of it. We only wish to act the part of a faithful watchman, agreeable to the word of the Lord to Ezekiel the prophet (Ezekiel chap. 33, verses 2, 3, 4, 5), and leave it for others to do as seemeth them good."[17]

"It is one of the first principles of my life, and one that I have cultivated from my childhood, having been taught it by my father, to allow every one the liberty of conscience. . . . In my feelings I am always ready to die for the protection of the weak and oppressed in their just rights."[18]

"Meddle not with any man for his religion: all governments ought to permit every man to enjoy his religion unmolested. No man is authorized to take away life in consequence of difference of religion, which all laws and governments ought to tolerate and protect, right or wrong."[19]

"We will . . . cultivate peace and friendship with all, mind our own business, and come off with flying colors, respected, because, in respecting others, we respect ourselves."[20]

"Although I never feel to force my doctrine upon any person, I rejoice to see prejudice give way to truth, and the traditions of men dispersed by the pure principles of the Gospel of Jesus Christ."[21]

Suggestions for Study and Teaching

Consider these ideas as you study the chapter or as you prepare to teach. For additional help, see pages vii–xii.

- Review the story of Joseph Smith speaking with members of the militia (pages 339–41). Why do you think the Prophet was able to stay calm in this situation? Consider other examples you have seen of people remaining calm and peaceful in difficult situations. What resulted from the actions of these people?
- Review pages 342–43, looking for words and phrases the Prophet used to describe peace and peacemakers. What characteristics can help us be peacemakers in our homes and communities?
- Read the second paragraph on page 344. How do you feel when you look for others' faults? How do you feel when you look for the virtuous qualities in others? How do you think other people feel when you take time to acknowledge their virtuous qualities?
- Read the third paragraph on page 344. In what ways can we build up one another? What have other people done to build you up? In what ways do such actions lead to peace?
- Review pages 344–46, looking for the Prophet's teachings about how we should treat people whose religious beliefs differ from our own. What are ways we can honor the rights of others to "worship how, where, or what they may"?
- Read the last paragraph on page 346. How can we share the restored gospel with others while also showing respect for their beliefs?

Related Scriptures: Ephesians 4:31–32; Mosiah 4:9–16; 4 Nephi 1:15–16; D&C 134:2–4, 7

Notes

1. Lucy Mack Smith, "The History of Lucy Smith, Mother of the Prophet," 1844–45 manuscript, book 15, pp. 8–10, Church Archives, The Church of Jesus Christ of Latter-day Saints, Salt Lake City, Utah.
2. *History of the Church*, 6:245–46; punctuation and grammar modernized; from "A Friendly Hint to Missouri," an article written under the direction of Joseph Smith, Mar. 8, 1844, Nauvoo, Illinois, published in

Times and Seasons, Mar. 15, 1844, p. 473.

3. Letter from Joseph Smith and others to Church members in Thompson, Ohio, Feb. 6, 1833, Kirtland, Ohio; Letter Book 1, 1829–35, p. 26, Joseph Smith, Collection, Church Archives.
4. *History of the Church,* 6:219–20; paragraph divisions altered; from "Pacific Innuendo," an article written under the direction of Joseph Smith, Feb. 17, 1844, Nauvoo, Illinois, published in *Times and Seasons,* Feb. 15, 1844, p. 443; this issue of the *Times and Seasons* was published late.
5. *History of the Church,* 2:122; from a letter from Joseph Smith and others to John Lincoln and others, June 21, 1834, Clay County, Missouri, published in *Evening and Morning Star,* July 1834, p. 176.
6. *History of the Church,* 1:368; from a letter from Joseph Smith and his counselors in the First Presidency to William W. Phelps and the brethren in Missouri, June 25, 1833, Kirtland, Ohio.
7. *History of the Church,* 1:444; from a Joseph Smith journal entry, Nov. 19, 1833, Kirtland, Ohio.
8. *History of the Church,* 5:388; from a discourse given by Joseph Smith on May 14, 1843, in Yelrome, Illinois; reported by Wilford Woodruff.
9. *History of the Church,* 3:383–84; from a discourse given by Joseph Smith on July 2, 1839, in Montrose, Iowa; reported by Wilford Woodruff and Willard Richards.
10. *History of the Church,* 4:226; from a letter from Joseph Smith and Hyrum Smith to the Saints in Kirtland, Ohio, Oct. 19, 1840, Nauvoo, Illinois.
11. Articles of Faith 1:11.
12. *History of the Church,* 2:6–7; from "The Elders of the Church in Kirtland, to Their Brethren Abroad," Jan. 22, 1834, published in *Evening and Morning Star,* Feb. 1834, p. 135.
13. Letter from Joseph Smith to Isaac Galland, Mar. 22, 1839, Liberty Jail, Liberty, Missouri, published in *Times and Seasons,* Feb. 1840, pp. 55–56.
14. *History of the Church,* 5:498–99; from a discourse given by Joseph Smith on July 9, 1843, in Nauvoo, Illinois; reported by Willard Richards; see also appendix, page 562, item 3.
15. *History of the Church,* 3:303–4; from a letter from Joseph Smith and others to Edward Partridge and the Church, Mar. 20, 1839, Liberty Jail, Liberty, Missouri.
16. *History of the Church,* 5:156; punctuation modernized; paragraph divisions altered; from a letter from Joseph Smith to James Arlington Bennet, Sept. 8, 1842, Nauvoo, Illinois; James Bennet's last name is incorrectly spelled "Bennett" in *History of the Church.*
17. *History of the Church,* 4:45, footnote; punctuation and grammar modernized; from a letter from the First Presidency and high council to the Saints living west of Kirtland, Ohio, Dec. 8, 1839, Commerce, Illinois, published in *Times and Seasons,* Dec. 1839, p. 29.
18. *History of the Church,* 6:56–57; from a discourse given by Joseph Smith on Oct. 15, 1843, in Nauvoo, Illinois; reported by Willard Richards; see also appendix, page 562, item 3.
19. *History of the Church,* 6:304; from a discourse given by Joseph Smith on Apr. 7, 1844, in Nauvoo, Illinois; reported by Wilford Woodruff, Willard Richards, Thomas Bullock, and William Clayton; see also appendix, page 562, item 3.
20. *History of the Church,* 6:221; from a letter from Joseph Smith to the editor of the *Nauvoo Neighbor,* Feb. 10, 1844, Nauvoo, Illinois, published in *Nauvoo Neighbor,* Feb. 21, 1844; this letter is incorrectly dated Feb. 19, 1844, in *History of the Church.*
21. *History of the Church,* 6:213; punctuation modernized; from a letter from Joseph Smith to Joseph L. Heywood, Feb. 13, 1844, Nauvoo, Illinois.

CHAPTER 30

Valiant in the Cause of Christ

"I am a lover of the cause of Christ."

From the Life of Joseph Smith

In October 1838, conflict between the Saints living in northern Missouri and the local mobs and militia reached a critical point. On the 27th of that month, Missouri governor Lilburn W. Boggs issued an infamous order to a commander of the state militia: "The Mormons must be treated as enemies and *must be exterminated* or driven from the state, if necessary for the public good. Their outrages are beyond all description."[1] Three days later, a large group of armed militia encamped near Far West, Missouri, the location of Church headquarters, and prepared to attack the city.

Gravely concerned for the safety of the Latter-day Saints, Joseph Smith and other Church leaders agreed to meet with officers of the militia on October 31 to negotiate for peace. However, as they approached the camp of the militia, the Prophet and his companions were suddenly arrested. They were then marched into the camp, where they were forced to lie all night on the cold ground in a freezing rainstorm while the guards shouted and cursed at them. When the officers decided to take the prisoners to Independence, Missouri, Joseph and his companions begged to be allowed to see their families.

"I found my wife and children in tears," the Prophet wrote, "who feared we had been shot by those who had sworn to take our lives, and that they would see me no more. . . . Who can realize the feelings which I experienced at that time, to be thus torn from my companion, and leave her surrounded with monsters in the shape of men, and my children, too, not knowing how their wants would be supplied; while I was to be taken far from them in order that my enemies might destroy me when they thought

In Richmond, Missouri, a group of imprisoned Church leaders listened for hours as their guards boasted of attacks on the Saints. Suddenly Joseph Smith rose and said, "In the name of Jesus Christ I rebuke you, and command you to be still."

proper to do so. My partner wept, my children clung to me, until they were thrust from me by the swords of the guards."[2]

After a short detainment in Independence, the Prophet and several other Church leaders were taken to Richmond, Missouri, where they were confined in an old log house, chained together, and kept under heavy guard. The Prophet would remain imprisoned in Richmond for about three weeks before being transferred to the jail in Liberty, Missouri. Although the circumstances were grim, the Prophet wrote to Emma shortly after arriving in Richmond: "We are prisoners in chains and under strong guards, for Christ's sake and for no other cause. . . . Brother [George W.] Robinson is chained next to me; he has a true heart and a firm mind. Brother [Lyman] Wight is next, Brother [Sidney] Rigdon next, Hyrum [Smith] next, Parley [P. Pratt] next, Amasa [Lyman] next, and thus we are bound together in chains as well as the cords of everlasting love. We are in good spirits and rejoice that we are counted worthy to be persecuted for Christ's sake."[3]

During one of the cold, tedious nights, the men lay on the floor until past midnight, unable to sleep because the guards were boasting of their recent attacks on the Saints, including acts of robbery, rape, and murder. Elder Parley P. Pratt recounted: "I had listened till I became so disgusted, shocked, horrified, and so filled with the spirit of indignant justice that I could scarcely refrain from rising upon my feet and rebuking the guards; but had said nothing to Joseph, or any one else, although I lay next to him and knew he was awake. On a sudden he arose to his feet, and spoke in a voice of thunder, or as the roaring lion, uttering, as near as I can recollect, the following words:

" '*SILENCE*. . . . In the name of Jesus Christ I rebuke you, and command you to be still; I will not live another minute and hear such language. Cease such talk, or you or I die *THIS INSTANT!*'

"He ceased to speak. He stood erect in terrible majesty. Chained, and without a weapon; calm, unruffled and dignified as an angel, he looked upon the quailing guards, whose weapons were lowered or dropped to the ground; whose knees smote together, and who, shrinking into a corner, or crouching at his feet, begged his pardon, and remained quiet till a change of guards."[4]

Teachings of Joseph Smith

The valiant cheerfully do all they can, even during times of trouble.

In September 1839, when the Saints were beginning the difficult work of building the city of Nauvoo, Illinois, the Prophet wrote to a Church member in Kirtland, Ohio: "As to the situation of the Church here, matters go with us as well as can reasonably be expected. . . . There have quite a number of families gathered up here already; and we anticipate a continuance, especially as upon inquiry we have found that we have not had more than [the usual] ratio of sickness here, notwithstanding the trials we have had, and the hardships to which we have been exposed. Calculating as we do, upon the mercy and power of God in our behalf, we hope to persevere on in every good and useful work, even unto the end, that when we come to be tried in the balance we may not be found wanting."[5]

In September 1842, the Prophet wrote the following in a letter to the Church, later recorded in Doctrine and Covenants 128:19, 22: "Now, what do we hear in the gospel which we have received? A voice of gladness! A voice of mercy from heaven; and a voice of truth out of the earth; glad tidings for the dead; a voice of gladness for the living and the dead; glad tidings of great joy. . . . Brethren, shall we not go on in so great a cause? Go forward and not backward. Courage, brethren; and on, on to the victory! Let your hearts rejoice, and be exceedingly glad."[6]

The Prophet said about the progress of the Church in 1831: "It was clearly evident that the Lord gave us power in proportion to the work to be done, and strength according to the race set before us, and grace and help as our needs required."[7]

The valiant love the cause of Christ and strive to develop Christlike qualities.

"I am a lover of the cause of Christ and of virtue, chastity, and an upright, steady course of conduct, and a holy walk."[8]

"I believe in living a virtuous, upright and holy life before God and feel it my duty to persuade all men in my power to do the same, that they may cease to do evil and learn to do well, and break off their sins by righteousness."[9]

"Strengthening our faith by adding every good quality that adorns the children of the blessed Jesus, we can pray in the season of prayer; we can love our neighbor as ourselves, and be faithful in tribulation, knowing that the reward of such is greater in the kingdom of heaven. What a consolation! What a joy! Let me live the life of the righteous, and let my reward be like his!

". . . Righteousness must be the aim of the Saints in all things, and when the [Doctrine and Covenants is] published, they will learn that great things must be expected from them. Do good and work righteousness with an eye single to the glory of God, and you shall reap your reward when the Lord recompenses every one according to his work. . . . In the name of Jesus Christ, we entreat you to live worthy of the blessings that shall follow after much tribulation, to satiate the souls of them that hold out faithful to the end."[10]

"From henceforth, let truth and righteousness prevail and abound in you; and in all things be temperate; abstain from drunkenness, and from swearing, and from all profane language, and from everything which is unrighteous or unholy; also from enmity, and hatred, and covetousness, and from every unholy desire. Be honest one with another, for it seems that some have come short of these things, and some have been uncharitable, and have manifested greediness. . . . Such characters God hates—and they shall have their turn of sorrow in the rolling of the great wheel, for it rolleth and none can hinder. Zion shall yet live, though she seem to be dead."[11]

"As one that greatly desires the salvation of men, let me remind you all to strive with godly zeal for virtue, holiness, and the commandments of the Lord. Be good, be wise, be just, be liberal; and above all, be charitable, always abounding in all good works. And may health, peace and the love of God our Father, and the grace of Jesus Christ our Lord be and abide with you all, is the sincere prayer of your devoted brother and friend in the everlasting Gospel."[12]

"Be meek and lowly, upright and pure; render good for evil. . . . Be humble and patient in all circumstances of life; we shall then triumph more gloriously."[13]

"We feel to exhort our brethren with boldness, to be humble and prayerful, to walk indeed as children of the light and of the day, that they may have grace to withstand every temptation, and to overcome every evil in the worthy name of our Lord Jesus Christ."[14]

The valiant strive to improve themselves while in this life.

"The reflection that everyone is to receive according to his own diligence and perseverance while in the vineyard, ought to inspire everyone who is called to be a minister of these glad tidings, to so improve his talent that he may gain other talents, that when the Master sits down to take an account of the conduct of His servants, it may be said, Well done, good and faithful servant: thou hast been faithful over a few things; I will now make thee ruler over many things: enter thou into the joy of thy Lord [Matthew 25:21]. . . .

". . . No consideration whatever ought to deter us from showing ourselves approved in the sight of God, according to His divine requirement. Men not unfrequently forget that they are dependent upon heaven for every blessing which they are permitted to enjoy, and that for every opportunity granted them they are to give an account. You know, brethren, that when the Master in the Savior's parable of the stewards called his servants before him he gave them several talents to improve on while he should tarry abroad for a little season, and when he returned he called for an accounting [see Matthew 25:14–30]. So it is now. Our Master is absent only for a little season, and at the end of it He will call each to render an account; and where the five talents were bestowed, ten will be required; and he that has made no improvement will be cast out as an unprofitable servant, while the faithful will enjoy everlasting honors. Therefore we earnestly implore the grace of our Father to rest upon you, through Jesus Christ His Son, that you may not faint in the hour of temptation, nor be overcome in the time of persecution."[15]

"He that has made no improvement will be cast out as an unprofitable servant, while the faithful will enjoy everlasting honors."

"After this instruction, you will be responsible for your own sins; it is a desirable honor that you should so walk before our heavenly Father as to save yourselves; we are all responsible to God for the manner we improve the light and wisdom given by our Lord to enable us to save ourselves."[16]

The valiant endure faithfully to the end and will receive a crown of celestial glory.

"Our trust is in God, and we are determined, His grace assisting us, to maintain the cause and hold out faithful unto the end, that we may be crowned with crowns of celestial glory, and enter into the rest that is prepared for the children of God."[17]

"Fight the good fight of faith that ye may gain the crown which is laid up for those that endure faithful unto the end of their probation [see 2 Timothy 4:7–8]. Therefore hold fast that which ye have received so liberally from the hand of God so that when the times of refreshing shall come ye may not have labored in vain, but that ye may rest from all your labors and have fulness of joy in the kingdom of God."[18]

"You cannot be too good. Patience is heavenly, obedience is noble, forgiveness is merciful, and exaltation is godly; and he that holds out faithful to the end shall in no wise lose his reward. A good man will endure all things to honor Christ, and even dispose of the whole world, and all in it, to save his soul."[19]

Suggestions for Study and Teaching

Consider these ideas as you study the chapter or as you prepare to teach. For additional help, see pages vii–xii.

- Read the story of Joseph Smith rebuking the guards on page 351. How does this story influence your feelings about Joseph Smith?
- Joseph Smith said that the gospel is a "voice of gladness" and declared, "Let your hearts rejoice, and be exceedingly glad" (page 352). In what ways can our knowledge of the gospel help us to rejoice and be "exceedingly glad" even during times of hardship?
- Read the third paragraph on page 352. What do you think it means to receive "power in proportion to the work to be done"? What examples can you recall that illustrate this truth?
- Review the fourth paragraph on page 352. What are some characteristics you would expect in someone who says he is "a lover of the cause of Christ"? (For some examples, see pages 352–54.)
- As you study the Prophet Joseph's counsel on pages 354–55, think about something in your life that needs to improve. Determine what you will do to take responsibility for that improvement.

- Review the last two paragraphs of the chapter (page 356). What are some of the rewards of those who "fight the good fight of faith"? How do some people try to persuade us not to be "too good"? How can we respond to such pressures?

Related Scriptures: Deuteronomy 31:6; 2 Timothy 1:7–8; 2 Nephi 31:19–20; Mosiah 5:15; D&C 59:23

Notes

1. Lilburn W. Boggs, quoted in *History of the Church,* 3:175; from orders given to John B. Clark, Oct. 27, 1838, Jefferson City, Missouri.
2. *History of the Church,* 3:193; from "Extract, from the Private Journal of Joseph Smith Jr.," *Times and Seasons,* Nov. 1839, p. 6.
3. Letter from Joseph Smith to Emma Smith, Nov. 12, 1838, Richmond, Missouri; Community of Christ Archives, Independence, Missouri.
4. Parley P. Pratt, *Autobiography of Parley P. Pratt,* ed. Parley P. Pratt Jr. (1938), pp. 210–11; italics deleted.
5. *History of the Church,* 4:8–9; bracketed words in original; grammar modernized; paragraph divisions altered; from a letter from Joseph Smith to Isaac Galland, Sept. 11, 1839, Commerce, Illinois.
6. Doctrine and Covenants 128:19, 22; a letter from Joseph Smith to the Saints, Sept. 6, 1842, Nauvoo, Illinois.
7. *History of the Church,* 1:176; from "History of the Church" (manuscript), book A-1, p. 118, Church Archives, The Church of Jesus Christ of Latter-day Saints, Salt Lake City, Utah.
8. Letter from Joseph Smith to William W. Phelps, July 31, 1832, Hiram, Ohio; Joseph Smith, Collection, Church Archives.
9. Letter from Joseph Smith to the editor of the *Chester County Register and Examiner,* Jan. 22, 1840, Brandywine, Pennsylvania; original in private possession; the letter was published in the newspaper on Feb. 11, 1840.
10. *History of the Church,* 2:229–30, footnote; from "To the Saints Scattered Abroad," *Messenger and Advocate,* June 1835, pp. 137–38.
11. *History of the Church,* 3:233; from a letter from Joseph Smith to Church members in Caldwell County, Missouri, Dec. 16, 1838, Liberty Jail, Liberty, Missouri.
12. *History of the Church,* 5:417; from a letter of recommendation issued by Joseph Smith to Brigham Young, June 1, 1843, Nauvoo, Illinois.
13. *History of the Church,* 6:411; from a discourse given by Joseph Smith on May 26, 1844, in Nauvoo, Illinois; reported by Thomas Bullock.
14. Letter from Joseph Smith and high priests to the brethren in Geneseo, New York, Nov. 23, 1833, Kirtland, Ohio, Church Archives.
15. *History of the Church,* 2:6, 23–24; from "The Elders of the Church in Kirtland, to Their Brethren Abroad," Jan. 22, 1834, published in *Evening and Morning Star,* Feb. 1834, p. 135; Apr. 1834, p. 152.
16. *History of the Church,* 4:606; from a discourse given by Joseph Smith on Apr. 28, 1842, in Nauvoo, Illinois; reported by Eliza R. Snow; see also appendix, page 562, item 3.
17. *History of the Church,* 1:450; from a letter from Joseph Smith to Edward Partridge and others, Dec. 5, 1833, Kirtland, Ohio.
18. Letter from Joseph Smith and John Whitmer to the Saints in Colesville, New York, Aug. 20, 1830, Harmony, Pennsylvania; in Newel Knight, Autobiography and Journal, ca. 1846–47, pp. 129–30, Church Archives.
19. *History of the Church,* 6:427; from a letter from Joseph Smith and Hyrum Smith to Abijah Tewksbury, June 4, 1844, Nauvoo, Illinois; Abijah Tewksbury's last name is incorrectly spelled "Tewkesbury" in *History of the Church.*

While the Prophet Joseph Smith was imprisoned in Liberty Jail, he wrote a number of letters to his family and to the Saints, in which he testified of God's power to triumph over evil and to stand by His Saints "forever and ever."

"God Shall Be with You Forever and Ever": The Prophet in Liberty Jail

"In His Almighty name we are determined to endure tribulation as good soldiers unto the end."

From the Life of Joseph Smith

On December 1, 1838, the Prophet Joseph Smith, his brother Hyrum, and other brethren were taken from Richmond, Missouri, where they had been incarcerated in a log home, to the jail in Liberty, Missouri. There they would remain for more than four months, awaiting trial on false charges arising from the persecution of the Saints in Missouri. During this time, Church members were being driven from their homes in Missouri by their persecutors, causing tremendous suffering. The trials of the Saints were a source of great anxiety to the Prophet and his companions during their long imprisonment.

Liberty Jail was divided into an upper room and a 14-foot-square lower dungeon, where the prisoners were kept. The Prophet described their situation: "We are kept under a strong guard, night and day, in a prison of double walls and doors, proscribed in our liberty of conscience. Our food is scant, uniform, and coarse; we have not the privilege of cooking for ourselves; we have been compelled to sleep on the floor with straw, and not blankets sufficient to keep us warm; and when we have a fire, we are obliged to have almost a constant smoke. The Judges have gravely told us from time to time that they knew we were innocent, and ought to be liberated, but they dare not administer the law unto us, for fear of the mob."[1]

The room was not tall enough to allow the men to stand upright, and Alexander McRae, one of the prisoners, said the food was "very coarse, and so filthy that we could not eat it until we were driven to it by hunger."[2]

Mercy Fielding Thompson, a Church member who visited the brethren in the jail, later wrote: "It would be beyond my power to describe my feelings when we were admitted into the jail by the keeper and the door was locked behind us. We could not help feeling a sense of horror on realizing that we were locked up in that dark and dismal den, fit only for criminals of the deepest dye; but there we beheld Joseph, the Prophet—the man chosen of God, in the dispensation of the fullness of time to hold the keys of His kingdom on the earth, with power to bind and to loose as God should direct—confined in a loathsome prison for no other cause or reason than that he claimed to be inspired of God to establish His church among men."[3]

During the Prophet's imprisonment, his wife, Emma, was able to visit him only three times. Their only other communication was through letters. On April 4, 1839, the Prophet wrote: "Dear and affectionate wife. Thursday night, I sit down just as the sun is going down, as we peek through the grates of this lonesome prison, to write to you, that I may make known to you my situation. It is, I believe, now about five months and six days since I have been under the grimace of a guard night and day, and within the walls, grates, and screeching iron doors of a lonesome, dark, dirty prison. With emotions known only to God do I write this letter. The contemplations of the mind under these circumstances defy the pen or tongue or angels to describe or paint to the human being who never experienced what we experience. . . . We lean on the arm of Jehovah and none else for our deliverance."[4]

From Liberty Jail, the Prophet also wrote letters to the Saints, expressing his love for them and his faith that God will always support those who trust in Him. Most of the following material comes from a letter to the members of the Church, dated March 20, 1839, containing the Prophet's counsel to the Saints, his pleadings with God, and God's answers to his prayers. Portions of this letter later became sections 121, 122, and 123 of the Doctrine and Covenants.

Teachings of Joseph Smith

No affliction can separate us from the love of God and fellowship with one another.

"Your humble servant, Joseph Smith, Jun., prisoner for the Lord Jesus Christ's sake, and for the Saints, taken and held by the power of mobocracy, under the exterminating reign of his excellency, the governor, Lilburn W. Boggs, in company with his fellow prisoners and beloved brethren, Caleb Baldwin, Lyman Wight, Hyrum Smith, and Alexander McRae, send unto you all greeting.[5] May the grace of God the Father, and of our Lord and Savior Jesus Christ, rest upon you all, and abide with you forever. May knowledge be multiplied unto you by the mercy of God. And may faith and virtue, and knowledge and temperance, and patience and godliness, and brotherly kindness and charity be in you and abound, that you may not be barren in anything, nor unfruitful [see 2 Peter 1:5–8].

"For inasmuch as we know that the most of you are well acquainted with the wrongs and the high-handed injustice and cruelty that are practiced upon us; whereas we have been taken prisoners charged falsely with every kind of evil, and thrown into prison, enclosed with strong walls, surrounded with a strong guard, who continually watch day and night as indefatigable as the devil does in tempting and laying snares for the people of God:

"Therefore, dearly beloved brethren, we are the more ready and willing to lay claim to your fellowship and love. For our circumstances are calculated to awaken our spirits to a sacred remembrance of everything, and we think that yours are also, and that nothing therefore can separate us from the love of God and fellowship one with another [see Romans 8:39]; and that every species of wickedness and cruelty practiced upon us will only tend to bind our hearts together and seal them together in love.

"We have no need to say to you that we are held in bonds without cause, neither is it needful that you say unto us, We are driven from our homes and smitten without cause. We mutually understand that if the inhabitants of the state of Missouri had let the Saints alone, and had been as desirous of peace as they were, there would have been nothing but peace and quietude in the state unto this day; we should not have been in this hell, . . . where we are compelled to hear nothing but blasphemous oaths, and witness a scene of blasphemy, and drunkenness and hypocrisy, and debaucheries of every description. And again, the cries of orphans and widows would not have ascended up to God against them. Nor would innocent blood have stained the soil of Missouri. . . . It is a tale of woe; a lamentable tale; yea, a sorrowful tale; too much to tell; too much for contemplation; too much for human beings. . . .

"[Our persecutors] practice these things upon the Saints, who have done them no wrong, who are innocent and virtuous; who loved the Lord their God, and were willing to forsake all things for Christ's sake. These things are awful to relate, but they are verily true. It must needs be that offenses come, but woe unto them by whom they come [see Matthew 18:7]."[6]

Adversity lasts only a small moment; if we endure well, we will be exalted in the presence of God.

"O God! where art Thou? And where is the pavilion that covereth Thy hiding place? How long shall Thy hand be stayed, and Thine eye, yea Thy pure eye, behold from the eternal heavens, the wrongs of Thy people, and of Thy servants, and Thy ear be penetrated with their cries?

"Yea, O Lord, how long shall they suffer these wrongs and unlawful oppressions, before Thine heart shall be softened towards them, and Thy bowels be moved with compassion towards them?

"O Lord God Almighty, Maker of Heaven, Earth and Seas, and of all things that in them are, and who controllest and subjectest the devil, and the dark and benighted dominion of Sheol! Stretch forth Thy hand, let Thine eye pierce; let Thy pavilion be taken up; let Thy hiding place no longer be covered; let Thine ear be inclined; let Thine heart be softened, and Thy bowels moved with compassion towards us. Let Thine anger be kindled against our enemies; and in the fury of Thine heart, with Thy sword avenge us of our wrongs; remember Thy suffering Saints, O our God! and Thy servants will rejoice in Thy name forever. . . .

". . . My son, peace be unto thy soul; thine adversity and thine afflictions shall be but a small moment; and then if thou endure it well, God shall exalt thee on high; thou shalt triumph over all thy foes."[7] [The paragraphs in this section are also found in D&C 121:1–8.]

God's power is greater than any evil, and the truths of the gospel will ultimately triumph.

"I beg leave to say unto you, brethren, that ignorance, superstition and bigotry placing itself where it ought not, is oftentimes in the way of the prosperity of this Church, like the torrent of rain from the mountains that floods the most pure and crystal stream with mire, and dirt, and filthiness, and obscures everything that was clear before, and all rushes along in one general deluge; but time weathers tide; and notwithstanding we are rolled in the mire of the flood for the time being, the next surge peradventure, as time rolls on, may bring to us the fountain as clear as crystal, and as pure as snow; while the filthiness, floodwood and rubbish is left and purged out by the way.

"How long can rolling water remain impure? What power shall stay the heavens? As well might man stretch forth his puny arm to stop the Missouri river in its decreed course, or to turn it up stream, as to hinder the Almighty from pouring down knowledge from heaven, upon the heads of the Latter-day Saints. [This paragraph is also found in D&C 121:33.]

"What is [Governor Lilburn W.] Boggs or his murderous party, but wimbling willows upon the shore to catch the flood-wood? As well might we argue that water is not water, because the mountain torrents send down mire and roil the crystal stream, although afterwards render it more pure than before; or that fire is not fire, because it is of a quenchable nature, by pouring on the flood; as to say that our cause is down because renegades, liars, priests, thieves and murderers, who are all alike tenacious of their crafts and creeds, have poured down, from their spiritual wickedness in high places, and from their strongholds of the devil, a flood of dirt and mire and filthiness . . . upon our heads.

"No! God forbid. Hell may pour forth its rage like the burning lava of mount Vesuvius, or of Etna, or of the most terrible of the burning mountains; and yet shall 'Mormonism' stand. Water, fire, truth and God are all realities. Truth is 'Mormonism.' God is the author of it. He is our shield. It is by Him we received our birth. It was by His voice that we were called to a dispensation of His Gospel in the beginning of the fullness of times. It was by Him we received the Book of Mormon; and it is by Him that we remain unto this day; and by Him we shall remain, if it shall be for our glory; and in His Almighty name we are determined to endure tribulation as good soldiers unto the end.

". . . You will learn by the time you have read this, and if you do not learn it, you may learn it, that walls and irons, doors and creaking hinges, and half-scared-to-death guards and jailers . . . are calculated in their very nature to make the soul of an honest man feel stronger than the powers of hell. . . .

". . . We are your brethren and fellow-sufferers, and prisoners of Jesus Christ for the Gospel's sake, and for the hope of glory which is in us."[8]

The Savior understands all our suffering, and He will be with us forever and ever.

The Lord comforted the Prophet with the following words: "The ends of the earth shall inquire after thy name, and fools shall have thee in derision, and hell shall rage against thee, while the pure in heart, and the wise, and the noble, and the virtuous, shall seek counsel, and authority and blessings constantly from under thy hand, and thy people shall never be turned against thee by the testimony of traitors; and although their influence shall cast thee into trouble, and into bars and walls, thou shalt be had in honor, and but for a small moment and thy voice shall be more terrible in the midst of thine enemies, than the fierce lion, because of thy righteousness; and thy God shall stand by thee forever and ever.

"If thou art called to pass through tribulations; if thou art in perils among false brethren; if thou art in perils among robbers; if thou art in perils by land or by sea; if thou art accused with all

The Savior before Pilate.
"The Son of Man hath descended below them all; art thou greater than he?"

manner of false accusations; if thine enemies fall upon thee; if they tear thee from the society of thy father and mother and brethren and sisters; and if with a drawn sword thine enemies tear thee from the bosom of thy wife, and of thine offspring, and thine elder son, although but six years of age, shall cling to thy garments, and shall say, My father, my father, why can't you stay with us? O, my father, what are the men going to do with you? and if then he shall be thrust from thee by the sword, and thou be dragged to prison, and thine enemies prowl around thee like wolves for the blood of the lamb; and if thou shouldst be cast into the pit, or into the hands of murderers, and the sentence of death passed upon thee; if thou be cast into the deep; if the billowing surge conspire against thee; if fierce winds become thine enemy; if the heavens gather blackness, and all the elements combine to hedge up the way; and above all, if the very jaws of hell shall gape open the mouth wide after thee, know thou, my son, that all these things shall give thee experience, and shall be for thy good.

"The Son of Man hath descended below them all; art thou greater than he?

"Therefore, hold on thy way, and the Priesthood shall remain with thee, for their bounds are set, they cannot pass. Thy days are known, and thy years shall not be numbered less; therefore, fear not what man can do, for God shall be with you forever and ever."[9] [The paragraphs in this section are also found in D&C 122:1–9.]

The still, small voice whispers consolation to our souls in the depths of sorrow and distress.

Shortly after the Prophet had been allowed to escape his captors in Missouri, he recalled the feelings he had during his imprisonment: "During the time I was in the hands of my enemies, I must say, that although I felt great anxiety respecting my family and friends, who were so inhumanly treated and abused, . . . yet as far as I was concerned, I felt perfectly calm, and resigned to the will of my Heavenly Father. I knew my innocence as well as that of the Saints, and that we had done nothing to deserve such treatment from the hands of our oppressors. Consequently, I could look to that God who has the lives of all men in His hands, and who had saved me frequently from the gates of death, for deliverance; and notwithstanding that every avenue of escape seemed to be entirely closed, and death stared me in the face, and that my destruction was determined upon, as far as man was concerned, yet, from my first entrance into the camp, I felt an assurance that I, with my brethren and our families, should be delivered.

"Yes, that still small voice, which has so often whispered consolation to my soul, in the depths of sorrow and distress, bade me be of good cheer, and promised deliverance, which gave me great comfort. And although the heathen raged, and the people imagined vain things, yet the Lord of Hosts, the God of Jacob was my refuge; and when I cried unto Him in the day of trouble, He delivered me [see Psalms 46:7; 50:15]; for which I call upon my soul, and all that is within me, to bless and praise His holy name. For although I was 'troubled on every side, yet [I was] not distressed; perplexed, but not in despair; persecuted, but not forsaken; cast down, but not destroyed.' [See 2 Corinthians 4:8–9.]"[10]

Suggestions for Study and Teaching

Consider these ideas as you study the chapter or as you prepare to teach. For additional help, see pages vii–xii.

- Review the description of the jail in Liberty, Missouri (pages 359–60). As you study and discuss this chapter, think about the Prophet's circumstances when he wrote the words recorded in this chapter. Review the third paragraph on page 363. How is the account of the Prophet in Liberty Jail an example of this truth?
- Study the third paragraph on page 361. How do difficult circumstances sometimes "awaken our spirits to a sacred remembrance"? In what ways can trials and persecution "bind our hearts" to family members and friends? What experiences have you had that relate to these truths?
- Joseph Smith declared that nothing could separate him and his brethren from the love of God (page 361). What are your thoughts or feelings as you ponder this statement? In what ways can we become separated from God's love? What are some things we must do to abide in God's love?
- Read the first paragraph on page 363. What can we do to receive the peace that the Lord offers us? What do you gain from the Lord's assurance that Joseph Smith's adversity and afflictions would be "but a small moment"?
- Review Joseph Smith's assurances to the Saints that the enemies of the Church could do nothing to hinder the power of God (pages 363–64). Why do we sometimes forget this truth? What can we do to remember it?
- Study the words of the Lord to the Prophet on pages 364–66. How might our lives change as we remember that trials can

give us experience and be for our good? What does it mean to you to know that the Savior has descended below all things? What do you think it means to "hold on thy way"?

- Read the last paragraph of the chapter (pages 366–67). Think about when the Holy Ghost has comforted you in a time of difficulty. Have you had any such experiences that would be appropriate to share?

Related Scriptures: Philippians 3:8–9; Mosiah 23:21–24; Alma 7:11; 36:3

Notes

1. Letter from Joseph Smith to Isaac Galland, Mar. 22, 1839, Liberty Jail, Liberty, Missouri, published in *Times and Seasons,* Feb. 1840, p. 52; punctuation modernized.
2. Alexander McRae, quoted in *History of the Church,* 3:257; from a letter from Alexander McRae to the editor of the *Deseret News,* Oct. 9, 1854, Salt Lake City, Utah, published in *Deseret News,* Nov. 2, 1854, p. 1.
3. Mercy Fielding Thompson, "Recollections of the Prophet Joseph Smith," *Juvenile Instructor,* July 1, 1892, p. 398; punctuation modernized.
4. Letter from Joseph Smith to Emma Smith, Apr. 4, 1839, Liberty Jail, Liberty, Missouri; Beinecke Library, Yale University, New Haven, Connecticut; copy in Church Archives, The Church of Jesus Christ of Latter-day Saints, Salt Lake City, Utah. In this letter, when the Prophet referred to being imprisoned for over five months, he was counting the time he was imprisoned in Independence and Richmond, Missouri, as well as in Liberty.
5. Sidney Rigdon was incarcerated in Liberty Jail with the other brethren on December 1, 1838. However, on January 25, 1839, about two months before the Prophet wrote this letter, Sidney was given permission to leave the jail on bail because he was severely ill. Because continued threats made him afraid to leave the security of the jail, Sidney chose to remain in jail until February 5.
6. *History of the Church,* 3:289–91; punctuation and grammar modernized; paragraph divisions altered; from a letter from Joseph Smith and others to Edward Partridge and the Church, Mar. 20, 1839, Liberty Jail, Liberty, Missouri; parts of this letter were later included in the Doctrine and Covenants as sections 121, 122, and 123.
7. *History of the Church,* 3:291, 293; spelling modernized; paragraph divisions altered. A number of minor changes in punctuation, capitalization, and grammar were made to prepare portions of the Prophet's letter for publication in the Doctrine and Covenants. Therefore, there are a number of small differences between Doctrine and Covenants 121, 122, and 123, and the material presented in this chapter.
8. *History of the Church,* 3:296–98; spelling and punctuation modernized.
9. *History of the Church,* 3:300–301; paragraph divisions altered.
10. *History of the Church,* 3:328–29; paragraph divisions altered; from "Extract, from the Private Journal of Joseph Smith Jr.," *Times and Seasons,* Nov. 1839, pp. 7–8.

CHAPTER 32

Responding to Persecution with Faith and Courage

"Fear not, but be strong in the Lord and in the power of his might."

From the Life of Joseph Smith

In the winter of 1838–39, the Missouri state militia was under orders from the governor to drive the Latter-day Saints from the state, and the Prophet Joseph Smith was imprisoned in Liberty Jail. That winter and the following spring, a scene of terrible suffering unfolded as thousands of Saints were forced to flee their homes in Missouri. Leaving much of their property behind, they began making their way 200 miles eastward to western Illinois, under the direction of Brigham Young and other Church leaders. Few of the Saints had good wagons and horses, and many slept unsheltered in the rain and snow. Some who did not have shoes wrapped their feet in rags as they walked across the snow.

In February 1839, a kind neighbor helped Emma Smith place her four children and her few belongings into a wagon lined with straw. When their party came to the frozen Mississippi River, Emma walked across the ice with her children, carrying the manuscripts of the Prophet's Bible translation in two cloth bags tied around her waist under her skirt. She and many other destitute Saints took refuge in the community of Quincy, Illinois, where they continued to suffer from hunger, cold, and sickness, though these sufferings were alleviated by many acts of kindness from a caring community.

Although the Prophet Joseph yearned to help the Saints, he could do little but pray and give direction through letters to Brigham Young and the other brethren who were leading the Saints in his absence. In these desperate circumstances, he wrote

In February 1839, while Joseph Smith was imprisoned in Liberty Jail, Emma Smith and her children walked across the frozen Mississippi River, fleeing their Missouri persecutors.

words of encouragement and peace to Church members: "Dearly beloved brethren, let us cheerfully do all things that lie in our power; and then may we stand still, with the utmost assurance, to see the salvation of God, and for his arm to be revealed" (D&C 123:17).

On April 6, 1839, the Prophet and his fellow prisoners were transferred on a change of venue from Liberty Jail to Gallatin, Daviess County, Missouri. After a court appearance there, the brethren were given another change of venue from Gallatin to Columbia, Boone County, Missouri. But in mid-April, while the Prophet and the other prisoners were being taken to Columbia, the guards allowed them to escape. Within a week, the brethren had joined the body of the Saints in Quincy, Illinois. Elder Wilford Woodruff wrote in his journal of his reunion with the Prophet: "We . . . once more had the happy privilege of taking Brother Joseph by the hand. . . . He greeted us with great joy. He had just received deliverance from prison and the hand of his enemies and returned to the bosom of his family and friends. . . . Joseph was frank, open, and familiar as usual. Sister Emma was truly happy."[1]

The Prophet later paid tribute to his fellow Saints, who, with him, valiantly endured so much for the sake of their faith in the restored gospel of Jesus Christ: "The conduct of the Saints, under their accumulated wrongs and sufferings, has been praise-worthy; their courage in defending their brethren from the ravages of the mobs; their attachment to the cause of truth, under circumstances the most trying and distressing which humanity can possibly endure; their love to each other; their readiness to afford assistance to me and my brethren who were confined in a dungeon; their sacrifices in leaving Missouri, and assisting the poor widows and orphans, and securing them houses in a more hospitable land; all conspire to raise them in the estimation of all good and virtuous men, and has secured them the favor and approbation of Jehovah, and a name as imperishable as eternity."[2]

Teachings of Joseph Smith

The enemy of truth opposes the servants of the Lord, especially as they grow closer to the Lord.

"Persecution has rolled upon our heads from time to time, . . . like peals of thunder, because of our religion."[3]

"Our religious principles are before the world ready for the investigation of all men, yet we are aware that all the persecution against our friends has arisen in consequence of calumnies [false charges] and misconstructions without foundation in truth and righteousness. This we have endured in common with all other religious societies at their first commencement."[4]

"Marvel not, then, if you are persecuted; but remember the words of the Savior: 'The servant is not above his Lord; if they have persecuted me, they will persecute you also' [see John 15:20]; and that all the afflictions through which the Saints have to pass, are the fulfillment of the words of the Prophets which have spoken since the world began."[5]

"When I do the best I can—when I am accomplishing the greatest good, then the most evils and wicked surmisings are got up against me. . . . The enemies of this people will never get weary of their persecution against the Church, until they are overcome. I expect they will array everything against me that is in their power to control, and that we shall have a long and tremendous warfare. He that will war the true Christian warfare against the corruptions of these last days will have wicked men and angels of devils, and all the infernal powers of darkness continually arrayed against him. When wicked and corrupt men oppose, it is a criterion to judge if a man is warring the Christian warfare. When all men speak evil of you falsely, blessed are ye, etc. [see Matthew 5:11]. Shall a man be considered bad, when men speak evil of him? No. If a man stands and opposes the world of sin, he may expect to have all wicked and corrupt spirits arrayed against him.

"But it will be but a little season, and all these afflictions will be turned away from us, inasmuch as we are faithful, and are not overcome by these evils. By seeing the blessings of the endowment rolling on, and the kingdom increasing and spreading from sea to sea, we shall rejoice that we were not overcome by these foolish things."[6]

"It is thought by some that our enemies would be satisfied with my destruction; but I tell you that as soon as they have shed my blood they will thirst for the blood of every man in whose heart dwells a single spark of the spirit of the fullness of the Gospel. The opposition of these men is moved by the spirit of the adversary of all righteousness. It is not only to destroy me, but every man and woman who dares believe the doctrines that God hath inspired me to teach to this generation."[7]

"I have learned by experience that the enemy of truth does not slumber, nor cease his exertions to bias the minds of communities against the servants of the Lord, by stirring up the indignation of men upon all matters of importance or interest."[8]

Those who love God will bear persecution with courage and faith.

"All Saints! profit by this important *Key*—that in all your trials, troubles, temptations, afflictions, bonds, imprisonments and death, see to it, that you do not betray heaven; that you do not betray Jesus Christ; that you do not betray the brethren; that you do not betray the revelations of God, whether in the Bible, Book of Mormon, or Doctrine and Covenants, or any other that ever was or ever will be given and revealed unto man in this world or that which is to come. Yea, in all your kicking and flounderings, see to it that you do not this thing, lest innocent blood be found upon your skirts, and you go down to hell."[9]

In the spring of 1830 the Saints were being persecuted as a result of the Book of Mormon being published: "The Book of Mormon (the stick of Joseph in the hands of Ephraim,) had now been published for some time, and as the ancient prophet had predicted of it, 'it was accounted as a strange thing.' [See Hosea 8:12.] No small stir was created by its appearance. Great opposition and much persecution followed the believers of its authenticity. But it had now come to pass that truth had sprung out of the earth, and righteousness had looked down from heaven [see Psalm 85:11; Moses 7:62], so we feared not our opponents, knowing that we had both truth and righteousness on our side, that we had both the Father and the Son, because we had the doctrines of Christ, and abided in them; and therefore we continued to preach and to give information to all who were willing to hear."[10]

In July 1839, Wilford Woodruff recorded: "Joseph addressed us in few words and said, 'Remember, brethren, that if you are imprisoned, Brother Joseph has been imprisoned before you. If you are placed where you can only see your brethren through the grates of a window while in irons because of the gospel of Jesus Christ, remember Brother Joseph has been in like circumstances.' "[11]

In 1841 Joseph Smith and his counselors in the First Presidency wrote: "The truth, like the sturdy oak, has stood unhurt amid the contending elements, which have beat upon it with tremendous force. The floods have rolled, wave after wave, in quick succession, and have not swallowed it up. 'They have lifted up their voice, O Lord; the floods have lifted up their voice; but the Lord of Hosts is mightier than the mighty waves of the sea' [see Psalm 93:3–4]; nor have the flames of persecution, with all the influence of mobs, been able to destroy it; but like Moses' bush, it has stood unconsumed, and now at this moment presents an important spectacle both to men and angels.

"Where can we turn our eyes to behold such another? We contemplate a people who have embraced a system of religion, unpopular, and the adherence to which has brought upon them repeated persecutions. A people who, for their love to God, and attachment to His cause, have suffered hunger, nakedness, perils, and almost every privation. A people who, for the sake of their religion, have had to mourn the premature death of parents, husbands, wives, and children. A people who have preferred death to slavery and hypocrisy, and have honorably maintained their characters, and stood firm and immovable, in times that have tried men's souls."[12]

During the winter of 1838–39, thousands of Latter-day Saints were forced to flee from their homes in Missouri, traveling 200 miles to Illinois.

God's mighty power will sustain those who are persecuted for righteousness' sake.

While imprisoned in Liberty Jail, Joseph Smith wrote to the Saints: "Do not think that our hearts faint, as though some strange thing had happened unto us [see 1 Peter 4:12], for we have seen and been assured of all these things beforehand, and have an assurance of a better hope than that of our persecutors. Therefore God hath made broad our shoulders for the burden. We glory in our tribulation, because we know that God is with us, that He is our friend, and that He will save our souls. We do not care for them that can kill the body; they cannot harm our souls [see Matthew 10:28]. We ask no favors at the hands of mobs, nor of the world, nor of the devil, nor of his emissaries the dissenters, and those who love, and make, and swear falsehoods, to take away our lives. We have never dissembled, nor will we for the sake of our lives. . . . We know that we have been endeavoring with all our mind, might, and strength, to do the will of God, and all things whatsoever He has commanded us. . . .

". . . The Savior said, 'It must needs be that offenses come, but woe unto them by whom they come.' [See Matthew 18:7.] And again, 'Blessed are ye when men shall revile you, and persecute you, and shall say all manner of evil against you falsely for my sake; rejoice and be exceeding glad, for great is your reward in heaven, for so persecuted they the Prophets which were before you.' [Matthew 5:11–12.]

"Now, dear brethren, if any men ever had reason to claim this promise, we are the men; for we know that the world not only hate us, but they speak all manner of evil of us falsely, for no other reason than that we have been endeavoring to teach the fullness of the Gospel of Jesus Christ. . . .

"And now, dear and well beloved brethren—and when we say brethren, we mean those who have continued faithful in Christ, men, women and children—we feel to exhort you in the name of the Lord Jesus, to be strong in the faith in the new and everlasting covenant, and nothing frightened at your enemies. . . . Hold on even unto death; for 'he that seeks to save his life shall lose it; and he that loses his life for my sake, and the Gospel's, shall find it,' saith Jesus Christ [see Mark 8:35]."[13]

Also from Liberty Jail, the Prophet and his counselors in the First Presidency wrote to Church leaders: "Brethren, fear not, but be strong in the Lord and in the power of his might. What is man that the servant of God should fear him, or the son of man that he should tremble at him? Neither think it strange concerning the fiery trials with which we are tried, as though some strange thing had happened unto us. Remember that all have been partakers of like afflictions. [See 1 Peter 4:12–13.] Therefore, rejoice in our afflictions, by which you are perfected and through which the captain of our salvation was perfected also. [See Hebrews 2:10.] Let your hearts and the hearts of all the Saints be comforted with you, and let them rejoice exceedingly, for great is our reward in heaven, for so persecuted the wicked the prophets which were before us [see Matthew 5:11–12]."[14]

Suggestions for Study and Teaching

Consider these ideas as you study the chapter or as you prepare to teach. For additional help, see pages vii–xii.

- Review the account on pages 369–71. What impresses you about the way Joseph Smith and his fellow Saints responded to persecution? Why do you think they were willing to endure persecution?
- Read pages 372–73, in which the Prophet Joseph teaches that righteous people will often face persecution. Why do you think this is so? How is persecution today similar to persecution in Joseph Smith's day? How is it different today?
- On page 373, Joseph Smith shared a key to help the Saints. What experiences have shown you the value of this key? What other counsel might you give to someone who is facing persecution because of his or her faith? (For some examples, see pages 373–74.)
- Review pages 375–76, in which Joseph Smith assures us that the Lord will sustain us when we respond to persecution with faith and courage. What do you think it means to say that God has "made broad our shoulders for the burden"? How can we "glory in our tribulation" and "rejoice in our afflictions"? In what ways do you think our afflictions can help us become perfected?

Related Scriptures: Matthew 5:43–44; Romans 8:35–39; 2 Nephi 26:8; Mosiah 24:8–16; 3 Nephi 6:13

Notes

1. Wilford Woodruff, Journals, 1833–98, entry for May 3, 1839, Church Archives, The Church of Jesus Christ of Latter-day Saints, Salt Lake City, Utah.
2. *History of the Church,* 3:329–30; from "Extract, from the Private Journal of Joseph Smith Jr.," *Times and Seasons,* Nov. 1839, p. 8.
3. *History of the Church,* 6:210; from a discourse given by Joseph Smith on Feb. 8, 1844, in Nauvoo, Illinois; reported by Wilford Woodruff.
4. *History of the Church,* 2:460; from a letter from Joseph Smith and others to John Thornton and others, July 25, 1836, Kirtland, Ohio, published in *Messenger and Advocate,* Aug. 1836, p. 358.
5. *History of the Church,* 3:331; punctuation modernized; from "Extract, from the Private Journal of Joseph Smith Jr.," *Times and Seasons,* Nov. 1839, pp. 8–9.

6. *History of the Church,* 5:140–41; paragraph divisions altered; from a discourse given by Joseph Smith on Aug. 31, 1842, in Nauvoo, Illinois; reported by Eliza R. Snow; see also appendix, page 562, item 3.
7. *History of the Church,* 6:498; from a discourse given by Joseph Smith on June 18, 1844, in Nauvoo, Illinois. The compilers of *History of the Church* combined verbal reports by several eyewitnesses into a single account of the discourse.
8. *History of the Church,* 2:437; from a letter from Joseph Smith to Oliver Cowdery, Apr. 1836, Kirtland, Ohio, published in *Messenger and Advocate,* Apr. 1836, p. 289.
9. *History of the Church,* 3:385; from a discourse given by Joseph Smith on July 2, 1839, in Montrose, Iowa; reported by Wilford Woodruff and Willard Richards.
10. *History of the Church,* 1:84; from "History of the Church" (manuscript), book A-1, p. 41, Church Archives.
11. Wilford Woodruff, reporting a statement made by Joseph Smith on July 7, 1839, in Commerce, Illinois; Wilford Woodruff, Journals, 1833–98, Church Archives.
12. *History of the Church,* 4:337; punctuation modernized; paragraph divisions altered; from a report from Joseph Smith and his counselors in the First Presidency, Apr. 7, 1841, Nauvoo, Illinois, published in *Times and Seasons,* Apr. 15, 1841, pp. 384–85.
13. *History of the Church,* 3:227–29, 232–33; punctuation modernized; paragraph divisions altered; from a letter from Joseph Smith to Church members in Caldwell County, Missouri, Dec. 16, 1838, Liberty Jail, Liberty, Missouri.
14. Letter from Joseph Smith and his counselors in the First Presidency to Heber C. Kimball and Brigham Young, Jan. 16, 1839, Liberty Jail, Liberty, Missouri, Church Archives.

CHAPTER 33

The Spiritual Gifts of Healing, Tongues, Prophecy, and Discerning of Spirits

"No man can be a minister of Jesus Christ except he has the testimony of Jesus; and this is the spirit of prophecy."

From the Life of Joseph Smith

Following a brief period of refuge in Quincy, Illinois, during the early months of 1839, the Saints began moving about 50 miles north to the settlement of Commerce, Illinois. After his escape from his Missouri imprisonment, the Prophet had begun purchasing tracts of land in and around Commerce as gathering places for the thousands who had fled Missouri and now needed a place to rebuild their lives. By July 1839, hundreds of Saints were camping in tents and wagons on the east side of the Mississippi River in Commerce, while others had found shelter in abandoned military barracks on the opposite side of the river in Montrose, Iowa. In this new home, the Saints worked to clear and drain the swampy land near the river. Many Church members were bitten by mosquitoes and fell seriously ill with malaria and other diseases. Some of the Saints died, and others were near death. Joseph and Emma Smith took so many into their log home to nurse that the Prophet gave up his bed to sleep outside in a tent.

On July 22, in the midst of the sickness that afflicted so many, the Saints witnessed what Elder Wilford Woodruff would call "a day of God's power."[1] That morning the Prophet arose, called upon the Lord in prayer, and, being filled with the Spirit of the Lord, administered to the sick in his house, in the yard outside, and down by the river. He crossed the river and visited the home of Brigham Young in Montrose to give him a healing blessing. Then, in company with Sidney Rigdon, Brigham Young, and other

On July 22, 1839, Elijah Fordham rose from the "sleep of death" after Joseph Smith entered his home and declared, "Elijah, I command you, in the name of Jesus of Nazareth, to arise and be made whole!"

members of the Twelve, he continued on his mission of mercy among other Iowa Saints. Elder Woodruff recalled one of the most memorable healings of that day:

"We crossed the public square, and entered Brother [Elijah] Fordham's house. Brother Fordham had been dying for an hour, and we expected each minute would be his last. I felt the power of God that was overwhelming his Prophet. When we entered the house, Brother Joseph walked up to Brother Fordham, and took him by the right hand. . . . He saw that Brother Fordham's eyes were glazed, and that he was speechless and unconscious.

"After taking hold of his hand, [the Prophet] looked down into the dying man's face and said: 'Brother Fordham, do you not know me?' At first he made no reply; but we could all see the effect of the Spirit of God resting upon him.

"[Joseph] again said: 'Elijah, do you not know me?' With a low whisper, Brother Fordham answered, 'Yes!' The Prophet then said, 'Have you not faith to be healed?'

"The answer, which was a little plainer than before, was: 'I am afraid it is too late. If you had come sooner, I think I might have been.' He had the appearance of a man awaking from sleep. It was the sleep of death. Joseph then said: 'Do you not believe that Jesus is the Christ?' 'I do, Brother Joseph,' was the response.

"Then the Prophet of God spoke with a loud voice, as in the majesty of the Godhead: 'Elijah, I command you, in the name of Jesus of Nazareth, to arise and be made whole!'

"The words of the Prophet were not like the words of man, but like the voice of God. It seemed to me that the house shook from its foundation. Elijah Fordham leaped from his bed like a man raised from the dead. A healthy color came to his face, and life was manifested in every act. His feet were done up in [cornmeal] poultices. He kicked them off his feet, scattering the contents, and then called for his clothes and put them on. He asked for a bowl of bread and milk, and ate it; then put on his hat and followed us into the street, to visit others who were sick."[2]

In a time of dire need, the Saints experienced an outpouring of the gift of healing at the hands of the Prophet Joseph Smith.

Teachings of Joseph Smith

The sick may be healed through faith and the exercise of priesthood power, according to the Lord's will.

"What is the sign of the healing of the sick? The laying on of hands is the sign or way marked out by James, and the custom of the ancient Saints as ordered by the Lord, and we cannot obtain the blessing by pursuing any other course except the way marked out by the Lord [see James 5:14–15]."[3]

In July 1839, when the Saints had recently moved to Commerce, Illinois, and there was much sickness among them, Joseph Smith recorded: "Much sickness began to manifest itself among the brethren, as well as among the inhabitants of the place, so that this week and the following were generally spent in visiting the sick and administering to them; some had faith enough and were healed; others had not. . . .

"Sunday 28.—Meeting was held as usual. . . . I spoke, and admonished the members of the Church individually to set their houses in order, to make clean the inside of the platter, and to meet on the next Sabbath to partake of the Sacrament, in order that by our obedience to the ordinances, we might be enabled to prevail with God against the destroyer, and that the sick might be healed. All this week chiefly spent among the sick, who in general are gaining strength, and recovering health."[4]

"Many of the righteous shall fall a prey to disease, to pestilence, etc., by reason of the weakness of the flesh, and yet be saved in the Kingdom of God. So that it is an unhallowed principle to say that such and such have transgressed because they have been preyed upon by disease or death, for all flesh is subject to death; and the Savior has said, 'Judge not, lest ye be judged.' [See Matthew 7:1.]"[5]

The purpose of the gift of tongues is to teach the gospel to others.

The Prophet spoke at an 1834 conference of elders: "Joseph Smith then gave an explanation of the gift of tongues, that it was particularly instituted for the preaching of the Gospel to other

"The gift of tongues by the power of the Holy Ghost in the Church, is for the benefit of the servants of God to preach to unbelievers."

nations and languages, but it was not given for the government of the Church."[6]

"As to the gift of tongues, all we can say is, that in this place, we have received it as the ancients did: we wish you, however, to be careful lest in this you be deceived. . . . Satan will no doubt trouble you about the gift of tongues, unless you are careful; you cannot watch him too closely, nor pray too much. May the Lord give you wisdom in all things."[7]

"I read the 13th chapter of First Corinthians [at a meeting held on December 26, 1841], also a part of the 14th chapter, and remarked that the gift of tongues was necessary in the Church; . . . the gift of tongues by the power of the Holy Ghost in the Church, is for the benefit of the servants of God to preach to unbelievers, as on the day of Pentecost."[8]

"Tongues were given for the purpose of preaching among those whose language is not understood; as on the day of Pentecost, etc., and it is not necessary for tongues to be taught to the Church particularly, for any man that has the Holy Ghost, can speak of the things of God in his own tongue as well as to speak in another; for faith comes not by signs, but by hearing the word of God."[9]

"Be not so curious about tongues, do not speak in tongues except there be an interpreter present; the ultimate design of tongues is to speak to foreigners, and if persons are very anxious to display their intelligence, let them speak to such in their own tongues. The gifts of God are all useful in their place, but when they are applied to that which God does not intend, they prove an injury, a snare and a curse instead of a blessing."[10]

"We have also had brethren and sisters who have had the gift of tongues falsely; they would speak in a muttering, unnatural voice, and their bodies be distorted . . . ; whereas, there is nothing unnatural in the Spirit of God."[11]

"Speak not in the gift of tongues without understanding it, or without interpretation. The devil can speak in tongues; the adversary will come with his work; he can tempt all classes; can speak in English or Dutch. Let no one speak in tongues unless he interpret, except by the consent of the one who is placed to preside; then he may discern or interpret, or another may."[12]

"If you have a matter to reveal, let it be in your own tongue; do not indulge too much in the exercise of the gift of tongues, or the devil will take advantage of the innocent and unwary. You may speak in tongues for your own comfort, but I lay this down for a rule, that if anything is taught by the gift of tongues, it is not to be received for doctrine."[13]

Though only one man speaks as the prophet of the Church, the spirit of prophecy enables all to testify of Jesus Christ.

"No man is a minister of Jesus Christ without being a Prophet. No man can be a minister of Jesus Christ except he has the testimony of Jesus; and this is the spirit of prophecy [see Revelation 19:10]."[14]

"John the Revelator says that the testimony of Jesus is the spirit of prophecy [see Revelation 19:10]. Now if any man has the testimony of Jesus, has he not the spirit of prophecy? And if he has the spirit of prophecy, I ask, is he not a prophet? And if a prophet, will he not receive revelation? And any man that does not receive revelation for himself must be damned, for the testimony of Jesus is the spirit of prophecy. For Christ says, ask and you shall receive; and if he happens to receive anything, I ask, will it not be a revelation? And if any man has not the testimony of Jesus or the spirit of God, he is none of his, namely Christ's. And if not his, he must be damned."[15]

A visitor to Nauvoo recorded that Joseph Smith taught the following during a conversation: "The Prophet Joseph [said that] . . . to be a minister of Jesus, a man must testify of Jesus; and to testify of Jesus, a man must have the spirit of prophecy; for, according to John, the testimony of Jesus is the spirit of prophecy.

"If a man professes to be a minister of Jesus and has not the spirit of prophecy, he must be a false witness, for he is not in possession of that gift which qualifies him for that office; and the difference between [Joseph Smith] and the clergy of this generation is, he claims to be in possession of that spirit of prophecy which qualifies him to testify of Jesus and the Gospel of salvation; and the clergy deny that spirit, even the spirit of prophecy, which alone could constitute them true witnesses or testators of the Lord Jesus, and yet claim to be true ministers of salvation."[16]

"Faith comes by hearing the word of God, through the testimony of the servants of God; that testimony is always attended by the Spirit of prophecy and revelation."[17]

The gift of discerning of spirits allows the faithful to distinguish between the influence of good and evil spirits.

In the early days of the restored Church, members of the Church, as well as members of other religious groups, sometimes acted upon influences from evil or false spirits, believing they were under the influence of the Holy Ghost. The Prophet Joseph Smith taught: "Recent occurrences that have transpired amongst us render it an imperative duty devolving upon me to say something in relation to the spirits by which men are actuated.

"It is evident from the Apostles' writings [in the New Testament], that many false spirits existed in their day, and had 'gone forth into the world,' and that it needed intelligence which God alone could impart to detect false spirits, and to prove what spirits were of God [see 1 John 4:1–4]. The world in general have been grossly ignorant in regard to this one thing, and why should they be otherwise—'for no man knows the things of God, but by the Spirit of God.' [See 1 Corinthians 2:11.] . . .

"There always did, in every age, seem to be a lack of intelligence pertaining to this subject. Spirits of all kinds have been manifested, in every age, and almost amongst all people. . . . All have their spirits, all have a supernatural agency, and all contend that their spirits are of God. Who shall solve the mystery? 'Try the spirits,' says John [1 John 4:1], but who is to do it? The learned, the eloquent, the philosopher, the sage, the divine—all are ignorant. . . . Who can drag into daylight and develop the hidden mysteries of the false spirits that so frequently are made manifest among the Latter-day Saints? We answer that no man can do this without the Priesthood, and having a knowledge of the laws by which spirits are governed; for as 'no man knows the things of God, but by the Spirit of God,' so no man knows the spirit of the devil, and his power and influence, but by possessing intelligence which is more than human, and having unfolded through the medium of the Priesthood the mysterious operations of his devices. . . .

"A man must have the discerning of spirits before he can drag into daylight this hellish influence and unfold it unto the world in all its soul-destroying, diabolical, and horrid colors; for nothing is a greater injury to the children of men than to be under the influence of a false spirit when they think they have the Spirit of God. Thousands have felt the influence of its terrible power and baneful effects. . . .

"As we have noticed before, the great difficulty lies in the ignorance of the nature of spirits, of the laws by which they are governed, and the signs by which they may be known; if it requires the Spirit of God to know the things of God; and the spirit of the devil can only be unmasked through that medium, then it follows as a natural consequence that unless some person or persons have a communication, or revelation from God, unfolding to them the operation of the spirit, they must eternally remain ignorant of these principles; for I contend that if one man cannot understand these things but by the Spirit of God, ten thousand men cannot; it is alike out of the reach of the wisdom of the learned, the tongue of the eloquent, the power of the mighty. And we shall at last have to come to this conclusion, whatever we may think of revelation, that without it we can neither know nor understand anything of God, or the devil; and however unwilling the world may be to acknowledge this principle, it is evident from the multifarious creeds and notions concerning this matter that they understand nothing of this principle, and it is equally as plain that without a divine communication they must remain in ignorance. . . .

"A man must have the discerning of spirits, as we before stated, to understand these things, and how is he to obtain this gift if there are no gifts of the Spirit? And how can these gifts be obtained without revelation? 'Christ ascended into heaven, and gave gifts to men; and He gave some Apostles, and some Prophets, and some Evangelists, and some Pastors and Teachers' [see Ephesians 4:8, 11]. And how were Apostles, Prophets, Pastors, Teachers and Evangelists chosen? By prophecy (revelation) and by laying on of hands:—by a divine communication, and a divinely appointed ordinance—through the medium of the Priesthood, organized according to the order of God, by divine appointment. The Apostles in ancient times held the keys of this Priesthood—of the mysteries of the kingdom of God, and consequently were enabled to unlock and unravel all things pertaining to the government of the Church, the welfare of society, the future destiny of men, and the agency, power and influence of spirits; for they could control them at pleasure, bid them depart in the name of Jesus, and detect their mischievous and mysterious operations when trying to palm themselves upon the Church in a religious garb, and militate against the interest of the Church and spread of truth. . . .

". . . Our Savior, the Apostles, and even the members of the Church were endowed with this gift, for, says Paul, 'To one is given the gift of tongues, to another the interpretation of tongues, to another the working of miracles, to another prophecy, to another the discerning of spirits.' [See 1 Corinthians 12:10.] All these proceeded from the same Spirit of God, and were the gifts of God. . . . No man nor set of men without the regularly constituted authorities, the Priesthood and discerning of spirits, can tell true from false spirits."[18]

"Lying spirits are going forth in the earth. There will be great manifestations of spirits, both false and true. . . . Every spirit, or vision, or singing, is not of God. . . . The gift of discerning spirits will be given to the Presiding Elder. Pray for him that he may have this gift."[19]

Suggestions for Study and Teaching

Consider these ideas as you study the chapter or as you prepare to teach. For additional help, see pages vii–xii.

- Review the account on pages 379–81. How can this account help Melchizedek Priesthood holders prepare to administer to the sick? How can it help us when we need a priesthood blessing? Why do you think it was important for Brother Fordham to express his faith in Jesus Christ at that time?
- Review the Prophet Joseph's teachings on page 382. What experiences have helped you understand the power of the priesthood in the healing of the sick? What principles should guide us in sharing our experiences with healing of the sick? Why are some people not healed, even when they exercise faith and receive priesthood blessings?
- Joseph Smith said that the gift of tongues "was particularly instituted for the preaching of the Gospel to other nations and languages" (pages 382–84). How has this gift helped in spreading the gospel throughout the world? How have you or someone you know received the gift of tongues to help preach the gospel?
- Review the Prophet's teachings about the spirit of prophecy (pages 384–85). What does it mean to you to know that each member of the Church can have the spirit of prophecy?
- Review the Prophet's teachings about the gift of discerning of spirits (pages 385–88). What is the gift of discerning of spirits? How can we avoid being deceived by evil influences? How do our current prophet and other Church leaders help us discern evil influences?

Related Scriptures: 1 Corinthians 12:1–31; 14:1–6, 22–28; James 5:14–15; Moroni 10:8–17; D&C 46:1–33; 50:1–36, 40–44; 52:14–19

Notes

1. Wilford Woodruff, Journals, 1833–98, entry for July 22, 1839, Church Archives, The Church of Jesus Christ of Latter-day Saints, Salt Lake City, Utah.
2. Wilford Woodruff, "Leaves from My Journal," *Millennial Star,* Oct. 17, 1881, p. 670; capitalization modernized; paragraph divisions altered.
3. *History of the Church,* 4:555; from a discourse given by Joseph Smith on Mar. 20, 1842, in Nauvoo, Illinois; reported by Wilford Woodruff.
4. *History of the Church,* 4:3–5; paragraph divisions altered; italics deleted; from Joseph Smith journal entries, July 8–10, 28, 1839, Commerce, Illinois.
5. *History of the Church,* 4:11; from instructions given by Joseph Smith on Sept. 29, 1839, in Commerce, Illinois; reported by James Mulholland.
6. *History of the Church,* 2:162; from the minutes of a conference of elders held on Sept. 8, 1834, in New Portage, Ohio; reported by Oliver Cowdery.
7. *History of the Church,* 1:369; from a letter from Joseph Smith and his counselors in the First Presidency to the brethren in Missouri, July 2, 1833, Kirtland, Ohio.
8. *History of the Church,* 4:485; from a discourse given by Joseph Smith on Dec. 26, 1841, in Nauvoo, Illinois; reported by Willard Richards.
9. *History of the Church,* 3:379; from a discourse given by Joseph Smith on June 27, 1839, in Commerce, Illinois; reported by Willard Richards.
10. *History of the Church,* 5:31–32; from "Gift of the Holy Ghost," an editorial published in *Times and Seasons,* June 15, 1842, pp. 825–26; Joseph Smith was the editor of the periodical.
11. *History of the Church,* 4:580; punctuation modernized; from "Try the Spirits," an editorial published in *Times and Seasons,* Apr. 1, 1842, p. 747; Joseph Smith was the editor of the periodical.
12. *History of the Church,* 3:392; from a discourse given by Joseph Smith about July 1839 in Commerce, Illinois; reported by Willard Richards.
13. *History of the Church,* 4:607; from a discourse given by Joseph Smith on Apr. 28, 1842, in Nauvoo, Illinois; reported by Eliza R. Snow.
14. *History of the Church,* 3:389; from a discourse given by Joseph Smith about July 1839 in Commerce, Illinois; reported by Willard Richards.
15. Quoted by James Burgess, in compilation of excerpts from Joseph Smith's discourses; James Burgess, Journals, 1841–48, vol. 2, Church Archives.
16. *History of the Church,* 5:407–8; punctuation modernized; paragraph divisions altered; from instructions given by Joseph Smith about Jan. 1843 in Nauvoo, Illinois; reported in a letter by an unidentified *Boston Bee* correspondent, Mar. 24, 1843, Nauvoo, Illinois, published in *Times and Seasons,* May 15, 1843, p. 200.
17. *History of the Church,* 3:379; from a discourse given by Joseph Smith on June 27, 1839, in Commerce, Illinois; reported by Willard Richards.
18. *History of the Church,* 4:571–75, 580; punctuation and grammar modernized; paragraph divisions altered; from "Try the Spirits," an editorial published in *Times and Seasons,* Apr. 1, 1842, pp. 743–45, 747; Joseph Smith was the editor of the periodical.
19. *History of the Church,* 3:391–92; paragraph divisions altered; from a discourse given by Joseph Smith about July 1839 in Commerce, Illinois; reported by Willard Richards.

The Savior showing compassion toward a woman taken in adultery (see John 8:1–11). "Christ said He came to call sinners to repentance, to save them," Joseph Smith declared.

CHAPTER 34

The Power of Forgiving

"Come on, dear brother, since the war is past,
For friends at first, are friends again at last."

From the Life of Joseph Smith

In the summer of 1839, the Prophet gave the name *Nauvoo* to the site where the Saints were gathering on the Illinois side of the Mississippi River. The name was of Hebrew origin, signifying "a beautiful situation, or place, carrying with it, also, the idea of rest."[1] Under the Prophet's direction, the Saints began transforming the village of Commerce into a lovely city. They first replaced their huts and tents with frontier log homes, and then numbers of frame houses and substantial brick homes began to appear. They planted fruit and shade trees and vines and bushes to beautify their large lots. In their beautiful Nauvoo, the Saints hoped to find a peaceful place of refuge where they could put the persecutions of Missouri behind them.

During this time of building, Joseph Smith had an experience that showed his merciful temperament and willingness to forgive others, allowing them to move beyond the wrongs of the past. Daniel Tyler recounted the experience:

"A man who had stood high in the Church while in Far West [Missouri], was taken down with chills or ague and fever. While his mind as well as body was weak, disaffected parties soured his mind and persuaded him to leave the Saints and go with them. He gave some testimony against the Prophet. While the Saints were settling in Commerce, having recovered from his illness, he removed from Missouri to Quincy, Illinois. There he went to work chopping cordwood to obtain means to take himself and family to Nauvoo, and [give] a present to the injured man of God if, peradventure, he would forgive and permit him to return to the fold. . . . He felt that there was salvation nowhere else for him and if that was denied him all was lost as far as he was concerned. He started with a sorrowful heart and downcast look.

"While [the man was] on the way the Lord told Brother Joseph he was coming. The Prophet looked out of the window and saw him coming up the street. As soon as he turned to open the gate the Prophet sprang up from his chair and ran and met him in the yard, exclaiming, 'O Brother ——, how glad I am to see you!' He caught him around the neck and both wept like children.

"Suffice it to say that proper restitution was made and the fallen man again entered the Church by the door, received his Priesthood again, went upon several important missions, gathered with the Saints in Zion and died in full faith."[2]

George Q. Cannon, who served as a counselor in the First Presidency, gave further evidence of Joseph Smith's forgiving nature: "With his staunch advocacy of truth, and his unyielding adherence to the commandments of God, Joseph was ever merciful to the weak and the erring. During the summer of 1835, he was laboring in councils and meetings in Kirtland and vicinity, and was chosen to take part in the proceedings against several members who were to be tried for utterances made against the Presidency of the Church. Whether it fell to his lot to plead the cause of the accused or to prosecute, though he himself might have been the one who was wronged, he acted with so much tenderness and justice that he won the love of all."[3]

Teachings of Joseph Smith

We are to exercise the principle of mercy and forgive our brothers and sisters.

"One of the most pleasing scenes that can occur on earth, when a sin has been committed by one person against another, is, to forgive that sin; and then according to the sublime and perfect pattern of the Savior, pray to our Father in heaven to forgive [the sinner] also."[4]

"Ever keep in exercise the principle of mercy, and be ready to forgive our brother on the first intimations of repentance, and asking forgiveness; and should we even forgive our brother, or even our enemy, before he repent or ask forgiveness, our heavenly Father would be equally as merciful unto us."[5]

"Bear and forbear one with another, for so the Lord does with us. Pray for your enemies in the Church and curse not your foes without: for vengeance is mine, saith the Lord, and I will repay [see Romans 12:19]. To every ordained member, and to all, we say, be merciful and you shall find mercy. Seek to help save souls, not to destroy them: for verily you know, that 'there is more joy in heaven, over one sinner that repents, than there is over ninety and nine just persons that need no repentance.' [See Luke 15:7.]"[6]

Eliza R. Snow reported these words of the Prophet: "[The Saints] should be armed with mercy, notwithstanding the iniquity among us. Said he had been instrumental in bringing iniquity to light—it was a melancholy thought and awful that so many should place themselves under the condemnation of the devil, and going to perdition. With deep feeling he said that they are fellow mortals, we loved them once, shall we not encourage them to reformation? We have not [yet] forgiven them seventy times seven, as our Savior directed [see Matthew 18:21–22]; perhaps we have not forgiven them once. There is now a day of salvation to such as repent and reform."[7]

"Suppose that Jesus Christ and holy angels should object to us on frivolous things, what would become of us? We must be merciful to one another, and overlook small things."[8]

Willard Richards, a member of the Quorum of the Twelve, reported: "Joseph remarked that all was well between him and the heavens; that he had no enmity against any one; and as the prayer of Jesus, or his pattern, so prayed Joseph—'Father, forgive me my trespasses as I forgive those who trespass against me' [see Matthew 6:12, 14], for I freely forgive all men. If we would secure and cultivate the love of others, we must love others, even our enemies as well as friends."[9]

Forgiving restores unity of feeling.

"It grieves me that there is no fuller fellowship; if one member suffer all feel it; by union of feeling we obtain power with

God. Christ said He came to call sinners to repentance, to save them. Christ was condemned by the self-righteous Jews because He took sinners into His society; He took them upon the principle that they repented of their sins. . . . If [sinners] repent, we are bound to take them, and by kindness sanctify and cleanse them from all unrighteousness by our influence in watching over them. . . . Nothing is so much calculated to lead people to forsake sin as to take them by the hand, and watch over them with tenderness."[10]

The Prophet Joseph Smith wrote to a group of Church leaders: "Now, brethren, let me tell you, that it is my disposition to give and forgive, and to bear and to forbear, with all long-suffering and patience, with the foibles, follies, weaknesses, and wickedness of my brethren and all the world of mankind; and my confidence and love toward you is not slackened, nor weakened. And now, if you should be called upon to bear with us a little in any of our weaknesses and follies, and should, with us, receive a rebuke to yourselves, don't be offended. . . . When you and I meet face to face, I anticipate, without the least doubt, that all matters between us will be fairly understood, and perfect love prevail; and the sacred covenant by which we are bound together, have the uppermost seat in our hearts."[11]

The Prophet Joseph Smith said the following at a meeting with his counselors in the First Presidency and the Twelve: "I have sometimes spoken too harshly from the impulse of the moment, and inasmuch as I have wounded your feelings, brethren, I ask your forgiveness, for I love you and will hold you up with all my heart in all righteousness, before the Lord, and before all men; for be assured, brethren, I am willing to stem the torrent of all opposition, in storms and in tempests, in thunders and in lightnings, by sea and by land, in the wilderness or among false brethren, or mobs, or wherever God in His providence may call us. And I am determined that neither heights nor depths, principalities nor powers, things present or things to come, or any other creature, shall separate me from you [see Romans 8:38–39].

"And I will now covenant with you before God, that I will not listen to or credit any derogatory report against any of you, nor condemn you upon any testimony beneath the heavens, short of that testimony which is infallible, until I can see you face to face, and know of a surety; and I do place unremitted confidence in your word, for I believe you to be men of truth. And I ask the same of you, when I tell you anything, that you place equal confidence in my word, for I will not tell you I know anything that I do not know."[12]

In the fall of 1835, the Prophet's brother William disagreed with a decision the Prophet had made, became enraged, and began to treat the Prophet with contempt and encourage others to do the same. This behavior grieved the Prophet, and he wrote the following to William: "I desire, Brother William, that you will humble yourself. I freely forgive you, and you know my unshaken and unchangeable disposition; I know in whom I trust; I stand upon the rock; the floods cannot, no, they shall not, overthrow me. You know the doctrine I teach is true, you know that God has blessed me. . . . You know that it is my duty to admonish you, when you do wrong. This liberty I shall always take, and you shall have the same privilege. I take the liberty to admonish you, because of my birthright; and I grant you the privilege, because it is my duty to be humble, and receive rebuke and instruction from a brother, or a friend. . . .

"And now may God have mercy upon my father's house; may God take away enmity from between me and thee; and may all blessings be restored, and the past be forgotten forever. May humble repentance bring us both to Thee, O God, and to Thy power and protection, and a crown, to enjoy the society of father, mother, Alvin, Hyrum, Sophronia, Samuel, Catherine, Carlos, Lucy, the Saints, and all the sanctified in peace, forever, is the prayer of your brother."[13]

On January 1, 1836, the Prophet said the following about his efforts to resolve this difficulty in his family: "Notwithstanding the gratitude that fills my heart on retrospecting the past year, and the multiplied blessings that have crowned our heads, my heart is pained within me, because of the difficulty that exists in my father's family. . . . I am determined that nothing on my part shall be lacking to adjust and amicably dispose of and settle all family difficulties on this day, that the ensuing year and years, be they few or many, may be spent in righteousness before God. . . .

"Brothers William and Hyrum, and Uncle John Smith, came to my house, and we went into a room by ourselves, in company with father and Elder Martin Harris. Father Smith then opened our interview by prayer, after which he expressed himself on the occasion in a very feeling and pathetic manner, even with all the sympathy of a father, whose feelings were deeply wounded on account of the difficulty that was existing in the family; and while he addressed us, the Spirit of God rested down upon us in mighty power, and our hearts were melted. Brother William made a humble confession and asked my forgiveness for the abuse he had offered me. And wherein I had been out of the way, I asked his forgiveness.

"And the spirit of confession and forgiveness was mutual among us all, and we covenanted with each other, in the sight of God, and the holy angels, and the brethren, to strive thenceforward to build each other up in righteousness in all things, and not listen to evil reports concerning each other; but, like brothers indeed, go to each other, with our grievances, in the spirit of meekness, and be reconciled, and thereby promote our happiness, and the happiness of the family, and, in short, the happiness and well-being of all. My wife and mother and my scribe were then called in, and we repeated the covenant to them that we had entered into; and while gratitude swelled our bosoms, tears flowed from our eyes. I was then requested to close our interview, which I did, with prayer; and it was truly a jubilee and time of rejoicing."[14]

By showing long-suffering, patience, and mercy to the repentant, we can help bring them into "the liberty of God's dear children."

In late 1838, William W. Phelps, who had been a trusted Church member, was among those who bore false testimony against the Prophet and other Church leaders, leading to their imprisonment in Missouri. In June 1840, Brother Phelps wrote to Joseph Smith, pleading for forgiveness. The Prophet Joseph replied: "I must say that it is with no ordinary feelings I endeavor to write

*William W. Phelps, portrayed here with Joseph Smith after returning to full fellowship with the Saints, wrote of the Prophet who had so freely forgiven him: "Praise to the man who communed with Jehovah!" (*Hymns*, no. 27).*

a few lines to you in answer to yours of the 29th [of last month]; at the same time I am rejoiced at the privilege granted me.

"You may in some measure realize what my feelings, as well as Elder Rigdon's and Brother Hyrum's were, when we read your letter—truly our hearts were melted into tenderness and compassion when we ascertained your resolves, etc. I can assure you I feel a disposition to act on your case in a manner that will meet the approbation of Jehovah, (whose servant I am), and agreeable to the principles of truth and righteousness which have been revealed; and inasmuch as long-suffering, patience, and mercy have ever characterized the dealings of our heavenly Father towards the humble and penitent, I feel disposed to copy the example, cherish the same principles, and by so doing be a savior of my fellow men.

"It is true, that we have suffered much in consequence of your behavior—the cup of gall, already full enough for mortals to drink, was indeed filled to overflowing when you turned against us, one with whom we had oft taken sweet counsel together, and enjoyed many refreshing seasons from the Lord—'had it been an enemy, we could have borne it.' [See Psalm 55:12–14.] 'In the day that thou stoodest on the other side, in the day when strangers carried away captive his forces, and foreigners entered into his gates, and cast lots upon [Far West], even thou wast as one of them; but thou shouldest not have looked on the day of thy brother, in the day that he became a stranger, neither shouldest thou have spoken proudly in the day of distress.' [See Obadiah 1:11–12.]

"However, the cup has been drunk, the will of our Father has been done, and we are yet alive, for which we thank the Lord. And having been delivered from the hands of wicked men by the mercy of our God, we say it is your privilege to be delivered from the powers of the adversary, be brought into the liberty of God's dear children, and again take your stand among the Saints of the Most High, and by diligence, humility, and love unfeigned, commend yourself to our God, and your God, and to the Church of Jesus Christ.

"Believing your confession to be real, and your repentance genuine, I shall be happy once again to give you the right hand of fellowship, and rejoice over the returning prodigal.

"Your letter was read to the Saints last Sunday, and an expression of their feeling was taken, when it was unanimously resolved, that W. W. Phelps should be received into fellowship.

" 'Come on, dear brother, since the war is past,
For friends at first, are friends again at last.' "[15]

Suggestions for Study and Teaching

Consider these ideas as you study the chapter or as you prepare to teach. For additional help, see pages vii–xii.

- This chapter includes several accounts of Joseph Smith forgiving others. Review these accounts on pages 391–92, 395–96, and 396–98. In what ways might these stories help someone who is struggling to forgive another?
- What blessings come into our lives when we forgive those who have offended us? Why do we sometimes have difficulty forgiving others? What can we do to develop a more forgiving spirit?
- Page 393 contains brief, wise statements about forgiving others. For example: "Bear and forbear one with another, for so the Lord does with us." "Be merciful and you shall find mercy." "Seek to help save souls, not to destroy them." "We must be merciful to one another, and overlook small things." What do you gain from each of these statements?
- In the paragraph that begins on the bottom of page 393, review the Prophet Joseph Smith's words about the effect of kindness and tenderness. Why do you think this counsel is true? How have you experienced these principles in your own life?
- Review the paragraph that begins on the bottom of page 394. What problems might we avoid as we follow this counsel? Why is this counsel sometimes difficult to follow? How can we overcome the temptation to believe negative reports about others?
- In his efforts to forgive others, the Prophet spoke of his desire to "copy the example" of Heavenly Father (page 398) and live "according to the sublime and perfect pattern of the Savior" (page 392). As we strive to follow the example of Heavenly Father and Jesus Christ, what are some characteristics we should strive to develop?

Related Scriptures: Psalm 86:5; Matthew 18:21–35; 1 Nephi 7:16–21; Mosiah 26:29–31; D&C 64:9–11

Notes

1. *History of the Church,* 4:268; from a letter from Joseph Smith and his counselors in the First Presidency to the Saints, Jan. 15, 1841, Nauvoo, Illinois, published in *Times and Seasons,* Jan. 15, 1841, pp. 273–74.
2. Daniel Tyler, in "Recollections of the Prophet Joseph Smith," *Juvenile Instructor,* Aug. 15, 1892, p. 491; punctuation modernized; paragraph divisions altered.
3. George Q. Cannon, *The Life of Joseph Smith, the Prophet* (1888), pp. 190–91.
4. *History of the Church,* 6:245; from "A Friendly Hint to Missouri," an article written under the direction of Joseph Smith, Mar. 8, 1844, Nauvoo, Illinois, published in *Times and Seasons,* Mar. 15, 1844, p. 473.
5. *History of the Church,* 3:383; from a discourse given by Joseph Smith on July 2, 1839, in Montrose, Iowa; reported by Wilford Woodruff and Willard Richards.
6. *History of the Church,* 2:230, footnote; from "To the Saints Scattered Abroad," *Messenger and Advocate,* June 1835, p. 138.
7. *History of the Church,* 5:19–20; bracketed word "yet" in original; paragraph divisions altered; from a discourse given by Joseph Smith on May 26, 1842, in Nauvoo, Illinois; reported by Eliza R. Snow.
8. *History of the Church,* 5:23; from a discourse given by Joseph Smith on June 9, 1842, in Nauvoo, Illinois; reported by Eliza R. Snow.
9. *History of the Church,* 5:498; punctuation modernized; from a discourse given by Joseph Smith on July 9, 1843, in Nauvoo, Illinois; reported by Willard Richards.
10. *History of the Church,* 5:23–24; from a discourse given by Joseph Smith on June 9, 1842, in Nauvoo, Illinois; reported by Eliza R. Snow.
11. Letter from Joseph Smith to Edward Partridge and others, Mar. 30, 1834, Kirtland, Ohio; in Oliver Cowdery Letterbook, pp. 34–35, Huntington Library, San Marino, California; copy in Church Archives, The Church of Jesus Christ of Latter-day Saints, Salt Lake City, Utah.
12. *History of the Church,* 2:374; paragraph divisions altered; from the minutes of a council meeting of the First Presidency and the Twelve held on Jan. 16, 1836, in Kirtland, Ohio; reported by Warren Parrish.
13. *History of the Church,* 2:343; from a letter from Joseph Smith to William Smith, Dec. 18, 1835, Kirtland, Ohio.
14. *History of the Church,* 2:352–54; paragraph divisions altered; from a Joseph Smith journal entry, Jan. 1, 1836, Kirtland, Ohio.
15. *History of the Church,* 4:162–64; second set of bracketed words in third paragraph in original; punctuation and capitalization modernized; paragraph divisions altered; italics deleted; from a letter from Joseph Smith to William W. Phelps, July 22, 1840, Nauvoo, Illinois.

C H A P T E R 3 5

Redemption for the Dead

"The great Jehovah . . . knows the situation of both the living and the dead, and has made ample provision for their redemption."

From the Life of Joseph Smith

Early in the Prophet Joseph Smith's ministry, he had an experience that would help to prepare him for the time when the doctrine of salvation for the dead would be revealed. In November 1823, Alvin Smith, the oldest child of Lucy Mack Smith and Joseph Smith Sr., suddenly became seriously ill and lay near death. Alvin was 25 years old, a strong and capable young man whose hard work contributed greatly to the family's financial stability. His mother described him as "a youth of singular goodness of disposition," whose "nobleness and generosity" blessed those around him "every hour of his existence."[1]

Knowing he was dying, Alvin called his brothers and sisters to him and spoke to each of them. To Joseph, who was almost 18 years old and had not yet received the gold plates, Alvin said, "I want you to be a good boy and do everything that lies in your power to obtain the records. Be faithful in receiving instruction and keeping every commandment that is given you. Your brother Alvin must now leave you, but remember the example which he has set for you, and set a good example for the children that are younger than you."[2]

When Alvin died, the family asked a Presbyterian minister in Palmyra, New York, to officiate at his funeral. As Alvin had not been a member of the minister's congregation, the clergyman asserted in his sermon that Alvin could not be saved. William Smith, Joseph's younger brother, recalled: "[The minister] . . . intimated very strongly that [Alvin] had gone to hell, for Alvin

"As the kingdom of God is established on the earth, and the ancient order of things restored, the Lord has manifested to us this duty and privilege, and we are commanded to be baptized for our dead."

was not a church member, but he was a good boy and my father did not like it."[3]

In January 1836, many years after Alvin's death, Joseph Smith received a vision of the celestial kingdom, in which he saw that Alvin, as well as his mother and father, would someday inherit that kingdom. Joseph "marveled how it was that [Alvin] had obtained an inheritance in that kingdom, seeing that he had departed this life before the Lord had set his hand to gather Israel the second time, and had not been baptized for the remission of sins" (D&C 137:6). The voice of the Lord then came to Joseph, declaring:

"All who have died without a knowledge of this gospel, who would have received it if they had been permitted to tarry, shall be heirs of the celestial kingdom of God; also all that shall die henceforth without a knowledge of it, who would have received it with all their hearts, shall be heirs of that kingdom; for I, the Lord, will judge all men according to their works, according to the desire of their hearts" (D&C 137:7–9).

On August 15, 1840, the Prophet Joseph Smith preached at a funeral in Nauvoo and, for the first time in public, taught the doctrine of salvation for the dead. According to Simon Baker, who was present, the Prophet began by testifying that the "gospel of Jesus Christ brought glad tidings of great joy." He read most of 1 Corinthians 15 and explained that "the Apostle was talking to a people who understood baptism for the dead, for it was practiced among them." He then declared that "people could now act for their friends who had departed this life, and that the plan of salvation was calculated to save all who were willing to obey the requirements of the law of God."[4]

One month after the funeral address, the Prophet visited his father, who was very ill and near death. The Prophet discussed with his father the doctrine of baptism for the dead, and Father Smith's thoughts turned to his beloved son Alvin. Father Smith asked that the work be done for Alvin "immediately." Just minutes before he died, he declared that he saw Alvin.[5] In the latter part of 1840, the Smith family rejoiced as Hyrum received the ordinance of baptism for his brother Alvin.

Teachings of Joseph Smith

God loves all His children and will judge all people according to the law they have received.

"The great designs of God in relation to the salvation of the human family, are very little understood by the professedly wise and intelligent generation in which we live. Various and conflicting are the opinions of men concerning the plan of salvation, the [requirements] of the Almighty, the necessary preparations for heaven, the state and condition of departed spirits, and the happiness or misery that is consequent upon the practice of righteousness and iniquity according to their several notions of virtue and vice. . . .

". . . While one portion of the human race is judging and condemning the other without mercy, the Great Parent of the universe looks upon the whole of the human family with a fatherly care and paternal regard; He views them as His offspring, and without any of those contracted feelings that influence the children of men, causes 'His sun to rise on the evil and on the good, and sendeth rain on the just and on the unjust.' [Matthew 5:45.] He holds the reins of judgment in His hands; He is a wise Lawgiver, and will judge all men, not according to the narrow, contracted notions of men, but, 'according to the deeds done in the body whether they be good or evil,' or whether these deeds were done in England, America, Spain, Turkey, or India. He will judge them, 'not according to what they have not, but according to what they have'; those who have lived without law, will be judged without law, and those who have a law, will be judged by that law. We need not doubt the wisdom and intelligence of the Great Jehovah; He will award judgment or mercy to all nations according to their several deserts, their means of obtaining intelligence, the laws by which they are governed, the facilities afforded them of obtaining correct information, and His inscrutable designs in relation to the human family; and when the designs of God shall be made manifest, and the curtain of futurity be withdrawn, we shall all of us eventually have to confess that the Judge of all the earth has done right [see Genesis 18:25]."[6]

"God judges men according to the use they make of the light which He gives them."[7]

"Men will be held accountable for the things which they have and not for the things they have not. . . . All the light and intelligence communicated to them from their beneficent creator, whether it is much or little, by the same they in justice will be judged, and . . . they are required to yield obedience and improve upon that and that only which is given, for man is not to live by bread alone but by every word that proceeds out of the mouth of God."[8]

The Savior, Jesus Christ, offers the opportunity for forgiveness and deliverance to both the living and the dead.

"The situation of the Christian nations after death, is a subject that has called forth all the wisdom and talent of the philosopher and the divine, and it is an opinion which is generally received, that the destiny of man is irretrievably fixed at his death, and that he is made either eternally happy, or eternally miserable; that if a man dies without a knowledge of God, he must be eternally damned, without any mitigation of his punishment, alleviation of his pain, or the most latent hope of a deliverance while endless ages shall roll along. However orthodox this principle may be, we shall find that it is at variance with the testimony of Holy Writ, for our Savior says, that all manner of sin and blasphemy shall be forgiven men wherewith they shall blaspheme; but the blasphemy against the Holy Ghost shall not be forgiven, neither in this world, nor in the world to come, evidently showing that there are sins which may be forgiven in the world to come, although the sin of blasphemy [against the Holy Ghost] cannot be forgiven [see Matthew 12:31–32; Mark 3:28–29].

"Peter, also, in speaking concerning our Savior, says, that 'He went and preached unto the spirits in prison, which sometimes were disobedient, when once the long suffering of God waited in the days of Noah' (1 Peter 3:19, 20). Here then we have an account of our Savior preaching to the spirits in prison, to spirits that had been imprisoned from the days of Noah; and what did He preach to them? That they were to stay there? Certainly

In the spirit world, the Savior organized the righteous spirits "and commissioned them to go forth and carry the light of the gospel to them that were in darkness" (D&C 138:30).

not! Let His own declaration testify. 'He hath sent me to heal the broken hearted, to preach deliverance to the captives, and recovering of sight to the blind, to set at liberty them that are bruised.' (Luke 4:18.) Isaiah has it—'To bring out the prisoners from the prison, and them that sit in darkness from the prison house.' (Isaiah 42:7.) It is very evident from this that He not only went to preach to them, but to deliver, or bring them out of the prison house. . . .

"The great Jehovah contemplated the whole of the events connected with the earth, pertaining to the plan of salvation, before it rolled into existence, or ever 'the morning stars sang together' for joy [Job 38:7]; the past, the present, and the future were and are, with Him, one eternal 'now;' He knew of the fall of Adam, the iniquities of the antediluvians [those who lived before the Great Flood], of the depth of iniquity that would be connected with the human family, their weakness and strength, their power and glory, apostasies, their crimes, their righteousness and iniquity; He comprehended the fall of man, and his redemption; He knew the plan of salvation and pointed it out; He was acquainted with the situation of all nations and with their destiny; He ordered all things according to the counsel of His own will; He knows the situation of both the living and the dead, and has made ample provision for their redemption, according to their several circumstances, and the laws of the kingdom of God, whether in this world, or in the world to come."[9]

God is perfectly just and merciful to all people, living and dead.

"The idea that some men form of the justice, judgment, and mercy of God, is too foolish for an intelligent man to think of: for instance, it is common for many of our orthodox preachers to suppose that if a man is not what they call converted, if he dies in that state he must remain eternally in hell without any hope. Infinite years in torment must he spend, and never, never, never have an end; and yet this eternal misery is made frequently to rest upon the merest casualty [chance]. The breaking of a shoe-string, the tearing of a coat of those officiating, or the peculiar location in which a person lives, may be the means, indirectly, of his damnation, or the cause of his not being saved.

"I will suppose a case which is not extraordinary: Two men, who have been equally wicked, who have neglected religion, are both of them taken sick at the same time; one of them has the good fortune to be visited by a praying man, and he gets converted a few minutes before he dies; the other sends for three different praying men, a tailor, a shoemaker, and a tinman; the tinman has a handle to solder to a pan, the tailor has a button-hole to work on some coat that he needed in a hurry, and the shoemaker has a patch to put on somebody's boot; they none of them can go in time, the man dies, and goes to hell: one of these is exalted to Abraham's bosom, he sits down in the presence of God and enjoys eternal, uninterrupted happiness, while the other, equally as good as he, sinks to eternal damnation, irretrievable misery and hopeless despair, because a man had a boot to mend, the button-hole of a coat to work, or a handle to solder on to a saucepan.

"The plans of Jehovah are not so unjust, the statements of holy writ so [illusory], nor the plan of salvation for the human family so incompatible with common sense; at such proceedings God would frown with indignance, angels would hide their heads in shame, and every virtuous, intelligent man would recoil.

"If human laws award to each man his deserts, and punish all delinquents according to their several crimes, surely the Lord will not be more cruel than man, for He is a wise legislator, and His laws are more equitable, His enactments more just, and His decisions more perfect than those of man; and as man judges his fellow man by law, and punishes him according to the penalty of the law, so does God of heaven judge 'according to the deeds done in the body.' [See Alma 5:15.] To say that the heathens would be damned because they did not believe the Gospel would be preposterous, and to say that the Jews would all be damned that do not believe in Jesus would be equally absurd; for 'how can they believe on him of whom they have not heard, and how can they hear without a preacher, and how can he preach except he be sent' [see Romans 10:14–15]; consequently neither Jew nor heathen can be culpable for rejecting the conflicting opinions of sectarianism, nor for rejecting any testimony but that which is sent of God, for as the preacher cannot preach except he be sent, so the hearer cannot believe [except] he hear a 'sent' preacher, and cannot be condemned for what he has not heard, and being without law, will have to be judged without law."[10]

It is our duty and privilege to be baptized and confirmed for those who have died without the gospel.

"When speaking about the blessings pertaining to the Gospel, and the consequences connected with disobedience to the requirements, we are frequently asked the question, what has become of our fathers? Will they all be damned for not obeying the Gospel, when they never heard it? Certainly not. But they will possess the same privilege that we here enjoy, through the medium of the everlasting priesthood, which not only administers on earth, but also in heaven, and the wise dispensations of the great Jehovah. Hence those characters referred to by Isaiah [see Isaiah 24:21–22] will be visited by the Priesthood, and come out of their prison upon the same principle as those who were disobedient in the days of Noah were visited by our Savior [who possessed the everlasting Melchizedek Priesthood] and had the Gospel preached to them, by Him in prison. And in order that they might fulfill all the [requirements] of God, living friends were baptized for their dead friends, and thus fulfilled the requirement of God, which says, 'Except a man be born of water and of the Spirit, he cannot enter into the kingdom of God.' [John 3:5.] They were baptized of course, not for themselves, but for their dead. . . . Paul, in speaking of the doctrine, says, 'Else what shall they do which are baptized for the dead, if the dead rise not at all? Why are they then baptized for the dead?' (1 Cor. 15:29). . . .

"And now as the great purposes of God are hastening to their accomplishment, and the things spoken of in the Prophets are fulfilling, as the kingdom of God is established on the earth, and the ancient order of things restored, the Lord has manifested to us this duty and privilege, and we are commanded to be baptized for our dead, thus fulfilling the words of Obadiah, when speaking of the glory of the latter-day: 'And saviors shall come upon Mount Zion to judge the remnant of Esau, and the kingdom shall be the Lord's.' [See Obadiah 1:21.] A view of these things reconciles the Scriptures of truth, justifies the ways of God to man, places the human family upon an equal footing, and harmonizes with every principle of righteousness, justice and truth. We will conclude with the words of Peter: 'For the time past of our life may suffice us to have wrought the will of the Gentiles.' 'For, for this cause was the Gospel preached also to them that are dead, that they might be judged according to men in the flesh, but live according to God in the spirit.' [1 Peter 4:3, 6.]"[11]

Suggestions for Study and Teaching

Consider these ideas as you study the chapter or as you prepare to teach. For additional help, see pages vii–xii.

- Review pages 401–3, noting how the doctrine of salvation for the dead affected Joseph Smith and his family. What effect has this doctrine had on you and your family?

- On pages 404–7, review the Prophet Joseph's teachings about God the Father and Jesus Christ. In what ways do these teachings influence your thoughts and feelings about our Father in Heaven and the Savior? In what ways do these teachings relate to salvation for the dead?
- Review the Prophet's teachings on pages 404–5 and 407–8. How does God judge His children?
- Joseph Smith said that baptism for the dead is a "duty and privilege" (page 409). In what ways is this work a duty? What experiences have you had in which you have felt that it is a privilege? What can you do to further the work of the Lord for those who have died? How can parents help their children participate in this work?
- How does the doctrine of salvation for the dead show God's justice? How does it show His mercy? After reading this chapter, how would you explain this doctrine to someone of another faith?

Related Scriptures: Isaiah 49:8–9; 61:1–3; John 5:25; D&C 138:11–37

Notes

1. Lucy Mack Smith, "The History of Lucy Smith, Mother of the Prophet," 1844–45 manuscript, book 4, pp. 5–6, Church Archives, The Church of Jesus Christ of Latter-day Saints, Salt Lake City, Utah.
2. Alvin Smith, quoted in Lucy Mack Smith, "The History of Lucy Smith, Mother of the Prophet," 1844–45 manuscript, book 4, p. 4, Church Archives.
3. William Smith, interview by E. C. Briggs and J. W. Peterson, Oct. or Nov. 1893, originally published in *Zion's Ensign* (periodical published by the Reorganized Church of Jesus Christ of Latter Day Saints, now called Community of Christ); reprinted in *Deseret Evening News,* Jan. 20, 1894, p. 2.
4. Simon Baker, reporting a discourse given by Joseph Smith on Aug. 15, 1840, in Nauvoo, Illinois; in Journal History of The Church of Jesus Christ of Latter-day Saints, Aug. 15, 1840. See also *History of the Church,* 4:231.
5. Joseph Smith Sr., quoted in Lucy Mack Smith, "The History of Lucy Smith, Mother of the Prophet," 1845 manuscript, pp. 296, 301, Church Archives.
6. *History of the Church,* 4:595–96; punctuation modernized; from "Baptism for the Dead," an editorial published in *Times and Seasons,* Apr. 15, 1842, p. 759; Joseph Smith was the editor of the periodical.
7. *History of the Church,* 5:401; from a discourse given by Joseph Smith on May 21, 1843, in Nauvoo, Illinois; reported by Willard Richards.
8. Letter from Joseph Smith to his uncle Silas Smith, Sept. 26, 1833, Kirtland, Ohio; in Lucy Mack Smith, "The History of Lucy Smith, Mother of the Prophet," 1845 manuscript, pp. 228–29, Church Archives.

9. *History of the Church,* 4:596–97; first set of bracketed words in first paragraph in original; spelling and punctuation modernized; paragraph divisions altered; from "Baptism for the Dead," an editorial published in *Times and Seasons,* Apr. 15, 1842, pp. 759–60; Joseph Smith was the editor of the periodical. A revelation received by President Joseph F. Smith in October 1918 clarified that while the Savior was in the spirit world, He visited the righteous spirits and appointed messengers to go to the wicked spirits with the gospel message (see D&C 138:18–23, 28–32).
10. *History of the Church,* 4:597–98; punctuation modernized; paragraph divisions altered; from "Baptism for the Dead," an editorial published in *Times and Seasons,* Apr. 15, 1842, p. 760; Joseph Smith was the editor of the periodical.
11. *History of the Church,* 4:598–99; second set of bracketed words in first paragraph in original; spelling and punctuation modernized; paragraph divisions altered; from "Baptism for the Dead," an editorial published in *Times and Seasons,* Apr. 15, 1842, pp. 760–61; Joseph Smith was the editor of the periodical.

The reconstructed Nauvoo Temple, standing on the site of the original temple. While the original Nauvoo Temple was being built, the Prophet Joseph Smith declared, "We need the temple more than anything else."

CHAPTER 36

Receiving the Ordinances and Blessings of the Temple

The temple is a place where God can "reveal unto His people the ordinances of His house and the glories of His kingdom, and teach the people the way of salvation."

From the Life of Joseph Smith

From the earliest days of the Restoration, the Lord had taught the Prophet Joseph Smith the importance of building temples. Although the Prophet had been forced to move many times and had constantly faced urgent demands on his time and attention, he had never lost sight of the need to build a house of the Lord. A site for a temple had been dedicated in Independence, Missouri. A beautiful temple had been completed and dedicated in Kirtland, Ohio. In Far West, Missouri, cornerstones for a temple had been laid, only to be abandoned. Now, as Church members began rebuilding their lives in Nauvoo—many of them without adequate food, shelter, or employment—Joseph Smith knew that the Saints' most important work was once again to build a temple.

In response to the Lord's command, the Prophet and the Saints moved forward as quickly as possible to begin building a house of the Lord. But the Prophet realized that the construction would take years, and he knew that the Saints needed the full blessings of the temple. Consequently, on May 4, 1842, even though the temple was not complete, Joseph Smith administered the endowment to a small group of faithful brethren.

The group met in the large upper room of the Prophet's Red Brick Store, which had been "arranged representing the interior of a temple as much as the circumstances would permit."[1] Franklin D. Richards, of the Quorum of the Twelve Apostles, wrote: "When the Spirit prompted [Joseph Smith] that his life's work was drawing to a close, and when he saw that his earthly days might be ended before the completion of the temple, he called a chosen few, and conferred upon them the ordinances of the holy endowments, so that the divine treasures of his mind might not perish from the world with his death."[2]

The Prophet's history records: "I spent the day in the upper part of the store, . . . in council with General James Adams, of Springfield, Patriarch Hyrum Smith, Bishops Newel K. Whitney and George Miller, and President Brigham Young and Elders Heber C. Kimball and Willard Richards, instructing them in the principles and order of the Priesthood, attending to washings, anointings, endowments and the communication of keys pertaining to the Aaronic Priesthood, and so on to the highest order of the Melchizedek Priesthood, setting forth the order pertaining to the Ancient of Days, and all those plans and principles by which anyone is enabled to secure the fullness of those blessings which have been prepared for the Church of the First Born, and come up and abide in the presence of the Eloheim in the eternal worlds. In this council was instituted the ancient order of things for the first time in these last days.

"And the communications I made to this council were of things spiritual, and to be received only by the spiritually minded: and there was nothing made known to these men but what will be made known to all the Saints of the last days, so soon as they are prepared to receive, and a proper place is prepared to communicate them, even to the weakest of the Saints; therefore let the Saints be diligent in building the Temple, and all houses which they have been, or shall hereafter be, commanded of God to build."[3]

While the majority of the Saints would receive the temple endowment after the Nauvoo Temple was completed, a limited number of men and women received this blessing in the months following the May 1842 meeting. Mercy Fielding Thompson was one of these. At the time she received her endowment, the Prophet said to her, "This will bring you out of darkness into marvelous light."[4]

Teachings of Joseph Smith

The Saints are commanded by God to build temples.

In January 1833 in Kirtland, Ohio, the Prophet wrote: "The Lord commanded us, in Kirtland, to build a house of God; . . . this is the word of the Lord to us, and we must, yea, the Lord helping us, we will obey: as on conditions of our obedience He has promised us great things; yea, even a visit from the heavens to honor us with His own presence. We greatly fear before the Lord lest we should fail of this great honor, which our Master proposes to confer on us; we are seeking for humility and great faith lest we be ashamed in His presence."[5]

In September 1840, the Prophet and his counselors in the First Presidency declared that the time had come to build the Nauvoo Temple: "Believing the time has now come, when it is necessary to erect a house of prayer, a house of order, a house for the worship of our God [see D&C 88:119], where the ordinances can be attended to agreeable to His divine will, in this region of country—to accomplish which, considerable exertion must be made, and means will be required—and as the work must be hastened in righteousness, it behooves the Saints to weigh the importance of these things, in their minds, in all their bearings, and then take such steps as are necessary to carry them into operation; and arming themselves with courage, resolve to do all they can, and feel themselves as much interested as though the whole labor depended on themselves alone. By so doing they will emulate the glorious deeds of the fathers, and secure the blessings of heaven upon themselves and their posterity to the latest generation."[6]

In January 1841, the Prophet and his counselors in the First Presidency wrote: "The Temple of the Lord is in process of erection here [in Nauvoo], where the Saints will come to worship the God of their fathers, according to the order of His house and the powers of the Holy Priesthood, and will be so constructed as to enable all the functions of the Priesthood to be duly exercised, and where instructions from the Most High will be received, and from this place go forth to distant lands. Let us then concentrate all our powers . . . and strive to emulate the action of the ancient covenant fathers and patriarchs, in those things which are of such vast importance to this and every succeeding generation."[7]

In early 1841, Joseph Smith taught the following, as recorded by William P. McIntire: "Joseph said the Lord said that we should build our house to his name, that we might be baptized for the dead. But if we did it not, we should be rejected, and our dead with us, and this Church should not be accepted [see D&C 124:32]."[8]

In April 1842, the Prophet said: "The Church is not fully organized, in its proper order, and cannot be, until the Temple is completed, where places will be provided for the administration of the ordinances of the Priesthood."[9]

In July 1842, the Prophet declared: "The Lord has told us to build the [Nauvoo] Temple . . . ; and that command is as binding upon us as any other; and that man who engages not in these things is as much a transgressor as though he broke any other commandment; he is not a doer of God's will, not a fulfiller of His laws."[10]

In October 1843, the Prophet admonished the Saints: "Hasten the work in the Temple, renew your exertions to forward all the work of the last days, and walk before the Lord in soberness and righteousness."[11]

In March 1844, the Prophet met with the Twelve and the Nauvoo Temple committee to discuss how to allocate the Church's meager resources. In this meeting, the Prophet said: "We need the temple more than anything else."[12]

In the temple we learn the things of eternity and receive ordinances of salvation for ourselves and our ancestors.

"What was the object of gathering the . . . people of God in any age of the world? . . . The main object was to build unto the Lord a house whereby He could reveal unto His people the ordinances of His house and the glories of His kingdom, and teach the people the way of salvation; for there are certain ordinances and principles that, when they are taught and practiced, must be done in a place or house built for that purpose.

". . . Ordinances instituted in the heavens before the foundation of the world, in the priesthood, for the salvation of men, are not to be altered or changed. All must be saved on the same principles.

"It is for the same purpose that God gathers together His people in the last days, to build unto the Lord a house to prepare them for the ordinances and endowments, washings and anointings, etc. One of the ordinances of the house of the Lord is baptism for the dead. God decreed before the foundation of the world that that ordinance should be administered in a font prepared for that purpose in the house of the Lord. . . .

"The doctrine of baptism for the dead is clearly shown in the New Testament; . . . it was the reason why Jesus said unto the Jews, 'How oft would I have gathered thy children together, even as a hen gathereth her chickens under her wings, and ye would not!' [Matthew 23:37]—that they might attend to the ordinances of baptism for the dead as well as other ordinances of the priesthood, and receive revelations from heaven, and be perfected in the things of the kingdom of God—but they would not. This was the case on the day of Pentecost: those blessings were poured out on the disciples on that occasion. God ordained that He would save the dead, and would do it by gathering His people together. . . .

". . . Why gather the people together in this place? For the same purpose that Jesus wanted to gather the Jews—to receive the ordinances, the blessings, and the glories that God has in store for His Saints. I will now ask this assembly and all the Saints if you will now build this house and receive the ordinances and blessings which God has in store for you; or will you not build unto the Lord this house, and let Him pass by and bestow these blessings upon another people?"[13]

"As soon as the [Nauvoo] Temple and baptismal font are prepared, we calculate to give the Elders of Israel their washings and anointings, and attend to those last and more impressive ordinances, without which we cannot obtain celestial thrones. But there must be a holy place prepared for that purpose. There was a proclamation made during the time that the foundation of

The Cardston Alberta Temple. In holy temples, the Lord reveals to His people "the glories of His kingdom" and "the way of salvation."

the Temple was laid to that effect, and there are provisions made until the work is completed, so that men may receive their endowments and be made kings and priests unto the Most High God. . . . There must, however, be a place built expressly for that purpose, and for men to be baptized for their dead. . . .

"The Lord has an established law in relation to the matter: there must be a particular spot for the salvation of our dead. I verily believe there will be a place, and hence men who want to save their dead can come and bring their families, do their work by being baptized and attending to the other ordinances for their dead."[14]

"The question is frequently asked, 'Can we not be saved without going through with all those ordinances, etc.?' I would answer, No, not the fullness of salvation. Jesus said, 'There are many mansions in my Father's house, and I will go and prepare a place for you.' [See John 14:2.] *House* here named should have been translated kingdom; and any person who is exalted to the highest mansion has to abide a celestial law, and the whole law too."[15]

"If a man gets a fulness of the priesthood of God, he has to get it in the same way that Jesus Christ obtained it, and that was by keeping all the commandments and obeying all the ordinances of the house of the Lord. . . .

"All men who become heirs of God and joint-heirs with Jesus Christ will have to receive the fulness of the ordinances of his kingdom; and those who will not receive all the ordinances will come short of the fulness of that glory."[16]

"Could we read and comprehend all that has been written from the days of Adam, on the relation of man to God and angels in a future state, we should know very little about it. Reading the experience of others, or the revelation given to *them*, can never give *us* a comprehensive view of our condition and true relation to God. Knowledge of these things can only be obtained by experience through the ordinances of God set forth for that purpose. Could you gaze into heaven five minutes, you would know more than you would by reading all that ever was written on the subject. . . . I assure the Saints that truth . . . can and may be known through the revelations of God in the way of His ordinances, and in answer to prayer."[17]

"The order of the house of God has been, and ever will be, the same, even after Christ comes; and after the termination of the thousand years it will be the same; and we shall finally enter into the celestial Kingdom of God, and enjoy it forever."[18]

The temple is a place of holiness where we receive the greatest blessings God has for His children.

As part of the dedicatory prayer for the Kirtland Temple, given to the Prophet Joseph Smith by revelation and later recorded in Doctrine and Covenants 109, the Prophet prayed: "And now, Holy Father, we ask . . . that thy glory may rest down upon thy people, and upon this thy house, which we now dedicate to thee, that it may be sanctified and consecrated to be holy, and that thy holy presence may be continually in this house; and that all people who shall enter upon the threshold of the Lord's house may feel thy power, and feel constrained to acknowledge that thou hast sanctified it, and that it is thy house, a place of thy holiness.

"And do thou grant, Holy Father, that all those who shall worship in this house may be taught words of wisdom out of the best books, and that they may seek learning even by study, and also by faith, as thou hast said; and that they may grow up in thee, and receive a fulness of the Holy Ghost, and be organized according to thy laws, and be prepared to obtain every needful thing; and that this house may be a house of prayer, a house of fasting, a house of faith, a house of glory and of God, even thy house. . . .

"And we ask thee, Holy Father, that thy servants may go forth from this house armed with thy power, and that thy name may be upon them, and thy glory be round about them, and thine angels have charge over them; and from this place they may bear exceedingly great and glorious tidings, in truth, unto the ends of the earth, that they may know that this is thy work, and that thou hast put forth thy hand, to fulfil that which thou hast spoken by the mouths of the prophets, concerning the last days.

"We ask thee, Holy Father, to establish the people that shall worship, and honorably hold a name and standing in this thy house, to all generations and for eternity; that no weapon formed against them shall prosper; that he who diggeth a pit for them shall fall into the same himself; that no combination of wickedness shall have power to rise up and prevail over thy people upon whom thy name shall be put in this house."[19]

Suggestions for Study and Teaching

Consider these ideas as you study the chapter or as you prepare to teach. For additional help, see pages vii–xii.

- Review the last two paragraphs on page 414. In what ways does temple work "bring [us] out of darkness into marvelous light"? What do you think it means to be "spiritually minded"? Why must we be "spiritually minded" in order to receive the light that is available to us in the temple?
- When the Saints in Nauvoo were working to build a temple, the Prophet Joseph Smith told them, "We need the temple more than anything else" (page 416). Review pages 413–16,

looking for reasons why this statement is true. In what ways is the Prophet's statement true in your life?

- Study Joseph Smith's teachings about the command to build temples (pages 415–16). Why do you think the Church would not be "fully organized" without temples and temple ordinances? What can we do today to "hasten the work in the Temple"? Why do we need to "weigh the importance" of temple work?
- Review the Prophet's teachings about the sacred temple ordinances and what we learn from them (pages 416–19). Which of these teachings is particularly helpful to you in understanding the importance of temple ordinances?
- Read the third paragraph on page 419. If you have received temple ordinances, reflect on how your experiences have taught you about your "condition and true relation to God." If you have never been to the temple or if you have not returned for some time, think about how you can prepare to attend the temple.
- What are some blessings we can receive when we attend the temple? (For some examples, see pages 419–20.) From what you have read in this chapter, how can you make your temple attendance more meaningful?

Related Scriptures: Psalm 24:3–5; Isaiah 2:2–3; D&C 124:25–28, 39–41

Notes

1. Lucius N. Scovil, *Deseret News: Semi-Weekly,* Feb. 15, 1884, p. 2.
2. Franklin D. Richards, "A Tour of Historic Scenes," *Contributor,* May 1886, p. 301; punctuation and capitalization modernized.
3. *History of the Church,* 5:1–2; spelling and grammar modernized; paragraph divisions altered; from "History of the Church" (manuscript), book C-1, pp. 1328–29, Church Archives, The Church of Jesus Christ of Latter-day Saints, Salt Lake City, Utah.
4. Mercy Fielding Thompson, "Recollections of the Prophet Joseph Smith," *Juvenile Instructor,* July 1, 1892, p. 400.
5. *History of the Church,* 1:316–17; from a letter from Joseph Smith to William W. Phelps, Jan. 11, 1833, Kirtland, Ohio; this letter is incorrectly dated Jan. 14, 1833, in *History of the Church.*
6. *History of the Church,* 4:186; grammar modernized; from a letter from Joseph Smith and his counselors in the First Presidency to the Saints, Sept. 1840, Nauvoo, Illinois, published in *Times and Seasons,* Oct. 1840, pp. 178–79.

7. *History of the Church,* 4:269; from a letter from Joseph Smith and his counselors in the First Presidency to the Saints, Jan. 15, 1841, Nauvoo, Illinois, published in *Times and Seasons,* Jan. 15, 1841, p. 274.
8. William P. McIntire, reporting a discourse given by Joseph Smith in early 1841 in Nauvoo, Illinois; William Patterson McIntire, Notebook 1840–45, Church Archives.
9. *History of the Church,* 4:603; from a discourse given by Joseph Smith on Apr. 28, 1842, in Nauvoo, Illinois; reported by Eliza R. Snow; see also appendix, page 562, item 3.
10. *History of the Church,* 5:65; from "The Government of God," an editorial published in *Times and Seasons,* July 15, 1842, pp. 857–58; Joseph Smith was the editor of the periodical.
11. *History of the Church,* 6:52; from a discourse given by Joseph Smith on Oct. 9, 1843, in Nauvoo, Illinois; reported by Willard Richards and *Times and Seasons,* Sept. 15, 1843, pp. 331–32; this issue of the *Times and Seasons* was published late.
12. *History of the Church,* 6:230; from a Joseph Smith journal entry, Mar. 4, 1844, Nauvoo, Illinois.
13. *History of the Church,* 5:423–25, 427; paragraph divisions altered; from a discourse given by Joseph Smith on June 11, 1843, in Nauvoo, Illinois; reported by Wilford Woodruff and Willard Richards; see also appendix, page 562, item 3.
14. *History of the Church,* 6:319; from a discourse given by Joseph Smith on Apr. 8, 1844, in Nauvoo, Illinois; reported by Wilford Woodruff, Willard Richards, Thomas Bullock, and William Clayton; see also appendix, page 562, item 3.
15. *History of the Church,* 6:184; punctuation modernized; from a discourse given by Joseph Smith on Jan. 21, 1844, in Nauvoo, Illinois; reported by Wilford Woodruff.
16. *History of the Church,* 5:424; spelling modernized; from a discourse given by Joseph Smith on June 11, 1843, in Nauvoo, Illinois; reported by Wilford Woodruff and Willard Richards; see also appendix, page 562, item 3.
17. *History of the Church,* 6:50–51; paragraph divisions altered; from a discourse given by Joseph Smith on Oct. 9, 1843, in Nauvoo, Illinois; reported by Willard Richards and *Times and Seasons,* Sept. 15, 1843, p. 331; this issue of the *Times and Seasons* was published late.
18. *History of the Church,* 2:309; from a discourse given by Joseph Smith on Nov. 12, 1835, in Kirtland, Ohio; reported by Warren Parrish.
19. Doctrine and Covenants 109:10, 12–16, 22–26; prayer offered by Joseph Smith on Mar. 27, 1836, at the dedication of the temple in Kirtland, Ohio.

CHAPTER 37

Charity, the Pure Love of Christ

"Love is one of the chief characteristics of Deity, and ought to be manifested by those who aspire to be the sons of God."

From the Life of Joseph Smith

In a revelation given through Joseph Smith in 1841, the Lord designated the stake in Nauvoo, Illinois, a "cornerstone of Zion, which shall be polished with the refinement which is after the similitude of a palace" (D&C 124:2). Under the Prophet's direction, Nauvoo became a thriving center of commerce, education, and the arts. Many people worked their farms, while those who had an acre of land in the city grew fruits and vegetables in home gardens. Sawmills, brickyards, printing offices, flour mills, and bakeries sprang up in the city, as well as shops for carpenters, potters, tinsmiths, jewelers, blacksmiths, and cabinetmakers. In Nauvoo, the Saints could enjoy the theater, balls, and concerts. Hundreds of students were enrolled in schools throughout the community, and plans were under way for a university.

As Nauvoo grew rapidly, several brickyards produced the red bricks that gave Nauvoo buildings their distinctive look. One of these buildings was the Prophet's Red Brick Store. The store was built to serve both as an office for the Prophet and the First Presidency and as a business to help the Prophet support his family. An incident that occurred in the Red Brick Store shows the charitable nature that made the Prophet so beloved.

James Leach was an Englishman who had come to Nauvoo with his convert sister and her husband, Agnes and Henry Nightingale. After looking for work without success, James and Henry determined to ask the Prophet for help. James recalled:

The reconstructed Red Brick Store in Nauvoo. This building served as an office for the Prophet Joseph Smith and as a business to help him support his family. Many Church meetings and social activities were held in the store.

"We . . . found [the Prophet] in a little store selling a lady some goods. This was the first time I had had an opportunity to be near him and get a good look at him. I felt there was a superior spirit in him. He was different to anyone I had ever met before; and I said in my heart, he is truly a Prophet of the most high God.

"As I was not a member of the Church I wanted Henry to ask him for work, but he did not do so, so I had to. I said, 'Mr. Smith, if you please, have you any employment you could give us both, so we can get some provisions?' He viewed us with a cheerful countenance, and with such a feeling of kindness, said, 'Well, boys, what can you do?' We told him what our employment was before we left our native land.

"Said he, 'Can you make a ditch?' I replied we would do the best we could at it. 'That's right, boys,' and picking up a tape line, he said, 'Come along with me.'

"He took us a few rods from the store, gave me the ring to hold, and stretched all the tape from the reel and marked a line for us to work by. 'Now, boys,' said he, 'can you make a ditch three feet wide and two and a half feet deep along this line?'

"We said we would do our best, and he left us. We went to work, and when it was finished I went and told him it was done. He came and looked at it and said, 'Boys, if I had done it myself it could not have been done better. Now come with me.'

"He led the way back to his store, and told us to pick the best ham or piece of pork for ourselves. Being rather bashful, I said we would rather he would give us some. So he picked two of the largest and best pieces of meat and a sack of flour for each of us, and asked us if that would do. We told him we would be willing to do more work for it, but he said, 'If you are satisfied, boys, I am.'

"We thanked him kindly, and went on our way home rejoicing in the kind-heartedness of the Prophet of our God."

James Leach was baptized that same year and recorded that he "often had the privilege of seeing [the Prophet's] noble face lit up by the Spirit and power of God."[1]

Teachings of Joseph Smith

A person filled with the love of God is anxious to bless others.

"Love is one of the chief characteristics of Deity, and ought to be manifested by those who aspire to be the sons of God. A man filled with the love of God, is not content with blessing his family alone, but ranges through the whole world, anxious to bless the whole human race."[2]

Lucy Meserve Smith recorded the following: "[Joseph Smith] said, 'Brethren and sisters, love one another; love one another and be merciful to your enemies.' He repeated these words in a very emphatic tone of voice with a loud amen."[3]

In July 1839, the Prophet spoke to a group of Church leaders: "I then addressed them and gave much instruction . . . touching upon many subjects of importance and value to all who wish to walk humbly before the Lord, and especially teaching them to observe charity, wisdom and fellow-feeling, with love one towards another in all things, and under all circumstances."[4]

We have a special obligation to love and care for those in need.

"It is a duty which every Saint ought to render to his brethren freely—to always love them, and ever succor them. To be justified before God we must love one another: we must overcome evil; we must visit the fatherless and the widow in their affliction, and we must keep ourselves unspotted from the world; for such virtues flow from the great fountain of pure religion [see James 1:27]."[5]

"[A member of the Church] is to feed the hungry, to clothe the naked, to provide for the widow, to dry up the tear of the orphan, to comfort the afflicted, whether in this church, or in any other, or in no church at all, wherever he finds them."[6]

"The rich cannot be saved without charity, giving to feed the poor when and how God requires."[7]

"Consider the state of the afflicted and try to alleviate their sufferings; let your bread feed the hungry, and your clothing cover the naked; let your liberality dry up the tear of the orphan, and cheer the disconsolate widow; let your prayers, and presence, and kindness, alleviate the pains of the distressed, and your liberality contribute to their necessities; do good unto all men, especially unto the household of faith, that you may be harmless and blameless, the sons of God without rebuke. Keep the commandments of God—all that he has given, does give, or will give, and an halo of glory will shine around your path; the poor will rise up and call you blessed; you will be honored and respected by all good men; and your path will be that of the just, which shineth brighter and brighter until the perfect day [see Proverbs 4:18]."[8]

"The Holy Spirit . . . shall be poured out at all times upon your heads, when you are exercised with those principles of righteousness that are agreeable to the mind of God, and are properly affected one toward another, and are careful by all means to remember those who are in bondage, and in heaviness, and in deep affliction for your sakes. And if there are any among you who aspire after their own aggrandizement, and seek their own opulence, while their brethren are groaning in poverty, and are under sore trials and temptations, they cannot be benefited by the intercession of the Holy Spirit, which maketh intercession for us day and night with groanings that cannot be uttered [see Romans 8:26].

"We ought at all times to be very careful that such high-mindedness shall never have place in our hearts; but condescend to men of low estate, and with all long-suffering bear the infirmities of the weak."[9]

Charity is long-suffering, merciful, and kind.

Eliza R. Snow reported an address given by the Prophet: "He then commenced reading the 13th chapter [of 1 Corinthians]—'Though I speak with the tongues of men and angels, and have not charity, I am become as sounding brass, or a tinkling cymbal;' and said, don't be limited in your views with regard to your neighbor's virtue, but beware of self-righteousness, and be limited in the estimate of your own virtues, and not think yourselves more righteous than others; you must enlarge your souls towards each other, if you would do like Jesus, and carry your fellow-creatures to Abraham's bosom. He said he had manifested long-suffering, forbearance and patience towards the Church, and also to his enemies; and we must bear with each other's failings, as an indulgent parent bears with the foibles of his children.

". . . As you increase in innocence and virtue, as you increase in goodness, let your hearts expand, let them be enlarged towards others; you must be long-suffering, and bear with the faults and errors of mankind. How precious are the souls of men! . . .

". . . Don't envy the finery and fleeting show of sinners, for they are in a miserable situation; but as far as you can, have mercy on them, for in a short time God will destroy them, if they will not repent and turn unto him."[10]

"Wise men ought to have understanding enough to conquer men with kindness. 'A soft answer turneth away wrath,' says the wise man [Proverbs 15:1]; and it will be greatly to the credit of the Latter-day Saints to show the love of God, by now kindly treating those who may have, in an unconscious moment, done wrong; for truly said Jesus, Pray for thine enemies [see Matthew 5:44]."[11]

"I do not dwell upon your faults, and you shall not upon mine. Charity, which is love, covereth a multitude of sins [see 1 Peter 4:8], and I have often covered up all the faults among you; but the prettiest thing is to have no faults at all. We should cultivate a meek, quiet and peaceable spirit."[12]

Eliza R. Snow reported another address given by the Prophet: "When persons manifest the least kindness and love to me, O what power it has over my mind, while the opposite course has a tendency to harrow up all the harsh feelings and depress the human mind.

"It is one evidence that men are unacquainted with the principles of godliness to behold the contraction of affectionate feelings and lack of charity in the world. The power and glory of godliness is spread out on a broad principle to throw out the mantle of charity. God does not look on sin with allowance, but when men have sinned, there must be allowance made for them. . . . The nearer we get to our heavenly Father, the more we are disposed to look with compassion on perishing souls; we feel that we want to take them upon our shoulders, and cast their sins behind our backs. . . .

". . . How oft have wise men and women sought to dictate Brother Joseph by saying, 'Oh, if I were Brother Joseph, I would do this and that;' but if they were in Brother Joseph's shoes they would find that men or women could not be compelled into the kingdom of God, but must be dealt with in long-suffering, and at last we shall save them. The way to keep all the Saints together, and keep the work rolling, is to wait with all long-suffering, till God shall bring such characters to justice. There should be no license for sin, but mercy should go hand in hand with reproof."[13]

We express charity through simple acts of service and kindness.

"I am your servant, and it is only through the Holy Ghost that I can do you good. . . . We do not present ourselves before you as anything but your humble servants, willing to spend and be spent in your service."[14]

Edwin Holden recalled: "In 1838, Joseph and some of the young men were playing various out-door games, among which was a game of ball. By and by they began to get weary. He saw it, and calling them together he said: 'Let us build a log cabin.' So off they went, Joseph and the young men, to build a log cabin for a widow woman. Such was Joseph's way, always assisting in whatever he could."[15]

Lucy Mack Smith, the Prophet Joseph Smith's mother, said of the time when the Saints were first settling in Commerce, Illinois, later called Nauvoo: "As the season advanced, the brethren who had settled here began to feel the effects of their hardships, which, joined to the unhealthiness of the climate, brought them down with agues and bilious fevers to such an extent that there were some whole families in which there was not one who was able to give another a drink of cold water or even to help themselves. Hyrum's family were mostly sick. My youngest daughter, Lucy, was also very sick, and there were, in fact, but few of the inhabitants of the place who were well.

"Off they went, Joseph and the young men, to build a log cabin for a widow woman. Such was Joseph's way, always assisting in whatever he could."

"Joseph and Emma had the sick brought to their house and took care of them there. And they continued to have them brought as fast as they were taken down until their house, which consisted of four rooms, was so crowded that they were under the necessity of spreading a tent in the yard for the reception of that part of the family who were still on their feet. Joseph and Emma devoted their whole time and attention to the care of the sick during this time of distress."[16]

John L. Smith, the Prophet's cousin, recalled the following incident that occurred in this same period of time: "The Prophet Joseph and cousin Hyrum, his brother, visited us. We were all sick but Mother with the fever and ague, and Father was out of his head the greatest part of the time. Joseph took the shoes from his feet when he saw our destitute condition and put them on Father's feet, as he was barefoot, and rode home without any himself. He sent and took Father home to his house and saved his life and supplied us with many comforts so we recovered."[17]

Elizabeth Ann Whitney recalled: "Early in the Spring of 1840 we went up to Commerce, as the upper portion of the city of Nauvoo continued to be called. We rented a house belonging to Hiram Kimball. . . . Here we were all sick with ague, chills and fever, and were only just barely able to crawl around and wait upon each other. Under these trying circumstances my ninth child was born. Joseph, upon visiting us and seeing our change of circumstances, urged us at once to come and share his accommodations. We felt the climate, the water, and the privations we were enduring could not much longer be borne; therefore we availed ourselves of this proposal and went to live in the Prophet Joseph's yard in a small cottage; we soon recruited in health, and the children became more like themselves. My husband was employed in a store Joseph had built and fitted up with such goods as the people were in actual need of.

"One day while coming out of the house into the yard the remembrance of a prophecy Joseph Smith had made to me, while living in our house in Kirtland, flashed through my mind like an electric shock; it was this: that even as we had done by him, in opening our doors to him and his family when he was without a home; even so should we in the future be received by him into his house."[18]

Mosiah L. Hancock reported the following experience that occurred in Nauvoo while he was a youth: "This summer [1841] I played my first game of ball with the Prophet. We took turns knocking and chasing the ball, and when the game was over the Prophet said, 'Brethren, hitch up your teams,' which we did, and we all drove to the woods. I drove our one-horse wagon standing on the front bolster, and Brother Joseph and father rode on the hounds behind [the *bolster* and *hounds* are structural parts of a wagon]. There were 39 teams in the group and we gathered wood until our wagons were loaded. When our wagon was loaded, Brother Joseph offered to pull sticks with anyone—and he pulled them all up one at a time—with anyone who wanted to compete with him.

"Afterwards, the Prophet sent the wagons out to different places of people who needed help; and he told them to cut the

During a time of much sickness in Commerce, Illinois, Joseph and Emma Smith brought the sick to their home and cared for them there.

wood for the Saints who needed it. Everybody loved to do as the Prophet said, and even though we were sickly, and death was all around us, folks smiled and tried to cheer everyone up."[19]

On January 5, 1842, the Prophet wrote the following in a letter to Edward Hunter, who later served as Presiding Bishop: "Our assortment [at the Red Brick Store] is tolerably good—very good, considering the different purchases made by different individuals at different times, and under circumstances which controlled their choice to some extent; but I rejoice that we have been enabled to do as well as we have, for the hearts of many of the poor brethren and sisters will be made glad with those comforts which are now within their reach.

"The store has been filled to overflowing, and I have stood behind the counter all day, dealing out goods as steady as any clerk you ever saw, to oblige those who were compelled to go without their usual Christmas and New Year's dinners, for the want of a little sugar, molasses, raisins, etc., etc.; and to please myself also, for I love to wait upon the Saints, and be a servant to all, hoping that I may be exalted in the due time of the Lord."[20]

Suggestions for Study and Teaching

Consider these ideas as you study the chapter or as you prepare to teach. For additional help, see pages vii–xii.

- As you review the stories on pages 423–25 and pages 429–32, ponder your feelings toward the Prophet Joseph Smith. What do these stories teach about him? In what ways do you think his actions influenced the people around him? In what ways has your life been touched by the kindness of others?
- Review the first three paragraphs on page 426. Why do you think that a person filled with the love of God wants to bless all mankind? How can our acts of love and kindness help to bless all people?
- What are some responsibilities we have in caring for those in need? (For some examples, see pages 426–27.) How do these responsibilities relate to people's temporal needs? How do they relate to spiritual needs? What examples have you seen of people caring for those in need?
- Read the paragraph that begins at the bottom of page 427. What can we do to grow in our appreciation of others' virtues? Why do you think we should "beware of self-righteousness, and be limited in the estimate of [our] own virtues"?
- The Prophet Joseph expressed concern about "the contraction of affectionate feelings . . . in the world" (page 428). In contrast, he said that we should "enlarge [our] souls towards each other" and "let [our] hearts expand, let them be enlarged towards others" (pages 427–28). What do you think it means to enlarge our hearts and souls toward each other?
- Read the fifth full paragraph on page 428. In what ways can we apply this teaching as we interact with our family members?

Related Scriptures: 1 Corinthians 13:1–13; Mosiah 4:14–16, 26–27; Ether 12:33–34; Moroni 7:45–48; D&C 121:45–46

Notes

1. James Leach, in "Recollections of the Prophet Joseph Smith," *Juvenile Instructor,* Mar. 1, 1892, pp. 152–53; punctuation modernized; paragraph divisions altered.
2. *History of the Church,* 4:227; from a letter from Joseph Smith to the Twelve, Dec. 15, 1840, Nauvoo, Illinois, published in *Times and Seasons,* Jan. 1, 1841, p. 258; this letter is incorrectly dated Oct. 19, 1840, in *History of the Church.*
3. Lucy Meserve Smith, in "Recollections of the Prophet Joseph Smith," *Juvenile Instructor,* Aug. 1, 1892, p. 471.
4. *History of the Church,* 3:383; from a Joseph Smith journal entry, July 2, 1839, Montrose, Iowa.
5. *History of the Church,* 2:229, footnote; from "To the Saints Scattered Abroad," *Messenger and Advocate,* June 1835, p. 137.
6. Editor's reply to a letter from Richard Savary, *Times and Seasons,* Mar. 15, 1842, p. 732; Joseph Smith was the editor of the periodical.
7. *History of the Church,* 4:608; from a discourse given by Joseph Smith on May 1, 1842, in Nauvoo, Illinois; reported by Willard Richards.
8. "To the Saints of God," an editorial published in *Times and Seasons,* Oct. 15, 1842, p. 952; Joseph Smith was the editor of the periodical.
9. *History of the Church,* 3:299; punctuation modernized; from a letter from Joseph Smith and others to Edward Partridge and the Church, Mar. 20, 1839, Liberty Jail, Liberty, Missouri.
10. *History of the Church,* 4:606–7; paragraph divisions altered; from a discourse given by Joseph Smith on Apr. 28, 1842, in Nauvoo, Illinois; reported by Eliza R. Snow; see also appendix, page 562, item 3.
11. *History of the Church,* 6:219; paragraph divisions altered; from "Pacific Innuendo," an article written under the direction of Joseph Smith, Feb. 17, 1844, Nauvoo, Illinois; published in *Times and Seasons,* Feb. 15, 1844, p. 443; this issue of the *Times and Seasons* was published late.
12. *History of the Church,* 5:517; from a discourse given by Joseph Smith on July 23, 1843, in Nauvoo, Illinois; reported by Willard Richards; see also appendix, page 562, item 3.
13. *History of the Church,* 5:24; spelling modernized; paragraph divisions altered; from a discourse given by Joseph Smith on June 9, 1842, in Nauvoo, Illinois; reported by Eliza R. Snow.
14. *History of the Church,* 5:355; paragraph divisions altered; from a discourse given by Joseph Smith on Apr. 13, 1843, in Nauvoo, Illinois; reported by Willard Richards.
15. Edwin Holden, in "Recollections of the Prophet Joseph Smith," *Juvenile Instructor,* Mar. 1, 1892, p. 153; punctuation modernized.
16. Lucy Mack Smith, "The History of Lucy Smith, Mother of the Prophet," 1844–45 manuscript, book 17, p. 7, Church Archives, The Church of Jesus Christ of Latter-day Saints, Salt Lake City, Utah.
17. John Lyman Smith, Autobiography and Diaries, 1846–95, photocopy, vol. 1, entry for Sept. 1839, Church Archives.
18. Elizabeth Ann Whitney, "A Leaf from an Autobiography," *Woman's Exponent,* Nov. 15, 1878, p. 91.
19. Mosiah Lyman Hancock, Autobiography, typescript, p. 22, Church Archives.
20. *History of the Church,* 4:492; from a letter from Joseph Smith to Edward Hunter, Jan. 5, 1842, Nauvoo, Illinois.

CHAPTER 38

The Wentworth Letter

The Wentworth Letter is the Prophet Joseph Smith's account of "the rise, progress, persecution, and faith of the Latter-day Saints," including the statements known as the Articles of Faith.

From the Life of Joseph Smith

In addition to being President of the Church, Joseph Smith had many other responsibilities in Nauvoo. In May 1842, he became mayor of Nauvoo, which meant that he was also chief judge of the Nauvoo Municipal Court. He was a lieutenant general and commander of the Nauvoo Legion. And in February 1842, he assumed the role of editor of the *Times and Seasons,* a Church periodical that was published twice a month. The *Times and Seasons* provided a way for Church leaders to communicate with the Saints, publish revelations and important discourses, and share news of the Church. John Taylor, a member of the Quorum of the Twelve, was appointed to handle many aspects of the publication under the Prophet's direction.

In the first edition published while he was editor, the Prophet wrote that the periodical would provide articles on "the important events that are daily transpiring around us; the rapid advance of truth; the many communications that we are receiving, daily, from elders abroad; both in this country, in England, from the continent of Europe, and other parts of the world; the convulsed state of the nations; the epistles and teachings of the Twelve; and the revelations which we are receiving from the Most High."[1]

While the Prophet served as editor, the *Times and Seasons* published documents of great importance. The text of the book of Abraham and two of the facsimiles were published in March 1842, with the third facsimile published in May. Also in March,

"At the request of Mr. John Wentworth, . . . I have written the following sketch of the rise, progress, persecution, and faith of the Latter-day Saints, of which I have the honor, under God, of being the founder."

the Prophet began publishing the "History of Joseph Smith," the account that would later become *History of the Church.*

In the *Times and Seasons* issue dated March 1, 1842, the Prophet published what has come to be known as the Wentworth Letter. Describing his reasons for producing this document, the Prophet explained: "At the request of Mr. John Wentworth, Editor and Proprietor of the *Chicago Democrat,* I have written the following sketch of the rise, progress, persecution, and faith of the Latter-day Saints, of which I have the honor, under God, of being the founder. Mr. Wentworth says that he wishes to furnish Mr. [George] Barstow, a friend of his, who is writing the history of New Hampshire, with this document. As Mr. Barstow has taken the proper steps to obtain correct information, all that I shall ask at his hands, is, that he publish the account entire, ungarnished, and without misrepresentation."[2]

George Barstow ultimately did not include the Prophet's account in his history because he decided to cover events only through the year 1819 in his book.[3] But the Wentworth Letter has immense value to Latter-day Saints. It is an original account by Joseph Smith testifying of his sacred call from God, his visions, and his ministry and teachings. It recounts the rise and growth of the Church and the persecutions of the Saints. It contains a prophetic declaration of the Church's future success in the earth under the protective hand of the Great Jehovah. It also contains several important details not found elsewhere in the Prophet's teachings, including a description of the gold plates and a sketch of the contents of the Book of Mormon. Significantly, it is the first time that Joseph Smith himself published an account of his First Vision.

Concluding with the 13 declarations of Church doctrine now called the Articles of Faith, it stands as a powerful witness of the divine calling of the Prophet Joseph Smith.

Teachings of Joseph Smith

God the Father and Jesus Christ appeared to Joseph Smith in answer to his prayer.

"I was born in the town of Sharon, Windsor County, Vermont, on the 23rd of December, A.D. 1805. When [I was] ten years old, my parents removed to Palmyra, New York, where we resided about four years, and from thence we removed to the town of Manchester. My father was a farmer and taught me the art of husbandry. When about fourteen years of age, I began to reflect upon the importance of being prepared for a future state, and upon inquiring [about] the plan of salvation, I found that there was a great clash in religious sentiment; if I went to one society they referred me to one plan, and another to another; each one pointing to his own particular creed as the *summum bonum* of perfection. Considering that all could not be right, and that God could not be the author of so much confusion, I determined to investigate the subject more fully, believing that if God had a Church it would not be split up into factions, and that if He taught one society to worship one way, and administer in one set of ordinances, He would not teach another, principles which were diametrically opposed.

"Believing the word of God, I had confidence in the declaration of James—'If any of you lack wisdom, let him ask of God, that giveth to all men liberally, and upbraideth not; and it shall be given him.' [James 1:5.] I retired to a secret place in a grove, and began to call upon the Lord; while fervently engaged in supplication, my mind was taken away from the objects with which I was surrounded, and I was enwrapped in a heavenly vision, and saw two glorious personages, who exactly resembled each other in features and likeness, surrounded with a brilliant light which eclipsed the sun at noon day. They told me that all religious denominations were believing in incorrect doctrines, and that none of them was acknowledged of God as His Church and kingdom: and I was expressly commanded 'to go not after them,' at the same time receiving a promise that the fullness of the Gospel should at some future time be made known unto me.

The Book of Mormon was written anciently upon gold plates and delivered to Joseph Smith by a divinely sent messenger.

"On the evening of the 21st of September, A.D. 1823, while I was praying unto God, and endeavoring to exercise faith in the precious promises of Scripture, on a sudden a light like that of day, only of a far purer and more glorious appearance and brightness, burst into the room; indeed the first sight was as though the house was filled with consuming fire; the appearance produced a shock that affected the whole body; in a moment a personage stood before me surrounded with a glory yet greater than that with which I was already surrounded. This messenger proclaimed himself to be an angel of God, sent to bring the joyful tidings that the covenant which God made with ancient Israel was at hand to be fulfilled, that the preparatory work for the second coming of the Messiah was speedily to commence, that the time was at hand for the Gospel in all its fullness to be preached in power, unto all nations that a people might be prepared for the Millennial reign. I was informed that I was chosen to be an instrument in the hands of God to bring about some of His purposes in this glorious dispensation.

"I was also informed concerning the aboriginal inhabitants of this country and shown who they were, and from whence they came; a brief sketch of their origin, progress, civilization, laws, governments, of their righteousness and iniquity, and the blessings of God being finally withdrawn from them as a people, was made known unto me; I was also told where were deposited some plates on which were engraven an abridgment of the records of the ancient Prophets that had existed on this continent. The angel appeared to me three times the same night and unfolded the same things. After having received many visits from the angels of God unfolding the majesty and glory of the events that should transpire in the last days, on the morning of the 22nd of September, A.D. 1827, the angel of the Lord delivered the records into my hands.

"These records were engraven on plates which had the appearance of gold; each plate was six inches wide and eight inches long, and not quite so thick as common tin. They were filled with

"On the morning of the 22nd of September, A.D. 1827, the angel of the Lord delivered the records into my hands."

engravings, in Egyptian characters, and bound together in a volume as the leaves of a book, with three rings running through the whole. The volume was something near six inches in thickness, a part of which was sealed. The characters on the unsealed part were small, and beautifully engraved. The whole book exhibited many marks of antiquity in its construction, and much skill in the art of engraving. With the records was found a curious instrument, which the ancients called 'Urim and Thummim,' which consisted of two transparent stones set in the rim of a bow fastened to a breast plate. Through the medium of the Urim and Thummim I translated the record by the gift and power of God.

". . . This book . . . tells us that our Savior made His appearance upon this continent after His resurrection; that He planted the Gospel here in all its fulness, and richness, and power, and blessing; that they had Apostles, Prophets, Pastors, Teachers, and Evangelists, the same order, the same priesthood, the same ordinances, gifts, powers, and blessings, as were enjoyed on the eastern continent; that the people were cut off in consequence of their transgressions; that the last of their prophets who existed among them was commanded to write an abridgment of their prophecies, history, etc., and to hide it up in the earth, and that it should come forth and be united with the Bible for the accomplishment of the purposes of God in the last days. For a more particular account I would refer to the Book of Mormon, which can be purchased at Nauvoo, or from any of our Traveling Elders.

"As soon as the news of this discovery was made known, false reports, misrepresentation and slander flew, as on the wings of the wind, in every direction; the house was frequently beset by mobs and evil designing persons. Several times I was shot at, and very narrowly escaped, and every device was made use of to get the plates away from me; but the power and blessing of God attended me, and several began to believe my testimony.

Although persecution may rage against the Church, nothing can stop the progress of truth.

"On the 6th of April, 1830, the 'Church of Jesus Christ of Latter-day Saints' was first organized in the town of Fayette, Seneca county, state of New York. Some few were called and ordained by the Spirit of revelation and prophecy, and began to preach as the Spirit gave them utterance, and though weak, yet were they strengthened by the power of God, and many were brought to repentance, were immersed in the water, and were filled with the Holy Ghost by the laying on of hands. They saw visions and prophesied, devils were cast out, and the sick healed by the laying on of hands. From that time the work rolled forth with astonishing rapidity, and churches were soon formed in the states of

New York, Pennsylvania, Ohio, Indiana, Illinois, and Missouri; in the last named state a considerable settlement was formed in Jackson county: numbers joined the Church and we were increasing rapidly; we made large purchases of land, our farms teemed with plenty, and peace and happiness were enjoyed in our domestic circle, and throughout our neighborhood; but as we could not associate with our neighbors (who were, many of them, of the basest of men, and had fled from the face of civilized society, to the frontier country to escape the hand of justice,) in their midnight revels, their Sabbath breaking, horse racing and gambling; they commenced at first to ridicule, then to persecute, and finally an organized mob assembled and burned our houses, tarred and feathered and whipped many of our brethren, and finally, contrary to law, justice and humanity, drove them from their habitations; who, houseless and homeless, had to wander on the bleak prairies till the children left the tracks of their blood on the prairie. This took place in the month of November, and they had no other covering but the canopy of heaven, in this inclement season of the year; this proceeding was winked at by the government, and although we had warranty deeds for our land, and had violated no law, we could obtain no redress.

"There were many sick, who were thus inhumanly driven from their houses, and had to endure all this abuse and to seek homes where they could be found. The result was, that a great many of them being deprived of the comforts of life, and the necessary attendances, died; many children were left orphans, wives [were left] widows, and husbands, widowers; our farms were taken possession of by the mob, many thousands of cattle, sheep, horses and hogs were taken, and our household goods, store goods, and printing press and type were broken, taken, or otherwise destroyed.

"Many of our brethren removed to Clay county, where they continued until 1836, three years; there was no violence offered, but there were threatenings of violence. But in the summer of 1836 these threatenings began to assume a more serious form, from threats, public meetings were called, resolutions were passed, vengeance and destruction were threatened, and affairs again assumed a fearful attitude; Jackson county was a sufficient precedent, and as the authorities in that county did not interfere, they [the Clay county authorities] boasted that they would not in this; which on application to the authorities we found to be too true, and after much privation and loss of property, we were again driven from our homes.

"We next settled in Caldwell and Daviess counties, where we made large and extensive settlements, thinking to free ourselves from the power of oppression, by settling in new counties, with very few inhabitants in them; but here we were not allowed to live in peace, but in 1838 we were again attacked by mobs, an exterminating order was issued by Governor Boggs, and under the sanction of law, an organized banditti ranged through the country, robbed us of our cattle, sheep, hogs, etc., many of our people were murdered in cold blood, the chastity of our women was violated, and we were forced to sign away our property at the point of the sword; and after enduring every indignity that could be heaped upon us by an inhuman, ungodly band of marauders, from twelve to fifteen thousand souls, men, women, and children, were driven from their own firesides, and from lands to which they had warranty deeds, houseless, friendless, and homeless (in the depths of winter) to wander as exiles on the earth, or to seek an asylum in a more genial clime, and among a less barbarous people. Many sickened and died in consequence of the cold and hardships they had to endure; many wives were left widows, and children [were left] orphans, and destitute. It would take more time than is allotted me here to describe the injustice, the wrongs, the murders, the bloodshed, the theft, misery and woe that have been caused by the barbarous, inhuman, and lawless proceedings of the state of Missouri.

"In the situation before alluded to, we arrived in the state of Illinois in 1839, where we found a hospitable people and a friendly home: a people who were willing to be governed by the principles of law and humanity. We have commenced to build a city called 'Nauvoo,' in Hancock county. We number from six to eight thousand here, besides vast numbers in the county around, and in almost every county of the state. We have a city charter granted us, and charter for a Legion, the troops of which now number 1,500. We have also a charter for a University, for an Agricultural and Manufacturing Society, have our own laws and administrators, and possess all the privileges that other free and enlightened citizens enjoy.

"Persecution has not stopped the progress of truth, but has only added fuel to the flame, it has spread with increasing rapidity. Proud of the cause which they have espoused, and conscious of our innocence, and of the truth of their system, amidst calumny and reproach, have the Elders of this Church gone forth, and planted the Gospel in almost every state in the Union; it has penetrated our cities, it has spread over our villages, and has caused thousands of our intelligent, noble, and patriotic citizens to obey its divine mandates, and be governed by its sacred truths. It has also spread into England, Ireland, Scotland, and Wales, where, in the year 1840, a few of our missionaries were sent, and over five thousand joined the Standard of Truth; there are numbers now joining in every land.

"Our missionaries are going forth to different nations, and in Germany, Palestine, New Holland [Australia], the East Indies, and other places, the Standard of Truth has been erected; no unhallowed hand can stop the work from progressing; persecutions may rage, mobs may combine, armies may assemble, calumny may defame, but the truth of God will go forth boldly, nobly, and independent, till it has penetrated every continent, visited every clime, swept every country, and sounded in every ear, till the purposes of God shall be accomplished, and the Great Jehovah shall say the work is done.

The Articles of Faith describe fundamental doctrines and principles of our religion.

"We believe in God the eternal Father, and in His Son Jesus Christ, and in the Holy Ghost.

"We believe that men will be punished for their own sins, and not for Adam's transgression.

"We believe that through the atonement of Christ all mankind may be saved by obedience to the laws and ordinances of the Gospel.

"We believe that the first principle and ordinances of the Gospel are: (1) Faith in the Lord Jesus Christ; (2) Repentance; (3) Baptism by immersion for the remission of sins; (4) Laying on of hands for the gift of the Holy Ghost.

"We believe that a man must be called of God by prophecy and by the laying on of hands, by those who are in authority, to preach the Gospel and administer in the ordinances thereof.

"We believe in the same organization that existed in the primitive Church, viz.: apostles, prophets, pastors, teachers, evangelists, etc.

"We believe in the gift of tongues, prophecy, revelation, visions, healing, interpretation of tongues, etc.

"We believe the Bible to be the word of God, as far as it is translated correctly; we also believe the Book of Mormon to be the word of God.

"We believe all that God has revealed, all that He does now reveal, and we believe that He will yet reveal many great and important things pertaining to the kingdom of God.

"We believe in the literal gathering of Israel and in the restoration of the Ten Tribes; that Zion will be built upon this [the American] continent; that Christ will reign personally upon the earth; and that the earth will be renewed and receive its paradisiacal glory.

"We claim the privilege of worshiping Almighty God according to the dictates of our own conscience, and allow all men the same privilege, let them worship how, where, or what they may.

"We believe in being subject to kings, presidents, rulers and magistrates, in obeying, honoring, and sustaining the law.

"We believe in being honest, true, chaste, benevolent, virtuous, and in doing good to *all men;* indeed we may say that we follow the admonition of Paul, We believe all things, we hope all things, we have endured many things, and hope to be able to endure all things. If there is anything virtuous, lovely, or of good report, or praiseworthy, we seek after these things. [See Articles of Faith 1:1–13.]

"Respectfully, etc.,

"JOSEPH SMITH."[4]

Suggestions for Study and Teaching

Consider these ideas as you study the chapter or as you prepare to teach. For additional help, see pages vii–xii.

- Joseph Smith wrote the Wentworth Letter in response to a request from John Wentworth and George Barstow (page 437). When have people asked you about the history or beliefs of the Church? As you study or discuss this chapter, think about how you might respond to such questions in the future. What can we learn from Joseph Smith's words in the Wentworth Letter about how to respond to such questions?
- Read what the Prophet said about his First Vision (page 438). The next time you tell someone about the First Vision, how might you help that person understand the First Vision and what it means to you?
- Read the Prophet's description of the coming forth of the Book of Mormon (pages 439–41). What difference has the Book of Mormon made in your life? What are some ways we can share our testimonies of the Book of Mormon?
- On pages 441–44, Joseph Smith gives a brief history of the beginnings of the Church and then testifies of the Church's destiny. What are your feelings as you study the second full paragraph on page 444? Why do you think persecution is unable to stop the Church's progress? What are some examples of people progressing despite opposition? (Consider examples from the scriptures, Church history, and your own life.)
- Review the Articles of Faith (pages 444–46). In what ways have the Articles of Faith helped you? Why do you think we ask Primary children to memorize them? Consider organizing a schedule so you can study or memorize the Articles of Faith.

Related Scriptures: Joseph Smith—History 1:1–75

Notes

1. "To Subscribers," an editorial published in *Times and Seasons,* Feb. 15, 1842, p. 696; capitalization modernized; Joseph Smith was the editor of the periodical.
2. *History of the Church,* 4:535–36; from a letter from Joseph Smith written at the request of John Wentworth and George Barstow, Nauvoo, Illinois, published in *Times and Seasons,* Mar. 1, 1842, p. 706. Mr. Barstow's last name is incorrectly spelled "Bastow" in *History of the Church* and *Times and Seasons.*
3. Though the letter was apparently never published by John Wentworth or George Barstow, the same account, with some additions and revisions, was published nationally in 1844 by I. Daniel Rupp in "Latter Day Saints," *He Pasa Ekklesia [The Whole Church]: An Original History of the Religious Denominations at Present Existing in the United States,* pp. 404–10.
4. *History of the Church,* 4:536–41; bracketed word "about" in first paragraph on p. 438 in original; bracketed words in eighth paragraph on p. 445 in original; spelling and punctuation modernized; from a letter from Joseph Smith written at the request of John Wentworth and George Barstow, Nauvoo, Illinois, published in *Times and Seasons,* Mar. 1, 1842, pp. 706–10. On several different occasions the Prophet Joseph Smith wrote or dictated a detailed account of the First Vision. The account in the Wentworth Letter is one of these accounts. The official scriptural account is found in Joseph Smith—History in the Pearl of Great Price. Also, a number of minor changes were made to prepare the Articles of Faith for publication in the 1981 edition of the Pearl of Great Price. Therefore, there are a number of small differences between the current version of the Articles of Faith and the version published in this chapter.

On March 17, 1842, the Prophet Joseph Smith organized the Female Relief Society of Nauvoo. "The Church was never perfectly organized until the women were thus organized," the Prophet declared.

CHAPTER 39

Relief Society: Divine Organization of Women

"If you live up to your privileges, the angels cannot be restrained from being your associates."

From the Life of Joseph Smith

In the spring of 1842, members of the Church in Nauvoo were busily occupied with the work of building the Nauvoo Temple. Two such members were Sarah Granger Kimball and her seamstress, Margaret A. Cook, who, while talking together one day, decided to combine their efforts in order to help the temple workmen. Sister Kimball said that she would provide fabric so that Sister Cook could make shirts for the men. The two women decided to invite other sisters to join them in forming a ladies' society to further their benevolent efforts. Sarah Granger Kimball recalled: "The neighboring sisters met in my parlor and decided to organize. I was delegated to call on Sister Eliza R. Snow and ask her to write for us a Constitution and By-laws, and submit them to President Joseph Smith prior to our next Thursday's meeting."

After looking over the proposed constitution and bylaws, the Prophet pronounced them the best he had ever seen but then said: " 'This is not what you want. Tell the sisters their offering is accepted of the Lord, and he has something better for them than a written Constitution. I invite them all to meet with me and a few of the brethren . . . next Thursday afternoon.' "[1]

Accordingly, on March 17, the Prophet, accompanied by Elders John Taylor and Willard Richards, met with 20 women of all ages in the upstairs room of the Red Brick Store. The Prophet officially organized the Female Relief Society of Nauvoo and taught those present about the purposes of the new organization. The sisters elected Emma Smith as president of the Relief Society, and Emma selected her two counselors. The Prophet then read a revelation received 12 years earlier in which the Lord assigned Emma to collect hymns for publication and designated her as an "elect lady" (D&C 25:3). Emma Smith rose to speak, emphasizing the society's vast potential: "We are going to do something extraordinary. . . . We expect extraordinary occasions and pressing calls."[2]

Emma Smith, the first Relief Society general president, had always had a strong desire to serve others and build God's kingdom, once declaring that she wanted to be "a blessing to all who may in any wise need aught at my hands."[3] In New York, she sewed clothing for the four missionaries called to preach the gospel to the Lamanites. In Kirtland, she worked with other women to collect blankets, food, and clothing for the Zion's Camp marchers to take to distressed Saints in Missouri. She helped prepare meals and make stockings, pantaloons, and jackets for the workmen building the Kirtland Temple. She took in so many temple workmen as boarders that she and Joseph had to sleep on the floor. In the early days of Nauvoo, she devoted much of her time and attention to nursing the many malaria victims camped outside her home on the banks of the Mississippi River. In these and other ways, she exemplified the service given by many sisters in her day. Polly Angell recalled that when the Prophet saw a group of women busily sewing the veils used to partition areas in the Kirtland Temple, he said, "Well, sisters, . . . you are always on hand. The sisters are always first and foremost in all good works."[4]

Since those early days of the Relief Society, the women of the Church have remained a tremendous force for good. At a meeting held a week after the Relief Society was organized, Lucy Mack Smith, the Prophet's mother, gave the sisters counsel that extends to millions of women in the Church today: "We must cherish one another, watch over one another, comfort one another and gain instruction, that we may all sit down in heaven together."[5]

Teachings of Joseph Smith

The Relief Society, organized under the priesthood and after its pattern, is an essential part of the Church.

Sarah Granger Kimball recalled that shortly before the Prophet Joseph Smith organized the Relief Society, he said: "I will organize the women under the priesthood after the pattern of the priesthood. . . . The Church was never perfectly organized until the women were thus organized."[6]

The Prophet's history for March 24, 1842, records: "[The] organization [of the Female Relief Society] was completed this day. Mrs. Emma Smith takes the presidential chair; Mrs. Elizabeth Ann Whitney and Sarah M. Cleveland are her counselors; Miss Elvira [Cowles] is treasurer, and our well-known and talented poetess, Miss Eliza R. Snow, secretary."[7]

Eliza R. Snow reported: "President Joseph Smith arose. Spoke of the organization of the Female Relief Society; said he was deeply interested, that it might be built up to the Most High in an acceptable manner."[8]

Eliza R. Snow also reported: "[Joseph Smith] exhorted the sisters always to concentrate their faith and prayers for, and place confidence in . . . those faithful men whom God has placed at the head of the Church to lead His people; that we should arm and sustain them with our prayers. . . . If this Society listen to the counsel of the Almighty, through the heads of the Church, they shall have power to command queens in their midst."[9]

"This Society is to get instruction through the order which God has established—through the medium of those appointed to lead—and I now turn the key to you in the name of God, and this Society shall rejoice, and knowledge and intelligence shall flow down from this time—this is the beginning of better days to this Society."[10]

The Relief Society enables women to act according to their benevolent natures, giving care to those in need.

"This is a charitable Society, and according to your natures; it is natural for females to have feelings of charity and benevolence.

You are now placed in a situation in which you can act according to those sympathies which God has planted in your bosoms."[11]

"Said Jesus, 'Ye shall do the work, which ye see me do.' [See 2 Nephi 31:12.] These are the grand key-words for the society to act upon."[12]

Willard Richards reported: "The [Female Relief Society] meeting was addressed by President Joseph Smith, to illustrate the object of the Society—that the Society of Sisters might provoke the brethren to good works in looking to the wants of the poor—searching after objects of charity, and in administering to their wants—to assist by correcting the morals and strengthening the virtues of the community."[13]

"I attended by request, the Female Relief Society, whose object is the relief of the poor, the destitute, the widow and the orphan, and for the exercise of all benevolent purposes. . . . There was a very numerous attendance at the organization of the society, and also at the subsequent meetings, of some of our most intelligent, humane, philanthropic and respectable ladies; and we are well assured from a knowledge of those pure principles of benevolence that flow spontaneously from their humane and philanthropic bosoms, that with the resources they will have at command, they will fly to the relief of the stranger; they will pour in oil and wine to the wounded heart of the distressed; they will dry up the tears of the orphan and make the widow's heart to rejoice.

"Our women have always been signalized for their acts of benevolence and kindness; . . . in the midst of their persecution, when the bread has been torn from their helpless offspring by their cruel oppressors, they have always been ready to open their doors to the weary traveler, to divide their scant pittance with the hungry, and from their robbed and impoverished wardrobes, to divide with the more needy and destitute; and now that they are living upon a more genial soil, and among a less barbarous people, and possess facilities that they have not heretofore enjoyed, we feel convinced that with their concentrated efforts, the condition of the suffering poor, of the stranger and the fatherless will be ameliorated."[14]

"This is a charitable Society. . . . You are now placed in a situation in which you can act according to those sympathies which God has planted in your bosoms."

The Relief Society encourages women to practice holiness and to instruct one another.

"The Ladies' Relief Society is not only to relieve the poor, but to save souls."[15]

"Now beloved sisters, . . . we desire you to do your part, and we will do ours, for we wish to keep the commandments of God in all things, as given directly from heaven to us, living by every word that proceedeth out of the mouth of the Lord. May God add his blessing upon your heads and lead you in all the paths of virtue, purity and grace."[16]

"The [Relief] Society have done well: their principles are to practice holiness. God loves you, and your prayers in my behalf shall avail much: let them not cease to ascend to God continually in my behalf."[17]

"You must put down iniquity, and by your good examples, stimulate the Elders to good works."[18]

Willard Richards reported: "President Joseph Smith read the revelation to Emma Smith, from the book of Doctrine and Covenants

[D&C 25]; and stated that she was . . . to expound the scriptures to all; and to teach the female part of the community; and that not she alone, but others, may attain to the same blessings."[19]

Eliza R. Snow reported: "As [the Prophet Joseph Smith] had this opportunity, he was going to instruct the ladies of this Society, and point out the way for them to conduct themselves, that they might act according to the will of God. . . .

"If you live up to these principles, how great and glorious will be your reward in the celestial kingdom! If you live up to your privileges, the angels cannot be restrained from being your associates. Females, if they are pure and innocent, can come in the presence of God; for what is more pleasing to God than innocence; you must be innocent, or you cannot come up before God: if we would come before God, we must keep ourselves pure, as He is pure."[20]

The Relief Society encourages women to follow the example of the Savior in showing mercy and avoiding strife.

"If you would have God have mercy on you, have mercy on one another. . . . We are full of selfishness; the devil flatters us that we are very righteous, when we are feeding on the faults of others. We can only live by worshiping our God; all must do it for themselves; none can do it for another. How mild the Savior dealt with Peter, saying, 'When thou art converted, strengthen thy brethren.' [Luke 22:32.] At another time, He said to him, 'Lovest thou me?' and having received Peter's reply, He said, 'Feed my sheep.' [John 21:15–17.] If the sisters [love] the Lord, let them feed the sheep, and not destroy them. . . .

"Sisters of the society, shall there be strife among you? I will not have it. You must repent, and get the love of God. Away with self-righteousness. The best measure or principle to bring the poor to repentance is to administer to their wants."[21]

Eliza R. Snow reported the following words of the Prophet: "Notwithstanding the unworthy are among us, the virtuous should not, from self importance, grieve and oppress needlessly, those unfortunate ones—even these should be encouraged to hereafter live to be honored by this society, who are the best portions of the community. Said he had two things to recommend to the members of this society, to put a double watch over the tongue: no organized body can exist without this at all. . . . The object is to make those not so good reform and return to the path of virtue that they may be numbered with the good. . . .

". . . Search yourselves—the tongue is an unruly member—hold your tongues about things of no moment—a little tale will set the world on fire."[22]

"The little foxes spoil the vines—little evils do the most injury to the Church. If you have evil feelings, and speak of them to one another, it has a tendency to do mischief."[23]

"Do not injure the character of anyone. If members of the Society shall conduct themselves improperly, deal with them, and keep all your doings within your own bosoms, and hold all characters sacred."[24]

Suggestions for Study and Teaching

Consider these ideas as you study the chapter or as you prepare to teach. For additional help, see pages vii–xii.

- Read the statement by Emma Smith at the top of page 450. Why do you think Relief Society sisters are able to accomplish extraordinary things? In what ways have you and your family been blessed through the efforts of Relief Society sisters? Read the counsel from Lucy Mack Smith at the bottom of page 450. In what ways do Relief Society sisters follow this counsel today?
- The Prophet Joseph Smith organized the Relief Society "under the priesthood after the pattern of the priesthood" (page 451). How does this set them apart from other service organizations in the world? (For some examples, see page 451.) Why do you think the Church was "never perfectly organized" until Joseph Smith organized the Relief Society?
- How do the responsibilities of Relief Society sisters today compare to the assignments the sisters received from Joseph Smith? (For some examples, see pages 451–54.) Read the first

full paragraph on page 452. In what ways do opportunities to give service help us become more like the Savior?

- Read the first paragraph on page 453. What do you think it means to save a soul? In what ways do members of the Relief Society fulfill this responsibility, both temporally and spiritually?
- Review the second full paragraph on page 452 and the fourth paragraph on page 453. What can Relief Society sisters do to stimulate good works among priesthood holders? What can priesthood holders do to support Relief Society sisters in their work?
- Read the paragraph that begins at the bottom of page 453. What can we learn from this statement about each sister's responsibilities and opportunities?
- The Prophet warned against "feeding on the faults of others" (page 454). What do you think this means? How might this attitude hinder the efforts of the Relief Society—or any quorum or group in the Church? What can we do to feed the Lord's sheep rather than feed ourselves on their faults?

Related Scriptures: Proverbs 31:10–31; 1 Corinthians 13:8; D&C 25:1–16; 88:125

Notes

1. Sarah Granger Kimball, "Auto-biography," *Woman's Exponent,* Sept. 1, 1883, p. 51.
2. Emma Smith, quoted in Relief Society, Minute Book Mar. 1842–Mar. 1844, entry for Mar. 17, 1842, p. 12, reported by Willard Richards, Church Archives, The Church of Jesus Christ of Latter-day Saints, Salt Lake City, Utah.
3. Emma Hale Smith, Blessing, 1844, typescript, Church Archives.
4. Quoted by Polly Angell, in Edward W. Tullidge, *The Women of Mormondom* (1877), p. 76.
5. Lucy Mack Smith, quoted in Relief Society, Minute Book Mar. 1842–Mar. 1844, entry for Mar. 24, 1842, pp. 18–19, reported by Eliza R. Snow, Church Archives.
6. Quoted in Sarah Granger Kimball, "Auto-biography," *Woman's Exponent,* Sept. 1, 1883, p. 51.
7. *History of the Church,* 4:567; from "Ladies' Relief Society," an editorial published in *Times and Seasons,* Apr. 1, 1842, p. 743; Joseph Smith was the editor of the periodical.
8. *History of the Church,* 4:570; from a discourse given by Joseph Smith on Mar. 30, 1842, in Nauvoo, Illinois; reported by Eliza R. Snow.
9. *History of the Church,* 4:604–5; paragraph divisions altered; from a discourse given by Joseph Smith on Apr. 28, 1842, in Nauvoo, Illinois; reported by Eliza R. Snow; see also appendix, page 562, item 3.

10. Discourse given by Joseph Smith on Apr. 28, 1842, in Nauvoo, Illinois; reported by Eliza R. Snow, in Relief Society, Minute Book Mar. 1842–Mar. 1844, p. 40, Church Archives.
11. *History of the Church,* 4:605; from a discourse given by Joseph Smith on Apr. 28, 1842, in Nauvoo, Illinois; reported by Eliza R. Snow.
12. *History of the Church,* 5:20; from a discourse given by Joseph Smith on May 26, 1842, in Nauvoo, Illinois; reported by Eliza R. Snow.
13. Discourse given by Joseph Smith on Mar. 17, 1842, in Nauvoo, Illinois; reported by Willard Richards, in Relief Society, Minute Book Mar. 1842–Mar. 1844, p. 7, Church Archives.
14. *History of the Church,* 4:567–68; from "Ladies' Relief Society," an editorial published in *Times and Seasons,* Apr. 1, 1842, p. 743; Joseph Smith was the editor of the periodical.
15. *History of the Church,* 5:25; from a discourse given by Joseph Smith on June 9, 1842, in Nauvoo, Illinois; reported by Eliza R. Snow.
16. Letter from Joseph Smith and other Church leaders to the Nauvoo Relief Society, 1842, Nauvoo, Illinois; in Relief Society, Minute Book Mar. 1842–Mar. 1844, p. 88, Church Archives.
17. *History of the Church,* 5:141; from a discourse given by Joseph Smith on Aug. 31, 1842, in Nauvoo, Illinois; reported by Eliza R. Snow.
18. *History of the Church,* 4:605; from a discourse given by Joseph Smith on Apr. 28, 1842, in Nauvoo, Illinois; reported by Eliza R. Snow.
19. Discourse given by Joseph Smith on Mar. 17, 1842, in Nauvoo, Illinois; reported by Willard Richards, in Relief Society, Minute Book Mar. 1842–Mar. 1844, p. 8, Church Archives.
20. *History of the Church,* 4:604–5; from a discourse given by Joseph Smith on Apr. 28, 1842, in Nauvoo, Illinois; reported by Eliza R. Snow; see also appendix, page 562, item 3.
21. *History of the Church,* 5:24–25; paragraph divisions altered; from a discourse given by Joseph Smith on June 9, 1842, in Nauvoo, Illinois; reported by Eliza R. Snow.
22. *History of the Church,* 5:20; from a discourse given by Joseph Smith on May 26, 1842, in Nauvoo, Illinois; reported by Eliza R. Snow; see also appendix, page 562, item 3.
23. *History of the Church,* 5:140; from a discourse given by Joseph Smith on Aug. 31, 1842, in Nauvoo, Illinois; reported by Eliza R. Snow.
24. Discourse given by Joseph Smith on Mar. 17, 1842, in Nauvoo, Illinois; reported by Willard Richards, in Relief Society, Minute Book Mar. 1842–Mar. 1844, p. 10, Church Archives.

Hyrum Smith was a continuing source of strength and support to his brother Joseph. "Brother Hyrum," the Prophet declared, "what a faithful heart you have got!"

CHAPTER 40

How Glorious Are Faithful, Just, and True Friends

"Friendship is one of the grand fundamental principles of 'Mormonism.' . . . It unites the human family with its happy influence."

From the Life of Joseph Smith

In August of 1842, civil authorities from Missouri were making repeated efforts to capture the Prophet Joseph Smith. Fearing he would be killed if he were arrested and taken to Missouri, the Prophet went into hiding. On August 11, he sent word to several loyal family members and friends to meet him on an island in the Mississippi River, not far from Nauvoo. That night, Emma Smith, Hyrum Smith, Newel K. Whitney, and others gathered near the edge of the river and traveled in a small boat to the appointed meeting place. Joyfully, the Prophet took each one by the hand, grateful for the aid and comfort of true friendship. He later wrote at length in his journal about his feelings of gratitude for his family members and friends. Some of these journal entries are included in this chapter. Several weeks later, the Prophet closed a letter to the Saints with words that expressed his feelings for them: "I am, as ever, your humble servant and never deviating friend, Joseph Smith" (D&C 128:25).

The Saints returned the Prophet's feelings, considering him not only their Prophet but also their friend. A close friend and personal secretary of Joseph Smith, Benjamin F. Johnson, recalled: " 'Joseph the Prophet'—as a friend he was faithful, long-suffering, noble and true. . . . As a companion, socially, he was highly endowed—was kind, generous, mirth loving. . . . For amusement he would sometimes wrestle with a friend, or oftener would test strength with others by sitting upon the floor with feet together and stick grasped between them. But he never found his match. Jokes, rebuses [using pictures to portray words], matching couplets in rhymes, etc., were not uncommon. But to call for the singing of one or more of his favorite songs was more frequent. . . . And yet, although so social and even convivial at times, he would allow no arrogance or undue liberties."[1]

Joseph Smith was as tenderhearted as he was sociable, as one young man remembered: "I was at Joseph's house; he was there, and several men were sitting on the fence. Joseph came out and spoke to us all. Pretty soon a man came up and said that a poor brother who lived out some distance from town had had his house burned down the night before. Nearly all of the men said they felt sorry for the man. Joseph put his hand in his pocket, took out five dollars and said, 'I feel sorry for this brother to the amount of five dollars; how much do you all feel sorry?' "[2]

Perhaps Joseph Smith's great love for his friends made the betrayals of some of those friends especially hard to bear. In Nauvoo, friends whom the Prophet had taken into his confidence turned against him. However, many friends returned the Prophet's loyalty, standing with him to the end.

One such friend was Willard Richards, a member of the Quorum of the Twelve, who was jailed with Joseph and Hyrum Smith and John Taylor in Carthage, Illinois. While being held in the jail, the men were allowed to move from a cell on the first floor to a more comfortable bedroom on the second floor of the jailhouse. Then, shortly before the martyrdom, the jailer suggested that the prisoners would be safer in an iron-barred cell next to the bedroom. Joseph asked Elder Richards, who was called "doctor" by his friends because he had practiced medicine: " 'If we go into the cell, will you go in with us?' The doctor answered, 'Brother Joseph, you did not ask me to cross the river with you—you did not ask me to come to Carthage—you did not ask me to come to jail with you—and do you think I would forsake you now? But I will tell you what I will do; if you are condemned to be hung for treason, I will be hung in your stead, and you shall go free.' Joseph said, 'You cannot.' The doctor replied, 'I will.' "[3]

Teachings of Joseph Smith

True friends ease one another's sorrows and remain faithful even in times of adversity.

Joseph Smith wrote the following about the family members and friends who visited him on August 11, 1842, while he was in hiding: "How good and glorious it has seemed unto me, to find pure and holy friends, who are faithful, just, and true, and whose hearts fail not; and whose knees are confirmed and do not falter, while they wait upon the Lord, in administering to my necessities, in the day when the wrath of mine enemies was poured out upon me. . . .

"How glorious were my feelings when I met that faithful and friendly band, on the night of the eleventh, on Thursday, on the island at the mouth of the slough [swamp], between Zarahemla and Nauvoo: with what unspeakable delight, and what transports of joy swelled my bosom, when I took by the hand, on that night, my beloved Emma—she that was my wife, even the wife of my youth, and the choice of my heart. Many were the reverberations of my mind when I contemplated for a moment the many scenes we had been called to pass through, the fatigues and the toils, the sorrows and sufferings, and the joys and consolations, from time to time, which had strewed our paths and crowned our board. Oh, what a commingling of thought filled my mind for the moment, again she is here, . . . undaunted, firm, and unwavering—unchangeable, affectionate Emma!

"There was Brother Hyrum who next took me by the hand—a natural brother. Thought I to myself, Brother Hyrum, what a faithful heart you have got! Oh, may the Eternal Jehovah crown eternal blessings upon your head, as a reward for the care you have had for my soul! Oh, how many are the sorrows we have shared together; and again we find ourselves shackled with the unrelenting hand of oppression. Hyrum, thy name shall be written in the Book of the Law of the Lord, for those who come after thee to look upon, that they may pattern after thy works.

"Said I to myself, Here is Brother Newel K. Whitney also. How many scenes of sorrows have strewed our paths together; and yet we meet once more to share again. Thou art a faithful friend in whom the afflicted sons of men can confide, with the most perfect safety. Let the blessings of the Eternal also be crowned upon his head. How warm that heart! how anxious that soul! for the welfare of one who has been cast out, and hated of almost all men. Brother Whitney, thou knowest not how strong those ties are that bind my soul and heart to thee. . . .

"I do not think to mention the particulars of the history of that sacred night, which shall forever be remembered by me; but the names of the faithful are what I wish to record in this place. These I have met in prosperity, and they were my friends; and I now meet them in adversity, and they are still my warmer friends. These love the God that I serve; they love the truths that I promulgate; they love those virtuous, and those holy doctrines that I cherish in my bosom with the warmest feelings of my heart, and with that zeal which cannot be denied. . . .

". . . I hope I shall see [my friends] again, that I may toil for them, and administer to their comfort also. They shall not want a friend while I live; my heart shall love those, and my hands shall toil for those, who love and toil for me, and shall ever be found faithful to my friends. Shall I be ungrateful? Verily no! God forbid!"[4]

On August 23, 1842, the Prophet continued: "I find my feelings . . . towards my friends revived, while I contemplate the virtues and the good qualities and characteristics of the faithful few, which I am now recording in the Book of the Law of the Lord,—of such as have stood by me in every hour of peril, for these fifteen long years past,—say, for instance, my aged and beloved brother, Joseph Knight, Sen., who was among the number of the first to administer to my necessities, while I was laboring in the commencement of the bringing forth of the work of the Lord, and of laying the foundation of the Church of Jesus Christ of Latter-day Saints. For fifteen years he has been faithful and true, and even-handed and exemplary, and virtuous and kind, never deviating to the right hand or to the left. Behold he is a righteous man, may God Almighty lengthen out the old man's days; and may his trembling, tortured, and broken body be renewed, and in the vigor of health turn upon him, if it be Thy will, consistently, O God; and it shall be said of him, by the sons of Zion, while there is one of them remaining, that this man was a faithful man in Israel; therefore his name shall never be forgotten. . . .

". . . While I remember the faithful few who are now living, I would remember also the faithful of my friends who are dead, for they are many; and many are the acts of kindness—paternal and brotherly kindnesses—which they have bestowed upon me; and since I have been hunted by the Missourians, many are the scenes which have been called to my mind. . . .

"There are many souls whom I have loved stronger than death. To them I have proved faithful—to them I am determined to prove faithful, until God calls me to resign up my breath."[5]

Friendship unites the human family, dispelling hatred and misunderstanding.

"I don't care what a man's character is; if he's my friend—a true friend, I will be a friend to him, and preach the Gospel of salvation to him, and give him good counsel, helping him out of his difficulties.

"Friendship is one of the grand fundamental principles of 'Mormonism'; [it is designed] to revolutionize and civilize the world, and cause wars and contentions to cease and men to become friends and brothers. . . .

". . . Friendship is like Brother [Theodore] Turley in his blacksmith shop welding iron to iron; it unites the human family with its happy influence."[6]

"That friendship which intelligent beings would accept as sincere must arise from love, and that love grow out of virtue, which is as much a part of religion as light is a part of Jehovah. Hence the saying of Jesus, 'Greater love hath no man than this, that a man lay down his life for his friends.' [John 15:13.]"[7]

In March 1839, while the Prophet Joseph Smith and several companions were imprisoned in the jail at Liberty, Missouri, the Prophet wrote to members of the Church: "We received some letters last evening—one from Emma, one from Don C. Smith [Joseph's brother], and one from Bishop [Edward] Partridge—

all breathing a kind and consoling spirit. We were much gratified with their contents. We had been a long time without information; and when we read those letters they were to our souls as the gentle air is refreshing, but our joy was mingled with grief, because of the sufferings of the poor and much injured Saints. And we need not say to you that the floodgates of our hearts were lifted and our eyes were a fountain of tears, but those who have not been enclosed in the walls of prison without cause or provocation, can have but little idea how sweet the voice of a friend is; one token of friendship from any source whatever awakens and calls into action every sympathetic feeling; it brings up in an instant everything that is past; it seizes the present with the avidity [eagerness] of lightning; it grasps after the future with the fierceness of a tiger; it moves the mind backward and forward, from one thing to another, until finally all enmity, malice and hatred, and past differences, misunderstandings and mismanagements are slain victorious at the feet of hope."[8]

Saints of God are true friends to one another.

The Prophet wrote the following note to a Church member in August 1835: "We remember your family, with all the first families of the Church, who first embraced the truth. We remember your losses and sorrows. Our first ties are not broken; we participate with you in the evil as well as the good, in the sorrows as well as the joys. Our union, we trust, is stronger than death, and shall never be severed."[9]

The Prophet said about a feast he attended in January 1836 in Kirtland: "Attended a sumptuous feast at Bishop Newel K. Whitney's. This feast was after the order of the Son of God—the lame, the halt, and the blind were invited, according to the instructions of the Savior [see Luke 14:12–13]. . . . The company was large, and before we partook we had some of the songs of Zion sung; and our hearts were made glad by a foretaste of those joys that will be poured upon the heads of the Saints when they are gathered together on Mount Zion, to enjoy one another's society for evermore, even all the blessings of heaven, when there will be none to molest or make us afraid."[10]

Many Saints arriving at the wharf in Nauvoo remembered the Prophet Joseph Smith coming to meet them as they disembarked, welcoming them to their new home.

Sister Presendia Huntington Buell tried to visit Joseph Smith while he was imprisoned in Liberty Jail in 1839, but she was turned away by the jailer. The Prophet later wrote to her: "Oh, what joy it would be to us to see our friends! It would have gladdened my heart to have had the privilege of conversing with you, but the hand of tyranny is upon us. . . . I want [your husband] and you to know that I am your true friend. . . . No tongue can tell what inexpressible joy it gives a man, after having been enclosed in the walls of a prison for five months, to see the face of one who has been a friend. It seems to me that my heart will always be more tender after this than ever it was before. My heart bleeds continually when I contemplate the distress of the Church. Oh, that I could be with them! I would not shrink at toil and hardship to render them comfort and consolation. I want the blessing once more of lifting my voice in the midst of the Saints. I would pour out my soul to God for their instruction."[11]

Speaking in Nauvoo, Illinois, where many Church members had arrived with few worldly possessions, the Prophet taught: "We should cultivate sympathy for the afflicted among us. If there is a place on earth where men should cultivate the spirit and pour in the oil and wine in the bosoms of the afflicted, it is in this place; and this spirit is manifest here; and although [a person is] a stranger and afflicted when he arrives, he finds a brother and a friend ready to administer to his necessities.

"I would esteem it one of the greatest blessings, if I am to be afflicted in this world, to have my lot cast where I can find brothers and friends all around me."[12]

George A. Smith, the Prophet's cousin, recalled: "At the close of the conversation, Joseph wrapped his arms around me, and squeezed me to his bosom and said, 'George A., I love you as I do my own life.' I felt so affected, I could hardly speak."[13]

Suggestions for Study and Teaching

Consider these ideas as you study the chapter or as you prepare to teach. For additional help, see pages vii–xii.

- Review the first paragraph on page 459. Then turn to pages 461–63 and note the characteristics Joseph Smith appreciated in Emma Smith, Hyrum Smith, Newel K. Whitney, and Joseph Knight Sr. Why do you think their friendship was such a comfort to him during difficult times? In what ways have you been supported by friends when you have faced adversity? What can we do to support others when they experience trials?
- Most of the stories in this chapter are about the value of true friendship in times of difficulty. But in the paragraph that begins on the bottom of page 459, Benjamin F. Johnson tells of Joseph Smith's friendly ways in times of peace. What do you gain from this description? How do our friendships and family relationships benefit when we take time to laugh and play together?
- Study the fourth full paragraph on page 463. Why do you think Joseph Smith would say that friendship is "one of the grand fundamental principles of 'Mormonism' "? In what ways can the restored gospel help people see each other as friends? How have other Presidents of the Church been examples of friendship with all people?

- Review the fifth full paragraph on page 463. How is friendship like welding iron to iron?
- Read the paragraph that begins at the bottom of page 465 and the following paragraph. Note the reference to "oil and wine," from the parable of the good Samaritan (Luke 10:34). What are some specific things we can do to follow the Prophet's counsel? to follow the example of the good Samaritan?

Related Scriptures: 1 Samuel 18:1; Proverbs 17:17; 2 Nephi 1:30; Mosiah 18:8–10; Alma 17:2; D&C 84:77; 88:133

Notes

1. Letter from Benjamin F. Johnson to George F. Gibbs, 1903, pp. 6–8; Benjamin Franklin Johnson, Papers, 1852–1911, Church Archives, The Church of Jesus Christ of Latter-day Saints, Salt Lake City, Utah.
2. Andrew J. Workman, in "Recollections of the Prophet Joseph Smith," *Juvenile Instructor,* Oct. 15, 1892, p. 641.
3. *History of the Church,* 6:616; punctuation modernized; from a Willard Richards journal entry, June 27, 1844, Carthage, Illinois.
4. *History of the Church,* 5:107–9; spelling, punctuation, and capitalization modernized; from a Joseph Smith journal entry, Aug. 16, 1842, near Nauvoo, Illinois.
5. *History of the Church,* 5:124–25, 127; from a Joseph Smith journal entry, Aug. 23, 1842, near Nauvoo, Illinois; this entry is incorrectly dated Aug. 22, 1842, in *History of the Church.*
6. *History of the Church,* 5:517; first set of bracketed words in original; from a discourse given by Joseph Smith on July 23, 1843, in Nauvoo, Illinois; reported by Willard Richards; see also appendix, page 562, item 3.
7. *History of the Church,* 6:73; from a letter from Joseph Smith to James Arlington Bennet, Nov. 13, 1843, Nauvoo, Illinois; James Bennet's last name is incorrectly spelled "Bennett" in *History of the Church.*
8. *History of the Church,* 3:293; spelling modernized; from a letter from Joseph Smith and others to Edward Partridge and the Church, Mar. 20, 1839, Liberty Jail, Liberty, Missouri.
9. Joseph Smith postscript in letter from Joseph Smith and others to Hezekiah Peck, Aug. 31, 1835, Kirtland, Ohio; in "The Book of John Whitmer," pp. 80–81, Community of Christ Archives, Independence, Missouri; copy of "The Book of John Whitmer" in Church Archives.
10. *History of the Church,* 2:362–63; from a Joseph Smith journal entry, Jan. 7, 1836, Kirtland, Ohio.
11. *History of the Church,* 3:285–86; spelling modernized; from a letter from Joseph Smith to Presendia Huntington Buell, Mar. 15, 1839, Liberty Jail, Liberty, Missouri; Sister Buell's last name is incorrectly spelled "Bull" in *History of the Church.*
12. *History of the Church,* 5:360–61; punctuation modernized; from a discourse given by Joseph Smith on Apr. 16, 1843, in Nauvoo, Illinois; reported by Wilford Woodruff and Willard Richards.
13. George A. Smith, quoted in *History of the Church,* 5:391; from George A. Smith, "History of George Albert Smith by Himself," p. 1, George Albert Smith, Papers, 1834–75, Church Archives.

The baptistry in the reconstructed Nauvoo Temple. In baptismal fonts such as this, Saints receive the ordinance of baptism for those who have died.

CHAPTER 41

Becoming Saviors on Mount Zion

"How are they to become saviors on Mount Zion? By building their temples, erecting their baptismal fonts, and going forth and receiving all the ordinances . . . in behalf of all their progenitors who are dead."

From the Life of Joseph Smith

For Church members living in Nauvoo in the 1840s, doing proxy work for their kindred dead was a major focus. Ever since the first proxy baptisms in this dispensation had been performed in 1840, the Saints had searched for genealogical information about their ancestors, and many had entered the waters of baptism vicariously for these deceased loved ones.

At first, baptisms for the dead had been performed in the Mississippi River or in local streams. But in January 1841, when the Saints were making plans for the Nauvoo Temple, the Lord declared: "A baptismal font there is not upon the earth, that they, my saints, may be baptized for those who are dead—for this ordinance belongeth to my house, and cannot be acceptable to me, only in the days of your poverty, wherein ye are not able to build a house unto me" (D&C 124:29–30).

Proxy baptisms in the river were discontinued on October 3, 1841, when the Prophet announced: "There shall be no more baptisms for the dead, until the ordinance can be attended to in the Lord's House. . . . *For thus saith the Lord!*"[1] The Saints quickly began building a temporary wooden font in the newly excavated basement of the Nauvoo Temple. The font, built of Wisconsin pine, rested on the backs of 12 wooden oxen. It was dedicated on November 8, for use "until the Temple shall be finished, when a more durable one will supply its place."[2] On November 21, 1841, six members of the Quorum of the Twelve performed baptisms for 40 people who had died, the first baptisms for the dead performed in the font.

The Saints' early experiences with baptism for the dead taught them the importance of record keeping in the Lord's Church. Though proxy baptisms in local rivers had been performed by proper priesthood authority, they had not been officially recorded. Consequently, those baptisms had to be performed again. In an address given on August 31, 1842, the Prophet explained: "All persons baptized for the dead must have a recorder present, that he may be an eyewitness to record and testify of the truth and validity of his record. . . . Therefore let the recording and witnessing of baptisms for the dead be carefully attended to from this time forth."[3] The Prophet discussed this matter at greater length in a letter he wrote to the Saints the next day, and in another letter written on September 6. These two letters are now sections 127 and 128 of the Doctrine and Covenants.

In section 127, the Prophet recorded the following instructions from the Lord: "When any of you are baptized for your dead, let there be a recorder, and let him be eye-witness of your baptisms; let him hear with his ears, that he may testify of a truth, saith the Lord; that in all your recordings it may be recorded in heaven. . . . And again, let all the records be had in order, that they may be put in the archives of my holy temple, to be held in remembrance from generation to generation" (D&C 127:6–7, 9).

As the Saints moved forward with this sacred work, "it soon became apparent that some had long records of their dead, for whom they wished to administer," recalled Elder George A. Smith, a member of the Quorum of the Twelve. "This was seen to be but the beginning of an immense work, and that to administer all the ordinances of the Gospel to the hosts of the dead was no light task. Some of the Twelve asked Joseph if there could not be some shorter method of administering for so many. Joseph in effect replied: 'The laws of the Lord are immutable; we must act in perfect compliance with what is revealed to us. We need not expect to do this vast work for the dead in a short time.' "[4]

Teachings of Joseph Smith

The doctrine of salvation for the dead shows the greatness of God's wisdom and compassion.

"All those who have not had an opportunity of hearing the Gospel, and being administered unto by an inspired man in the flesh, must have it hereafter, before they can be finally judged."[5]

"It is no more incredible that God should *save* the dead, than that he should *raise* the dead.

"There is never a time when the spirit is too old to approach God. All are within the reach of pardoning mercy, who have not committed the unpardonable sin, which hath no forgiveness, neither in this world, nor in the world to come. There is a way to release the spirits of the dead; that is by the power and authority of the Priesthood—by binding and loosing on earth. This doctrine appears glorious, inasmuch as it exhibits the greatness of divine compassion and benevolence in the extent of the plan of human salvation.

"This glorious truth is well calculated to enlarge the understanding, and to sustain the soul under troubles, difficulties and distresses. For illustration, suppose the case of two men, brothers, equally intelligent, learned, virtuous and lovely, walking in uprightness and in all good conscience, so far as they have been able to discern duty from the muddy stream of tradition, or from the blotted page of the book of nature.

"One dies and is buried, having never heard the Gospel of reconciliation; to the other the message of salvation is sent, he hears and embraces it, and is made the heir of eternal life. Shall the one become the partaker of glory and the other be consigned to hopeless perdition? Is there no chance for his escape? Sectarianism answers 'none.' . . .

"This doctrine presents in a clear light the wisdom and mercy of God in preparing an ordinance for the salvation of the dead, being baptized by proxy, their names recorded in heaven and they judged according to the deeds done in the body. This doctrine was the burden of the scriptures. Those Saints who neglect it in behalf of their deceased relatives, do it at the peril of their own salvation."[6]

In December 1840 Joseph Smith wrote to members of the Quorum of the Twelve and other priesthood leaders who were serving missions in Great Britain: "I presume the doctrine of 'baptism for the dead' has ere this reached your ears, and may have raised some inquiries in your minds respecting the same. I cannot in this letter give you all the information you may desire on the subject; but . . . I would say that it was certainly practiced by the ancient churches; and St. Paul endeavors to prove the doctrine of the resurrection from the same, and says, 'Else what shall they do which are baptized for the dead, if the dead rise not at all? Why are they then baptized for the dead?' [1 Corinthians 15:29.]

"I first mentioned the doctrine in public when preaching the funeral sermon of Brother Seymour Brunson; and have since then given general instructions in the Church on the subject. The Saints have the privilege of being baptized for those of their relatives who are dead. . . . Without enlarging on the subject, you will undoubtedly see its consistency and reasonableness; and it presents the Gospel of Christ in probably a more enlarged scale than some have imagined it."[7]

We become saviors on Mount Zion by performing sacred ordinances for the dead.

"If we can, by the authority of the Priesthood of the Son of God, baptize a man in the name of the Father, of the Son, and of the Holy Ghost, for the remission of sins, it is just as much our privilege to act as an agent, and be baptized for the remission of sins for and in behalf of our dead kindred, who have not heard the Gospel, or the fullness of it."[8]

"The Bible says, 'I will send you Elijah the Prophet before the coming of the great and dreadful day of the Lord; and he shall turn the hearts of the fathers to the children, and the hearts of the children to the fathers, lest I come and smite the earth with a curse.' [Malachi 4:5–6.]

"Now, the word *turn* here should be translated *bind,* or seal. But what is the object of this important mission? or how is it to

"The greatest responsibility in this world that God has laid upon us is to seek after our dead."

be fulfilled? The keys are to be delivered, the spirit of Elijah is to come, the Gospel to be established, the Saints of God gathered, Zion built up, and the Saints to come up as saviors on Mount Zion [see Obadiah 1:21].

"But how are they to become saviors on Mount Zion? By building their temples, erecting their baptismal fonts, and going forth and receiving all the ordinances, baptisms, confirmations, washings, anointings, ordinations and sealing powers upon their heads, in behalf of all their progenitors who are dead, and redeem them that they may come forth in the first resurrection and be exalted to thrones of glory with them; and herein is the chain that binds the hearts of the fathers to the children, and the children to the fathers, which fulfills the mission of Elijah. . . .

"The Saints have not too much time to save and redeem their dead, and gather together their living relatives, that they may be saved also, before the earth will be smitten, and the consumption decreed falls upon the world.

"I would advise all the Saints to go to with their might and gather together all their living relatives to [the temple], that they may be sealed and saved, that they may be prepared against the day that the destroying angel goes forth; and if the whole Church should go to with all their might to save their dead, seal their posterity, and gather their living friends, and spend none of their time in behalf of the world, they would hardly get through before night would come, when no man can work."[9]

"There is baptism, etc., for those to exercise who are alive, and baptism for the dead who die without the knowledge of the Gospel. . . . It is not only necessary that you should be baptized for your dead, but you will have to go through all the ordinances for them, the same as you have gone through to save yourselves. . . .

". . . There should be a place where all nations shall come up from time to time to receive their endowments; and the Lord has said this shall be the place for the baptisms for the dead. Every man that has been baptized and belongs to the kingdom has a right to be baptized for those who have gone before; and as soon as the law of the Gospel is obeyed here by their friends who act as proxy for them, the Lord has administrators there to set them free. A man may act as proxy for his own relatives; the ordinances of the Gospel which were laid out before the foundations of the world have thus been fulfilled by them, and we may be baptized for those whom we have much friendship for."[10]

"All those who die in the faith go to the prison of spirits to preach to the dead in body, but they are alive in the spirit; and those spirits preach to the spirits [who are in prison] that they may live according to God in the spirit, and men do minister for them in the flesh; . . . and they are made happy by these means [see 1 Peter 4:6]. Therefore, those who are baptized for their dead are the saviors on Mount Zion, and they must receive their washings and their anointings for their dead the same as for themselves."[11]

God has placed upon us a great responsibility to seek after our dead.

"I will open your eyes in relation to the dead. All things whatsoever God in his infinite wisdom has seen fit and proper to reveal to us, while we are dwelling in mortality, in regard to our mortal bodies, are revealed to us in the abstract, and independent of affinity of this mortal tabernacle, but are revealed to our spirits precisely as though we had no bodies at all; and those revelations which will save our spirits will save our bodies. God reveals them to us in view of no eternal dissolution of the body, or tabernacle. Hence the responsibility, the awful responsibility, that rests upon us in relation to our dead; for all the spirits who have not obeyed the Gospel in the flesh must either obey it in the spirit or be damned. Solemn thought!—dreadful thought! Is there nothing to be done?—no preparation—no salvation for our fathers and friends who have died without having had the opportunity to obey the decrees of the Son of Man? . . .

"What promises are made in relation to the subject of the salvation of the dead? and what kind of characters are those who can be saved, although their bodies are moldering and decaying in the grave? When His commandments teach us, it is in view of eternity; for we are looked upon by God as though we were in eternity; God dwells in eternity, and does not view things as we do.

"The greatest responsibility in this world that God has laid upon us is to seek after our dead. The apostle says, 'They without us cannot be made perfect' [see Hebrews 11:40]; for it is necessary that the sealing power should be in our hands to seal our children and our dead for the fulness of the dispensation of times—a dispensation to meet the promises made by Jesus Christ before the foundation of the world for the salvation of man.

". . . It is necessary that those who are going before and those who come after us should have salvation in common with us; and thus hath God made it obligatory upon man. Hence, God said, 'I will send you Elijah the prophet before the coming of the great and dreadful day of the Lord: he shall turn the heart of the fathers to the children, and the heart of the children to their fathers, lest I come and smite the earth with a curse.' [Malachi 4:5–6.]"[12]

The Prophet Joseph Smith wrote the following in a letter to the Saints, later recorded in Doctrine and Covenants 128:15–18, 22, 24: "And now, my dearly beloved brethren and sisters, let me assure you that these are principles in relation to the dead and the living that cannot be lightly passed over, as pertaining to our salvation. For their salvation is necessary and essential to our salvation, as Paul says concerning the fathers—that they without us cannot be made perfect—neither can we without our dead be made perfect.

"And now, in relation to the baptism for the dead, I will give you another quotation of Paul, 1 Corinthians 15:29: *Else what shall they do which are baptized for the dead, if the dead rise not at all? Why are they then baptized for the dead?*

"And again, in connection with this quotation I will give you a quotation from one of the prophets, who had his eye fixed on the restoration of the priesthood, the glories to be revealed in the last days, and in an especial manner this most glorious of all subjects belonging to the everlasting gospel, namely, the baptism for the dead; for Malachi says, last chapter, verses 5th and 6th: *Behold, I will send you Elijah the prophet before the coming of the great and dreadful day of the Lord: And he shall turn the heart of the fathers to the children, and the heart of the children to their fathers, lest I come and smite the earth with a curse.*

"I might have rendered a plainer translation to this, but it is sufficiently plain to suit my purpose as it stands. It is sufficient to know, in this case, that the earth will be smitten with a curse unless there is a welding link of some kind or other between the fathers and the children, upon some subject or other—and behold what is that subject? It is the baptism for the dead. For we without them cannot be made perfect; neither can they without us be made perfect. . . .

". . . Let your hearts rejoice, and be exceedingly glad. Let the earth break forth into singing. Let the dead speak forth anthems of eternal praise to the King Immanuel, who hath ordained, before the world was, that which would enable us to redeem them out of their prison; for the prisoners shall go free. . . .

". . . Let us, therefore, as a church and a people, and as Latter-day Saints, offer unto the Lord an offering in righteousness; and let us present in his holy temple, when it is finished, a book containing the records of our dead, which shall be worthy of all acceptation."[13]

Suggestions for Study and Teaching

Consider these ideas as you study the chapter or as you prepare to teach. For additional help, see pages vii–xii.

- Review pages 469–70, noting how Joseph Smith and the early Saints grew in their understanding of the doctrine of baptism for the dead. Think about how the Saints might have felt when they first learned of salvation for the dead. What were your feelings when you first participated in ordinances for the dead?
- Read the third and fourth paragraphs on page 471. How does the doctrine of salvation for the dead show God's compassion and mercy? In what ways can this doctrine "enlarge the understanding" and "sustain the soul"?
- What does it mean to be a savior on Mount Zion? (For some examples, see pages 472–74.) Why do you think it is impossible for our deceased ancestors to be made perfect without us? Why do you think it is impossible for us to be made perfect without them?
- Review some of the Prophet Joseph Smith's teachings about our great responsibility to "seek after our dead" (pages 475–77). What experiences have you had as you have learned about your ancestors? How has your love for your family and your faith in God been strengthened as you learned about your ancestors? How has performing temple ordinances for your ancestors influenced your feelings about them?
- What can we do to help children appreciate their family heritage? What can we do to help children participate in temple and family history work?

Related Scriptures: Romans 14:9; D&C 128:8–11

Notes

1. *History of the Church,* 4:426; from the minutes of a Church conference held on Oct. 3, 1841, in Nauvoo, Illinois, published in *Times and Seasons,* Oct. 15, 1841, p. 578.
2. *History of the Church,* 4:446–47; from "History of the Church" (manuscript), book C-1, addenda, p. 44, Church Archives, The Church of Jesus Christ of Latter-day Saints, Salt Lake City, Utah.
3. *History of the Church,* 5:141; from a discourse given by Joseph Smith on Aug. 31, 1842, in Nauvoo, Illinois; reported by Eliza R. Snow; see also appendix, page 562, item 3.
4. George A. Smith, discourse given on Dec. 25, 1874, in St. George, Utah; in St. George Stake, General Minutes, vol. 4, Church Archives.
5. *History of the Church,* 3:29; from an editorial published in *Elders' Journal,* July 1838, p. 43; Joseph Smith was the editor of the periodical.
6. *History of the Church,* 4:425–26; from the minutes of a Church conference held on Oct. 3, 1841, in Nauvoo, Illinois, published in *Times and Seasons,* Oct. 15, 1841, pp. 577–78.
7. *History of the Church,* 4:231; paragraph divisions altered; from a letter from Joseph Smith to the Twelve, Dec. 15, 1840, Nauvoo, Illinois; this letter is incorrectly dated Oct. 19, 1840, in *History of the Church.*
8. *History of the Church,* 4:569; from a discourse given by Joseph Smith on Mar. 27, 1842, in Nauvoo, Illinois; reported by Wilford Woodruff; see also appendix, page 562, item 3.
9. *History of the Church,* 6:183–84; from a discourse given by Joseph Smith on Jan. 21, 1844, in Nauvoo, Illinois; reported by Wilford Woodruff.
10. *History of the Church,* 6:365–66; paragraph divisions altered; from a discourse given by Joseph Smith on May 12, 1844, in Nauvoo, Illinois; reported by Thomas Bullock.
11. Quoted by George Laub, in compilation of excerpts from Joseph Smith's discourses, ca. 1845; George Laub, Reminiscences and Journal Jan. 1845–Apr. 1857, p. 21, Church Archives.
12. *History of the Church,* 6:312–13; spelling modernized; from a discourse given by Joseph Smith on Apr. 7, 1844, in Nauvoo, Illinois; reported by Wilford Woodruff, Willard Richards, Thomas Bullock, and William Clayton.
13. Doctrine and Covenants 128:15–18, 22, 24; a letter from Joseph Smith to the Saints, Sept. 6, 1842, Nauvoo, Illinois.

C H A P T E R 4 2

Family: The Sweetest Union for Time and for Eternity

"The sweetest union and happiness pervaded our house. No jar nor discord disturbed our peace, and tranquility reigned in our midst." (Lucy Mack Smith)

From the Life of Joseph Smith

By 1843, although the Nauvoo Temple was not yet finished, the Prophet had announced the doctrine of salvation for the dead, and he had administered the temple endowment to a group of faithful Saints. But an important part of the sacred work of temples had yet to be put in place. On May 16, 1843, the Prophet traveled from Nauvoo to Ramus, Illinois, where he stayed at the home of his close friend Benjamin F. Johnson. That evening, he taught Brother and Sister Johnson and a few close friends about the "new and everlasting covenant of marriage." He explained that this covenant was the "order of the priesthood" necessary to obtain the highest degree of the celestial kingdom. (See D&C 131:1–4.) He also taught that unless a man and a woman enter into the covenant of eternal marriage, "they will cease to increase when they die; that is, they will not have any children after the resurrection." Those who do enter into this covenant and remain faithful "will continue to increase and have children in the celestial glory."[1]

Two months later, on July 12, 1843, in the upstairs office of his Red Brick Store, the Prophet dictated to William Clayton a revelation about the doctrine of eternal marriage (see D&C 132). The Prophet had known and taught this doctrine for some time before. In this revelation, the Lord declared that if a husband and wife are not sealed by the power of the holy priesthood, "they cannot be enlarged, but remain separately and singly, without exaltation, in their saved condition, to all eternity" (see D&C

Parley P. Pratt declared: "It was Joseph Smith who taught me how to prize the endearing relationships of father and mother, husband and wife; of brother and sister, son and daughter."

132:15–18). To receive exaltation, husbands and wives must be sealed by priesthood power and then remain faithful to their covenants:

"Verily I say unto you, if a man marry a wife by my word, which is my law, and by the new and everlasting covenant, and it is sealed unto them by the Holy Spirit of promise, by him who is anointed, unto whom I have appointed this power and the keys of this priesthood; . . . it shall be done unto them in all things whatsoever my servant hath put upon them, in time, and through all eternity; and shall be of full force when they are out of the world; and they shall pass by the angels, and the gods, which are set there, to their exaltation and glory in all things, as hath been sealed upon their heads, which glory shall be a fulness and a continuation of the seeds forever and ever.

"Then shall they be gods, because they have no end; therefore shall they be from everlasting to everlasting, because they continue; then shall they be above all, because all things are subject unto them. Then shall they be gods, because they have all power, and the angels are subject unto them. Verily, verily, I say unto you, except ye abide my law ye cannot attain to this glory" (D&C 132:19–21).

For Elder Parley P. Pratt of the Quorum of the Twelve, a knowledge of this doctrine deepened his love for his family: "It was Joseph Smith who taught me how to prize the endearing relationships of father and mother, husband and wife; of brother and sister, son and daughter. It was from him that I learned that the wife of my bosom might be secured to me for time and all eternity; and that the refined sympathies and affections which endeared us to each other emanated from the fountain of divine eternal love. It was from him that I learned that we might cultivate these affections, and grow and increase in the same to all eternity; while the result of our endless union would be an offspring as numerous as the stars of heaven, or the sands of the sea shore. . . . I had loved before, but I knew not why. But now I loved—with a pureness—an intensity of elevated, exalted feeling, which would lift my soul from the transitory things of this grovelling sphere and expand it as the ocean. . . . In short, I could now love with the spirit and with the understanding also."[2]

Teachings of Joseph Smith

Husbands and wives honor each other by showing love, kindness, and affection.

"Marriage [is] an institution of heaven, instituted in the garden of Eden."[3]

"It is the duty of a husband to love, cherish, and nourish his wife, and cleave unto her and none else [see D&C 42:22]; he ought to honor her as himself, and he ought to regard her feelings with tenderness, for she is his flesh, and his bone, designed to be an help unto him, both in temporal, and spiritual things; one into whose bosom he can pour all his complaints without reserve, who is willing (being designed) to take part of his burden, to soothe and encourage his feelings by her gentle voice.

"It is the place of the man, to stand at the head of his family, . . . not to rule over his wife as a tyrant, neither as one who is fearful or jealous that his wife will get out of her place, and prevent him from exercising his authority. It is his duty to be a man of God (for a man of God is a man of wisdom,) ready at all times to obtain from the scriptures, the revelations, and from on high, such instructions as are necessary for the edification, and salvation of his household."[4]

At a meeting of Relief Society sisters, Joseph Smith said: "You need not be teasing your husbands because of their deeds, but let the weight of your innocence, kindness and affection be felt, which is more mighty than a millstone hung about the neck; not war, not jangle [quarreling], not contradiction, or dispute, but meekness, love, purity—these are the things that should magnify you in the eyes of all good men. . . .

". . . When a man is borne down with trouble, when he is perplexed with care and difficulty, if he can meet a smile instead of an argument or a murmur—if he can meet with mildness, it will calm down his soul and soothe his feelings; when the mind is going to despair, it needs a solace of affection and kindness. . . . When you go home, never give a cross or unkind word to your husbands, but let kindness, charity and love crown your works henceforward."[5]

Eliza R. Snow reported: "[The Prophet Joseph Smith] exhorted the sisters always to concentrate their faith and prayers for, and place confidence in their husbands, whom God has appointed for them to honor."[6]

Children honor their parents by expressing gratitude to them and cherishing them throughout their lives.

For several days in October 1835, the Prophet made daily visits to his gravely ill father, attending to him "with great anxiety." The Prophet's journal records: "Waited on my father again, who was very sick. In secret prayer in the morning, the Lord said, 'My servant, thy father shall live.' I waited on him all this day with my heart raised to God in the name of Jesus Christ, that He would restore him to health, that I might be blessed with his company and advice, esteeming it one of the greatest earthly blessings to be blessed with the society of parents, whose mature years and experience render them capable of administering the most wholesome advice. At evening Brother David Whitmer came in. We called on the Lord in mighty prayer in the name of Jesus Christ, and laid our hands on him, and rebuked the disease. And God heard and answered our prayers—to the great joy and satisfaction of our souls. Our aged father arose and dressed himself, shouted, and praised the Lord."[7]

"Blessed is my mother, for her soul is ever filled with benevolence and philanthropy; and notwithstanding her age, yet she shall receive strength, and shall be comforted in the midst of her house, and she shall have eternal life. And blessed is my father, for the hand of the Lord shall be over him, for he shall see the affliction of his children pass away; and when his head is fully ripe, he shall behold himself as an olive tree, whose branches are bowed down with much fruit; he shall also possess a mansion on high."[8]

"I have remembered scenes of my childhood. I have thought of my father who is dead. . . . He was of noble stature and possessed a high, and holy, and exalted, and virtuous mind. His soul soared above all those mean and groveling principles that are so congenial to the human heart. I now say that he never did a

Joseph Smith was raised in a family in which parents and children loved and respected one another. This painting shows the Smith family being reunited with their father in 1816 after he had preceded them in their move to Palmyra, New York.

mean act, that might be said was ungenerous in his life, to my knowledge. I love my father and his memory; and the memory of his noble deeds rests with ponderous weight upon my mind, and many of his kind and parental words to me are written on the tablet of my heart.

"Sacred to me are the thoughts which I cherish of the history of his life, that have rolled through my mind, and have been implanted there by my own observation, since I was born. Sacred to me is his dust, and the spot where he is laid. Sacred to me is the tomb I have made to encircle o'er his head. Let the memory of my father eternally live. . . . May the God that I love look down from above and save me from my enemies here, and take me by the hand that on Mount Zion I may stand, and with my father crown me eternally there.

"Words and language are inadequate to express the gratitude that I owe to God for having given me so honorable a parentage.

"My mother also is one of the noblest and the best of all women. May God grant to prolong her days and mine, that we may live to enjoy each other's society long."[9]

"When we reflect with what care, and with what unremitting diligence our parents have striven to watch over us, and how many hours of sorrow and anxiety they have spent, over our cradles and bed-sides, in times of sickness, how careful we ought to be of their feelings in their old age! It cannot be a source of sweet reflection to us, to say or do anything that will bring their gray hairs down with sorrow to the grave."[10]

Love among brothers and sisters can be sweet and enduring.

Of two of his brothers, both of whom had died as young men, the Prophet wrote: "Alvin, my oldest brother—I remember well the pangs of sorrow that swelled my youthful bosom and almost burst my tender heart when he died. He was the oldest and the noblest of my father's family. He was one of the noblest of the sons of men. . . . In him there was no guile. He lived without spot from the time he was a child. . . . He was one of the soberest of men, and when he died the angel of the Lord visited him in his last moments. . . .

"My brother Don Carlos Smith . . . also was a noble boy; I never knew any fault in him; I never saw the first immoral act, or the first irreligious or ignoble disposition in the child from the time that he was born till the time of his death. He was a lovely, a good-natured, a kind-hearted and a virtuous and a faithful, upright child; and where his soul goes, let mine go also."[11]

Joseph Smith wrote the following in a letter to his older brother Hyrum: "My Dearly Beloved Brother Hyrum, I have had much concern about you, but I always remember you in my prayers, calling upon God to keep you safe in spite of men or devils. . . . God protect you."[12]

Of Hyrum, the Prophet wrote: "I could pray in my heart that all my brethren were like unto my beloved brother Hyrum, who possesses the mildness of a lamb, and the integrity of a Job, and in short, the meekness and humility of Christ; and I love him with that love that is stronger than death."[13]

Parents who love, support, and pray for their children bring immeasurable blessings into their children's lives.

After his visit to the Hill Cumorah in September 1823, Joseph Smith related his experience to his family and then continued to share his experiences with them. The Prophet's mother recorded: "Every evening we gathered our children together. I think that we presented the most peculiar aspect of any family that ever lived upon the earth, all seated in a circle, father, mother, sons, and daughters listening in breathless anxiety to the religious teachings of a boy [seventeen] years of age. . . .

"We were convinced that God was about to bring to light something that we might stay our minds upon, something that we could get a more definite idea of than anything which had been taught us heretofore, and we rejoiced in it with exceeding great joy. The sweetest union and happiness pervaded our house. No jar nor discord disturbed our peace, and tranquility reigned in our midst."[14]

Near the end of the march of Zion's Camp, in June 1834, Joseph and Hyrum Smith, among many others, were afflicted with cholera. Their mother recounted the following about their experience: "Hyrum and Joseph's . . . joy at meeting us again in health was exceeding great, above measure, because of the perils which they had escaped during their absence. They sat down, one on each side of me, Joseph holding one of my hands and Hyrum the other, and they related the following: . . .

" 'The disease instantly fastened itself upon us, and in a few minutes we were in awful distress. We made mute signals to each other and left the house for the purpose of going into some

"Every evening we gathered our children together," Lucy Mack Smith recalled, "father, mother, sons, and daughters listening in breathless anxiety to the religious teachings of a boy [seventeen] years of age."

secluded place to join in prayer that God would deliver us from this awful influence. But before we could get a sufficient distance to be secure from interruption, we were scarcely able to stand upon our feet and we were greatly alarmed, fearing that we should die in this western wilderness so far from our families, without even the privilege of blessing our children or of giving them one word of parting counsel. Hyrum cried out, "Joseph, what shall we do? Must we be cut off from the face of the earth by this horrid curse?" "Let us," said [Joseph], "get down upon our knees and pray to God to remove the cramp and other distress and restore us to health, that we may return to our families." We did so but without receiving any benefit, but still grew worse. . . .

" 'We soon came to the resolution of appealing again to God for mercy and not to rise from our knees until one or the other got a testimony that we should be healed. . . . We prayed some time, first one and then the other, and soon perceived that the cramp began to loose its hold. And in a short time afterwards, Hyrum sprang to his feet and exclaimed, "Joseph, we shall return, for I have seen an open vision in which I saw Mother on her knees under an apple tree praying for us, and she is even now asking in tears for God to spare our lives that she may behold us again in the flesh. And the Spirit testifies to me that her prayers and ours shall be heard." And from that moment we were healed and went on our way rejoicing.'

" 'Oh, my Mother,' said Joseph, 'how often have your prayers been a means of assisting us when the shadows of death encompassed us.' "[15]

The love of Lucy Mack Smith for her sons is illustrated by her account of the Prophet and his brother Hyrum being taken as prisoners from Far West, Missouri, in November 1838, to Independence and then Richmond, Missouri, where they would be imprisoned. The family feared that Joseph and Hyrum would be killed: "When the news came to us that our sons were to be taken away, the messenger told us that if we ever saw our sons again alive, we would have to go to them, as they were in the wagon to be driven away and would be gone in a few minutes. My husband was then too ill to be able to go, but I and Lucy [a daughter] started alone, for we were the only well ones of the family.

"When we came within about 400 yards of the wagon, we could go no farther because of the men with which they were surrounded. 'I am the mother of the Prophet,' I cried, 'and is there not a gentleman here who will assist me through this crowd to that wagon that I may take a last look at my children and speak to them once more before they die?' One individual volunteered to make a pathway through the army, and we went on through the midst of swords, muskets, pistols, and bayonets, threatened with death at every step, until at last we arrived there. The man who accompanied me spoke to Hyrum, who sat in front, and told him his mother was there and wished him to reach his hand to her. He did so, but I was not permitted to see them, for the cover of the wagon was made of very heavy cloth and tied closely down in front and nailed fast at the sides. . . .

"Our friend then conducted us to the hinder part of the wagon, where Joseph was, and spoke to him, saying, 'Mr. Smith, your mother and sister are here and wish to shake hands with you.' Joseph crowded his hand through between the wagon and cover where it was nailed down to the end board. We caught hold of his hand, but he did not speak to us. I could not bear to leave him without hearing his voice. 'Oh, Joseph,' said I, 'do speak to your poor mother once more. I cannot go until I hear you speak.'

" 'God bless you, Mother,' he said, and then a cry was raised and the wagon dashed off, tearing my son from us just as Lucy was pressing his hand to her to bestow upon it a sister's last kiss, for we knew that they were sentenced to be shot.

"We succeeded in getting to the house again, although we were scarcely able to support ourselves. . . . For some time nothing was heard in the house but sighs and groans, as we did not then know but we had seen Joseph and Hyrum for the last time. But in the midst of my grief, I found consolation that surpassed all earthly comfort. I was filled with the Spirit of God and received the following by the gift of prophecy: 'Let your heart be comforted concerning your children, for they shall not harm a hair of their heads.' . . . 'My children,' said I, 'do not cry any more. The mob will not kill them, for the Lord has signified to me that he will deliver them out of the hands of their enemies.' This was a great comfort to us all, and we were not so much distressed afterwards as to their lives being taken."[16]

Suggestions for Study and Teaching

Consider these ideas as you study the chapter or as you prepare to teach. For additional help, see pages vii–xii.

- Review Elder Parley P. Pratt's description of how a knowledge of the doctrine of eternal marriage blessed his life (page 481). In what ways can this doctrine influence the way we feel about our families? the way we treat one another at home?
- Read Joseph Smith's counsel to husbands and wives (pages 482–83). Consider how some of this counsel applies to both women and men. Why is it important for both fathers and mothers to study the scriptures and receive revelations to guide the family? What are some things a man can do when he sees that his wife is "borne down with trouble"? Why do both husbands and wives need to avoid using "a cross or unkind word"?
- As an adult, the Prophet Joseph continued to enjoy being with his parents, to seek their advice, and to honor them (pages 483–85). Which of the Prophet's statements about his parents particularly impress you? What examples have you seen of the enduring influence for good that parents can have on their children? Think about what you can do to better honor your parents.
- Review the Prophet's statements about his brothers Alvin, Don Carlos, and Hyrum (pages 485–86). Why do you think the relationship between brothers and sisters can be so lasting and strong? What can parents do to encourage their sons and daughters to be good friends? What can brothers and sisters do to nurture their friendship with one another?
- Review Lucy Mack Smith's recollection of her son Joseph teaching the family (page 486). What experiences can you share in which you have felt "union and happiness" with family members? What can parents learn from the experience Joseph and Hyrum had with being healed from cholera? (See pages 486–88.)

Related Scriptures: Exodus 20:12; 1 Corinthians 11:11; Ephesians 6:1–4; Mosiah 4:14–15; Moses 3:18, 21–24

Notes

1. *History of the Church,* 5:391; from instructions given by Joseph Smith on May 16, 1843, in Ramus, Illinois; reported by William Clayton.
2. Parley P. Pratt, *Autobiography of Parley P. Pratt,* ed. Parley P. Pratt Jr. (1938), pp. 297–98; paragraph divisions altered.
3. *History of the Church,* 2:320; from a Joseph Smith journal entry, Nov. 24, 1835, Kirtland, Ohio.
4. "On the Duty of Husband and Wife," an editorial published in *Elders' Journal,* Aug. 1838, p. 61; paragraph divisions altered; Joseph Smith was the editor of the periodical.
5. *History of the Church,* 4:605–7; spelling modernized; paragraph divisions altered; from a discourse given by Joseph Smith on Apr. 28, 1842, in Nauvoo, Illinois; reported by Eliza R. Snow; see also appendix, page 562, item 3.
6. *History of the Church,* 4:604; from a discourse given by Joseph Smith on Apr. 28, 1842, in Nauvoo, Illinois; reported by Eliza R. Snow; see also appendix, page 562, item 3.
7. *History of the Church,* 2:289; from Joseph Smith journal entries, Oct. 8 and 11, 1835, Kirtland, Ohio.
8. *History of the Church,* 1:466; paragraph divisions altered; from a Joseph Smith journal entry, Dec. 18, 1833, Kirtland, Ohio.
9. *History of the Church,* 5:125–26; from a Joseph Smith journal entry, Aug. 23, 1842, near Nauvoo, Illinois; this entry is incorrectly dated Aug. 22, 1842, in *History of the Church.*
10. *History of the Church,* 2:342; from a letter from Joseph Smith to William Smith, Dec. 18, 1835, Kirtland, Ohio.
11. *History of the Church,* 5:126–27; from a Joseph Smith journal entry, Aug. 23, 1842, near Nauvoo, Illinois; this entry is incorrectly dated Aug. 22, 1842, in *History of the Church.*
12. Letter from Joseph Smith to Hyrum Smith, Mar. 3, 1831, Kirtland, Ohio; Joseph Smith, Collection, Church Archives, The Church of Jesus Christ of Latter-day Saints, Salt Lake City, Utah.
13. *History of the Church,* 2:338; from a Joseph Smith journal entry, Dec. 18, 1835, Kirtland, Ohio.
14. Lucy Mack Smith, "The History of Lucy Smith, Mother of the Prophet," 1844–45 manuscript, book 4, p. 1, Church Archives.
15. Lucy Mack Smith, "The History of Lucy Smith, Mother of the Prophet," 1844–45 manuscript, book 13, pp. 12–14, Church Archives.
16. Lucy Mack Smith, "The History of Lucy Smith, Mother of the Prophet," 1844–45 manuscript, book 16, pp. 3–6, Church Archives.

"The people loved to hear [the Prophet Joseph Smith], because he was full of revelation," Lorenzo Snow declared. "According to the promise of the Lord, those who accepted the principles he taught received from the Lord a testimony of their truth."

"He Was a Prophet of God": Contemporaries of Joseph Smith Testify of His Prophetic Mission

"I feel like shouting, hallelujah, all the time, when I think that I ever knew Joseph Smith, the Prophet." (Brigham Young)

From the Life of Joseph Smith

In Nauvoo, the Saints often gathered together to hear the Prophet Joseph Smith speak to them. Because there was no building in Nauvoo large enough to hold all the Saints, the Prophet often spoke outside. He frequently spoke in a grove located just west of the temple, where thousands could assemble. A portable platform was constructed for Church leaders and speakers, and the congregation sat on the grass or on logs or bricks. The Prophet also spoke in other locations in Nauvoo, including the unfinished temple and private homes. A visitor to Nauvoo in early 1843 reported seeing meetings held "on the rough floor of the basement of the Temple, and then the Prophet frequently preaches."[1]

When the Prophet spoke outdoors, he often began his talks by asking the Saints to pray for the wind or rain to be calmed until he got through speaking. At a conference held in Nauvoo on April 8, 1843, the Prophet began an address by saying: "I have three requests to make of the congregation: The first is, that all who have faith will exercise it and pray the Lord to calm the wind; for as it blows now, I cannot speak long without seriously injuring my health; the next is that I may have your prayers that the Lord will strengthen my lungs, so that I may be able to make you all hear; and the third is, that you will pray for the Holy Ghost to rest upon me, so as to enable me to declare those things that are true."[2]

The Prophet's appointments to speak were very important to members of the Church, and he sometimes spoke to congregations numbering several thousand. "None listened to him that were ever weary with his discourse," recalled Parley P. Pratt. "I have even known him to retain a congregation of willing and anxious listeners for many hours together, in the midst of cold or sunshine, rain or wind, while they were laughing at one moment and weeping the next."[3] Alvah J. Alexander, who was a boy during the Nauvoo years, recalled that "no amusements or games were as interesting to me as to hear him talk."[4]

Amasa Potter recalled being present at a powerful sermon the Prophet Joseph Smith preached to a large group of Saints in Nauvoo:

"When [the Prophet] had spoken about thirty minutes there came up a heavy wind and storm. The dust was so dense that we could not see each other any distance, and some of the people were leaving when Joseph called out to them to stop and let their prayers ascend to Almighty God that the winds may cease blowing and the rain stop falling, and it should be so. In a very few minutes the winds and rain ceased and the elements became calm as a summer's morning. The storm divided and went on the north and south of the city, and we could see in the distance the trees and shrubs waving in the wind, while where we were it was quiet for one hour, and during that time one of the greatest sermons that ever fell from the Prophet's lips was preached on the great subject of the dead."[5]

The Saints who heard the Prophet Joseph Smith speak bore powerful and vivid testimonies of his prophetic mission. Many of them recorded their memories of discourses they heard him give and experiences they had with him, for they wanted the generations that followed them to know, as they knew, that Joseph Smith was truly a prophet of God.

Testimonies of Joseph Smith

Like the early Saints, we can know that Joseph Smith is the prophet through whom the Lord restored the fulness of the gospel.

Brigham Young, the second President of the Church: "I feel like shouting, hallelujah, all the time, when I think that I ever knew Joseph Smith, the Prophet whom the Lord raised up and ordained, and to whom he gave keys and power to build up the kingdom of God on earth and sustain it. These keys are committed to this people, and we have power to continue the work that Joseph commenced."[6]

Eliza R. Snow, the general president of the Relief Society from 1866 to 1887: "In the cause of truth and righteousness—in all that would benefit his fellow man, his integrity was as firm as the pillars of Heaven. He knew that God had called him to the work, and all the powers of earth and hell combined, failed either to deter or divert him from his purpose. With the help of God and his brethren, he laid the foundation of the greatest work ever established by man—a work extending not only to all the living, and to all the generations to come, but also to the dead.

"He boldly and bravely confronted the false traditions, superstitions, religions, bigotry and ignorance of the world—proved himself true to every heaven-revealed principle—true to his brethren and true to God, then sealed his testimony with his blood."[7]

Bathsheba W. Smith

Bathsheba W. Smith, the general president of the Relief Society from 1901 to 1910: "I know him to be what he professed to be—a true prophet of God, and the Lord through him restored the everlasting gospel and every ordinance and endowment that will lead us into the celestial kingdom."[8]

Wilford Woodruff, the fourth President of the Church: "I have felt to rejoice exceedingly in what I saw of Brother Joseph, for in his public and private career he carried with him the Spirit of the Almighty, and he manifested a greatness of soul which I had never seen in any other man."[9]

Daniel D. McArthur, an early Church member who later led one of the first handcart companies to Salt Lake City: "My testimony is that he was a true Prophet of the living God; and the more I heard his sayings and saw his doings the more I was convinced that he had of a truth seen God the Father and His Son Jesus Christ, as also the holy angels of God. . . . It always seemed to me that if I ever did know anything on this earth I surely knew that he was a Prophet."[10]

Alexander McRae, one of those imprisoned in Liberty Jail with Joseph Smith: "Such was our confidence in [Joseph Smith] as a Prophet, that when he said, 'Thus saith the Lord,' we were confident it would be as he said; and the more we tried it, the more confidence we had, for we never found his word to fail in a single instance."[11]

Lyman O. Littlefield, a member of Zion's Camp: "The whole energies of his soul were absorbed in the glorious latter-day work to which he had been called by his Divine Master."[12]

Mary Alice Cannon Lambert

Mary Alice Cannon Lambert, an English convert who emigrated to Nauvoo in 1843: "I first saw Joseph Smith in the Spring of 1843. When the boat in which we came up the Mississippi River reached the landing at Nauvoo, several of the leading brethren were there to meet the company of saints that had come on it. Among those brethren was the Prophet Joseph Smith. I knew him the instant my eyes rested upon him, and at that moment I received my testimony that he was a Prophet of God. . . . He was not pointed out to me. I knew him from all the other men, and, child that I was (I was only fourteen) I knew that I saw a Prophet of God."[13]

Angus M. Cannon, a Church member who lived in Nauvoo as a youth and later became a stake president in Salt Lake City:

"On one occasion especially do I remember Brother Joseph as he addressed an assembly of the Saints, in the spring of 1844. It was under some large oak trees, in a hollow south of the Temple, near to Parley street. He was discoursing upon the fact that God, in establishing His Church, had provided that only one man was authorized, of God, to receive revelations that should be binding upon the Church. . . . It was on this same occasion that I heard the Prophet declare he had received the Melchizedek Priesthood, under the administration of Peter, James and John.

"The impression created upon my young mind in the inspired utterances of Joseph Smith has accompanied me throughout my subsequent life; and when darkness would otherwise have beclouded my mind, his testimony has come up vividly before me, giving me evidence that the Church of Jesus Christ of Latter-day Saints has been established and governed by the manifest power and authority of God."[14]

Hyrum Smith, the Prophet's brother and the Patriarch to the Church: "There were prophets before, but Joseph has the spirit and power of all the prophets."[15]

Joseph Smith was an example we can follow in developing a Christlike character.

Parley P. Pratt

Parley P. Pratt, a member of the Quorum of the Twelve Apostles from 1835 to 1857: "President Joseph Smith was in person tall and well built, strong and active; of a light complexion, light hair, blue eyes, very little beard, and of an expression peculiar to himself. . . . His countenance was ever mild, affable, beaming with intelligence and benevolence; mingled with a look of interest and an unconscious smile, or cheerfulness, and entirely free from all restraint or affectation of gravity; and there was something connected with the serene and steady penetrating glance of his eye, as if he would penetrate the deepest abyss of the human heart, gaze into eternity, penetrate the heavens, and comprehend all worlds. He possessed a noble boldness and independence of character; his manner was easy and familiar; his rebuke terrible as the lion; his benevolence unbounded as the ocean; his intelligence universal."[16]

John Needham, an early English convert: "Joseph Smith is a great man, a man of principle, a straight forward man; no saintish long-faced fellow, but quite the reverse. Indeed some stumble because he is such a straight forward, plain spoken, cheerful man, but that makes me love him the more."[17]

Emmeline B. Wells, the general president of the Relief Society from 1910 to 1921: "I . . . testify that he was the greatest man and the greatest prophet and the greatest personage of this generation, the greatest, I feel safe in saying, since the days of the Savior. His majesty in appearance was something wonderful. You would think that he was much taller and much larger even than he was. Perhaps many of you have noticed men who have such a bearing when they rise up and walk. This was the way with the Prophet Joseph. There are no pictures of him extant that I know of, that compare with the beauty and majesty of his presence."[18]

Mary Alice Cannon Lambert: "The love the saints had for him was inexpressible. They would willingly have laid down their lives for him. If he was to talk, every task would be laid aside that they might listen to his words. He was not an ordinary man. Saints and sinners alike felt and recognized a power and influence which he carried with him. It was impossible to meet him and not be impressed by the strength of his personality and influence."[19]

John M. Bernhisel

John M. Bernhisel, a medical doctor who boarded in Joseph and Emma's home in Nauvoo for several months during 1843 and 1844: "Joseph Smith is naturally a man of strong mental powers, and is possessed of much energy and decision of character, great penetration, and a profound knowledge of human nature. He is a man of calm judgment, enlarged views, and is eminently distinguished by his love of justice. He is kind and obliging, generous and benevolent, sociable and cheerful, and is possessed of a mind of a contemplative and reflective character. He is honest, frank, fearless and independent, and as free from dissimulation [false appearances] as any man to be found. . . . As a religious teacher, as well as a man, he is greatly beloved by this people."[20]

Jesse N. Smith, a cousin of Joseph Smith: "[The Prophet was] incomparably the most God-like man I ever saw. . . . I know that by nature he was incapable of lying and deceitfulness, possessing the greatest kindness and nobility of character. I felt when in his presence that he could read me through and through. I know he was all that he claimed to be."[21]

William Clayton

William Clayton, an English convert who served as a clerk to Joseph Smith: "The more I am with him, the more I love him; the more I know of him, the more confidence I have in him."[22]

Joseph F. Smith, the sixth President of the Church: "He was brimming over with the noblest and purest of human nature, which often gave vent in innocent amusements—in playing ball, in wrestling with his brothers and scuffling with them, and enjoying himself; he was not like a man with a stake run down his back, and with his face cast in a brazen mold that he could not smile, that he had no joy in his heart. Oh, he was full of joy; he was full of gladness; he was full of love, and of every other noble attribute that makes men great and good, and at the same time simple and innocent, so that he could descend to the lowest condition; and he had power, by the grace of God, to comprehend the purposes of the Almighty too. That was the character of the Prophet Joseph Smith."[23]

As the prophet through whom the gospel was restored, Joseph Smith taught God's plan of salvation with clarity and power.

Brigham Young: "The excellency of the glory of the character of Brother Joseph Smith was that he could reduce heavenly things to the understanding of the finite. When he preached to the people—revealed the things of God, the will of God, the plan of salvation, the purposes of Jehovah, the relation in which we stand to him and all the heavenly beings—he reduced his teachings to the capacity of every man, woman and child, making them as plain as a well defined pathway. This should have convinced every person, that ever heard him, of his divine authority and power, for no other man was able to teach as he could, and no person can reveal the things of God, but by the revelations of Jesus Christ."[24]

Howard Coray, a clerk to Joseph Smith: "I have studied the Gospel as revealed by Joseph Smith and wondered if it were possible for anyone unaided by the Spirit of God to have revealed such a system of salvation and exaltation for man. My conclusion is in the negative. I sat and listened to his preaching at the stand in Nauvoo a great many times when I have been completely carried away with his indescribable eloquence—power of expression—speaking as I have never heard any other man speak."[25]

Joseph L. Robinson

Joseph L. Robinson, a counselor in a bishopric in Nauvoo: "We have long since believed and verily known that Joseph Smith was a true and humble Prophet of God, but now our eyes do see him, and our ears hear his voice, which is like the voice of the mighty thunders of Heaven, yet his language is meek and instructive, edifying much. But there is a power and majesty that attends his words and preaching that we never beheld in any man before, for he is a mighty Prophet, a holy man of God. He truly had been educated in the things pertaining to the kingdom of God and was highly charged with the Holy Ghost, which was a constant companion."[26]

Orson Spencer, a Baptist minister who joined the Church in 1841: "In doctrine Mr. Smith is eminently scriptural. I have never known him to deny or depreciate a single truth of the Old and New Testaments; but I have always known him to explain and defend them in a masterly manner. Being anointed of God, for the purpose of teaching and perfecting the church, it is needful that he should know how to set in order the things that are wanting to bring forth things new and old, as a scribe well instructed. This office and apostleship he appears to magnify; at his touch the ancient prophets spring into life, and the beauty and power of their revelations are made to commend themselves with thrilling interest to all that hear."[27]

Jonah R. Ball, a member of the Church who lived in Nauvoo: "Went to meeting. Heard the Prophet preach on the temple floor. There were several thousand to hear him. There is no mistake. The way he unfolds the scriptures is beyond calculation or controversy. His text was the 1st chapter of 2 Peter. He explained it as clear as the [noonday] sun."[28]

William Clayton: "We have had the privilege of conversing with Joseph Smith Jr. and we are delighted with his company. . . . He is . . . a man of sound judgment and possessed of an abundance of intelligence, and whilst you listen to his conversation you receive intelligence which expands your mind and causes your heart to rejoice. He is very familiar and delights to instruct the poor saint. I can converse with him just as easily as I can with you, and with regard to being willing to communicate instruction he says, 'I receive it freely and I will give it freely.' He is willing to answer any question I have put to him and is pleased when we ask him questions. He seems exceedingly well versed in the scriptures, and whilst conversing upon any subject, such light and beauty is revealed as I never saw before. If I had come from England purposely to converse with him a few days I should have considered myself well paid for my trouble."[29]

Mercy Fielding Thompson

Mercy Fielding Thompson, a British convert whose husband, Robert B. Thompson, served as a clerk to Joseph Smith: "I have . . . listened to his clear and masterly explanations of deep and difficult questions. To him all things seemed simple and easy to be understood, and thus he could make them plain to others as no other man could that I ever heard."[30]

Like the early Saints, we can treasure up the words of Joseph Smith and live the principles he taught.

Emmeline B. Wells

Emmeline B. Wells: "In the Prophet Joseph Smith, I believed I recognized the great spiritual power that brought joy and comfort to the Saints. . . . The power of God rested upon him to such a degree that on many occasions he seemed transfigured. His expression was mild and almost childlike in repose; and when addressing the people, who loved him it seemed to adoration, the glory of his countenance was beyond description. At other times the great power of his manner, more than of his voice (which was sublimely eloquent to me), seemed to shake the place on which we stood and penetrate the inmost soul of his hearers, and I am sure that then they would have laid down their lives to defend him. I always listened spell-bound to his every utterance—the chosen of God in this last dispensation."[31]

Lorenzo Snow

Lorenzo Snow, the fifth President of the Church: "The first time I saw the Prophet Joseph was when I was a boy [about 17 years old]. He was talking to a small congregation. He told them of the visits of the angel to him. . . . The people loved to hear him, because he was full of revelation. . . . According to the promise of the Lord, those who accepted the principles he taught received from the Lord a testimony of their truth."[32]

Edward Stevenson, a member of the Seventy from 1844 to 1897: "I first saw him in 1834 at Pontiac [Michigan] and the impression made upon my mind by him at that time causes me now much pleasure in presenting the picture to his many friends. The love for him, as a true Prophet of God, was indelibly impressed upon my mind, and has always been with me from that time, although nearly sixty years have since passed away. In that same year, 1834, in the midst of many large congregations, the Prophet testified with great power concerning the visit of the Father and the Son, and the conversation he had with them. Never before did I feel such power as was manifested on these occasions."[33]

Mary Ann Stearns Winters, a stepdaughter of Elder Parley P. Pratt: "I stood close by the Prophet while he was preaching to the Indians in the Grove by the Temple. The Holy Spirit lighted up his countenance till it glowed like a halo around him, and his words penetrated the hearts of all who heard him. . . .

"I saw the dead bodies of Brothers Joseph and Hyrum as they lay in the Mansion House after they were brought from Carthage, and also saw some of the clothing they had worn, tinged with their life's blood. I know they were men of God, Prophet and Patriarch, true and faithful. May we be worthy to meet them in the world to come!"[34]

Wilford Woodruff, reporting an April 6, 1837, sermon: "President Joseph Smith Jr. arose and addressed the congregation for the term of three hours, clothed with the power, spirit, and image of God. He unbosomed his mind and feelings in the house of his friends. He presented many things of vast importance to the minds of the elders of Israel. Oh, that they might be written upon our hearts as with an iron pen to remain forever that we might practice them in our lives [see Job 19:23–24]. That fountain of light, principle, and virtue that came forth out of the heart and mouth of the Prophet Joseph, whose soul like Enoch's swelled wide as eternity—I say, such evidences presented in such a forcible manner ought to drive into oblivion every particle of unbelief and dubiety from the mind of the hearers, for such language, sentiment, principle, and spirit cannot flow from darkness. Joseph Smith Jr. is a prophet of God raised up for the deliverance of Israel as true as my heart now burns within me."[35]

Brigham Young: "From the first time I saw the Prophet Joseph I never lost a word that came from him concerning the kingdom. And this is the key of knowledge that I have to-day, that I did hearken to the words of Joseph, and treasured them up in my heart, laid them away, asking my Father in the name of his Son Jesus to bring them to my mind when needed. I treasured up the things of God, and this is the key that I hold to-day. I was anxious to learn from Joseph and the Spirit of God."[36]

Suggestions for Study and Teaching

Consider these ideas as you study the chapter or as you prepare to teach. For additional help, see pages vii–xii.

- Read the testimonies about the Prophet Joseph Smith on pages 495–97. What impresses you about these testimonies? What is the foundation of your own testimony of Joseph Smith? How did you obtain this testimony? You may wish to write your testimony in your journal or share it with your family.
- Pages 497–99 contain statements describing Joseph Smith's appearance, personality, and character. How do these statements influence your feelings about Joseph Smith? Think about ways you might develop some of these same character traits.
- Study the testimonies about the way the Prophet Joseph taught the gospel and explained the scriptures (pages 499–501). How can these testimonies help us as we study and teach the gospel?
- Review the final section of this chapter (pages 502–4). How can you follow the examples of Wilford Woodruff and Brigham Young in your study of this book? How can you follow their examples as you study the teachings of the living prophets? What do you think it means to allow the truth to be "written upon our hearts as with an iron pen"?

Related Scriptures: 2 Nephi 3:6–19; D&C 24:1–9; 124:1

Notes

1. Quoted in *History of the Church,* 5:408; capitalization modernized; from a letter by an unidentified *Boston Bee* correspondent, Mar. 24, 1843, Nauvoo, Illinois, published in *Times and Seasons,* May 15, 1843, p. 200.
2. *History of the Church,* 5:339; from a discourse given by Joseph Smith on Apr. 8, 1843, in Nauvoo, Illinois; reported by Willard Richards and William Clayton.
3. Parley P. Pratt, *Autobiography of Parley P. Pratt,* ed. Parley P. Pratt Jr. (1938), p. 46.

4. Alvah J. Alexander, in "Joseph Smith, the Prophet," *Young Woman's Journal,* Dec. 1906, p. 541.
5. Amasa Potter, "A Reminiscence of the Prophet Joseph Smith," *Juvenile Instructor,* Feb. 15, 1894, p. 132.
6. Brigham Young, *Deseret News,* Oct. 31, 1855, p. 268.
7. Eliza R. Snow, "Anniversary Tribute to the Memory of President Joseph Smith," *Woman's Exponent,* Jan. 1, 1874, p. 117; punctuation modernized.
8. Bathsheba W. Smith, in "Recollections of the Prophet Joseph Smith," *Juvenile Instructor,* June 1, 1892, p. 344.
9. Wilford Woodruff, *Deseret News,* Jan. 20, 1858, p. 363; capitalization modernized.
10. Daniel D. McArthur, in "Recollections of the Prophet Joseph Smith," *Juvenile Instructor,* Feb. 15, 1892, p. 129.
11. Alexander McRae, quoted in *History of the Church,* 3:258; from a letter from Alexander McRae to the editor of the *Deseret News,* Nov. 1, 1854, Salt Lake City, Utah, published in *Deseret News,* Nov. 9, 1854, p. 1; punctuation and grammar modernized.
12. Lyman O. Littlefield, *Reminiscences of Latter-day Saints* (1888), p. 35.
13. Mary Alice Cannon Lambert, in "Joseph Smith, the Prophet," *Young Woman's Journal,* Dec. 1905, p. 554.
14. Angus M. Cannon, in "Joseph Smith, the Prophet," *Young Woman's Journal,* Dec. 1906, p. 546; spelling and grammar modernized.
15. Hyrum Smith, quoted in *History of the Church,* 6:346; from a discourse given by Hyrum Smith on Apr. 28, 1844, in Nauvoo, Illinois.
16. Parley P. Pratt, *Autobiography of Parley P. Pratt,* ed. Parley P. Pratt Jr. (1938), pp. 45–46; paragraph divisions altered.
17. Letter from John Needham to his parents, July 7, 1843, Nauvoo, Illinois, published in *Millennial Star,* Oct. 1843, p. 89.
18. Emmeline B. Wells, "The Prophet Joseph," *Young Woman's Journal,* Aug. 1912, pp. 437–38; paragraph divisions altered.
19. Mary Alice Cannon Lambert, in "Joseph Smith, the Prophet," *Young Woman's Journal,* Dec. 1905, p. 554.
20. John M. Bernhisel, quoted in *History of the Church,* 6:468; paragraph divisions altered; from a letter from John M. Bernhisel to Thomas Ford, June 14, 1844, Nauvoo, Illinois.
21. Jesse N. Smith, in "Recollections of the Prophet Joseph Smith," *Juvenile Instructor,* Jan. 1, 1892, pp. 23–24; paragraph divisions altered.
22. Letter from William Clayton to William Hardman, Mar. 30, 1842, Nauvoo, Illinois, published in *Millennial Star,* Aug. 1, 1842, p. 76.
23. Joseph F. Smith, in "Joseph, the Prophet," *Salt Lake Herald Church and Farm Supplement,* Jan. 12, 1895, p. 211; spelling and punctuation modernized.
24. Brigham Young, *Deseret News,* Nov. 28, 1860, p. 305; capitalization modernized.
25. Letter from Howard Coray to Martha Jane Lewis, Aug. 2, 1889, Sanford, Colorado, pp. 3–4, Church Archives, The Church of Jesus Christ of Latter-day Saints, Salt Lake City, Utah.
26. Joseph Lee Robinson, Autobiography and Journals, 1883–92, folder 1, p. 22, Church Archives.
27. Letter from Orson Spencer to unknown person, Nov. 17, 1842, Nauvoo, Illinois, published in *Times and Seasons,* Jan. 2, 1843, pp. 56–57; punctuation modernized.
28. Letter from Jonah R. Ball to Harvey Howard, May 19, 1843, Nauvoo, Illinois; Jonah Randolph Ball, Letters 1842–43, to Harvey Howard, Shutesbury, Massachusetts, Church Archives.
29. Letter from William Clayton to Church members in Manchester, England, Dec. 10, 1840, Nauvoo, Illinois, Church Archives.
30. Mercy Fielding Thompson, "Recollections of the Prophet Joseph Smith," *Juvenile Instructor,* July 1, 1892, p. 399; paragraph divisions altered.
31. Emmeline B. Wells, in "Joseph Smith, the Prophet," *Young Woman's Journal,* Dec. 1905, p. 556; punctuation modernized; paragraph divisions altered.

32. Lorenzo Snow, *Deseret Weekly,* Apr. 13, 1889, p. 487.
33. Edward Stevenson, *Reminiscences of Joseph, the Prophet, and the Coming Forth of the Book of Mormon* (1893), p. 4; paragraph divisions altered.
34. Mary Ann Stearns Winters, in "Joseph Smith, the Prophet," *Young Woman's Journal,* Dec. 1905, p. 558; paragraph divisions altered.
35. Wilford Woodruff, reporting a discourse given by Joseph Smith on Apr. 6, 1837, in Kirtland, Ohio; Wilford Woodruff, Journals, 1833–98, Church Archives.
36. Brigham Young, *Deseret News,* June 6, 1877, p. 274; capitalization modernized.

CHAPTER 44

The Restoration of All Things: The Dispensation of the Fulness of Times

"[This] is truly the dispensation of the fullness of times, when all things which are in Christ Jesus, whether in heaven or on the earth, shall be gathered together in Him, and when all things shall be restored."

From the Life of Joseph Smith

The Prophet Joseph Smith loved the Nauvoo Temple and yearned to see it completed. Nauvoo resident Martha Coray was present at an address where she saw the Prophet stretch his hand toward the temple and say in a melancholy tone, "If it should be . . . the will of God that I might live to behold that temple completed and finished from the foundation to the top stone, I will say, 'O Lord, it is enough. Lord, let thy servant depart in peace.' "[1]

George Q. Cannon, who later became a counselor in the First Presidency, recalled: "Previous to his death, the Prophet Joseph manifested great anxiety to see the [Nauvoo] temple completed, as most of you who were with the Church during his day, well know. 'Hurry up the work, brethren,' he used to say,—'let us finish the temple; the Lord has a great endowment in store for you, and I am anxious that the brethren should have their endowments and receive the fullness of the priesthood.' He urged the Saints forward continually, preaching unto them the importance of completing that building, so that therein the ordinances of life and salvation might be administered to the whole people, but especially to the quorums of the holy priesthood; 'then,' said he, 'the Kingdom will be established, and I do not care what shall become of me.' "[2]

The Prophet Joseph Smith yearned to see the Nauvoo Temple completed. " 'Hurry up the work, brethren,' he used to say,—'let us finish the temple; the Lord has a great endowment in store for you.' "

The plans for the Nauvoo Temple called for an edifice that would be larger and even more beautiful than the Kirtland Temple. Situated on the summit of a bluff overlooking the Mississippi River, the completed Nauvoo Temple would be one of the most magnificent buildings in Illinois. It was made of limestone obtained from quarries near Nauvoo and lumber floated down the river from pineries in Wisconsin. When finished, it would be 128 feet long, 88 feet wide, and 165 feet high at the top of the spire. The exterior was ornamented with intricately carved moonstones, sunstones, and starstones, while sunlight streaming through the many windows illuminated the interior.

Joseph Smith did not live to see the Nauvoo Temple completed, but after his death, thousands of Saints received sacred ordinances in the temple under the direction of Brigham Young. After the Saints were forced to leave Nauvoo, their beautiful temple was destroyed. It was gutted by fire in 1848, and in 1850 a tornado leveled some of the walls, leaving the remaining walls so weakened that they had to be razed. Some 150 years later, construction began on a new Nauvoo Temple, built on the original site. The reconstructed temple was dedicated on June 27, 2002, becoming one of more than a hundred temples throughout the world. Each of these temples is a symbol that the fulness of God's blessings to His children, living and dead, has been restored in this last dispensation.

The Prophet Joseph Smith was called of God to restore these great blessings to earth and to stand at the head of the dispensation of the fulness of times. During the Prophet's ministry, all things were restored that were necessary to lay the foundation of the greatest dispensation of all time. The priesthood, with its essential keys, was restored; the Book of Mormon was translated; the Church was organized; and doctrines, ordinances, and covenants were revealed, including the ordinances and covenants of the endowment and the marriage sealing. The Lord declared that He had committed unto Joseph Smith "the keys of my kingdom, and a dispensation of the gospel for the last times; and for the fulness of times, in the which I will gather together in one all things, both which are in heaven, and which are on earth" (D&C 27:13).

Teachings of Joseph Smith

In this last dispensation, all the authority, ordinances, and knowledge of earlier dispensations have been restored.

"It is in the order of heavenly things that God should always send a new dispensation into the world when men have apostatized from the truth and lost the priesthood."[3]

On September 6, 1842, the Prophet Joseph Smith wrote the following to the Saints, later recorded in Doctrine and Covenants 128:18: "It is necessary in the ushering in of the dispensation of the fulness of times, which dispensation is now beginning to usher in, that a whole and complete and perfect union, and welding together of dispensations, and keys, and powers, and glories should take place, and be revealed from the days of Adam even to the present time. And not only this, but those things which never have been revealed from the foundation of the world, but have been kept hid from the wise and prudent, shall be revealed unto babes and sucklings in this, the dispensation of the fulness of times."[4]

"Truly this is a day long to be remembered by the Saints of the last days,—a day in which the God of heaven has begun to restore the ancient order of His kingdom unto His servants and His people,—a day in which all things are concurring to bring about the completion of the fullness of the Gospel, a fullness of the dispensation of dispensations, even the fullness of times; a day in which God has begun to make manifest and set in order in His Church those things which have been, and those things which the ancient prophets and wise men desired to see but died without beholding them; a day in which those things begin to be made manifest, which have been hid from before the foundation of the world, and which Jehovah has promised should be made known in His own due time unto His servants, to prepare the earth for the return of His glory, even a celestial glory, and a kingdom of Priests and kings to God and the Lamb, forever, on Mount Zion."[5]

"The dispensation of the fullness of times will bring to light the things that have been revealed in all former dispensations;

also other things that have not been before revealed. He shall send Elijah, the Prophet, etc., and restore all things in Christ."[6]

" 'Having made known unto us the mystery of His will, according to His good pleasure which He hath purposed in Himself: that in the dispensation of the fullness of times He might gather together in one all things in Christ, both which are in heaven, and which are on earth; even in him.' [Ephesians 1:9–10.]

"Now the purpose in Himself in the winding up scene of the last dispensation is that all things pertaining to that dispensation should be conducted precisely in accordance with the preceding dispensations.

"And again. God purposed in Himself that there should not be an eternal fullness until every dispensation should be fulfilled and gathered together in one, and that all things whatsoever, that should be gathered together in one in those dispensations unto the same fullness and eternal glory, should be in Christ Jesus. . . .

". . . All the ordinances and duties that ever have been required by the Priesthood, under the directions and commandments of the Almighty in any of the dispensations, shall all be had in the last dispensation, therefore all things had under the authority of the Priesthood at any former period, shall be had again, bringing to pass the restoration spoken of by the mouth of all the Holy Prophets."[7]

Joseph Smith holds the keys of the dispensation of the fulness of times.

"I . . . hold the keys of the last kingdom, in which is the dispensation of the fullness of all things spoken by the mouths of all the holy Prophets since the world began, under the sealing power of the Melchizedek Priesthood."[8]

"Every man who has a calling to minister to the inhabitants of the world was ordained to that very purpose in the Grand Council of heaven before this world was. I suppose that I was ordained to this very office in that Grand Council. It is the testimony that I want that I am God's servant, and this people His people. The ancient prophets declared that in the last days the

God of heaven should set up a kingdom which should never be destroyed, nor left to other people. . . .

"I calculate to be one of the instruments of setting up the kingdom of Daniel by the word of the Lord, and I intend to lay a foundation that will revolutionize the whole world."[9]

"I have the whole plan of the kingdom before me, and no other person has."[10]

Lucy Mack Smith was present when Joseph Smith preached in Kirtland, Ohio, in 1832. She recalled these words of the Prophet: "I myself hold the keys of this last dispensation, and I forever will hold them in time and in eternity. So set your hearts at rest, for all is well."[11]

This final dispensation is of such vast importance that it requires the complete, unselfish dedication of the Saints.

In September 1840, Joseph Smith and his counselors in the First Presidency made the following declaration to the members of the Church: "The work of the Lord in these last days, is one of vast magnitude and almost beyond the comprehension of mortals. Its glories are past description, and its grandeur unsurpassable. It is the theme which has animated the bosom of prophets and righteous men from the creation of the world down through every succeeding generation to the present time; and it is truly the dispensation of the fullness of times, when all things which are in Christ Jesus, whether in heaven or on the earth, shall be gathered together in Him, and when all things shall be restored, as spoken of by all the holy prophets since the world began; for in it will take place the glorious fulfilment of the promises made to the fathers, while the manifestations of the power of the Most High will be great, glorious, and sublime. . . .

". . . We feel disposed to go forward and unite our energies for the upbuilding of the Kingdom, and establishing the Priesthood in their fullness and glory. The work which has to be accomplished in the last days is one of vast importance, and will call into action the energy, skill, talent, and ability of the Saints, so that it may roll forth with that glory and majesty described by the prophet [see Daniel 2:34–35, 44–45]; and will consequently require the concentration of the Saints, to accomplish works of such magnitude and grandeur.

"The work of the gathering spoken of in the Scriptures will be necessary to bring about the glories of the last dispensation. . . .

"Dear brethren, feeling desirous to carry out the purposes of God, to which work we have been called; and to be co-workers with Him in this last dispensation; we feel the necessity of having the hearty cooperation of the Saints throughout this land, and upon the islands of the sea. It will be necessary for the Saints to hearken to counsel and turn their attention to the Church, the establishment of the Kingdom, and lay aside every selfish principle, everything low and groveling; and stand forward in the cause of truth, and assist to the utmost of their power, those to whom has been given the pattern and design. . . .

"Here, then, beloved brethren, is a work to engage in worthy of archangels—a work which will cast into the shade the things which have been heretofore accomplished; a work which kings and prophets and righteous men in former ages have sought, expected, and earnestly desired to see, but died without the sight; and well will it be for those who shall aid in carrying into effect the mighty operations of Jehovah."[12]

"The building up of Zion is a cause that has interested the people of God in every age; it is a theme upon which prophets, priests and kings have dwelt with peculiar delight; they have looked forward with joyful anticipation to the day in which we live; and fired with heavenly and joyful anticipations they have sung and written and prophesied of this our day; but they died without the sight; we are the favored people that God has made choice of to bring about the Latter-day glory; it is left for us to see, participate in and help to roll forward the Latter-day glory, 'the dispensation of the fullness of times, when God will gather together all things that are in heaven, and all things that are upon the earth, even in one' [see Ephesians 1:10], when the Saints of God will be gathered in one from every nation, and kindred, and people, and tongue, when the Jews will be gathered together into one, the wicked will also be gathered together to be destroyed, as spoken of by the prophets; the Spirit of God

Full-time missionaries at the Missionary Training Center in Provo, Utah. Joseph Smith declared that in the last dispensation, "it will be necessary for the Saints to hearken to counsel and . . . stand forward in the cause of truth."

will also dwell with His people, and be withdrawn from the rest of the nations, and all things whether in heaven or on earth will be in one, even in Christ.

"The heavenly Priesthood will unite with the earthly, to bring about those great purposes; and whilst we are thus united in the one common cause, to roll forth the kingdom of God, the heavenly Priesthood are not idle spectators, the Spirit of God will be showered down from above, and it will dwell in our midst. The blessings of the Most High will rest upon our tabernacles, and our name will be handed down to future ages; our children will rise up and call us blessed; and generations yet unborn will dwell with peculiar delight upon the scenes that we have passed through, the privations that we have endured, the untiring zeal that we have manifested, the all but insurmountable difficulties that we have overcome in laying the foundation of a work that brought about the glory and blessing which they will realize; a work that God and angels have contemplated with delight for generations past; that fired the souls of the ancient patriarchs and prophets; a work that is destined to bring about the destruction of the powers of darkness, the renovation of the earth, the glory of God, and the salvation of the human family."[13]

Suggestions for Study and Teaching

Consider these ideas as you study the chapter or as you prepare to teach. For additional help, see pages vii–xii.

- Review pages 507–9. Why are temples so important in the accomplishment of the Lord's work?
- Why do you think ancient prophets and wise men looked forward to our day? (For some examples, see pages 510–11.) Ponder the privilege of being a member of The Church of Jesus Christ of Latter-day Saints in the dispensation of the fulness of times.
- Study the paragraph that begins on the bottom of page 511. As you ponder this statement, what are your thoughts and feelings about your callings to serve in the Church?
- Read the first three full paragraphs on page 512. How do these statements strengthen your testimony of the mission of the Prophet Joseph Smith?
- The Prophet Joseph Smith said, "The work of the Lord in these last days, is one of vast magnitude" (page 512). Study pages 512–15, pondering our responsibility to help accomplish the Lord's work in the last dispensation. Why must we "unite our energies" if we are to accomplish this work? Why must we "lay aside every selfish principle"? Think about how you can use your "energy, skill, talent, and ability" to contribute to the Lord's work.

Related Scriptures: D&C 27:12–13; 90:2–3; 112:30–32; 124:40–41

Notes

1. Quoted by Martha Jane Knowlton Coray, reporting a discourse given by Joseph Smith in Nauvoo, Illinois; Martha Jane Knowlton Coray, Notebook, Church Archives, The Church of Jesus Christ of Latter-day Saints, Salt Lake City, Utah; this discourse is dated July 19, 1840, in Sister Coray's notebook, but the discourse was probably given at a later date.
2. George Q. Cannon, *Deseret News: Semi-Weekly,* Dec. 14, 1869, p. 2.
3. *History of the Church,* 6:478–79; from a discourse given by Joseph Smith on June 16, 1844, in Nauvoo, Illinois; reported by Thomas Bullock; see also appendix, page 562, item 3.
4. Doctrine and Covenants 128:18; a letter from Joseph Smith to the Saints, Sept. 6, 1842, Nauvoo, Illinois.
5. *History of the Church,* 4:492–93; from a Joseph Smith journal entry, Jan. 6, 1842, Nauvoo, Illinois.
6. *History of the Church,* 4:426; from the minutes of a Church conference held on Oct. 3, 1841, in Nauvoo, Illinois, published in *Times and Seasons,* Oct. 15, 1841, p. 578.
7. *History of the Church,* 4:208, 210–11; from a discourse prepared by Joseph Smith and read at a Church conference held on Oct. 5, 1840, in Nauvoo, Illinois.
8. *History of the Church,* 6:78; spelling modernized; from a letter from Joseph Smith to James Arlington Bennet, Nov. 13, 1843, Nauvoo, Illinois; James Bennet's last name is incorrectly spelled "Bennett" in *History of the Church*.
9. *History of the Church,* 6:364–65; from a discourse given by Joseph Smith on May 12, 1844, in Nauvoo, Illinois; reported by Thomas Bullock.
10. *History of the Church,* 5:139; from a discourse given by Joseph Smith on Aug. 29, 1842, in Nauvoo, Illinois; reported by William Clayton.
11. Quoted by Lucy Mack Smith, reporting a discourse given by Joseph Smith in early 1832 in Kirtland, Ohio; Lucy Mack Smith, "The History of Lucy Smith, Mother of the Prophet," 1844–45 manuscript, book 13, p. 5, Church Archives.
12. *History of the Church,* 4:185–87; punctuation modernized; from a letter from Joseph Smith and his counselors in the First Presidency to the Saints, Sept. 1840, Nauvoo, Illinois, published in *Times and Seasons,* Oct. 1840, pp. 178–79.
13. *History of the Church,* 4:609–10; punctuation modernized; paragraph divisions altered; from "The Temple," an editorial published in *Times and Seasons,* May 2, 1842, p. 776; Joseph Smith was the editor of the periodical.

C H A P T E R 4 5

Joseph Smith's Feelings about His Prophetic Mission

"I have no desire but to do all men good."

From the Life of Joseph Smith

From the beginning of the Prophet Joseph Smith's ministry, his life was often in peril. Though the Lord delivered him many times from his enemies, the Prophet knew that once he had completed his earthly mission, he could die. "Some have supposed that Brother Joseph could not die," he said at a funeral in Nauvoo in 1842, "but this is a mistake: it is true there have been times when I have had the promise of my life to accomplish such and such things, but, having now accomplished those things, I have not at present any lease of my life. I am as liable to die as other men."[1]

The Prophet was well aware that he and all of the Saints living in Nauvoo were in an increasingly dangerous situation. As Nauvoo grew larger, some of the people who lived in the area began to fear the growing political and economic power of the Saints, and mobs began again to harass them. The Prophet was in particular danger, for authorities from Missouri made repeated efforts to capture him, and apostates from the Church became increasingly hostile in their efforts to destroy him. On August 6, 1842, the Prophet declared that the time would come when Church members would be forced to leave Nauvoo:

"I prophesied that the Saints would continue to suffer much affliction and would be driven to the Rocky Mountains, many would apostatize, others would be put to death by our persecutors or lose their lives in consequence of exposure or disease, and some of you will live to go and assist in making settlements and build cities and see the Saints become a mighty people in the midst of the Rocky Mountains."[2]

Joseph Smith found time to show that he cared for the Saints individually. Margarette McIntire Burgess remembered the Prophet, whom she called "the loving friend of children," helping her and her brother when they were stuck in the mud.

In the sermons and writings of the last few years of the Prophet's life, there is a sense of urgency in his words. Knowing that his time was short, he labored earnestly to teach the Saints the things that God had revealed to him and encouraged them to prepare to receive these truths. He also expressed his great love for the Saints, even declaring that he was willing to lay down his life for them: "I am ready to be offered up a sacrifice in that way that can bring to pass the greatest benefit and good."[3]

It is remarkable that while the Prophet was enduring so much persecution and was pressured by the constant demands of the growing Church, he found time to show that he cared for each Church member as an individual. Many Saints in later years remembered the love and kindness the Prophet Joseph showed to them.

Aroet L. Hale recalled: "The Prophet . . . frequently used to come out of the Mansion [House] and play ball with us boys, his son Joseph being near my age. [The Prophet] Joseph would always conform to the rules. He would catch till it came his turn to take the club, then, being a very stout [strong] man, would knock the ball so far that we used to holler to the boy that was going for the ball to take his dinner. This used to make the Prophet laugh. Joseph was always good natured and full of fun."[4]

Margarette McIntire Burgess recalled another experience with the Prophet in Nauvoo: "My older brother and I were going to school, near to the building which was known as Joseph's brick store. It had been raining the previous day, causing the ground to be very muddy, especially along that street. My brother Wallace and I both got fast in the mud, and could not get out, and of course, child-like, we began to cry, for we thought we would have to stay there. But looking up, I beheld the loving friend of children, the Prophet Joseph, coming to us. He soon had us on higher and drier ground. Then he stooped down and cleaned the mud from our little, heavy-laden shoes, took his handkerchief from his pocket and wiped our tear-stained faces. He spoke kind and cheering words to us, and sent us on our way to school rejoicing. Was it any wonder that I loved that great, good and noble man of God?"[5]

Teachings of Joseph Smith

Prophets teach what God reveals to them; we strive to understand and give heed to their words.

"It is my meditation all the day, and more than my meat and drink, to know how I shall make the Saints of God comprehend the visions that roll like an overflowing surge before my mind. Oh! how I would delight to bring before you things which you never thought of! But poverty and the cares of the world prevent. . . .

"Hosanna, hosanna, hosanna to Almighty God, that rays of light begin to burst forth upon us even now. I cannot find words in which to express myself. I am not learned, but I have as good feelings as any man. Oh, that I had the language of the archangel to express my feelings once to my friends! But I never expect to in this life."[6]

"There has been a great difficulty in getting anything into the heads of this generation. It has been like splitting hemlock knots with a corn-dodger [a piece of corn bread] for a wedge, and a pumpkin for a beetle [a wooden mallet]. Even the Saints are slow to understand.

"I have tried for a number of years to get the minds of the Saints prepared to receive the things of God; but we frequently see some of them, after suffering all they have for the work of God, will fly to pieces like glass as soon as anything comes that is contrary to their traditions: they cannot stand the fire at all. How many will be able to abide a celestial law, and go through and receive their exaltation, I am unable to say, as many are called, but few are chosen [see D&C 121:40]."[7]

"I am not like other men. My mind is continually occupied with the business of the day, and I have to depend entirely upon the living God for everything I say on such occasions as these [a funeral]. . . .

"Had I inspiration, revelation, and lungs to communicate what my soul has contemplated in times past, there is not a soul in this congregation but would go to their homes and shut their mouths in everlasting silence on religion till they had learned something.

"Why be so certain that you comprehend the things of God, when all things with you are so uncertain? You are welcome to all the knowledge and intelligence I can impart to you."[8]

"Some people say I am a fallen Prophet, because I do not bring forth more of the word of the Lord. Why do I not do it? Are we able to receive it? No! not one in this room."[9]

"I will from time to time reveal to you the subjects that are revealed by the Holy Ghost to me. All the lies that are now hatched up against me are of the devil, and the influence of the devil and his servants will be used against the kingdom of God. The servants of God teach nothing but principles of eternal life, by their works ye shall know them. A good man will speak good things and holy principles, and an evil man evil things. I feel, in the name of the Lord, to rebuke all such bad principles, liars, etc., and I warn all of you to look out whom you are going after. I exhort you to give heed to all the virtue and the teachings which I have given you. . . .

"I enjoin for your consideration—add to your faith virtue, love, etc. I say, in the name of the Lord, if these things are in you, you shall be fruitful [see 2 Peter 1:5–8]. I testify that no man has power to reveal it but myself—things in heaven, in earth and hell. . . . I commend you all to God, that you may inherit all things; and may God add His blessing."[10]

Although prophets are men with human frailties, they are called of God to teach and lead His people.

The Prophet's journal for November 6, 1835, records: "I was this morning introduced to a man from the east. After hearing my name, he remarked that I was nothing but a man, indicating by this expression, that he had supposed that a person to whom the Lord should see fit to reveal His will, must be something more than a man. He seemed to have forgotten the saying that fell from the lips of St. James, that [Elijah] was a man subject to like passions as we are, yet he had such power with God, that He, in answer to his prayers, shut the heavens that they gave no rain for the space of three years and six months; and again, in answer to his prayer, the heavens gave forth rain, and the earth gave forth fruit [see James 5:17–18]. Indeed, such is the darkness and ignorance of this generation, that they look upon it as incredible that a man should have any [dealings] with his Maker."[11]

"When did I ever teach anything wrong from this stand? When was I ever confounded? I want to triumph in Israel before I depart hence and am no more seen. I never told you I was perfect; but there is no error in the revelations which I have taught. Must I, then, be thrown away as a thing of naught?"[12]

"Although I do wrong, I do not the wrongs that I am charged with doing: the wrong that I do is through the frailty of human nature, like other men. No man lives without fault. Do you think that even Jesus, if He were here, would be without fault in your eyes? His enemies said all manner of evil against Him—they all watched for iniquity in Him."[13]

Joseph Smith's journal for October 29, 1842, records: "I . . . went over to the store [in Nauvoo, Illinois], where a number of brethren and sisters were assembled, who had arrived this morning from the neighborhood of New York. . . . I told them I was but a man, and they must not expect me to be perfect; if they expected perfection from me, I should expect it from them; but if they would bear with my infirmities and the infirmities of the brethren, I would likewise bear with their infirmities."[14]

Despite opposition, prophets fulfill the missions given to them by God.

"I am happy and thankful for the privilege of being present on this occasion. Great exertions have been made on the part of our enemies to carry me to Missouri and destroy my life; but the Lord has hedged up their way, and they have not, as yet, accomplished their purpose. God has enabled me to keep out of their hands. I have warred a good warfare. . . .

"I shall triumph over my enemies: I have begun to triumph over them at home, and I shall do it abroad. All those that rise up against me will surely feel the weight of their iniquity upon their own heads."[15]

"I speak boldly and faithfully and with authority. . . . I know what I say; I understand my mission and business. God Almighty is my shield; and what can man do if God is my friend? I shall not be sacrificed until my time comes; then I shall be offered freely. . . . I thank God for preserving me from my enemies; I have no enemies but for the truth's sake. I have no desire but to do all men good. I feel to pray for all men."[16]

"If I had not actually got into this work and been called of God, I would back out. But I cannot back out: I have no doubt of the truth."[17]

"I am a rough stone. The sound of the hammer and chisel was never heard on me until the Lord took me in hand. I desire the learning and wisdom of heaven alone."[18]

"I prophesy and bear record this morning that all the combined powers of earth and hell shall not and cannot ever overthrow or overcome this boy, for I have a promise from the eternal God. If I have sinned, I have sinned outwardly; but surely I have contemplated the things of God."[19]

"When men come out and build upon other men's foundations, they do it on their own responsibility, without authority from God; and when the floods come and the winds blow, their foundations will be found to be sand, and their whole fabric will crumble to dust.

"Did I build on any other man's foundation? I have got all the truth which the Christian world possessed, and an independent revelation in the bargain, and God will bear me off triumphant."[20]

Prophets love those they serve and desire to lead them well, even if doing so requires reproving them.

"There is no greater love than this, that a man lay down his life for his friends [see John 15:13]. I discover hundreds and thousands of my brethren ready to sacrifice their lives for me.

"The burdens which roll upon me are very great. My persecutors allow me no rest, and I find that in the midst of business and care the spirit is willing, but the flesh is weak. Although I was called of my Heavenly Father to lay the foundation of this great work and kingdom in this dispensation, and testify of His revealed will to scattered Israel, I am subject to like passions as other men, like the prophets of olden times. . . .

"I see no faults in the Church, and therefore let me be resurrected with the Saints, whether I ascend to heaven or descend to hell, or go to any other place. And if we go to hell, we will turn the devils out of doors and make a heaven of it. Where this people are, there is good society."[21]

"The Saints need not think because I am familiar with them and am playful and cheerful, that I am ignorant of what is going on. Iniquity of any kind cannot be sustained in the Church, and it will not fare well where I am; for I am determined while I do lead the Church, to lead it right."[22]

"If I am so fortunate as to be the man to comprehend God, and explain or convey the principles to your hearts, so that the Spirit seals them upon you, then let every man and woman henceforth sit in silence, put their hands on their mouths, and never lift their hands or voices, or say anything against the man of God or the servants of God again. . . . If I am bringing you to a knowledge of Him, all persecutions against me ought to cease. You will then know that I am His servant; for I speak as one having authority. . . .

"I have intended my remarks for all, both rich and poor, bond and free, great and small. . . . I love all men, especially these my brethren and sisters."

". . . I can taste the principles of eternal life, and so can you. They are given to me by the revelations of Jesus Christ; and I know that when I tell you these words of eternal life as they are given to me, you taste them, and I know that you believe them. You say honey is sweet, and so do I. I can also taste the spirit of eternal life. I know that it is good; and when I tell you of these things which were given me by inspiration of the Holy Spirit, you are bound to receive them as sweet, and rejoice more and more. . . .

"I have intended my remarks for all, both rich and poor, bond and free, great and small. I have no enmity against any man. I love you all; but I hate some of your deeds. I am your best friend, and if persons miss their mark it is their own fault. If I reprove a man, and he hates me, he is a fool; for I love all men, especially these my brethren and sisters.

". . . You don't know me; you never knew my heart. No man knows my history. I cannot tell it: I shall never undertake it. I don't blame any one for not believing my history. If I had not experienced what I have, I would not have believed it myself. I never did harm any man since I was born in the world. My voice is always for peace.

"I cannot lie down until all my work is finished. I never think any evil, nor do anything to the harm of my fellow-man. When I am called by the trump of the archangel and weighed in the balance, you will all know me then. I add no more. God bless you all."[23]

Suggestions for Study and Teaching

Consider these ideas as you study the chapter or as you prepare to teach. For additional help, see pages vii–xii.

- On page 517, read about the persecution Joseph Smith faced in Nauvoo. Then turn to page 519 and review the stories of him serving and playing with the children in Nauvoo. Why do you think he was able to maintain such a cheerful, caring attitude? Think about what you can do to remain happy and loving during times of trial.

- Read the third and fourth paragraphs on page 520, noting the Prophet Joseph's disappointment when the Saints were not ready to receive all he wanted to teach them (see pages 520–21). What can interfere with our ability to receive more truth? What can we do to be "prepared to receive the things of God"?
- Review the paragraph that begins on the bottom of page 521 and the two following paragraphs. What counsel could you give someone who refuses to follow a Church leader because the leader has some kind of character flaw? Read the third full paragraph on page 522, and think about how this statement applies in all our relationships.
- Joseph Smith expressed faith that God would protect him and enable him to accomplish his mission in life (pages 522–23). What experiences have you had in which God has helped you to fulfill your responsibilities in your family or in a Church calling?
- Study the first two paragraphs on page 525. When have you tasted the sweetness of the truth? How can we rejoice in the words of a prophet or other Church leader even when he reproves us for our misdeeds?
- Quickly review the entire chapter, looking for one or two statements that are particularly helpful for you. What do you appreciate about the statements you have chosen? How has this chapter influenced your testimony of the Prophet Joseph Smith?

Related Scriptures: Daniel 2:44–45; 2 Timothy 4:6–8; Jacob 1:17–19; Mosiah 2:9–11; Mormon 9:31

Notes

1. *History of the Church,* 4:587; punctuation modernized; from a discourse given by Joseph Smith on Apr. 9, 1842, in Nauvoo, Illinois; reported by Wilford Woodruff.
2. *History of the Church,* 5:85; from "History of the Church" (manuscript), book D-1, p. 1362, Church Archives, The Church of Jesus Christ of Latter-day Saints, Salt Lake City, Utah.
3. *History of the Church,* 5:159; from a letter from Joseph Smith to James Arlington Bennet, Sept. 8, 1842, Nauvoo, Illinois; James Bennet's last name is incorrectly spelled "Bennett" in *History of the Church.*
4. Aroet L. Hale, "First Book or Journal of the Life and Travels of Aroet L. Hale," pp. 23–24; Aroet Lucius Hale, Reminiscences, ca. 1882, Church Archives.

5. Margarette McIntire Burgess, in "Recollections of the Prophet Joseph Smith," *Juvenile Instructor,* Jan. 15, 1892, pp. 66–67.
6. *History of the Church,* 5:362; spelling and punctuation modernized; paragraph divisions altered; from a discourse given by Joseph Smith on Apr. 16, 1843, in Nauvoo, Illinois; reported by Wilford Woodruff and Willard Richards.
7. *History of the Church,* 6:184–85; from a discourse given by Joseph Smith on Jan. 21, 1844, in Nauvoo, Illinois; reported by Wilford Woodruff.
8. *History of the Church,* 5:529–30; spelling and punctuation modernized; from a discourse given by Joseph Smith on Aug. 13, 1843, in Nauvoo, Illinois; reported by Willard Richards.
9. *History of the Church,* 4:478; from a discourse given by Joseph Smith on Dec. 19, 1841, in Nauvoo, Illinois; reported by Wilford Woodruff.
10. *History of the Church,* 6:366–67; from a discourse given by Joseph Smith on May 12, 1844, in Nauvoo, Illinois; reported by Thomas Bullock.
11. *History of the Church,* 2:302; from a Joseph Smith journal entry, Nov. 6, 1835, Kirtland, Ohio.
12. *History of the Church,* 6:366; from a discourse given by Joseph Smith on May 12, 1844, in Nauvoo, Illinois; reported by Thomas Bullock.
13. *History of the Church,* 5:140; from a discourse given by Joseph Smith on Aug. 31, 1842, in Nauvoo, Illinois; reported by Eliza R. Snow.
14. *History of the Church,* 5:181; paragraph divisions altered; from a Joseph Smith journal entry, Oct. 29, 1842, Nauvoo, Illinois.
15. *History of the Church,* 5:139–40; from a discourse given by Joseph Smith on Aug. 31, 1842, in Nauvoo, Illinois; reported by Eliza R. Snow; see also appendix, page 562, item 3.
16. *History of the Church,* 5:257, 259; paragraph divisions altered; from a discourse given by Joseph Smith on Jan. 22, 1843, in Nauvoo, Illinois; reported by Wilford Woodruff; see also appendix, page 562, item 3.
17. *History of the Church,* 5:336; from a discourse given by Joseph Smith on Apr. 6, 1843, in Nauvoo, Illinois; reported by Willard Richards.
18. *History of the Church,* 5:423; from a discourse given by Joseph Smith on June 11, 1843, in Nauvoo, Illinois; reported by Wilford Woodruff and Willard Richards; see also appendix, page 562, item 3.
19. *History of the Church,* 5:554; paragraph divisions altered; from a discourse given by Joseph Smith on Aug. 27, 1843, in Nauvoo, Illinois; reported by Willard Richards and William Clayton.
20. *History of the Church,* 6:479; from a discourse given by Joseph Smith on June 16, 1844, in Nauvoo, Illinois; reported by Thomas Bullock; see also appendix, page 562, item 3.
21. *History of the Church,* 5:516–17; from a discourse given by Joseph Smith on July 23, 1843, in Nauvoo, Illinois; reported by Willard Richards; see also appendix, page 562, item 3.
22. *History of the Church,* 5:411; from instructions given by Joseph Smith on May 27, 1843, in Nauvoo, Illinois; reported by Wilford Woodruff.
23. *History of the Church,* 6:304–5, 312, 317; paragraph divisions altered; from a discourse given by Joseph Smith on Apr. 7, 1844, in Nauvoo, Illinois; reported by Wilford Woodruff, Willard Richards, Thomas Bullock, and William Clayton; see also appendix, page 562, item 3.

On the afternoon of June 27, 1844, a mob stormed the jail in Carthage, Illinois, killing the Prophet Joseph Smith and Hyrum Smith.

C H A P T E R 4 6

The Martyrdom: The Prophet Seals His Testimony with His Blood

"He lived great, and he died great in the eyes of God and his people."

From the Life of Joseph Smith

The winter and spring of 1843–44 was a time of great tension in Nauvoo, as Joseph Smith's enemies increased their efforts to destroy him and the Church. Knowing his mortal ministry would soon come to a close, the Prophet met frequently with members of the Quorum of the Twelve Apostles to instruct them and to give them the priesthood keys necessary to govern the Church. These preparations culminated in a meeting with the Apostles and a few other close associates in March 1844. In this extraordinary council, the Prophet charged the Twelve to govern the Church after his death, explaining that he had conferred upon them all the ordinances, authority, and keys necessary to do so. "I roll the burden and responsibility of leading this church off from my shoulders on to yours," he declared. "Now, round up your shoulders and stand under it like men; for the Lord is going to let me rest awhile."[1]

On June 10, 1844, Joseph Smith, who was the mayor of Nauvoo, and the Nauvoo city council ordered the destruction of the *Nauvoo Expositor* and the press on which it was printed. The *Nauvoo Expositor* was an anti-Mormon newspaper that slandered the Prophet and other Saints and called for the repeal of the Nauvoo Charter. City officials feared that this publication would lead to mob action. As a result of the action by the mayor and city council, Illinois authorities brought an unfounded charge of riot against the Prophet, his brother Hyrum, and other Nauvoo city officials. The governor of Illinois, Thomas Ford, ordered the men to stand trial in Carthage, Illinois, the county seat, and promised them protection. Joseph knew that if he went to Carthage, his life would be in great danger from the mobs who were threatening him.

Believing that the mobs wanted only them, Joseph and Hyrum decided to leave for the West to preserve their lives. On June 23, they crossed the Mississippi River, but later that day, brethren from Nauvoo found the Prophet and told him that troops would invade the city if he did not surrender to the authorities in Carthage. This the Prophet agreed to do, hoping to appease both government officials and the mobs. On June 24, Joseph and Hyrum Smith bade farewell to their families and rode with other Nauvoo city officials toward Carthage, voluntarily surrendering themselves to county officials in Carthage the next day. After the brothers had been released on bail for the initial charge, they were falsely charged with treason against the state of Illinois, arrested, and imprisoned in Carthage Jail to await a hearing. Elders John Taylor and Willard Richards, the only members of the Twelve who were not then serving missions, voluntarily joined them.

On the afternoon of June 27, 1844, the little group of brethren sat silent and disconsolate in the jail. One of the men asked Elder Taylor, who had a rich tenor voice, to sing to them. Soon his voice was raised: "A poor wayfaring Man of grief hath often crossed me on my way, who sued so humbly for relief that I could never answer nay."[2] Elder Taylor recollected that the hymn "was very much in accordance with our feelings at the time for our spirits were all depressed, dull and gloomy."[3]

Shortly after five o'clock in the afternoon, a large group of attackers stormed the jail, firing their guns at the men inside. Within a few minutes, the foul deed was done. Hyrum Smith was shot first and died almost immediately. Elder Richards miraculously received only a superficial wound; and Elder Taylor, though severely wounded, survived and later became the third President of the Church. The Prophet Joseph ran to the window and was fatally shot. The Prophet of the Restoration and his brother Hyrum had sealed their testimonies with their blood.

Teachings of Joseph Smith

God protected Joseph Smith until his earthly mission was complete.

In August 1842, Joseph Smith said: "My feelings at the present time are that, inasmuch as the Lord Almighty has preserved me until today, He will continue to preserve me, by the united faith and prayers of the Saints, until I have fully accomplished my mission in this life, and so firmly established the dispensation of the fullness of the priesthood in the last days, that all the powers of earth and hell can never prevail against it."[4]

In October 1843, the Prophet said: "I defy all the world to destroy the work of God; and I prophesy they never will have power to kill me till my work is accomplished, and I am ready to die."[5]

In May 1844, the Prophet said: "God will always protect me until my mission is fulfilled."[6]

In June 1844, the Prophet said: "I do not regard my own life. I am ready to be offered a sacrifice for this people; for what can our enemies do? Only kill the body, and their power is then at an end. Stand firm, my friends; never flinch. Do not seek to save your lives, for he that is afraid to die for the truth, will lose eternal life. Hold out to the end, and we shall be resurrected and become like Gods, and reign in celestial kingdoms, principalities, and eternal dominions."[7]

Early on June 27, 1844, in Carthage Jail, Joseph Smith wrote in a hasty letter to Emma Smith: "I am very much resigned to my lot, knowing I am justified and have done the best that could be done. Give my love to the children and all my friends . . . ; and as for treason, I know that I have not committed any, and they cannot prove one appearance of anything of the kind, so you need not have any fears that any harm can happen to us on that score. May God bless you all. Amen."[8]

Before his death, Joseph Smith conferred upon the Twelve Apostles every priesthood key and power that the Lord had sealed upon him.

Wilford Woodruff, the fourth President of the Church, recalled: "[Joseph Smith] spent the last winter of his life, some three or four months, with the quorum of the Twelve teaching them. It was not merely a few hours ministering to them the ordinances of the gospel; but he spent day after day, week after week and month after month, teaching them and a few others the things of the kingdom of God."[9]

Wilford Woodruff said about Joseph Smith's meeting with the Apostles in March 1844: "I remember the last speech that [Joseph Smith] ever gave us before his death. . . . He stood upon his feet some three hours. The room was filled as with consuming fire, his face was as clear as amber, and he was clothed upon by the power of God. He laid before us our duty. He laid before us the fullness of this great work of God; and in his remarks to us he said: 'I have had sealed upon my head every key, every power, every principle of life and salvation that God has ever given to any man who ever lived upon the face of the earth. And these principles and this Priesthood and power belong to this great and last dispensation which the God of Heaven has set His hand to establish in the earth. Now,' said he, addressing the Twelve, 'I have sealed upon your heads every key, every power, and every principle which the Lord has sealed upon my head.' And continuing, he said, 'I have lived so long—up to the present time—I have been in the midst of this people and in the great work and labor of redemption. I have desired to live to see this Temple built. But I shall never live to see it completed; but you will—you will.' . . .

"After addressing us in this manner he said: 'I tell you, the burden of this kingdom now rests upon your shoulders; you have got to bear it off in all the world, and if you don't do it you will be damned.' "[10]

Members of the Quorum of the Twelve recorded: "We, the [Twelve], . . . were present at a council in the latter part of the month of March last [1844], held in the City of Nauvoo. . . .

Wilford Woodruff recalled that the Prophet Joseph Smith "spent the last winter of his life, some three or four months, with the quorum of the Twelve teaching them. . . . He spent day after day, week after week and month after month."

"In this council, Joseph Smith seemed somewhat depressed in spirit, and took the liberty to open his heart to us . . . : 'Brethren, the Lord bids me hasten the work in which we are engaged. . . . Some important scene is near to take place. It may be that my enemies will kill me. And in case they should, and the keys and power which rest on me not be imparted to you, they will be lost from the earth. But if I can only succeed in placing them upon your heads, then let me fall a victim to murderous hands if God will suffer it, and I can go with all pleasure and satisfaction, knowing that my work is done, and the foundation laid on which the kingdom of God is to be reared in this dispensation of the fulness of times.

" 'Upon the shoulders of the Twelve must the responsibility of leading this church henceforth rest until you shall appoint others to succeed you. Your enemies cannot kill you all at once, and should any of you be killed, you can lay your hands upon others and fill up your quorum. Thus can this power and these keys be perpetuated in the earth.' . . .

"Never shall we forget his feelings or his words on this occasion. After he had thus spoken, he continued to walk the floor, saying: 'Since I have rolled the burden off from my shoulders, I feel as light as a cork. I feel that I am free. I thank my God for this deliverance.' "[11]

Parley P. Pratt, a member of the Quorum of the Twelve, wrote: "This great and good man was led, before his death, to call the Twelve together, from time to time, and to instruct them in all things pertaining to the kingdom, ordinances, and government of God. He often observed that he was laying the foundation, but it would remain for the Twelve to complete the building. Said he, 'I know not why; but for some reason I am constrained to hasten my preparations, and to confer upon the Twelve all the ordinances, keys, covenants, endowments, and sealing ordinances of the priesthood, and so set before them a pattern in all things pertaining to the sanctuary [the temple] and the endowment therein.'

"Having done this, he rejoiced exceedingly; for, said he, the Lord is about to lay the burden on your shoulders and let me rest awhile; and if they kill me, continued he, the kingdom of God will roll on, as I have now finished the work which was laid upon me, by committing to you all things for the building up of the kingdom according to the heavenly vision, and the pattern shown me from heaven."[12]

Brigham Young, the second President of the Church, taught: "Joseph conferred upon our heads all the keys and powers belonging to the Apostleship which he himself held before he was taken away, and no man or set of men can get between Joseph and the Twelve in this world or in the world to come.

How often has Joseph said to the Twelve, 'I have laid the foundation and you must build thereon, for upon your shoulders the kingdom rests.' "[13]

The Prophet Joseph Smith and his brother Hyrum lived great and died great for their testimonies of the gospel.

As recorded in Doctrine and Covenants 135:1–6, John Taylor, while serving as a member of the Quorum of the Twelve, wrote: "To seal the testimony of this book and the Book of Mormon, we announce the martyrdom of Joseph Smith the Prophet, and Hyrum Smith the Patriarch. They were shot in Carthage jail, on the 27th of June, 1844, about five o'clock p.m., by an armed mob—painted black—of from 150 to 200 persons. Hyrum was shot first and fell calmly, exclaiming: *I am a dead man!* Joseph leaped from the window, and was shot dead in the attempt, exclaiming: *O Lord my God!* They were both shot after they were dead, in a brutal manner, and both received four balls.

"John Taylor and Willard Richards, two of the Twelve, were the only persons in the room at the time; the former was wounded in a savage manner with four balls, but has since recovered; the latter, through the providence of God, escaped, without even a hole in his robe.

"Joseph Smith, the Prophet and Seer of the Lord, has done more, save Jesus only, for the salvation of men in this world, than any other man that ever lived in it. In the short space of twenty years, he has brought forth the Book of Mormon, which he translated by the gift and power of God, and has been the means of publishing it on two continents; has sent the fulness of the everlasting gospel, which it contained, to the four quarters of the earth; has brought forth the revelations and commandments which compose this book of Doctrine and Covenants, and many other wise documents and instructions for the benefit of the children of men; gathered many thousands of the Latter-day Saints, founded a great city, and left a fame and name that cannot be slain. He lived great, and he died great in the eyes of God and his people; and like most of the Lord's anointed in ancient times, has sealed his mission and his works with his own blood; and so has his brother Hyrum. In life they were not divided, and in death they were not separated!

"When Joseph went to Carthage to deliver himself up to the pretended requirements of the law, two or three days previous to his assassination, he said: 'I am going like a lamb to the slaughter; but I am calm as a summer's morning; I have a conscience void of offense towards God, and towards all men. I shall die innocent, and it shall yet be said of me—he was murdered in cold blood.'—The same morning, after Hyrum had made ready to go—shall it be said to the slaughter? yes, for so it was—he read the following paragraph, near the close of the twelfth chapter of Ether, in the Book of Mormon, and turned down the leaf upon it:

"And it came to pass that I prayed unto the Lord that he would give unto the Gentiles grace, that they might have charity. And it came to pass that the Lord said unto me: If they have not charity it mattereth not unto thee, thou hast been faithful; wherefore thy garments shall be made clean. And because thou hast seen thy weakness, thou shalt be made strong, even unto the sitting down in the place which I have prepared in the mansions of my Father. And now I . . . bid farewell unto the Gentiles; yea, and also unto my brethren whom I love, until we shall meet before the judgment-seat of Christ, where all men shall know that my garments are not spotted with your blood. [Ether 12:36–38.] The testators are now dead, and their testament is in force.

"Hyrum Smith was forty-four years old in February, 1844, and Joseph Smith was thirty-eight in December, 1843; and henceforward their names will be classed among the martyrs of religion; and the reader in every nation will be reminded that the Book of Mormon, and this book of Doctrine and Covenants of the church, cost the best blood of the nineteenth century to bring them forth for the salvation of a ruined world; and that if the fire can scathe a green tree for the glory of God, how easy it will burn up the dry trees to purify the vineyard of corruption. They lived for glory; they died for glory; and glory is their eternal reward. From age to age shall their names go down to posterity as gems for the sanctified."[14]

Joseph Smith fulfilled his earthly mission and sealed his testimony with his blood.

Brigham Young declared: "Though the enemy had power to kill our prophet, that is, kill his body, did he not accomplish all that was in his heart to accomplish in his day? He did, to my certain knowledge."[15]

Brigham Young

Brigham Young also taught: "Who delivered Joseph Smith from the hands of his enemies to the day of his death? It was God; though he was brought to the brink of death time and time again, so that to all human appearance there could be no prospect of his being saved. When he was in jail in Missouri, and no person expected that he would ever escape from their hands, I had the faith of Abraham, and told the Brethren as the Lord God lived, he shall come out of their hands. Though he had prophesied that he would not live to be 40 years of age, yet we all cherished hopes that that would be a false prophecy, and we should keep him forever with us. We thought our faith would outreach it, but we were mistaken—he at last fell a martyr to his religion. I said it is all right; now the testimony is in full force; he has sealed it with his blood."[16]

Wilford Woodruff testified: "I used to have peculiar feelings about his death and the way in which his life was taken. I felt that if . . . Joseph could have had his desire, he would have pioneered the way to the Rocky Mountains. But since then I have been fully reconciled to the fact that it was according to the programme, that it was required of him, as the head of this dispensation, that he should seal his testimony with his blood, and go hence to the spirit world, holding the keys of this dispensation, to open up the mission that is now being performed by way of preaching the Gospel to the 'spirits in prison.' "[17]

Joseph F. Smith, the sixth President of the Church, taught: "What does the martyrdom [of Joseph and Hyrum Smith] teach us? The great lesson that 'where a testament is, there must also of necessity be the death of the testator' (Heb. 9:16) to make it of force. Moreover, that the blood of martyrs is indeed the seed of the Church. The Lord permitted the sacrifice that the testimony of those virtuous and righteous men should stand as a witness against a perverse and unrighteous world. Then, again, they were examples of the wonderful love of which the Redeemer speaks: 'Greater love hath no man than this, that a man lay down his life for his friends.' (John 15:13.) This wonderful love they manifested to the Saints and to the world; for both realized and expressed their conviction, before starting on the journey to Carthage, that they were going to their death. . . . Their courage, their faith, their love for the people were without bounds, and they gave all that they had for their people. Such devotion and love left no doubt in the minds of those who enjoyed the companionship of the Holy Spirit that these good men and true, were indeed the authorized servants of the Lord.

"This martyrdom has always been an inspiration to the people of the Lord. It has helped them in their individual trials; has given them courage to pursue a course in righteousness and to know and to live the truth, and must ever be held in sacred memory by the Latter-day Saints who have learned the great truths that God revealed through His servant, Joseph Smith."[18]

George Albert Smith

George Albert Smith, the eighth President of the Church, declared: "Joseph Smith performed his mission; and when the time came that he was face to face with death, he said, 'I am going like a lamb to the slaughter, but I am calm as a summer morning. I have a conscience void of offense toward God and toward all men. If they take my life, I shall die an innocent man, and my blood shall cry from the ground for vengeance, and it shall yet be said of me, "He was murdered in cold blood." ' [See D&C 135:4.] He was not afraid to stand before the pleasing bar of our Father in heaven and answer for the deeds done in the body. He was not afraid to meet the charge that had been made against him, that he was deceiving the people and dealing unjustly with them. He was not afraid of the result of his life's mission, and of the final triumph of the work which he knew was of divine origin, and for which he gave his life."[19]

Gordon B. Hinckley, the fifteenth President of the Church, testified: "So certain was [Joseph Smith] of the cause he led, so sure of his divinely given calling, that he placed them above the value of his own life. With prescient knowledge of his forthcoming death, he surrendered himself to those who would deliver him defenseless into the hands of a mob. He sealed his testimony with his life's blood."[20]

Suggestions for Study and Teaching

Consider these ideas as you study the chapter or as you prepare to teach. For additional help, see pages vii–xii.

- Shortly before Joseph and Hyrum Smith were killed, Elder John Taylor sang "A Poor Wayfaring Man of Grief" (page 530). Read or sing the words of this hymn (*Hymns,* no. 29), and think about how they relate to the life of the Prophet Joseph Smith. Why was this a fitting hymn under the circumstances?
- Review the statements testifying that Joseph Smith conferred priesthood keys on the Twelve Apostles (pages 532–35). Why do you think the Apostles felt it was important to testify of these experiences? What is your testimony of succession in the Presidency of the Church?
- Study John Taylor's account of the martyrdom of Joseph and Hyrum Smith (pages 535–36). How might you defend the statement that Joseph Smith "has done more, save Jesus only, for the salvation of men in this world, than any other man that ever lived in it"? Before going to Carthage Jail, Hyrum read Ether 12:36–38 and turned down the page. In what ways did this passage apply to Joseph and Hyrum? What are your feelings as you think about the sacrifices Joseph and Hyrum Smith made for their testimonies of Jesus Christ?

- Read the testimonies of latter-day prophets on pages 537–39. What words of gratitude and testimony can you add to theirs?

Related Scriptures: Hebrews 9:16–17; D&C 5:21–22; 98:13–14; 112:30–33; 136:37–40

Notes

1. Quoted in declaration of the Twelve Apostles (undated draft), reporting Mar. 1844 meeting; in Brigham Young, Office Files 1832–78, Church Archives, The Church of Jesus Christ of Latter-day Saints, Salt Lake City, Utah.
2. "A Poor Wayfaring Man of Grief," *Hymns,* no. 29.
3. John Taylor, quoted in *History of the Church,* 7:101; from John Taylor, "The Martyrdom of Joseph Smith," in Historian's Office, History of the Church ca. 1840s–1880, p. 47, Church Archives.
4. *History of the Church,* 5:139–40; from a discourse given by Joseph Smith on Aug. 31, 1842, in Nauvoo, Illinois; reported by Eliza R. Snow; see also appendix, page 562, item 3.
5. *History of the Church,* 6:58; from a discourse given by Joseph Smith on Oct. 15, 1843, in Nauvoo, Illinois; reported by Willard Richards; see also appendix, page 562, item 3.
6. *History of the Church,* 6:365; from a discourse given by Joseph Smith on May 12, 1844, in Nauvoo, Illinois; reported by Thomas Bullock.
7. *History of the Church,* 6:500; from a discourse given by Joseph Smith on June 18, 1844, in Nauvoo, Illinois. The compilers of *History of the Church* combined verbal reports by several eyewitnesses into a single account of the discourse.
8. Letter from Joseph Smith to Emma Smith, June 27, 1844, Carthage Jail, Carthage, Illinois; Community of Christ Archives, Independence, Missouri; copy in Church Archives.
9. Wilford Woodruff, *Deseret News: Semi-Weekly,* Dec. 21, 1869, p. 2.
10. Wilford Woodruff, *Deseret Semi-Weekly News,* Mar. 15, 1892, p. 2; punctuation modernized.
11. Declaration of the Twelve Apostles (undated draft), reporting Mar. 1844 meeting; in Brigham Young, Office Files 1832–78, Church Archives.
12. Parley P. Pratt, "Proclamation to The Church of Jesus Christ of Latter-day Saints," *Millennial Star,* Mar. 1845, p. 151.
13. Brigham Young, quoted in *History of the Church,* 7:230; paragraph divisions altered; from a discourse given by Brigham Young on Aug. 7, 1844, in Nauvoo, Illinois.
14. Doctrine and Covenants 135:1–6.
15. Brigham Young, *Deseret News,* Apr. 30, 1853, p. 46; italics deleted.
16. Brigham Young, discourse given on Aug. 1, 1852, in Salt Lake City, Utah; in Historian's Office, Reports of Speeches ca. 1845–85, Church Archives.
17. Wilford Woodruff, *Deseret News,* Mar. 28, 1883, p. 146.
18. Joseph F. Smith, "The Martyrdom," *Juvenile Instructor,* June 1916, p. 381; punctuation modernized; paragraph divisions altered.
19. George Albert Smith, in Conference Report, Apr. 1904, p. 64; spelling modernized.
20. Gordon B. Hinckley, in Conference Report, Oct. 1981, pp. 6–7; or *Ensign,* Nov. 1981, p. 7.

CHAPTER 47

"Praise to the Man": Latter-day Prophets Bear Witness of the Prophet Joseph Smith

"The Prophet Joseph Smith . . . was called of God, by the voice of God Himself, to open up the dispensation of the Gospel to the world for the last time." (Joseph F. Smith)

From the Life of Joseph Smith

Following the death of the Prophet Joseph Smith and his brother Hyrum, the members of the Quorum of the Twelve who had been on missionary journeys in the United States returned as quickly as possible to Nauvoo. The members of the Twelve called a meeting of the Saints for August 8, 1844, at which Brigham Young, the President of the Quorum of the Twelve, spoke. As he did so, an extraordinary event occurred that was witnessed by many Saints. President Young was miraculously made to appear and sound like Joseph Smith. "If Joseph had risen from the dead and again spoken in their hearing," George Q. Cannon recalled, "the effect could not have been more startling than it was to many present at that meeting. It was the voice of Joseph himself; and not only was it the voice of Joseph which was heard; but it seemed in the eyes of the people as though it was the very person of Joseph which stood before them. A more wonderful and miraculous event than was wrought that day in the presence of that congregation we never heard of. The Lord gave His people a testimony that left no room for doubt as to who was the man He had chosen to lead them."[1]

At the conclusion of this meeting, the Saints voted to have the Twelve preside over them. A little over three years later, in December 1847, the First Presidency was again organized, with Brigham Young sustained as the President of the Church.

"It was decreed in the councils of eternity," Brigham Young declared, "long before the foundations of the earth were laid, that [Joseph Smith] should be the man, in the last dispensation of this world, to bring forth the word of God to the people."

Since the time of Brigham Young, each of the prophets who has presided over the Church has testified of the remarkable mission of the Prophet Joseph Smith. Joseph Smith was chosen in the Council in Heaven to be the great prophet and seer of the latter days. His mission was so important that it was foretold by ancient prophets, including the Old Testament prophet Joseph, who was sold into Egypt. Joseph of Egypt was himself a seer, and he prophesied at length about Joseph Smith:

"A seer shall the Lord my God raise up, who shall be a choice seer unto the fruit of my loins. . . . And his name shall be called after me; and it shall be after the name of his father. And he shall be like unto me; for the thing, which the Lord shall bring forth by his hand, by the power of the Lord shall bring my people unto salvation" (2 Nephi 3:6, 15; see also 2 Nephi 3:6–22).[2]

In December 1834, Joseph Smith Sr. gave the Prophet Joseph a blessing, confirming that he was the seer of whom Joseph of old had prophesied: "I bless thee with the blessings of thy fathers Abraham, Isaac and Jacob; and even the blessings of thy father Joseph, the son of Jacob. Behold, he looked after his posterity in the last days . . . ; he sought diligently to know from whence the son should come who should bring forth the word of the Lord, by which they might be enlightened and brought back to the true fold, and his eyes beheld thee, my son; his heart rejoiced and his soul was satisfied, and he said, . . . 'From among my seed, scattered with the Gentiles, shall a choice seer arise . . . , whose heart shall meditate great wisdom, whose intelligence shall circumscribe and comprehend the deep things of God, and whose mouth shall utter the law of the just.' . . . Thou shalt hold the keys of this ministry, even the presidency of this church, both in time and in eternity."[3]

Through Joseph Smith, the choice seer of the latter days, the doctrines and saving ordinances of the gospel were revealed, and the true Church of Jesus Christ was once again established on the earth. The testimonies of ancient and modern prophets join together to proclaim that Joseph Smith was the instrument through whom God restored the fulness of the gospel for the blessing of "the whole human family, from eternity to eternity."[4]

Testimonies of Latter-day Prophets

Joseph Smith was foreordained to his prophetic calling.

President Brigham Young

President Brigham Young: "It was decreed in the councils of eternity, long before the foundations of the earth were laid, that [Joseph Smith] should be the man, in the last dispensation of this world, to bring forth the word of God to the people and receive the fullness of the keys and power of the Priesthood of the Son of God. The Lord had his eye upon him, and upon his father, and upon his father's father, and upon their progenitors clear back to Abraham, and from Abraham to the flood, from the flood to Enoch and from Enoch to Adam. He has watched that family and that blood as it has circulated from its fountain to the birth of that man. [Joseph Smith] was foreordained in eternity to preside over this last dispensation."[5]

President Joseph Fielding Smith: "Joseph Smith was chosen to stand at the head of the work of the Lord in the last days, and his work was assigned to him through the fore-knowledge of our Eternal Father in the eternities before he was born. He came in the spirit of Elias to prepare the way for the coming of our Lord. No prophet since the days of Adam, save, of course, our Redeemer, has been given a greater mission."[6]

President Ezra Taft Benson

President Ezra Taft Benson: "To get a vision of the magnitude of the Prophet's earthly mission we must view it in the light of eternity. He was among 'the noble and great ones' whom Abraham described as follows:

" 'Now the Lord had shown unto me, Abraham, the intelligences that were organized before the world was; and among all these there were many of the noble and great ones; and God saw these souls that they were good, and he stood in the midst of them, and he said: These I will make my rulers; for he stood among those that were spirits, and he saw that they were good; and he said unto me: Abraham, thou art one of them; thou wast chosen before thou wast born.' (Abraham 3:22–23.)

"So it was with Joseph Smith. He too was there. He too sat in council with the noble and great ones. Occupying a prominent place of honor and distinction he unquestionably helped in the planning and execution of the great work of the Lord to 'bring to pass the immortality and eternal life of man,' the salvation of all our Father's children [Moses 1:39]. His mission had had, and was to have, impact on all who had come to earth; all who then dwelt on earth and the millions yet unborn. . . .

"The Prophet Joseph Smith was not only 'one of the noble and great ones,' but he gave and continues to give attention to important matters here on the earth even today from the realms above. For in the eyes of the Lord . . . it is all one great eternal program in which the Prophet Joseph plays an important role—all through the eternal priesthood and authority of God."[7]

Joseph Smith's First Vision is a fundamental part of our individual testimonies.

President Joseph F. Smith: "The greatest event that has ever occurred in the world since the resurrection of the Son of God from the tomb, and his ascension on high, was the coming of the Father and of the Son to that boy Joseph Smith, to prepare the way for the laying of the foundation of [God's] kingdom—not the kingdom of man—never more to cease nor to be overturned.

"Having accepted this truth, I find it easy to accept of every other truth that he enunciated and declared during his mission . . . in the world. He never taught a doctrine that was not true. He never practiced a doctrine that he was not commanded to practice. He never advocated error. He was not deceived. He saw; he heard; he did as he was commanded to do; and, therefore, God is responsible for the work accomplished by Joseph Smith—not Joseph Smith. The Lord is responsible for it, and not man."[8]

President Heber J. Grant

President Heber J. Grant: "Either Joseph Smith did see God and did converse with Him, and God Himself did introduce Jesus Christ to the boy Joseph Smith, and Jesus Christ did tell Joseph Smith that he would be the instrument in the hands of God of establishing again upon the earth the true Gospel of Jesus Christ—or Mormonism, so-called, is a myth. And Mormonism is not a myth! It is the power of God unto salvation; it is the Church of Jesus Christ, established under His direction, and all the disbelief of the world cannot change the fundamental facts connected with the Church of Jesus Christ of Latter-day Saints."[9]

President Howard W. Hunter

President Howard W. Hunter: "I am grateful for my membership in the Church; and my testimony of its divinity hinges upon the simple story of the lad under the trees kneeling and receiving heavenly visitors—not one God, but two separate, individual personages, the Father and the Son, revealing again to the earth the personages of the God-head. My faith and testimony hinge upon this simple story, for if it is not true, Mormonism falls. If it is true—and I bear witness that it is—it is one of the greatest single events in all history."[10]

President David O. McKay: "The appearing of the Father and the Son to Joseph Smith is the foundation of this Church. Therein lies the secret of its strength and vitality. This is true, and I bear witness to it. That one revelation answers all the queries of science regarding God and His divine personality. Don't you see what that means? What God is, is answered. His relation to His children is clear. His interest in humanity through authority delegated to man is apparent. The future of the work is assured. These and other glorious truths are clarified by that glorious First Vision."[11]

President Ezra Taft Benson: "The First Vision of the Prophet Joseph Smith is bedrock theology to the Church. The adversary knows this and has attacked Joseph Smith's credibility from the day he announced the visitation of the Father and the Son. . . . You should always bear testimony to the truth of the First Vision. Joseph Smith did see the Father and the Son. They conversed with him as he said they did. It is the most glorious event since the resurrection of our Lord. Any leader who, without reservation, cannot declare his testimony that God and Jesus Christ appeared to Joseph Smith can never be a true leader, a true shepherd. If we do not accept this truth, . . . if we have not received a witness about this great revelation, we cannot inspire faith in those whom we lead."[12]

President George Albert Smith

President George Albert Smith: "When the boy prophet, in the woods of Palmyra, saw the Father and the Son, and realized that they were indeed personages, that they could hear and reply to what he said, it began a new era in this world, and laid a foundation for the faith of the children of men. They could now pray to our Father in heaven and realize that he could hear and answer their prayers, that there was a connection between the heavens and the earth."[13]

The Prophet Joseph Smith was taught by God and angels.

President John Taylor

President John Taylor: "Who was Joseph Smith? The Book of Mormon tells us he was of the seed of Joseph that was sold into Egypt, and hence he was selected as Abraham was to fulfil a work upon the earth. God chose this young man. He was ignorant of letters as the world has it, but the most profoundly learned and intelligent man that I ever met in my life, and I have traveled hundreds of thousands of miles, been on different continents and mingled among all classes and creeds of people, yet I have never met a man so intelligent as he was. And where did he get his intelligence from? Not from books; not from the logic or science or philosophy of the day, but he obtained it through the revelations of God made known to him through the medium of the everlasting gospel."[14]

President Wilford Woodruff

President Wilford Woodruff: "I have never read anywhere, that I know of, of the same power manifested in any dispensation to the children of men, which was manifested to the Prophet of God in the organization of this Church, when the Father and the Son both appeared to the Prophet Joseph in answer to his prayer, and when the Father said, 'This is My Beloved Son; behold Him; hear ye Him.' This was an important revelation, which has never been manifested in the same manner in any dispensation of the world, that God has given concerning His work. So in its organization, the Prophet of God was administered to by the angels of heaven. They were his teachers, they were his instructors, and all that he did, and all that he performed from the commencement, from that day to the day of his martyrdom, was by the revelation of Jesus Christ."[15]

President Lorenzo Snow

President Lorenzo Snow: "Joseph Smith, whom God chose to establish this work, was poor and uneducated, and belonged to no popular denomination of Christians. He was a mere boy, honest, full of integrity. . . . Like Moses he felt incompetent and unqualified for the task, to stand forth as a religious reformer, in a position the most unpopular, to battle against opinions and creeds which had stood for ages, having had the sanction of men, the most profound in theological obedience; but God had called him to deliver the poor and honest-hearted of all nations from their spiritual and temporal thraldom [bondage]. And God promised him that whosoever should receive and obey his message, and whosoever would receive baptism for remission of sins, with honesty of purpose, should receive divine manifestations, should receive the Holy Ghost, should receive the same gospel and blessings as were promised and obtained through the gospel, as preached by the ancient apostles, and this message, this promise, was to be in force wherever and to whomsoever it should be carried by the Elders, God's authorized messengers. So said Joseph Smith, the uneducated, the unsophisticated, the plain, simple, honest boy."[16]

President Harold B. Lee

President Harold B. Lee: "Joseph Smith, the young man not schooled in the theologies of the day, not schooled in the high schools of learning of his day, . . . [was] one who could be submissive to the teachings and whisperings of the Spirit. Joseph Smith could not have established this Church. He could not have brought forth the work of the Lord, the Book of Mormon. They may scoff at the Prophet Joseph Smith as a man. They may question how this Church began, but here the thing stands as a monument—the Book of Mormon itself. Joseph, the man, could not have done this, but Joseph, actuated by the power of Almighty God, could and did perform the miraculous service of bringing forth the kingdom out of obscurity in the restored gospel of Jesus Christ."[17]

President David O. McKay

President David O. McKay: "It is of Joseph Smith, not only as a great man, but as an inspired servant of the Lord that I desire to speak on this occasion. Indeed, Joseph Smith's greatness *consists* in divine inspiration. . . .

" 'How knoweth this man letters, having never learned?' questioned the Jews as they marveled at the wisdom of Jesus [John 7:15]. So may we repeat the question regarding Joseph Smith, as we consider his outstanding accomplishments during the brief span of [fourteen] years between the organization of the Church and his martyrdom; as we contemplate the perfect harmony of the Restored Gospel with that of the primitive Church established by Jesus and his Apostles; as we note his penetrating insight into principles and doctrines; and as we see the incomparable plan and efficiency of the Church, established by the inspiration of the Christ whose name it bears. The answer to the question 'Whence hath this man wisdom?' is given in the stirring stanza:

"Praise to the man who communed with Jehovah!
Jesus anointed that Prophet and Seer.
Blessed to open the last dispensation,
Kings shall extol him, and nations revere."[18]

President Howard W. Hunter: "We praise [Joseph Smith] for his capacity to commune not only with Jehovah but also with other personages of heaven. So many visited, gave keys, and tutored that 'choice seer' raised up in the latter days. . . . We praise Joseph Smith, too, for his diligence and capacity to translate and to receive hundreds of pages of revealed scripture. He was the revealing conduit. Through him, it has been estimated, more marvelous pages of scripture passed than through any other human in history."[19]

The Prophet Joseph Smith was called of God to open the final dispensation and restore the fulness of the gospel.

President Spencer W. Kimball

President Spencer W. Kimball: "I bear witness to the world today that more than a century and a half ago the iron ceiling was shattered; the heavens were once again opened, and since that time revelations have been continuous.

"That new day dawned when [a] soul with passionate yearning prayed for divine guidance. A spot of hidden solitude was found, knees were bent, a heart was humbled, pleadings were voiced, and a light brighter than the noonday sun illuminated the world—the curtain never to be closed again.

"A young lad . . . , Joseph Smith, of incomparable faith, broke the spell, shattered the 'heavens of iron' and reestablished communication. Heaven kissed the earth, light dissipated the darkness, and God again spoke to man, revealing anew 'his secret unto his servants the prophets.' (Amos 3:7.) A new prophet was in the land and through him God set up his kingdom, never to be destroyed nor left to another people—a kingdom that will stand forever.

"The foreverness of this kingdom and the revelations which it brought into existence are absolute realities. Never again will the sun go down; never again will all men prove totally unworthy of communication with their Maker. Never again will God be hidden from his children on the earth. Revelation is here to remain."[20]

President Gordon B. Hinckley

President Gordon B. Hinckley: "The story of Joseph's life is the story of a miracle. He was born in poverty. He was reared in adversity. He was driven from place to place, falsely accused, and illegally imprisoned. He was murdered at the age of 38. Yet in the brief space of 20 years preceding his death, he accomplished what none other has accomplished in an entire lifetime. He translated and published the Book of Mormon, a volume which has since been retranslated into scores of languages and which is accepted by millions across the earth as the word of God. The revelations he received and other writings he produced are likewise scripture to these millions. The total in book pages constitutes approximately twice the volume of the entire New Testament of the Bible, and it all came through one man in the space of a few years. In this same period he established an organization which . . . has withstood every adversity and challenge and is as effective today in governing a worldwide membership . . . as it was in governing a membership of 300 in 1830. There are those doubters who have strained to explain this remarkable organization as the product of the times in which he lived. That organization, I submit, was as peculiar, as unique, and as remarkable then as it is today. It was not the product of the times. It came as a revelation from God. . . .

"Within the space of that 20 years preceding his death, Joseph Smith set in motion a program for carrying the gospel to the nations of the earth. I marvel at the boldness with which he moved. Even in the infant days of the Church, in times of dark adversity, men were called to leave homes and families, to cross the sea, to proclaim the Restoration of the gospel of Jesus Christ. The Prophet's mind, his vision encompassed the entire earth.

"For our general conference meetings twice each year, members gather in North, Central, and South America; in the British Isles and Africa; in the nations of Europe; in the islands and continents of the Pacific; and in the ancient lands of Asia. These are the flowering of the vision of Joseph Smith, the prophet of God. He was indeed a mighty seer who saw this day and greater days yet to come as the work of the Lord moves over the earth."[21]

President Joseph F. Smith

President Joseph F. Smith: "Whatever else the Prophet Joseph Smith may have done or may have been, we must not forget the fact that he was the man out of the millions of human beings that inhabited this earth at the time—the only man, that was called of God, by the voice of God Himself, to open up the dispensation of the Gospel to the world for the last time; and this is the great thing to bear in mind, that he was called of God to introduce the Gospel to the world, to restore the holy priesthood to the children of men, to organize the Church of Jesus Christ of Latter-day Saints in the world, and to restore all the ordinances of the Gospel, for the salvation not only of the living, but also of the dead, and he was called to this mission by God Himself. . . .

". . . There have been other prophets, and great prophets, too, who have had angels minister to them, and others who have seen the finger of God, and who have been favored more or less; but where is the circumstance, and who is the man unto whom the Father and the Savior have appeared together in person, and declared themselves unto him? Where is that man? Nowhere that history records, except the Prophet Joseph Smith, and that while he was a youth. He was only a youth, comparatively in fact, when he was martyred, being only 38 years of age.

". . . The Prophet Joseph Smith . . . communed with the Father and the Son and spoke with angels, and they visited him, and conferred blessings and gifts and keys of power upon him that were never before bestowed upon any human being other than the Son of God Himself. No man yet that ever lived upon the earth had all the keys of the Gospel and of the dispensations bestowed upon him as were bestowed upon the Prophet Joseph Smith in the temple at Kirtland when he was visited there by the Son of God, by Moses, and by Elias and Elijah, and when the heavens were opened unto him and he received the keys of power and authority by which he could lay the foundation of the work of God, broad and deep, to cover the earth with the knowledge of God, and with His power and glory."[22]

The work of Joseph Smith blesses those who have lived on the earth, those who are now living, and those who will yet be born.

President Joseph F. Smith: "The work in which Joseph Smith was engaged was not confined to this life alone, but it pertains as well to the life to come and to the life that has been. In other words, it relates to those that have lived upon the earth, to those that are living and to those that shall come after us. It is not something which relates to man only while he tabernacles in the flesh, but to the whole human family from eternity to eternity. Consequently, as I have said, Joseph Smith is held in reverence, his name is honored; tens of thousands of people thank God in their heart and from the depths of their souls for the knowledge the Lord has restored to the earth through him, and therefore they speak well of him and bear testimony of his worth. And this is not confined to a village, nor to a State, nor to a nation, but this extends to every nation, kindred, tongue and people where the Gospel, up to the present time, has been preached."[23]

President Joseph Fielding Smith

President Joseph Fielding Smith: "In the same way that I know Jesus is the Christ—and that is by revelation from the Holy Spirit—I know that Joseph Smith is and was and everlastingly shall be a prophet of God.

"I revere and honor his holy name. With his brother, my grandfather, Patriarch Hyrum Smith, he sealed his testimony with his blood in Carthage Jail. And I, for one, want to be an instrument in the Lord's hands of letting the ends of the earth know that salvation is again available because the Lord raised up a mighty seer in this day to reestablish his kingdom on earth.

"In a spirit of testimony and thanksgiving, I close with these inspired words from the Doctrine and Covenants: 'Joseph Smith, the Prophet and Seer of the Lord, has done more, save Jesus only, for the salvation of men in this world, than any other man that ever lived in it.' (D&C 135:3.)"[24]

President Gordon B. Hinckley, speaking in Carthage, Illinois, on June 26, 1994, in honor of the 150th anniversary of the Prophet Joseph Smith's martyrdom: "The glorious work, begun by him who was killed at Carthage, has grown in a miraculous and wonderful way. . . . This marvelous work, which has sprung from the prophetic calling of the boy of Palmyra, has 'come forth out of the wilderness of darkness,' and is shining 'forth fair as the moon, clear as the sun, and terrible as an army with banners,' as the Prophet prayed it would (D&C 109:73). . . .

"We pause in reverence here this evening. We reflect on the miracle of the life begun in the green hills of Vermont and ended here in the jail of Carthage. That life was not long. But the fruits of that life have been something almost beyond comprehension.

"This great cause of The Church of Jesus Christ of Latter-day Saints has been more precious than life itself to thousands upon thousands who have died in its service. Witnesses have gone into the world by the hundreds of thousands to bear testimony of Joseph Smith's calling as a Prophet of God. The holy priesthood restored through him has fallen as a mantle upon uncounted numbers of men of integrity and virtue who have been clothed with this divine power. The Book of Mormon is going across the earth as another testament of the Lord Jesus Christ.

"To quote a truism uttered long ago and in different circumstances, 'the blood of the martyrs has become the seed of the Church.' The testimonies which were sealed here in these very precincts, on this ground where we meet tonight, that hot and sultry day 150 years ago, now nurture the faith of people around the world."[25]

Suggestions for Study and Teaching

Consider these ideas as you study the chapter or as you prepare to teach. For additional help, see pages vii–xii.

- Read the experience described on page 541. Think about how the people might have felt when they received the witness that Brigham Young was to succeed Joseph Smith as the leader of the Church. How can we receive a witness that the Lord has called the President of the Church today?
- Joseph of Egypt and other ancient prophets prophesied of Joseph Smith and his mission (page 543). As shown in this chapter, latter-day prophets have continued to emphasize the importance of Joseph Smith. Why do you think Joseph Smith has received such attention, both before his earthly ministry and after?
- Study the testimonies on pages 544–45 about the foreordination of Joseph Smith. How does our understanding of Joseph Smith's earthly mission change when we "view it in the light of eternity"?
- Read the testimonies on pages 545–47 about the First Vision. What makes this event "the greatest event that has ever occurred

in the world since the resurrection of the Son of God"? How is the First Vision "the foundation of this Church" and "the secret of its strength and vitality"? What has helped you gain a testimony of the First Vision?

- President Joseph F. Smith declared, "God is responsible for the work accomplished by Joseph Smith—not Joseph Smith" (page 545). Why do you think this is an important point to make about Joseph Smith's mission?
- Of Joseph Smith, President John Taylor said, "I have never met a man so intelligent as he was" (page 548). However, President Taylor and other Presidents of the Church have pointed out that Joseph Smith did not have many opportunities for schooling. Why was the Prophet Joseph able to grow so much in his intelligence? (For some examples, see pages 547–50.) As we seek spiritual knowledge, how can we follow Joseph Smith's example?
- Review pages 550–55, noting the truths and ordinances that the Lord restored through Joseph Smith. Think about how your life would be different if you did not know of the restored gospel. Why are you thankful for Joseph Smith and his mission?

Related Scriptures: 2 Nephi 3:6–19; 27:6–26; 3 Nephi 21:9–11; D&C 1:17; 5:9–10; 21:1–6

Notes

1. George Q. Cannon, "Joseph Smith, the Prophet," *Juvenile Instructor,* Oct. 29, 1870, pp. 174–75.
2. Another account of ancient Joseph's prophecies is given in the Joseph Smith Translation of the Bible, Genesis 50:24–36.
3. Joseph Smith Sr., blessing given to Joseph Smith on Dec. 9, 1834, in Kirtland, Ohio; in Patriarchal Blessings 1833–2005, Church Archives, The Church of Jesus Christ of Latter-day Saints, Salt Lake City, Utah.
4. Joseph F. Smith, *Deseret News,* Mar. 7, 1883, p. 98; punctuation modernized.
5. Brigham Young, *Deseret News,* Oct. 26, 1859, p. 266.
6. Joseph Fielding Smith, "The Historical Background of the Prophet Joseph Smith," *Improvement Era,* Dec. 1941, p. 717.
7. Ezra Taft Benson, "Joseph Smith—Man of Destiny," address given on Dec. 3, 1967, in Logan, Utah, pp. 3–4; in *Annual Joseph Smith Memorial Sermons* (no date); punctuation and capitalization modernized; paragraph divisions altered.
8. Joseph F. Smith, *Deseret Evening News,* July 14, 1917, p. 9; punctuation modernized; paragraph divisions altered.
9. Heber J. Grant, "Some Things We Must Believe," *Improvement Era,* Sept. 1938, p. 519.

10. Howard W. Hunter, "Joseph—The Seer," address given on Dec. 15, 1960, in Logan, Utah; in *Annual Joseph Smith Memorial Sermons* (1966), 2:197–98; spelling, punctuation, capitalization, and grammar modernized.
11. David O. McKay, "Joseph Smith—Prophet, Seer, and Revelator," *Improvement Era,* Jan. 1942, p. 54.
12. Ezra Taft Benson, address given on May 20, 1984, in Salt Lake City, Utah, p. 2; Ezra Taft Benson, Addresses 1943–89, Church Archives.
13. George Albert Smith, in Conference Report, Apr. 1917, p. 37.
14. John Taylor, *Deseret News,* June 2, 1880, p. 275.
15. Wilford Woodruff, *Millennial Star,* Apr. 28, 1890, p. 258; capitalization modernized.
16. Lorenzo Snow, *Deseret News,* Apr. 13, 1870, pp. 115–16.
17. Harold B. Lee, *Teachings of Harold B. Lee,* ed. Clyde J. Williams (1996), p. 372.
18. David O. McKay, "The Prophet Joseph Smith—On Doctrine and Organization," address given on Dec. 10, 1944, in Logan, Utah; in *Annual Joseph Smith Memorial Sermons* (1966), 1:9, 14; punctuation and capitalization modernized.
19. Howard W. Hunter, "The Temple of Nauvoo," *Ensign,* Sept. 1994, p. 63; paragraph divisions altered.
20. Spencer W. Kimball, in Conference Report, Apr. 1977, pp. 114–15; or *Ensign,* May 1977, p. 77.
21. Gordon B. Hinckley, "Joseph Smith Jr.—Prophet of God, Mighty Servant," *Ensign,* Dec. 2005, pp. 4–6.
22. Joseph F. Smith, in "Joseph, the Prophet," *Salt Lake Herald Church and Farm Supplement,* Jan. 12, 1895, pp. 210–11; capitalization modernized.
23. Joseph F. Smith, *Deseret News,* Mar. 7, 1883, p. 98; punctuation modernized.
24. Joseph Fielding Smith, "The First Prophet of the Last Dispensation," *Ensign,* Aug. 1971, p. 7.
25. Gordon B. Hinckley, "Joseph, the Seer," *Ensign,* Sept. 1994, p. 71; paragraph divisions altered.

Appendix: Sources Used in This Book

There are a variety of sources from which the teachings of the Prophet Joseph Smith are drawn, including the *History of the Church*. The following material is provided to help you understand these sources.

Sources of the Prophet's Teachings

The teachings of the Prophet Joseph Smith included in this book are drawn from the following types of sources.

Sermons. This book quotes extensively from the discourses given by the Prophet Joseph Smith. The way in which these sermons were recorded is very different from the way sermons were recorded for later Presidents of the Church. Church Presidents who came after Joseph Smith used scribes to record in shorthand their addresses to Church members. When electronic recording devices, such as tape recorders and motion picture film, became available, these were used to record the precise words delivered by Church leaders.

During the lifetime of Joseph Smith, however, shorthand was not in widespread use. Therefore, the sermons he delivered were recorded imprecisely in longhand, generally by scribes, Church leaders, and other Church members. Almost all of Joseph Smith's addresses were given extemporaneously, without prepared texts, so the notes taken by those who listened to him constitute the only record of the discourses. While some lengthy reports of his addresses exist, most are summarizations of the messages delivered by the Prophet. Unfortunately, there is no record for many of the discourses given by Joseph Smith. Of the more than 250 sermons he is known to have delivered, reports or notes taken by scribes or others cover only about 50 of the sermons given.

Articles. Some of the Prophet's teachings in this book are drawn from articles that Joseph Smith designed for publication in Church periodicals, including the *Evening and Morning Star, Latter Day Saints' Messenger and Advocate, Elders' Journal,* and *Times and Seasons.*[1] Joseph Smith wrote or dictated some material for publication. Also, he frequently directed a scribe, another member of the First Presidency, or another trusted individual to write an article regarding specific matters he wished addressed. The Prophet would then endorse the text, having approved it as representing his thinking, and publish it under his name. For example, this book quotes from several editorials published in the *Times and Seasons* in 1842. During an eight-month period of that year, from February to October, Joseph Smith served as the editor of this periodical and frequently published articles signed "Ed." Though others helped to write many of these articles, the Prophet approved them and published them in his name.

Letters. This book quotes from many letters written or dictated by Joseph Smith. This book also quotes from letters approved and signed by Joseph Smith that were partially or completely prepared by others under his direction.

Journals. The Prophet's journals are a rich source of his teachings. Though his journals are extensive, he actually wrote in them himself infrequently. Instead, he directed that his journals be kept by scribes, under his supervision, allowing him to focus on the pressing responsibilities of his calling. Just prior to his martyrdom he stated, "For the last three years I have a record of all my acts and proceedings, for I have kept several good, faithful, and efficient clerks in constant employ: they have accompanied me everywhere, and carefully kept my history, and they have written down what I have done, where I have been, and what I have said."[2] The Prophet's scribes recorded journal entries in third person and in first person, as if Joseph Smith himself were writing.

Remembrances of others. This book quotes from the recollections of those who heard the Prophet speak and later recorded his words in their journals and other writings. After the Prophet's death, Church leaders and historians made great efforts to collect and preserve such writings and to record previously unwritten recollections about the Prophet. Such sources have been used only when the person actually heard the words that he or she recorded.

Scriptures. This book quotes from Joseph Smith's teachings and writings that were later canonized as scripture in the Doctrine and Covenants and Pearl of Great Price. Such canonized writings include instructions he gave on doctrinal subjects, visions he recorded, and letters and other documents he wrote. This book quotes from these canonized teachings and writings when they provide insight into doctrines presented in this book.

History of the Church

Many of the Prophet Joseph Smith's sermons and writings included in this book are quoted from the *History of The Church of Jesus Christ of Latter-day Saints,* which is referred to in this book as the *History of the Church.*[3] The first six volumes of the *History of the Church* present the history of The Church of Jesus Christ of Latter-day Saints from its beginnings until the death of Joseph Smith. This history primarily describes events and experiences connected with the life and ministry of Joseph Smith. It is one of the most important sources of historical information about the Prophet's life and teachings and about the development of the early Church.

Joseph Smith began preparing the history that ultimately became the *History of the Church* in the spring of 1838 to counter false reports being published in newspapers and elsewhere. The completion of his history was a subject of great concern to him. In 1843 he said, "There are but few subjects that I have felt a greater anxiety about than my history, which has been a very difficult task."[4]

The *History of the Church* is based on the Prophet's recollections, journals, and other personal records. It presents a daily narrative of the Prophet's activities and significant events in Church history. It also includes reports of the Prophet's discourses, copies of revelations he received, articles from Church periodicals, minutes of conferences, and other documents.

Joseph Smith remained involved in preparing and reviewing his history until his death. However, he directed that most of the work be done by others, under his supervision. Reasons for this include his lifelong preference for speaking or dictating his thoughts, rather than writing them down, and the constant demands of his ministry. The Prophet's history for July 5, 1839, records, "I was dictating history, I say dictating, for I seldom use the pen myself."[5]

By June 1844 the history was written through August 5, 1838. In Carthage Jail, shortly before he died, the Prophet charged Elder Willard Richards, his chief scribe at that time, to continue the plan of compiling the history.[6] Elder Richards and other men who had been close to the Prophet continued the history as directed until Elder Richards's death in 1854. Then the work of compiling the history was done or directed primarily by Elder George A. Smith, a cousin and close friend of the Prophet, who was ordained an Apostle in 1839 and became Church Historian in 1854. Many others who worked in the Church Historian's Office also assisted with the compilation.

One important task of the compilers of the *History of the Church* was editing and preparing original documents for inclusion in the history. Their work involved making light editorial revisions to almost all original documents included in the *History of the Church*. The compilers corrected misspelled words and standardized punctuation, capitalization, and grammar. Additionally, in some cases, the compilers of the history made other changes to original documents. These changes can be divided into three categories:

1. *Combining accounts.* Many of Joseph Smith's discourses were recorded by more than one observer. In some instances, the compilers of the *History of the Church* combined two or more accounts of the same discourse into a single version.
2. *Changing accounts from third person to first person.* Many accounts of the Prophet's teachings and activities were recorded in third person. These accounts were written primarily by his scribes, but some accounts were taken from the writings of others who knew the Prophet and from newspaper articles.

As the compilers of the *History of the Church* worked, they wrote the history in the first person, as if the Prophet were writing. This required that some third-person accounts be changed into first-person accounts.

3. *Adding or changing words or phrases.* Many of the original notes taken of the Prophet's sermons are brief, incomplete, and disconnected. In some of these instances, Church historians reconstructed the Prophet's sermons based on the available records, drawing also upon their memories and experiences with the Prophet. This work sometimes involved adding or changing words or phrases to fill in gaps and clarify meaning.

All of the compiling and writing of the *History of the Church* was done under apostolic supervision and review. The history was read to members of the First Presidency, including President Brigham Young, and the Quorum of the Twelve Apostles, some of whom had been intimately acquainted with the Prophet and had heard the original addresses. These leaders approved the manuscript for publication as the history of the Church for the period of time it covers.

In August 1856 the history was completed through the time of Joseph Smith's death. The history was published in serial form in Church periodicals in the 19th century as the "History of Joseph Smith."[7] Later, the history was edited by Elder B. H. Roberts, a member of the Presidency of the Seventy, and was published between 1902 and 1912 in six volumes. It was titled *History of The Church of Jesus Christ of Latter-day Saints.*

The men who compiled the history attested to the accuracy of the work. Elder George A. Smith said: "The greatest care has been taken to convey the ideas in the Prophet's style as near as possible; and in no case has the sentiment been varied that I know of, as I heard the most of his discourses myself, was on the most intimate terms with him, have retained a most vivid recollection of his teachings, and was well acquainted with his principles and motives."[8]

Elder George A. Smith and Elder Wilford Woodruff declared: "The History of Joseph Smith is now before the world, and we are satisfied that a history more correct in its details than this, was never published. To have it strictly correct, the greatest possible pains have been taken by the historians and clerks engaged in the work. They were eye and ear witnesses of nearly all the transactions recorded in this history, most of which were reported as they transpired, and, where they were not personally present, they have had access to those who were. Moreover, since the death of the Prophet Joseph, the History has been carefully revised under the strict inspection of President Brigham Young, and approved of by him.

"We, therefore, hereby bear our testimony to all the world, unto whom these words shall come, that the History of Joseph Smith is true, and is one of the most authentic histories ever written."[9]

In this book, the Prophet Joseph Smith's discourses and writings are quoted from the *History of the Church* unless the original discourse or writing was not included in it. When this book quotes from the *History of the Church,* the endnotes include information about the original discourse or writing, including the names of those who recorded the Prophet's sermons. The endnotes also indicate when the compilers of the *History of the Church* drew upon their memories and experiences with Joseph Smith to change words or add words or phrases to the original report. Such additions or changes are noted only when they affect the meaning of the quotation. Minor editing changes are not noted.

The book titled Joseph Smith—History, as recorded in the Pearl of Great Price, is an excerpt from the first five chapters of the first volume of the *History of the Church*.

Notes

1. The *Evening and Morning Star* was published in Independence, Missouri, from 1832 to 1833, and in Kirtland, Ohio, from 1833 to 1834. The *Latter Day Saints' Messenger and Advocate* was published in Kirtland from 1834 to 1837. The *Elders' Journal* was published in Kirtland in 1837, and in Far West, Missouri, in 1838. The *Times and Seasons* was published in Nauvoo, Illinois, from 1839 to 1846.
2. *History of the Church,* 6:409; from a discourse given by Joseph Smith on May 26, 1844, in Nauvoo, Illinois; reported by Thomas Bullock.
3. The *History of the Church* has been referred to as the *Documentary History of the Church.*

4. *History of the Church,* 6:66; from "History of the Church" (manuscript), book E-1, p. 1768, Church Archives, The Church of Jesus Christ of Latter-day Saints, Salt Lake City, Utah.
5. *History of the Church,* 4:1; from "History of the Church" (manuscript), book C-1, p. 963, Church Archives.
6. See letter from George A. Smith to Wilford Woodruff, Apr. 21, 1856, Salt Lake City, Utah; in Historical Record Book, 1843–74, p. 219, Church Archives.
7. The "History of Joseph Smith" was published in the *Times and Seasons* from Mar. 15, 1842, to Feb. 15, 1846. It was continued in the *Deseret News* from Nov. 15, 1851, to Jan. 20, 1858. It was reprinted in the *Millennial Star* from June 1842 to May 1845; and from Apr. 15, 1852, to May 2, 1863.
8. Letter from George A. Smith to Wilford Woodruff, Apr. 21, 1856, Salt Lake City, Utah; in Historical Record Book, 1843–74, p. 218, Church Archives.
9. George A. Smith and Wilford Woodruff, *Deseret News,* Jan. 20, 1858, p. 363; paragraph divisions altered.

List of Visuals

Index

C

G

K

Q

R

S

T

U